D1214252

ALL·IN·ONE

CEA-CompTIA DHTI+ ™
Digital Home Technology Integrator

EXAM GUIDE
Second Edition

Ron Gilster
Helen Heneveld

New York • Chicago • San Francisco • Lisbon
London • Madrid • Mexico City • Milan • New Delhi
San Juan • Seoul • Singapore • Sydney • Toronto

The **McGraw·Hill** Companies

Cataloging-in-Publication Data is on file with the Library of Congress

McGraw-Hill books are available at special quantity discounts to use as premiums and sales promotions, or for use in corporate training programs. To contact a special sales representative, please visit the Contact Us page at www.mhprofessional.com.

CEA-CompTIA DHTI+™ Digital Home Technology Integrator All-in-One Exam Guide, Second Edition

1 2 3 4 5 6 7 8 9 0   DOC DOC   0 1 9 8

ISBN: Book p/n 978-0-07-154679-9 and CD p/n 978-0-07-154680-5
of set 978-0-07-154665-2

MHID: Book p/n 0-07-154679-0 and CD p/n 0-07-154680-4
of set 0-07-154665-0

Sponsoring Editor	**Contributing Editor**	**Production Supervisor**
Tim Green	*Helen Heneveld*	*Jim Kussow*
Editorial Supervisor	**Technical Editors**	**Composition**
Jody McKenzie	*Josh Lehman, Jason White*	*International Typesetting and Composition*
Project Manager	**Copy Editor**	
Vastavikta Sharma, International Typesetting and Composition	*Sally Engelfried*	**Illustration**
	Proofreader	*International Typesetting and Composition*
Acquisitions Coordinators	*Carol Shields*	
Jennifer Housh	**Indexer**	**Art Director, Cover**
Carly Stapleton	*Broccoli Information Management*	*Jeff Weeks*

CompTIA Authorized Quality Curriculum

The logo of the CompTIA Authorized Quality Curriculum (CAQC) program and the status of this or other training material as "Authorized" under the CompTIA Authorized Quality Curriculum program signifies that, in CompTIA's opinion, such training material covers the content of CompTIA's related certification exam.

The contents of this training material were created for the CEA-CompTIA DHTI+ exam covering CompTIA certification objectives that were current as of 2008.

CompTIA has not reviewed or approved the accuracy of the contents of this training material and specifically disclaims any warranties of merchantability or fitness for a particular purpose. CompTIA makes no guarantee concerning the success of persons using any such "Authorized" or other training material in order to prepare for any CompTIA certification exam.

How to Become CompTIA Certified

This training material can help you prepare for and pass a related CompTIA certification exam or exams. In order to achieve CompTIA certification, you must register for and pass a CompTIA certification exam or exams. In order to become CompTIA certified, you must:

1. Select a certification exam provider. For more information please visit www.comptia.org/certification/general_information/exam_locations.aspx.

2. Register for and schedule a time to take the CompTIA certification exam(s) at a convenient location.

3. Read and sign the Candidate Agreement, which will be presented at the time of the exam(s). The text of the Candidate Agreement can be found at www.comptia.org/certification/general_information/candidate_agreement.aspx.

4. Take and pass the CompTIA certification exam(s).

For more information about CompTIA's certifications, such as its industry acceptance, benefits or program news, please visit www.comptia.org/certification.

CompTIA is a not-for-profit information technology (IT) trade association. CompTIA's certifications are designed by subject matter experts from across the IT industry. Each CompTIA certification is vendor-neutral, covers multiple technologies, and requires demonstration of skills and knowledge widely sought after by the IT industry.

To contact CompTIA with any questions or comments, please call (630) 678-8300 or e-mail questions@comptia.org.

ABOUT THE AUTHOR

Ron Gilster is the author of many best-selling books on networking, PC hardware, and IT career certifications. He holds a variety of IT certifications and has worked in computing and networking for over 20 years. Ron has also served in a variety of small business and corporate technical, management, and executive positions. He is currently a college administrator in Spokane Valley, Washington, and remains in high demand as a speaker/presenter at conferences worldwide.

About the Contributing Editor

Helen Heneveld, MBA, CEDIA Installer I, HTI+ is a recognized industry expert who speaks, trains, and consults worldwide in the converging home systems industry. Helen is a former CEDIA board member and former Chair of CEDIA's Systems Integration Council.

About the Technical Editors

Jason White is one of the leading home theater/electronics engineers in the business, and has an electrical engineering degree from Georgia Tech. Jason also holds ISF and HAA Certifications, as well as many CEDIA certifications.

Josh Lehman is considered one of the leading home theater/electronics experts in the business today. He is a THX-Certified Level II Engineer and holds master certifications in ISF and HAA Level II. Josh was a contributing writer for McGraw-Hill's *How to Do Everything with TiVo*.

CONTENTS AT A GLANCE

CONTENTS

To my father George; I'm his biggest fan.

—Ron Gilster

ACKNOWLEDGMENTS

I'd like to thank several individuals whose support and contributions have helped to create this book:

- Helen Heneveld, the guru of home automation
- Markus H. Burns for his photography and insights
- Connie J Price for her photographs
- Neilfred Picciotto for his photographs
- Joel Silver and Bob Fucci of Imaging Science Foundation, Inc. for their input on imaging technology and products
- Scott Lohraff of The Symphony House for his input on audio
- Mark Stiving of Destiny Networks for his contributions on home control systems and programming
- Gordon van Zuiden of cyberManor for his contributions on integrated home network systems
- Frank White of Custom Metrics, for his help outlining video knowledge areas
- Tom Lyga and Pass & Seymour/Legrand (www.passandseymour.com) for general support and for providing an image for the cover of the book.

I also wish to acknowledge the contributions of information, art, and guidance from the following companies:

2Wire, Inc.   www.2wire.com
3Com Corporation   www.3com.com
Absolute Automation, Inc.   www.absoluteautomation.com
Accell Corporation   www.accellcables.com
Access Lighting, Inc.   www.accesslighting.com
Ademco (Honeywell)   www.ademco.com
ALLNET GmbH   www.allnet.de
Almex Ltd   www.almexltd.com
American Fluorescent Corporation
    www.americanfluorescent.com
American Power Conversion Corporation   www.apcc.com
Amerillum Corporation.   www.amerillum.com

Amtel Security Systems, Inc.   www.amtel-security.com
AMX Corporation   www.amx.com
Asante Technologies, Inc.   www.asante.com
ATI Technologies, Inc.   www.ati.com
AudioControl   www.audiocontrol.com
Audio, Security & Automation Providers, Inc.
    www.automation-providers.com
AverMedia Technologies, Inc.   www.aver.com
AwoX   www.awox.com
BEAMEX   www.beamex.com
Belden, Inc.   www.belden.com
Berk-Tek, a Nexans Company   www.nexans.us

Boca Automation, Inc/S D Synder & Associates
http://home.earthlink.net/bocasite
Broan-NuTone, LLC   www.broan.com
Brookstone Company, Inc.   www.brookstone.com
Cabinet Tronix   www.cabinet-tronix.com
Cadet Manufacturing   www.cadetco.com
Canadian Standards Authority   www.csa.ca
Canare Corporation   www.canare.com
Channel Vision   www.channelvision.com
Cisco Systems, Inc.   www.cisco.com
Cisco Systems, Inc. (LinkSys)   www.linksys.com
Cogency Semiconductor, Inc.   www.cogency.com
Crestron Electronics, Inc.   www.crestron.com
Crutchfield New Media, LLC.   www.crutchfield.com
cyberManor   www.cybermanor.com
Dell Corporation   www.dell.com
Delphi Technologies, Inc.   www.delphi.com
Destiny Networks, Inc.   www.destinynetworks.com
Digital Rapids Corporation   www.digital-rapids.com
DITEK Corporation   www.ditekcorp.com
Dynacom Corporation   www.dynacom-usa.com
Dynaquip Controls   www.dynaquip.com
Elan Home Systems, LLC   www.elanhomesystems.com
Embedded Automation, Inc.
www.embeddedautomation.com
Everest Communications   www.everest-communications.com
EVVA-WERK GmbH & Co.   www.evva.com
FBII (Honeywell)   www.fbii.com
Fiber Connections, Inc.   www.fiberconnectionsinc.com
FiberSource Inc.   www.fibersource.net
Fluke Networks   www.flukenetworks.com
Fujitsu Siemens Computers   www.fujitsu-siemens.com
FutureSmart Systems, Inc. (Honeywell)
www.futuresmart.com
GE Interlogix   www.ge-interlogix.com
General Electric Company   www.ge.com
Gepco International   www.gepco.com
Harris Corporation   www.harris.com
HDCI, Heneveld Dynamic Consulting, Inc.
www.hheneveld.com
Hewlett Packard Company   www.hp.com
HID Corporation   www.hidcorp.com
Home Automation, Inc.   www.homeauto.com
Honeywell International, Inc.   www.honeywell.com
Hwan Ming Enterprise Co., Ltd   www.hme.com.tw
IBASE Technology, Inc.   www.ibase-usa.com
Ingersoll-Rand Co., Ltd   http://company.ingersollrand.com
Intellikey Corporation   www.intellikey.com
Intrigue Technologies, Inc.   www.harmonyremote.com
Invensys Building Systems, PLC   www.invensysibs.com
Jablotron s.r.o.   www.jablotron.cz
JVC Professional Products Company   www.jvc.com
Klipsch Audio Technologies   www.klipsch.com
Koninklijke Philips Electronics NV (Philips USA)
www.philipsusa.com
Lamson & Sessions (Carlon)   www.carlon.com
Lantronix Corporation   www.lantronix.com
Leviton Manufacturing Company (Voice & Data
Division)   www.levitonvoicedata.com
Leviton Manufacturing Company (Lighting Division)
www.leviton.com
Lexicon, a division of Harman Specialty Group
www.harman.com
LG Electronics   www.lge.com
Lindows.com, Inc.   www.linspire.com

LiteTouch, Inc.   www.litetouch.com
Lowes Corporation   www.lowes.com
Lutron Lighting Controls   www.lutron.com
Marantz America, Inc.   http://us.marantz.com
Mediatrix Telecom, Inc.   www.mediatrix.com
Megger Group Limited   www.megger.com
Mier Products, Inc.   www.mierproducts.com
Molex, Inc.   www.molex.com
Monster Cable Products, Inc.   www.monstercable.com
Mordaunt-Short   www.mordaunt-short.co.uk
NetComm Limited   www.netcomm.com.au
NetGear, Inc.   www.netgear.com
New Frontier Electronics, Inc.   www.frontierelec.com
Niles Audio Corporation   www.nilesaudio.com
Onkyo USA Corporation   www.onkyousa.com
OnQ Technologies   www.onqtech.com
Pacific Digital Corporation   www.pacificdigitalcorp.com
Paladin Tools, Inc.   www.paladin-tools.com
Panasonic USA   www.panasonic.com
Pegasus Communications Corporation
www.pegasuscom.com
Pelco   www.pelcom.com
Philex Electronic, Ltd   www.philex.co.uk
Precise Biometrics   www.precisebiometrics.com
ProjectorPeople.com   www.projectorpeople.com
RAB Lighting   www.rabweb.com
Rain Bird Corporation   www.rainbird.com
RCI Automation, LLC   http://ourworld.compuserve.com/
homepages/rciautomation/
Residential Control Systems, Inc.   www.resconsys.com
Ronfell Lighting Group   www.ronfell.com
Russound   www.russound.com
Rutherford Controls International Corporation
www.rutherfordcontrols.com
Scan Technology, Inc.   www.scantec.com
Seatek Company   www.seatek.com
Siemens Information and Communication Mobile,
LLC   www.siemens.com
The Siemon Company   www.siemon.com/
SignaMax Connectivity Systems   www.signamax.com
Silent Witness Enterprises, Ltd. (Honeywell Video
Systems)   www.silentwitness.com
Skylink Group   www.skylinknet.com
Smarthome, Inc.   www.smarthome.com
Sonance   www.sonance.com
Sony Electronics, Inc.   www.sony.com
Sound Advance Systems, Inc.   www.soundadvance.com
SpeakerCraft   www.speakercraft.com
Streamzap   www.streamzap.com
Tecra Tools, Inc.   www.tecratools.com
Telect, Inc.   www.telect.com
Toro Company   www.toro.com
TriangleCables.com   www.trianglecables.com
Underwriters Laboratories, Inc.   www.ul.com
Universal Electronics, Inc.   www.uei.com
Universal Remote Controls, Inc.   www.universal-remote.com
UStec   www.ustecnet.com
Vantage/Legrand   www.vantagecontrols.com
Velux Group   www.velux.com
Videx, Inc.   www.videx.com
ViewSonic Corporation   www.viewsonic.com
Voyetra Turtle Beach, Inc.   www.voyetra-turtle-beach.com
Vutec Corporation   www.vutec.com
Weiser Lock   www.weiserlock.com
X-10 Wireless Technology, Inc.   www.x10.com

The Benefits of Certification

The Computing Technology Industry Association (CompTIA) and the Consumer Electronics Association (CEA) have collaborated to create a certification exam that verifies the knowledge, training, and experience of a home technology integrator who has been working in this field for at least six months. The fact that the Digital Home Technology Integrator+ (CompTIA DHTI+) certification exam exists is a clear indication that the home automation market is rapidly expanding, and these two organizations have combined to provide the consumer with a baseline to which all professionals in the home technology industry can be measured.

The CompTIA DHTI+ certification provides benefits to the technician and the employer, as well as the homeowner.

The benefits to the technician include:

- Proof of his or her professional achievement and knowledge
- A clear career path
- Improved job opportunities
- A foundation for additional higher-level certifications

The benefits to the employer and the homeowner include:

- Verified skills of job candidates simplifies recruitment and hiring
- Reduced entry-level training costs
- Measurable job performance and competency standards
- Increased customer satisfaction and repeat and follow-up business
- Reduced warranty repair work and costs
- Increased competitive advantage over companies without certified technicians

CEA and CompTIA

CEA and CompTIA are computing and electronics industry associations that promote the development of workplace and product standards.

CEA

CEA, the Consumer Electronics Association, is a worldwide trade association of over 2,200 companies that design, manufacture, distribute, sell, and install residential electronic systems. In addition to the DHTI+ certification, the CEA has developed and sponsors a wide variety of certification tests for electronics technicians.

 NOTE For more information on CEA and other certification programs it sponsors, visit its website at www.ce.org.

CompTIA

CompTIA, the Computing Technology Industry Association, was founded in 1982 with a focus on advancing the growth of the information technology (IT) industry and to improve the skills and knowledge of IT professionals. Because CompTIA has over 20,000 individual and institutional members in more than 102 countries, it has become one of the more influential IT trade associations in the world.

CompTIA's commitment is to help facilitate the growth and quality of the IT industry through the development of IT industry standards, the skills and expertise of IT professionals, and the development of ongoing skills education. The areas of focus for CompTIA are currently convergence technology, e-commerce, IT training, software services, IT career certification, and workforce development.

 NOTE For more information on CompTIA and its certification programs, visit its website at www.comptia.org.

The DHTI+ Certification

The DHTI+ certification provides a comprehensive evaluation of the knowledge and skills that are required to perform well on a home integration job. DHTI+ is a vendor-neutral, international certification (although only available in English at this time) that verifies a home technology integration technician's capabilities to perform the design, configuration, integration, maintenance, diagnosis, and troubleshooting of digital electronic home automation and control systems.

CEA and CompTIA have worked in partnership to provide a credible and recognized certification for home technology integrators who have at least 18–24 months of experience in some area of home technology integration, which includes security system technicians, communications and audio/video installers, HVAC technicians, low-voltage electricians, and network administrators.

The DHTI+ certification covers a broad range of the basic knowledge required of a home technology installer/integrator at the entry level. The exam assesses the candidate on the balance of skills and knowledge that are required to perform the tasks inherent

Domain	Subject Area	Percentage of Exam
1.0	Networking	20%
2.0	Audio/Video	22%
3.0	Telephone/VoIP	10%
4.0	Security and Surveillance	15%
5.0	Home Control Management	15%
6.0	Documentation and Troubleshooting	18%
	TOTAL	100%

Table 1   DHTI+ Subject Area Domains

in any home integration job. The objectives of the DHTI+ certification examination upon which the exam questions are based was developed by a panel of nationally recognized subject matter experts (SMEs) from each of the different subsystem areas.

There aren't any required prerequisites for taking the DHTI+ certification exams. However, it's highly recommended that you have both on-the-job experience and specific training before spending the money to attempt the exam. The technician that earns DHTI+ certification demonstrates that he or she has the equivalent knowledge and skill levels of a working professional, with at least 18–24 months of hands-on experience in each of the objective areas.

Table 1 lists the subject matter areas of the DHTI+ exam along with the percentage of the exam dedicated to each area.

NOTE   These certification objectives are subject to change. For the most current information, visit www.comptia.org.

About the CD-ROM

The CD-ROM located in the back of this book includes a practice exam for the DHTI+ certification exam to help you get a feel for the type of questions you may face on the actual certification exams. Though the practice exam provides no guarantee for your performance on the actual exam, it may be a valuable tool for making sure you understand the knowledge in this book and that you have some familiarity with electronic exams before taking the real exam.

Updates and Errata

Though every effort has been made to provide complete and accurate information, digital home technology integration is a complex and ever-changing area, and it is possible that corrections may be identified after publication. Please visit www.mhprofessional .com, click Computing at the top, and then click Errata on the left to access any confirmed fixes.

PART I

Home Technology Installation Basics

Wire and Cable Basics

In this chapter, you will learn about:
- Wire types, insulation, and jacket materials
- Cable types, construction, and characteristics
- Cable performance, attenuation, cancellation, and interference

Just like a house is built on its foundation, a home automation network is built on its wiring. Home networks of all types, and yes, even wireless networks, are built on a network of electrical, communications, and audio/visual wiring.

The myriad standards, guidelines, and cable and wire types can be a bit confusing, but when you organize them by the various systems in a house, it's really not all that complicated. This chapter focuses on the different cable types used in computer networking and their construction, performance, specifications, and how each is typically used in a home automation project. This chapter provides you with the basic construction, use, and performance characteristics of the cable used in each of these different networking applications that could be installed a home.

Electrical Wiring and Cable

Residential electrical wiring actually includes all of the wiring in a home, but for now we'll focus on the low-voltage wiring. If you plan on using any of this wiring as a component of a home network of any kind, it is important for this wiring to conform to certain standards and codes.

Low-Voltage versus High-Voltage

When installing wire and cable in a home, you must be aware of the voltage specification of the cable in use. There are certain cable types that are specified as low voltage and others as high voltage. Low-voltage cable is designed to carry lower levels of alternating current (AC) and direct current (DC) voltages than high voltage. I know that may sound like a no-brainer, but there is enough of a difference between these two cabling types that electricians are certified separately for installing one or the other. Table 1-1 lists the basic cable categories and the voltage range each is specified to carry.

Cable Type	DC Voltage	AC Voltage	Usage
Extra Low-Voltage (ELV)	<120 volts (V)	<50V	Audio, video, telephone, data cables
Low-Voltage	120V – 750V	50V – 500V	Standard household electrical wiring
High-Voltage	>1.5 kV	>1 kV	Power lines to a home

Table 1-1   Wire Voltage Specifications

Low-Voltage Wiring

No specific definition exists for what is generally called low-voltage wiring. In some references, low-voltage is circuit wiring of less than 30 volts (V) of AC or 60V of DC. Another reference defines it as being less than 50V AC, and yet another defines it as being between 0 and 150V AC and DC. In effect, the term *low-voltage wiring*, which typically is used to describe communications, speaker, security and control signal wiring, is more of a slang term than a specific reference. However, in common usage, electricians use low voltage to refer to less than 50V and wire gauges less than 16 AWG (American Wire Gauge).

Low-voltage wiring is defined as being one of five types of circuits:

- **Communication circuits**   Circuits that carry data signals between devices, typically connected to a network of devices. Communication circuits, such as data networking, telephone, and in some cases, electrical cabling, are explained in detail in Chapters 3 and 10.

- **Signal circuits**   An electrical circuit that supplies power to an appliance or electrical device that produces a visual light signal or audible sound signal. Examples of signals circuits are doorbells, buzzers, signal lights, fire or smoke detectors, alarm systems, and other types of security systems.

- **Remote control circuits**   An electrical circuit that controls one or more other circuits, motor controllers, magnet contacts, or electrical relays. A remote control circuit controls the supply of power to electrical equipment like appliances, lighting, and heating devices, or provides command signals to control their operation.

- **Motor control circuits**   A circuit that carries electric signals that control the function of a device or motor controller, but not the main electrical power service.

- **Power-limited circuits**   Circuits that aren't used for signaling or remote control where the power on the line is limited. A low-voltage lighting circuit that includes 120V to 12V transformers to drive 12V lamps is an example of a power-limited circuit. Power-limited circuits are limited to 30V.

Low-Voltage Classes

Low-voltage circuits are separated into four circuit classes, as listed in Table 1-2. Class 1 is divided into two subclasses: Class 1 power-limited and Class 1 remote control and

Class	Type	Volts	Volt-Amps (Power)
1	Power-limited	30	1000
1	Remote control and signaling	600	No limits
2	DC	30	100
3	DC	>30V	>0.5, but not more than 100 VA

Table 1-2   Low-Voltage Circuit Classes

signaling. Class 2 and 3 circuits are commonly found in residential wiring. A few examples of Class 2 circuits are low-voltage lighting controls, thermostats, security systems, intercoms, audio systems, and computer networks. Some security systems, intercoms, and audio systems can also be Class 3 circuits.

Each circuit class also defines the cable class that must be used. On Class 2 and 3 circuits, the cable must be rated for Class 2 and 3 circuits, respectively. The manufacturer's specifications should indicate the rating class of each cable it sells, and the class rating should be marked on the cable as CL2 (Class 2) or CL3 (Class 3).

Electrical Wiring

Generally, home automation projects rarely have to deal with electrical wiring except to plug a controller or network adapter into an outlet. However, if you are installing home network wiring into open walls or retrofitting wiring into an existing wall, you should be able to at least recognize common electrical service wiring and its characteristics.

 NOTE   Most of these electrical wire characteristics are also found in low-voltage wiring.

The following are the most common electrical wiring used in home construction today:

- **Modern nonmetallic (NM)**   This wire is made up of two solid copper or aluminum core wires insulated with plastic vinyl and a bare copper ground wire sheathed with a paper layer and an outer vinyl jacket. Modern NM wiring, commonly called Romex (a brand name), is flexible, durable, and moisture-resistant, which is why it is the most popular choice for residential electric wiring. See Figure 1-1.

Figure 1-1
The construction of modern nonmetallic electrical wiring

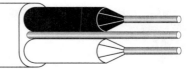

- **Underground feeder (UF)**   This wire, is very much like NM cable, except that the three copper wires (two insulated and one bare) are embedded in solid plastic vinyl sheathing. UF wire is the best choice for damp or buried installations.

- **Zip wire**   This wire type is lighter duty than most residential wiring and has very limited use. Most lamp cords are zip wire, which gets its name from the fact that the two conductors are molded together, but can be easily separated by pulling them apart manually. Figure 1-2 illustrates the construction of zip wire.

Some older wire types you may encounter in a house are

- **Flexible armored cable**   This two-wire type of electric cable, which is also called Greenfield or BX wire (see Figure 1-3), was very popular from the 1920s to the 1940s. The metallic armoring around the outside of the cable provides the grounding.

- **Metal conduit**   From the 1940s to the 1970s, two insulated wires were installed in rigid metal conduit tubing. The metal of the conduit provided the grounding. Metal conduit installation is still required in some areas for bare wire installations in basements, foundation crawl space, attics, and garages. It is also required in some cities. Check your local codes.

- **Early NM**   This two-wire cable was popular from the 1930s to the mid-1960s. It is made up of a flexible rubberized fabric jacket that surrounds two solid copper wires with rubber insulation and paper sheathing inside the outer jacket. Early NM wire had no grounding wire.

Figure 1-2
A cutaway view
of zip wire

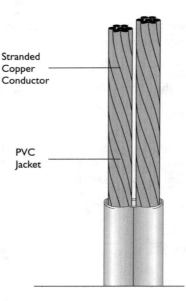

Stranded
Copper
Conductor

PVC
Jacket

Figure 1-3
BX cable is a type
of armored cable

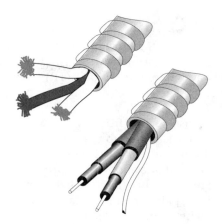

- **Knob and tube** Wires covered with a rubberized fabric material, called "loom," was strung over ceramic insulators (knobs) and ceramic tubes through studs and joists. This is a very old and obsolete wiring system found in homes constructed before 1940.

Residential Wire Gauge and Characteristics

The wire gauge used in a home depends on the number of amperes on a particular circuit. For example, if a circuit has 20 amps, a 12-gauge wire should be used. See Table 1-3 for a listing of a few of the common circuit amps and the appropriate wire gauge to use. Remember that a smaller gauge means a bigger and less flexible wire. For wire runs longer than 100 feet, placed inside a conduit, or installed in a bundle with other wires, the next heavier gauge wire should be used to avoid voltage drops and to overcome heat problems.

AWG/B&S*	CSA*	Circuit Amps	Ohms per 1K feet	Common Usage
24 /Cat 5e	0.205	2.1	28.6	Communications
18 – 22	0.0480 – 0.0280	10 – 8	6.386 – 16.200	Thermostats, doorbells, security systems
16	0.051	12	4.016	Audio
14	0.0800	15	2.524	Light fixtures, receptacles
12	0.1040	20	1.619	Light fixtures, receptacles
10	0.1280	30	1.018	Air conditioners (AC), clothes dryers
8	0.1600	40	0.641	Electric ranges, central AC
6	0.1920	60	0.403	Central AC, electric furnaces

*AWG (American Wire Gauge); B&S (Brown and Sharpe) – equivalent to AWG; CSA (Canadian Standards Association)

Table 1-3 Wire Gauge to Circuit Amperes

Twisted-Pair Cable

Twisted-pair wiring is by far the most popularly installed media for networking in just about any type of network for many reasons, including that it is inexpensive, easy to handle, and readily available. Twisted-pair (TP) wire is the de facto standard for both Ethernet and Token Ring networks, with Ethernet being the most commonly used networking standard.

Twisted-pair wire gets its name from its construction. Pairs of 24-gauge (or heavier) wire are twisted around each other to reduce cancellation between the two wires. Most TP cables have multiple pairs of wire, typically two or four pairs. Each wire pair is wrapped or twisted around one another to help protect the wires from interference and crosstalk. The more twists in the wires, the better the protection.

Two types of twisted-pair wire are available: unshielded and shielded. Unshielded twisted-pair (UTP) wire, shown in Figure 1-4, doesn't include any electromagnetic interference (EMI) shielding to speak of, while shielded twisted-pair (STP) wire, shown in Figure 1-5, has an extra wrapping of foil to help protect the inner wires from EMI and cancellation effects.

Figure 1-4
The construction of unshielded twisted-pair (UTP) wire

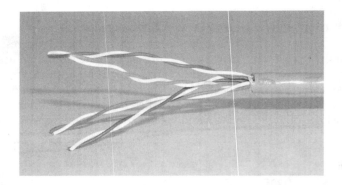

Figure 1-5
Shielded twisted-pair (STP) wire has a foil wrapper that shields the inner wires from EMI.

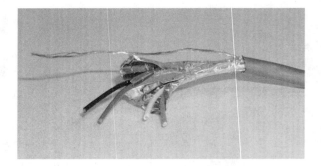

AWG and Metric Wire Sizes

Wire, including the wires bundled into a cable, is measured in a variety of sizes throughout the world. In the U.S., wire is measured using the American Wire Gauge (AWG) standard, which measures the diameter of a wire using a formula. Essentially, the formula says that for each drop of six gauges (or 6 AWG), the wire doubles in diameter.

Many countries around the world use a metric wire sizing system that states a wire's size (gauge) as ten times its diameter in millimeters. For example, a 40-gauge metric wire has a 4 mm diameter. In the metric wire gauge system, wire gauge increases as the diameter of the wire gets bigger. This can be somewhat confusing because as the AWG of a wire is getting smaller, its metric wire gauge is increasing. To avoid this confusion, metric wire sizes are typically stated in millimeters and not wire gauge. Table 1-4 shows a comparison of AWG wire sizes and the equivalent metric wire diameter of wire sizes commonly used in home automation systems.

Table 1-4
Comparison of AWG and Metric Wire Sizes

AWG	Metric Wire Size (in millimeters)
10	2.588
12	2.304
14	1.628
16	1.290
18	1.024
20	0.081
22	0.065
24	0.511
26	0.404
28	0.320

UTP cable is designated for a variety of uses using a specification that divides its various grades into a series of categories. Each of the seven categories specified so far defines a specific number of wire pairs, a number of radial twists per foot (or twists per inch), the bandwidth rating, the maximum segment (run) length for performance, and its recommended networking application. Table 1-5 details the various UTP wire categories, which are referred to as "Cats." The most common cable categories used in home networking are Cat 5, Cat 5e, and Cat 6. The cable categories listed in Table 1-5 are defined by the American National Standards Institute (ANSI) and recognized by the Electronic Industries Alliance (EIA) and the Telecommunication Industry Association (TIA), who co-author a number of the standards used in home and commercial networking.

Category	Frequency	Bandwidth	Wire Pairs	Applications
Cat 1	16 MHz	128 Kbps	2	Not currently recognized in TIA/EIA cabling standards. Previously used for telephone lines and doorbell wiring.
Cat 2	16 MHz	4 Mbps	4	Not currently recognized in TIA/EIA cabling standards. Previously used for 4 Mbps Token Ring networks.
Cat 3	16 MHz	10 Mbps	4	Defined in TIA/EIA 568B and 10BaseT standards. Used in 10 Mbps Ethernet networks.
Cat 4	20 MHz	10 – 16 Mbps	4	Not currently recognized in TIA/EIA cabling standards. Previously used for 16 Mbps Token Ring networks and 10 Mbps Ethernet.
Cat 5	100 MHz	100 Mbps	4	Not currently recognized in TIA/EIA cabling standards. Previously used for 100 Mbps Ethernet networks (100BaseT).
Cat 5e	100 MHz	1 Gbps	4	Current TIA/EIA 568B cable standard. Used for 100 Mbps and 1 Gbps Ethernet networks.
Cat 6	250 MHz	1 Gbps	4	Current TIA/EIA 568B cable standard. Used for 1 Gpbs Ethernet networks (1000BaseT).
Cat 6a	500 MHz	10 Gbps	4	Future specification for 10 Gbps Ethernet networks.
Cat 7	600 MHz	10 Gbps	4	Designed to be backward compatible with Cat 5 and Cat 6. Each wire pair is insulated.

Table 1-5   ANSI/TIA/EIA UTP Cabling Standards

Frequency and Bandwidth

There is a relationship between a copper cable's frequency rating and its bandwidth. In each of the Institute of Electrical and Electronics Engineers (IEEE) cable standards you can find one or more formulas that convert a cable's frequency in megahertz (MHz) to its bandwidth in bits per seconds (bps). However, the short version is that the amount of current a cable is capable of carrying translates into the amount of data the cable can transmit. As shown in Table 1-5, as the frequency increases on a cable, so does its bandwidth rating.

Figure 1-6
Foil-wrapped
twisted-pair
(FTP) cabling

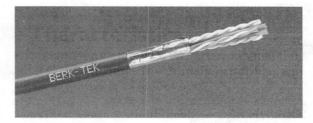

Photo courtesy of Berk-Tek.

In North America, UTP is the most commonly used networking cable. However, outside of North America, shielded twisted-pair (STP), and its two variations, screened twisted-pair (ScTP) and foil twisted-pair (FTP) wiring (see Figure 1-6) are commonly used. ScTP and FTP include an overall shielding layer, but don't provide as much protection from interference as STP.

UTP cable, like nearly all cable and wiring, carries a variety of rating codes, which are assigned by the product performance and safety authorities and testing laboratories to indicate the fire safety rating of a cable. These rating codes, listed in Table 1-6, are defined by the National Electric Code (NEC) that is published by the National Fire Protection Association (NFPA).

NOTE Virtually all twisted-pair cable used in networking applications is terminated with an RJ-45 connector. See Chapter 2 for information on cable connectors.

Coaxial Cable

Coaxial cable is constructed of a single-core wire conductor that is encased in a layer of dielectric insulation, which is then wrapped by a wire mesh outer conductor and shield. A plastic sheathing encases the entire cable assembly. Some manufacturers also add additional layers of mesh or foil shielding between the mesh and the outer jacket. Figure 1-7 illustrates the construction of a common coaxial cable.

Rating	Description
CM	General building cables suitable for nonplenum and riser application
CMP	Horizontal cabling that is suitable for installation in ducts and plenums without conduit
CMR	Riser (vertical) cabling that is suitable for use in vertical shaft installations

Table 1-6 The NEC Cable Ratings

Figure 1-7
The layers of an
RG6 coaxial cable

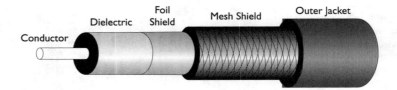

Coaxial cable is called single-ended cable because it has a single signal path and a single return path. The core wire carries the positive signals and the braided mesh layer of the cable carries any return signals.

The classes of coaxial cabling commonly used in residential systems are

- **RG6** This type of coaxial cable is a 75-ohm cable commonly used with digital satellite systems, analog television, video cassette recorders (VCRs), closed-circuit television (CCTV), and community antenna (cable) television (CATV). RG6 coaxial cable is the minimum requirement for many digital television systems and for television antenna systems. RG6 cables are typically terminated with F-type connectors.

CROSS-REFERENCE   See Chapter 2 for information on cable connectors.

- **RG11** This type of coaxial cable is fairly stiff and difficult to work with. It was once fairly popular with Ethernet data networks and is included in the IEEE 802.3 Ethernet specifications as 10Base2. RG11 coaxial cabling is most commonly terminated with Bayonet Neill-Concelman (BNC) connectors. This cable is also occasionally used for long cable runs for digital television feeds.

- **RG58** This type of low-loss coaxial cable is a 50-ohm cable with a diameter of 0.195 inches, which makes it a good general-purpose cable commonly used for security systems and video display applications. RG58 cables are commonly terminated with BNC connectors.

- **RG59** This coaxial cable type is a low-loss 100-ohm cable with a diameter of just under 1/4 inch and is a general purpose cable that can carry about 20 percent higher frequencies and a bit longer attenuation limit than RG58 cable. RG59 cable is suitable for basic analog television antennas in homes and for CCTV on short cable runs. RG59 cable is commonly terminated with F-type connectors.

Fiber Optic Cable

Fiber optic cabling (see Figure 1-8) is certainly an option for installing a home network, but it's not usually a particularly practical one. While fiber optic is extremely fast, it can be difficult to work with, its interface devices are relatively expensive, and copper wire technologies have advanced to the point that they are capable of transmitting multiple CD- or DVD-quality streams simultaneously. Installing fiber optic cabling can help to future-proof a home, but it's not likely it will be connected and used at the time of the installation.

Figure 1-8
A multistrand
fiber optic cable

Fiber optic cable is either single-mode or multimode. Single-mode cable carries a single system, but over very long distances. Multimode fiber optic cable is capable of carrying multiple signals, but over a relatively shorter distance, which is still far beyond the requirements of just about any home network. However, if you or your customer insists on installing fiber optic cabling, the type most commonly used in home installations is multimode.

NOTE Fiber optic cables are terminated with a variety of connectors, depending on the type of cable and the application. See Chapter 2 for more information on fiber optic connectors.

Audio and Video Wire and Cable

If you understand how water flows through a hose, then you essentially understand the physics of how electrical waveforms travel through an audio/video cable. Just like a hose stores and releases water, when an audio signal is transmitted, the audio/video cable stores (voltage) and releases (current) an electrical wave at certain frequencies and amplitudes. The voltage and current transmitted through the cable are generally combined under the term *frequency*. An audio/video signal consists of a collection of high- and low-frequency waves.

Another function of an audio/video cable is its ability to release or pass the audio signal to the next component (amplifier, speaker, or the like) at the right time, without slowing down the signal. A cable with the ability to release the signal at the right time is called in-phase. Not all cables are able to efficiently carry (store and release) audio signals at all frequencies. Virtually every audio cable can carry high frequencies (above 1 kHz) fairly efficiently. However, the ability for a cable to remain in-phase diminishes as the frequencies drop below 450 Hz. When this happens, the lower frequencies are produced out-of-phase, or reproduced later than the higher frequencies.

Balanced Audio Cables

Like a coaxial cable, a balanced audio cable uses both positive and negative carriers, but it also adds a grounding carrier. In an unbalanced cable, the grounding signals are combined on the negative carrier.

Figure 1-9
Samples of
balanced audio
cables

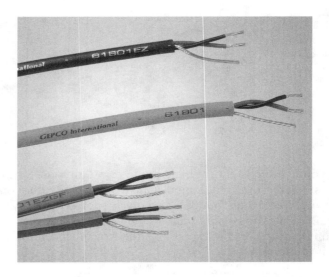

A balanced audio cable is used in high-end or professional microphone, line-level balanced analog audio, extended distance runs, and wiring connected to a patch panel. A balanced audio cable is made up of two twisted-pair insulated wires, commonly copper, and a separate grounding wire or mesh shield (see Figure 1-9).

Parallel Pair Wiring

This type of wiring, which resembles a lamp cord, is made up of two separate conductors (a positive and a negative) that are encased in a single plastic or rubber insulating

Frequency, Amplitude, and Hertz

No, this isn't the name of an audio industry law firm; these are the properties that characterize the parts of an audio signal:

- **Frequency** The number of cycles (waves) for a sound in a second. Frequency translates to the pitch of a sound. Every sound has pitch: a tiny bell has high pitch and a high frequency, and a bass drum has low pitch and a low frequency. Frequency is measured in hertz (Hz).

- **Amplitude** The height of an audio signal, which translates into the volume of each part of the signal.

- **Hertz** The measurement of the number of cycles occurring in an audio wave in one second. One wave, measured from the center of the raise in amplitude to the center of the decline in amplitude is 1 Hz, which is named after Heinrich Hertz, the discoverer of this phenomenon.

Figure 1-10
Parallel pair wire
is commonly used
for speaker wire

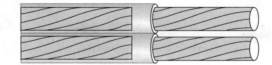

jacket (see Figure 1-10). This type of wiring is inexpensive, but doesn't provide much protection from external interference. Parallel pair wiring is commonly referred to as speaker wire.

Parallel wire is available in a variety of wire gauges, ranging from 8-gauge on the high end to 24-gauge on the low end. However, the gauge that should be used is dependent on a number of factors. A cable with conductors too thin for the signals generated by the amplifier will produce a degraded sound quality with loss in the lower frequencies. In contrast, a cable that is too heavy may be too awkward to work with easily and will definitely cost more.

CROSS-REFERENCE   Chapters 11, 12, and 13 discuss audio and video cabling in detail.

NOTE   Speaker wire and parallel cable are often advertised as "oxygen-free." This means that the cable has no corrosion. As a cable is exposed to the air, it can begin to darken in color, which means it is oxidizing. In fact, if a copper wire is green, it is likely fully oxidized.

Speaker Wire

There is a wide range of speaker wire available that falls into several categories of performance, application, and cost. Typically, 16-gauge stranded twisted-pair wire or 14- to 18-gauge audio cable is used for an average length speaker run, with heavier wiring used for very long runs. The twist in the wire helps reduce the amount of electromagnetic interference (EMI) the wiring picks up.

The following terms are commonly used to describe speaker wire and its characteristics:

- **Cable ratings**   The cable designed for a specific use is rated for that use. For example, a cable designed for installation inside a wall carries a premise wiring rating, which means that a cable complies with the NEC and its fire safety standards. Most speaker cable is not rated for use as premise wiring.

- **Gauge**   The wire gauge selected for a home A/V system should be chosen based on its properties and the distance of the wiring runs. Speakers have low impedance (4 to 8 ohms), which means the resistance in the wiring is key to determining how much of the audio signal will reach the speaker. For example, a 100-foot run of 16-gauge twisted-pair wiring has a round-trip resistance of 0.8 ohms. When this wire is used with a 4-ohm speaker, 17 percent of the signal is lost to the resistance on the wire, which means only 83 percent of the sound signal actually reaches the speaker. The solution to this is the use of heavier wire.

Speaker Ohms	Decibel Loss	Signal Loss	16 AWG Max. Run (feet)	14 AWG Max. Run (feet)
4	0.5	11%	60	100
4	1	21%	130	210
4	2	37%	290	460
4	3	50%	500	790
8	0.5	11%	120	190
8	1	21%	260	410
8	2	37%	580	930
8	3	50%	990	1580

Table 1-7   Speaker Wire Signal Loss

The wire size typically used for home A/V systems is 16 or 14 AWG; both sizes provide good compromises against signal loss, cost, and ease of installation. Plus, the connectors on most audio devices are designed for these wiring sizes.

- **Signal (power) loss**   Table 1-7 lists the maximum cable run distances for 16- and 14-gauge speaker wiring, given the percentage of power lost to the cable due to line resistance. If you know the speaker's impedance and acceptable loss numbers, you should be able to look up the right size wire to use and its maximum run length.

Video Cables

There are a variety of cables that can be used with video systems. The primary types of video cable are

- **Coaxial**   The standard cable used for cable television connections. Coaxial cable can be terminated with either a BNC or an RCA connector (see Chapter 2). Although it is developing other applications, such as transmission of IR signals, coaxial cable is used primarily for antenna and cable inputs and video distribution.

- **Component (also called digital component)**   The newest of the cable and connector types that provides the best picture quality. The video signal is separated into individual red, green, and blue (RGB) color components, which results in better color and clarity. The connection for a 3-channel component cable has three plugs, one for each color component. Component cable is available in 3-, 4-, or 5-channel configurations as well. Figure 1-11 shows a component video cable with four coaxial cable channels.

Figure 1-11
A video component cable with four channels

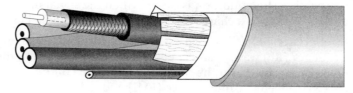

HTI

Figure 1-12
A composite video cable with RCA connectors

Photo courtesy of Canare Corporation of America.

- **Composite**   A standard video signal format that contains the color, brightness, and synchronization information. Virtually all VCRs and other legacy video equipment have a composite video input or output. Composite video cables are a single cable carrying only the video signal component. Composite A/V cables that also carry the right and left channels of the audio are terminated with three connectors that are typically color coded with a yellow jack for the video, a white jack for left-side audio, and a red jack for right-side audio. The jack and plug used for composite video are RCA connectors, F-type connectors, or BNC coaxial connectors. Figure 1-12 shows a terminated composite video cable.

Wire and Cable Characteristics

All wire and cable have performance properties and characteristics that limit the use of a particular wire or cable in a given situation. The primary performance properties of metallic (meaning copper typically) wire are as follows:

- **Attenuation**   As an electrical signal moves through a wire, it eventually reaches a point where it begins to lose its strength—the attenuation point. Beyond this point, the signal may become distorted or lost altogether. Every cable type is rated with an attenuation distance, which indicates its maximum run or segment length.

- **Cancellation**   When two wires are not properly insulated or are placed too closely together, the signal in each wire can be significantly impacted (cancelled) by the signal in the other wire. This is also referred to as phase cancellation.

- **Crosstalk** This condition is caused when the signal in one conductor, which is also referred to as a channel, leaks into another channel and distorts its signal.

- **Interference** Electrical signals, in the form of electromagnetic (EM) or radio frequency (RF) waves, can penetrate a cable and distort or disrupt the signals being transmitted over the cable. The two most common types of interference are electromagnetic interference (EMI) and radio frequency interference (RFI). EMI is caused by strong electromagnetic fields emanating from nearby electrical devices, such as electrical motors, magnetic ballasts, and the like. RFI is caused by radio frequency electromagnetic waves, like radio and TV signals, that travel through the air and are picked up by the conductors or shielding of a cable.

- **Inductance** Signals carried on a wire typically have a varying current that produces a varying magnetic field. This field, if strong enough, can create additional current in the same cable or a nearby cable. In a twisted-pair cable, the wires in each wire pair are twisted around each other to reduce electromagnetic induction between the wires.

Control Wiring

There are many different types of control systems in an automated home: lighting control, climate control, security, and perhaps even water control (as in controlling landscape sprinklers).

The wiring that is commonly used to interconnect a control system's elements, generally 22-gauge wiring or Cat 3 UTP cable, is readily available, inexpensive, and easily installed, especially in a new construction situation. Installing new control system wiring in an existing house can be more difficult, but there are alternatives to new wiring in these situations, such as power line carrier (PLC) and phone line systems, discussed in Part VII of this book.

Bundled Cable

Structured wiring involves the installation of wire homeruns to each room, zone, or area of a home. There are two ways this can be accomplished: pulling each individual cable required separately or pulling in a cable bundle that includes all of the cabling runs required to support the needs of the room, zone, or area.

Using a structured cable bundle eliminates the guesswork of pulling individual cable runs to areas of the home in an attempt to provide future capability to the home. A cable bundle pulled throughout a home provides additional capability and expandability to all areas of a home and can save on installation time.

Some cable bundles are enclosed inside a plastic outer sheathing to facilitate pulling the cable through the walls. Others connect the wires together in a zip wire form and others wrap the bundle with strands of plastic ribbons that can be easily removed to terminate the cables in the bundle at the distribution panel or the room outlets. Figure 1-13 illustrates some of the different cable bundle enclosures available.

Figure 1-13
Examples of
bundled cable
enclosures

Photo courtesy of Smarthome, Inc.

2+2 Bundled Cabling

A standard cable bundle is the 2+2 cable that includes two runs of UTP Cat 5e cable and two runs of RG6 coaxial cable. Since these four cable runs typically satisfy the distributed system needs of most homes, it is a very popular cable bundle for structured wiring.

2+2+2 Bundled Cabling

Another popular cable bundle, called 2+2+2, adds two runs of fiber optic cable to the 2+2 bundle to provide for even more current capability and future proofing to a home. The two fiber optic cables are multimode strands that can be used for a wide range of current and certainly future applications.

Control Wire Bundles

There are several specialized structured wiring cable bundles, each designed for a specific purpose. Some are variations of the 2+2 bundle with an additional run or UTP or coaxial cable included. However, one special purpose cable bundle is the control wire bundle.

Control wire bundles typically include a single run each of RG59 or RG6 coaxial cable and Cat 5e cable and two runs of 18-gauge stranded wire, which are used to cable keypads, room controls, and intercoms with video and for supplying power.

Subsystem	Usage	AWG	Conductors	Conductor Type	Shielded?	Cable Color
Audio	LV audio	22	4	Stranded	Shielded	Yellow
	Speakers, security siren	14	2	Stranded	None	Green
	Speakers	16	4	Stranded	None	Blue
Baseband video	Composite video (cameras)	RG6/RG59	1	Solid	Shielded	Black/white
Communications	Telephone and data	25 (Cat 5e)	8	Solid	None	Blue
Fire detection	Smoke and heat detectors	18	4	Solid	None	Red
IR control	IR, LV wiring	22	4	Stranded	None	Pink
Security	Door and window contacts	22	2	Stranded	None	Gray
	Motion sensor, glass break	22	4	Stranded	None	Gray
	Keypads	22	4	Stranded	None	Gray
	Advanced keypad with voice pickup and playback	18	2	Stranded	Shielded	Pink
	Driveway probe	18	3	Stranded	Direct burial	Black
Video	Video signal	RG6	1	Shielded solid	Shielded	Black/white

Table 1-8   Recommended Structured Wiring Cable Applications

Common Home Automation Wire Types

For reference purposes, Table 1-8 lists some industry designations for common audio and video cable and wire types. There are no industry standards for the colors of the individual wires or the outer sheathing of structured wiring cables. Category UTP wiring (such as Cat 5e) has the same eight wire colors in four matched pairs, but the outer covering of other types of wire is available in a rainbow of colors. For best results, use one color wire or cable for a particular purpose throughout a home and a different color for each specific application. This makes installation and troubleshooting a lot easier. Table 1-8 also includes guidelines on which wiring type is recommended for particular subsystems, including a suggested outer jacket color.

Test the Wiring

After what typically seems like miles of cable and wiring have been pulled into the walls, under the floor, or above the ceiling; the connectors are attached; and the wall plates are mounted, a second round of testing should be performed. Yes, a second round. The first round of continuity and attenuation testing is done immediately after each cable segment is pulled into place. After all of the cabling and wiring has been installed, it's time to perform a full set of tests.

Even if you are absolutely sure of the quality of your work in attaching the connectors to the cable or wire and the terminations made at the punch down block, you should always test the cable runs again at this point in the process. This is especially true in new construction where a cable can be "nailed" or "screwed" when the drywall is attached to the wall studs.

The testing process includes two steps: a visual inspection and a "buzz-out" of the wire. Of course, a visual inspection must be done either before new walls are completed or from down in the basement or crawl space or up in the attic. You are looking for the obvious: nails or screws piercing the cable or cuts, gashes, bends, kinks, and breaks in the cable.

A buzz-out test of the cabling involves the use of a cable tester, which sends an electrical signal through the cable. Some testers require connectors to work; others use a vibrating electrical noise that is placed on the wire by a transmitting device and, hopefully, detected by a receiving device. This is generally a two-person job, but there are testers available into which you can connect one end of the cable and then use the receiving device at the other end to identify the cable and its continuity. Of course, you labeled all of the cables and documented them on a wire chart during installation, so you shouldn't need to "find" each cable end as you test, right? Completely test all wiring before beginning the fix-it process, if needed.

For RG6 coaxial cabling, the testing should include tests for shorts, cable length, continuity, and cable termination. For Cat 5e or Cat 6 cables, testers are available that will verify compliance of your wiring runs and terminations to these standards.

 CROSS-REFERENCE   Chapter 3 covers cable installation and testing in more detail.

Chapter Review

When installing wire and cable in a home, you must be aware of the characteristics and specifications of the cable or wire in use. The most common types of electrical wiring used for home construction today are modern nonmetallic (NM), underground feeder (UF), and zip wire. Some older wire types you may encounter in a home are flexible armored cable, metal conduit, early NM, and knob and tube.

The wire gauge used in a home depends on the number of amperes on a particular circuit. Remember that a smaller gauge means a bigger and less flexible wire. Heavier gauge wire should be used to avoid voltage drops and to overcome heat problems.

Twisted-pair (TP) wiring is by far the most popularly installed media for networking in just about any type of network for many reasons, including that it is inexpensive, easy to handle, and readily available. TP wire, Cat 5, is the de facto standard for both Ethernet and Token Ring networks.

UTP cable carries a variety of rating codes, which are assigned by the product performance and safety authorities and testing laboratories. The primary rating codes for UTP cable are defined by the NEC (National Electric Code), published by the National Fire Protection Association, as CM, CMP, or CMR. Twisted-pair cable is available as shielded twisted pair (STP) and unshielded twisted pair (UTP).

Coaxial cable is constructed of a single inner core wire conductor that is encased in a layer of dielectric insulation, which is then wrapped by a wire mesh outer conductor and shield. A plastic sheathing covers the cable. Coaxial cable is single-ended cable with a single signal path and a single return path. RG6 is the most common coaxial cable installed in homes.

When an audio signal is transmitted, A/V cable stores (voltage) and releases (current) an electrical wave at certain frequencies and amplitudes and is generally combined under the term frequency. An audio/video signal consists of a collection of high- and low-frequency waves. An audio/video releases or passes an audio signal to the next component without slowing down the signal. A cable with the ability to release the signal at the right time is called in-phase.

A balanced audio cable uses both positive and negative carriers with a grounding carrier added. In an unbalanced cable, the grounding signals are combined onto the negative carrier.

Parallel or speaker wire is available in a variety of wire gauges, ranging from 8-gauge on the high end to 24-gauge on the low end.

The primary performance properties of metallic wire are attenuation, cancellation, crosstalk, interference, and inductance.

There are a variety of cables that can be used with video systems. The primary types of video cable are coaxial, component, and composite. Typically, 16-gauge stranded twisted-pair wire or 14- to 18-gauge audio cable is used for an average length speaker run.

Structured wiring involves the installation of wire homeruns to each room, zone, or area of a home. Structured wiring can be installed in two ways: pulling each individual cable separately or pulling a cable bundle. A 2+2 cable includes two runs of UTP Cat 5e cable and two runs of RG6 coaxial cable. The 2+2+2 cable adds two runs of fiber optic cable to 2+2 bundle.

Control wire bundles typically include a single run each of RG59 coaxial cable and Cat 5e cable and two runs of 18-gauge stranded wire, which are used to cable keypads, room controls, and intercoms with video and for supplying power.

Questions

1. Which of the following is not a home circuit type?

    A. Communication circuits

    B. Signal circuits

    C. Wireless communication circuits

    D. Power-limited circuits

2. What is the term that describes the metallic core of a wire?

    A. Armor

    B. Conductor

    C. Insulator

    D. Jacket

3. What is the general name used for common household electric cable?

    A. Modern NM/Romex

    B. NMC

    C. UF

    D. Zip wire

4. According to Table 1-2, what wire gauge should be used for a circuit with 30 amperes?

    A. 20 AWG

    B. 18 AWG

    C. 14 AWG

    D. 10 AWG

5. When an audio cable is able to release all audio frequencies without adding delay, the cable is said to be

    A. Out-of-phase

    B. In-sync

    C. In-phase

    D. Synchronous

6. Which cable type has a single inner core wire conductor and a wire mesh outer conductor?

    A. UTP

    B. STP

    C. Coaxial

    D. 16g-4

7. Which type of audio/video cable includes carriers for both positive and negative signals, but also includes a grounding carrier as well?

    A. Coaxial

    B. Balanced

    C. UTP

    D. Parallel pair

8. Which cable type resembles a lamp cord?

    A. Coaxial

    B. Balanced

    C. UTP

    D. Parallel pair

9. What is the cable property that states the distance at which the signal traveling on a cable begins to weaken?

   A. Attenuation

   B. Cancellation

   C. Crosstalk

   D. Interference

10. What is the common used term that describes a bundled cable with two runs of UTP and two runs of coaxial cable?

   A. UC cable

   B. Structured bundle

   C. 2+2

   D. 2+2+2

Answers

1. **C.** Because they are wireless communication circuits, these systems are not part of a house's wiring structure.

2. **B.** A conductor has the ability to store and release an electrical current.

3. **A.** Modern nonmetallic (NM) or Romex cable is the currently accepted standard for general household electrical wiring.

4. **D.** 10 AWG wire is rated for a 30-amp, 240-volt system.

5. **C.** The opposite, out-of-phase, is true when a cable releases lower frequencies later than its higher frequencies.

6. **C.** Both the inner core (positive) and the outer conductor (negative) carry signals in a coaxial cable.

7. **B.** The balance comes from having conductors for both positive and negative signals and a separate conductor for grounding, but on other cables may be combined onto the negative carrier.

8. **D.** Parallel pair cable looks very much like a lamp cord and is also referred to as rip cable for the ease with which the two conductors can be separated.

9. **A.** Attenuation can be overcome with shorter cable runs or a signal extender, such as a repeater.

10. **C.** 2+2 cable combines two runs of UTP and two runs of coaxial cable into a single cable bundle that is easier to install and provides for future expansion of the home system.

Connector Types and Uses

- Structured wiring connectors
- Specialized connectors
- Cable preparation and connector installation

Connectors are a major part of home technology integration and home automation. Properly installing the right connector on the right cable is very important to the success of a home's system. Connectors (and their receptacles) create the interfaces that allow electrical signals to flow over the cables between devices. Without them there would be no data, sound, images, or control on the network.

In the structured wiring environment, not that many different types of cable and wiring are used. Typically, the majority of the cabling is twisted-pair (TP) and coaxial, with some quad wire and speaker wire used as required. As a result, the number and types of connectors used is also fairly limited. However, in different applications, you have connector choices based on the type of connection or interface a particular system may require.

This chapter focuses on the connectors commonly used with the cable and wire used in a structured wiring system and the processes used for their installation.

Connector Terminology

There is a definite set of terms used to specify, describe, and name connectors. Some of these terms represent the name of the standards authority that defined a certain connector; others are shorthand or abbreviations for technical terms; and still others are names that describe the shape, use, or application of a connector or are names that have just caught on.

Here is a list of terms common to just about all connectors that describes parts and components of connectors in general:

- **Backboard**   A plywood panel mounted on the wall of a telecom or distribution where a cross-connect device is mounted.

- **Connector**   A device that allows electrical signals to flow from one wire or cable to another.

Figure 2-1

Examples of female (right) and male (left) DB-9 connectors

- **DB-*n* connector**   Also called D-shell connector; this type of connector facilitates parallel signal transfers. The housing is D-shaped and contains either a male or female plug. The *n* in DB-*n* represents the number of pins or contacts (male or female) in the connector. For example, a DB-9 connector has nine pins or contacts and a DB-25 has 25 pins or contacts. Figure 2-1 shows an example of a data bus (DB) connector.

- **Female**   A type of connector plug that has pin receptacles in its housing (see Figure 2-2).

- **Male**   A type of connector plug that has one or more pins extending from its housing (see Figure 2-2).

- **Mass termination**   Although gruesome sounding, this means that all of the wires in a cable are terminated into a connector in a single operation.

- **Molded cable**   A cable assembly that has molded connectors terminating one or both of its ends. Figures 2-2 and 2-3 show molded cables.

Figure 2-2

Examples of connectors with male (right) and female (left) contacts.

Photo courtesy of Canare Corporation of America.

Figure 2-3   An example of a molded cable

- **Plug**   A male connector housing with either male or female contacts.
- **Receptacle**   A female connector housing with either male or female contacts.
- **Strain relief**   A molded sleeve or a clamping device that is either incorporated into the connector body or can be attached during termination. This device provides mechanical support to ensure the cable and wires are not pulled out of the connector and the contacts are not broken during installation, handling, or from the weight of the cable itself (see Figure 2-4).

Figure 2-4
The strain relief
on a molded
audio cable

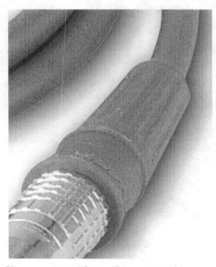

Photo courtesy of Canare Corporation of America.

CROSS-REFERENCE The glossary in Appendix B of this book contains additional connector, cable, and wiring terms, and their meanings.

Power Connectors

When installing some systems in a home technology project, it may be necessary to connect to the AC power system. As a part of this activity, you may need to use one or more power connectors.

The basic types of power connectors are

- **Lug** Also called a compression lug, this connector is attached to the end of a power cable. When used with stranded wire, a lug is crimped onto the wire; when used with solid core wire, the lug should be soldered to the wire. Lugs come in a variety of types: single-hole or dual-hole flat connectors, ring connectors, forked connectors, and spade connectors. Figure 2-5 shows a selection of a variety of lug connectors. Lugs have different ratings for use with different wire sizes and some require specialized crimping tools.

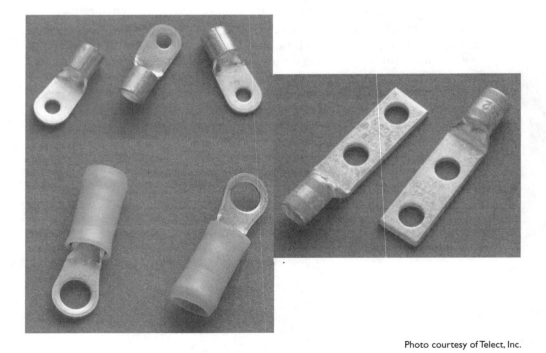

Photo courtesy of Telect, Inc.

Figure 2-5 Single-hole and dual-hole lug connectors

Figure 2-6
A standard
three-contact U.S.
electrical plug

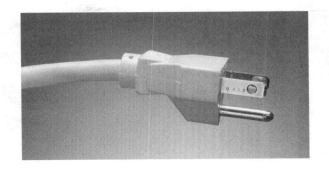

- **Plug**   As shown in Figure 2-6, the standard three-contact electrical plug is commonly attached to the power cord of virtually all electrical appliances, control systems, and power supplies in North America. Lamps and other low-voltage devices use only a two-contact plug. There are several types of electrical plugs used in the United States, with different plugs used for different applications. Around the world, electrical plug patterns, shapes, and sizes vary by country and region (see the next section, "Electrical Plugs").

- **Receptacle**   A device with female contacts that makes an electrical contact with an inserted plug.

- **Terminal strip**   Not to be confused with a plug strip, a terminal strip is used to make multiple connections by either soldering a wire to a contact, connecting with a lug style connector, or connecting with a screw terminal. Figure 2-7 shows an example of a solder terminal strip. Terminal strips are used in a variety of systems, including AC and DC power and telecom cabling.

Figure 2-7
A terminal
strip on which
connecting wires
are anchored
with set screws

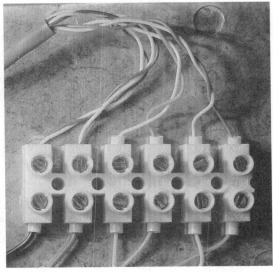

Photo courtesy of Molex, Inc.

Figure 2-8
A sampling of the different electrical plugs used around the world

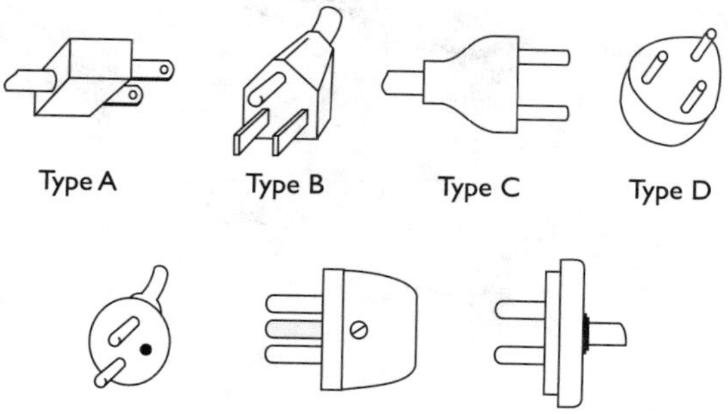

Type A Type B Type C Type D

Type E Type K Type I

Electrical Plugs

As I discussed in the preceding section, electrical plugs vary from country to country, depending on the electrical system in use. Figure 2-8 illustrates some of the various types of plugs used throughout the world. In the United States and Canada, Type A and B plugs are used. Table 2-1 lists the power characteristics and electrical plugs used in a sample of other countries.

Country	Voltage	Frequency	Plug Type
Australia	230V	50 Hz	I
China	220V	50 Hz	A and I
Colombia	110V	60 Hz	A and B
Czech Republic	230V	50 Hz	E
Denmark	220V	50 Hz	C and K
Egypt	220V	50 Hz	C
France	230V	50 Hz	E
Germany	230V	50 Hz	C
India	240V	50 Hz	C and D
Ireland	230V	50 Hz	E
Japan	100V	50/60 Hz	A and B
Mexico	127V	60 Hz	A
Russian Federation	220V	50 Hz	C
Sweden	220V	50 Hz	C

Table 2-1 Electrical Characteristics and Electrical Plugs in Use Around the World

Coaxial Cable Connectors

A wide variety of coaxial cables are available, but in a structured wiring system, the primary coaxial cable types used are RG6 and RG59 ("RG" stands for Radio Guide).

F-Type Connectors

The F-type connector is the most commonly used connector for home systems that apply coaxial cabling. F-type connectors are available as either a screw-on or a crimp-on type connector.

F-Type Twist-On Connectors

To terminate a coaxial cable with a crimp-on F-type connector (see Figure 2-9), use the following steps:

1. Use a knife to cut around the plastic outer layer about 1 inch (25 millimeters) from the end of the cable. Take care not to cut the mesh or braided copper shielding under the outer jacket of the cable. Remove the cutaway outer covering and separate wires of the braided shielding so that they can be twisted together to create a "pigtail."

2. After removing the braided shielding, a metal foil layer should be exposed. Cut off the exposed portion of the foil shielding.

3. Use a knife to cut off the white dielectric material, leaving about 1/8 inch (3 mm) of the dielectric material extending out onto the center core to serve as an insulator that prevents the metallic braided pigtail from making contact with the center conductor. Be careful not to cut into or through the center conductor wire.

4. Pull the shielding pigtail back over the uncut portion of the cable's outer jacket and twist or screw the F-type connector plug over the cable end as far as it can go. The sleeve of the connector should also cover a portion of the pigtail, trapping it against the outside of the cable. Cut off any exposed portion of the pigtail.

5. Use wire cutters to cut the end of the exposed center conductor wire at a 45-degree angle, leaving about 1/8 inch (3 mm) extending beyond the end of the F-type jack body. Be careful when handling the terminated cable and jack; the end of the center wire should be a very sharp point.

Figure 2-9
An F-type twist-on connector for coaxial cabling

NOTE If the F-type connector is to be used outside the home, such as to an antenna or satellite dish, it must be sealed to prevent water from getting inside the cable or connector body. The recommended way to seal the cable against water seepage is to wrap the connector sleeve and a portion of the cable with waterproofing or self-amalgamating tape.

F-Type Crimp-On Connectors

Some technicians believe that a crimp-on style F-type connector (see Figure 2-10) provides a tighter and more secure connection. To terminate a coaxial cable with a crimp-on F-type connector, follow these steps:

1. Use a knife to cut away about 3/8 inch (9.5 mm) of the cable's outer covering, exposing the braided metal shielding. Be careful not to cut the braided shielding.

2. Fold the braided shielding back over the outer jacket of the cable.

3. Cut away the metal foil shielding and cut the white dielectric material so that only 1/4 inch (6.3 mm) of the dielectric material is exposed (and 1/8 inch of the center conductor wire is exposed). Take care not to nick, cut, or ding the center conductor wire when cutting the dielectric material. Clean away any dielectric material dust or fuzz that may be on the center wire.

4. Slide the crimp ring over the folded back, braided metal shielding and over the cable's outer jacket.

5. Check the exposed edge of the foil shielding that was cut away earlier and ensure that it is lying flat against the dielectric material under the edge of the outer jacket. If any burrs or flags are sticking up, they need to be smoothed down by twisting them flat against the dielectric material.

6. Push the connector sleeve (mandrel) back under the uncut portion of the cable so that the mandrel is placed between the braided shielding and the foil shielding inside the uncut cable.

7. Slide the crimp ring towards the stripped end of the cable so that it fits over the mandrel inside the cable.

8. Use a coaxial crimping tool to secure the connector to the cable.

Coaxial Cable Strippers and Crimpers

When working with coaxial cable, or any cable or wire for that matter, it's best to use tools specifically designed for use with that particular cable type. Several specialized

Figure 2-10
An F-type crimp-on connector for coaxial cabling

Figure 2-11
A handheld
coaxial cable
stripper

Photo courtesy of Paladin Tools, Inc.

tools are available for stripping and terminating coaxial cable. However, not every tool is designed to work with every type of coaxial cable, so you need to be sure that your tools are specifically designed for RG58, RG59, or RG6, depending on which coaxial cable you are installing.

Strippers   Coaxial cable strippers are designed to cut through the outer jacket and dielectric layers of a cable, leaving the proper amount of conductor wire for installing any of the various coaxial cable connectors. Figures 2-11 and 2-12 show the two most common types of coaxial cable strippers. Remember that cable strippers are specified to a certain cable type, so be sure you match the tool to the cable and the task.

Figure 2-12
A pliers-type
coaxial cable
stripper

Photo courtesy of Harris Corp.

Figure 2-13
A coaxial cable
F-type crimping
tool

Photo courtesy of Graber Bender.

Coaxial Cable Crimpers   Crimpers are used to clamp a metal connector to a cable. Coaxial cable crimp-on connectors require the use of a crimper tool, but not just any crimper. Crimpers are typically designed to work with a specific type of cable and, in many cases, a special type of connector. Typically, when you are working with coaxial cabling in a home system, the crimper you use is a specialized coaxial cable F-type connector crimper like the one shown in Figure 2-13.

Coaxial Cable Termination Kits   Several cable and connector vendors have prepared connector kits for use with coaxial cable. A typical kit includes all of the pieces and tools commonly needed to terminate coaxial cable in a home system, including a number of professional grade F-type plugs, a coaxial cable stripping tool, an F-type connector crimping tool, and a small tone testing device. In most cases, the tools are specialized for either RG59 or RG6 cable.

BNC Connector

Another type of coaxial connector that could be used in a residential system on RG58 and RG6 cable in data networking and some audio/visual applications is the Bayonet Neill Concellman (BNC) connector. The male portion (plug) of a BNC connector has a bayonet-like shell with two small pins that fit into spiral slots located on the female portion (receptacle) of the connector. The plug is inserted into the receptacle and twisted into a locked position.

There are two styles of BNC connectors: a BNC-T connector and a BNC barrel connector. The BNC-T connector is commonly used for Ethernet data networks to interconnect a computer's network adapter to the coaxial cable. However, a BNC barrel connector can also be used with some network adapters. When used with video and community antenna television (CATV, which is better known as cable TV) systems, the barrel style connector is the most common. Figure 2-14 shows a BNC-T connector and Figure 2-15 shows a barrel-style BNC connector.

Figure 2-14
A BNC-T
connector
assembly

Figure 2-15
A BNC barrel
connector

Twisted-Pair Cable Connectors

Depending on the application, Category (Cat) 3, 5, 5e, 6, or higher twisted-pair cable use one of the following modular registered jack (RJ) connectors:

- **RJ-11**   This is the standard two- or four-conductor telephone connector used to connect telephone handsets to telephone outlets. Figure 2-16 shows an RJ-11 plug.

- **RJ-31x**   This is the connection type used to interface a security system into a home's telephone system. Figure 2-17 shows an RJ-31x modular jack.

- **RJ-45**   This is the standard twisted-pair connector used for data networking. Figure 2-18 shows an RJ-45 connector.

Figure 2-16
An RJ-11 plug

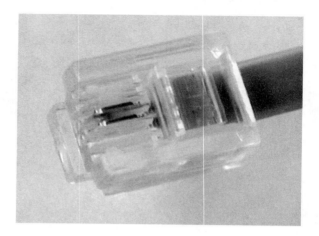

Figure 2-17
An RJ-31x
modular jack

Figure 2-18
An RJ-45 plug

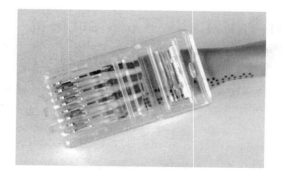

NOTE RJ connectors are also called keystone connectors because of the shape of their plugs and jacks.

The jack and plug of a registered jack conforms to the standards specified in the Universal Service Order Code (USOC), published by the U.S. Federal Communications Commission (FCC). The USOC specifies the standard telephone and data communications jacks and plugs used in the U.S. Table 2-2 lists the most common USOC jacks. Although the standard refers mostly to jacks, it also includes the plugs that fit the jacks.

NOTE The registered jacks listed in Table 2-2 commonly include a suffix of C, W, or X. The C refers to desk sets; the W refers to wall sets; and the X refers to special-purpose jacks. This suffix refers to the type of connection and equipment for which each jack is most commonly used.

Wiring RJ-11 Jacks and Plugs

To attach an RJ-11 jack or plug to a run of twisted-pair wiring, the first thing you must know is how many lines the jack will be supporting. If the jack and plug are being used to connect a single telephone line, then only two conductors are needed to make the connection; however, it is always best to connect four or more conductors to provide for expansion of the telephone system in the future. As listed in Table 2-2, two-line connections use four conductors (which is technically an RJ-14 configuration) and three-line connections use six conductors (RJ-25).

Registered Jack	Contacts	Conductors Used	Usage
RJ-11	6	2	Single-line telephone
RJ-12	6	4	Single-line telephone on key system
RJ-13	6	6	Single-line telephone on key system
RJ-14	6	4	Two-line telephones
RJ-15	3	3	Single-line weatherproof telephone connections
RJ-17	6	2	Medical equipment
RJ-21x	50	50	Amphenol connector for 25-pair 66-style punch-down blocks
RJ-22	4	4	Telephone handset connector
RJ-25	6	6	Three-line telephones
RJ-31x	8	4 or 6	Security system to telephone interface
RJ-45	8	4 or 8	Data networking connector
RJ-48	8	4 or 8	T-1 networking connections
RJ-61x	8	8	Eight-conductor version of RJ-45

Table 2-2 Common USOC Registered Jacks

Figure 2-19
The wiring
diagram for an
RJ-11 connector

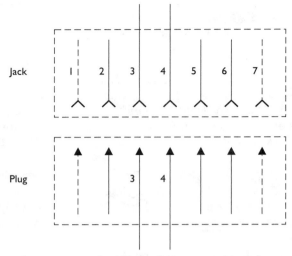

The reason each line requires two conductors is that two contacts are required for telephone communications. These two lines, which are referred to as *tip* and *ring* are the modern-day equivalents of the plugs used by switchboard operators years ago. When the operator inserted the plug into the jack to complete a circuit between an incoming call and a telephone in her office or building, the tip of the plug completed one loop and the metal ring around the shaft of the plug completed the other, linking the incoming circuit to a particular line and handset.

To terminate twisted-pair wire in an RJ-11 configuration, one wire pair (typically the blue and white-blue) is connected to the center two contacts (pins) 3 and 4 of the jack and plug, as illustrated in Figure 2-19.

Most RJ-11 jacks and plugs use a 66-type punch-down receptacle, which is also called an insulation displacement connector (IDC). Each of a cable's wires is inserted using a punch-down or impact tool fitted with a 66-type blade (see Figure 2-20). The punch-down

Figure 2-20
A punch-down
(impact) tool is
used to install
wire in an IDC.

tool pushes an individual wire into an IDC slot and, in the process, pierces the wire's insulation and places the core wire in contact with the IDC's tines.

> **NOTE** The 66-type punch-down blade is used for telephone and other voice connections. If data networking connections use an IDC-type connector, they use a 110-type punch-down blade. Some manufacturers now make a combination 66/110 blade.

RJ-11 jacks and plugs can also be attached to twisted-pair wiring using a crimper with the proper attachments. After the appropriate wires are placed into the slots corresponding to the proper pins on the jack or plug, the crimper is used to cinch clasping material on the connector to hold the wire in place. Figure 2-21 shows a twisted-pair wiring crimping tool.

Wiring RJ-31x Jacks and Plugs

An RJ-31x jack can be connected to one of the outside phone lines of a home and optionally to the home's inside phone lines. It seizes an outgoing phone line, alerting the monitoring station when there is a security event. If you wish to allow the security system to seize more than one line to prevent interruptions, separate RJ-31x jacks can be connected to each of the inside phone lines.

Photo courtesy of Tecra Tools, Inc.

Figure 2-21   A crimping tool is used to attach RJ jacks and plugs to a cable.

Wire	Source	Inside Phone Line #1	Inside Phone Line #1	Outside Phone Line #2	Outside Phone Line #2
White (TP)	Jack	Tip			
Blue (TP)	Jack	Ring			
White-Blue (TP)	Internal wiring		Tip		
Blue (TP)	Internal wiring		Ring		
Red (Quad)	Telco central office (CO)			Tip	
Green (Quad)	CO			Ring	
Red (Quad)	Jack				Tip
Green (Quad)	Jack				Ring

Table 2-3   RJ-31x Wire Connections

If the RJ-31x is only being connected to the outside lines, then only two of its conductors need be connected. However, if one inside line is to be made available for line seizure by the security system, two additional conductors are connected for that line. If more than one inside line is to be connected to the security system, multiple RJ-31x jacks are required.

RJ-31x jacks have a small 66-type punch-down block inside the housing of the jack. Punch-down blocks make it easy to connect inside lines to outside lines. Assuming an RJ-31x jack has eight inside IDCs and eight outside IDCs in the punch-down block, Table 2-3 lists the configuration of the punch-down to connect the jack to the telephone lines, and Figure 2-22 illustrates this connection.

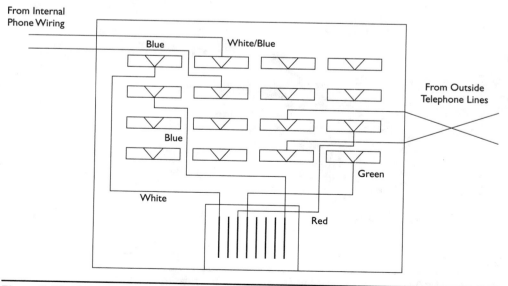

Figure 2-22   A wiring diagram for a single telephone line in an RJ-31x jack

Figure 2-23
The EIA/
TIA 568A
specification
for an RJ-45
connector

TIA/EIA 568A Wiring

1	White and Green
2	Green
3	White and Orange
4	Blue
5	White and Blue
6	Orange
7	White and Brown
8	Brown

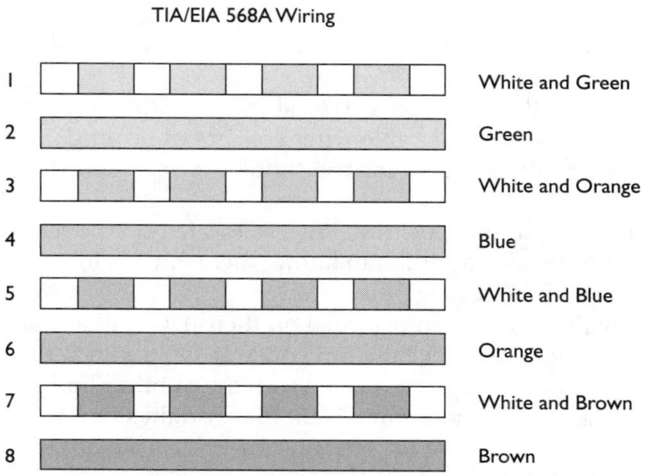

Wiring RJ-45 Jacks and Plugs

The RJ-45 jacks and plugs are the standards for terminating twisted-pair cable used for data networks. However, these connectors are more commonly known by the networking standards (EIA/TIA 568A and 568B) that are used to configure the jack and plug connections. While RJ-45 describes the USOC jack and plug used to make the connections in a data network, other standards are used to describe the actual wiring of the jack and plug.

Twisted-pair Wire Color

In a standard four-pair unshielded twisted-pair (UTP) cable (Cat 5, Cat 5e, Cat 6, and Cat 7), each pair of wires shares a base color. As shown in Figures 2-23 and 2-24, the base colors are orange, blue, green, and brown. One of the wires in each pair has a solid color jacket and one has a jacket with a color strip alternating with a white strip.

Figure 2-24
The EIA/TIA
568B specification
for an RJ-45
connector

TIA/EIA 568B Wiring

1	White and Orange
2	Orange
3	White and Green
4	Blue
5	White and Blue
6	Green
7	White and Brown
8	Brown

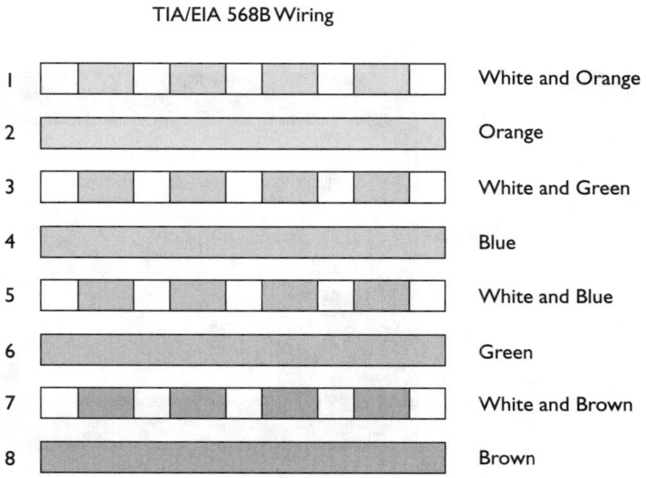

The color coding on the wires provides you with end-to-end consistency when you are terminating a cable with connectors. If the wires were all one color, it would be easy to get your wires crossed.

Installing an RJ-45 plug on a UTP cable is a matter of orientation and color. Orienting the plug to receive the cable wires consists of turning the plug so that the locking tab, or what the Telco people call the "hook," is on the bottom and the open end of the connector is towards you.

With the plug in this position, Pin 1 is located on the left side and Pin 8 is located on the right side. It's important to know where Pin 1 is located so that the correct wires are inserted into the correct pins.

Most quality jacks are color-coded on their IDC contacts or if the jack is a crimp-on type, on a bar located above the pin contacts. On a punch-down block, looking at the jack from the front, Pin 1 is indicated with the number 1 and on a crimp-style jack, Pin 1 is on the far-left side, and Pin 8 is on the far-right side.

Twisted-pair Wiring Standards

The two wiring standards used to define how twisted-pair cable is attached to an RJ-45 jack or plug are Electronics Industry Association/Telecommunications Industry Association (EIA/TIA) 568A and 568B.

The primary difference between these two cable standards is the sequence and placement of the green and orange wire pairs on the plug or receptacle. Actually, for a computer network installation, there is no difference in performance between the two standards because the color of a wire's jacket has no bearing on the signal being transmitted. However, if the cable is intended to carry both data and voice (telephone) traffic, the 568A standard (Figure 2-25) is backward compatible with the older USOC telephone standards; EIA/TIA 568B (Figure 2-26) doesn't support voice signals.

Figure 2-25
The EIA/TIA 568A cable termination standard for twisted-pair cable also supports voice signals.

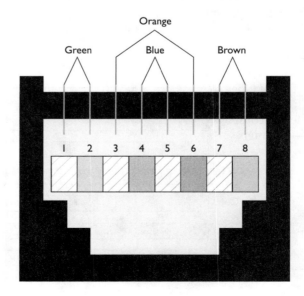

Figure 2-26
The EIA/TIA 568B cable termination standard for twisted-pair cable

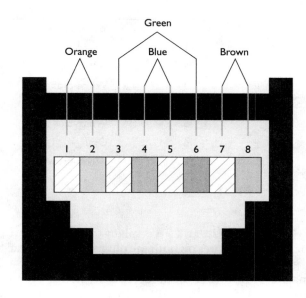

NOTE Although 568B has been the most commonly used of the two 568 standards, especially in commercial installations in the United States, most technical and trade organizations generally agree that all future installations should use the 568A configuration to avoid problems with integrated voice and data systems in the future.

Twisted-pair EIA/TIA 568 Pinouts

When you install an RJ-45 jack or plug on the end of a UTP cable, it is very important that you match the correct pin to the correct wire color. However, beyond the differences between 568A and 568B, there are also variations in the pinout (which pin is connected to which wire) patterns used for the different types of connections made between different types of hardware. The pattern you use depends on the requirements of the equipment to which the cable is to be attached. Table 2-4 lists the types of wiring patterns used in common network situations.

The pinout patterns listed in Table 2-4 are discussed in the following sections.

Table 2-4
Pinout Patterns for Different Connection Types

Connection Type	Pattern
Computer-to-hub/hub-to-computer	Straight-through
Computer-to-computer	Cross-connect (crossover)
Computer-to-Internet gateway	Cross-connect (crossover)

Table 2-5

The Pinout for a
Straight-Through
EIA/TIA 568A
Connection

Pin	Wire Color
I	White-green
2	Green
3	White-orange
4	Blue
5	White-blue
6	Orange
7	White-brown
8	Brown

Straight-Through Pinout A straight-through pinout on an RJ-45 connector matches the same color wires on both the plug and the receptacle. In other words, the orange, blue, green, and brown wires on the plug match up with and connect to the orange, blue, green, and brown wires on the receptacle. Tables 2-5 and 2-6 list the pinouts for straight-through EIA/TIA 568A and EIA/TIA 568B connections, respectively. Figures 2-25 and 2-26 showed these two configurations.

Cross-Connect/Crossover Pinout Cross-connect connector configuration is used when the cable is installed between a computer (actually, the computer's network adapter) and a network hub. The 568A and 568B crossover patterns reverse two of the wire pairs to connect the transmit pins at one end of the cable to the receive pins at the other end. Tables 2-7 and 2-8 list the pinouts for the jacks and plugs at each end of a cross-connect or crossover connection for EIA/TIA 568A and 568B, respectively, and Figures 2-27 and 2-28 illustrate these wiring patterns.

Table 2-6

The Pinout for a
Straight-Through
EIA/TIA 568B
Connection

Pin	Wire Color
I	White-orange
2	Orange
3	White-green
4	Blue
5	White-blue
6	Green
7	White-brown
8	Brown

Table 2-7
The Pinout
for an EIA/TIA
568A Crossover
Connection

Connector A Pin	Wire Color	Connector B Pin
1	White-green	3
2	Green	6
3	White-orange	1
4	Blue	7
5	White-blue	8
6	Orange	2
7	White-brown	4
8	Brown	5

Table 2-8
The Pinout
for an EIA/TIA
568B Crossover
Connection

Connector A Pin	Wire Color	Connector B Pin
1	White-orange	3
2	Orange	6
3	White-green	1
4	Blue	7
5	White-blue	8
6	Green	2
7	White-brown	4
8	Brown	5

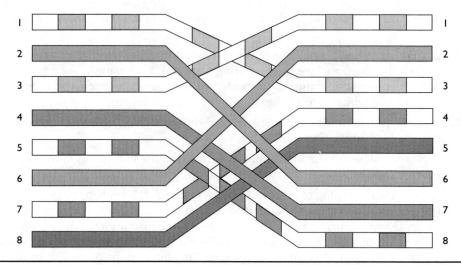

Figure 2-27   A diagram of the pinout for an EIA/TIA 568A crossover connection

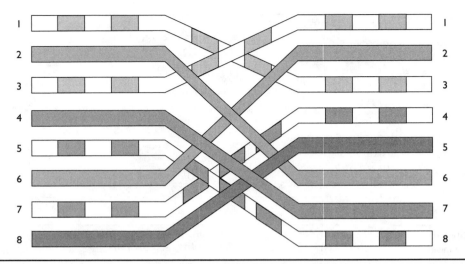

Figure 2-28   A diagram of the pinout for an EIA/TIA 568B crossover connection

Attaching an RJ-45 Connector

To attach an RJ-45 plug to a UTP cable, follow these steps:

1. Strip away about 1.25 inches of the outer jacket of the UTP cable. Use a Cat*X* (the *X* represents Cat 3 and above) cable stripper, if one's available. The cable sheathing should not be stripped more than 1.25 inches from the connection end of the cable, and one inch is best.

2. Untwist the exposed wire pairs, but avoid untwisting the wires at the end of the jacket. UTP wire should not be untwisted more than 0.5 inch, and 0.375 inch is best.

3. Arrange the wires in a flat row in the order that matches the pinout pattern for the cable purpose (see the preceding sections). For example, for a straight-through connector, arrange the wires left to right as white-green, green, white-orange, blue, white-blue, orange, white-brown, and brown.

4. Use wire-cutters to trim the length of the wires to 0.5 inch. There is no need to strip the individual wires.

5. Insert the wires into the RJ-45 plug, ensuring that the wires remain in the required pattern.

6. Use an RJ-45 crimping tool (refer back to Figure 2-21) to push the gold insulation displacement contacts into contact with the wires. The crimper also pushes down a hinged tab that presses against the insulation of the wire to hold it into the plug and create a strain relief. Some crimper tools, when used with special connectors, also cut the wires extending beyond the other side of the connector.

NOTE Actually, you can buy UTP cables with RJ-45 connectors attached. This can be very expensive for longer run cables. However, it is a good option for patch cords and cables.

Punch-downs and IDC Connectors

In many networking situations, centralizing the network resources provides for better control, maintenance, and security. Not all home networks are large enough to require centralization, but in a larger home with several networked subsystems, having the servers, controllers, and source devices in a central location is generally a good idea.

Using a central wiring closet or panel simplifies network maintenance, troubleshooting, and expansion. The central wiring panel terminates all of the network cabling and provides an interface for all of the controlling devices to the entire home automation network as is needed.

For the twisted-pair cable part of a home network, a patch panel can be used as the clustering device. A patch panel looks, and in many ways functions, like the old operator-controlled telephone switchboards (see Figure 2-29). Cable homeruns terminate to the back of the patch panel using IDC contacts. A patch cord is then used to connect each run to the next upstream device as appropriate. For example, the patch panel can interconnect a networked computer to a network switch that supports both voice and data services.

Figure 2-29
A patch panel
with RJ-45 jacks

Photo courtesy of SignaMax Connectivity Systems.

The two most common types of IDC contacts are the 66 block and the 110 block. The 66 block is used primarily in telephone and voice system connections. The 110 is used for data networks. The wires of the twisted-pair cable are pressed into the IDC contacts using a punch-down tool, shown earlier in Figure 2-20.

Fiber Optic Connectors

Fiber optic cable is included in several types of structured wiring cable bundles and often installed in homes for two reasons: for its speed and bandwidth and to future-proof the home. Few home system devices currently exist that connect to fiber optic cable.

Fiber optic cable is terminated using one of three general types of connectors:

- **Interface connectors** Connectors that connect a fiber optic cable to a networking device
- **Inline connectors** Connectors that mates two glass or plastic fibers from separate cable runs to form a temporary joint
- **Splices** Connectors that create a permanent joint between two fiber optic cable runs

In each of these connections, the termination must use an approved connector that is properly installed to minimize light loss and protect the cable from dirt or being damaged. More than 75 different interface and inline connectors are available on the market that can be installed in several different ways, but luckily only a few are commonly used in most residential applications. And fortunately, there are only two ways to splice a cable.

As discussed in Chapter 1, fiber optic cable is single-mode or multimode,. Different connectors and splicing methods are used for each type of fiber optic cable. When connecting or splicing fiber optic cable, you must first know which type of cable you are working with. The standard for fiber optic cabling and connectors is ANSI/EIA/TIA 568A and 568B.

Fiber Optic Connector Basics

The two basic types of fiber optic connectors are butt-jointed and expanded-beam connectors.

Butt-jointed connectors align two prepared fiber ends into very close proximity or in contact with one another. There are two types of butt-jointed connectors: ferrule and biconical.

- **Ferrule connectors** This type of butt-jointed fiber optic connector uses two cylindrical ceramic plugs (called ferrules) and an alignment sleeve. The exposed and prepared fiber strand is inserted into precision holes through the center of each ferrule, which aligns it properly. The quality of this type of connection is dependent on how accurately the center holes of each ferrule are in alignment.

Epoxy resin adhesive is used to permanently hold the fiber strand in the ferrule. The ends of the fiber strands must be polished so that they are flush with the end of the ferrule to prevent light loss in the connection. The ferrules are inserted into the alignment sleeve, which by aligning the ferrules, aligns the fiber strands. This is the method used for straight tip (ST) connectors.

- **Biconical connectors**   This type of butt-jointed connector uses two cone-shaped plugs that are inserted into a double cone-shaped alignment sleeve. Springs in each plug provide the tension that joins the two fiber strands. Epoxy resin is used to secure the plugs into the alignment sleeve. A threaded outer shell is then used to lock in the alignment of the fibers.

Expanded-beam connectors use lenses to expand and refocus light from one fiber to another. Like butt-jointed connectors, expanded-beam connectors are made up of two plugs and a coupling alignment device.

Fiber Optic Connectors

When choosing a fiber optic connector for residential structured wiring, there are four criteria to consider:

- **Availability**   Is the connector a standard connector and will it be readily available for future expansion or repair work?
- **Compatibility**   Is the connector compatible with the bridging and source equipment?
- **Tools**   Are special tools required to install or test the connector?
- **Reliability**   Is the connector reliable and subject to certain environmental conditions?

 NOTE   Of the connectors listed in this section, the ST connector is considered to be the most reliable, available, and compatible of the fiber optic connectors.

The most common fiber optic connectors that should be used in a residential situation are

- **SC**   This connector, shown in Figure 2-30, is a push-pull snap on and off connector. It is very similar to audio and video connectors in that it is small enough to allow multiple connectors to connect into a patch panel or other networking devices. SC (568SC) is the connector currently specified by EIA/TIA 568 for both single-mode and multimode fiber cable.
- **Straight tip (ST)**   The ST connector (see Figure 2-31) was the original standard for fiber optic connections, but is no longer recommended by TIA for new installations. It has been replaced by the SC (568SC) connector in the current standards.

Figure 2-30
An SC fiber optic
plug

- **Lucent connector (LC)**   The LC connector (see Figure 2-32) looks just like an SC connector but is one-half its size. The size of the LC is based on the size of the RJ-45 connector and is designated as a small form factor (SFF) connector for fiber optic cable.

- **Face contact (FC)**   The FC connector (see Figure 2-33) uses a threaded plug and sockets to create a secure connection.

- **SMA**   The SMA connector uses a threaded plug and socket that is the first connector standardized in the industry. (See Figure 2-34.)

- **Physical contact (PC)**   PC describes the end-face polishing used in a connector. The most common of the PC connectors is the FC/PC. A variation of PC is the angled polished connector (APC).

- **MT-RJ**   A small form factor two-fiber connector, the MT-RJ connector (see Figure 2-35) is based on the form and size of the RJ-45 connector, which accounts for the RJ in its name.

Figure 2-31
An ST fiber optic
plug

Photo courtesy of Fiber Connections, Inc.

Figure 2-32
LC fiber optic
connectors

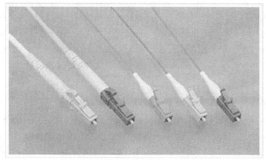

Photo courtesy of FiberSource Inc.

Figure 2-33
FC fiber optic
connectors

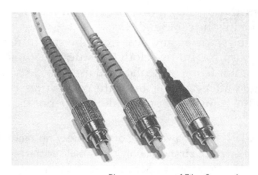

Photo courtesy of FiberSource Inc.

Figure 2-34
An SMA fiber
optic connector

Photo courtesy of FiberSource Inc.

Figure 2-35
An MT-RJ fiber
optic connector

Photo courtesy of Fiber Connections, Inc.

NOTE I've tried to provide a definition for the acronyms or abbreviations used for the different fiber optic connectors. However, some definitions, such as MT and SMA, are lost to history, assuming that they existed at some point.

Fiber Optic Cable Preparation

For fiber optic connections to be secure, the fiber strands must be cleaned before they are mated. Even at the size of a fiber optic strand, dust particles can cause up to 1 dB of signal loss if the cable ends aren't properly cleaned. Dust can be easily removed from the cable and its glass or plastic strands with a blast from a can of compressed air.

Any time a cable connection is unmated (disconnected), a rubber or plastic boot should be immediately placed over the ends of the cable or its ferrule to prevent dust from contaminating the cable end.

In addition to removing any dust from the end of the cable, the cable end should also be cleaned using a lint-free cloth or tissue, denatured alcohol, and canned dry air. Saturate the cloth or tissue in alcohol and use it to clean the sides of the connector ferrule. Immediately after cleaning, make the connection. Use the compressed air to clean the outside of the connector housing and receiver ports, if any.

 NOTE Here's a very important safety tip: *Never* look directly into the end of a fiber optic strand. It only takes milliseconds for the intense light in the cable to damage your eye permanently. You should also never touch the end of a fiber strand, but this has more to do with cleanliness.

Stripping a Fiber Optic Cable

To strip a fiber optic cable, you should perform these steps:

1. Remove the outer jacket of the cable using an electrical stripping tool.

2. Use a knife or scissors to remove the Kevlar (the same stuff used in bullet-proof vests) strength member. Avoid cutting too deeply into the buffer, coating, and sealing layers around the glass or plastic fiber strand.

3. Carefully remove the buffer, coating, and sealing layers around the fiber strand using a special fiber stripper tool to avoid creating surface flaws or scratches, which could cause the cable to fail.

Figure 2-36 shows the construction of a fiber optic cable and the layers you must carefully cut through to strip a fiber cable.

Each fiber optic connector has a unique and required process when it comes to installing the components of the connector. Follow the manufacturer's instructions to the letter to ensure a proper connection that minimizes light loss.

Figure 2-36
The construction of a fiber optic cable

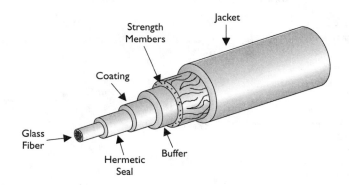

Jacket

Strength Members

Coating

Glass Fiber

Hermetic Seal

Buffer

Fiber Optic Connector Standards

Like twisted-pair cabling, the standard for cabling and connectors for fiber optic cabling is defined in American National Standards Institute/Electronics Industry Association/Telecommunications Industry Association (ANSI/EIA/TIA) 568A, and in a new section for the ANSI/EIA/TIA 568B standard recently released. At present, the 568A standard specifies the SC connector as the 568SC connector, but TIA has published a standard called the Fiber-Optic Cable Intermatability Standard (FOCIS) that recognizes, among others, the fiber optic connectors, listed in Table 2-9 with their standard commercial names.

Computer Data and Cable Connectors

In addition to the RJ connectors I described earlier in the chapter, personal computers (PCs) use a variety of other connectors. These connectors are used to connect to peripheral and other devices, such as printers, scanners, and the like.

Three basic types of physical connectors are most commonly used with PCs:

- Data bus (DB) series connectors
- Universal Serial Bus (USB) connectors
- Institute of Electrical and Electronic Engineers (IEEE)-1394 connectors

Table 2-9
FOCIS Fiber Optic Connectors

Connector Type	FOCIS Designation
FC	FOCIS-4
SC	FOCIS-3
SMA	FOCIS-1
ST	FOCIS-2

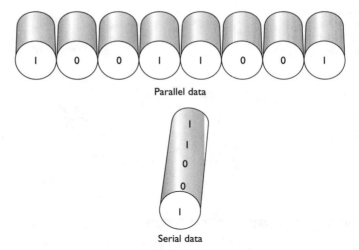

Figure 2-37
Serial data is transmitted one bit at a time over a single line (bottom), and parallel data is transmitted as bit streams on multiple parallel lines (top).

Parallel data

Serial data

Serial versus Parallel

External connections made to a PC use either serial or parallel data transmission modes. Serial transmissions transfer data one bit at a time in series using a form of single-file transmission over a single transmission line. Parallel transmissions transfer data in waves that are made up of several parallel bits moving on separate transmission lines. Figure 2-37 illustrates the basic difference between these two transmission modes.

DB Series Connectors

As I defined earlier in the chapter, a DB connector is a computer and device connector that transfers data between two serial or parallel interface devices. Typically, the number of pins available in its plug and the matching number of receptacles in its jack are used to specify a DB connector. For example, a DB-25 connector (see Figure 2-1 earlier in the chapter) has 25 pins and 25 receptacles in its plug and jack, respectively. Likewise, a DB-9 connector has nine pins and receptacles.

USB Connectors

The USB provides a high-speed data bus that provides an easy way to connect peripheral devices to a PC. A USB port supports data transfer at speeds of 12 million bits per second (Mbps), which is much faster than the interface available on a standard serial port. USB ports are standard to most new PCs. Figure 2-38 illustrates a USB connection being made on a PC.

The USB Implementers Forum (USB-IF), which is an industry standards group that includes such companies as Apple, Hewlett-Packard, Intel, Microsoft, and NEC, publishes a standard that currently includes three data transmission rates:

Figure 2-38
A USB plug being inserted into a USB jack on a PC

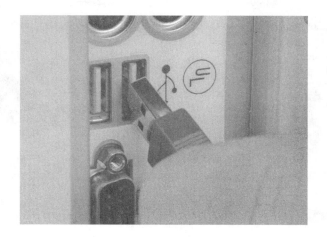

- **USB 1.0 (Low Speed)** This standard has a data rate of 1.5 Mbps, which is about 192 Kilobytes per second (Kbps) and is used primarily for human interface devices (HID), such as keyboards and mice.

- **USB 1.1 (Full Speed)** This standard has a data rate of 12 Mbps (or 1.5 Megabytes per second [MBps]) and is the default standard used on many devices.

- **USB 2.0 (Hi-Speed)** This standard has a data rate of 480 Mbps (60 Mbps).

There are two types of USB connectors (see Figure 2-39). These connectors, which are commonly referred to as Mini-A (Type A) and Mini-B (Type B) connectors are found on PCs and some device interfaces. Type A connectors are most commonly found on devices that connect directly to a PC or hub, and Type B connectors are used at the device end of peripheral devices that connect to a PC over a USB connection.

In addition to the Type A and Type B USB connectors, shown in Figure 2-39, new USB connectors are emerging. The latest of the USB connectors is the Micro-USB that was introduced in early 2007 by the USB-IF for use in smaller devices, such as personal digital assistants (PDAs), mobile phones, and digital cameras. Where the Mini-A connector is about 4 mm in height and about 12 mm in width, the Micro-A connector is about 7 mm by 8 mm.

Figure 2-39
USB cables can have Type A connectors (left) or Type B connectors (right), or both.

Photo courtesy of Belkin Corporation.

Figure 2-40
IEEE 1394 plugs:
4-pin connector
(left) and 6-pin
connector (right)

Photo courtesy of Accell Corporation.

IEEE 1394 Connectors

IEEE 1394 connectors are more commonly known by the brand or model names given to them by manufacturers. Perhaps the best known commercial names for IEEE 1394 connections are FireWire, which is the name used by Apple Computer, and i.Link, the name used by the Sony Corporation.

IEEE 1394 transfers data in speeds up to 800 Mbps and a single 1394 port can support up to 63 additional external devices. IEEE 1394 uses a transfer technology that is similar to USB, but these two data bus technologies are more complementary than competitive. The connectors for IEEE 1394 are also similar to the USB connectors (see Figure 2-40) and, like USB, IEEE 1394 is hot swappable, which means it can be connected and disconnected from the PC without shutting down the PC.

The IEEE 1394AA standard defines two connectors: a four- and six-pin connector (also called FireWire 400). The 1394A standard supports three transfer modes (S100, S200, and S400) that have data transfer rates of 100, 200, and 400 Mbps, respectively. The IEEE 1394A specification limits the cable segment length of the six-pin connector to 15 feet, but 16 cables can be connected in series using hubs or repeaters to a total cable length of 72 meters (about 236 feet). The primary difference between the 4-pin and 6-pin versions of the 1394A connector is that the 6-pin configuration includes power connectors, but otherwise the two configurations are compatible.

The IEEE 1394B (aka FireWire 800) standard defines a 9-pin connector that supports data rates of up to 786 Mbps at present, but is capable of connections of 100 meters in length and data rates of 3.2 Gbps.

Audio/Video Cable Connectors

The connectors used to terminate the various wire and cable types used on audio systems are fairly standardized. Some systems have multiple connector choices, like the system shown in Figure 2-41.

Figure 2-41
The back panel
of an audio/video
device showing
a variety of jack
types

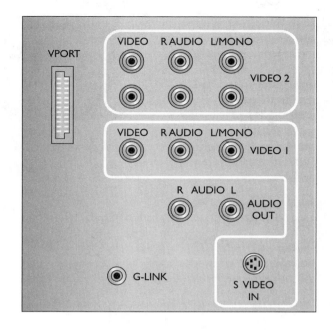

Audio Connectors

Audio connections use many of the same connectors as data networks and video systems. However, while the connection is very much the same, the application is different. The primary connectors used for audio systems are

- **Bayonet Neill Concellman (BNC)**   This connector type provides a mechanically solid twist-lock connection. Although it's most commonly used with coaxial cable, this connector can be used with other cable types as well. BNC connectors are used in high-end installations for high-quality audio and video systems. See Figure 2-15 earlier in the chapter for an example of a BNC connector.

- **IEEE 1394 (High Performance Serial Bus [HPSB])**   Although originally developed for graphics and video transfer, IEEE 1394, discussed earlier in "IEEE 1394 Connectors" is becoming a popular audio connection as well.

- **Radio Corporation of America (RCA) connector**   RCA connectors are a plug and jack combination designed for use with coaxial cable. This connector style is designed to carry a wide range of audio frequency (AF) signals, from very low to several megahertz. RCA connectors are also called phono plugs and jacks. Figure 2-42 shows a crimp-on RCA plug.

Figure 2-42
A crimp-on RCA plug

Photo courtesy of Canare Corporation of America.

- **TosLink (aka Optical Digital Audio Output)** If "Tos" has a meaning, it's lost forever. However, TosLink is a fiber optic digital audio interface commonly used to connect a digital source (typically a DVD or CD player) to a digital receiver or pre-amplifier. Data is passed as laser (light) pulses that minimize interference and signal degradation. Figure 2-43 shows an example of a TosLink cable.

- **Triple RCA** An enhanced version of component video and standard RCA connectors, this connector type is used for component video signals (red, green, and blue). High-definition television (HDTV) uses this special type of component video cable (see Figure 2-44).

Figure 2-43
A TosLink optical digital audio cable

Photo courtesy of Monster Cable Products, Inc.

Figure 2-44
A triple RCA
cable

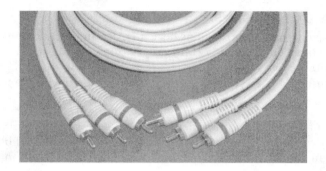

- **USB** As discussed earlier in the chapter (see "USB Connectors"), USB is a
  high-speed digital serial interface that allows USB CD, DVD, speakers, and other
  audio devices to be connected to a computer using what is called hot-swap.

- **XLR** XLR connectors are primarily used for professional-level analog audio
  connections. XLR cables use positive and negative ground carriers, as do RCA
  cables, but the XLR cable adds a ground circuit. Figure 2-45 shows an XLR
  connector.

Preparing Audio Cable

In a structured wiring environment, audio signals can be distributed over speaker wire,
coaxial cable, or fiber optic cable. Twisted-pair cable may also be used, but that is generally not a good first choice for this purpose unless it is digital audio.

CROSS-REFERENCE See Chapter 11 for information on installing RCA and
other audio connectors.

NOTE To prepare coaxial, fiber optic, or twisted-pair cabling for termination
with an audio connector, the process is the same as described earlier in the
chapter for each of these cable types.

Figure 2-45
The female and
male components
of an XLR
connector

Video Connectors

Video systems and audio systems have many connector types in common. In fact, what may be classified as a video connector is often an audio/video connector in that the connection services both media.

The primary video connectors used in a structured wiring environment are

- **Component (also called digital component)** The newest of the cable and connector types, component connectors provide the best picture quality. The video signal is separated into individual red, green, and blue (RGB) color components, which results in better color and clarity. The connection for a component cable has three plugs, one for each color component. Make sure the colors are matched to the device jack colors. The connectors for a component video connection are shown in Figure 2-46.

- **Composite** A standard video signal format that contains color, brightness, and synchronization information. Virtually all VCRs and other legacy video equipment have a composite video input or output. The most commonly used jacks and plugs for composite video are RCA connectors. This signaling and connection format is distinctive in that it uses a yellow jack for video, a white jack for left-side audio, and a red jack for right-side audio.

- **Digital Video Interface (DVI)** This interface connector provides connections for both analog and digital monitors on a single cable. There are three standards for DVI connectors, each of which is designed to accommodate either analog (DVI-A), digital (DVI-D), or integrated (DVI-I), shown in Figure 2-47, signals. When a DVI connector and port are used, the digital signal sent to an analog monitor is converted to an analog signal. If the monitor is a digital monitor, such as a flat panel display, no conversion is performed.

  Because Hollywood and the movie industry fears the image quality possible with DVI may make it possible to illegally copy and distribute high-quality bootlegs of their films, the High-Bandwidth Digital Content Protection (HDCP) standard has been developed to work with DVI circuits. HDCP circuitry is added to the DVI connection on both the transmitter (DVD player, cable box, and

Figure 2-46
A component
video cable

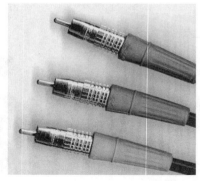

Photo courtesy of Accell Corporation.

Figure 2-47
A DVI-I
connector

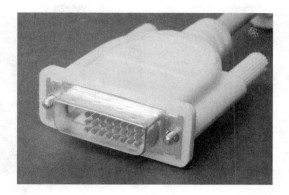

the like) and the receiver (projector, LCD TV, and so on). The HDCP circuits encrypt the video content, which prevents a copy of the original content from being played.

- **F-type connector**   This is the common connector used for video signals, such as connecting a cable television service or an Internet connection service to a TV set, receiver, or Internet gateway using coaxial cable. This connector is secured by screwing its locking cap onto a threaded jack.

- **High-Definition Multimedia Interface (HDMI)**   An improvement over the DVI interface, HDMI (see Figure 2-48) supports either RGB or YcbCr (RGB encoding) digital video at rates well above the 2.2 Gbps required by HDTV. HDMI also supports up to eight channels of digital audio.

- **Super Video (S-Video)**   The signal is split into two color groups: chrominance and luminance. Chrominance carries color information, and luminance carries brightness and lighting information. S-Video is used primarily to transmit video signals to a television from a VCR or game device. The pin configuration on the jack and plug (see Figure 2-49) on an S-Video connection prevents the connection from being made incorrectly.

Figure 2-48
An HDMI plug

Figure 2-49
An S-video plug

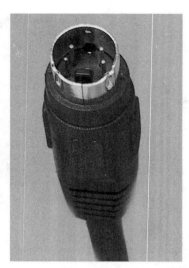

Photo courtesy of Crutchfield New Media, LLC.

Speaker Connectors

Speaker wire is typically connected to a speaker using one of six common attachment methods:

- **Banana plug**   The single prong on this connector is slightly bulged in the center, which gives it a banana look. A banana plug (see Figure 2-50) is attached to the stripped end of a speaker wire inserted through a hole in the body of the connector using a set screw. Banana plugs can be used on either end of a speaker patch cord, and a banana jack can terminate the distributed speaker wire in a wall outlet.

Figure 2-50
A pair of banana
connectors

Figure 2-51
Binding post
connectors

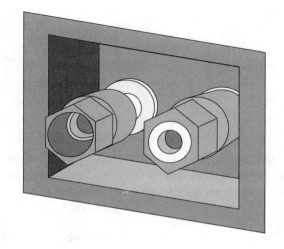

- **Binding post** Binding posts (see Figure 2-51) are available in three- and five-way configurations to which a speaker wire can be attached in two primary ways. Its most commonly used connection method is its threaded shaft on which a screw knob can be tightened to anchor a spade lug or a loop of bare wire. However, the post shaft is hollow and will accept a banana plug or, like a banana plug, there is a horizontal hole in the shaft through which a speaker wire can be inserted and anchored with the knob. The shaft is also sized to accept a pin connector.

- **Pin connector** Although they're most commonly used for test equipment, pin connectors, like the one in Figure 2-52, can be attached to a speaker wire and connect to a binding post by inserting the pin of the connector into the top of the binding post's shaft.

- **Screw terminal** Some older speakers may have screw terminals, which are used to anchor a speaker wire terminated with a spade lug or a loop of bare wire. The setscrew is either a screw that is tightened with a screwdriver or a metal or plastic knob that can be tightened by hand.

Figure 2-52
A screw-on pin
connector can be
used to connect
speaker wire to a
binding post.

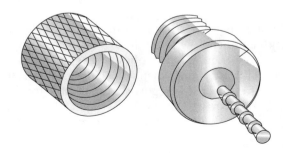

Figure 2-53
A spade
connector

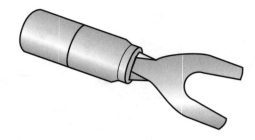

- **Spade (lug)**   Spades (see Figure 2-53) and other types of lug connectors are connections commonly used for terminating a speaker wire at the speaker. Spades are crimped or soldered on individual speaker wire conductors. Spades, also called Y-posts, and other lugs are placed at the end of the patch cord that connects a wall outlet to a speaker (the other end of the patch cord is usually a banana plug).

- **Spring clip**   This connector, which is also called a push terminal, is a very common connector on lower-end speakers. A stripped speaker wire is inserted in the hole of the connector while a spring-loaded lever is pressed down. When the lever is released, gripping teeth on the inside of the connector clamp on the wire.

Chapter Review

The basic types of power connectors are lugs, plugs, receptacles, and terminal strips. Electrical plugs and electrical power characteristics vary from country to country.

In a structured wiring system, the primary coaxial cable types used are RG6 and RG59, and the common coaxial connector is the F-type connector. The two methods used to attach an F-type connector are crimp-on and twist-on.

Cat 3, 5, 5e, 6, and higher twisted-pair cable typically use one of the following modular connectors: RJ-11, RJ-31x, or RJ-45. The connector used depends on the number of lines the jack is supporting and its application. These modular connectors are standardized in the USOC, which defines the standard telephone and data communications jacks and plugs.

RJ-11 jacks and plugs use a 66-type punch-down with IDC contacts into which wire is inserted with a punch-down tool. RJ-31X jacks are connected to outside phone lines and optionally to a home's inside phone lines to allow a security system to seize the line and prevent interruptions when it is alerting a monitoring service. RJ-45 jacks and plugs are standard for terminating twisted-pair cable for data networks.

In a standard four-pair UTP cable, each pair of wires shares a base color: orange, blue, green, and brown. One of the wires in each pair has a solid color and the other wire is marked with its color alternated with a white strip. The two wiring standards used to define twisted-pair cable connections in a network are EIA/TIA 568A and 568B. The 568A standard is backward compatible with the older USOC telephone standards, and 568B doesn't support voice signals.

To install an RJ-45 jack or plug, it is very important that you match the correct pin to the correct wire color. Which wiring pattern you use depends on the requirements of the networking equipment. A straight-through pattern is used to connect computers to hubs and a crossover pattern is used to link computers to other computers.

The use of a central wiring closet or panel simplifies maintenance, troubleshooting, and expansion for a network. The central wiring panel terminates all of the network cabling and provides an interface for all of the controlling devices to the entire home automation network as needed. A patch panel can be used as a clustering device. Cable homeruns terminate to the back of the patch panel using IDC contacts. A patch cord is then used to connect each run to the next upstream device as appropriate. The two most common types of IDC contacts are the 66 block and the 110 block. The 66 block is used primarily in telephone and voice system connections; the 110 block is used for data networks.

Fiber optic cable is included in several types of structured wiring cable bundles and is being installed in homes for two reasons: its speed and bandwidth and to future-proof the home. Fiber optic cable is terminated using one of three general types of connectors: interface connectors, inline connectors, and splices.

The two basic types of fiber optic connectors are butt-jointed and expanded-beam connectors. Butt-jointed connectors align two prepared fiber ends into very close proximity or in contact with one another. There are two types of butt-jointed connectors: ferrule and biconical. Expanded-beam connectors use lenses to expand and refocus light from one fiber to another. The most common fiber optic connectors and those that should be used in a residential situation are SC, ST, LC, FC, SMA, and MT-RJ. Fiber strands must be clean before being mated. The standard for fiber optic cabling and connectors is ANSI/EIA/TIA 568A and 568B.

The three basic types of physical connectors most commonly used with PCs are the DB series, USB, and IEEE-1394 connectors. External connections made to a PC use either serial or parallel data transmission modes. USB provides a high-speed data bus that provides an easy way to connect peripheral devices to a PC. IEEE-1394 connectors are known as FireWire and i.Link. USB and IEEE-1394 connections are hot swappable.

Audio connections use many of the same connectors as data networks and video systems. The primary connectors used for audio systems are BNC, IEEE 1394, RCA, TosLink, USB, and XLR. Audio signals can be distributed over either coaxial cable or fiber optic cable. The primary video connectors are component, composite, DVI, F-type, HDMI, and S-video.

Speaker wire is typically connected to a speaker using one of six common attachment methods: banana plug, binding post, pin connector, screw terminal, spade lug, and spring clip.

Questions

1. A connector plug that has one or more pins extending from its housing is commonly called a

   A. Female plug

   B. Male plug

   C. Negative connector

   D. Positive connector

2. Which of the following is the most commonly used connector for terminating coaxial cable as a part of a structured wiring system in a home?

   A. RJ-11

   B. F-type

   C. RJ-45

   D. Spade

3. What connector type is used to interconnect telephone lines with a security system?

   A. RJ-11C

   B. RJ-21x

   C. RJ-31x

   D. RJ-45

4. Which type of punch-down block is used to terminate data networking cable?

   A. 66 block

   B. 88 block

   C. 110 block

   D. 240 block

5. What tool is used to connect a Cat 5e cable wire to an IDC contact?

   A. Punch-down

   B. Screwdriver

   C. Spring clip

   D. Twist-on

6. What are the four wire colors used in a Cat 5e cable?

   A. Blue, green, red, black

   B. Orange, blue, green, brown

    C. Orange, blue, green, yellow

    D. White, black, red, green

7. What is the wiring and connector standard that governs data networking?

    A. EIA/TIA 568

    B. NEC 411

    C. USOC

    D. NFSB

8. Which of the following is not a commonly used fiber optic connector?

    A. RJ

    B. SC

    C. SMA

    D. ST

9. What type of video signal interface separates the video images into RGB color components using three plugs, one for each color component?

    A. Composite

    B. Component

    C. DVI

    D. S-Video

10. What type of speaker wire connection is a five-way connector that can be used to anchor a lug, bare wire loops, stripped wire, a banana plug, and a pin connector?

    A. Binding post

    B. Screw terminal

    C. Spade

    D. Spring clip

Answers

1. **B.** A plug that has one or more receptacles in its housing is referred to as a female.

2. **B.** F-type connectors are commonly used in home systems for coaxial cable terminations. RJ-45 and RJ-11 connectors require multiple wires, and a spade connector may not provide the contact required for high-speed signal transmissions.

3. **C.** RJ-11 and RJ-21 are other telephone line connections, and an RJ-45 is used with data networking.

4. **C.** A 66 block is used in telephone applications. An 88 block terminates up to 256 wire pairs in large telephone applications, such as a telephone company. As far as I know, I made up the 240 block.

5. **A.** This tool is especially made to strip, cut, and insert a wire into an IDC contact.

6. **B.** The only other choice listed that you may actually encounter is yellow, black, red, and green, which are the colors in telephone quad wire.

7. **A.** The standards are 568A and 568B. The newer EIA/TIA 570 also specifies residential wiring standards. National Electric Code (NEC) Article 411 governs electrical connections. The other choices are not relevant at all.

8. **A.** RJs (registered jacks) are communication connectors for twisted-pair wiring.

9. **B.** Composite breaks the signal into two audio channels and one video channel, DVI is a Digital Video Interface, and S-Video breaks the signal into two components for chrominance and luminance.

10. **A.** Screw terminals can anchor lugs or bare wire, a spade is a type of lug, and a spring clip connector only terminates bare wire.

Wiring Installation Practices

In this chapter, you will learn about:
- Planning for a wiring installation
- Pre-wiring activities
- Cable and wire installation
- Structured wiring trim-out

The performance of a network wiring in a home is determined more by the quality of the installation than the quality of the actual wire or cable installed to support the network. Not that the quality of the cabling isn't important, but even the very best quality cable can't overcome a poor or shoddy installation.

This chapter provides an overview of the installation practices and processes that should be used when installing wire and cable in a new construction environment to support an integrated home network. However, these same practices and processes should also be applied to remodeling and retrofit projects to ensure that the end result provides a high-quality wiring infrastructure for the new network.

Pre-Wire Planning

As entertainment, networking, and communication technologies continue to evolve and merge, homeowners are seeing the value of pre-wiring new homes not only for existing services, but also for those yet to come. In fact, the pre-wiring phase of a new home construction project has essentially become as much a part of standard building practices as the plumbing, electrical wiring, and heating and ventilation systems.

Before the actually wiring can be performed, you and the builder or homeowners, or both, should meet to plan out the network wiring system and address some common installation issues, including:

1. What types of Internet service are available to the home and to what type of Internet service(s) do the homeowners wish to connect initially?

2. What type(s) of video and television service is available to the home and to which type do the homeowners wish to connect initially?

3. How many telephone lines do the homeowners plan to install?

4. Is a distributed audio or video system planned for the home, now or in the future?

5. What type of security system is planned?

6. What type of HVAC (heating, ventilation, air conditioning) system is planned? Is automated control desired?

7. How do the homeowners see the house being zoned for each system (audio, security, HVAC, and so on)?

8. Do the homeowners want systems integrated and controlled by a central control system?

This list is hardly all-inclusive for every situation, but it does cover the basics. Be sure to discuss every subsystem that is to be supported by the network infrastructure. The subsystems that should be considered for inclusion or elimination from the wiring plan is likely some or all of the following (among others):

- Structured wiring
- Whole-house music system
- Telephone/intercom system
- Security system
- Lighting control system
- HVAC interface control system
- Motorized devices
- Integrated control system
- Surge protection

The primary objective of pre-wiring planning is for you and the homeowners to develop a shared vision of what the finished system is to be and the networking infrastructure necessary to ensure its successful functionality. The result of your meeting(s) should be a rough sketch of the home that clearly identifies the locations of the networked devices and the cabling and wiring required to interconnect these devices. Figure 3-1 shows one example of what this sketch might look like. In new construction situations, a walking tour of the home may be impossible, but in remodeling situations walking through the home with the floor plan in hand will save time and money later.

NOTE The pre-wiring plan should also include any wiring that can be installed as a part of the current project to provide support for a feature that may be added in the future.

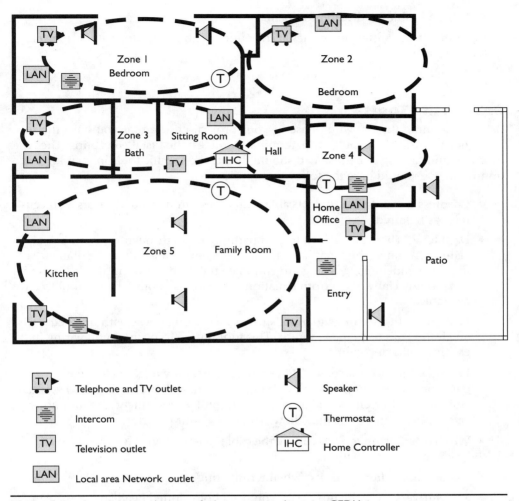

Zone 1
Bedroom

Zone 2

Bedroom

Zone 3   Sitting Room

Bath   Hall   Zone 4

Home
Office

Zone 5   Family Room

Kitchen   Patio

Entry

TV▶	Telephone and TV outlet	◁		Speaker
🔲 Intercom		Ⓣ	Thermostat
TV	Television outlet	IHC	Home Controller
LAN	Local area Network outlet		

Figure 3-1   A preliminary diagram of a home wiring plan using CEDIA icons

The Pre-Wire Process

The process of pre-wiring a house or building for a digital network consists of the following major activities:

1. Determine the locations of the distribution panel, outlets, and devices.
2. Create a wire chart.
3. Place outlet boxes or mud rings at each location.
4. Pull the appropriate type and number of cable runs to each outlet and device location.

5. Label all cables at distribution panel.

6. Terminate or protect the cables at the outlets with the appropriate connecters or bagging.

7. Test all cable runs and connections.

Pre-Wiring Tools

Before beginning the pre-wire phase of your project, ensure that you have the tools you'll need to drill holes, pull, strip, terminate, and test the installed cabling. The types of wiring and cabling to be installed should dictate the specific tools in your kit, but at minimum you should have the following:

- **Cordless hand drill** To drill cable path holes through studs, floors, and ceilings, as required.

- **Drill bits** These are needed to drill pathway holes through studs, floors, or ceilings. You need bits that have a diameter slightly larger than the diameter of the cable and are long enough to eliminate the need to drill multiple holes in a surface, especially in a retrofit situation. A flex bit is another handy tool to have available.

- **Fish tape** In a retrofit situation, such as an existing house with finished walls, an electrician's fish tape is a must. This tool is used to push or pull wiring into existing walls or conduit.

- **Fiberglass push/pull rods** These can be very handy in either a new construction or retrofit situation. Wire push/pull rods are sectional, so you can lengthen or shorten the rod as you push or pull. I recommend the luminous "glow-in-the-dark" type that allows you to see your progress.

- **Wire cutter/stripper** For cutting the cable to length and stripping its outer jacket during termination.

- **Needle-nose pliers** For use when terminating all cable types.

- **Screwdrivers** For the most part, you need both slotted head and crosshead recessed (Phillips) screwdrivers.

- **Volt meter/continuity tester** For testing each cable run before termination and trim out.

Wire Chart

Table 3-1 shows an example of a wire chart that should be created during the planning phase of a structured wiring project and used as a guide for the pre-wiring, rough in, and trim out of the structured wiring of a home. The information in the wire chart should be taken directly from the project design and planning documents. If abbreviations are used on the wire chart, a legend should be created to ensure that everyone associated with the project understands their meaning. The format shown in Table 3-1 is only an example, and you may want to include additional columns for other information, but the columns shown represent the minimum information needed during the complete wiring project.

Pulled	Tested	Run #	Type	Source	Destination	Device	Length	Special Instructions
		1	Cat 5e	House feed	Control center (CC)	Phone feed		Phone feed
		2	Cat 5e	House feed	CC	Future		Future
		4	RG6	Attic	CC	Future TV antenna		Loop extra cable
		6	RG6	Roof	CC	DSS feed		Satellite TV
		8	Cat 5e	CC	Studio A	Phone jack		
		9	Cat 5e	CC	Studio A	Data jack		
		10	RGRG6	CC	Studio A	TV jack		
		11	Cat 5e	CC	Studio B	Phone jack		
		12	Cat 5e	CC	Studio B	Data jack		
		13	RG6	CC	Studio B	TV jack		
		14	Cat 5e	CC	Family room	Phone jack		
		15	Cat 5e	CC	Family room	Data jack		
		16	RG6	CC	Family room	TV jack		
		17	Cat 5e	CC	Up bedroom	Phone jack		
		18	Cat 5e	CC	Up bedroom	Data jack		
		19	RG6	CC	Up bedroom	TV jack		
		20	Cat 5e	CC	Living room	Phone jack		
		21	Cat 5e	CC	Living room	Data jack		
		22	Cat 5e	CC	Up hallway	Phone jack		
		23	Cat 5e	CC	Up hallway	Data jack		
		24	Cat 5e	CC	Master bedroom	Phone jack		
		25	Cat 5e	CC	Master bedroom	Data jack		
		28	Cat 5e	CC	Kitchen	Wall phone		Mount high on wall
		30	16-4	Living room	Living room, stairway wall	Speakers		Pre-wire for speakers located on stairway wall, either side of opening

Table 3-1   A Sample Home System Wire Chart. Format used with permission from Heneveld Dynamic Consulting, Inc.

The columns included in this wire chart example are

- **Pulled**   After each cable run is installed (pulled) from the source indicated in the Source column to the location listed in the Destination column, this column can be checked off and initialed by both the installer and whomever inspects his or her work. A double-check of the work is highly recommended to prevent oversight, errors, and omissions.

- **Tested**   During trim out and after each cable run is terminated and tested, the corresponding box in this column for the cable run can be checked off and initialed by the tester and the person verifying the test. Again, a double-check of the work is highly recommended to prevent oversight, errors, and omissions.

- **Run #**   This column is used to create a unique identity and reference number for each cable run. The number or code assigned in this column can later be used in cable documentation and when labeling each cable. Cable number labeling systems provide self-adhesive numbered labels that can be affixed to each cable run at the distribution panel or control center (CC) end.

- **Type**   The type of cable to be used is entered into this column for each cable run.

- **Source**   The location of the starting point from where the cable run is to begin is entered into this column.

- **Destination**   The location of the ending point to where the cable run is to be pulled is entered into this column.

- **Device**   The source, distribution, control, or outlet device to which the cable run is to be connected or will support is identified in this column. When a cable run is being installed for future-proofing purposes (see Chapter 5), this information should be recorded as well.

- **Length**   This is an optional column, but can be helpful when comparing wire usage estimates to the actual installation. After estimating or length testing is completed on each cable run, record the length in this column. Wire types used can be totaled up and compared to total usage wire estimates for the project. The information in the Length column may come in handy later when you are troubleshooting a cable for possible attenuation problems.

- **Special Instructions**   Because it is common for one technician to design and plan a structured wiring job and another technician to install its cable, this column can prove valuable in noting any issues or instructions, such as device height, that the installer should know before beginning his or her work. Any problems encountered by the installer should also be recorded should yet another technician perform the cable testing. This column can also be used to record any other information relating to a particular cable run that may be valuable for future reference.

Wall Outlets

The system plan that was developed earlier in the project (and discussed earlier in this chapter) reflects where you and the homeowners have decided the connections, speakers, and controls for the home's integrated system should be placed. However, it's one thing to mark it on a floor plan and quite another to religiously follow the plan exactly. Sometimes the wall studs, pipes, vents, or another room feature may not support the original placement of a system device. In these cases, you should coordinate with the homeowner to decide on a new location for the device.

Locate Outlets

The first step in the pre-wiring process is to install the outlet boxes and mud rings or plaster rings. In each location, an outlet box or mud ring should be nailed to a wall stud at the same height from the floor as the electrical outlets placed by the rough-in electricians and should be 12 inches or 300 millimeters above the floor. The boxes should also be from 12 to 16 inches from any nearby electrical outlets. A standard recommendation is to locate low-voltage outlets at least one wall-stud cavity away from an electrical outlet.

The outlet box (see Figure 3-2), backless outlet box, or mud ring should be of appropriate size to accommodate the size and amount of cabling that is to terminate or pass through that location, as well as the number of connectors and jacks to be installed. Outlet boxes should be placed so that when the drywall is installed they are flush with the front edge of the drywall. A mud ring will be stuck to the back of the drywall by joint compound.

Figure 3-2
A standard electrical outlet box can be used to mount connectors and faceplates.

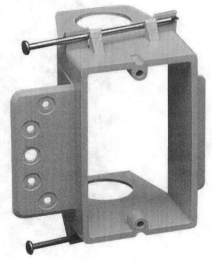

Photo courtesy of Lamson & Sessions.

Outlet boxes for other devices that may be included in the home vary in their placement. For example, the boxes used for control panels, volume controls, or keypads depend on their type and, in many cases, the homeowners' preferences. The rule of thumb is to place outlet boxes for pushbutton devices at light switch height (generally shoulder height). Outlet boxes for touch-screen inputs/displays should be at eye-level, but the homeowners may have a preference for their placement. Most input or display devices fit into either a single or double outlet box, but some also come with their own in-wall or surface-mount boxes, which is why it is always good practice to know what specific equipment is to be installed so that outlet and mounting boxes are placed appropriately.

Sidecar Brackets

Several manufacturers make specialized low-voltage boxes and brackets that are able to service both AC electrical power lines and low-voltage structured wiring lines. The double-gang box shown in Figure 3-3 includes a separator panel in the center that meets the requirements of the NEC and EIA/TIA standards 568 and 570 for the separation of these lines.

Another box type attaches to the side of an electrical service outlet box to create a tandem box that will appear, after the drywall is installed, to be a two-gang box. Add-on or sidecar brackets (see Figure 3-4) allow the outlet box to be paired with an electrical outlet, creating the finished look of a two-gang box rather than two separate outlets a short distance from each other on the same wall.

Figure 3-3
A double-gang outlet box uses a separator panel to segregate AC power lines from network cabling.

Photo courtesy of Lamson & Sessions.

Figure 3-4
A sidecar bracket
can be attached
to the side of an
electrical box.

Photo courtesy of Lamson & Sessions.

If you use a sidecar bracket, be sure to wire the low-voltage wire as far away as possible from the electrical wires. For example, the electrical wiring comes down the stud that the electrical box is mounted on, so wire the low-voltage wire down the opposite stud of that stud opening, wiring into the two-gang box at a right angle to the electrical wiring.

Cable

A variety of composite cable systems, like the one shown in Figure 3-5, is available; these systems that combine coaxial cable and Cat 5e cables into a single bundle, called a 2 + 2 bundled cable. Some manufacturers also offer what amounts to a 2 + 2 + 2 that includes an additional two runs of fiber optic cable.

CROSS-REFERENCE   See Chapter I for more information on network cabling.

Cable Schemes

Table 3-2 lists the recommended cables that should be installed for a variety of structured wiring applications. Remember that this is only a recommendation, but it does adhere closely to most of the recognized standards.

Cable Installation

After the outlet boxes and mud rings have been installed, the next step in the pre-wire process is to install the cabling. In a new construction pre-wire situation, the structured

Figure 3-5
An example of a composite cable that includes two RG6 and two Cat 5e lines

Photo courtesy of Smarthome, Inc.

cable runs through holes drilled in the wall studs and runs parallel to the electrical wiring that should already be in place.

As a general rule, the path through the wall studs used for the structured cable should not be placed too close to the electrical power lines to avoid the possibility of electrical interference on the structured cabling. The general guidelines for how far a structured cable should be placed from an electrical line vary from 6 to 24 inches (with 6 inches the absolute minimum distance). However, the generally accepted standard and convention is that 12 inches is the minimum that should be used, unless for some reason the structure doesn't permit it. If the electrical cable in question is a high-voltage line, such as a 240 V line, the minimum distance moves out to 24 inches. If an electrical cable must be crossed, the structured cabling should do so at a 90-degree angle.

Nearly all structured wiring cable products are designed for installation in residential settings, so by and large, the bend radii required to pull a cable down between two

Space	Wire Types	Number of Runs Data/Audio-Video	Applications
Typical room	Cat 5e/RG6	2/2	Phone/TV/data/satellite
Media center	Cat 5e/RG6	3/3	Phone/TV/AV/data
Home office	Cat 5e/RG6	3/3	Phone/TV/data/AV

Table 3-2   Cable Recommendations for Room Types as Included in the EIA/TIA Standards

wall studs is well within its specifications. However, sharp bends or kinks should be completely avoided.

The primary concern for pulling cable into an existing structure is to spread the runs of the various cable types over as wide a space as possible. If it is absolutely necessary to cross cabling, there are standards and guidelines for the installation of low-voltage cabling that covers overlap, separation, and crossing angles.

In general, structured wiring cable should be installed using the following guidelines:

- Use no more than 25 pounds of pull on the cable.

- Use at least 12 inches of separation between 120 V power and structured wiring cables, and at least 24 inches of separation for 240 V lines.

- If a low-voltage cable crosses a power cable, it must do so at a 90-degree angle.

- The low-voltage cable should avoid fluorescent light fixtures, and if you must run a cable by a fluorescent fixture, treat it like a 240 V electrical line.

- Cable sheathing should not be stripped more than 1.25 inches from the connection end of the cable, and one inch is better.

- Unshielded twisted-pair (UTP) wire pairs should not be untwisted more than 0.5 inches and 0.375 inches is even better.

- The bend radius of a cable should be at least one inch, but some cable types are more sensitive than others.

- Between a transmitting source and a terminating (receiving device), a UTP cable segment should not be longer than 100 meters (a bit more than 300 feet).

 NOTE In North America, UTP is the most commonly used cable for low-voltage (LV) data networking installations. However, outside of North America, shielded twisted-pair (STP) and screened twisted-pair (ScTP) wiring are commonly used.

Cable Path

In a structured cabling environment, one or more separate cable runs are strung between the outlet location and the central distribution panel so that each outlet has its own homerun of cable back to the panel.

When routing the structured cable through a wall stud, you should use a 5/8-inch auger drill bit to drill a hole in the horizontal center of the stud. This provides both a hole big enough for most cable bundles and composite cabling and leaves enough wood in the stud on each side (at least one inch) of the hole to retain the strength of the stud. If you are concerned that the dry wall installers may penetrate your cable when they screw on the dry wall, place a nail plate on the front edge of the stud even with the cable hole. Minimize the number of holes drilled through a wall stud to maintain the integrity of the stud.

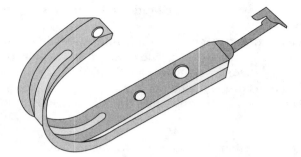

Figure 3-6
A J-hook creates
a cable path in
open spaces.

An alternative cable path is to pass the cable through a hole drilled in the header of the wall (the boards to which the studs are fastened) and run the cable through the attic or crawl space above or below the house. Using this path, the cable can be placed on J-hooks (see Figure 3-6) or tie wraps that hold the cable in place without the threat of damage from nails, staples, or other fasteners used to secure the cable to wall studs.

Service Loops

At the outlet end of the structured cable pulled through the walls, leave at least two feet of cable length to work with during the trim-out phase of the cabling project. At the distribution panel have at least two feet of cable after the panel location, or better yet, have all cables reach the floor. Having ample cable in a service loop provides some flexibility when you are terminating the cable at an outlet or the distribution panel.

Tuck the service loop into the outlet opening of the wall in such a way that it can later be pulled out through the outlet or mud ring after the wallboard is installed.

It is beneficial to protect the distribution panel cable by putting a large piece of cardboard to fit in the panel opening to cover all the cables.

Cable Handling

Cat 5e and RG6 are high-frequency cables and must not be damaged during installation. This means that staples or any other type of cable fastener that dents, pierces, or crimps the cable in any way shouldn't be used. Also avoid bending these cable types too sharply when entering or exiting a wall stud cavity. The minimum bend radius for Cat 5e or Cat 6 is 1 inch, or 25.4 millimeters (mm), and for RG6 is 2.5 inches, or 63.5 mm (see Figure 3-7).

Another important part of cable handling is to label or tag each run of cable per the wire chart. Each cable should be numbered per the wire chart and the number recorded on its labeling. This identification links the cable back to the cable plan created during the design and planning phases. Should a problem develop in the future on a specific cable run, knowing its cable number and being able to identify and locate the cable labeled with this number can be a real time saver.

Figure 3-7
The recommended maximum bend radii of Cat 5e and RG6 cables.

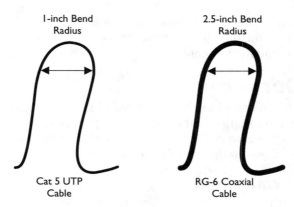

1-inch Bend Radius

Cat 5 UTP Cable

2.5-inch Bend Radius

RG-6 Coaxial Cable

Cable Trays, Conduits, and Chases and Other Cable Supports

Most often, residential cables are routed through stud walls. However, if the cable has to be routed through an attic, basement, or other open space, the cables must be supported and organized, so typically they are routed through cable (J-) hooks (see Figure 3-6) or tie-wraps attached to the rafters.

Cable Trays   In residential settings, it is rare that you would need to install cable trays, which look something like a ladder installed horizontally. A cable tray is used to bridge cable runs that must run over areas that have no natural support features. For example, if you were to run cable through an attic, a cable tray hung from the roof rafters would provide a secure and safe pathway for the cabling.

Conduits   Conduits can be rigid aluminum tubing or plastic piping or flexible plastic tubing. In most areas, conduit is not required for home structured wiring, but can be a wise choice when the pathway available for the structured cable is too close to electrical wiring or other interference sources.

EIA/TIA 570, the standard for residential cabling, recommends that data cabling is segregated into its own pathway, which has been interpreted in some municipalities as requiring conduit for all wiring, especially data network cabling. So be sure to check your local building and electrical codes.

Some technicians, especially those working with fiber optic cable, recommend the use of conduits for a variety of reasons, including ease of cable installation, cable upgrades, and new outlet installation, as well as protection of the cable from damage.

Chases   A chase is a tube or a three-sided frame placed horizontally on a wall or in a slot cut into a floor. A chase permits cabling to be suspended and protected along a wall or beneath a floor. Chases are commonly used in multistory buildings in the space between the floors. Typically, a lid or cap is placed over the chase to protect the wire. There are vertical chases as well, which are on walls or in shafts to provide a protective path for riser cables, something that is rare in most home-wiring installations.

As a part of future-proofing a home, it's wise to install 2-inch plastic pipe (conduit or chase) between the distribution panel and some key areas of a home, such as the attic, home office, and media center.

Trim-Out

The final step in the wiring process is called *trim-out*, during which the cable runs are terminated and installed in the distribution panel and the appropriate connectors and outlets at the in-room end are installed. The trim-out phase is done after the wallboard installers have put up the drywall to cover the wall studs and the painters are finished.

Cable Termination

During the trim-out phase, the cables that have been pulled into place are terminated at both the outlet and distribution panel or intermediate device (such as a patch panel or hub) ends. The type of termination applied depends on the cable and its intended use at the outlet. For example, coaxial cabling being terminated at an outlet to provide a connection for distributed video or a Cat 5e cable being terminated for a data network connection will each be connected to the outlet connections with a device and method specific to the cable and its application.

CROSS-REFERENCE   See Chapter 2 for more information on cable connectors and terminations.

Telephone Cable

The trim-out work for a home telephone system involves the termination of Cat 5e UTP cabling at both the telephone block, either inside or outside of the central distribution panel, and the telephone outlets.

Telephone Block   The cabling installed to provide telephone links throughout a home are connected into the telephone system using a telephone panel or block located inside or very near the structured wiring distribution panel.

The telephone block, shown in Figure 3-8, is commonly referred to as a 110 punch-down block and consists of two columns of 50 IDC contacts. Each row of contacts, which can be connected to one another as one circuit of the panel, consists of one contract from

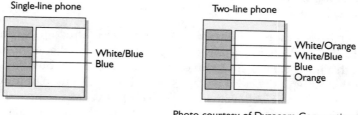

Photo courtesy of Dynacom Corporation.

Figure 3-8   A telephone connection block

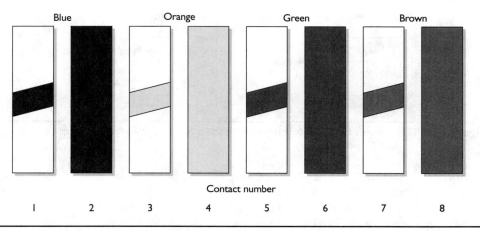

Contact number

| 1 | 2 | 3 | 4 | 5 | 6 | 7 | 8 |

Figure 3-9 The wire color scheme used for Cat 5e cabling for a 110-type punch-down block

each column. On some blocks, the pairs are internally linked and on others a bridging clip must be inserted over the inner two contacts to bridge the outer contacts.

When terminating Cat 5e cabling for a telephone system, a 110-type block should be used. Typically, a 66-type block is used in telephone systems where quad wire is in use, but the 110-type IDC contacts, which have shorter contacts, are better suited to Cat 5e cable.

An impact punch-down tool is used to press unstripped wire strands of the Cat 5e cable into an IDC contact. The tool pushes the wire down into the IDC and its tines cut through the wire's insulation to allow the tines to make contact with the wire's copper core. The standard wire pattern, meaning the color sequence of the wire as it is placed into the 110 block, is shown in Figure 3-9 and listed in Table 3-3.

 NOTE If you consistently reverse one or more of the wire colors, don't worry. As long as the wire pattern is exactly the same on each end of a terminated cable, everything should still work. However, following the standard removes all guesswork about how consistent you've been.

Wire Color	Pair	Contact
White/Blue	1	1
Blue or Blue/White	1	2
White/Orange	2	3
Orange or Orange/White	2	4
White/Green	3	5
Green/Green/White	3	6
White/Brown	4	7
Brown or Brown/White	4	8

Table 3-3 Cat 5e Wire Color Scheme for Use in 110-type Punch-down Blocks

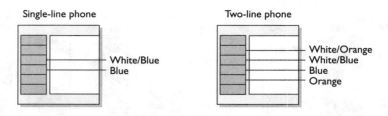

Figure 3-10 The pinouts for a one-pair (single line) and a two-pair (two line) connection

Telephone Outlets Telephone cabling should be terminated at the wall outlet with an RJ-11 jack, using a one-, two-, or three wire-pair configuration, depending on the number of lines to be connected through the wall outlet. Figure 3-10 illustrates the wire configuration of the RJ-11 terminations at a wall outlet and Table 3-4 lists the wire configurations for RJ-11 wall jacks.

Audio Cable

Most audio cabling is actually speaker wire and can be terminated in one of two ways: directly at an in-wall or an in-ceiling speaker, or at a wall outlet for hookup with external speakers. To directly connect a speaker, the speaker wire is terminated to the speaker itself. If you choose to terminate the speaker wire at a wall outlet, it can be either a standalone outlet or a part of a multiple-connection outlet that may include other connector types. In situations where the audio cable or speaker wire terminates directly on a speaker, the wire must be prepared or terminated to connect to the connection type or types available on the speaker.

CROSS-REFERENCE Chapter 13 covers the specifics of terminating speaker cable and the various connector types that may be used.

Speaker Outlets Figure 3-11 shows an example of a speaker outlet with four 5-way binding post connectors where local freestanding or bookshelf speakers can be connected. Binding post connectors are the most commonly used connector for audio

Wire Pair	Function	Position	UTP Wire Color	Quad Wire Color
1	Tip	Pin/Slot 4	White/Blue	Green
	Ring	Pin/Slot 3	Blue (Blue/White)	Red
2	Tip	Pin/Slot 2	White/Orange	Black
	Ring	Pin/Slot 5	Orange (Orange/White)	Yellow
3	Tip	Pin/Slot 1	White/Green	n/a
	Ring	Pin/Slot 6	Green (Green/White)	n/a

Table 3-4 RJ-11 Pinouts for UTP Cable

Figure 3-11
A multiconnector
speaker outlet

Photo courtesy of Niles Audio Corporation.

system outlets. Speaker wire is secured to a binding post connector using its setscrew. Care should be taken to ensure that the right and left speaker wires are connected properly and the plugs on the face of the outlet are labeled properly. Audio cabling can also be terminated on simple screw connectors as well.

Audio Cable Termination   To properly terminate audio cabling, follow these guidelines:

- Split the insulation between the conductors of the audio cable about one inch.

- Remove ½ inch of insulation from each conductor.

- When using screw-type or binding post connectors, wrap the stripped wire 180 degrees around the screw post in a clockwise direction and then tighten the setscrew. Don't wrap the bare wire completely around the post, because when the setscrew is tightened, the wires could be damaged or broken—keep some of the insulation under the screw post.

Coaxial Cable

Coaxial cabling, meaning RG59 or RG6 cable, is terminated at an outlet box using a variety of connector types. The most common connector used is the F-type connector,

Figure 3-12
Coaxial cable
is commonly
terminated with
an F-type jack.

Photo courtesy of Channel Vision.

shown in Figure 3-12. Many coaxial outlet connectors require the cable to be terminated before it is connected to the back of the outlet. In others, the coaxial connection terminator is attached to the cable and then inserted into the outlet faceplate. On some, the connector is a permanent part of the faceplate and the cable must be terminated to the rear of the connection.

Coaxial connectors are attached to the cable using a variety of methods, including crimp-on, compression lock, threaded or twist-on, and several proprietary types of connectors. Some require standard crimper tools, and other require a crimper made specifically for a particular brand or style of connector.

 CROSS-REFERENCE   See Chapter 2 for more information on coaxial cable terminations and connectors.

Data Outlets

Twisted-pair (TP) wiring, such as Cat 5e or Cat 6, is most commonly terminated with an 8-pin RJ-45 connector using an impact punch-down tool. However, RJ-45 connectors that can be attached to the cable with a crimper or merely clamp down on the individual wires with a snap close are available and becoming popular.

 CROSS-REFERENCE   See Chapter 2 for more information on twisted-pair cable terminations and connectors.

Figure 3-13
A modular
faceplate with
angular snap-
in connector
mounts

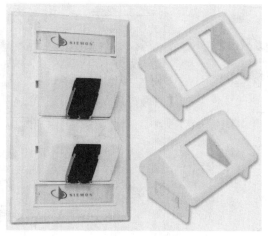

Photo courtesy of The Siemon Company.

The best practice is to terminate TP and coaxial cabling with what are called modular connectors that can be snapped into an open slot faceplate (see Figure 3-13).

Video Outlets

Coaxial cabling is the most commonly used and recommended wiring for distributed video service lines. The best connectors to use when terminating video cabling are either compression lock or threaded male F-type coaxial connectors. The best practice is to use snap-in connectors that can be inserted into an open-slot faceplate at the outlet.

CROSS-REFERENCE   Chapter 2 includes more information about coaxial and twisted-pair cable termination.

Faceplates

If modular faceplates are used to hold multiple cable termination jacks, a consistent pattern of placement should be used in every location. A fairly commonly used convention (for a 4-slot faceplate) is to place the RJ-11 telephone jack in the upper-left position, the data network RJ-45 jack in the upper-right position, the video coaxial F-type jack in the lower-left position, and, if used, a video out coaxial F-type connector in the lower-right position. Figure 3-14 illustrates this arrangement.

Jacks are inserted into a modular faceplate by inserting them from the rear of the faceplate, as shown in Figure 3-15. Although this figure shows only a single jack being inserted, the process is essentially the same for multiple jacks.

Figure 3-14
An illustration of a commonly used convention for modular jack placement on a faceplate

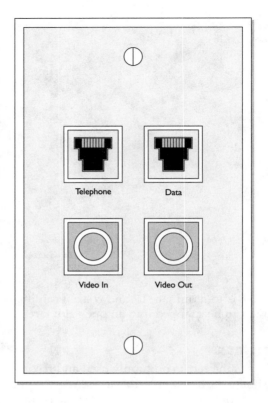

Figure 3-15
Modular jacks are inserted into a faceplate from the rear.

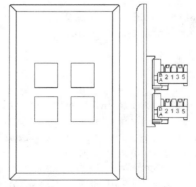

Original image courtesy of Smarthome, Inc.

The Distribution Panel

Whether the network cabling scheme is anchored by a small distribution panel, like the one shown in Figure 3-16, or a large fully integrated panel, the cabling scheme becomes a structured installation when the homerun cable pulls all terminate in this one location.

The distribution panel is the central hub for the communications lines and connections in a home. It serves as the interconnection point between service lines that enter the home and the cabling that distributes the various services to the rooms, areas, and zones of the house. The panel also provides an interconnection point for the data networking cabling throughout the home.

A distribution panel doesn't have to be a commercial device like the one shown in Figure 3-8; the various interconnecting devices could actually be mounted on a sheet of plywood and hung on a wall. However, commercially available distribution panels typically have basic service connections included and a variety of optional modules for different connection types and quantities. A common distribution panel supports a coaxial signal splitter, a telephone distribution block, and a data networking distribution block. Other devices, such as a telecom distribution block, audio distribution, and a video distribution block can be added to the panel, as required.

Distribution Panel Trim-Out

The distribution panel provides the interconnectivity of a structured network wiring system, not to mention versatility and flexibility. It also provides a single access point for all of the various home technology systems and communication services integrated into a home.

Typically, the only distribution panel found in an average home is the electrical panel. The electrical panel is the central point for incoming and service wiring in the home's electrical system. In the same way, a distribution panel simplifies and centralizes the design, installation, and perhaps more importantly, maintenance for the home's network cabling.

The distribution panel should ideally be centrally located in a home. However, it's far more important that it be central to the cabling scheme to minimize the lengths of cable runs as much as possible. On the other hand, if a home has a natural location for its distribution panel, cable is relatively inexpensive. Figure 3-17 illustrates how a room in the center of a home serves as a central distribution panel for the structured wiring installed throughout the home.

Figure 3-16

A residential structured wiring distribution panel

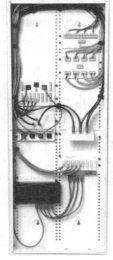

Photo courtesy of ChannelVision.

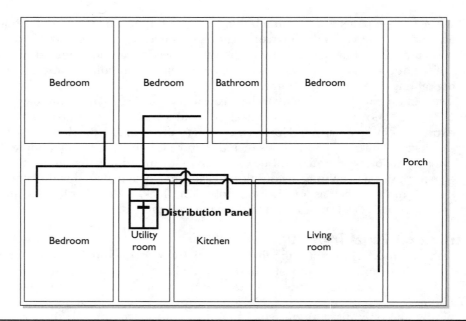

Figure 3-17   The ideal location for a network cabling distribution panel is a central point in the home.

Distribution Panel Installation

The distribution panel should be mounted on a wall at a safe distance from possible interference sources and at about eye level. If the panel is mounted too low or too high, access to the panel could be cumbersome later. Distribution panels are either flush-mount, which means they are mounted into the wall (this type should be installed during rough-in), or surface-mount. In either case, if multiple panels are installed, they should be set side-by-side on the same level. If the distribution panel is a flush mount, run conduit between the multiple panels to allow for easy hookup.

Following the manufacturer's documentation, remove the appropriate knockouts or plugs from the top or sides of the distribution panel's cabinet. If the cabinet has metal knockouts, you should install protective grommets in each hole to protect the cabling that will pass through them.

All cabling in the distribution panel should be labeled about 6 to 10 inches below where the cable enters the cabinet. This step is included in the TIA/EIA standards, which state that each cable should be individually identified both at the termination point and on the cable.

The cables terminating in the distribution panel should be organized by room, zone, or system using Velcro ties, cable ties, or another form of cable management. A bit of organization now will save time during troubleshooting or system reconfiguration later.

Distribution Panel Components Installation

Structured wiring distribution panels are available from empty panel shells that contain none of the modules needed to terminate and distribute the systems attached to the structured wiring all the way to fully populated distribution panels (see Figure 3-16). In most residential installations, a typical distribution panel should contain the following modules:

- **Bridged telephone module**   Used to bridge the telephone line connections from the telephone company's network interface device (NID) to the telephone lines in a home. The telephone module should have the capacity to bridge at least the number of incoming lines to at least the number of telephone lines being installed in the home.

- **Data network module**   Interconnects the incoming Internet service connection (DSL, ISDN, or cable) to the residential gateway and the distributed network outlets in the home. The connections supported should include RJ-45 and 110-type IDC contacts.

- **Video splitter module**   Combines off-air antenna, cable television, or satellite receiver services to the distributed video outlets in the home.

 NOTE   Extra capacity in these modules, in the form of connections for additional incoming and distributed lines beyond a home's current requirements, helps to future-proof a home.

Additional modules can also be installed, such as telephone or data security modules, video surveillance splitters, audio distribution modules, security system, and electrical surge suppressors or power line filters.

If the distribution panel modules must be installed into the distribution panel independently, a logical layout must be used to support cable management, ease of connection and troubleshooting, and perhaps most important, fit.

Placing Modules in the Distribution Panel   If the distribution panel is not preconfigured with the basic modules, or if additional modules are being added to a preconfigured panel, the modules should be placed into the panel in the location where it can be easily attached and which provides the shortest path to the cabling to which it will connect. There is really no standard way to configure a distribution panel, but typically the modules are added starting at the top of the panel to simplify the cable management inside the panel.

Mounting Distribution Panel Modules   Distribution panel modules typically include a mounting bracket kit that can be adjusted to fit the openings available in the panel back and allow some flexibility in their placement inside the panel. However, some add-in modules have screw-type connectors that are fixed in place (see Figure 3-18). Snap-in standoffs are commonly used to mount add-in modules into a distribution panel.

Figure 3-18
An audio distribution module with fixed-position mounting screws

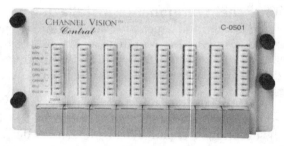

Photo courtesy of Channel Vision.

Distribution Panel Connections

The cable terminations made at the distribution panel mirror those made at the outlet end of each cable. Twisted-pair cabling is most commonly terminated using 110-style punch-down connections, and coaxial connections are made using F-type connectors. For audio connections that terminate into a distribution panel, screw-down terminals are usually used in the distribution panel.

Depending on the complexity of the systems being installed in a home, the distribution panel may connect to other distribution devices. For example, the data network lines may first connect to a hub or bridge before connecting into the distribution panel. In this case, patch cords, shorter runs of TP cable, are used to connect the hub into the distribution panel. The same goes for coaxial cabling for the video and Cat 5 cabling for a telephone system, where the distribution panel may connect into the video cable head-in or the telephone system demarcation point using patch cords.

When installing the AC power for the distribution panel, the appropriate national, state, and local electrical codes must be followed. For best results, the distribution panel should be wired into a dedicated 15-amp circuit using standard high-voltage electrical wiring. Many brands and models of structured wiring distribution panels void their warranties if their electrical guidelines aren't followed exactly.

Distribution Panel Grounding

It is important that the distribution panel be grounded to an earth ground. The panel itself, a power module, or a surge suppression module should each have a grounding connection (typically a screw) that can be connected to the earth ground of the main power line to the panel. Grounding the panel's AC power input provides grounded power distribution to any of the modules connecting to it, including DC power converters.

Cable and Outlet Testing

When installing network cabling in any situation, it is vital to both inspect and test the cable at each milestone in the process, such as after pulling the cable, after terminating the cable, and after mounting the terminations into outlets or faceplates.

The first test that should be performed is a visual test. A visual test should be performed during the rough-in phase as the cabling is installed and immediately after it is installed. This visual inspection should examine every inch of the installed cable and carefully examine the cable ends. If the ends have become damaged (meaning unusable in a quality connection), they should be trimmed before the cable is terminated. This is also the best time to ensure that the cables have been properly labeled and identified in your wire chart.

Standards Testing

The only way you can assure yourself and demonstrate to the customer that the network's wiring and infrastructure supports the network to be installed on it is with a planned and formal test procedure that incorporates the TIA/EIA TSB-67, the Transmission Performance Specifications for Field-Testing of Unshielded Twisted-Pair Cabling Systems (TSB-67 for short), and the TSB-95, which provides additional test parameters for Cat 5e cable.

A number of handheld devices are available to perform the tests prescribed in these two TSB standards. In fact, Cat 5e testers perform what is called a certified test that should assure your customer that his or her network wiring is installed per specification and is ready to support any network-capable devices attached to the network. Certifying the cable provides a benchmark for any future network or cable problems. However, you should know that Cat 5e testing devices can be quite expensive. Cable testing units, like the one shown in Figure 3-19, commonly include a master unit and a slave unit that are attached to the ends of the cable segment being tested and an auto-test function that measures the results of the test as either a pass or a fail.

Essentially, Cat 5e testing units perform two tests: a link test and a channel test. The link test measures the end-to-end connectivity (continuity) of a cable segment and is typically performed on the cable with the master unit at the distribution panel end

Figure 3-19

A multifunction cable tester with a master and a slave device

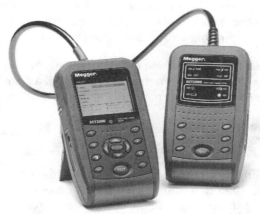

Photo courtesy of Megger Group Limited.

and the slave at the wall outlet end of the cable. A channel test extends the link test to include devices attached to the cable segment.

A Cat 5e link (cable only) should not be more than 295 feet (90 meters) in length. A Cat 5e channel shouldn't be more than 328 feet (100 meters) in length. The difference of 33 feet or 10 meters between a link and a channel represents the cables used to connect a computer or other device to a link. What this boils down to is that the cable running between the patch panel and the wall jack can only be 90 meters in length, and all of the cables used to connect a computer to a central device (like a gateway or router) cannot exceed 100 meters in length.

TSB Tests

The EIA/TIA TSB-95 standards specify the following standard testing procedures:

- **Attenuation test**   Measures the attenuation affect on a signal transmitted on a cable. A series of frequencies up to 100 MHz is transmitted on each wire pair at one end of a link and the strength of the signal received at the other end of the cable is measured.

- **Length test**   Measures the length of a cable segment. In addition to displaying the distance of the cable in feet or meters (at least to the point where the signal is reflected in the cable), this test checks the links and channels of a cable using time domain reflectometry (TDR) technology. TDR emits a signal pulse and then calculates the length of the cable based on what is called nominal velocity of propagation (NVP), which in essence is the speed of a signal through a cable. If the test fails, the cable is too long to meet standards.

- **Near-end crosstalk (NEXT) test**   Places a test signal on one pair of wires and then measures all of the other wire pairs for signal presence to see how much crosstalk the cable is allowing. Crosstalk is electromagnetic signals on one wire being picked up by another wire.

- **Wire-map test**   Tests each individual wire in the cable and whether or not it maps to the same pin at each end of the cable. This test is used to identify connector and pinning errors on a cable segment.

Any link that fails one of these tests should be replaced, rewired, reconnected, or, in the case of the length test, shortened or replaced. If a channel fails, you need to test the patch cords used to connect a particular networked device to the link being tested.

Chapter Review

Before beginning the pre-wire process, you should meet with the homeowners and discuss room use issues that impact the installation of the wiring and its connectors. This action ensures a shared vision of the home's structured wiring environment and should result in a rough sketch of the home, the devices, and the home's wiring requirements.

The process of pre-wiring a house consists of several major activities: determining the locations of the distribution plan and the outlets, creating a wire chart, placing outlet boxes or mud rings at each location, pulling the appropriate type and number of cable runs to each outlet location, labeling all cables at the distribution panel, terminating or protecting the cables at the outlets with the appropriate connecters, connecting the cable runs into the home's distribution panel, and testing all cable runs and connections.

The first step in the pre-wiring process is to install the outlet boxes and mud rings or plaster rings. Outlet boxes or mud rings are nailed or screwed to wall studs at 12 inches or 300 millimeters above the floor and 12 to 16 inches from any nearby electrical outlets. The outlet box or mud ring should be of appropriate size to accommodate the size and amount of cabling that is to terminate or pass through it. Sidecar brackets allow for two-gang boxes with both electrical and low-voltage wiring. Be sure to follow installation practices to avoid interference.

Four standard types of wiring are typically used to pre-wire a home in a structured wiring scheme: Cat 5e, coaxial, fiber optic, and quad wire. Bundled cables are commonly used. A bundled cable combines coaxial cable and Cat 5e cables into a single cable bundle. Bundles are also available that also include one or more runs of fiber optic cable.

Structured cable should not be placed less than 12 inches to electrical power lines to avoid the possibility of electrical interference. If an electrical cable must be crossed, the structured cabling should do so at a 90-degree angle. One or more separate cable runs are used to connect an outlet to the distribution panel using a home run or dedicated cable scheme. At least two feet of extra cable length should be left at the outlet end of the cable during rough-in to provide working cable for trim out. At least two feet of cable beyond the distribution panel location, or down to the floor, should be left at the distribution panel location.

Each cable run should be labeled per the wire chart to identify its cable type and intended use. Each cable should also be numbered and the number recorded on its labeling and the wiring plan diagram. Cable hooks can be used to bridge cable runs over areas with no support features, such as across an attic. Aluminum tubing or plastic piping conduits are not required for most home structured wiring, but should be used when the pathway available is too close to electrical wiring or other interference sources. Include a chase of 2-inch plastic piping for future use from key areas.

The structured wiring distribution panel is the central hub for the communications lines and connections in a home. It serves as the interconnection point between service lines that enter the home and the cabling that distributes the various services to the rooms of the house.

Performing continuity testing checks each cable for any crimps, breaks, or other installation problems that may have been introduced when the cable was pulled into the walls or when the drywall was hung. A cable with poor or no continuity should be replaced; it is just not good practice to leave a spliced cable in the wall of a structured wiring installation. A voltage meter or cable tester is used for this testing.

A formal test procedure that incorporates the TIA/EIA TSB-67 and TSB-95 should be used to test all structured wiring cable installed for use with a data network. The TSB-95 standards specify the following standard testing procedures: attenuation test, length test, NEXT test, and wire-map test.

The distribution panel provides the interconnectivity of the structured wiring system, along with versatility and flexibility. It also provides for a single access point for all of the various home technology systems and communication services integrated into a home.

Questions

1. Before beginning the process of pre-wiring a home, what document, form, or chart should be completed?

   A. Materials list

   B. System documentation

   C. User training guide

   D. Wire chart

2. What is the recommended minimum separation distance between a structured wiring cable and an AC electrical cable?

   A. 6 inches

   B. 18 inches

   C. 24 inches

   D. 12 inches

3. Which of the following cable types is not commonly used for home networking?

   A. Cat 5e

   B. Cat 3

   C. RG6

   D. Fiber optic

4. What is the central device in a structured wiring scheme that provides an interconnection between external services and internal cabling?

   A. Hub

   B. Switch

   C. Distribution panel

   D. Outlet box

5. What cable test should be performed immediately after installing a structured cable, typically before the cable is terminated?

    A. Fox and hound

    B. Attenuation

    C. Crosstalk feedback

    D. Continuity

6. Twisted-pair cabling for a data network is terminated with what type of connector?

    A. RJ-11

    B. RJ-45

    C. IEEE 1394

    D. EIA/TIA 568

7. What termination method is used to terminate twisted-pair cabling at the distribution panel?

    A. 66-style

    B. 110-style

    C. EIA/TIA 570

    D. Telco standard

8. Which standard should be used when terminating twisted-pair cabling for residential data networking use?

    A. IEEE 802.3

    B. EIA/TIA 568a

    C. EIA/TIA 568b

    D. EIA/TIA 570

9. Which of the following EIA/TIA standards specifies transmission performance standards testing UTP cable?

    A. 568a

    B. 568b

    C. TSB 67

    D. 570

10. Which of the following tests measures how much of a transmitted signal is present on other wire pairs in the same cable?

   A. Attenuation

   B. Length

   C. NEXT

   D. Wire-map

Answers

1. **D.** The wire chart summarizes the cabling to be installed and identifies the placement and purpose of each cable run, something that should be understood clearly before beginning the pre-wiring of a home.

2. **C.** Although the recommended distance is 6 to 24 inches between structured wiring and electrical lines, the minimum distance should be 24 inches to avoid interference from 240 V lines.

3. **B.** Cat 3 cable doesn't provide enough bandwidth to handle today and tomorrow's system requirements. The other cable types listed as choices are structured wiring cable types.

4. **C.** Hubs and switches are connectivity devices used primarily for data networking. Outlet boxes are used to mount terminators and connectors to cable runs.

5. **D.** A continuity check verifies that the cable is free of breaks and shorts end-to-end. The other choices are cable tests that are used for locating, identifying, and verifying cable performance capabilities.

6. **B.** An RJ-11 connector is used with standard telephone (2-wire) connections; IEEE 1394 is commonly known as FireWire; and EIA/TIA 568 is a business environment cabling standard.

7. **B.** The 110-style punch-down type block is used to connect TP cable to RJ-45 connectors as well as distribution panels and patch panels.

8. **B.** EIA/TIA 568a is the cabling standard recommended by the residential data network cabling standard, EIA/TIA 570.

9. **C.** TSB 67, along with TSB 95, are the testing standards required by EIA/TIA 568 and 570.

10. **C.** Near-end crosstalk (NEXT) tests to see if pairs or wires in the same cable are interfering with a signal transmitted on a wire in the same cable.

Troubleshooting Basics

In this chapter, you will learn about:
- Standard troubleshooting steps
- Problem identification and diagnostics
- Testing procedures
- Testing devices

The wiring system installed in a home should be something homeowners can take for granted. Homeowners can't be faulted for believing that if the system is properly installed, it should never break or have problems. In fact, that was the basic idea behind all of the precautions and extra steps you took during the installation.

However, it is possible for a wiring system to develop problems. Assuming the cabling was properly installed and all of the appropriate standards were observed and implemented, rarely will a problem be with the cable itself. That is, unless something has happened to the wire, such as a nail or screw being driven through it or a wire tugged on a bit too much, or if the system has plainly been abused. There is also the possibility that a connector or termination wasn't installed exactly right or the cable was installed improperly.

Nonetheless, should one or more of a home's systems stop performing or perform oddly, a primary candidate for consideration should be the wiring and cabling. This chapter focuses on the troubleshooting processes and tools used to identify and isolate a cabling problem, should one exist.

General Troubleshooting Procedure

There are six steps in a generalized troubleshooting procedure. While not every step is necessarily required in all problems, for the most part, you should apply each of these steps as a general rule. The steps of a general troubleshooting procedure are:

1. Prepare to troubleshoot.
2. Determine the symptoms.
3. Reproduce the problem.

4. Apply the fix.

5. Test the fix.

6. Document the maintenance activity.

Prepare to Troubleshoot

When you approach a problem that requires some troubleshooting and diagnostic work, you should have the appropriate tools (physical and software, as appropriate) to do the job. Your tools should include an appropriate work space, the system and component documentation, and, of course, you—your knowledge, abilities, skills, and approach to the job.

While the other tools may be fairly obvious, your approach to the job should be one of confidence, a can-do attitude, and a willingness to see the process through to its end. Your ability to successfully troubleshoot any problem is equal to how complete and thorough your troubleshooting process is.

Before beginning your actual troubleshooting process, you should review the safety requirements prescribed by your employer, the state, and even your own common sense. The first and foremost rule of troubleshooting is that you should do no harm.

Determine the Symptoms

First of all, remember that most homeowners are not technicians and cannot give a technical description of what they believe to be a problem with the system beyond the fact that something isn't working as they believe it should. With this in mind, listen carefully to their description of the symptoms without interrupting and, very importantly, without jumping to conclusions.

It is a good practice to create a symptom report that includes the pertinent information surrounding the problem being reported by the customer. In the symptom report, you should include such information as:

- The date
- The name of the person reporting and describing the problem
- The suspected system or component
- A brief yet complete description of the symptoms being reported
  - If the problem is intermittent, you should describe:
    - The frequency with which it occurs
    - The time(s) of the day it occurs
    - Any particular environmental situations when it occurs
    - The method used to temporarily eliminate it
  - If the problem is reproducible, include:
    - A brief statement as to your ability to reproduce the symptoms
- A detail of the work performed, including any parts, components, or systems repaired, replaced, or taken offline to correct the problem

When interviewing a customer, it is best to use direct questions that cannot be answered yes or no. You should ask questions that require a specific answer. Questions that start with who, which, when, how, where, and what that request information about the problems experienced, are best.

After you've completed a symptom report, you should have the customer review it for concurrence that you understand the symptoms and have recorded them accurately. You may even want to get the customer to sign or initial the report.

Reproduce the Problem

If you can't reproduce the exact symptoms the customer is experiencing, then fixing the problem will likely be a shot in the dark. If you have prior knowledge of similar problems from vendor bulletins or other troubleshooting situations, you may be able to exact the fix. However, unless you can witness the exact symptoms for a problem, you may or may not be applying the appropriate fix. The ability to reproduce the symptoms ensures you that you can't be blamed for making the problems worse.

Apply the Fix

Most system, component, or wiring problems have at least a few alternative remedies, with the possible exception of plugging in the electrical cord to fix a component that won't power on. You should apply the most appropriate fix first, which is the fix that is the least invasive, costs the least, and can be applied in the least amount of time.

Test the Fix

The best way to satisfy your customer is to demonstrate that the symptoms are no longer present. To achieve this result, you must test the system in question. There are three questions that you should be able to answer "no" if your repair and its testing are successful.

- Are the symptoms recurring?
- Have other symptoms appeared?
- Is further corrective maintenance required to permanently eliminate the problem?

Document the Maintenance Activity

Every troubleshooting, diagnostic, and repair activity performed on any part of a system should be formally recorded in the system's maintenance log. The more detail provided in the maintenance log, the better the next technician will be able to continue working on the same issues or determine the causes of new issues.

 NOTE Remember that most system problems occur as the result of a change made to some part of the system.

A written record should be maintained of any and all problems reported or even suspected about the structured wiring system of a home. Actually, this maintenance record should have been created at the end of the trim-out phase of the installation project when cable verification testing was performed to create a benchmark against which later testing can be compared.

Any time a technician responds to a customer or visit's a home to diagnose, troubleshoot, or resolve a cabling problem, he or she should record in a maintenance log the suspected problem, the actions taken to diagnose the problem, the steps used to isolate the problem, and the solution applied. Often, any problems that develop after one problem has been solved are because of changes made to the system or a problem introduced during the testing or resolution of the earlier problem. This documentation makes it much easier to troubleshoot the next problem.

Troubleshooting Cable Problems

A suspected cabling problem must be identified and isolated before an appropriate solution can be applied. Each type of system, which means each type of cable, has its own unique potential problems, and each potential cable problem should be eliminated through a methodical diagnostics process.

Here is a recommended approach for identifying a cabling problem:

1. **Listen**   Unless you have witnessed the symptoms of a problem firsthand, you must rely on information provided by the homeowner. Listen carefully and actively to their description of the problem and interact with the customer enough to fully understand what he or she believes to be the issues.

2. **Look**   Ask the homeowner to re-create the problem for you. If the customer is able to re-create the problem for you, make a note of exactly what you observe, hear, or smell. Your senses are your best fact-gathering tools. From what you have learned, you should be able to determine what your next diagnostic steps should be. If the problem cannot be re-created, a test procedure should still be performed, but its nature will be more generic.

3. **Inspect**   Starting at the malfunctioning device, begin checking the integrity of all visible components and connections of the system. Check connections for fit and snugness, watching for loose wires, broken or pierced insulation, smashed or kinked cable, and any other obvious conditions that could be causing the problem. In many cases, the problem can be found on an exterior (patch cord) cable rather than in the wall.

   If no problems can be found with the existing patch or connector cabling, you can replace or remove them to minimize the variables that could be the source of the problem. Next, your diagnostics should move to the distribution or patch panel. If possible, connect the incoming suspected cable to a different port on the distribution panel or source device to see if the problem may be with the jack on that device. If the problem still exists, check the termination of the cable very closely and verify the connector pinout (the placement of the cable wires in the connector). See Chapter 2 for details of connectors and termination. If the termination of the cable is good, the problem is likely within the cable run.

4. **Test**   If the source of the problem hasn't been identified to this point, the cable run should be tested for shorts, crosstalk, and attenuation. These tests are discussed later in this chapter.

Cable Testing

In a residential structured wiring installation, typically the runs are not long enough to develop attenuation problems and, because of the shorter runs, the signal tends to be stronger so crosstalk and signal return loss aren't typically problems either. However, this doesn't mean that these issues can't happen; it just means that in a typical structured wiring installation they are usually uncommon.

Cable Diagnostics

Cable problems in structured wiring systems are more likely to be caused by damage to the cable, improper termination, or improper installation caused during rough-in and trim-out. The construction crew can also damage a cable during their finish work, when a cable can be nailed, stapled, cut, crimped, or crushed.

Testing Twisted-Pair TP Cable

Common TP cable problems include the following:

- **Cable impedance**   If the wrong type or quality of cabling is installed, the cable may not support the proper impedance levels required to correctly transmit signals over the cable.

- **Cross-pinning**   If the pinout (wiring pattern) of a TP cable is incorrect at one or both ends of the cable (for example, the receive pin on one end of the cable is connected to the receive pin on the other end of the cable), the transmitted signal will not be transmitted or received correctly, resulting in a crossed or switched pinning condition. Figure 4-1 illustrates wire pairs crossed to create a reversed pair fault.

- **Open**   An open circuit lacks continuity between the pins on each end of the cable, indicating that a wire has been broken or one of the pins is not properly attached (see Figure 4-2).

- **Short**   A short occurs when two or more conductor wires in a cable are in contact or if a metal object, such as a nail or staple penetrates the cable and creates a contact between two or more conductors (see Figure 4-3).

- **Split pair**   If one conductor of a wire pair is connected to the wrong pin at each end of the wire, which in effect splits the pair, the cable will not function properly. Figure 4-4 illustrates this condition.

Figure 4-1
Two pairs of
a twisted-pair
cable have been
reversed.

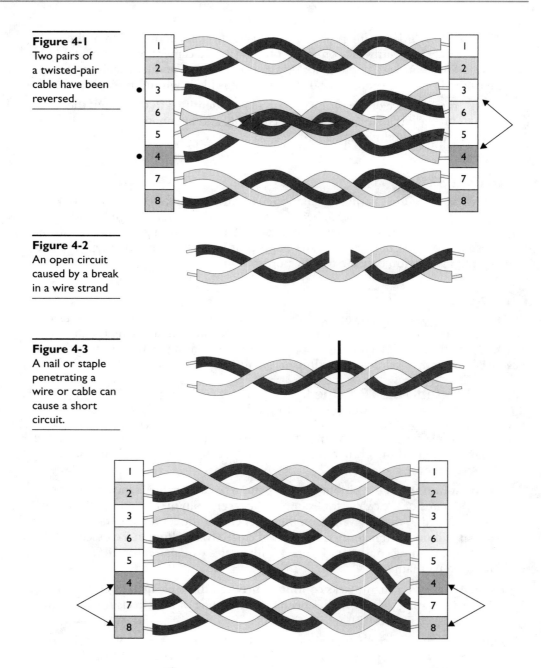

Figure 4-2
An open circuit
caused by a break
in a wire strand

Figure 4-3
A nail or staple
penetrating a
wire or cable can
cause a short
circuit.

Figure 4-4   A split wire pair results in a poor termination and likely a nonfunctioning link.

- **Termination**   If a cable termination changes the impedance of the cable, which should be 100 ohms on a TP cable and 75 ohms on a coaxial cable, the transmitted signal may be reflected by the terminator and cause data loss.

Diagnosing TP Cable

When a cable is suspected to have a fault, you must be able to locate it in order to fix it. You need to be able to identify whether or not the fault is on a certain pin or at some distance along the cable, or even as far away as the far-end connector.

The two test procedures that can be helpful in determining where a fault may exist on a cable, if one exists at all, are wire map and time domain reflectometry (TDR) testing. To accomplish these tests you need a digital multimeter and a tone/probe tester.

Wire Map Testing   When a cable fault is first suspected as the source of a problem, perhaps the most useful and informative test that can be performed on residential structured wiring, especially TP cable, is a wire map test.

Wire map testers are often incorporated into a TDR tester. The tester shown in Figure 4-5 verifies the pin-to-pin connectivity between the ends of a cable and, in doing so, eliminates or finds any of the problems described in the preceding section.

TDR Testing   A time domain reflectometer (TDR) transmits a signal on a conductor and measures the time required for the signal or some part of the signal to return. If a fault exists on a conductor, the signal is reflected at the point of the fault. The amount of time required for this to take place is then converted into a distance using a formula that involves the speed of light, the velocity of propagation, and some simple arithmetic.

Figure 4-5
A data communication cable tester that performs wire map and TDR testing

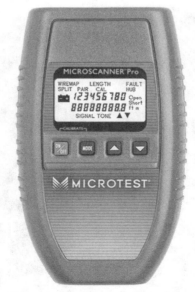

Photo courtesy of Everett Communications.

A TDR tester can tell you only where a problem may be, meaning at what distance from the test point, and not what type of problem may exist. Any cable that has two metal conductors can be tested using TDR, which makes it perfect for testing twisted-pair cabling (refer to Figure 4-5).

Multimeter   A commonly used tool for testing cable is a multimeter, shown in Figure 4-6, which can be used for testing voltage, current, resistance, and continuity on a copper wire. The most common problem with copper wire cabling is an open circuit. Using the resistance test (or ohm test) of a multimeter is the easiest way to test for this problem.

Toner/Probe Testing   Another common testing procedure uses a tone generator and probe to identify one cable from a bundle, or find a cable inside a wall or under a floor. This test is also referred to as "fox and hound." The tone generator generates a specific signal on the cable and the probe converts it to an audible tone. The closer the probe is placed to the cable carrying the generated signal, the louder the audible tone is sounded. Figure 4-7 shows both a tone generator and probe.

Testing Coaxial Cable

Testing coaxial cabling is less complex than testing TP cable. First of all, there is only one conductor, so the tests performed by a tone generator and probe, a multimeter, and a TDR are typically sufficient for tracking down any problem.

Although coaxial cable is generally more durable than TP cable, they can exhibit many of the same faults, except, of course, those involving wire pairs specifically. However, problems on a coaxial cable are typically caused by improper termination or damage to

Figure 4-6
A handheld digital
multimeter

Figure 4-7
A tone generator
and probe are
used to locate
and identify
cables and wires.

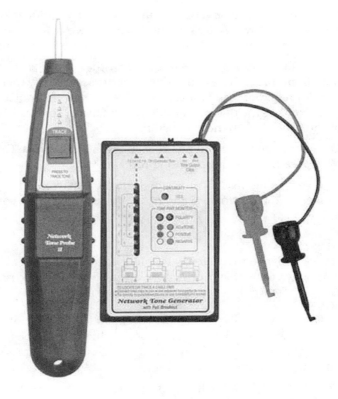

the cable. Also, although a coaxial cable has only one center conductor, remember that the metallic shielding on the cable also carries current and between these two conductors some faults can occur.

When troubleshooting a coaxial cable, here are some physical conditions to check for:

- The coaxial cable must match the impedance requirements of the equipment to which it is attached. Coaxial cable with a cable TV system must be 75 ohm. The coaxial cable for a data network must be 50 ohm. If 75-ohm cable is used for a data network, intermittent data errors, which are very hard to track down, are likely to occur.

- Be sure the connectors and terminators attached to the cable are the correct size and match the impedance of the cable. Using the wrong connectors or terminators can cause signal faults on the cable.

- Make sure that each end of the cable is properly terminated and, although this is somewhat obvious, be sure that there are two connectors or terminators on each cable segment.

- Avoid using twist-on connectors because they can loosen easily and cause intermittent problems. Use crimp-on connectors and apply them with a good quality crimping tool made for coaxial cable. Be sure the tool and the connectors are fitted for the type of coaxial cable you are using, such as RG6. Don't use pliers or the like to attach the connectors.

- Ensure that only one end of a coaxial cable is grounded. Grounding both can cause intermittent transmission problems.

- If you are using BNC-T connectors with a PC network, make sure the "T" is connected directly to a PC and not connected to a patch cord that connects to the PC.

Cable Tests

Cable testers designed to test coaxial cable specifically are available, but a better investment is usually a tester that is capable of testing both TP and coaxial cabling. The standard tests used for troubleshooting coaxial cable are as follows:

- **Attenuation**   Coaxial cable has a segment length limit of 185 meters (about 607 feet) when used in a data network, which should be more than adequate for any home network. However, attenuation can be a problem for coaxial cabling that is run to exterior cameras and other devices.

- **Crosstalk**   If the cable has been crushed or otherwise damaged, the inner conductor and the outer conductor energies can cause crosstalk between the two conductors.

- **Impedance**   The impedance of the cable should match the requirements of the equipment to which it's connected, and the impedance of the connectors must match that of the cable.

- **TDR**   The TDR testing of a coaxial cable measures the length of the cable to a reflection point, which (one hopes) is the terminator or connector on the end of the cable. If the TDR test detects a short or open circuit that causes the test signal to reflect before the termination, the point in the cable where the problem exists is returned.

Chapter Review

There are six steps in a generalized troubleshooting procedure: prepare to troubleshoot, determine the symptoms, reproduce the problem, apply the fix, test the fix, and document the maintenance activity.

It is a good practice to create a symptom report that includes the pertinent information surrounding the problem being reported by the customer. After you've completed a symptom report, you should have the customer review it for concurrence that you understand the symptoms and have recorded them accurately.

 NOTE Every troubleshooting, diagnostic, and repair activity performed on any part of a system should be formally recorded in the system's maintenance log.

A suspected cabling problem must be identified and isolated before an appropriate solution can be applied. A recommended approach for identifying a cabling problem involves the following steps: listen, look, inspect, and test.

Cable problems are most likely caused by damage to the cable, improper termination, or improper installation that may have been introduced during rough-in, trim-out, or during construction. The cable may have been nailed, stapled, cut, crimped, or crushed. Common TP cable problems include cable impedance, crossed pinning, open circuit, short circuit, split pair, and improper termination.

Two test procedures can be helpful in determining where a fault exists on a cable: time domain reflectometry (TDR) and wire mapping. The most commonly used tool for testing cable is a multimeter, which is used for testing voltage, current, resistance, and continuity on a copper wire. Wire map testers verify the pin-to-pin connectivity between the ends of a cable. A tone generator and probe are used to identify one cable in a bundle or to find a cable inside a wall.

Questions

1. Which of the following is not a step in the troubleshooting procedure described in this chapter?

   A. Determine the symptoms.

   B. Call for help.

   C. Test the fix.

   D. Document the maintenance activity.

2. Which of the following is not listed in this chapter as an approach for identifying a cable problem?

   A. Listen

   B. Look

   C. Replace suspected cable runs

   D. Test

3. When should a record be created that documents the testing and performance of a structured wiring system?

   A. On the first visit to investigate a problem

   B. During trim-out

    C. After solving a problem

    D. Only after fixing "real" problems

4. Which of the following problems is not a common issue with a structured wiring system?

    A. Attenuation

    B. Reversed pairs

    C. Open circuits

    D. Improper termination

5. After completing the trim-out and finish work of a structured wiring system, the homeowner calls to complain that one of the PCs attached to the data networking system cannot be reached from other PCs in the home for file sharing. After diagnostic testing, you discover that the fault is a short about 20 feet up the TP cable connecting the PC to the patch panel. What diagnostic test was likely used to determine this information?

    A. Ohm (resistance) test

    B. Tone generator/probe test

    C. Wire map test

    D. TDR test

6. The pinout of the connector on a TP cable is incorrect at one end of the cable and the transmitted signal is not being received correctly. What type of problem does this describe?

    A. Impedance

    B. Cross pinning

    C. Open circuit

    D. Short circuit

7. What impedance level should a TP cable have?

    A. 50 ohms

    B. 75 ohms

    C. 100 ohms

    D. 150 ohms

8. Which type of test device is able to verify the pin-to-pin connectivity between two ends of a cable?

    A. TDR

    B. Multimeter

    C. Tone generator/probe

    D. Wire map

9. Which type of cable testing device can be used to locate a single cable in a wall that is a part of a cable bundle?

    A. TDR

    B. Multimeter

    C. Tone generator/probe

    D. Wire map

10. Which of the following is not a common cable fault of a coaxial cable?

    A. Improper termination

    B. Cable damage

    C. Impedance of 35 ohms

    D. Split pairs

Answers

1. **B.** Before you respond to a customer call, you should ensure you have the right tools and people to do the job.

2. **C.** During diagnostics, replacing suspected cable runs may be wasteful and unnecessary. First gather some facts and then act.

3. **B.** The first testing cycles performed on the cable should begin the record into which all maintenance activities are recorded.

4. **A.** Because the cable runs tend to be less than the maximum segment length for TP cabling, attenuation is rarely an issue in residential systems.

5. **D.** A TDR test is able to locate the position of a fault on a cable and report the distance from the test point to the fault.

6. **B.** Because of the size of the wires and the connectors, cross pinning is a common problem for TP cabling.

7. **C.** A TP cable that tests for less than 100 ohms may be of insufficient quality or a termination error may be causing the problem.

8. **D.** A multimeter is also able to test for continuity, but not to identify the pins in question; wire mapping can do both.

9. **C.** The probe uses induction amplification to sense the tone generator's signal and sound an audible tone when the cable carrying the signal is located.

10. **D.** A coaxial cable has only a single conductor wire.

PART II

Home Computer Networks

Wiring Documentation

In this chapter, you will learn about:
- Essential components of a complete wiring documentation set
- When to document the components of the wiring installation

One of the more important components of any wiring installation is a full set of documentation for the wiring design and installation. Wiring documentation is not only important to have in case of wiring problems and troubleshooting, it also provides information necessary should, at some future point, the wiring needs to be updated or repurposed for future systems or devices.

A complete set of wiring documentation for a home system can help to minimize any system or network downtime; increase the useful life of the wiring installation; allow any technician, in addition to than the technician who installed the wiring, to troubleshoot and diagnose wiring problems; and significantly reduce the time needed to make changes to the wiring.

Wiring Documentation Components

A complete set of wiring documentation should include certain specific components. There are degrees of completeness in wiring documentation sets, but at minimum the documentation for a home system's wiring should include:

- A diagram or floor plan of the home or building showing a map of the installed wiring and its terminations
- A logical system diagram
- A wiring plan
- Manufacturer documentation for wiring, terminations, and supported devices
- A maintenance log
- Contact information

Wiring Diagram

Regardless of the complexity of the wiring installation, during the planning and installation phases (rough-in and trim-out), a diagram was created and possibly updated with adjustments made to the plan during installation. Figure 5-1 is an illustration of what such a diagram looks like. The wiring diagram included in the final wiring documentation should be complete and reflect the installation as completed.

Logical System Diagram

The logical system diagram identifies the devices attached to each run of wiring. As shown in the sample logical system diagram in Figure 5-2, each of the devices supported by the installed wiring is identified.

Figure 5-1

A sample diagram of a wiring installation for an audio/video system

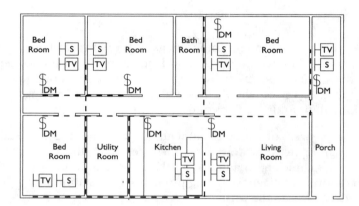

Figure 5-2

A simple logical system diagram for an audio/video system

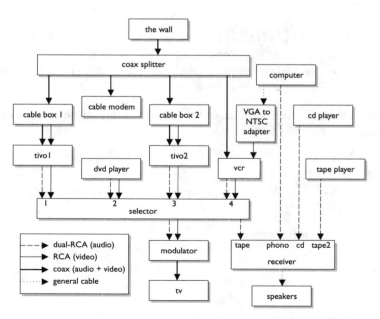

Image courtesy of Neilfred Picciotto.

Wiring Plan

The wiring plan (see Table 5-1), as its name implies, is developed during the preinstallation phase of the wiring project. However, as the installation proceeds, the wiring plan must be updated to reflect the actual installation of the wiring. The wiring plan identifies not only the wiring type used, but its termination point and the device each wire run supports.

Notice that the completed wiring chart shown in Table 5-1 identifies each cable or wire segment with a label or identification number. Labeling wire runs is discussed later in the chapter (see "Identifying Wire Segments," later in this chapter).

Manufacturer Documentation

For each type of wire or cable installed and for each terminator and supported device, you should include its specifications, installation instructions, and other manufacturer or vendor supplied documentation in your wiring documentation package. This information should include, at minimum:

- Manufacturer or vendor name
- Date of purchase
- Purchase documentation identification numbers
- Make and model numbers
- Serial numbers, if applicable
- Warranty information

Label/ID#	Type	Source	Destination	Device	Use/Comments
1	Cat 5	House feed	Distribution panel (DP)	Phone feed	Phone feed
2	Cat 5	House feed	DP	Future	Future
3	RG6	House feed	DP	Future	Cable feed—future
4	RG6	Attic	DP	Future TV antenna	Loop extra cable
5	RG6	Attic	DP	Future FM antenna	Loop extra cable
6	RG6	Roof	DP	DSS feed	Satellite TV
7	RG6	Roof	DP	DSS feed	Future satellite service
8	Cat 5	CC	Living room	Phone jack	
9	Cat 5	CC	Living room	Data jack	
10	RG6	CC	Living room	TV jack	

Table 5-1   A Sample Wiring Planning Chart

Maintenance Log

The maintenance log for a wiring plant should include an entry for any troubleshooting, repair, upgrade, change, to any wire segment in the system beginning at the point where the installation is completed. Table 5-2 shows a sample of the maintenance log for a wiring installation.

A detailed record of the actions taken on the wiring plant will provide valuable information for the next technician who responds to a trouble call, even if it's you. Knowing the last action taken on a suspected wire segment may be all the information you need to focus your corrective actions and not have to troubleshoot and diagnose the problem.

A written record should be maintained of any and all problems reported or even suspected about the structured wiring system of a home. As mentioned in Chapter 4, this maintenance record should have been created at the end of the trim-out phase of the installation project when cable verification testing was performed to create a benchmark against which later testing can be compared.

Anytime a technician comes to a customer's premises to diagnose, troubleshoot, or resolve a cabling problem, the suspected problem, the actions taken to diagnose the problem, the steps used to isolate the problem, and the solution applied should be recorded in a maintenance log. Often, any problems that develop after one problem has been solved are the cause of changes made to the system or a problem introduced during the testing or resolution of the earlier problem. This documentation makes it much easier to troubleshoot the next problem.

Contact Information

The wiring documentation should include the names, telephone numbers, e-mail addresses, and other pertinent contact information for any and all technicians who participated in the planning, design, installation, and maintenance of the wiring system. In addition, if not already available in the vendor information, the name, address, contact name, phone numbers, e-mail addresses, and website addresses for the manufacturers whose materials, devices, or components are installed in the system should also be included.

Label/ID#	Date	Technician	Action	Results
16	12/10/07	RG	Test RJ-45 termination at distribution panel	Connector replaced
32	12/21/07	HH	Perform continuity test	Tested okay
33	12/21/07	HH	Perform continuity test	Connector 28 identified as bad and replaced
5	1/15/08	RG	RJ-45 connectors replaced with Class 7 connectors	Tested and operational

Table 5-2 A Sample Wire Maintenance Log

Identifying Wire Segments

Perhaps more important than any other identifying information about a wire plant is the identity of each separate wire segment, connector, and device integrated into the home's system. There are far too many unstructured wiring systems installed in buildings and homes. When the need arises to determine which particular wire or connector may be faulty, the difficulty factor of the task can be exponential. If you arrive at a home to troubleshoot a problem and find that minimal or no documentation exists and none of the cable or wiring is labeled, you will first need to identify the particular segment you need before you can begin any other testing.

Simply identifying each wire segment, connector, and device as it is installed in the system and recording its identity in the wire plan, logical diagram, and physical diagram ensures that whoever arrives to perform maintenance work on the system will be able to proceed logically and efficiently.

Wire Labels

By far, the most important part of any wiring system or network to physically label is the wiring itself. More than likely each type of cabling or wiring installed is the same color and has the same outer jacket markings on it. When you need to troubleshoot a line problem on an audio cable that terminates in the far bedroom, it can save time if you are able to locate that cable by name (or number) readily.

An industry standard (TIA/EIA-606) prescribes that all network components must have a label that assigns a unique identifier to each. To meet this standard, most cabling and termination device manufacturers include a space for a label on the product. Labels specifically designed for use to identify cable and wiring segments, like those shown in Figure 5-3, are available in a variety of sizes, shapes, and colors.

Each end of a wire or cable should be labeled to assign an identity and indicate the purpose or use of that segment. The coding scheme used should be as simple and consistent as possible so that no special decoders are needed to identify each segment.

Figure 5-3
Cable labels
applied to cable
segments

Photo courtesy of Brady Worldwide, Inc.

Table 5-3	Room	Outlet	Type	Label Number
A Sample	Theater (T)	2	Video (V)	0102
Cable or Wire				
Identification	Theater (T)	3	Audio (A)	0103
Scheme	Theater (T)	5	Audio (A)	0104

If a more complex scheme is used, an explanation and legend for the scheme should be included in the wiring documentation package.

One example of a cable and wire segment identification scheme includes the termination point of the wire segment (room), the cable purpose or type, and the cable number. Table 5-3 shows the details of this particular scheme.

As shown in Table 5-3, a particular wire segment is identified by the room in which it terminates, the outlet it terminates at, the use or purpose of the cable, and the unique number assigned to the cable. The label placed on the cable represented in the first entry should read "T2-V-0102," which indicates the cable terminates in the home theater at outlet 2 as a video cable assigned the number 0102. Whatever scheme is used, this level of identification should be used.

As each cable is labeled, the identity of the cable should be recorded in the wiring documentation where appropriate.

Termination Labels

Like each of the wire segments in the system, each termination point should also be labeled and identified. This includes outlets, patch panel connections, hubs, splitters, and all source devices. Identifying all termination points in a wiring system helps to identify the wire segment as well as the far connection point of the wire.

Chapter Review

The documentation for a home system's wiring should include a floor plan showing the wiring and terminations, a logical system diagram, a wiring plan, manufacturer documentation, a maintenance log, and contact information.

The wiring diagram included in the final wiring documentation should be complete and reflect the installation as completed. The logical system diagram identifies the devices attached to each run of wiring. The wiring plan identifies not only the wiring type used, but its termination point and the device each wire run supports. The specifications, installation instructions, and other manufacturer-supplied documentation for each type of wire installed should be included in the wiring documentation package.

The maintenance log for a wiring plant should include an entry for any troubleshooting, repair, upgrade, or change to any wire segment in the system, beginning at the point where the installation is completed. The wiring documentation should include the names, telephone numbers, e-mail addresses, and other pertinent contact information for any and all technicians who participated in the planning, design, installation, and maintenance of the wiring system.

Each separate wire segment, connector, and device integrated into the home's system should be identified and labeled. Industry standard TIA/EIA-606 prescribes that network components be labeled with a unique identifier. As each cable is labeled, the identity of the cable should be recorded in the wiring documentation where appropriate.

Questions

1. Which of the following is not normally included in the wiring documentation of a home system?

   A. Floor plan

   B. Wiring plan

   C. List of recommended technicians

   D. Maintenance log

2. Which of the following doesn't necessarily include the identification information on wiring labels?

   A. Maintenance log

   B. Wiring plan

   C. Logical diagram

   D. Physical diagram

3. A record of all changes, troubleshooting, repairs, and other actions to the wiring is kept in the

   A. Maintenance log

   B. Wiring plan

   C. Logical diagram

   D. Physical diagram

4. What record illustrates the placement, path, and terminations of the system's wiring?

   A. Logical diagram

   B. Wiring plan

   C. Wiring diagram

   D. Manufacturer's documentation

5. What record depicts the relationships of the installed components and the wiring system?

   A. Logical diagram

   B. Wiring plan

   C. Wiring diagram

   D. Manufacturer's documentation

6. What component of the wiring documentation is initially created during the planning phase of a wiring system?

   A. Wiring plan

   B. Maintenance log

   C. Contact information

   D. Logical diagram

7. Which of the following elements of the manufacturer's documentation are important reasons to include the manufacturer's documentation in the wiring documentation?

   A. Wire and device specifications

   B. Troubleshooting guide

   C. Make and model

   D. Warranty information

   E. Answers A through D are all valid reasons to include a manufacturer's documentation in the wiring documentations.

8. What component of the wiring documentation allows a technician to learn all past actions of the system?

   A. Wiring plan

   B. Maintenance log

   C. Contact information

   D. Logical diagram

9. Using the sample wire identification method described in the chapter, what does the identification code of T6-A-0121 indicate?

   A. Terminal, Room 6, Audio, Cable segment 121

   B. Terminal 6, Run A, Outlet 121

   C. Theater, Outlet 6, Audio, Segment 121

   D. Theater, Segment 6, Audio, Outlet 121

10. Which of the following system components should be labeled for identification? (Choose all that apply.)

    A. Cable segments

    B. Outlets

    C. Interconnect jacks and plugs

    D. Electrical wiring

Answers

1. **C.** A list of technicians may be obsolete quickly, where the other choices provide the baseline of information needed by a technician.

2. **C.** While it could include the identification information on the wiring labels, the logical diagram is meant to depict the relationships of the system's components.

3. **A.** Granted, this one was kind of easy. However, it is important to understand the purpose and value of the maintenance log.

4. **C.** The key word is *illustrates*. The wiring diagram depicts the path of wire runs and where each is terminated.

5. **A.** The logical diagram illustrates the hierarchy and relationships of system components.

6. **A.** Although it may be adjusted during the installation phases, the wiring plan should be created prior to the wiring being installed.

7. **E.** All of the elements listed are valuable information that should be included in the wiring documentation.

8. **B.** If properly maintained, the maintenance log provides a history and chronology of all past repair, test, and modification actions to the system.

9. **C.** This sample identification method is not a standard, and each company or technician may have their own method. However, whatever method is used should be documented in the wiring documentation.

10. **A, B, C.** Labeling the outlets and interface devices clearly and distinctly should be enough for later identification and location.

PART II

Computer Network Hardware and Software

In this chapter, you will learn about:

- Common home networking devices
- Network cable and wiring media
- Network operating systems and protocols
- Network security measures
- Network addressing

A home computer network isn't really all that different from any other type of computer network. The only difference that may exist is one of scale; where a network in a business may involve dozens, if not hundreds, of computers and networked devices, a home network typically includes only a few computers and other devices. The number of nodes in any network affects only its size and the complexity of its physical layout. However, in terms of hardware, communications devices, cable and wiring, as well as its overall purpose, a network is a network.

Any network, whether in a business or home, is made up of two fundamental groups of components: hardware and software. The networking hardware establishes the physical network, but without software, the network has no life. Networking software prepares and presents data to the media for transmission. At the other end of the media, software intercepts, formats, and presents the data to a computer for processing. When the response is ready, the software performs its tasks to deliver the data to the requesting PC and assists the PC to display the data for the user. Without several types of network software, none of that would happen.

In this chapter, you'll learn about both the hardware and software components typically found in a home network. On the hardware side, this includes computers, cabling, network adapters, Internet gateways, and some of the more important communication/connectivity devices. On the software side, protocols, network operating systems, and a few networking utilities that can be used to test, debug, and troubleshoot a network are included in the discussion.

NOTE When I use the term *home network* in this chapter, I'm referring to a home computer network or a home data network and not the telephone, lighting, heating, security systems, or networks.

Network Hardware Components

As illustrated in Figure 6-1, a basic home network typically includes some standard hardware components:

- An Internet gateway device that provides a connection to an Internet service
- Two or more personal computers and peripheral devices
- Network adapters in each device connected to the network
- Network media (cabling or wireless)

In addition, a home network may also require some form of network clustering or connectivity devices. Regardless of the complexity of the network, these basic devices can be found in virtually all computer networks. Each of these component types is discussed in the sections that follow.

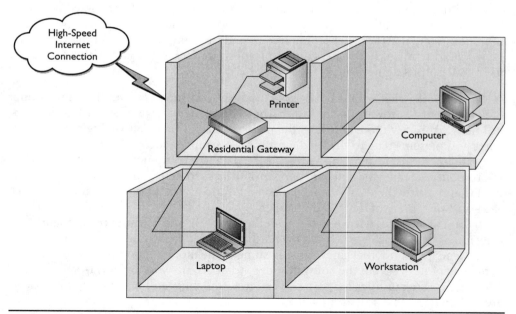

Figure 6-1 A simple home network using a communication service gateway to share access to an Internet link

Computers

By definition, a network interconnects at least two network-ready devices, whether they are desktop PCs, portable PCs, printers, or computerized home automation controllers or receivers. Virtually every PC on the market today is network-ready, meaning that its operating system provides network support "out-of-the-box" (OTB) and includes a built-in or preinstalled network adapter.

Technically, a PC doesn't connect to a network directly; the PC connects to its network adapter or interface, which is the device that connects to the network. Through the device drivers (software that interacts between the device and the operating system) and the operating system's networking support services, a PC is able to connect and communicate on a network. However, the most valuable device in establishing a network connection on a PC is the network adapter, whether the PC is connecting to a wired network or a wireless network.

NOTE Wired networks are discussed in this chapter. For more information on wireless networks, see Chapter 8.

Wired Network Adapters

As its name suggests, a network adapter, also commonly called a network interface, is the device that adapts (interfaces) a computer to a network. As mentioned earlier, it is technically the network adapter that connects to the network media; the PC is connected to the network adapter. The PC interacts with the network and its resources through the network adapter.

Network adapters come in a variety of styles. Until very recently, the most common form has been an expansion card, like the one shown in Figure 6-2, which is called a network interface card, or NIC. However, most new computers now include a built-in network adapter that is directly integrated into the motherboard and chipset. Regardless of whether a computer includes a NIC or an integrated network adapter, the default functions of the network adapter remain the same: to provide the interface and interconnect point between a PC and the network media.

Figure 6-2
An expansion card network interface card (NIC)

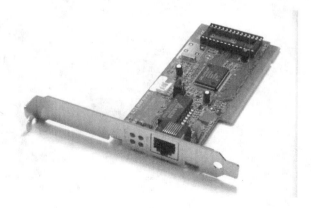

An expansion card NIC plugs into a PCI (Peripheral Component Interface) or PCI Express (PCIe) expansion card slot on the motherboard (see Figure 6-3). Those motherboards that have built-in Ethernet connectivity either integrate this capability into their chipsets or integrate a dedicated Ethernet chip on the motherboard and include an RJ-45 jack on their back panel. In either case, the network adapter is directly integrated into the PCI or PCIe bus, which allows it to move data onto the network media or into its host PC and serve as a translating interface between the two.

A network adapter (NIC) uses one of four different methods to communicate with and transfer data to and from the network media:

- **Direct Memory Access (DMA)**   Allows the network adapter to control the system bus and access memory directly without support from the system's processor. A network adapter that uses the DMA method of accessing a computer's memory directly to retrieve data to be transmitted or storing data received requires its own processor.

- **Interrupt-driven**   Works through the system resources and assigned interrupt and input/output (I/O) buffers. The host system's processor is notified that data stored in the I/O buffer needs to be transferred over the system bus either into memory or onto the transmission channel by the network adapter setting an interrupt.

- **Polling**   Involves the system processor checking the status of the network adapter at set intervals to learn if a data transfer operation is needed.

Figure 6-3
PCI slots on
a computer
motherboard

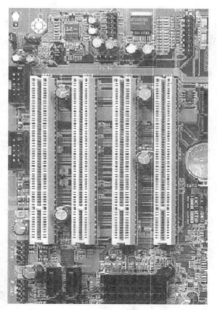

Photo courtesy of IBASE Technology, Inc.

- **Programmed I/O (also called memory-mapped I/O)**   The system processor maps the network adapter's memory into the processor's address space. Data to be transmitted onto the network media is moved to the network adapter's memory by the adapter's device driver. Data being received by the adapter is placed in a shared memory location to be copied into the system memory.

As discussed in Chapter 2, a network adapter is most commonly configured to connect to twisted-pair cables using an RJ-45 connector. However, there are network adapters configured to connect to coaxial cable through a BNC (Bayonet Neill Cancellman) or AUI (attachment unit interface) connector. Some even include connections for both.

Network Interface Card (NIC)

Most of today's expansion card NICs, like the one shown earlier in Figure 6-2, are typically designed for installation in either a PCI or PCIe slot on a computer's motherboard. After the NIC is installed, the Ethernet port is available through the slot bay at the back of the computer.

CROSS-REFERENCE   Chapter 7 covers the installation steps for Ethernet network adapters.

Older, or what are called "legacy," computers may include one or more ISA (Industry Standard Architecture), EISA (Enhanced ISA) slots or an ISA/EISA combination slot (that can take either a legacy ISA card or an EISA card). Although they're getting harder to find, ISA/EISA NIC cards are still available for use in legacy computers.

TIP   A wireless NIC is installed in a computer in the same manner as a wired NIC. The difference is that the wireless NIC has an antenna that fits through the slot bay and protrudes outside of the system case. See Chapter 8 for more information on wireless networking.

Integrated Network Adapters

Many new computers include several functions that in the past were added to the computer through an expansion board, such as a network adapter, a sound card, or a video card. In many cases, the integrated system is equal to or better than the average expansion card available for that function. This is especially true for network adapters.

The ports associated with the systems integrated in the motherboard's circuits are typically clustered on the back of the computer (as illustrated in Figure 6-4).

Figure 6-4
Connection jacks for integrated systems on a desktop computer

Photo courtesy of Dell Corporation.

Figure 6-5
Connections jack for integrated systems on a notebook computer

Photo courtesy of ASI Corp.

Regardless of whether the network adapter is installed on an NIC or through an integrated system, the de facto location for the connection jack for the network media is on the back panel of the computer.

The downside to an integrated network adapter is that should this particular system fail, you either have to replace the motherboard completely or, if you're lucky and the network adapter is integrated through its own circuit on the motherboard, replace the component(s) that provide the network adapter functionality and interface.

Portable PC Network Adapters

Like desktop PCs, portable PCs such as notebook and laptop computers either have an integrated network adapter or require the use a plug-in network adapter. Figures 6-5 through 6-7 show examples of the types of network adapters commonly used with notebook PCs. Figure 6-5 shows the integrated connectors on the rear panel of a notebook PC. Figure 6-6 shows a PC Card network adapter installed in a notebook PC. Figure 6-7 shows a USB (Universal Serial Bus) Ethernet adapter. The network adapter shown in Figure 6-7 uses a dongle that has an RJ-45 connector on one end.

PLC and HomePNA Network Adapters

The existing electrical and telephone wiring installed in a home can also be used as network media through the use of PLC (Power Line Control) and HomePNA (Home Phoneline Networking Alliance) technologies, which enable electrical wiring and

Figure 6-6
A PC Card Ethernet adapter installed in a notebook computer

Figure 6-7
A USB Ethernet
adapter

Photo courtesy of the Belkin International, Inc.

telephone wiring to be used to carry data networking signals, respectively. While technically a wired system, many refer to these technologies as "wireless" because no new wiring needs to be installed to create a network. These systems require special types of network adapters, such as the PLC network adapter shown in Figure 6-8.

Wireless Network Adapters

Wireless Ethernet networking continues to gain in popularity as an alternative to installing a wired network. The majority of new computers on the market today typically have a wireless Ethernet network adapter built in. This is especially true of notebook and other portable PCs. However, if you wish to add a wireless network adapter to a PC, you have the option of attaching an external wireless adapter or installing a wireless network NIC, like the one shown in Figure 6-9.

CROSS-REFERENCE   See Chapter 8 for a more information on wireless Ethernet networks.

Figure 6-8
A PLC network
adapter

Photo courtesy of ALLNET GmbH.

Figure 6-9
A wireless NIC
expansion card

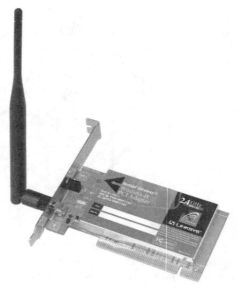

Photo courtesy of Cisco Systems, Inc.

Network Media

The technology used to provide a path for the electromagnetic signals transmitted between two (or more) points is the network medium; its plural reference is *network media*. Cable, wire, and even wireless radio frequency (RF) signals are all considered to be network media.

There are several factors to consider when choosing network media for a home network. They are listed here, in no particular order or priority:

- **New construction versus retrofit**   Just about any medium can be chosen in a new construction situation, but hardwired is best. It also depends on the homeowner's wishes and budget.

- **Existing network or new installation**   If an existing (and functioning) network is already in place with cable runs pulled throughout the house and the cable terminations remain in usable locations, there is little need to replace the existing network media. However, if the house is being remodeled extensively and the existing cable and its outlets will no longer be usable in a practical sense, then another medium should be considered.

- **Distance between network nodes**   Most media types have effective distance limitations. For all practical purposes, the distance limits for most cable types shouldn't be a problem in most houses, but in larger houses, the length of the cable pulls may be an issue for each medium being considered.

Characteristic	UTP Cable	Coaxial Cable	Wireless
Availability	Good	Good	Good
Expandability	Fair	Fair	Good
Transmission quality	Fair	Good	Fair
Security	Fair	Fair	Poor
Range	Good	Poor	Good
Environmental constraints	Fair	Good	Fair

Table 6-1 Comparison of Common Residential Network Media

- **Budget**   Each of the common network media types has its advantages and disadvantages that could translate into cost issues for a home network. The cost of the network hardware used with each medium can range from inexpensive to perhaps prohibitively expensive.

- **Homeowner's preferences**   Sometimes, if budget is not a concern, the medium choice may boil down to what the homeowner wishes to use. However, as a home automation professional, you should educate the user on the advantages and disadvantages of the alternative media types. Table 6-1 shows a comparison of the capabilities of the networking media most likely to be used in a residential setting.

Network Media Basics

Networks can be installed using either wired or wireless media. In a wired environment, new cabling, such as unshielded twisted-pair (UTP) Cat 5e or Cat 6 wire can be installed in the walls, above the ceiling, or under the floor. Or you can install wireless network access points throughout a home to create a totally flexible and cableless network. Or you can adapt the home's existing electrical or telephone wiring to create a network infrastructure. My point? You have a variety of alternative ways available to provide network media for a home network.

Network Media Standards   Network media and their electrical and mechanical specifications are defined on the physical layer of the OSI model. The OSI model's Layer 1 standards are developed by a variety of standards organizations, including the EIA/TIA (Electronic Industries Alliance/Telecommunication Industry Association), ANSI (American National Standards Institute), the IEEE (Institute of Electrical and Electronics Engineers), UL (Underwriters Laboratories), CSA (Canadian Standards Association), and others around the world.

 CROSS-REFERENCE   The major standards governing the use of physical media in a network are covered in Chapter 4.

Network Media Characteristics   There are a few characteristics that should be considered for any network medium before it is chosen for installation and use. The primary considerations are as follows:

- **Attenuation**   For nearly every media type, there is a distance at which a transmitted signal begins to weaken to the point that it may become incoherent. Several factors combine to degrade a signal, including impedance and resistance on wire transmissions and signal strength on wireless transmission, but every media type has an attenuation point. Because of attenuation, each media type specifies a maximum standard segment (cable run) length. For example, on twisted-pair copper cable, the maximum segment length is 100 meters (or 328 feet), which is the distance at which attenuation begins to degrade a transmitted signal on that medium. On wireless media, the effective communications range is essentially its attenuation point, which is affected by a variety of factors, including the materials and construction of the building and any radio frequency interference sources present.

- **Cancellation**   When two wires are placed too close to one another, there is a chance that their electromagnetic fields may cancel each other out. Generally, cancellation can be a good thing because it can help to control the signals being transmitted on the individual wires. However, too much cancellation can destroy the integrity of a signal being carried on either wire. For this reason, there are standards regarding how closely two cables can be placed and at what angle wires must cross each other.

- **Electromagnetic interference (EMI)**   Virtually every electrical device emits electromagnetic waves that can cause interference and impair the signals of other devices. EMI can result when a wire is placed too close to electrical wiring or some electrical lighting fixtures, especially fluorescent fixtures. Electrical appliances, such as refrigerators, freezers, and even vacuum cleaners can also create EMI. Too much EMI, regardless of its source, can lead to the bad kind of cancellation.

- **Radio frequency interference (RFI)**   Devices that broadcast wireless radio signals can cause interference with other wireless and wired transmissions. In a wireless transmission, RF signals that overlap or overpower a data transmission can scramble the signals (a condition called cancellation) to the point that the integrity of the original signal is destroyed. In the same manner that copper media absorbs EMI from nearby wires, the media can also absorb airborne RF signals.

Network Cabling Choices   If you choose to install a wired network in a home, the physical network media most commonly used is UTP, with coaxial cable a distant second. Fiber optic cabling can be used, but at this point in time this remains a fairly expensive way to go. However, installing fiber optic cabling for a home network should really future-proof the home.

CROSS-REFERENCE   See Chapter 1 and the other chapters in Part 1 for more information on home network cabling choices.

Network Connectivity Devices

Regardless of a network's topology (see Chapter 3), any device that is to be connected to the network must make its connection through some form of a network connectivity device. Only in the case of peer-to-peer networks (see "Peer-to-Peer Networks" later in the chapter), do network devices connect directly to the computers that make up the network.

While there are a wide variety of features and functions available on these devices, they basically boil down to a small number of choices: hubs, switches, routers, and repeaters.

Hubs

In the same manner that a hub is a central distribution point for an airline's routes, a network hub serves as a clustering device that allows several devices to interconnect to the network and each other. In a home network, a hub can be used to connect several computers and peripheral devices in two ways:

- To connect two or more network-ready devices (computers, printers, and other peripherals) to the network media and the main Internet service connection point
- To connect two or more computers to each other to create a peer-to-peer network

 NOTE While hubs have been a networking mainstay over the years, they are being replaced in networks with switches. A network switch provides the same functionality as a hub, but with additional features that help the network perform better at about the same price. Switches are discussed in the section that follows.

Hubs are either passive or active. A passive hub is really just a pass-along device in that it passes any signal it receives on any of its ports out to all of its ports. Active hubs are sometimes referred to as smart hubs. A smart hub includes embedded firmware that allows it to make basic Layer 2 decisions on where a signal should be forwarded, stopping short of the function of a switch.

One drawback to the use of a hub in a network is that it doesn't help to resolve the shared bandwidth nature of an Ethernet medium. In fact, because the signal must pass through a hub, there is additional latency (time delay) and signal loss as a result. So, when a hub is used in a network, it can serve to provide a connection and clustering point (creating a star topology) for several devices, but not without a small amount of network performance degradation.

Like all network connectivity devices, hubs must be matched to the bandwidth speed of the network. If a network is running a 10-megabit per second (10 Mbps) Ethernet, then its hubs must be 10 Mbps hubs. However, if the network is moving from 10 Mbps to 100 Mbps one segment at a time, or if it will in the future, there are speed-sensing hubs (called 10/100 or 10/100/1000 hubs) that can automatically detect the line speed and set the speed accordingly.

In situations in which more connections are required than an existing hub can handle, two hubs can be stacked (daisy-chained) to each other. Many Ethernet hubs include a special port for just this purpose.

Network Switches and Bridges

The primary differences between a switch or bridge and a hub are

- A bridge or switch determines the port on which a signal arrives and doesn't repeat the message to that port.
- A bridge or switch forwards a message only to the port on which the destination address of a message is located.
- A bridge or switch more efficiently uses the bandwidth of the network.

A network switch (see Figure 6-10), also known as a LAN (local area network) switch, packet switch, or an Ethernet switch, combines the functions of an active hub with those of a network bridge. A switch combines two important network message delivery functions, bridging and forwarding, into a single action commonly referred to as *switching*. In a home network environment, the functions of a switch or a bridge are essentially the same. However, on larger networks, these two devices have very discrete and unique functions and purposes.

Bridging   At its most basic level, a switch is a bridge, and vice versa. Both of these devices function basically on the Media Access Control (MAC) sublayer of the Data Link Layer of the OSI model, which means that they work with the MAC address of any networked devices. A bridge, which is not typically an intelligent device, creates a table that ties the MAC address of a transmitting device to the port (on the bridge) through which the bridge receives a message. For example, if node A sends a message to node B that must pass through a bridge or switch, the MAC address or node A is recorded in a table (called a bridging table) in the bridge's memory that ties node A to port Ethernet1, the port through which the bridge received node A's message. The information recorded in the bridging table indicates that node A is located on the network segment

Figure 6-10
An 8-port
Ethernet switch

Photo courtesy of Cisco Systems, Inc.

connected to Ethernet1. So, if any messages arrive at the bridge addressed to node A, the bridge knows to which of its ports it needs to forward the message. If node A and node C are located on the same network segment (in other words, communicate to the bridge through the same port), the bridge knows that it doesn't have to do anything because node C has already "seen" the message.

Where the primary function of a network bridge is to interconnect two dissimilar networks (such as an incoming DSL link to a home's local network) and essentially manage only a single path between two points on a network, switches can also provide services to reduce the amount of signal collisions on the network.

Forwarding

TIP   In a home networking situation, the functions of a network switch are often implemented by a converged device, such as an Internet gateway or router.

A switch, which is technically a marketing name for a smart bridge, adds intelligence to message forwarding, which helps to reduce the amount of unnecessary traffic on any particular network segment. Switches manufactured since 2004 incorporate the Rapid Spanning Tree Protocol (RSTP), defined in the IEEE 802.1d standard that extends the capability of the switch beyond its bridging table by applying one of four variations of message forwarding:

- **Cut-through**   A switch reads only as much of an incoming message as it needs to learn the hardware address (MAC address) of the destination node and then begins forwarding the message.

- **Store-and-forward**   A switch receives and buffers an entire incoming message before discerning its destination address and forwarding it. Using this method, the switch may also perform error checking on the message, such as a checksum, before forwarding it.

- **Fragment-free**   Combines the benefits of the store-and-forward and the cut-through forwarding methods by reading the first 64-bytes of an incoming message (which includes the destination address) and then forwarding the message. This method delegates any message length or integrity checking to the sending and receiving devices.

- **Adaptive switching**   More of a switching management scheme than a forwarding technique, in that it applies one of the other three forwarding methods as required by the status of the media or the switch itself. For example, if the port to which the switch needs to forward a message is busy at the time it is needed by the cut-through method, the switch will automatically move to store-and-forward to allow the port to become available.

NOTE   The forwarding method used by a switch is generally under the control of the switch and not the network administrator.

Routers

A network router, like the one in Figure 6-11, is the workhorse of high-speed communication connections. Routers embody all of the functionality of hubs, bridges, and switches and perform a very valuable service as well: routing.

Routing is the process used to forward messages from a local (home) network to a remote network, such as the Internet. Much like the way that the postal service routes a letter from one city to the next and delivers it to a particular address, routing ensures that network messages reach their destination. Where switching (message forwarding) is used to deliver a message to its destination within a local network (such as a network inside a home), routing is used to deliver a message to a remote local network, across town or around the world. And where switching uses the hardware address (MAC address) of the devices connected to the network, routing uses logical addressing, or what is referred to in the TCP/IP (Transmission Control Protocol/Internet Protocol) world of the Internet as IP addressing.

The primary function of routing is to forward a message along the best path possible to reach its destination. In business local area networks (LANs), routing is used to send a message out the best path of several outbound choices. Because there is typically only a single inbound or outbound choice on a home network, routing is used to direct messages to the router port to which a particular home network workstation is located. Yes, this is essentially what switching does as well, but routers perform a few other services, such as Network Address Translation (NAT) and security functions, which make them worth the investment.

To simplify the routing process, the router maintains a routing table (which contains a cross-reference that indicates for each of the router's own interface ports what network addresses should be forwarded to that port) that is maintained either by the network administrator, a routing protocol, or both. When a message arrives at the router, its destination address is looked up in the routing table that indicates to which of the router's ports the message should be forwarded. While very simplified, this is what routing is all about.

Repeaters

Should it be necessary to install a network device at a distance that exceeds the maximum segment distance of a particular network medium (such as beyond the 90-meter attenuation limit of UTP cabling), a repeater can be installed to extend the attenuation point of a cable segment. A repeater merely regenerates the signal on the line and retransmits it so the signal is strong enough to reach its destination and be usable.

Figure 6-11
A DSL gateway
router

Photo courtesy of NetGear, Inc.

TIP   The maximum segment length limit on a network medium includes all pieces of cabling between the signal source and the destination device.

Network Hardware Summary

What hardware is needed or installed in a home network depends on a variety of factors, but the most important factors are the complexity of the network's design and the functionality it must support. Figure 6-12 illustrates a home network structure that has been exaggerated to illustrate the relationships between the various hardware devices that can be installed in a home network.

A network that is used to connect only one or two computers to an Internet gateway requires little beyond the router, bridge, or modem that the Internet service provider (ISP) provided. However, a network that is installed to control the lighting, heating, security, audio, video, and data networking in the home requires far more connectivity, management, and availability, which translates to a variety of network hardware. This need and how a solution is determined and installed is the general topic of discussion throughout the remainder of this book.

Figure 6-12
The relationship of a router, switches, and hubs in a network

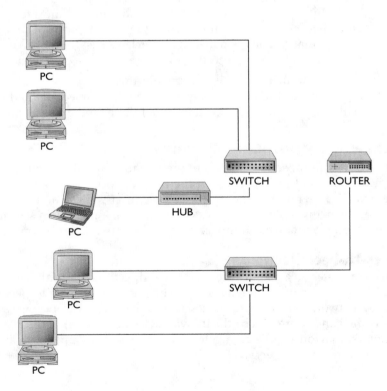

Software and the Network

As networking has become more popular, even in the home, the software tools available have made the task of installing and configuring network software relatively easy. Network operating systems, such as Windows 2008 Server, Windows 2003 Server, or Mac OS X, have made the task of configuring a network logically a fairly simple matter.

The general classifications of network software are as follows:

- **Network operating systems (NOS)**   An NOS, on the whole, operates outside of the OSI model. Typically, an NOS is installed on a network server and used to manage and control the network resources. Most NOS packages provide their strongest support to the network at the application layer. I'll talk again about the NOS when I discuss the client/server relationship later in this chapter. Some examples of NOS that can be used to manage a home network are Windows 2008 Server, Windows 2003 Server, and Mac OS X, which are perhaps overkill for a home network. Windows XP Professional, Windows Vista, and Linux are for the most part capable of managing a typical home network.

- **Network protocols**   A protocol is a set of rules that must be obeyed by the parties in a communication, whether it is on the phone, across the fence, or over a network. Without protocols, or a set of rules, data transmission would be chaos. In the Internet environment, TCP/IP is dominant, almost to the exclusion of any other protocol suite. Included in the TCP/IP protocol suite are a group of utilities that can be the network technician's best friend when a networked PC is having trouble communicating on the network (see Chapter 9).

- **Network security software**   Arguably, this group of software is very important, especially in the days of "always on" network connections and the demonstrated skill level and number of evildoers out there on the Internet.

Network Operating Systems

The primary purpose of a NOS is to provide for centralized control and management of a network and its resources. In the early days of networking, nearly all networks were peer-to-peer arrangements, where every user was the administrator of his or her part of the network. But, as networks have grown, especially in size and their ability to interoperate, centralized administration of the network has become a virtual necessity.

Peer-to-Peer Networks

Each computer on a peer-to-peer network is directly connected to the computers before and after it in a daisy-chained fashion. The purpose of a peer-to-peer network, like any type of network, is to share resources. However, on a peer-to-peer network, the resources are owned and controlled by the individual users (owners) of the PCs that make up the network. Obviously, this arrangement requires some cooperation and sharing among the network users to succeed.

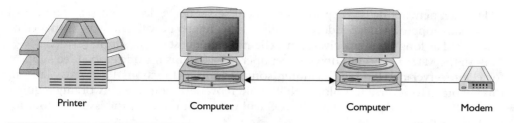

Figure 6-13 A two-computer peer-to-peer network sharing a printer and a modem.

Figure 6-13 depicts a very simple two-computer peer-to-peer network structure. On this network, one user has a nifty new laser printer and the other controls the access to the Internet through a modem. If User1 wishes to allow User2 to access and use his or her laser printer, he or she must grant permission to User2 to do so. The same goes for User2 allowing User1 access to the Internet connection via the modem.

Peer-to-peer networks are very common in home networking situations because the PCs are in relatively close proximity and the number of computers is typically much fewer than 8 to 10. Above this range, the administration of the individual computers is more efficient if transferred to a centralized activity.

Commonly, a home peer-to-peer network is created by installing a network adapter in each PC and connecting the computers to one another using a Cat 5e or Cat 6 cable and RJ-45 connections.

 TIP A crossover or a rolled cable is used to connect two network adapters directly. In this cable configuration, receive and transmit lines are crossed over to directly interface to each other. See Chapters 1 and 2 for more information on cable and connection standards.

A peer-to-peer network doesn't require an NOS. Most client operating systems, such as Windows 2000 Pro, Windows XP Pro, and Windows Vista, all include features that support peer-to-peer networking and file, print, and other resource sharing.

Client/Server Networks

The type of network most commonly found in more complex network settings is a client/server network. The elements of this network include the network client, which formulates and sends requests to a server for information and the use of software or hardware, and the server, which interprets and responds to the requests from the clients. Just as in a restaurant, where clients are the restaurant customers and the server is, well, the server.

Client/server networks are built on a network structure that includes one or more centralized servers. In the context of client/server, a server is a piece of software that runs on a centralized hardware "server." You might have a fax server, an e-mail server, a database server, and most likely a web server on your network. In fact, on most networks, there is probably only a single computer on which all or at least most of the server software is running.

Ethernet networking is very popular on client/server networks. Client/server networks are actually topology-independent. It really doesn't matter how the network is shaped or configured as long as, at any given time, clients can request services from servers.

Both the Mac OS and Windows Server operating systems include embedded support for client/server networking, including some advanced functions I'll discuss later in this chapter. However, a full-blown NOS is often overkill for home networking requirements. There is no doubt that a full NOS will work, but there are the issues of tool-to-the-task and cost.

Network Protocols

A network protocol is a set of rules that govern the interactions between two communicating entities, regardless of whether they are two computers, modems, routers, or other hardware or software. When one modem dials up another, the transmissions between them are governed by a common protocol. The same goes for two computers on a peer-to-peer network or two routers on a wide area network (WAN).

The TCP/IP protocol suite includes a collection of communications and networking protocols that can be used to initiate, facilitate, manage, maintain, and troubleshoot network communications, whether on a local area network (LAN) or a WAN. The best way to understand the purpose and application of the TCP/IP protocols is by their function. Table 6-2 groups the TCP/IP protocols by their general function or when they are applied and the OSI layer each operates on.

Here is a brief description of each of these protocols:

- **DNS** The TCP/IP service used to convert human-friendly domain names (such as comptia.org) to their IP address equivalents (such as 10.0.100.20).

- **DHCP** This protocol is used to automatically configure a networked PC each time the PC is booted (powered on or restarted). DHCP provides an IP address and other TCP/IP configuration data to enable a PC to connect and interact with its network.

- **FTP** Used to transfer entire files from one computer to another over the Internet.

Function	Protocol	OSI Layer
Application interface	Domain Name System (DNS) Dynamic Host Configuration Protocol (DHCP) File Transfer Protocol (FTP) Hypertext Transfer Protocol (HTTP) Internet Mail Access Protocol (IMAP) Post Office Protocol, version 3 (POP3) Simple Mail Transfer Protocol (SMTP)	Application and Presentation
Transmission of data	Transmission Control Protocol (TCP) User Datagram Protocol (UDP)	Transport
Addressing and delivery	Internet Protocol (IP) Internet Control Message Protocol (ICMP) Packet Internet Groper (PING) Trace Route (TRACERT)	Network

Table 6-2 The TCP/IP Protocols and Their Functions

- **HTTP** Defines how requests and response messages are formatted and transmitted and the actions Web servers and browser software take in response to the commands included in the transmitted messages and files. S-HTTP (or HTTPS) is an extension of HTTP that provides for secure transmission of data.

- **ICMP** Other protocols and devices that need to communicate with one another use this protocol.

- **IMAP** Allows e-mail to be accessed and read on a mail server and optionally transferred to a mail client.

- **IP** The workhorse protocol of the Internet, IP defines logical addressing (IP addresses) and how it is applied to networks and hosts across a network.

- **PING** Used to verify that two network nodes are able to communicate with each other.

- **POP3** Used to move e-mail from a mail server to a mail client.

- **SMTP** Used to transfer e-mail messages between mail servers.

- **TCP** A connection-oriented protocol that manages the transmission of data between two communicating stations. TCP includes processes that provide for reliable, guaranteed transmission and receipt of data between a source address and a destination address. TCP messages must be acknowledged as received before additional messages are sent.

- **TRACERT** Used to determine the routing path used by messages to move across a network from a source address to a destination address.

- **UDP** A connectionless protocol that transports messages across a network without mechanisms to provide for reliability or delivery guarantees. UDP messages are not acknowledged and are transmitted in a continuous stream.

Network Security

Security is a growing concern on all types of networks and perhaps the most important issue surrounding the use of networks, whether they are small networks in homes and offices or large international networks, such as the Internet.

Included in the TCP/IP protocol suite are a few utilities that help to create a secure environment for a home network. Most of the Internet gateways (modems, bridges, or routers) used with broadband communication services also provide services to help secure the devices attached to them. In addition, third-party software and hardware can be added to a home network to provide additional security.

TCP/IP Security

When a homeowner subscribes to an Internet service, the Internet service provider (ISP) provides the connection with an IP address. This address is assigned to the connection using DHCP and the IP address assigned will typically be different each time the user connects to the ISP's network. Dynamic addresses (those that change frequently) create a moving target for a network hacker looking to invade a home network. However, DHCP alone isn't enough to prevent an intrusion.

Network Address Translation (NAT)

Because the Internet world is only beginning to convert to the much larger addresses of IP version 6, IP version 4 addresses (there was no real version 5) are now in short supply; as a result, most Internet subscribers are issued only one or two IP addresses or are assigned an address through DHCP. However, if a home network has four computers and a printer to address, using one IP address (and a dynamic one no less) just won't work. This problem is solved using NAT.

A home that has subscribed to either cable or DSL must use an Internet gateway device to connect to the service. Many of these devices have switching or routing capabilities. This is good news in terms of network security. The NAT protocol is supported by most of the Internet gateways used by cable and DSL services. Even most dialup connections are protected behind a router (at the ISP) that is running NAT services.

What NAT does is translate the IP address of a computer on its internal network into a generic one that is sent out over the external network. This way, anyone wishing to access a specific network computer has only the generic IP address issued by the NAT device and not the IP address of a particular computer.

Access Lists

Another feature that may be available in the Internet gateway device is access lists, also called access control lists (ACLs). ACLs use a feature called packet filtering to scan the source and destination addresses included in network messages to determine if the sender has the authority or permission to send messages to the destination address—that is, if it can access the network at all.

When a packet-filtering device receives message packets from either an internal or an external source, it extracts the IP address of the sending station (source address) and compares it to an access control list created by the network administrator (the homeowner, in the DHTI+ world). Depending on the action prescribed by the information on the list, the message is either permitted access in or out, or denied access in or out.

Firewall

Internet gateways also provide basic firewall functions. A firewall works something like an access control list in that it performs packet filtering to deny access to a PC from external sources. However, on a firewall the filtering can occur on the type of application being accessed or the type of action requested, such as chat, e-mail, FTP, and so on.

PC Security

One of the primary issues that must be addressed for any home network, whether it be a data network or a control network, is security. Home network security must be designed and configured to protect against unauthorized physical access, unauthorized logical access, and malicious damage from software loaded to the system, intentionally or inadvertently. When designing security for the individual computers on a network, the following must be considered and incorporated into the plan:

- Passwords
- Antivirus software
- Encryption

Each of these components of a PC security system is discussed in the following sections.

Passwords

Any PC attached to a network should have a login process that includes a strong password to help limit physical access not only to the computer (in addition to locked doors, security cables, and the like), but to the network as well. A strong password is one that has sufficient length and complexity (content) to be difficult to hack by guess or process. The general guidelines for a strong password are that it should be not less than 8 characters and include at least one number, special character, and both upper- and lowercase letters.

Antivirus Software

Computer viruses can enter a PC using a variety of ways, virtually all of which involve the user doing something: opening e-mail, downloading files, opening a Web site and so on. Once a virus is on a system, it can then be activated to do whatever it was designed for: corrupting or removing files, accessing the network, or perhaps just displaying a screen as a prank. Whatever the evil intent of the computer virus, the best defense against it is to prevent it from entering the PC and, if it does gain entry, to identify and remove it.

Antivirus software should be installed on the PC (and perhaps the network server, if the network includes one) and used to scan the PC regularly. Antivirus software uses a signature database containing the signature (digital identity) of each of the known viruses and compares each of the files stored on the computer (even temporary files such as e-mail attachments) to this database. The scan results are then displayed for your action on each potentially dangerous file identified.

Although not technically antivirus software, malware (short for malicious and software) detection software can be used to supplement antivirus protection on a PC. Malware enters a PC as a part of an Internet download and then is used to report information back to a source about the use of the computer, most typically reporting on the Internet sites and any personal information found on the PC or entered to a website. Malware detection software, like Ad-Aware from Lavasoft and Microsoft's Malicious Software Removal Tool, are able to identify and remove any malware detected on a PC.

Encryption

Encryption transforms information stored in a file on a PC from a readable (open text) form to an unreadable (encrypted) form. The process used to encrypt (cipher) information involves a mathematical formula that is applied to the binary digits (bits) of a file to convert them systematically into a form that can be later unencrypted (deciphered) by any user who has the proper user credentials (passwords, user ID). Encrypting information on a PC adds an additional layer of security to the PC and the information it stores.

Network Addressing

Addressing is a very important part of networking. Just as a house or building must have an address so that postal and package services and friends and relatives can find it, each node on a network must also have a unique address. In fact, on a network most nodes have at least two addresses: a logical address and a physical address.

A networked computer is also identified with a variety of physical and logical addresses, including its MAC address, Internet Protocol (IP) address, and perhaps a Uniform Resource Locator (URL). For example, a networked computer can have an IP address, such as 172.168.10.10, for use on IP networks; a MAC address, such as 00-A0-CC-34-0A-CE, for use on a local network; and a URL, such as http://www .rongilster.com, so people can find its web page.

Logical versus Physical Addressing

IP addresses are logical addresses because each address is created in a logical pattern that ties one network device to others on the same network. What this means is that it is safe to assume that a networked device with an IP address of 192.168.20.15 is logically located on the same segment of a network as the device with the IP address of 192.168.20.14. IP addresses tend to be assigned in a series, one at a time, in a logical pattern. On the other hand, physical addresses (MAC addresses) are randomly assigned by a device's manufacturer.

Physical Addresses

When a networking device is manufactured, it is assigned a physical address that is a universally unique identification number permanently embedded in its electronic circuitry. This number, known as a Media Access Control (MAC) address is like a lifetime membership card to the networking club. On local networks, the MAC address is used to route messages to specific devices. In essence, a MAC address is the unique identifying number assigned to each network adapter or other networking device. MAC addresses are physical addresses.

A MAC address consists of a 48-bit or 6-byte hexadecimal number. It is represented in the form of six 2-digit numbers separated by dashes. The first 24 bits (3 bytes) of the MAC address contain a code assigned by the IEEE (Institute of Electrical and Electronics Engineers) to uniquely identify the manufacturer of the card, and the next 24 bits (3 bytes) are a number uniquely assigned by the manufacturer. For example, a MAC address of 00-A0-CC-34-0A-CE includes a manufacturer ID number of 00-A0-CC and a serialized ID number of 34-0A-CE. The segments of this number are hexadecimal numbers, but their specific values aren't important, only their uniqueness.

Every networked computer has a MAC address—the address burned into its network adapter during manufacturing. On a Windows PC, the MAC address assigned to its network adapter can be displayed using the TCP/IP command IPCONFIG that should look something like the display shown in Figure 6-14. On this computer, the MAC address is listed as the physical address.

Logical (IP) Addresses

The most commonly used logical network address is what is called an *IP address*. It gets its name from the Internet Protocol (IP), which controls and manages logical addressing on TCP/IP networks, both small (like a home network) and large (like the Internet).

IP addresses are 32 bits long (the equivalent of 4 bytes) and are represented as four 8-bit segments, called octets, which are arranged into a dotted-decimal notation scheme, as in 100.100.100.100.

NOTE The latest version of IP addressing is IP version 6 (IPv6), which provides a 128-bit address and supports a more complex numbering scheme than the currently popular IP version 4 (IPv4). IPv6 is backward compatible for IPv4, so don't worry too much about support for IPv6 in a home network.

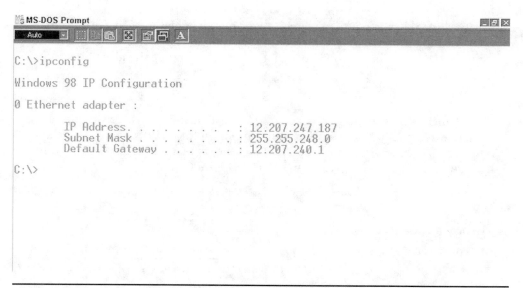

Figure 6-14 The display produced by the IPCONFIG command on a Windows PC

Binary Address Representation

Although IP addresses are represented in decimal numbers for human readability purposes, computers and networking devices see these addresses as a series of binary bits. The binary number system uses only two values (0 and 1) to represent numbers in powers of 2.

Most people are accustomed to thinking and working in the decimal system, which is based on the number 10. To most people, the number 124 represents $100 + 20 + 4$. To the computer, this number of 124 is 1111100, which is 64 (2^6) + 32 (2^5) + 16 (2^4) + 8 (2^3) + 4 (2^2) + 0 (2^1) + 0 (2^0). Each position in a binary number represents, right to left, a power of two beginning with 2^0 and increasing by one power of two as it moves left: 2^0, 2^1, 2^2, 2^3, 2^4, and so forth.

Perhaps we need a quick lesson in binary-to-decimal conversion. There are 8 bits in an octet, and each bit can only be a 1 or a 0. The highest binary number that can be expressed in an octet is 11111111. To convert this binary number to its decimal equivalent requires that we know the powers of two value of each position that has a 1, which in this case is all of them. The powers of two values for the 8 bits in an octet are

$$2^7 \ 2^6 \ 2^5 \ 2^4 \ 2^3 \ 2^2 \ 2^1 \ 2^0$$

When a 1 is placed in one of the binary positions, it means that the value of that position adds into the decimal value being represented. A zero (0) in any position indicates that the value of that position is not added into the decimal value.

Use Table 6-3 as a guide to convert the values assigned to each position in an octet into the total decimal value being represented. Using this table, the binary number 11111111 converts into a decimal value by adding up the individual values of each position, as

$$128 + 64 + 32 + 16 + 8 + 4 + 2 + 1 = 255$$

This means that the largest decimal number that can be represented in an IP address octet is 255. This is important information for reasons I will discuss a bit later in this chapter (see "Subnet Masks"). In the same manner, the decimal number 196 would be represented in an octet as 11000100 or

$$128 + 64 + 0 + 0 + 0 + 4 + 0 + 0 = 196$$

Binary Positional Value	2^7	2^6	2^5	2^4	2^3	2^2	2^1	2^0
Decimal Value	128	64	32	16	8	4	2	1

Table 6-3   The Binary Values Assigned to Each Bit of an IPv4 Octet

Table 6-4

IP Class Address Ranges

Class	Values in the First Octet
Class A	0–127
Class B	128–191
Class C	192–223

IP Address Classes

IP addresses are divided into five address classes; each is designated with a letter A to E. Classes D and E are not used for general IP addressing. Class D addresses are used for multicasting (or broadcasting a message or an audio/video stream to a preset list of addresses), and Class E addresses are reserved for testing and future, reserved usage. Table 6-4 lists the IP address ranges included in Classes A, B, and C.

Using the ranges in Table 6-4, the address class of an IP address can be determined by the value in its first octet. For example, an address with 120 in the first octet is a Class A address; an address with 155 in the first octet is a Class B address; and an address with 220 in its first octet is a Class C address. As I discuss later in this chapter (see the section "Subnet Masks"), knowing the address class of an IP address is key to setting subnet masks, if needed.

Networks and Hosts

The 32 bits and 4 octets of an IP address represent network and host IDs. The number of bits or octets used to identify the network ID and the host ID depends on the IP address class. Table 6-5 lists how each IP address class designates which octets are used to represent the network or host ID.

In the IP addressing scheme, every network is assigned a network address and every computer, node, device, or interface (such as a switch, bridge, or router port) is assigned a host address. In Figure 6-14, shown earlier in the chapter, the IP address assigned to the computer is 12.207.242.31. Based on what we know to this point, we can assume that this is a Class A IPv4 address, which means that the network address is 12.0.0.0 (zeros are used as placeholders) and the host ID portion is 207.242.31.

Assigning Network Addresses

In a typical home networking situation, the ISP assigns one dynamic IP address to the connection, which means that this address may be different each time the connection is established or reset. Some ISPs do assign a single static IP address (which remains the same at all times), but in most cases there is an extra charge for this and additional security is required at the connection link point (at the home).

Table 6-5

Network ID and Host ID Representations of IP Classes

Class	Octet1	Octet2	Octet3	Octet4
Class A	Network ID	Host ID	Host ID	Host ID
Class B	Network ID	Network ID	Host ID	Host ID
Class C	Network ID	Network ID	Network ID	Host ID

In a home network situation with, for example, four computers sharing an Internet connection, each of the computers must be assigned a unique IP address in order to communicate with the Internet gateway device (to which the IP address from the ISP is actually assigned). Typically, the address assigned by the ISP is either a Class C address or a subnet equivalent ("Subnet Masks," later in this chapter). The solution to stretching the single IP address across the four computers on the home network is to enable NAT and DHCP on the Internet gateway device and dynamically assign private addresses to the node of the internal network.

Public and Private IP Addresses

IP addresses are categorically divided into public and private addresses. A public IP address is used on a network like the Internet where all of the devices communicate directly with one another, such as one router transmitting to another. Private IP addresses are reserved for those networks where the networked devices don't interact with the Internet directly but communicate to the public network through an Internet gateway.

Three blocks of IP addresses (see Table 6-6) are set aside for use on private networks. The IP address range that is used on a particular network is a matter of choice because each range has enough available addresses for virtually every home networking situation. Where a public IP address can only be assigned to a single network node, private IP addresses can be reused over and over on literally every private network in existence.

Special Addresses

The IP address specifications set aside some addresses for use in special situations. These addresses fall into four categories:

- **Network addresses**   Any IP address where the host ID portion of the address is all zeros is a network address (as represented in binary value) and cannot be assigned to a host or node on a network.

- **Broadcast addresses**   Any IP address where the host ID portion of the address is all ones (as represented in binary value) is a broadcast address and cannot be assigned to a host or node on a network. Broadcast addresses are used to send messages to the network when the destination address of the target node is not known.

- **Loopback testing**   The address range 127.0.0.0 to 127.255.255.255 (the entire 127 address range) is reserved for loopback testing on any network. Loopback testing is used to test the connection and functionality of a network adapter.

	IP Address Class	Private IP Address Range
Table 6-6 Private IP Address Blocks	Class A	10.0.0.0 to 10.255.255.255
	Class B	172.16.0.0 to 172.31.255.255
	Class C	192.168.0.0 to 192.162.255.255

Subnet Masks

As mentioned earlier, an IP address has two parts: the network identification portion and the host identification portion. In order to route an address across a network, the network and host portions of a network address must be separately identified.

In most cases, if you know the address class, it's easy to separate the two portions. However, in certain cases where bits of the host ID have been used as a part of the network ID (called subnetting) a special tool, a subnet mask, must be applied to extract the network ID from an IP address.

The function of a subnet mask is to extract the network ID portion of an IP address. This function is performed, in the case of a home network, by the Internet gateway device to determine whether an IP address is on the local network or whether it must be routed outside the local network—to the Internet, for example.

Without going into the Boolean algebraic functions that are used when a subnet mask is applied, the value 255 in an octet indicates that all of the bits in that octet are used to identify the network ID. Table 6-7 lists the default subnet masks for Class A, B, and C addresses. A Class A address uses all of the bits in its first octet, a Class B address uses the bits in two octets, and a Class C address uses the bits in three octets for the network ID.

Let me illustrate how a subnet mask works: if a router receives a message addressed to IP address 12.207.242.31, it must extract the network ID from the address. The extracted network ID is then looked up in the routing table to determine to which of its interface ports the message is to be forwarded. By applying a Boolean algebra operation, the subnet mask is combined with the incoming IP address. The result of the Boolean algebra operation is that any address bit that corresponds to a one bit in the subnet mask is used intact; otherwise the address bit is ignored. So, in the following example, the subnet mask for a Class A address is applied and the result is 12.0.0.0.

```
              12      . 207     . 242     . 31
IP Address:   00000110  11001111  11110010  00011111
              255     . 0       . 0       . 0
Subnet Mask:  11111111  00000000  00000000  00000000
              12      . 0       . 0       . 0
Network ID:   00000110  00000000  00000000  00000000
```

Home networks shouldn't actually require much in the way of routing or subnetting internally, for the most part. However, who knows what the future holds and where routing or subnetting may come in useful.

Table 6-7

Standard IPv4 Default Subnet Masks

Address Class	Subnet Mask
A	255.0.0.0
B	255.255.0.0
C	255.255.255.0

Chapter Review

A home network consists of a few primary components: computers, network adapters, cabling, and typically, a network clustering or connectivity device. A network interconnects two or more devices, including desktop PCs, portable PCs, or computerized home automation controllers or receivers.

A network adapter or network interface card (NIC) connects a computer to a network. New computers, both desktop and portable, now include an integrated network adapter built into their motherboards. Network connections can also be made through existing electrical or telephone wiring installed in a home, but require special types of network adapters.

The term *network media* refers to the cabling that connects two communicating devices together, such as cable, wire, and even wireless RF signals. There are several factors to consider when choosing network media for a home network: new construction versus retrofit, existing network or new installation, distance between network nodes, budget, and the homeowner's preferences.

In the home network environment, the network media used includes a few choices not typically associated with business or industrial networking. The choices common to all computer networks are RG58 coaxial cable, Cat 5 UTP, fiber optic, and wireless RF. Cat 5e or Cat 6 UTP wire is the most commonly used cabling on Ethernet networks.

Network connectivity devices provide a means to share a communications link. The primary types of connectivity devices are hubs, switches, and routers. A network hub serves as a clustering device that allows several devices to interconnect to the network and each other. A switch is a hybrid device that combines the functions of an active hub with those of the bridge. A router combines the functionality of a hub, bridge, and switch and performs Internet routing.

The software building blocks of a home network are the network operating system (NOS), the network protocols, and the network security software. The purpose of the NOS is to provide for centralized control and management of a network and its resources. Network protocols provide the rules and guidelines that govern the transmission of data between two communicating entities. Security features, whether implemented through software or features of the networking hardware, prevent unauthorized users from accessing the network and protect data transmission around wired and wireless networks.

The two types of network structures are peer-to-peer and client/server. Peer-to-peer is the most commonly used type for home networks.

TCP/IP is the most commonly used protocol suite on local area networks (LANs) and wide area networks (WANs). Included in this protocol suite are protocols that perform virtually every step in the process used to transmit data across a network, including DNS, DHCP, HTTP, POP3, PING, and TRACERT.

Network security is applied to a home network through several tools. First, the ISP provides some level of security. However, at the home network location, security must be applied through such tools as DHCP, NAT, private IP addresses, access lists, a firewall, and security protocols.

On TCP/IP networks, there are two types of addressing: logical and physical. An IP address is a logical address. Each network device has a universally unique MAC address embedded into its electronics during manufacturing. DNS is used to resolve domain names to their IP address equivalents.

An IP address is expressed in four 8-bit octets. IP addressing is divided into address classes A, B, and C. Within the address classes, a range of addresses have been set aside for use by private networks. An IP address is made up of network and host IDs. A subnet mask is used to extract the network ID from an IP address. While IPv6 is available for use, most Ethernet networks, especially home networks, still employ the IPv4 addressing scheme.

Questions

1. The device integrated in, installed in, or connected to a PC that provides connection to a network's media is a

    A. Repeater

    B. Network adapter

    C. Hub

    D. Switch

2. The simple networking device that clusters networked devices and broadcasts an incoming signal to all of its ports is a

    A. Repeater

    B. Hub

    C. Network adapter

    D. Router

3. The most commonly used network cabling for Ethernet networks is

    A. Cat 3

    B. Cat 5e

    C. 10BaseF

    D. Cat 1

4. The connector type used for UTP cabling is

    A. BNC

    B. RJ-11

    C. RCA

    D. RJ-45

5. The expansion slot type used by most modern expansion card NICs is

   A. ISA

   B. EISA

   C. PCI

   D. USB

6. A specification of the rules and guidelines that govern the transmission of data between two communicating entities is called a

   A. Session

   B. Connection

   C. Protocol

   D. Handshake

7. The protocol suite that provides the foundation for the Internet as well as most home networks is

   A. PPTP

   B. TCP/IP

   C. PGP

   D. CSMA/CD

8. The protocol that is used to convert an IP address to a ghost IP address that hides its true identity and location is

   A. DNS

   B. TCP

   C. NAT

   D. PING

9. Which of the following IP addresses is *not* a private address?

   A. 10.220.0.115

   B. 172.32.10.1

   C. 192.162.0.253

   D. 172.31.254.250

10. What is the default Class C subnet mask?

   A. 255.0.0.0

   B. 255.255.0.0

   C. 127.0.0.0

   D. 255.255.255.0

Answers

1. **B.** A network adapter (NIC) is typically installed inside a PC's case as an expansion card. A repeater is a cable attenuation device; hubs are used to cluster devices to the network backbone; and a terminal adapter is used to terminate an ISDN line.

2. **B.** Okay, this may seem like a trick question, but it's not. The key is clustering and multiple ports, both key characteristics of a hub.

3. **B.** Cat 5e is the most commonly used media today; Cat 6 is rapidly becoming very popular. Cat 3 is also an Ethernet media, but has largely been replaced. There is no specification for 10BaseF, and Cat 1 is used for audio systems only, if at all.

4. **D.** BNC is the connector used with coaxial cabling; RJ-11 is the connector type on a standard telephone line; and RCA is an audio/video connector type.

5. **C.** PCI was introduced with the Pentium computer and has become the standard for expansion cards since then. ISA and EISA, while still supported on many computers, are disappearing more every year. USB may challenge PCI in the future and is an external connection type.

6. **C.** Network protocols are the guidelines that control communications between two devices. Connections, sessions, and handshakes are all part of the functions controlled under a protocol's guidelines.

7. **B.** TCP/IP was developed for the Internet, although home, office, and other local area networks also use it as their network protocol suite. The others are individual protocols in the TCP/IP protocol suite.

8. **C.** Network Address Translation is a service performed by many Internet gateways that allows multiple internal network nodes to share a single IP address on the Internet. TCP is a transport protocol; DNS translates domain names into their associated IP addresses; and PING is used to test network node connectivity.

9. **B.** Each of the other addresses fall within the range of one of the three private IP address ranges.

10. **D.** Remember that Class C (the third class) uses three octets to identify the network ID. The subnet masks 255.0.0.0 and 255.255.0.0 are Class A and B's subnet masks, respectively. The address 127.0.0.0 is a special IP address reserved for loopback testing.

Planning and Installing a Wired Network

In this chapter, you will learn about:

- Planning a home computer network
- Internet connection services
- Installing network cabling

In this chapter, we focus on the tasks performed to design and install a home computer network. At its most basic level, a home network may consist of only two computers connected together by a communications line. However, if the home computer network is also intended to provide a foundation for a home automation control network, there are a few additional design and installation issues, and tasks that must be considered before installation begins.

I won't go into too much detail regarding the components, functions, and configuration of a home automation control network in this chapter. More detailed information is provided in later chapters that specifically addresses each of these areas. Instead, this chapter primarily focuses on the considerations, issues, and installation procedures of a home computer (data) network. Part VIII of this book brings together all of the various control systems that can be integrated into a home network. However, since a data network and its infrastructure typically provides the fundamental structure for a home network, including control networks, what we discuss here also applies to the systems described in the chapters that follow.

Planning a Home Network

The most important part of planning, designing, and implementing a home network is to first gain an understanding of just what the network is intended to provide. If the network is to be only a data network, its design is much less complicated and far easier to implement. Beyond a few decisions on its topology, technologies, and media, a home data network can be simply and easily installed. However, if a home network is meant to provide the infrastructure of a home automation or control network, the planning, design, and implementation steps take on added importance.

Integrating several independent home automation or control systems requires not only a thorough understanding of each of the systems to be integrated, but also how the integration best meets and serves the design, functional requirements, and especially the expectations of the homeowners.

The major steps involved in planning and designing home automation networks are

1. **Identify current and future needs.** Identify the homeowner's current and future networking needs. While the focus is on current needs, also discuss network capabilities that the homeowner may wish to add to the network at a later time. The implemented design shouldn't prevent adding new systems or devices in the future. This foresight in the network design is called *future-proofing*.

2. **Conduct a project survey.** Certain issues must be addressed and solutions developed, including new construction or remodeling, structural changes needed, existing equipment, new systems compatibility, and others. The survey should identify all existing wiring and equipment or devices, how each is to be integrated into the new network, and any possible future use, if any.

3. **Define the project scope of work.** Before the customer can truly believe that you understand their requirements, wants, and needs, you need to state (preferably in writing) what the project entails and what the finished product is to be. The approved project scope provides the overarching statement of exactly what is to be included or not included in the project, as the case may be.

4. **Develop a preliminary design.** The preliminary design document is a work proposal that contains a project detail, equipment list, work plan, and budget.

5. **Document the network connectivity plan.** This stage creates the detailed wiring diagrams or wireless coverage diagrams (or both), schematics, equipment layouts, distribution centers, and the like, so the homeowner can approve it before the plan is finalized.

Communication Services

Often, the customer has already made an important decision for his or her home network: the type of Internet connection the network will use. But, if this decision remains to be made, the choice boils down to availability, bandwidth, and cost.

For most customers, availability is the most critical criterion. Not all Internet communication services are available in all areas. Only the provider of each service can tell you if its service is available to the customer's home.

Internet Services

The primary Internet connectivity or communication services available to home users are

- Cable
- Dialup

- DSL (Digital Subscriber Line)
- Fixed wireless services
- ISDN (Integrated Services Digital Network)
- Satellite broadband services

Each of these Internet service types is explained in the following sections.

Cable Service

Cable service to a home can be significant in that it may also be an integral part of an audio/video distribution system in the home. If the homeowner wishes to use cable television and audio feeds in their integrated home network, you should seriously consider using cable Internet service for the network.

Leveraging the bandwidth of the cable used to carry television signals to homes, the cable industry is able to provide high-speed broadband Internet service over the same coaxial cable system. A cable Internet system is easily installed in a home that already has cable television service. However, one potential problem with cable Internet service is that it is a shared system, meaning television and Internet customers share the line, and a busy line isn't able to provide the same speed as a lightly used line. Cable Internet service providers currently offer service with 1 Mbps upload speeds and 8 Mbps download speeds, but with improvements to technology and increasing competition, many cable Internet service providers are ready to launch a 2 Mbps/16 Mbps service in the near future.

The cable media used to distribute signals to a home is divided into 2 MHz and 6 MHz channels. The upstream (upload) channel uses a 2 MHz channel since less data is sent upstream by users; the downstream (download) channel is larger (6 MHz) because users download more data than they send.

Dialup Internet Service

While over 70 percent of the homes in the United States and other Tier 1 countries have access to cable or DSL services, there are still some homes that either prefer to or must use a dialup service because of its cost advantage. Dialup Internet service has been the primary baseband method (as opposed to broadband) for connecting to the Internet since its inception and, as a result, dialup service is mature, tested, and reliable, which is the good news. The bad news is that a standard dialup connection is limited to 56 Kbps in either direction.

However, accelerated dialup services are now available that increase the effective speed of the connection to as much as 100 percent. Although the telephone line over which the connection is made cannot change its speed (it is a telephone line, after all), service providers are able to decrease the wait time inherent in a slower speed line by applying caching and compression "acceleration" techniques that reduce the fetch and download time for requested content.

Those homes that cannot connect to cable or DSL because they are not available at the home have few options that are as cost effective as dialup for connecting to the Internet. The downside to dialup as the primary link for a home network is that its limited bandwidth may not be enough to support more than a single user at a time. However, there are operating system–based features, such as Microsoft's Internet Connection Sharing (ICS) service that can be used to share the line.

DSL

DSL (Digital Subscriber Line), also called xDSL, is a high-speed Internet service offered by the telephone company (Telco) over its existing copper POTS (Plain Old Telephone Service) lines. Only those homes that are connected to their local servicing central office (CO) over all copper lines and within the standard operating distances of the service have DSL services available to them. At the CO, a DSL Access Multiplexer (DSLAM) provides multiple DSL lines access to the Internet backbone.

DSL is transmitted as an analog signal to and from a home over the same line that provides voice communications services to the home. To do this, each service (voice and DSL) is assigned to different frequency channels on the line. Voice communications are carried on 4 KHz and below channels and DSL on 25 KHz and above channels, as illustrated in Figure 7-1. This allows the same telephone line to be used simultaneously for both services. At the home, each specific device (telephones and DSL gateways) uses a filter to extract the frequency it needs to operate. However, DSL filters are commonly needed on the telephone connections in a home connected to a DSL service to block the higher frequency signals from interfering with voice communications.

Although originally developed as an American standard, DSL is used throughout the world, and its standards now fall under the governance of the International Telecommunication Union. While the number of DSL subscribers is still growing, its growth has slowed because of the availability, and more importantly, the affordability of other faster services, such as cable.

DSL is available in three flavors:

- Asymmetrical DSL (ADSL)
- Symmetrical DSL (SDSL)
- ISDN over DSL (IDSL)

DSL Distance Limitations   The primary limitation for both DSL's availability and data speeds is distance. The distance between a subscriber's location and the Telco's CO determines 1) if the service is even available; 2) the type of service that is available; and

Figure 7-1

The channels used on a telephone line to support DSL services

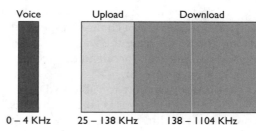

Table 7-1	Service	Maximum Distance Limit
DSL Maximum Distance Limitations	ADSL	12,000 – 18,000 feet
	SDSL	10,000 – 13,000 feet
	IDSL	25,000 – 28,000 feet

3) the data rate the service can provide. Because copper wiring has natural attenuation characteristics, DSL service is available only to a fairly limited range of distances. A subscriber located beyond a provider's service range won't have DSL service available.

Table 7-1 lists the general maximum distance limits for DSL services throughout the United States. Some providers are more strict on their distance limits than others, but nearly all providers fall somewhere in the distance limits shown.

As the distance grows between the subscriber's location and the CO, the speed of the service type available begins to decline. IDSL, which offers the greatest distance limitations of the standard DSL services offers a longer distance limit, but a much slower transmission rate, typically 128 Kbps. There are several SDSL types that offer speeds from 768 Kbps down to 192 Kbps for shorter and longer distances, respectively. However, for the most part, ADSL services and their different data rates are typically limited to a shorter distance limit. The fastest ADSL service, with 8 Mbps of download speed, is limited to less than 9,000 feet.

Understand that the measurement of the distance for the DSL line is not "as the crow flies." The distance measurement used is the total length of the copper wiring from the CO to the home, including any twists, turns, loops, and coils in the line. It often surprises people to learn that a CO that is only about a quarter-mile (1,320 feet) from their home (on a straight line) is, according to the Telco, about 5,000 feet from the CO in terms of wire distance.

ADSL   ADSL (Asymmetrical DSL) transmits data on two separate frequency bands—one for upload traffic and one for download traffic—on the copper lines that connect a home to the Telco's CO. The upload band carries data transmissions from the home to the CO and DSLAM, and to the Internet. The download band then carries data from the Internet through the DSLAM to the home. In either case, conventional copper telephone lines provide the connection between the home and the CO.

Like cable service, ADSL uses higher speeds for download and lower speeds for upload. These different upload and download speeds are the asymmetrical part of this service. Like all telephone services (and Internet services as well), there are a number of ADSL standards in use. Table 7-2 lists the more commonly available ADSL standards.

SDSL   SDSL uses the same line speeds for both upload and download transmissions, which makes it symmetrical. This type of service is better suited for applications that require constant speeds, such as commercial applications or Web servers. Besides the fact that it is symmetrical, SDSL uses the entire bandwidth of its medium, which means that it is not compatible with standard telephone voice service and must have its own wire pair.

Standard	Commercial Name	Download Speed	Upload Speed
ANSI T1.413	ADSL	8 Mbps	1 Mbps
ITU G.992.1 Annex A	ADSL over POTS	8 Mbps	1 Mbps
ITU G.992.1 Annex B	ADSL over ISDN	8 Mbps	1 Mbps
ITU G.992.2	ADSL Lite (G.Lite)	1.5 Mbps	500 Kbps
ITU G.992.3/4	ADSL2	12 Mbps	1 Mbps
ITU G.992.3/4 Annex L	RE-ADSL2	5 Mbps	800 Kbps
ITU G.992.5	ADSL2+	24 Mbps	1 Mbps

Table 7-2 ADSL Standards

A variation of SDSL that operates on either one wire pair or two wire pairs is Symmetric High-Bitrate DSL (SHDSL). SHDSL, which is not available in all areas of the U.S., provides up to 2.3 Mbps on one pair or up to 4.6 Mbps on two pairs. However, like all DSL flavors, SHDSL has distance limitations as well. The one-pair mode supports its 2.3 Mbps service up to 10,000 feet and can supply 192 Kbps at around 20,000 feet. The two-pair mode supports 4.6 Mbps at 10,000 feet and 2.3 Mbps to about 16,000 feet.

IDSL The biggest difference between IDSL and other types of DSL is that it transmits data in a digital format over ISDN (Integrated Services Digital Network) data lines. IDSL requires a separate copper wire pair to transmit on the Telco's existing ISDN network. While ISDN is limited to a data transfer rate of 128 Kbps, IDSL is able to transmit at 144 Kbps, using the entire bandwidth of the media. ISDN is an on-demand system and must connect (dial) for each transmission session; IDSL is an always-on system.

Feet, Miles, and Kilometers

Distances for telecommunications are being standardized internationally to the metric system. This means that wire distances and attenuation limits are typically stated in meters, kilometers, and the like. So, to help you make this transition, I've included the following table:

Measurement	Meters (m)	Kilometers (km)
1 foot	0.304 8	0.0003048
1 yard (3 feet)	0.9144	0.0009144
1 mile (5,280 feet)	1,609	1.609
10,000 feet	3,048	3.048
20,000 feet	6,096	6.096

Typically, xDSL distances that are stated in kilometers are rounded down. A distance of 10,000 feet is cited as 3 kilometers and 20,000 feet as 6 kilometers.

IDSL bypasses the Telco's voice network switching system and connects to the digital data equipment at the CO. Because of its lower speeds and dedicated wiring, IDSL is able to extend the distance limitations of DSL service to more than 25,000 feet. However, IDSL is not available in all local telephone systems.

Fixed Wireless Services

Essentially all wireless Internet services provide what the communications industry calls a "last mile" connection. This means that the final link between an Internet backbone and the home or business is provided by a subscribed communication connection, wireless or wired.

In a fixed wireless system, as its name implies, both the transmitting and receiving devices are fixed in place, as opposed to mobile wireless services, such as cell phones or mobile radio systems. A fixed wireless service uses a terrestrial (transmitted along the surface of the earth, rather than transmitting off a satellite) point-to-point microwave signal to deliver broadband services, eliminating the need for cabling, a telephone system, or even satellite dishes. For the most part, the fixed wireless systems available to the majority of homes operate in unlicensed bands of the radio frequency (RF) spectrum, but the new WiMAX (Worldwide Interoperability for Microwave Access) services operate on both unlicensed and licensed frequencies.

The equipment in a wireless broadband system consists of equipment at the WISP's (Wireless Internet Service Provider) location and at the home. In general, this equipment consists of a Wireless Internet Point-of-Presence, or WIPOP, operated by the WISP and the customer premise equipment (CPE) located at the subscriber's home. The WIPOP typically includes one or more access points and some form of bandwidth management. The access point antenna is the subscriber's central transmit and receive point with the Internet backbone. Bandwidth management attempts to evenly apply the available bandwidth to meet the WISP's subscriber demands.

The subscriber CPE consists of an antenna that includes an amplified radio, a non-amplified radio, or both. In most cases, the CPE of a fixed wireless system produces an Ethernet-compatible signal that can be connected into a wireless router or directly to a computer. However, the WIPOP and the CPE must have a substantially clear line-of-sight (LoS) to operate properly. Trees, buildings, mountains, signs, or any other terrestrial obstruction can either block or disrupt the service.

Like most transmitted signals, distance plays a huge role in the amount of bandwidth available to a particular location. Bandwidth varies from provider to provider, but generally available fixed wireless systems offer from 2 or 3 Mbps data rates at costs comparable to cable or DSL systems. Higher cost services can offer higher bandwidths, but these services aren't consistently available in all area. One good thing about microwave systems is that, for the most part, weather is not typically a factor to either link speed or signal quality.

Unlicensed Band Wireless   A variety of wireless Internet services are available in a growing number of urban and some rural areas of U.S., Canada, and Europe. With the advancements being made in the cellular telephone industry, wireless broadband services are becoming increasingly more commonplace.

The WISP services that operate on unlicensed RF bands are marketed under a variety of names, including Wireless DSL, Wireless Internet, and the like. Regardless of what name it goes by, unlicensed band wireless Internet links are spread-spectrum wireless systems that operate in the general 2.4 GHz RF band (also referred to as the Industrial, Scientific, and Medicine [ISM] band) and provide data transfer speeds of between 1 and 11 Mbps over distances of up to 25 miles. Of course, the actual data speeds realized by a home depend on the antenna technology in use and several other conditions, including distance, terrain, line-of-sight, transmitter power, and more.

CROSS-REFERENCE The 2.4 GHz RF band on which ISM operates is the same frequency used by the IEEE 802.11x wireless local area network (WLAN) devices inside a home. See Chapter 8 for more information on WLANs.

TIP The ISM standards have recently been expanded to include a 5.8 GHz band for use in wireless Internet services.

In addition to the ISM band, the UNII (Unlicensed National Information Infrastructure) band (pronounced as "you-nee") defines three service types: UNII 1 and UNII 2 (UNII Indoor), which are designed primarily for indoor high-speed wireless networks and operate in the 5.15 to 5.35 GHz and 5.25 to 5.35 GHz bands, respectively; and UNII 3, which operates in the 5.725 to 5.825 GHz band for use in wireless networks, such as a wireless Internet connection to a home.

Licensed Band Wireless   Over the past ten years or so, a variety of last-mile wireless services have been offered for home connections, including MMDS (Multichannel Multipoint Distribution System), which is used primarily for wireless cable TV services; LMDS (Local Multipoint Distribution System), a point-to-point limited distance service initially designed for delivering broadband video and voice; and WiMAX, designed specifically for the transmission of wireless data over long distances. Of these and a few others, WiMAX is emerging as the more promising service for home use.

WiMAX is a point-to-point microwave system defined by the 802.16d (Wireless Metropolitan Area Network [WMAN]) standard that provides both mobile and fixed-base wireless broadband connectivity as an alternative to a cable or DSL link to homes unable to access either of those services. WiMAX services currently offer bandwidth packages with download speeds of 768 Kbps, 1.5 Mbps, and 2.0 Mbps and with an upload speed of 256 Kbps.

ISDN

As described earlier, ISDN is a telephone system service that requires a dedicated wire pair to operate. ISDN is available to home users as BRI (Basic Rate Interface) ISDN, which combines the two wires to transmit data at 128 Kbps, with the remaining 16 Kbps of the media's bandwidth used for control and command signaling.

As its original name, Integrated Speech and Data Network, implies, ISDN was developed to support the transmission of voice and data signals needed for video conferencing as digital data rather than the analog signals transmitted on the POTS systems. ISDN offers about twice the throughput compared to a standard analog dialup modem for connecting to a network, but since higher rate products and services are now available, ISDN's popularity is waning except where other services aren't yet available.

Satellite Internet Service

Another type of wireless link available to homes is a satellite Internet service. Satellite Internet services can be used in areas where other systems are not generally available or where a home is too distant to connect to another service, wired or wireless.

A satellite Internet service is offered in one of three ways:

- **One-way multicast**   Transmits data, voice, and video, but since the system is only one way, many TCP/IP protocols will not operate properly without a return channel. While a one-way satellite system can be used to surf the Net, interactivity is either nonexistent or very limited.

- **One-way multicast with terrestrial link**   Adds a telephone line and dialup modem for uploads, allowing the one-way (download) satellite link to supply near wired broadband transfer speeds.

- **Two-way**   Provides just what its name implies: both upload and download communications links via a satellite service. The actual Internet backbone connection occurs at a hub site that communicates with the satellite to receive or send content from and to home-based systems. Two-way satellite Internet services use a VSAT (Very Small Aperture Terminal) ground station to provide up to 4 Mbps transfer speeds. A major benefit of a two-way satellite Internet service is that it doesn't have to be fixed in position or location. A homeowner can move the satellite dish receiver to a motor home or other recreational vehicle and take their service on the road.

Internet Gateways

Each of the various broadband services listed in the preceding section must provide some form of an interfacing device (CPE) to convert its broadband signaling into baseband signaling for use on the internal network. Typically, the CPE device provided with the service has the primary function of modulating the signal for interoperability with the internal home network.

In general, these devices are referred to as Internet gateways. Each type of communications link uses a different CPE because of the unique nature of the incoming signal. The common CPE devices used to connect a home system are

- **Cable**   The basic Internet gateway for a cable Internet service is a cable modem. Cable modems typically don't offer much more in the way of services. However, there are a wide variety of cable bridges, switches, and routers that can be used in place of a cable modem to gain several valuable control, security, and management functions.

Baseband versus Broadband

All high-speed Internet services are nominally broadband services. A broadband transmission carries multiple streams of audio, video, and data simultaneously over a single medium. Each distinct signal is transmitted on an individual, independent channel that is specific to the frequency of the signal.

Baseband is a networking technology that transmits data over a single medium channel without frequency shifting. In practical terms, a baseband network transmits only one signal at a time using the entire medium. Ethernet is a baseband networking technology.

- **Dialup**   Nearly every computer has a modem either installed as an expansion card or integrated into the motherboard and chipset. Modems simply provide modulation services and not much more.

- **DSL**   The type of Internet gateway used with a DSL service can vary with the DSL service in use. ADSL services use either a DSL modem or bridge. These products are limited in their capabilities and services, much like a cable modem, but do typically offer multiple ports that allow multiple computers to share the connection. SDSL services provide either a bridge or a router, with the router being the preferred device. A DSL router offers security, firewall, Network Address Translation (NAT), and other common router functions.

- **ISDN**   ISDN requires a terminal adapter that performs inverse multiplexing to split the outgoing signal onto the two lines and to combine incoming signals from the two lines for use by a computer or network device. Any additional services must be added through the installation of other network devices.

- **Fixed wireless and satellite Internet**   Like all broadband services, these wireless services require a wireless modem or bridge to modulate the broadband signal into a baseband signal for the internal network. This device is typically built into the CPE antenna system.

Network Cabling

In a home network, the quality of the cable installation is far more important than the quality of the wire. Don't misunderstand: the quality of the cable is important, but how well the cable is installed can have a major impact on the performance of the network. It is critical that standardized wiring practices and terminations be followed at all times.

New Construction

The type of network cable installed in a new home depends on the requirements the user defines for the network. The current cabling standards, EIA/TIA 568a, 568b, and 570, prescribe Cat 5e or Cat 6 cabling for both data and voice networks.

In a new construction situation, installing Cat 5e wire in the walls throughout the house, using a star topology (homeruns), provides an infrastructure that should support the networking needs of the home for years to come. As a rule of thumb, the rooms to be included in the home network should have at least two runs of Cat 5e cable—one each for voice and data—and more if you're attempting to future-proof the home.

Existing Structures

Retrofitting a home with Cat 5e wiring can prove to be a challenge. Pulling cable into existing walls, under floors, or over ceilings and avoiding existing electrical wiring and plumbing fixtures because of their interference problems can be very difficult.

In these situations, wireless systems, powerline control (PLC), or Home Phoneline Networking Alliance (HomePNA) should be seriously considered. The pros and cons of each of these network media needs to be discussed with the homeowner, and the right mix of media should be matched to the client's needs. Of course, the primary consideration is still how well these systems can support both the data and automation network requirements.

 CROSS-REFERENCE See Chapter 3 for a discussion of the processes and best practices that should be used to install network cabling in a home—new or existing.

Cable Installation Standards

The primary concern for pulling cable into an existing or new structure is to spread the runs of the various cable types over as wide a space as possible. If it is absolutely necessary to cross cabling, there are standards and guidelines for the installation of low voltage cabling that cover overlap, separation, and crossing angles.

Here are the low-voltage cable installation guidelines you should follow:

- Use no more than 25 pounds of pull on the cable.
- Use at least six inches of separation between power and data cables.
- If a data cable crosses a power cable, it must do so at a 90-degree angle.
- A data cable should avoid fluorescent light fixtures.
- Cable sheathing can be stripped off not more than 1.25 inches from the connection end of the cable; one inch is recommended.
- Unshielded twisted-pair (UTP) wire pairs should not be untwisted more than 0.5 inch; 0.375 inches is recommended.
- The bend radius of any network cable should not be more than one inch, but because some cable types are more sensitive than others, read the specifications of a cable before beginning installation.

When installing UTP cable, the total length of all cabling between a transmitting source and a terminating (receiving) device should not be more than 90 meters, or about 295 feet. This doesn't mean just the longest run of cable between two points; it means all of the cable segments used to create the run between two communicating devices.

CROSS-REFERENCE Chapter 3 lists the recommended pre-wiring guidelines for low-voltage cabling.

RFI and EMI Interference

The purpose for the rules, standards, and guidelines of cable installation is to protect the cable and its electrical signals from external interference. Virtually anything electrical has the potential to generate sufficient interference to degrade the signal being carried in low-voltage cable. This is especially true when standard unshielded wire is used. UTP is highly susceptible to interference from any number of sources, including appliance motors, televisions, vacuum cleaners, AC power lines, nearby radio or cellular transmitters, and just about any other electrical source.

Contrary to common belief, interference on a UTP cable is cumulative. Even if a cable picks up interference at only two points along a long cable run, the effect can be cumulatively damaging. Each time the cable picks up additional voltage from an interference source, the risk also increases for damage to or loss of the signal quality.

Choosing the Cable

As discussed in Chapter 1, there are two basic networking cable types used in home network situations: twisted-pair and coaxial cable (RG6 or RG58). Some homeowners may choose to install fiber optic cabling, but typically the expense of using fiber optic cabling is still fairly prohibitive.

UTP/STP Unshielded twisted-pair (UTP) cable is the most commonly used cabling for networks because it's the lightest, most flexible, least expensive, and easiest to install and maintain of any of the popular physical network media. On the other hand, UTP is very vulnerable to interference and has attenuation issues as well. However, for the most part, these issues can be overcome through proper use and installation.

Inside a shielded twisted-pair (STP) cable, the wire pairs are wrapped in a copper or foil shield to help reduce EMI and RFI interference. The shielding makes STP more expensive than UTP wire, which is why it is not frequently used in home networking situations. However, if an existing home has more interference sources than can be easily avoided, STP may be the better choice of the twisted-pair cables.

Coaxial Cable RG58 or RG6 coaxial cable is commonly found in many newer homes in the cable TV system that commonly have outlets in most of the rooms in the house. The primary differences between RG58 and RG6 are that RG58 has 100-ohm resistance and RG6 has 75-ohm resistance and that RG6 has about twice the maximum distance of RG58, which is why RG6 is becoming more popular for networking purposes.

Coaxial cable has built-in features that make it more reliable than UTP, but it does cost more and is less forgiving to install. In existing home or retrofit situations, attempting to install new runs of coaxial cable may prove very difficult, if not virtually impossible. However, there are situations in which coaxial cable makes sense for a home network. In cases where network cabling must pass through, over, or under damp, wet, or extremely electrically noisy areas, coaxial cable is a better choice than either twisted-pair cable types. Of course, in these situations and if the homeowner can afford it, fiber optic may be the better choice. However, on a cost-performance basis, coaxial cable is a good choice for less than ideal cabling situations.

Cable Standards

Chapter 4 discusses the various electrical, wiring, and cable standards that apply to the structured wiring systems in a house, but here is a bit more on cable standards, especially in the context of designing and installing a computer network.

EIA/TIA 568

The EIA/TIA standards 568a and 568b are the most widely used cabling standards for computer network media. Included in these two standards are specifications and guidelines for six elements of computer network cabling:

- Backbone cabling
- Equipment rooms
- Entrance facilities
- Horizontal cabling
- Telecommunications closets
- Work areas

The 568 standard that directly affects home networking is the standard for horizontal cabling. This part of the standard covers the network media (cable, connectors, and so on) that run horizontally from the distribution facility to each of a network's nodes.

The 568 standard specifies that for each network location there should be the following:

- At least two network connection outlets.
- A maximum distance of 90 meters (295 feet) for each cable segment of Cat 5e UTP cable in a horizontal run. Remember that Cat 5e cable is rated at a maximum segment length of 100 meters (328 feet), but the standard reduces the distance for performance purposes.
- Patch cords, the cables used to interconnect two devices at a horizontal cross-connect, should not exceed 6 meters (19.6 feet) in length.
- Patch cords used to connect a computer to a wall outlet should not exceed 3 meters (9.8 feet).
- If the square footage of a building floor exceeds 1,000 square meters (over 10,000 square feet), or if any run of the horizontal cable exceeds 90 meters, a second distribution facility should be added to the cable plant. Granted, this particular requirement is not likely to be a problem in most houses.

Distribution Panels

The primary distribution panel in an average house is the electrical panel. The electrical panel is the central point for the incoming electrical service and the service wiring of the home's electrical system. The electrical panel provides a central, single-point control and access unit for a home's electrical system.

In the same way, a single panel, closet, or center simplifies and centralizes the design, installation, and perhaps more importantly, the maintenance for the home's structured network cabling. The distribution panel should be centrally located in a house, but it is far more important that the distribution panel be central to the network to minimize the length of cable runs as much as possible. However, if the home has a natural or predesignated location for the distribution center, remember that cable is relatively inexpensive. Figure 7-2 illustrates how a laundry room on the rear of a home can serve as the location for a central distribution facility for the network cable installed in the home.

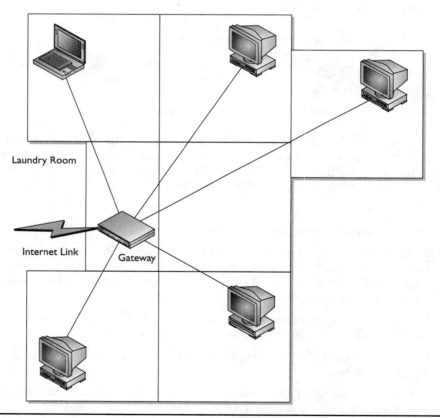

Figure 7-2 The distribution panel should be placed at a central point in the home.

Cross-Connects

Figure 7-3 illustrates the physical components of a typical Ethernet network. The computers are connected into the jacks of a wall outlet using patch cords. The wall outlet is terminated with a punch-down connection at a patch panel. The jack terminating the horizontal cable from the wall outlet is then interconnected into a hub, which provides connection to the network backbone.

Figure 7-4 illustrates the use of a patch panel as a system cross-connect. Officially, a cross-connect is used to bridge or interconnect two separate segments or subsystems of a network. One of the most common methods of creating network cross-connects is to use a patch panel. Each cable is terminated into the patch panel and then a patch cord is used to connect each of the patch panel's ports to the appropriate device or distribution facility.

 CROSS-REFERENCE   See Chapters 3 and 4 for more information on EIA/TIA 568 standards and connecting network cable to a punch-down jack.

Wall Outlets

Assuming a home network is using a wired installation, the cable plan must include wall jacks in those rooms where network access is to be provided. The type of jacks included on the outlet depends on exactly what service connections are to be supplied

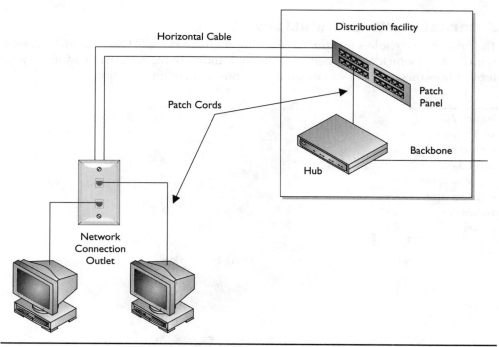

Figure 7-3   The physical components of a typical wired Ethernet network

Figure 7-4
A patch panel used as a network cross-connect to interconnect different network subsystems

through the outlet. If the outlet is to provide a connection to the UTP horizontal cabling, then an RJ-45 jack needs to be provided for each connection allowed in that outlet. However, if connections to other systems in the house are to be included on the outlet, the outlet could also include connection jacks for the telephones, video, audio, and television systems.

Figure 7-5 illustrates a wall jack with two data network connections, a telephone connection, and a video connection.

Alternative Wired Solutions

The primary two choices for structured wiring alternatives are PLC and HomePNA solutions, both of which are defined in Chapters 1 and 2. In the sections that follow, we'll look at how these systems can be used in a home networking solution.

Figure 7-5
Wall outlets can include connections for any or all of the wired services available to a room.

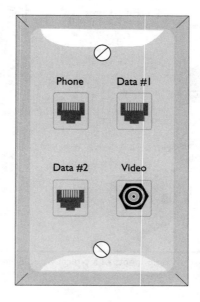

Power Line Technologies

There are three primary PLC (power line control) technologies that can be used in a home network: CEBus, HomePlug, and X-10. X-10 is not useful as a structured-wiring network element and is better suited to on/off control and monitoring functions. I'll talk more about X-10 in Chapter 25.

CEBus   EIA and the Consumer Electronics Association (CEA) developed CEBus (Consumer Electronics Bus), which is an open standard that is also known as EIA 600, as a home communications standard in the early 1990s as an extension to the X-10 standard. CEBus supports communication over 100V (volt) AC (alternating current) electrical line, UTP, coaxial cable, fiber optics, and radio frequency (RF) and infrared (IR) wireless media. The primary reason CEBus is not better known is the lack of product development and the high cost of the few products that do exist. However, more CEBus products are becoming available.

HomePlug   The HomePlug Powerline Alliance publishes a series of standards for the use of existing electrical lines in a variety of home network applications:

- **HomePlug 1.0**   Defines a 14 Mbps system for connecting home network devices over electrical power lines in a home.

- **HomePlug 1.0 Turbo**   Defines an unofficial standard that improves a HomePlug 1.0 system to as much as 85 Mbps data speeds.

- **HomePlug AV (audio/video)**   Defines a standard for the transmission of HDTV (high-definition television) and VoIP (voice over the Internet Protocol) signals at speeds as high as 200 Mbps. However, HomePlug AV is not backward-compatible with HomePlug 1.0 and requires a bridging device to interface the two standards.

- **HomePlug BPL (Broadband Power Line)**   This standard, currently under development, will define the use of outside power lines to deliver last-mile connections to a home.

- **HomePlug CC (Command and Control)**   Another standard currently under development to define a technology that adds advanced home automation control capabilities to the HomePlug 1.0 standard.

On a HomePlug network, each networked device must connect into a HomePlug adapter (see Figure 7-6). The HomePlug adapter serves as the network adapter to interface a connected device to the network media, which in this case are the home's electrical lines.

HomePNA

HomePNA (Home Phoneline Networking Alliance), also known as HPNA, is a standard for devices that provide networking communication support with speeds as high

Figure 7-6
A HomePlug
adapter used
to connect a
computer to a
home network

Photo courtesy of Cogency Semiconductor, Inc.

as 128 Mbps over coaxial or telephone lines in a home. HomePNA network adapters are available as PCI expansion cards and external USB devices and connect to network devices using standard telephone connectors (RJ-11) and wiring. The network adapter shown in Figure 7-7 connects to a computer through a USB port and connects to the HomePNA network using a standard phone cable and RJ-11 jack.

Figure 7-7
A HomePNA
USB network
adapter

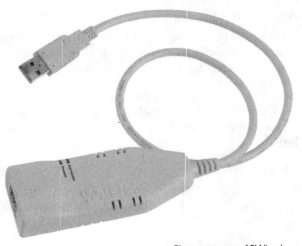

Photo courtesy of 2Wire, Inc.

The HomePNA 3.0 standard allows several computers to share a single Internet connection with or without a router. This standard also allows a client/server network to function as a peer-to-peer network for the sharing of locally connected peripherals and data files on client devices. Because HomePNA uses a different frequency band for data signals, there is no impact on voice or fax traffic on the network.

Configuring Network Clients

Perhaps the most important part of configuring a home network is the network configuration of each individual computer. Unless a computer is configured properly, it cannot communicate effectively across the network, regardless of whether it is connected on a peer-to-peer or a client/server network.

TCP/IP Configuration

Microsoft's Windows 2000, XP, and Vista have advanced network configurations to the point of it being almost automatic. If you are installing a Windows operating system on home computers, there typically isn't much in the way of configuration actions you need to perform. The XP and Vista installation procedure automatically configures a computer for DHCP (Dynamic Host Configuration Protocol) and the protocols, services, and clients needed to communicate on a network.

Internet Connection Sharing

As discussed in Chapter 5, the owners/users of computers connected into a peer-to-peer network have the ability to create shares on the peripheral devices connected directly to their computers and to files and folders located on their local hard disk drives. However, another resource that peer-to-peer networks can share is an Internet connection.

Microsoft Windows operating systems (Windows 2000, Windows XP, and Windows Vista) include a feature, Internet Connection Sharing (ICS), that can be used to share a single Internet connection with other computers on a network. In effect, ICS converts the central (host) computer into a network router. The host computer must have at least two network adapters installed: one to connect to the local network and one to connect to the Internet. Once enabled, ICS provides both DHCP and NAT services to the computers sharing the Internet connection.

NOTE   ICS is most commonly used for sharing a dialup connection rather than a broadband connection. DSL, cable, and wireless Internet services can be more easily shared using a gateway device like a bridge or a router.

TIP   The networking term for a computer with multiple network adapters is multihomed.

Chapter Review

The process of planning and designing a home network, especially one that will be integrated into a home automation network, is an essential part of a successful project.

The primary choices for high-speed Internet connection services for most homes are cable Internet, DSL, and wireless. Each of these services typically provides an Internet gateway device that is a modem, bridge, switch, or router.

The EIA/TIA 568 standards provide the working specification for UTP cabling, including termination and cross-connection. Alternative network media choices include PLC, CEBus, and HomePNA technologies.

Questions

1. What is the primary network cabling standard used in North America?

   A. RS 232

   B. EIA/TIA 432

   C. EIA/TIA 568

   D. IEC

2. After installing the wiring in a home network, you run your data cable certification testing and fail the length test on the cable segment that runs to a far upstairs bedroom. In checking out the problem, you discover that the cable link is 295 feet long and there is a 20-foot patch cord connecting the computer to the wall outlet and a 15-foot patch cord connecting the patch panel to the Internet gateway. Which of the following is likely the cause of the problem?

   A. The link cable is too long.

   B. The home run cabling is too long.

   C. The patch cord at the computer is too long.

   D. The patch cord at the patch panel is too long.

3. Which of the following is not an Internet connection service commonly used in home networking situations?

   A. DSL

   B. ISM

   C. ISDM

   D. Leased T-3 line

4. What Internet gateway device is generally used with an SDSL service?

   A. Modem

   B. Bridge

PART II

    C. Terminal adapter

    D. Router

5. Which two of the following networking media are coaxial cabling types?

    A. RG6

    B. RG58

    C. UTP

    D. ScTP

6. Which two of the following technologies define the use of electrical wiring as a networking medium?

    A. HomePlug

    B. CEBus

    C. HomePNA

    D. 802.11g

7. What standard defines the transmission of HDTV signals across a home's electrical service lines?

    A. HomePlug 1.0 Turbo

    B. CEBus

    C. HomePNA

    D. HomePlug AV

8. A network facility that is used to interconnect separate or dissimilar network subsystems or segments is called a

    A. Distribution panel

    B. Cross-connect

    C. Patch cord

    D. Horizontal cable

9. What Windows operating system feature allows a host computer to share a dialup connection to the Internet with other computers on the network?

    A. Printer and file sharing

    B. Network shares

    C. ICS

    D. Network bridging

10. Which of the following is a recommended cable installation guideline?

    A. Use no more than 25 pounds of pull on the cable.

    B. Use at least six inches of separation between power and data cables.

    C. If a data cable crosses a power cable, it must do so at a 90-degree angle.

    D. B and C only.

    E. A and B only.

    F. A, B, and C.

Answers

1. **C.** Let's hope you know this by now. You definitely need to know this for the exam. EIA/TIA 232 and EIA/TIA 432 are legacy cabling standards for serial connections. IEC is an international connection standard.

2. **B.** If you add up the lengths of the cables that make up the channel, the total comes to 335 feet. The specified total length for a Cat 5 channel is 328 feet. Remember that the channel length includes all cable segments used to connect a computer to its signal source. The cable link is only the portion between the patch panel and the wall outlet and it is at the maximum acceptable length.

3. **D.** DSL, ISM (wireless DSL), and ISDN are all common Internet connection services used with home networks. A T-3 communications line is a physical media technology that supplies bandwidth only.

4. **D.** A router is used with SDSL because its higher bandwidth and cost makes it generally only practical for use in larger networking situations. The other devices listed are used with dialup/cable, cable/wireless, and ISDN, respectively.

5. **A and B.** RG6 and RG58 are types of coaxial cable. The other choices are media that can be used in a home network.

6. **A and B.** HomePlug and CEBus define standards that use existing electrical wiring as a networking medium. HomePNA is a phone line networking technology, and 802.11g is a wireless Ethernet standard.

7. **D.** HomePlug AV is a standard for transmitting AV signals on electrical power lines in a home. None of the other choices specifically address this capability.

8. **B.** A cross-connect interconnects different network segments or subsystems. A patch panel is commonly used to create a cross-connect, within a distribution facility.

9. **C.** ICS (Internet Connection Sharing) converts a host computer into a gateway router for other computers on a network.

10. **F.** All of the options given are recommended cable installation guidelines.

Designing and Installing a Wireless Network

In this chapter, you will learn about:
- Wireless networking devices
- Wireless networking standards
- Wireless network design considerations

Wireless networking is a very viable option for a home network. Installing a wireless network eliminates a large portion, if not all, of the cabling and wiring requirements of a home network; not to mention providing more flexibility of use immediately and into the future. A wireless network allows a home network to adapt to the user and where the network's use is located, rather than vice versa.

This chapter covers the basics of wireless networking you need to know for the DHTI+ examination. In addition, I've included information that you should know to better serve your customer when considering the inclusion of a wireless network in a home environment.

Wired versus Wireless

When you compare a wireless network to a wired network in a home, there are really only two major differences: medium and security. However, they do have some major similarities as well: wired and wireless networks are likely to be Ethernet networks; both need to connect to an Internet gateway; and both require the same types of implementation considerations to address administration, reliability, and usability.

In general, a wired network is a better choice over a wireless network. A wired network can be much less expensive, more reliable, easier to manage, and, generally easier to troubleshoot. However, in situations where installing cable is impractical, the network nodes are likely to be moved or repositioned, or the network's physical configuration needs to be more dynamic, a wireless LAN can, in spite of its shortcomings, be a good choice.

Radio frequency (RF) communications, the medium used in wireless networking, has limitations and constraints that can keep a wireless network from being totally effective in some situations. The construction materials used in a home or building, interference from other RF devices, or the shape of the area in which the wireless network is to operate—among other factors—can reduce the effectiveness and efficiency of a wireless network. On the other hand, these factors aren't generally issues in a wired network, assuming it is installed properly.

The overall goal of any network is to support and fulfill the resource and data needs of the network's users. Deciding which network medium and technology best supports this goal requires the consideration of several issues, including cost and scalability.

Cost Considerations

Wireless networking is a wire replacement technology, which means that when you start adding up the cost savings of a wireless network in comparison to a wired network, the most obvious savings is the wiring. A wireless network is typically less expensive to install or modify because a) a wireless network eliminates the cost of cable runs between the network's workstations and peripheral devices to the Internet gateway, and b) a wireless network provides an immediate connection anywhere within the range of its access point, avoiding the incremental cost of moving or installing new network cabling.

Scalability

A network that has the capability to adapt to the changing needs of its users is scalable. A wireless network is generally more scalable than a wired network. While wireless networks do have distance limitations, these limitations are less restrictive than those associated with a wired network. For example, if a new PC needs to be installed at a location that is more than 100 meters from the nearest gateway on a wired network, additional equipment, such as a repeater or a switch, is required. Plus, the new PC must be located close to an outlet jack, which involves the expense of pulling wire into a wall and terminating it. On the other hand, a wireless connection can be created as simply as installing a wireless network adapter in the PC, providing the PC doesn't already have one built in.

Wireless Network Standards

The wireless networking standards that are appropriate for use in a home's wireless local area network (WLAN) are primarily those that have been developed by the IEEE (Institute of Electrical and Electronics Engineers) and the ETSI (European Telecommunications Standards Institute). The IEEE developed the 802.11x wireless network standards and the ETSI developed HIPERLAN (High Performance Radio LAN) and HIPERLAN/2. These standards and those published by the Wi-Fi Alliance are commonly grouped under wireless fidelity (Wi-Fi). The Wi-Fi standards define the functions of a wireless Ethernet network operating on the lower layers of the open systems interconnection (OSI) model.

The wireless networking standards typically considered for use in a home network are

- **IEEE 802.11a**   This wireless networking standard defines an RF technology in the 5 GHz band that offers very high bandwidth (as much as 54 Mbps) over short distances. However, with the popularity and expansion of the 802.11b and 802.11g standards and the release of the 802.11n standard, it is likely that 802.11a may be short-lived.

- **IEEE 802.11b**   This is the most commonly used of the 802.11x standards, at least for the time being. Virtually every wireless network gateway, access point, or PC Card produced is based on one variation of 802.11b or another. The 802.11b standard defines a 10 Mbps Ethernet network operating over a 2.4 GHz RF band.

- **IEEE 802.11g**   This wireless LAN standard is an extension of the 802.11b standard that increases data speeds from 11 Mbps to 54 Mbps on the 2.4 GHz band. The 802.11g standard is backward-compatible so 802.11b access points and upward are compatible with the 802.11g standard.

TIP   Many 802.11b devices can be upgraded to 802.11g through simple firmware upgrades.

- **IEEE 802.11n**   This is the newest of the 802.11 standards (although it's not completely finalized as of this writing). The 802.11n standard uses the MIMO (multiple inputs/multiple outputs) technology that works with multiple radios and antennas to handle multiple signals and up to 100 Mbps data speeds on either the 2.4 GHz or the 5 GHz bands or both. The 802.11n standard is backward-compatible with the 802.11b and 802.11g standards, but its multiple signals can cause interference with the older devices. Many 802.11n devices that are technically pre-802.11n devices are now available.

- **IEEE 802.11y**   This standard, scheduled for release in early 2008, allows Wi-Fi equipment to communicate with devices operating on licensed RF bands, such as the 3.65 to 3.7 GHz, 4.9 GHz, and 5 GHz bands, allocated to fixed satellite services (FSS) to provide long-range communications services to 2.4 GHz devices.

- **HIPERLAN**   This European standard provides for 10 Mbps wireless communications in a 50 meter (about 170 feet) range. This standard has been replaced in Europe by either the HIPERLAN/2 or the IEEE 802.11x standards, though HIPERLAN devices are still available.

- **HIPERLAN/2**   This European standard closely matches the performance of the 802.11a standard, with a data speed of 54 Mbps and a range of 50 meters.

Other wireless communications technologies that can be considered for a home WLAN are

- **Bluetooth**   An RF personal area networking (PAN) standard that also operates on the 2.4 GHz band. The benefit of Bluetooth, named after an ancient warrior king of Sweden, is that it is self-discovering and self-configuring among Bluetooth-capable devices, which means that you can roam freely within a Bluetooth range: when you leave one device's range, another Bluetooth device will automatically establish a connection. While Bluetooth may not yet be a totally viable option for home networking, as more products emerge its 10-meter range limit seems well suited for most homes.

- **Infrared (IR)**   Though not a commonly used wireless network technology, the Infrared Data Association (IrDA) has defined a series of IR standards that can produce up to 16 Mbps over a range of about 1 meter (slightly more than 3 feet). Because of its limited range, IrDA standards, including IrSimple and Very Fast IR (VFIR) are better suited for use in a PAN.

- **ZigBee**   This wireless RF standard was designed specifically for use in home automation, control, and monitoring applications, including such systems as home lighting, smoke detectors, HVAC controls, security, and other home systems.

- **Z-wave**   This standard implements a standard RF signal format for power line carrier (PLC) networks. Many of the PLC standards offer an optional RF signal (such as X-10), but the Z-wave standard is totally based on the RF signal format.

 NOTE   Both ZigBee and Z-wave networking standards are primarily designed for use in personal area networks (PANs) using the IEEE 802.15.4 standard.

Wireless Networking Devices

Arguably, the most important components of any network are those that provide and support the communications links between a network's nodes. A network's communications and connectivity devices provide the links that attach a node to the network, allow it to share its resources, and facilitate its capability to communicate with other nodes across its network and on other networks.

The wireless network connectivity devices commonly used in home networks are

- Network adapters
- Access points
- Bridges
- Routers
- Antennas
- Repeaters

Not all of these devices are found in every home WLAN, but a typical WLAN includes at least one access point and one or more network adapter, each with a built-in or attached RF radio transceiver and an antenna.

Wireless Network Adapters

In order for a computer—regardless of whether it's a desktop, notebook, tablet, or handheld computer—to communicate on a wireless network, it must be equipped with a wireless network adapter. The portable devices available today (such as notebook PCs, handheld PCs, personal digital assistants [PDAs], and some cell phones) typically have a built-in wireless network adapter. In fact, a majority of the desktop PCs available also include built-in wireless connectivity.

However, older computers and peripheral devices that don't have a built-in wireless adapter must have this capability added. A wireless network adapter can be connected to a computer as either an internal expansion card or an external peripheral device. An internally installed network adapter is typically in the form of an expansion card that is inserted into an expansion slot on a computer's motherboard. External network adapters connect most commonly through a USB interface or some other form of high-speed serial interface. Many older notebook computers use a PCMCIA (Personal Computer Memory Card International Association) PC Card interface, like the one shown in Figure 8-1.

When selecting a wireless network adapter, two primary characteristics must be considered: the wireless networking standard needed and the interface type. The only issue to be addressed when considering the network standard of a wireless network adapter is its compatibility with the network standard in use (or to be used) on the WLAN. However, the interface type of the network adapter can involve a bit more thought.

CROSS-REFERENCE   For more information on expansion card network adapters, see Chapter 6.

Figure 8-1
A PC Card wireless network adapter

Photo courtesy of Cisco Systems, Inc.

Network Adapter Type	Advantages	Disadvantages
PC Card (PCMCIA)	No open-case installation required PC Card (16-bit) and CardBus (32-bit) models available Easily removed	Not compatible with most desktop PCs Relatively high-power requirements Size and power of antenna commonly lower than other types Poor antenna orientation
PCI and mini-PCI expansion cards	Permanent installation	Requires open-case installation Antenna orientation can be weak
USB	No open-box installation required USB 2.0 features 480 Mbps peak transfer rate 802.11b operates at approximately the same speed as USB 1.1 USB devices can be easily removed Usable on either desktop or portable PCs	USB 1.0 features 12 Mbps peak transfer rate 802.11a/802.11g requires USB 2.0 Higher CPU usage More easily stolen

Table 8-1　Advantages and Disadvantages of Common Wireless NIC Types

Table 8-1 lists some of the advantages and disadvantages of the different 802.11*x* wireless network adapters readily available.

Like the one shown in Figure 8-2, expansion card network adapters are typically marked with the 802.11*x* standard they support with a label on the face of the card. When installing a wireless network interface card (NIC) in a computer, you should check, recheck, and then verify that the IEEE 802.11*x* standard of the card matches that

Figure 8-2
An IEEE 802.11b mini-PCI wireless NIC expansion card

Photo courtesy of Cisco Systems, Inc.

of the other devices included in the network. As simple as this may sound, this check can save you troubleshooting time and a lot of head scratching later.

Wireless Access Points

Basically, a wireless access point (see Figure 8-3) is a hub that clusters any wireless network adapters within its range and a bridge for the wireless network to a wired network. Because it is, in effect, an entry point to a network, an access point (AP) can also provide the first-line of security for the network, permitting only those wireless devices that have the appropriate identities and security codes to gain access to the network.

Access Point Considerations

Like all other 802.11x wireless network components, APs have distance limitations at which the signal range begins to weaken, slow down, and become unusable. IEEE 802.11b APs have a range of 29 meters (95 feet) in an enclosed area, 50 meters (163 feet) indoors (its nominal range), and a maximum of around 400 meters (or about ¼ mile) outdoors. However, an AP's actual range (its coverage) can vary depending on the network standard in use and its data rate, capacity, the presence of RF interference, the construction materials in its surroundings, and perhaps even the quality of the device itself. Table 8-2 lists the common indoor and outdoor coverage ranges for the different 802.11x standards.

Figure 8-3

A wireless access point

Photo courtesy of Cisco Systems, Inc.

Standard	Maximum Data Rage	Typical Throughput	Indoor Range	Outdoor Range
802.11a	54 Mbps	25 Mbps	35 feet	75 feet
802.11b	11 Mbps	6.5 Mbps	40 feet	150 feet
802.11g	54 Mbps	20 Mbps	40 feet	150 feet
802.11n	248 Mbps	74 Mbps	220 feet	500 feet
802.11y	54 Mbps	25 Mbps	32 feet	5000 feet

Table 8-2 Coverage Range and Characteristics of IEEE 802.11x Wireless Network Standards

Providing wireless coverage for an entire area, such as a home and its grounds, may require more than one AP. Just how many APs are needed in a network depends on a number of considerations:

- **Coverage**   The design goal of a WLAN should be first to provide linkage to every wireless node and second to create an overlapping pattern of coverage cells to allow location flexibility to roaming wireless devices.

- **Placement**   Typically, it is better to install APs in higher locations inside a room to minimize the opportunity for interference from walls, partitions, and any electrical or RF devices in use.

- **Network mode**   APs can be configured for ad hoc or infrastructure mode. If the AP is to support the roaming of the wireless devices in its vicinity, it should be configured to ad hoc mode. However, if the AP is installed to support a fairly stationary wireless network, it should be configured to infrastructure mode, the most common use and configuration of an AP. Even in infrastructure mode, there is still some flexibility for moving wireless devices within the range of the AP. When a station moves into the range of another AP, the network adapter's configuration may need to be modified with the connection identity of the new AP.

Multiradio Access Points

With the continual evolution of wireless standards, many manufacturers now offer upgradeable, multiple-radio access points capable of supporting two or more different WLAN standards simultaneously. Commonly, multiradio APs are used to service an existing WLAN on one standard, while also supporting new wireless devices on a different standard. For example, the Cisco 1200 AP and the Intermec MobileLAN WA22 (see Figure 8-4) both incorporate an 802.11b or 802.11g radio, as well as an 802.11a radio.

Bridging Access Points

The bridging function in a wireless AP is used to connect two or more WLANs together, allowing them to communicate and exchange messages. An AP that includes bridging (commonly referred to as a wireless bridge) supports point-to-point or

Figure 8-4
An access point
with multiple
built-in WLAN
radios

Photo courtesy of Intermec Technologies.

point-to-multipoint configurations. Point-to-point bridging provides an interconnecting midpoint between two WLANs.

Multipoint bridging connects multiple WLANs together by providing a link point for the AP in each network. A point-to-multipoint bridging AP is commonly used as a base service set (BSS), which provides the connection point for the WLANs to a wired network.

Not all APs provide bridging. For the most part, wireless bridges (see the section "Wireless Bridges" a bit later in this chapter) are not typically used in home networks and are more commonly used in larger corporate, campus, or commercial wireless networks.

Stealth Access Points

Most new wireless APs now include the ability to disable the broadcast of the AP's service set identifier (SSID). Any wireless device that knows, either through discovery or configuration, the SSID of an AP (and perhaps some additional security codes) is able to connect to the WLAN served by the AP. Blocking the clear transmission of the AP's SSID prevents its discovery, which can be a large part of preventing intruders from connecting to the WLAN. When the SSID broadcast is disabled, the AP operates in stealth mode, which requires the SSID to be configured into any wireless device attempting to connect to the network.

TIP Stealth mode access points are not defined in the 802.11x standards. This feature is identified by manufacturers with a variety of names, including stealth mode, closed mode, private network mode, SSID broadcasting feature, and others.

Configuring Access Points

Straight out of its box, a wireless access point is configured with a variety of default values, depending on the manufacturer. These default values generally allow the access point to work in most situations, but they may not be appropriate to the specific needs of any particular WLAN.

Important to the effective operation of the access point is that each of the major features and settings are configured to best support the needs of its WLAN. The process of configuring an access point can be divided into three general steps:

- Connection configuration
- Administrative configuration
- Networking configuration

Connection Configuration

The primary settings you should configure on an AP are (listed in alphabetical order because their sequence varies from device to device)

- **Administrative control** To prevent unauthorized access and protect the administrative settings on the AP, such as administrator login, password, SSID, and other important WLAN settings, configure the administrative control security settings. This is done in two ways: disabling the serial (console) port and resetting the administrative username and password. The default values are universal for a manufacturer's devices and easily obtained, which can enable an unauthorized person to reconfigure an access point to allow easy access to the network.

- **Authentication** If an AP offers Wi-Fi Protected Access (WPA), it should be enabled to provide a higher level of encryption and authentication. If it's available, SKA (Shared Key Authentication) should be enabled to provide a minimum level of security. The default authentication is typically OSA (Open System Authentication), which affords virtually no security. Another option is to enable a higher-level authentication, such as the 802.1x security or EAP (Extensible Authentication Protocol), LEAP (Lightweight EAP), or PEAP (Protected EAP), if available.

- **Encryption** There are some who say that WEP (Wired Equivalent Privacy) provides virtually no security at all. However, if it is all that's available, enable it. A better choice is WPA, or WPA2, which are much harder to crack.

- **IP address** Just like all other network devices, an access point must be configured with an IP address. In most cases, an access point is assigned a default IP address (such as 192.168.0.225 or similar) by the manufacturer, which should be changed to fit the IP addressing plan in use on the WLAN.

An access point can be configured with a static (unchanging) IP address or to obtain its IP address from a DHCP (Dynamic Host Configuration Protocol) server on a LAN or from an ISP (Internet service provider).

- **RF channel** In a WLAN that includes multiple APs, you may need to alter the default channel of the device, especially if the network is using the 802.11b standard. 802.11b channels can overlap, which can cause channel crosstalk. In this situation, adjacent APs should be set to use channels 1, 6, or 11 to ensure frequency separation. In most cases, this is not an issue for 802.11a, 802.11g, and 802.11n APs, in which the channels don't overlap.

 NOTE You should update the firmware of an access point before installing it in the WLAN and starting its configuration to ensure you have the latest updates and features. The best place to look for an update to the firmware of your access point is on the manufacturer's website.

Networking Configuration

The primary networking setting for an AP is its DHCP configuration. DHCP is used to automatically configure the IP settings of network nodes when they connect to the network, typically at startup.

In many installations, the AP is connected to the Internet gateway that connects to an ISP's network. While the AP will likely get its IP configuration from the DHCP server of the ISP, it can then provide this same service to the wireless nodes on the internal WLAN.

DHCP on a WLAN works in exactly the same way it does on a wired network. The access point acts as the DHCP server to the WLAN using a range of available IP addresses and the related information needed to configure DHCP clients (wireless nodes).

DHCP is almost a necessity on wireless networks, especially on those that support roaming. The utility gained from being wireless would be defeated if you had to manually reconfigure the IP settings of a PC each time you moved from one roaming domain to another or happened to move a wireless station from one access point to another. DHCP allows a wireless node to obtain the information it needs to join a network automatically.

 NOTE Virtually all wireless bridges, routers, and switches include an AP function, which is configured the same as a standalone AP. However, there are function-specific configurations that you need to set on these other devices.

Wireless Bridges

A wireless bridge (see Figure 8-5) is commonly used to provide a connection point between two or more WLANs located in separate buildings of a campus area network (CAN) and to allow the wireless network to jump over a street, a landscaped area, or another type of open area between buildings.

Figure 8-5
A wireless bridge

Photo courtesy of Cisco Systems, Inc.

A wireless bridge commonly has a maximum range of about two miles, but its range can vary depending on the capabilities of the bridge. A home network typically doesn't require a wireless bridge, but on a large estate or in a situation where workshops are located some distance from a home on the same property, the use of a wireless bridge may be appropriate.

Wireless Routers

In a purely technical sense, a wireless router isn't a totally wireless device. In most applications, a router integrated into a WLAN has the capability to communicate with wireless devices. However, in almost every case, the router is also being used as a wireless switch or bridge as it is also connected to either a wired network or an ISP's service connection.

A wireless router, like the one shown in Figure 8-6, performs the same basic function as any other network router: it routes network packets to the network path on which they can move closer to and, eventually, finds their destination addresses. A wireless router combines the functions of a wireless access point with the standard functions of an IP multipoint router, which is to provide connectivity to a wide area network (WAN)

Figure 8-6

A wireless router

Photo courtesy of Cisco Systems, Inc.

and possibly to stations on other network segments. In addition to the basic functions of routing and serving as a wireless access point, wireless routers commonly provide other LAN support features, including:

- **Network Address Translation (NAT)**   NAT allows network stations to share a single public IP address when communicating beyond the LAN and facilitates the use of private addresses within the LAN.

- **Port-based access control**   Transmission Control Protocol/User Datagram Protocol (TCP/UDP) port numbers can be used to allow or deny access to the WLAN (incoming) or to the WAN (outgoing) based on the port number associated with the application initiating a network packet. For example, if you want to block Telnet requests from outside the WLAN, port 23 traffic can be blocked from the forwarding process.

- **Firewall**   A firewall is a network mechanism that prefilters incoming packets before they reach the router or the network. While firewalls can be a standalone device or appliance on a network, most wireless routers incorporate a firewall.

WLAN Antennas

The dipole antennas built into most wireless network adapters, NICs, access points, routers, and so on, are generally adequate for home wireless networks. External antennas are available that can be used in place of a device's built-in antenna, often with increased power, range, and signal strength.

If you wish to "hot-spot" a portion of a house that may need a bit more signal support, installing an antenna can improve the performance of the network. An external antenna (see Figure 8-7) provides you with the capability to locate the antenna of a WLAN device where it has the best reception and interface to the wireless media and the AP, router, or other wireless device in an accessible location.

Firewalls

In networking, a firewall is a mechanism, either hardware or software, that is used to prevent certain inbound traffic from gaining access to a LAN or outbound traffic from gaining access to a WAN.

Although it is not commonly thought of as such, the most basic firewall service, and one of the most commonly implemented, is NAT. Even the most inexpensive routers include NAT, which eliminates an outside station from knowing any IP address other than that of the network gateway.

Another common router-based firewall function is Stateful Packet Inspection (SPI), which protects a LAN from network attacks. A router with SPI in its firewall functions looks at the packet header to determine if any special security handling is required. SPI routers have the capability to filter out advanced Denial of Service (DoS) attacks (see Chapter 11 for more information on DoS and other types of network attacks).

Two levels of firewalls can be implemented on a WLAN: personal software firewalls and dedicated hardware network firewalls.

A personal firewall is a software package most typically used in situations where a small network is connected to an open connection between the network and an Internet service provider (ISP). Because connection services like cable Internet and digital subscriber lines (DSL) are always on or available, the LAN is susceptible to hacker access. A personal firewall blocks incoming traffic not initiated from the network itself.

While nearly every wireless router includes an access point function, it's the router's more advanced routing, switching, and security functions that define its function as a wireless gateway. A popular use for wireless gateways is in support of hot spots, or areas of cities and buildings that are enabled for wireless station connections using a single base station.

When planning and designing a WLAN, you should consider several RF and antenna characteristics:

- An antenna's transmissions can be distorted by nearby metal and other objects, including walls and large furniture, as well as trees, buildings, and the like.

- Antennas both transmit and receive RF signals. Any nearby source of RF interference may be picked up and retransmitted by an antenna.

- Many RF antennas, such as cellular telephone antennas, may be polarized vertically, so an antenna with horizontal polarization may perform better in these situations.

- Any cable connections to an RF antenna should be free of splices, connectors, and other types of interconnections to minimize RF interference.

Figure 8-7

A desktop
wireless antenna

Photo courtesy of Belkin International, Inc.

 NOTE WLAN antennas are not included in the WLAN standards, so the good news is you are free to choose any antenna. However, the bad news is you're free to choose any antenna because with so many choices available, it is easy to mismatch the antenna to the router or access point.

Wireless Repeaters

Wireless network media has an effective range or distance (attenuation point) at which the quality of its transmitted signal begins to degrade. Attenuation degrades the transmitted signal because the strength of the electrical impulses can no longer overcome the resistance of the medium, be it the air or even copper cabling. Wireless RF network signals are generally limited to the broadcast range of the transmitter, the power of the antenna, and the amount of interference in the coverage area. Should it be necessary to extend the coverage range of a WLAN, a wireless repeater (see Figure 8-8), which is also called a signal extender or a range expander, can be used to filter and re-energize the signal to extend its quality, strength, and effective range.

A repeater isn't a complicated device. All a repeater does is receive a transmitted signal and retransmit the signal with its original strength restored and, in most cases, with much of the signal noise removed. However, the downside to repeaters and extenders is that they can add a small amount of delay (latency) to the signal. Including too many repeaters or extenders on a wireless system can cause timing issues, especially on high-speed networks.

Given that in a home networking environment today's wireless networking standards generally have the range to provide coverage to an entire home, it is unlikely that a repeater is needed. Adding a higher power antenna or even an additional access point may be a better solution.

Figure 8-8
A wireless
repeater

Photo courtesy of Cisco Systems, Inc.

WLAN Design Considerations

IEEE 802.11x WLANs have a number of limitations and performance issues that must be considered during the planning and design phases of a WLAN installation project. If these limitations and issues, some obvious and some rather subtle, are not addressed during the WLAN design process, they can cause the network to have intermittent problems or to fail altogether.

The issues that must be addressed during planning and design are, categorically:

- RF design issues
- Capacity and coverage
- Existing network issues

RF Design Issues

Perhaps the most important design issue in any WLAN design is that it communicates using radio frequency (RF) radio waves. RF transmissions are definitely affected by their environment and surroundings, which can cause a WLAN to develop operational problems.

You should never assume that any specific location is able to support RF communications. Wireless communications just don't work the same in every situation.

IEEE 802.11x WLANs operate primarily on the 2.4 GHz ISM frequency band, which can be both its boon and its bust. ISM has proven to be generally reliable, but some of its characteristics have also been known to affect a WLAN's performance:

- **Competing devices**   Because the ISM RF frequency band is unlicensed, many different types of wireless devices also use this band, such as Bluetooth devices, cordless telephones, emergency services (police and fire protection) radio communications, and even some baby monitors. For example, if a company incorporated Bluetooth headsets into its call center operations, it shouldn't be a huge surprise that its 802.11b 2.4 GHz WLAN might have intermittent problems in the call center area. If ISM interference is an issue in a home, consider using a 5 GHz standard, such as 802.11a.

- **Distance**   At some distance, all RF signals will lose at least some signal strength. This translates to a loss of bandwidth and signal integrity for a wireless network as the distance approaches the outside edges of a wireless device's effective range. Depending on an antenna's power (gain), the distance of its operating range may be longer or shorter, even in comparison to the same or similar devices in the same network. In a WLAN situation, 802.11b and 802.11g devices can only provide their full bandwidth over the first 30 meters (100 feet) around of its antenna, assuming everything else is okay. For each successive 30 meters in distance, about 50 percent of the bandwidth is lost. At a distance of 100 meters, the bandwidth available is only about 10 percent of the standard's nominal rating. Similarly, the 802.11a standard, which transmits on the 5 GHz frequency band, loses around one-third of its bandwidth every 25 meters. This reduction in bandwidth is caused by the APs automatically reducing data transfer speed as the signal begins to weaken. In a home wireless network, a single WLAN node placed at the outer fringe of an AP's range slows down the entire WLAN; the AP slows the network to service this node. The solution: ensure every node is placed in a proximity to an AP that allows it to operate at or as close as it can to its nominal speeds.

- **Metal boxes**   In RF terminology, a "metal box" is any metallic or magnetic object that blocks or absorbs a transmitted RF signal. A metal box can be a building, an air conditioning unit, a vault or large safe, a large machine, metal partitions, and the like. To avoid this condition, place APs and nodes so that they avoid having a metal box in a direct loss of signal (LoS) between devices.

- **Stationary objects**   Not only metal boxes can block or interfere with an RF transmission, but also the walls of a building, rock walls and fireplaces, trees and large bushes, and other large stationary objects can deflect or block RF signals. Different stationary objects create different levels of attenuation in the RF signal. Table 8-3 lists many common objects and their effect on an RF signal.

Obstruction	Degree of Attenuation	Example
Open space	None	Courtyard; clear LoS in a room
Wood	Low	Inner wall, door, floor
Plaster	Low	Inner wall (older plaster walls produce a shorter attenuation point than new plaster)
Synthetic materials	Low	Room partitions
Cinder block	Low	Inner wall, outer wall
Asbestos	Low	Ceiling (consider removing, if for no other reason than health issues)
Glass	Low	Nontinted window
Wire mesh in glass	Medium	Door, security windows
Metal tinted glass	Low	Tinted window
Human body	Medium	Large group of people
Water	Medium	Damp wood, aquarium
Bricks	Medium	Inner wall, outer wall, floor
Marble	Medium	Inner wall, outer wall, floor
Ceramic (metal content or backing)	High	Ceramic tile, ceiling, floor
Paper	High	Roll or stack of paper stock
Concrete	High	Floor, outer wall, support pillar
Silvering	Very High	Mirror
Metal	Very High	Desk, office partition, reinforced concrete, elevator shaft, filing cabinet, sprinkler system, ventilator

Table 8-3 Degree of Attenuation by Common Materials. Used with permission from Intel Corporation.

- **Shared bandwidth**   The bandwidth of WLAN devices is *shared bandwidth*, which means all active wireless devices are competing for the available bandwidth. The number of wireless nodes on a WLAN that must compete for the bandwidth can reduce the overall performance of the network.

Because of these issues and many others specific to a particular location, any proposed WLAN area may have spots in which wireless reception can change from outstanding to poor in only a few meters. Before a WLAN can be planned into an area, large or small, the area should be physically and carefully modeled using a site survey.

Capacity and Coverage

There are two primary considerations when designing a WLAN: ensuring both sufficient coverage and capacity. You need to strike a balance between the two because if the design provides only coverage, sufficient bandwidth won't be available to all nodes. If the design provides only capacity, there may not be sufficient signal strength to all nodes.

WLAN Coverage

To maximize the coverage of an AP, it should be placed in the center of or, at a minimum, in a location that provides the most coverage to the area it supports. In larger areas (areas that exceed the 100-meter coverage of a single access point), multiple APs, additional antennas, or repeaters should be planned into the network to provide overlap and seamless roaming within the WLAN's coverage area.

WLAN Capacity

The capacity of a WLAN is dependent on the capability of its APs to support the amount of data traffic at any given time. The capacity of an AP changes with the types and amounts of data its users are transmitting. For example, an 802.11b access point, which has up to 11 Mbps of bandwidth (within 10 meters), can support 50 nodes that are mostly idle, as many as 25 nodes accessing e-mail and midsized data files, or 10 to 15 nodes that are active on the network and transmitting or receiving mid- to large-sized data files. The general rule of 20 nodes per AP is based on the nodes transmitting a mix of traffic.

WLAN Site Survey

If the home network calls for a considerable number or wireless workstations or roaming devices, it is good practice to conduct a site survey before you designate the locations of the APs and fixed stations in the WLAN. While a full-blown commercial site survey can be expensive, both in terms of time and cost, it can be a relatively simple affair for a home network.

The purpose of the site survey is to verify the home's capability to support a WLAN. Unless there will be more than 20 wireless nodes in the WLAN, coverage is probably not an issue. Even though the 802.11x network's bandwidth is shared bandwidth, unless there are a large number of stations on the WLAN, there won't be significant bandwidth issues. So, the only thing you need to verify is the planned placement of the AP and devices. You want to avoid placing an AP or station in a dead zone that is affected by any of the conditions listed in Table 8-2.

To survey the possible AP and node locations, install a wireless router or AP at the gateway's designed location. Then carry a wireless-enabled portable computer around to the designed locations of the other devices to test the signal strength. You can use the Windows wireless utilities for this test or signal strength testing utilities available for nearly all network adapters or APs.

Where the signal strength is too low for consistent operations, move around the intended location to verify your findings. By moving only one or two feet, you may find a better spot in the same general location.

WLAN Modes and Topology

A WLAN can be configured into one of two basic operating modes and three standard topologies. WLANs operate in either ad hoc or infrastructure modes. An ad hoc operating mode establishes an Independent Basic Service Set (IBSS) topology. Infrastructure operating mode networks use either a Basic Service Set (BSS) or an Extended Service Set (ESS) topology.

Figure 8-9
An ad hoc WLAN is created from two or more IBSS devices.

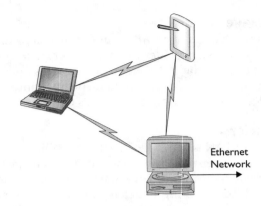

Ethernet
Network

Ad Hoc Mode

An ad hoc WLAN allows nodes to directly connect to each other. Just as a wired peer-to-peer network doesn't require a central server, an ad hoc WLAN doesn't require a central access point.

Each of the wireless nodes in an ad hoc WLAN is an IBSS. An IBSS (see Figure 8-9) can provide access to peripherals, a wired network, a modem connection, and other services, depending on the permissions granted by the IBSS's user. In a home setting, an ad hoc WLAN can provide the most flexibility. However, as we'll discuss later, it can also be less secure.

Infrastructure Mode

The most common mode used for larger WLANs is infrastructure, which requires the use of at least one base station AP that could be connected to a wired network or an Internet gateway. A WLAN implemented with 20 or less wireless nodes and a single access point creates a BSS topology (see Figure 8-10).

When multiple access points must interact to access a single wired network connection, an ESS topology is created. An ESS topology is a good choice for larger (in terms of both the number of nodes and the coverage area) networks.

Figure 8-10
A BSS requires the inclusion of an access point (base station).

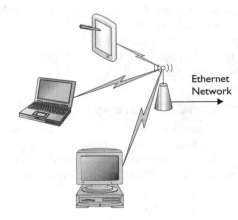

Ethernet
Network

Wireless LAN Security

Several protocols and methods can be used to secure WLAN transmissions and prevent unauthorized access to the network. The most commonly used methods are

- Wired Equivalent Privacy (WEP)
- Wi-Fi Protected Access (WPA) and WPA2
- MAC address filtering
- Authentication methods

These security methods and the specific protocols used to implement them are discussed in the following sections.

Wired Equivalent Privacy (WEP)

The need for security was apparent early in the development of the IEEE 802.11 standards, so a security protocol, WEP, was included in the 802.11b standard. WEP is designed to provide a WLAN with security and privacy equivalent to that expected on a wired Ethernet network. Although WEP offers only minimum security, it does provide more security than if it is not used at all. WEP was never intended to serve as the only security measure on a network, but many home wireless networks depend on it as the sole security mechanism on the network.

One fairly large flaw in the design of WEP is that much of the security surrounding a wired network is physical in nature, including such security elements as controlled building access, locked office doors, cables in the walls and floors, and the like. A wireless network is much harder to secure because radio waves are transmitted through the air and can pass through walls. Unfortunately, software programs like AirSnort and WebCrack are readily available and can be used to crack WEP encryption. Because WEP works on only the two lowest OSI layers (data link and physical layers), it can't provide end-to-end security for transmitted data.

WEP encrypts the payload of each transmitted packet, leaving the packet header unprotected. Figure 8-11 illustrates the process used by WEP to encrypt and transmit a single packet between a wireless node and an access point. The node (PC) prepares the data for transfer and passes it to its network adapter. The network adapter applies the WEP encryption process to the packet payload and then transmits the packet to the access point. The access point deciphers the encrypted data in the packet using an unencrypted key transmitted with the packet. If the packet is transmitted on to a wired

Figure 8-11

The WEP
encryption
process

1. Data passed to network adapter
2. IV+WEP key used to encrypt data
3. Encrypted data + IV sent to AP

1. Encrypted packet received by AP
2. IV used to decipher encrypted data

network or a WAN, the packet remains unencrypted, but if the packet is forwarded to another wireless node, the AP applies the WEP process before transmitting it.

Activating WEP is still better than nothing. WEP does a good job of keeping most people out, at least those who are easily deterred. But, true hackers can exploit the weaknesses of WEP and easily gain access to wireless networks depending only on WEP for security.

Wi-Fi Protected Access (WPA) and WPA2

Wi-Fi Protected Access (WPA) security was developed by the Wi-Fi Alliance to overcome the shortcomings of WEP. One of the major differences between WPA and WEP is that WPA uses a temporal key integrity protocol (TKIP) that alters the encryption key in use after certain time periods, where the WEP uses the same key throughout a session.

WPA includes other improvements over WEP as well, including the use of an extensible authentication protocol (EAP), which is a security model that has been adopted into a variety of different security protocols. At present the Wi-Fi Alliance certifies six EAPs for use with WPA security: EAP Transport Layer Security (EAP-TLS), EAP Tunneled Transport Layer Security (EAP-TTLS), Protected EAP (PEAP), and EAP for Global System for Mobile Communications (GSM) Subscriber Identifier Modules or EAP-SIM. Other implementations of the 802.11i standards are the Lightweight EAP (LEAP) and the EAP Flexible Authentication for Secure Tunneling (EAP-FAST), both proprietary method developed by Cisco Systems, Inc. New implementations of 802.11i standards are emerging rapidly as the use of wireless networks expands and the need for secure continues to increase.

The WPA2 standard adds the use of the advanced encryption standard (AES) to create an access method that is considered to be, for now anyway, fully secure.

Media Access Control (MAC) Address Filtering

Because of WEP's flaws, many early wireless access point manufacturers chose to develop an alternative security access method: MAC address filtering. Wireless network adapters and devices, like virtually all network devices, are identified using a MAC or Layer 2 address. Essentially MAC address filtering screens the MAC address of each device requesting access to the WLAN to see if it is on a permit list.

Beyond the fact that to use MAC address filtering the permit list must be manually managed on the AP, the upside to this access control method is that only those devices identified in the permit list are granted access to the media. However, there is one very large downside: the MAC address is transmitted in several of the administrative and association frames exchanged between two wireless nodes and, even if MAC filtering is used with encryption, a dedicated hacker can eventually learn one or more of the MAC addresses on a WLAN.

 NOTE MAC address filtering is not a part of the 802.11 standards and provides only marginal security to a wireless network.

WLAN Security Threats

Primarily because they are wireless, 802.11 networks are uniquely vulnerable to outside attacks and interception. Unlike a wired network, a wireless network's media cannot be physically secured and an attack can be launched from almost anywhere within the media's range, which could be the next cubicle, the next building, the parking lot, or even the street.

An attack on a wireless network can take a wide variety of forms and, unless you understand the different types of attacks that could be made, protecting against them is difficult. Not all attacks are particularly dangerous and devastating to a WLAN. Some are frivolous and harmless, but any attack, even those that are harmless, could lead to something far more dangerous. In designing and implementing the security for a WLAN, the more you know about the threats that exist, the better your chances are of protecting the network.

The threats a WLAN should be protected against the most are not much different than those that threaten a wired network. The most common and frequent of the attacks made on networks are

- **Client-to-client**   In ad hoc mode, the nodes of a WLAN must be protected because they don't have the security applied to the network through the AP. In the spirit of sharing, an ad hoc station may be too generous and essentially be an open door to hackers who gain access to the WLAN or to other users on the same network.

- **Denial of service (DoS)**   A DoS attack has only one objective: to prevent any access to a network's resources. The most common DoS attack involves flooding an Internet gateway, web server, or internal network server with packets or frames that must be processed, monopolizing the system's resources to the point that all other user functions are severely interrupted or prevented entirely.

- **Insertion or interception**   With the right information, gained through interception, a rogue device can insert itself into a WLAN, either spoofing as a valid station or merely eavesdropping on the network traffic, and begin capturing sensitive information.

Protecting a WLAN

The following is a list of suggested actions and configurations you can apply to a WLAN to help secure it from outside evildoers:

- Develop a WLAN security policy that defines exactly what is to be allowed and, more specifically, what is not to be allowed on the network. The policy should list the most secure level desired and the configuration elements of the APs and routers to be included in the network.

- Implement the 802.11x (802.11a, 802.11b, 802.11g, or 802.11n) standard that provides just enough range to support the network.

- Configure the network with dynamic privacy keys and 802.1x security. Avoid static privacy keys as they negate the role of 802.1x in the security scheme.

Wardriving and Warchalking

Back in the days when only dialup modems could be used to access a remote network for good or evil, hackers would dial a sequence of phone numbers looking to find one that would reach a modem. This practice became known as *wardialing,* a term based on the actions of the young computer hacker in the movie *War Games.*

In the wireless network world, there is no need to dial sequential numbers to gain access. To find a wireless network, all one has to do is carry a wireless networking–equipped laptop or notebook computer as they walk around (warwalking), drive around (wardriving), or fly over (warflying) residential neighborhoods to discover any number of unsecured wireless access points.

Wardrivers, -walkers, and -flyers then mark the house or building with one of three symbols, which were adapted from the symbols used in the past by hobos to indicate which houses would give food, drink, or shelter. The following illustrates these symbols. Where a word or acronym is used in a symbol, the actual value detected is inserted at that position.

Symbol	Meaning
SSID)(Bandwidth	Open Node
SSID ○	Closed Node
SSID Access (W) Contact Bandwidth	WEB Node

So, if you have a wireless network, you may want to check for any suspicious chalk marks around or on your home (called *warchalking*). An evildoer may have detected your network and be sharing his good fortune with fellow warriors.

Chapter Review

Wireless networking is a very viable option for a home network. Installing a wireless network eliminates the cost and management of cabling and wiring and provides scalability. Wireless networking is a wire replacement technology. A network that has the capability to adapt to the changing needs of its users is scalable.

The IEEE developed the 802.11x wireless network standards and the ETSI developed HIPERLAN (High Performance Radio LAN) and HIPERLAN/2. These standards and those published by the Wi-Fi Alliance define the functions of a wireless Ethernet network.

The wireless networking standards typically considered for use in a home network are 802.11a, 802.11b, 802.11g, 802.11n, and, in the future, 802.11y. In Europe, the standards in use are HIPERLAN and HIPERLAN/2. Other wireless communications technologies that can be considered for home use are Bluetooth, IrDA, and ZigBee.

The wireless network connectivity devices commonly used in home networks are network adapters, access points, bridges, routers, antennas, and repeaters. A wireless network adapter can be connected to a computer as either an internal expansion card or externally as a peripheral device. A wireless AP is a hub that clusters any wireless network adapters within its range and serves as a bridge to a wired network. A wireless bridge is used to connect two or more WLANs. A wireless router includes the functions of an AP and a bridge, but its basic function is to provide connectivity to a WAN. Router features include NAT, port-based access control, and firewall services. External antennas can be used to increase power, range, and signal strength. A repeater receives a transmitted signal and retransmits it with the signal strength restored.

The issues that must be addressed during planning and design are RF design issues, capacity and coverage, and existing network issues. A site survey should be performed before the AP locations and fixed stations of a WLAN are determined.

WLANs operate in either ad hoc or infrastructure modes. An ad hoc operating mode establishes an Independent Basic Service Set (IBSS) topology. Infrastructure operating mode networks use either a Basic Service Set (BSS) or an Extended Service Set (ESS) topology.

Several protocols and methods can be used to secure WLAN transmissions and prevent unauthorized access to the network. The most commonly used methods are WEP, WPA and WPA2, MAC address filtering, and authentication methods.

Questions

1. A network that has the capability to adapt to the changing needs of its users is _____.

   A. Scalable

   B. Interoperable

   C. Adaptable

   D. Convergent

2. Which of the following is not an organization that has published standards for a WLAN?

   A. IEEE

   B. CompTIA

   C. ETSI

   D. Wi-Fi Alliance

3. Which IEEE WLAN standard defines 54 Mbps speeds over a 2.4 GHz RF band?

   A. IEEE 802.11a

   B. IEEE 802.11b

   C. IEEE 802.11g

   D. IEEE 802.11y

4. What device must be installed on a PC before it is able to communicate on a wireless network?

   A. Router

   B. Network adapter

   C. Switch

   D. Access point

5. What is the basic wireless communications device that serves as a central hub to the wireless nodes within its range?

   A. Router

   B. Network adapter

   C. Switch

   D. Access point

6. What protocol allows multiple internal nodes to share a single external IP address?

   A. TCP

   B. IP

   C. NAT

   D. UDP

7. Which of the following is not a wireless network design consideration?

   A. RFI

   B. Metal boxes

   C. ISP

   D. Stationary or blocking objects

8. What wireless operating mode is associated with an IBSS topology?

   A. Ad hoc

   B. Infrastructure

   C. Mobile

   D. Fixed

9. What topology is most commonly associated with an infrastructure operating mode?

   A. IBSS

   B. BSS

   C. ESS

   D. XSS

10. Which of the following is not a WLAN security method?

    A. WEP

    B. WPA

    C. MAC filtering

    D. CSMA/CA

Answers

1. **A.** A network that is scalable is able to change with the needs of its users. Interoperable means that a device or protocol is compatible with another. Adaptable refers to a device that can be adapted to work in a situation. Convergence occurs when all components of a network are in synch.

2. **B.** CompTIA (Computer Technical Industry Association) is better known as a certification sponsor. IEEE, ETSI, and the Wi-Fi Alliance have each published wireless networking standards.

3. **C.** IEEE 802.11g is compatible with 802.11b. 802.11a also produces 54 Mbps, but on the 5 GHz band. 802.11y is an unreleased WWAN standard.

4. **B.** Whether installed as an external or internal device, computers and other devices must have a network adapter to communicate on the network. The other choices are all network connectivity devices.

5. **D.** Even a wireless router or switch has an access point capability built-in.

6. **C.** NAT is a router-based protocol that allows multiple nodes to use a single public IP address outside of the WLAN.

7. **C.** The ISP service to be used determines the type of gateway in use, but the other choices are design considerations that can affect the network's performance.

8. **A.** An IBSS creates a form of a peer-to-peer network.

9. **B.** BSS is the most commonly used infrastructure mode topology. An ESS is a grouping of BSS groups. As far as I know, there's no such thing as an XSS.

10. **D.** CSMA/CA (Carrier Sense Multiple Access/Collision Avoidance) is an Ethernet access management technology. All of the other choices are WLAN security methods.

Troubleshooting
a Home Network

In this chapter, you will learn about:
- Troubleshooting network connections
- Troubleshooting network cabling
- Troubleshooting a network PC's configuration

Tracking down a problem on a network is often more of an issue of where to begin looking than it is resolving the problem. Often a network problem is easily remedied once you're able to pinpoint its source.

Networks, including home networks, bring together several layers of technology—media, hardware, and software—all capable of causing or contributing to a network or a networked computer not performing properly.

In this chapter, we look at some of the ways you can diagnose and resolve problems on a network, including testing network media (cabling and wireless), network connections, and a networked computer's configuration.

Troubleshooting Network Connections

Any number of things can go wrong with network connections, but generally, and especially in a home environment, once they are configured properly and working, network connections tend to continue to work until something is changed on the computer or its network. So, the first thing to check if the network or a computer develops connection problems is whether or not anything has changed recently.

Troubleshooting Dialup Connections

If a dialup connection fails to connect, there are five areas to check:

- **Phone connections**   If there is no dial tone present, you should get an error message displayed on the computer to that effect. The sound produced by nearly all modems is there for the user to track the action of the connection (called a *handshake*, meaning the activities involved with two modems negotiating the connection) as it is being made. The first of these sounds is the dial tone from the phone line. If the modem is not connecting and you don't hear a dial tone, there is likely a problem with the phone service, wall jack, the wire, the RJ-11 connector, or the connection between the connector and the wall jack. Of course, this assumes that you are getting a dial tone on all other phone connections.

- **Modem problems**   If the modem is failing to complete the handshake with the modem at the other end and a timeout or connection failed message is displayed on the PC, it is likely that the modem is configured incorrectly in terms of its character length, start and stop bits, and speed. Check with the technical support people at the Internet service provider (ISP) to verify what the modem's settings should be. Depending on the modem, these settings can be made through software on the PC or may have to be made through toggle switches (DIP switches) on the modem. Set the modem configuration as required and retry the connection.

- **Protocols**   Protocol problems are common with new modems and, typically the modem's Transmission Control Protocol/Internet Protocol (TCP/IP) or another protocol has not been properly configured. Remember that dialup connections require the Point-to-Point Protocol (PPP). Verify that the proper TCP/IP protocols are enabled and that the proper bindings (protocols linked to one another) are set. If you aren't sure which protocols or bindings are required, contact the service provider's technical support for this information.

- **Remote responses**   The ISP network access server (NAS) to which you are attempting to connect may be down or having problems. The dialer may also be dialing an incorrect number or be configured improperly with other erroneous information. Before making any assumptions about why this may be happening, call the ISP's technical support people or have the customer call to verify these settings.

- **Telephone company or phone line problems**   Static or crosstalk on the telephone line can cause a modem to disconnect frequently and, typically, very soon after completing a connection. Line noise can also cause so many data retransmissions that the connection's data speed can appear exceptionally slow. Another common problem is call-waiting being active on the modem line because the signaling that is sent to indicate a call is waiting will interrupt the connection. If call-waiting is enabled on a line, you can temporarily suspend it by dialing *70 on the appropriate line before reattempting to dial out through the modem.

Troubleshooting a DSL or Cable Connection

The problems associated with a digital subscriber line (DSL) or cable connection are typically one of a set of common issues. DSL bridges and routers do have a few problems specific to them, just as cable modems have their unique problems. However, for the most part, connection issues for DSL and cable modems are very similar. The next few sections list the more common connection problems for these services and how to resolve them.

Common DSL and Cable Connection Problems

Here are the more common problems a customer could experience with a DSL connection:

- **Authentication** If the connection fails to establish during a startup, the username and password being used to log onto the system or the configuration settings on the computer or Internet gateway may be erroneous. Understand that although DSL (and cable) are "always on" services, should the customer shut down (power off) his computer, then when the computer is powered on, a boot-up and sign-on sequence occurs where these errors may appear.

- **Link control** If the connection link is established and then quickly dropped, the problem is likely one of configuration on the computer. Verify that the computer's settings match those indicated in the user documentation for the DSL or cable modem. If the computer's configuration is as it should be, contact the service provider for assistance.

- **Physical connection** If the connection is intermittent, there is something wrong with the physical connection. Verify the connections to the computer and Internet gateway and, if they are properly connected, have the customer call the service provider.

- **Sync** To work properly, DSL and cable lines must be "in sync," or in synchronization, which means that the Internet gateway is connected and receiving a signal over the phone or cable line. In other words, the line must have a link established even if no data is being transmitted. Use the owner's manual for the Internet gateway to determine from the status light-emitting diodes (LEDs) on the device whether or not a link is established and the link is in sync. If the connection is not in sync, power off the computer and then the Internet gateway device. Wait about 30 seconds and then power up the Internet gateway and then the computer. This should establish and sync-up the connection. If the problem persists, contact the service provider's technical support line.

DSL/Cable Troubleshooting Checklist

Before calling the technical support function or a service provider, here is a list of things to check so that you can be fairly confident of the source and nature of the problem:

1. Check the power connection on the Internet gateway device.

2. Check the cable/phone line connection on the Internet gateway device for snugness and to ensure that there are no free wires or cuts or breaks in the wiring connecting to the source.

3. Check the RJ-45 connection to the computer for snugness, free wires, cuts, or breaks in the patch cord.

4. Check the link lights on both the Internet gateway and the network adapter on the computer for activity and sync.

Troubleshooting Wireless Connections

If a computer equipped with a wireless network adapter is having a connection problem, the first step in troubleshooting the problem is to verify that the computer has recognized the wireless network adapter and that the appropriate device driver software has been properly installed. To troubleshoot this problem, follow these steps:

1. **Hardware check** To check the network adapter and the device driver software, use the Windows Device Manager. If a red "x" or a yellow "i" icon is displayed next to the wireless network adapter's name instead of a small icon of a network card, you need to reinstall the network adapter and driver after checking the Hardware Compatibility List (HCL) for the Windows version running on the computer.

2. **Settings check** If the network adapter and driver are properly installed, the next thing to check is the computer's network settings. Use the documentation for the network adapter and the network access point (NAP) to verify the settings for the adapter.

3. **Signal strength and link quality test** The procedure used to check the signal strength and the link quality varies by manufacturer, so reference the device documentation for the process used for the specific network adapter and NAP in use. If moving the computer closer to the NAP eliminates this problem, this is definitely the issue.

4. **Renew IP configuration** Under the heading of "if all else fails," use IPCONFIG to release and renew the Dynamic Host Configuration Protocol (DHCP) settings for the computer (see the following section for instructions on how to do this).

Troubleshooting DHCP Problems

If after booting or restarting a networked PC, no network connection is present, a good place to begin your diagnosis is by running the IPCONFIG command. Figure 9-1 shows a sample of the output produced by this command. Notice the entry for "IP Address." In Figure 9-1, the IP address is fine, reflecting an address has been assigned to the PC by a DHCP server on the network, either locally or at the ISP.

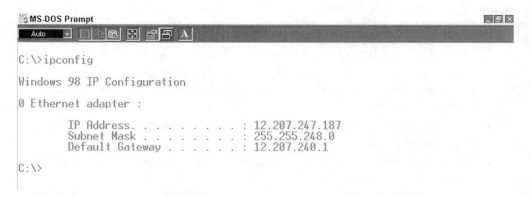

Figure 9-1 The output produced by the IPCONFIG command on a Windows computer

Should a networked computer boot up and not find a DHCP server available, the computer will complete its boot cycle by using an Automatic Private IP Addressing (APIPA), which is a nonfunctioning IP address from a range reserved by Microsoft for just this purpose. When this happens, unless the PC requesting an IP address is able to get one, it will continue to poll for an IP address from the DHCP server after waiting increasingly longer wait periods. This process continues until the networked PC finally gets an IP address from a DHCP server.

The address provided by APIPA allows the PC (DHCP client) to automatically configure itself with an IP address from the range of 169.254.0.1 to 169.254.254.255 using a Class B subnet mask of 255.255.0.0. Understand that this IP address is merely a placeholder and cannot be used to access the network.

Windows NT, 2000, and XP Computers

When a PC is unable to obtain an IP address from the DHCP server, check with the ISP to try to determine why this may be happening. The problem could very well be that the ISP's DHCP server is down. However, if the ISP indicates that there is no reason for a computer to not be able to get its IP configuration from its DHCP server, you should try releasing and renewing the DHCP "lease" using the following process (on Windows NT, 2000, and XP computers):

1. Click the Start button and choose Run from the Start menu.

2. In the Open box, enter **cmd** and click OK. This opens a command prompt window.

3. At the command prompt (C:\>), enter **ipconfig /release_all** and press the ENTER key. IPCONFIG will confirm the release with a display showing zeros in the IP Address and Subnet Mask fields.

4. At the command prompt, enter **ipconfig /renew_all** and press ENTER. IPCONFIG should confirm the renewal of the IP configuration data with values in the IP Address, Subnet Mask, and Default Gateway fields.

5. At the command prompt, enter **exit** and press ENTER to close the command prompt window.

Another process you might try is to right-click the network connection icon in the Task Bar tray and choose Repair from the pop-up menu. If either of these processes fails to correct the problem, you should reinstall the network adapter's device drivers and reconfigure the network protocols settings. Before retesting the connection, verify the network settings with the ISP's technical support.

Windows Vista Computers

On a computer running Microsoft Windows Vista, if the computer is unable to obtain an IP address from a DHCP server, the issue is most likely that the DHCP server doesn't support DHCP broadcast discovery packets. To cure this problem, you need to disable the DHCP broadcast flag in the system registry.

To disable the DHCP broadcast flag on a Vista PC, follow these steps:

1. Click the Start menu and enter **regedit** in the Start Search box.

2. From the Programs list that results, click regedit. You may be prompted for an administrator password to continue this action.

3. Expand the HKEY_LOCAL_MACHINE tree and locate the SYSTEM\ CurrentControlSet\Services\Tcpip\Parameters\Interfaces\{GUID} subkey.

4. Find the GUID subkey for the network adapter on which you are having a problem.

5. From the Edit menu, select New and then click DWORD (32-bit) Value to open a New Value #1 dialog box.

6. Enter **DhcpConnDisableBcastFlagToggle** and press ENTER.

7. Right-click DhcpConnDisableBcastFlagToggle and choose Modify from the pop-up menu.

8. In the Modify Value dialog box, enter a 1.

9. Click OK to save the setting.

10. Exit the regedit utility and restart the system.

Linux Computers

To troubleshoot a DHCP connection on a Linux computer, you should first execute the IFCONFIG command, which produces output similar to that of the IPCONFIG command, shown in Figure 9-1. As is the case on any computer, if the IP address shown is valid, then the problem is likely with the network connection. However, if the IP address is all zeros (there is no APIPA service on Linux), you should perform the following steps:

1. Locate the command dhclient, which is an open-source utility available from the Internet Software Consortium.

2. Execute the dhclient command for the network adapter you are using to connect to the network, such as dhclient eth0.

This should obtain a dhcp address and configure the computer for the network.

If any of these processes fail to complete a connection to the network, the problem is most likely in the connection itself.

Troubleshooting Network Connections

Another reason a PC may not be automatically configured by the network is that it can't make a network connection or for some reason the network has stopped communicating with it. There are two TCP/IP utilities that can be used to make an initial diagnosis of this problem.

PING

The first TCP/IP utility is PING. This command sends out a message that requests that a remote device with a specific IP address or domain reply with a message (an echo). If this activity succeeds, you know the connection between the two devices is valid. The PING command also times this process. A slow response time could indicate congestion or perhaps a mechanical problem along the way. Figure 9-2 shows the output produced by the PING command.

NOTE The Domain Name System (DNS) is used to identify the IP address of the domain name "osborne.com." This IP address is then used by the PING command to send its messages.

However, if the PING command cannot find or doesn't receive a response from the destination address or domain entered, an error message will indicate that.

TraceRoute

The second command that you can use to determine if there is a path problem between two network devices is the TraceRoute utility. This traces and tracks the path used by a message to reach a remote destination IP address by displaying each router or internetworking device the message passes through on its journey. The time used for each "hop" is also displayed to help diagnose possible bottlenecks on the network. Figure 9-3 shows the output produced by a TRACERT command.

TraceRoute is implemented on various systems as TRACEROUTE, TRACERT, or TRACE, with TRACERT used on Windows systems. This command displays the complete route from a source IP address to a destination IP address. TRACERT transmits probe packets one at a time to each router or switch on the path between the source and the destination. When an echo is received at the source, the round-trip time for

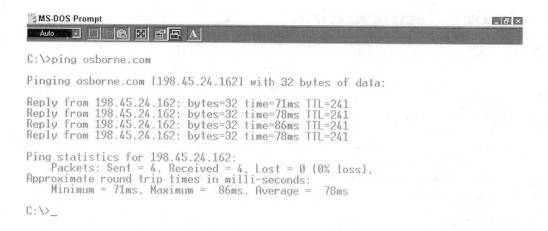

Figure 9-2 The results of a PING command

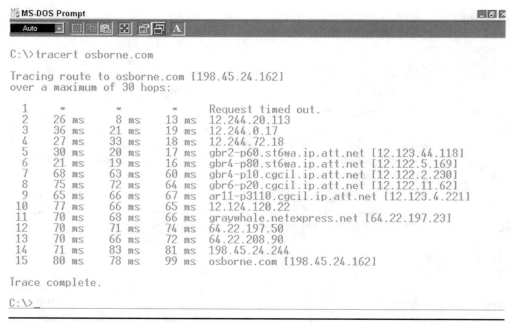

```
MS-DOS Prompt                                                    _ 🗗 ⊠
  Auto    ▾  □ 🖿🖺  ⊠  🖆🖺  A

C:\>tracert osborne.com

Tracing route to osborne.com [198.45.24.162]
over a maximum of 30 hops:

   1    *         *         *       Request timed out.
   2   26 ms     8 ms     13 ms    12.244.20.113
   3   36 ms    21 ms     19 ms    12.244.0.17
   4   27 ms    33 ms     18 ms    12.244.72.18
   5   30 ms    20 ms     17 ms    gbr2-p60.st6wa.ip.att.net [12.123.44.118]
   6   21 ms    19 ms     16 ms    gbr4-p80.st6wa.ip.att.net [12.122.5.169]
   7   68 ms    63 ms     60 ms    gbr4-p10.cgcil.ip.att.net [12.122.2.230]
   8   75 ms    72 ms     64 ms    gbr6-p20.cgcil.ip.att.net [12.122.11.62]
   9   65 ms    66 ms     67 ms    ar11-p3110.cgcil.ip.att.net [12.123.4.221]
  10   77 ms    66 ms     65 ms    12.124.120.22
  11   70 ms    68 ms     66 ms    graywhale.netexpress.net [64.22.197.23]
  12   70 ms    71 ms     74 ms    64.22.197.50
  13   70 ms    66 ms     72 ms    64.22.208.90
  14   71 ms    83 ms     81 ms    198.45.24.244
  15   80 ms    78 ms     99 ms    osborne.com [198.45.24.162]

Trace complete.

C:\>
```

Figure 9-3   The display produced by a TRACERT command

that hop is displayed. TRACERT displays only two different events: either that the time (called time-to-live or TTL) was exceeded or the destination was unreachable. This information is very helpful in determining if there is a breakdown or bottleneck in a particular route.

Testing Network Wiring

The benefit that comes from planning a network before installing it is that you and the customer both know what to expect when you are done. Once you and the customer both commit to the plan, you have to follow through on it. This isn't necessarily a bad thing, but you may have to revisit the plan and its objectives at several points during the installation, both to keep yourself on track and to keep the customer's expectations grounded.

The only way you can assure yourself and demonstrate to the customer that the network's wiring and infrastructure supports the network to be installed on it is with a planned and formal test procedure that incorporates the Transmission Performance Specifications for Field-Testing of Unshielded Twisted-Pair Cabling Systems (TIA/EIA TSB-67 for short) and TSB-95, which provides additional test parameters for Cat 5 wiring.

Cable Certification Testing

A number of handheld devices are available to perform the tests prescribed in these two TSB standards. In fact, a variety of category wire (Cat 5e/Cat 6) testers are available to perform what is called a certified test. By certifying the cable, the customer is assured that the network wiring is installed to specification and is ready to support any network-capable devices attached to the network. Certifying the cable also provides a benchmark for any future network or cable problems. However, category wire testing devices can be quite expensive. Cable testing units include a master unit and a slave unit, which are attached to the ends of the cable segment being tested, and an auto-test function that measures the results of the test as either a pass or a fail.

Essentially, category wire testing units perform two tests: a link test and a channel test. The link test measures the end-to-end connectivity of a cable segment and is typically run on the cable running from the distribution panel to a wall outlet. A channel test extends the link test to include devices attached to the cable segment.

A Cat 5e/Cat 6 link (cable only) should not be more than 295 feet (90 meters) in length. A Cat 5e/Cat 6 channel shouldn't be more than 328 feet (100 meters) in length. A link is a single cable run and a channel is all of the cable and connections between two communicating devices. The difference of 33 feet or 10 meters between a link and a channel represents the cables used to connect a computer or other device to a link. What this boils down to is that the cable running between a patch panel and a wall jack can only be 90 meters in length, and all of the cables used to complete the connection between a computer and a central device (such as a gateway or router) cannot exceed 100 meters in length.

TIA/EIA TSB Tests

The Telecommunications Industry Association/ Electronic Industries Alliance (TIA/EIA) TSB standards specify standard cable testing procedures. The standard TSB tests are

- **Attenuation test**   This test measures the attenuation effect on a signal transmitted on a cable. A series of frequencies up to 100 MHz is transmitted on each wire pair at one end of a link, and the strength of the signal received at the other end of the cable is measured.

- **Length test**   This test measures the length of a cable segment. It tests both links and channels using what is called *time domain reflectometry*, or TDR technology. TDR emits a signal pulse and then calculates the length of the cable based on what is called nominal velocity of propagation (NVP). The result of this test is the distance to a reflection point on the cable. On a good cable, the distance displayed should be the length of the actual cable run. However, if there is a problem on the cable, such as a break, kink, short, or the like, the length test will return the distance to that problem.

- **Near-end crosstalk test (NEXT)**   This test places a test signal on one pair of wires and then measures all of the other wire pairs for signal presence to see how much crosstalk the cable is allowing. Crosstalk is electromagnetic signals on one wire being picked up by another wire.

- **Wire-map test**   This test looks at each individual wire in the cable and whether or not it maps to the same pin at each end of the cable. This test is used to identify connector and pinning errors on a cable segment.

Figure 9-4
A multiple media
cable testing
system

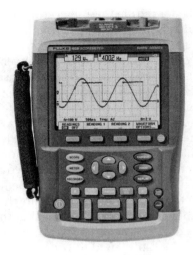

Photo courtesy of Fluke Networks.

Any link that fails one of these tests should be replaced or, in the case of the length test, shortened. If a channel fails, you may need to test the patch cords used to connect the networked device to the link to decide if the problem is in the cable link or patch cords.

TIP Wire testing should be performed in the pre-wire phase of a new construction project and then again before the network devices are attached.

If the network is to use a power line or phone line, any line problems should also be affecting the AC power or the telephone lines. If not, the problem is either with the media adapter or the patch cord used to connect a device to the adapter.

Simple Cable Testing Devices

It isn't totally necessary in every situation for the cable to be certified. Often, especially as part of a troubleshooting procedure, all that is needed is to perform a test for signal continuity, assuming the initial installation was properly tested. Whereas cable certification devices can cost thousands of dollars, quality cable testers range in capability from all-in-one devices to continuity testers and most are reasonably priced. For home automation networking, you should consider a multiple media tester, like the one shown in Figure 9-4.

Configuring Network Computers

In a majority of situations, a network connection problem typically occurs when something has changed on a networked computer. This doesn't mean that cable, connector, service provider, and Internet gateway problems don't occur, only that these components of a network continue to work until changes are made.

When I say changes to a network computer, I don't mean only changes to the computer's networking configuration or equipment. Changes can include new software or hardware and the conflicts they may create. The number one troubleshooting step when diagnosing a networked computer for connection problems is to determine if anything—and I mean *anything*—has changed on the computer and remove it to see if the problem goes away. Then you can deal with the issues being created and solve the larger issue of incompatibility.

Configuring a Windows Computer

When configuring a computer on a home network, you must check the installation of the network adapter and TCP/IP protocols and verify operations.

Checking the Network Adapter

Windows systems use Plug-and-Play (PnP) technology to detect and configure an internal network interface card (NIC) installed in a Peripheral Components Interconnect (PCI) slot. However, before you get too far along with connecting a computer to the network, you should verify the NIC's settings. To do this, follow these steps:

1. To open the properties window for the NIC, you have two navigation choices:

   - Click the Start button and choose Settings and then, from the Settings menu, choose Network and Dial-up Connections.

   - Right-click the My Network Places icon on the Desktop and choose Network and Dial-up Connections.

2. Right-click the network connection that is or will be connected to the network to display the properties window for the NIC (see Figure 9-5).

Figure 9-5

The properties dialog box for a network adapter in a Windows computer

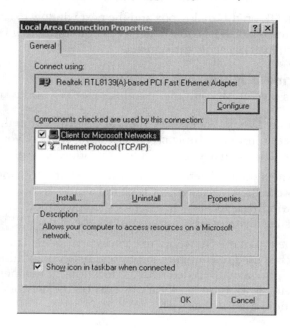

Figure 9-6

The Internet Protocol (TCP/IP) properties dialog box on a Windows computer

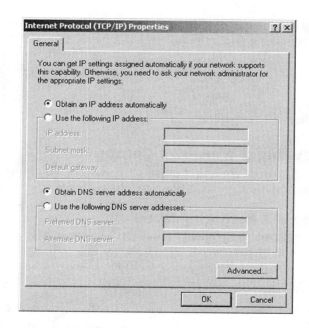

3. In the panel labeled "Components checked are used by this connection," highlight Internet Protocol (TCP/IP), and then click the Properties button. The TCP/IP Properties window (see Figure 9-6) will open.

4. Verify that the Obtain an IP address and the Obtain DNS server address are automatically selected and, if they are not, change the settings so that they are the only items with their radio buttons selected.

5. Click OK on this dialog box and the next window to configure the TCP/IP client. Use the IPCONFIG command (see "Troubleshooting DHCP Problems" earlier in the chapter) to verify the settings.

Configuring a Macintosh Computer

To enable a Macintosh computer running Mac OS X 10.x or later, follow these steps:

1. Start the System Preferences application from either the OS X Applications folder or from the Apple menu. On some systems, you may also find it in the Dock. The main System Preferences window is displayed.

2. On the System Preferences windows, click the Network icon to open the Network Preferences pane. Check the windows lock in the lower-left corner. If the window is locked, click the lock icon to unlock the preferences (you'll need the administrator password to unlock the window).

3. At the top of the Network Preferences pane is the Location pop-up menu, which is used to configure the current network location, create a new location, or remove any unneeded network locations. If the menu contains only the Automatic location, no locations exist on the network. Otherwise, any existing locations are listed as well.

4. You may elect to use the Automatic location if your Mac has a single Ethernet port (interface) that is always connected to the network.

5. If there are any special configuration needs, such as the interface is something other than Ethernet or you wish to define a wireless interface, you should click the Edit Locations option to display the Locations sheet. In addition to listing all existing locations, the Locations sheet includes the functions used to create, rename, delete, or copy an existing network location.

6. On the Locations sheet, click the plus (+) button to create a new location. The new location, named Untitled or Untitled *n* (if an Untitled already exists) is added to the locations list. Click the new location and rename it to something meaningful such as its physical location or use.

7. When you have completed the actions on the Location sheet, click the Done button to return to the Network Preferences pane.

8. Click Apply on the Network Preferences pane to save the new configuration.

9. If you unlocked the System Preferences window at the start of this process, click the lock icon to relock the window.

10. Choose the Quit System Preferences option from the System Preferences menu, or click the System Preferences window's Close button.

Chapter Review

Most computer problems occur immediately after a change is made to the computer's hardware, software, or configuration.

To diagnose a dialup connection, you should check the following: the phone connection, the modem settings, the protocol configuration on the computer, the service provider's NAS, and if there are technical issues on the phone line.

To troubleshoot a DSL or cable connection, you should check the following: authentication, link control, the physical connection, and if the system has synchronized (is in sync). To diagnose a connection problem on a DSL or cable connection, check the power connection on the Internet gateway, the phone or cable connection to the Internet gateway, the RJ-45 connection to the computer and the Internet gateway, and the link lights on the Internet gateway and the network adapter, and verify the integrity of all cables.

To troubleshoot a wireless connection, perform a hardware check on the computer using the Device Manager to verify that the network adapter is properly installed and functioning, check the network settings on the computer, test the signal strength and the link quality between the computer and the NAP, and release and renew the IP configuration on the computer.

Many networked computer issues are related to the network configuration on the computer, especially in the DHCP settings. A quick way to see if a computer is having DHCP problems is to run the IPCONFIG command; if the computer is assigned an IP in the range of 169.254.0.1 to 169.254.254.255, the DHCP is not functioning properly.

Two other tools that you can use to check a computer's connection are the PING command to ping the Internet gateway and TRACERT to see if there is a routing issue between the home network and the service provider.

If you suspect the connection problem may be in the network media, you can run the TIA/EIA TSB-67 tests on the cable to check its attenuation, length, NEXT, and wire-mapping. Cable testing devices are generally inexpensive and readily available.

A common source for connection problems on a computer is its network configuration. The Windows operating systems virtually auto-configure themselves to a network, but you should check the network adapter's settings as part of your troubleshooting. Mac computers running OS X 10.0 or higher are configured to a network through the System Preferences window.

Questions

1. Which of the following is not likely the source of a modem connection problem?

   A. Modem

   B. Phone line

   C. Network adapter

   D. PPP protocol settings

2. Which of the following can cause a DSL/cable connection to fail because of username and password issues?

   A. Authentication

   B. Synchronization

   C. Link control

   D. Bad physical connection

3. What is one of the first things you should check to see if a physical connection, link, and sync have been established on a DSL/cable connection?

   A. Temperature of the patch cord

   B. Link/activity lights

   C. Computer's TCP/IP settings

   D. Service provider technical help

4. Of the following, which troubleshooting step is not performed on a computer using a wireless network adapter to connect to a network?

   A. Hardware check

   B. Setting check

   C. Signal strength and link quality test

   D. Renewing the DHCP configuration

5. What command can be used to verify the IP configuration on a computer?

   A. PING

   B. TRACERT

   C. IPCONFIG

   D. DNS

6. When a network computer cannot find a DHCP server, what service is used to assign the computer an IP address?

   A. DNS

   B. RARP

   C. BOOTP

   D. APIPA

7. Which TCP/IP command is used to verify the connection between two network devices?

   A. TRACERT

   B. DHCP

   C. PING

   D. IPCONFIG

8. What TCP/IP command is used to determine if a problem exists on the routing path between two network devices?

   A. TRACERT

   B. DHCP

   C. PING

   D. IPCONFIG

9. What is the cable testing standard for Cat 5 wiring?

   A. EIA/TIA 232

   B. EIA/TIA 568

   C. EIA/TIA TSB-67

   D. IEEE 802.3

10. Which is the technology used to check the length of a cable?

    A. Attenuation

    B. TDR

    C. NEXT

    D. Wire-map

Answers

1. **C.** A modem connects to a computer through its serial port and not a network adapter. The other choices can each contribute to a modem connection problem.

2. **A.** This step verifies the username and password of the link attempting to log into the DSL/cable service provider's network. The other choices, with the exception of a bad physical connection of course, are aspects of the link established between the Internet gateway and the ISP.

3. **B.** If there are no lights on or flashing on the Internet gateway, then something is seriously wrong with the connection. There could be something wrong with the TCP/IP settings, but the other choices are just silly.

4. **C.** All of the other troubleshooting steps are performed on the computer.

5. **C.** DNS is used to translate domain names into their IP address equivalents. (See questions 7 and 8 for PING and IPCONFIG.)

6. **D.** This service assigns a temporary IP address that allows the computer to complete its startup. RARP and DNS are used to look up IP addresses, and the computer uses BOOTP to request its DHCP information.

7. **C.** PING sends out an echo request message and, if present or connected, the receiving station sends back an echo response.

8. **A.** TRACERT times the connection between each of the routers (hops) located on the path between two network devices.

9. **C.** The EIA/TIA TSB-67standard, along with TSB-95, establishes the testing procedures for Cat 5 wiring.

10. **B.** TDR emits a signal pulse and then calculates the length of the cable based on NVP.

PART III

Audio/Video Systems

Distributed Audio System Basics

In this chapter, you will learn about:
- Audio concepts and basic terminology
- Different types of distributed audio systems
- Audio system hardware and components
- Different types of audio source equipment

The ability to have high-fidelity (hi-fi) music in every room of a home is no longer limited to the owners of million-dollar mansions with unlimited budgets. With existing technology, the cost of installing a whole house audio system has fallen to the point where such a system can be a reality for virtually any homeowner.

Installing a distributed audio system, one that distributes audio throughout a house, allows the customer to virtually replicate his or her audio source equipment into every room of the house. The expense of actually installing hi-fi audio equipment in every room is prohibitive for most homeowners, but with a relatively modest investment in wiring, speakers, and controls, every room in the house can have radio and recorded music playback.

In this and the next few chapters, we look at the basics of a distributed audio systems; a more detailed examination of the hardware and wiring and installation procedures required; and a few troubleshooting techniques.

Audio Systems Basics

Audio systems have a language all their own, and when you help a homeowner choose the system and features that will work best for his or her needs and budget, you should be able to speak the language. The customer may have a number of questions about why one system may be a better choice than another or why one feature should be used over another; he or she may be an audiophile that really knows his or her stuff, or he or she may know the terms but not quite have the meanings down. In any of these cases, your being well-versed in the concepts of audio systems technology is sure to contribute to the design and installation of a system that satisfies the customer's wishes, wants, and needs.

The audio terms and concepts you should know at a minimum, are

- Sound characteristics
- Analog versus digital audio signals
- Line-level versus speaker-level
- Balanced versus unbalanced
- Electrical properties
- Surround sound

Sound Characteristics

An audio system reproduces sound that has been recorded on some form of analog or digital media, so before you can understand audio systems, you need to first understand sound and how it is generated, heard, and transmitted.

Sound is produced when an object creates vibrations in air, liquid, or something solid. I am going to deal with sound vibrations in the air first and discuss how sound is generated from a speaker later in the section titled "Speaker Basics."

Vibrating Air

When any object vibrates, it agitates the air around it, which makes the molecules in the air bounce around, and a chain reaction starts. The moving molecules cause other air molecules to begin moving, and so on. This movement of the air molecules is how sound moves through the air: one set of moving molecules causes others to move or vibrate. All of this vibration creates a pulsing wave of moving air molecules that travels through the air—something like ripples in a pond. The effect is a series of pulse waves with increased and decreased air pressure.

Your ears contain eardrums, which are thin membranes of skin. The eardrum catches the vibrating wave of air pressure and begins to vibrate. Your brain then interprets the vibrations of the eardrum into what we hear as sound.

A vibrating object creates a fluctuating wave of air pressure that moves through the air (or liquid or solids) to our ear, and our brain "hears" it as a voice, some music, or a whole range of other sounds. What causes one sound to be heard differently than another? Different sounds have different vibration patterns and air pressure fluctuations, which translate into a sound's frequency and amplitude.

Frequency and Amplitude

The frequency of a sound wave represents the number of times the air pressure of the wave fluctuates up and down in a certain period of time. Each fluctuation cycle (measured from the peak of one wave to the peak of the next wave, as shown in Figure 10-1) represents one sound wave and its wavelength.

Figure 10-1
The charac-
teristics of a
sound wave

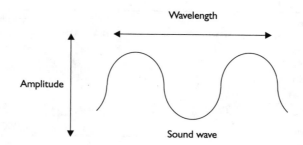

The number of waves that occur in a set period of time, such as a second or a fraction of a second, represents the sound wave's frequency, or how frequent the sound wave fluctuates over time. As is illustrated in Figure 10-2, sound waves can have a higher frequency, meaning there are more waves in a time period, or a lower frequency, meaning there are fewer waves in a time period. High-frequency sound waves are heard as higher pitched sounds and low-frequency sound waves are heard as lower pitched sounds. The frequency of a sound wave is equivalent to the sound's pitch.

Another characteristic of sound waves is amplitude, which translates into how loud the sound is heard. The height of a sound wave, as shown in Figure 10-1, is its amplitude. The amplitude of a sound wave also represents the amount of air pressure in the wave. Higher amplitudes hit the eardrum harder and are heard as louder sounds.

Decibels

There is a relationship between the volume level a speaker produces and the amount of power an amplifier produces. The loudness of the sound coming from a speaker is a fairly subjective thing, with each listener having his or her version of what is too loud or not loud enough. In order to set how loud a speaker should be, a scale is used to determine a level that's acceptable to everyone and serves as a standard setting. For the sound produced by a speaker (and sound produced by just about anything), the measurement used is the decibel (dB).

A dB measures the intensity or the level of a sound. This logarithmic scale is able to represent a wide range of sound level measurements with relatively simple numbers.

Figure 10-2
High-frequency
sound waves
(top) have a
higher pitch than
low-frequency
sound waves
(bottom).

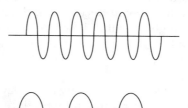

Table 10-1	dB Increase	Voltage Increase	Power Increase	Volume Increase
The Relationship of dB, Voltage, Power, and Volume in Sound Reproduction	3	1.4	2	1.2
	6	2.0	4	1.5
	10	3.2	10	2
	20	10.0	100	4
	40	100.0	10,000	16

However, because decibel measurements are logarithmic, they can also be confusing; for example, 2.0 dB is not twice as loud as 1.0 dB. Table 10-1 shows the relationship of different dB levels to line voltage (signal strength), power (watts of amplifier output), and volume (the loudness of a speaker's output).

Using the information in Table 10-1, to double the sound level produced by a speaker requires an increase of about three times the signal strength and a tenfold increase in the amplifier output, which equates to an increase of 10 dB.

Analog versus Digital Sound

Recorded or broadcasted sounds are either analog or digital. The quality of a reproduced sound isn't necessarily affected by whether it is analog or digital; the quality of a recorded analog or digital sound and the fidelity of its reproduction are directly dependent on the equipment in use.

Analog Sound

Analog sound is sound that is transmitted or recorded in its natural state, which means it was originally created in sound-wave form. Phonograph records were manufactured to cause the phonograph needle to vibrate and reproduce the analog sound etched into the plastic or vinyl on the record.

Analog sound can also be recorded onto audiotape. The record heads present the characteristics of the sound as electromagnetic impulses stored on the tape. When the tape is played, the record heads pick up these impulses and translate them into frequency, pitch, and amplitude, which are heard as a representation of the original sound.

The quality of the sound reproduction, which is determined partly by the recording of the sound and partly by the quality of the playback device, is its fidelity. High-fidelity (hi-fi) sound reproduction reproduces a sound quality that represents a sound that is very similar to the original sound. Low-fidelity sound is a poor reproduction of the original sound.

Digital Sound

The quest of the recorded sound industry has always been to create recording and playback devices that are able to record and reproduce sounds that are a perfect reproduction of the original sound; this has led to the development of digital recording and playback technologies.

Figure 10-3
An analog sound wave is divided into a series of samples.

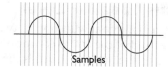

Samples

Converting Audio to Digital   Where analog recordings represent a sound by causing a pickup device to vibrate or emulate the vibrations of the original recording, digital recordings store a series of binary numbers that represent the characteristics of the original sound.

To do this, a sound wave is sliced into a number of samples, as illustrated in Figure 10-3. A piece of the sound is captured at different points along the wavelength. Each sample represents a different combination of frequency and amplitude in the sound, which can be converted to a numeric value and stored as a binary number on the recorded media.

Digital recordings and their playback mechanisms must be coordinated for the sampling rate (the number of samples taken per second of sound) and the sampling precision (the number of samples taken in a sound wave's vertical height).

The device used to convert an analog sound for digital recording is an analog-to-digital converter (ADC), which samples the sound and converts it to digital data. On the playback end, a digital-to-analog converter (DAC) is used to reconvert the digital values back into analog sound.

Sampling   Achieving perfect sound reproduction would be possible only with 100-percent sampling; taking samples as often as tens of thousands per second can capture the sound quality at a level that is able to fool most people's ears (and brains) into believing they are hearing the whole original sound.

Of course, the higher the sample rate and sampling precision are, the lower the probability that a sampling error (or failure to capture the true original sound) will occur. The sampling rate standard for a music compact disc (CD) is generally 44,100 samples per second with a sampling precision of 65,536. Table 10-2 lists some of the standard sampling rates of digital recording media. As listed in Table 10-2, sampling rates are normally stated in kilohertz (kHz), or thousands of samples per second.

Samples/Sec	Sampling Rate in kHz	Recording Media
8,000	8 kHz	Digital telephony
32,000	32 kHz	Extended play digital audio tape (DAT)
37,800	37.8 kHz	CD-ROM/XA standard
44,056	44.056 kHz	Video-embedded audio
44,100	44.1 kHz	Stereo music CD and MP3
48,000	48 kHz	Standard DAT
96,000	96 kHz	DVD-Audio

Table 10-2   Digital Recording Sampling Rates

Line Level versus Speaker Level

A line-level audio signal is a signal with one to two volts (V) of amplitude that is used as the normal interface level of the audio components in a system. The line-level signal, which is also referred to as the pre-amp level, is the level (amplitude) of an audio signal before it is amplified to drive speakers.

A speaker-level audio signal is essentially a line-level signal that has been amplified to a higher voltage level to facilitate the transmission of the audio signals to a speaker and provide a reasonable level of volume at the speaker.

Unbalanced versus Balanced Audio

Essentially the difference between unbalanced and balanced audio devices, cables, and connectors is the same difference you see between home-use and professional systems.

Unbalanced Audio

Most audio devices found in homes include unbalanced audio inputs and outputs. This means that the audio signals produced by these devices, whether stereophonic (left and right) or monophonic (mono), are transmitted on a single conductor cable that has a single shield.

While unbalanced audio systems are adequate for most residential systems, they are best when used with shorter line-level signals because of their susceptibility to line noise and interference. Over long distances, unbalanced cables and connectors are probably not the better choice.

The connectors commonly used with unbalanced audio systems are RCA connectors, DIN connectors, ¼-inch (6.3 millimeter [mm]) connectors, and 3.5 mm connectors.

Balanced Audio

Balanced audio uses at least two conductors to transmit audio signals that are in opposite phase to each other to prevent cross-feed between the conductors while transmitting audio signals. The two wires are the live conductor, which carries a positive signal, and the return conductor, which carries an equal but opposite negative signal.

Balanced audio has the capability to resist external interference as the audio signal is carried over the wire, something an unbalanced link can't and doesn't do. The most common connector used with balanced audio systems is the Canon, or 3-pin XLR, connector.

Electrical Properties

There are certain electrical properties that are very important for getting the best performance from an audio system, including:

- **Resistance** Every conductor resists the flow of an electrical current through it to some extent, depending on the type of conductor and the conductor's physical characteristics. Some conductors offer less resistance and others more. Resistance, or the amount of resistive force in a conductor, is measured in ohms.

- **Capacitance** The characteristic of a circuit to store an electrical charge, or the potential difference between two closely spaced conductors in the circuit. The unit of measure for capacitance is a farad.

PART III

- **Inductance**   The characteristic of a conductor or circuit that resists changes in the current. Inductance, which is measured in henrys, causes changes in the current on a circuit to occur after changes in voltage occur. Inductance increases with the frequency of the electrical current.

- **Impedance**   Where resistance is the amount of opposing force on a direct current (DC) electrical flow, impedance is the resistance a circuit, wire, cable, or electrical device has to an alternating current (AC). Impedance measures the cumulative impact of both resistance and reactance in the conductor to an AC flow.

- **Reactance**   The cumulative effect of capacitance and inductance on an AC electrical flow is reactance. Reactance, like inductance, varies with changes in the frequency in an electrical current. However, reactance decreases as the frequency increases.

Speaker Efficiency

A speaker's efficiency is normally equated with the speaker's sound quality. The efficiency of a speaker is determined by measuring its decibel (dB) output from the input power of 1 watt from a distance of 1 meter in front of the speaker. The dB measurement is then qualified by the speaker's impedance, which is measured in ohms. For example, a speaker could be producing 90 dB at an impedance of 8 ohms, which is commonly stated as 90 dB at 8 ohms.

A speaker's efficiency should be matched to the amplifier or audio controller driving it, in terms of the amount of power (in watts) the amplifier is sending to the speaker. For example, a speaker that produces 93 dB at 8 watts may produce 96 dB at 16 watts, which would be twice as loud. Remember that a 3 dB gain in efficiency requires twice as much power. So, if a speaker isn't rated for the power level produced by the amplifier, the sound quality, if any, would suffer from the mismatch.

Surround Sound

A surround sound system is used to enhance the experience of watching a video presentation. The goal of a surround sound system is what the movie makers call "suspended disbelief," which means that the visual and audio images and sound come together to create an experience in which the viewer suspends her awareness of her surroundings for a time.

Understanding Ohm's Law

Ohm's law, which is named for Georg Ohm, a nineteenth-century Bavarian mathematician, defines a relationship between power, voltage, current, and resistance. Ohm's law is the primary law electrical theory is based on.

Ohm's law says that when one volt is placed on a conductor, it has a resistance of one ohm and one ampere (amp) of current; with two volts you get two amps. However, if you have one volt with two ohms, you'll get one-half amp.

Technically, Ohm's law states that a steady increase in voltage should produce a constant and linear increase in current (amps) on a circuit that has constant resistance. However, it also says that a steady increase in resistance (ohms) will produce a nonlinearly weaker current (amps) on a circuit with constant voltage.

The formulas used to represent the relationships of voltage, current (amps), and resistance (ohms) are

$$V \text{ (voltage)} = I \text{ (current in amperes)} * R \text{ (resistance in ohms)}$$

or

$$I = V / R$$

or

$$R = V / I$$

The bottom line to all of this is that Volts = Amps * Resistance
Visit this website for a handy Ohm's Law Calculator:
www.thelearningpit.com/elec/tools/ohms_calc/ohms_calc.asp

Surround Sound Systems

A true surround sound system incorporates several speakers that separate the sound by frequency as well as physically to literally surround the listener. There are systems called surround sound that include one, two, and three speakers, but a true surround sound system has five, six, or seven speakers.

An unofficial designation system for surround sound systems has been created by Dolby Digital sound systems that designate the number of channels, full-range and sub-range, used in a particular system. Table 10-3 lists the three Dolby surround sound systems. Figure 10-4 illustrates the placement of the speakers in a 5.1 surround sound system.

System	Number of Full-range Speakers	Number of Low-frequency Effects (LFE) Speakers	System Description
5.1	Five	One	Six channels (front left, front center, front right, left surround, right surround, and LFE)
6.1	Six	One	Seven channels (front left, front center, front right, left surround, right surround, rear surround, and LFE)
7.1	Seven	One	Eight channels (front left, front center, front right, left surround, right surround, rear surround (x2), and LFE)

Table 10-3   Dolby Digital Surround Sound System Designators

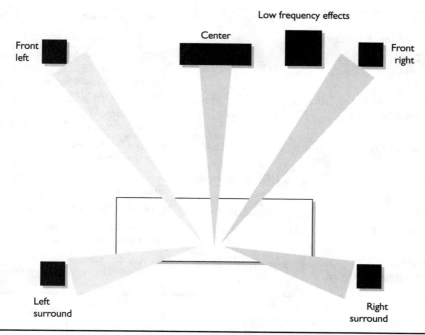

Figure 10-4 The arrangement of speakers in a 5.1 Dolby digital surround sound system

A low-frequency effects (LFE) speaker is a subwoofer speaker that reproduces the very lowest frequency sounds. LFE sounds are those that add impact to the sound used to emphasize certain actions in a film or video, such as a monster's footsteps, a bomb exploding, and the like.

The standard professional level surround sound is the 5.1 system, which Dolby specifies as including a 12-watt (W) root mean square (RMS) subwoofer for the LFE channel, a 2 W RMS center speaker, and four 2 W RMS front and rear speakers. RMS is the measurement for the maximum amount of amplified sound signals the speaker is designed to handle. More watts RMS mean more power. A surround sound system also needs an amplifier with enough built-in channels to drive the system. Amplifiers are rated using a couple of different rating scales, but a 5.1 surround sound system requires an amplifier with 6 built-in amplified channels that produces a 50 to 20,000 Hertz (Hz) frequency response. The frequency response of an amplifier indicates the lowest and highest frequencies the amplifier is able to amplify and retransmit.

Surround Sound Formats

Although there are virtual surround sound systems, such as the Sound Retrieval System (SRS) and others, that need only two left and two right speakers and "psycho-acoustic effects" that emulate true surround sound formats, they have not been developed to the point where they provide the same experience as a true surround sound format and the use of designated speakers.

Table 10-4 lists the most popular digital surround sound formats available.

Format	Systems	Channels	Media Supported
Dolby Surround Pro-Logic	5.1	Four	Hi-fi, VHS, and stereo analog TV
Dolby Digital (AC-3)	5.1	Six	DVD video, Laserdisc, high-definition television (HDTV), digital broadcast satellite (DBS), and pay-per-view and video-on-demand movies
DTS Digital Surround	5.1	Six	PC and console games, DVD-Video, DVD-Audio, and DVD-ROM software
Dolby Digital EX	5.1/6.1/7.1	Six/seven	Extends 5.1 surround systems with rear surround channels
Dolby TrueHD	5.1/6.1/7.1	Up to eight	Advanced lossless multichannel audio codec
DTS-HD Master Audio	7.1	Up to eight	Extends DTS to a lossless audio codec
THX Surround EX	5.1/6.1/7.1	Six/seven	Extends 5.1 surround systems with rear surround channels
Uncompressed PCM (pulse code modulation)	5.1	Six	Blu-Ray disc standard, not supported on HD-DVD; uncompressed standard 5.1 to 7.1 soundtrack

Table 10-4 Surround Sound Media Formats

Distributed Audio Systems

Depending on whom you ask, a distributed, or multiroom, audio system installed as a part of new home construction or during a major renovation of the home may or may not add value to the home. Whether or not a distributed audio system, as illustrated in Figure 10-5, is an investment that increases the value of a home, it certainly increases the enjoyment and perhaps livability of the home for its occupants.

Regardless of the investment issue, a distributed audio system provides an infrastructure where the entire house can share the latest audio technologies, including CDs, AM and FM radio, MiniDisc, satellite radio, hard disk drive systems, Internet music, and MP3 players. Depending on the investment made in the system, it is also possible for each room to control not only the local volume of the audio source, but also which source is distributed to that room.

Centralization is the key concept of any distributed audio system. The system and its audio source devices are centrally located, either hidden away or on display, with only speakers and controllers placed in each room. In addition, it is possible for locally placed playback units in any one room to be connected into the system for local playback in that room or in other rooms as well.

Audio System Types

A distributed audio system can be classified by one of two major characteristics and typically it will actually be some combination of both. An audio system can be classified by the type of amplifier it uses or by the number of zones it supports.

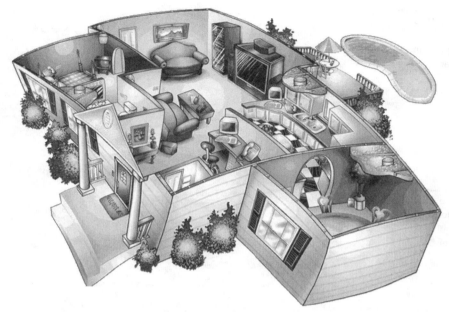

Original drawing courtesy of Hi Tech Homes, North Carolina.

Figure 10-5 A distributed audio system can be only one element of an automated home.

Audio Amplifiers

There are two types of audio amplifiers from which to choose:

- Constant current amplifiers
- Constant voltage amplifiers

Constant Current Amplifiers A constant current amplifier is able to support typically only one or two speakers because of its low impedance. The speakers must be directly connected to the amplifier and the minimum impedance load from the speakers cannot exceed the impedance load rating of the amplifier. A constant current amplifier can be used in a small, distributed audio system with several small speakers as long as the total impedance load of the speakers doesn't exceed that of the amplifier.

When using multiple speakers with a constant current amplifier, the speakers must be used in a "times two" configuration, which means one speaker, two speakers, four speakers, eight speakers, and so on. If more than one speaker is connected, the speakers must be configured in series or parallel connections. Figures 10-6 and 10-7 illustrate speaker configurations for a series configuration and a parallel configuration, respectively. Series connections are seldom used in a single-zone multiroom system, since it is typical to have individual stereo volume controls in each room. When two or more speakers are connected in a series, individual volume controls affect *all* speakers on the circuit, whereas parallel connections allow individual controls to be located between the amplifier and

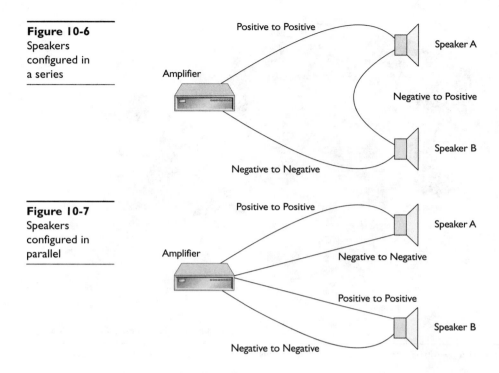

Figure 10-6
Speakers
configured in
a series

Figure 10-7
Speakers
configured in
parallel

each pair of speakers. For this reason, most single-zone audio systems with more than one or two pairs of speakers on a single amplifier use some sort of impedance protection system or an amplifier capable of driving extremely low impedance loads.

CROSS-REFERENCE   See Chapter 14 for information on series and parallel configurations.

Constant Voltage Amplifiers   Constant voltage amplifiers have a higher impedance output than constant current amplifiers, which allows them to support more speakers on longer runs of speaker wire. A constant voltage amplifier can support wire runs of up to several thousand feet, provided the speakers are mounted with line matching transformers that convert 8-ohm speakers to the higher impedance needed to match the speakers to the 70 V output of the amplifier. Figure 10-8 illustrates a common configuration for speakers connected to a constant voltage amplifier.

CROSS-REFERENCE   Chapter 14 covers design and installation considerations for using a constant voltage amplifier.

Centralized versus Distributed Amplification

The sound signals sent to speakers from centralized source equipment (such as DVD players, CD players, AM and FM radio, and so on) typically must be amplified to overcome

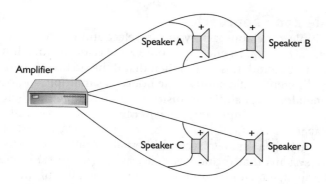

Figure 10-8
Speakers in a series/parallel configuration

the electrical characteristics of the cable and to supply adequate volume at the speaker. In a home audio system, you have two choices for amplifying audio signals:

- Centralized amplification
- Distributed amplification

Centralized Amplification   Depending on the design of the audio system and the characteristics of the cabling, the source devices, and the speakers, a single amplifier may be able to supply enough amplification to drive all of the speakers in a home that are connected to the audio system. In general, the use of a single amplification source can limit the number of speakers in the system because as more speakers are added (which means more speaker cables and possibly local controls), the amount of amplification produced may prove to be inadequate to expand the system too much.

Distributed Amplification   Several distributed audio amplifiers are available that have the capability to individually drive as many as 12 channels. In most situations, two channels are used to distribute stereo sound to each zone or rooms of a home. Distributed audio amplifiers also include several advanced features that allow the system to be adapted to a wide range of audio system requirements, including capabilities that allow the power output on individual channels to be controlled individually, allow channels to be bridged to increase the power to a particular area, and assign a channel to multiple source devices.

Audio Zones

Essentially, there are two general approaches to configuring a whole house audio system:

- Single zone
- Multiple zones

Single Zone Approach

In a single zone approach, all of the speakers in a house play the same sound supplied from a single source. The entire house is one large audio output zone. This has been a common approach to home audio systems, especially those simply added on in existing houses.

Multiple Zone Approach

In a multiple zone approach, you can select and listen to the audio from a different source in each room. In effect, an audio zone is an area of a home where all occupants hear the same sound. It is logical then that if the occupants of different parts of a house can hear different audio sources, the house has multiple audio zones.

In general, the capability to distribute different audio sources to different parts of a house requires multiple amplifiers/receivers, room controllers, source components, and speakers. A separate amp or receiver drives each zone. Some high-end amplifier/receivers include a separate second internal amplifier to drive a second zone. In fact, there are systems that include as many as six (or more) discrete amplifiers, a source distribution system, and a zone volume control, all built into a single piece of equipment designed especially for distributed audio systems. Figure 10-9 shows front and back views of a multizone system that can support up to six audio inputs and eight distributed audio zones.

A multiroom audio video (MRAV) system is one that allows a variety of centrally located audio (and video) source devices to be distributed throughout a home under the control of a single system controller. The use of an MRAV system can eliminate the need for duplicate or redundant audio devices in certain zones of a home and provides the home's occupants access to all of the audio devices and their recorded sound libraries in a single remotely controlled system.

Audio Cabling Alternatives

There are a few different approaches you can use to wiring a distributed audio system, but really only two basic approaches are commonly used: direct-run phono or audio cables or twisted-pair cabling. The first approach, using phono cabling, can provide a quality sound, but only over short distances. Phono cables are not intended for in-wall placement and, compared to twisted-pair alternatives, can be quite expensive to use on longer runs.

Figure 10-9
A multizone audio distribution controller

Photo courtesy of Niles Audio Corporation.

Figure 10-10
Audio connectors
for use with
category-rated
twisted-pair
cabling

Photo courtesy of Smarthome, Inc.

You have two basic choices for twisted-pair cabling recommended for use in a distributed audio system: category-rated twisted-pair cable (Cat 5e/Cat 6) or what is called XLR cable. While both cabling types carry a balanced signal, category-rated cabling has two primary advantages over XLR cabling: the devices needed to modulate the audio signal onto the cable are much less expensive than the same equipment used with XLR cable, and category-rated cabling is likely already in place throughout the home (or it should or will be) and can be terminated with relatively less expensive connections (like the one shown in Figure 10-10). Cat 5e/Cat 6 cabling can carry analog audio signals as far as 5,000 feet and digital audio up to 1,400 feet.

XLR cabling, which is most commonly used for microphone cabling in high-end audio applications, because of its cost primarily, is best used in shorter runs, perhaps within a single zone, such as a home theater. Like Cat 5e cabling, XLR cable (see Figure 10-11) carries a balanced signal on two wires twisted around each other to cancel any interference each of the wires produces.

It is possible to used both Cat 5e (or higher) and XLR cabling in the same system. Adapters are available that allow a signal distributed over a Cat 5e cable to be modulated onto an XLR cable at distributed points. These adapters, like the one in Figure 10-11, include a balun that modulates the signal for the media differences. XLR to Cat 5e adapters are placed at each end of the Cat 5e cable run. A balun is a transformer that converts the audio signal from unbalanced to balanced, or vice versa, so that it is compatible with the different wiring types.

Figure 10-11
An XLR to
Cat 5e adapter
allows audio to
be transmitted
over Cat 5e
cabling.

Figure 10-12
The source cards for a customizable multiple source receiver/amplifier distributed audio system

Photo courtesy of Niles Audio Corporation.

In situations where the constraints of a house prevent dedicated cable runs from individual source devices to speakers and controls in multiple zones of the house, systems like the Niles Audio IntelliControl ICS (see Figure 10-12) have the capacity to host several sources (through optional source cards installed in the unit). This allows sources to share a single amplifier and transmit over a shared wiring plant. Compared to some source devices, these types of systems can be more expensive. However, their usefulness more than compensates for the cost that would be incurred installing dedicated wire runs.

Audio System Components

Just about any distributed audio system has certain essential components: speakers, controls, and amplifiers/receivers. Each of these components is typically purchased separately, but even so, they must be matched to one another electrically and performance-wise.

Audio Source Equipment

Without some equipment to receive or reproduce sound from radio transmissions or from a CD or tape, a distributed audio system doesn't have much purpose.

For most home audio systems, the audio source devices (so-called because they are the source of the audio signals sent to the speakers) are generally one of the following:

- **AM/FM tuner**   This device receives AM/FM radio signals and amplifies them for distribution to speakers. For a single-zone audio system, a good quality AM/FM tuner/amplifier should be adequate to drive the system. For a multiple zone system, a remotely controlled AM/FM tuner without an amplifier built in is best when connected to amplifiers for each room.

- **CD/DVD player**   These digital devices read the digitally encoded data from the CD or DVD and convert it into analog audio signals. Most multiroom systems use a multidisc changer capable of holding at least five or more discs so the owner doesn't have to access the centralized system each time he wants to hear a new selection.

- **Digital multiplex (DMX) cable music receiver**   This digital form of music transmission is carried to a home on the cable or satellite television signals. The cable or satellite receiver converts these signals to analog audio signals.

- **MiniDisc player** This recording format digitally records audio signals on a small magneto-optical disc encased in a protective cassette. The MiniDisc player converts the digital signals to analog audio signals.

- **MP3 players** Although usually associated with computers and the Internet, MP3 recorders and players store the digital audio signals of a CD or another MP3 device on a hard disk drive or a compact flash card for digital to audio playback.

- **Hard drive–based music servers** These relatively new components allow music tracks to be stored on a hard drive for instant access. The music files can originate from the owners' CDs or MP3 files. It takes quite a bit of time to burn them into the hard drive, but there are services that will perform this task for a fee. They usually have a display that can be sent to a video display device and/or modulated so that the owner can use the local TV in each room to view the library of available music and access songs, albums, or playlists. Some music servers even have several zone outputs so different music zones can listen to different selections from the hard drive at the same time. Additionally, some of these devices can control high-capacity (200–400 discs) CD changers so the client can benefit from the convenience of the video display to access their entire library of recorded music. Some hard drive servers even allow playback of Internet radio stations!

- **Satellite radio tuners** Two new subscription services (Sirius and XM radio) that were originally developed for the automotive market deliver commercial-free music and other formats in a digital format much like satellite TV. Tuners are starting to become available, as well as adapters that allow car units to be played in the home. Some multiroom systems manufacturers are starting to offer these satellite radio tuners built into their tuners, pre-amp/controllers, or multiroom receivers.

- **Tape players** There are three types of audio tape players a customer may want in her home audio system:

  - **Audiocassette tape** This source device is still widely used, even given the popularity of the CD. Sound is recorded as analog audio signals and playback merely reproduces the original audio.

  - **DAT** DAT recorders and players are more common to professional systems, but this type of audio tape player records and reproduces very high-quality sound. DAT records audio signals digitally and in playback converts the digital signals to analog audio signals.

  - **Reel-to-reel tape** The technology in use on reel-to-reel tape recorders and players is essentially the same as that used on the audiocassette. The difference is in the size of the tape and that it is wound on open reels.

With the expansion of the bandwidth available to homes over broadband systems and the increasing number and quality of Internet radio and other music sources on the Internet, it definitely won't be long before Internet radio receivers find their way into multizone- and whole house–distributed audio systems. While not completely a must in a system currently being designed or installed, Internet radio is something to keep in mind for the future. Remember that a good multizone audio system should be able to be upgraded in the future without much work, redesign, or hassle.

Figure 10-13
A speaker showing its cone, surround, and voice coil

Speaker Basics

Audio system speakers translate electrical signal representations of audio sounds back into the vibrations that create the sound waves we hear.

Speaker Anatomy

A speaker (I discuss the different types of speakers beginning with the next section) consists of the following major components:

- **Driver**   This speaker component vibrates the cone (also known as the diaphragm) to create sound waves.

- **Cone/diaphragm/dome**   The concave cone or diaphragm is typically paper, plastic, or a flexible metal. The cone is vibrated by the speaker's driver mechanism to create sound waves. Some speakers have a dome, which extends outward from the speaker assembly. Figure 10-13 shows the cone/diaphragm of a speaker.

- **Suspension/surround**   The suspension or surround is a ring of flexible material that attaches the cone to the metal frame, called a basket, and allows it to move back and forth as it vibrates.

- **Voice coil**   Speakers have magnets at the bottom of the cone and at the top of the voice coil that, depending on the polarity of the power supplied from the voice coil, either attract or repel each other to move the cone in or out. By changing the polarity and amplitude of the voice coil (and its magnet), the magnet on the cone is pulled in or pushed out. Newer speaker models now include a dual voice coil (DVC) or twin voice coil (TVC) that allows both stereo channels to be played from a single speaker.

Frequency Range Speakers

Some speakers have specially adapted drivers that produce sound for a specific frequency range. The primary three frequency range speakers are

- **Woofers**   This type of speaker has a larger driver than other speaker types and is designed to produce sounds in the low frequencies and pitch.

- **Tweeters** This type of speaker has a smaller driver and is designed to produce sounds in the highest frequency ranges.

- **Midrange** This type of speaker is designed to produce sounds in a range of frequencies that are between those produced by tweeters and woofers.

Many home audio and home theater speakers include speakers of all three types in one enclosure. To separate the sound to be produced by each speaker type, a device called a speaker crossover is used. There are two types of speaker crossovers: passive and active. Passive crossovers, like the one in illustrated in Figure 10-14, are the most commonly used and get their operating power from the audio signal passing through it. Active crossovers (see Figure 10-15) are electronic devices that separate the frequency ranges before the signal passes through an amplifier. Each frequency range signal then must be amplified separately before being passed on to the appropriate speaker.

Speaker Enclosures

Essentially, a speaker enclosure is a box that houses the speaker and crossover. However, a speaker enclosure can be an important part of the sound produced by the driver. The first function of a speaker enclosure, beyond holding all of the speaker's parts, is to absorb the vibrations the driver produces. Quality speaker enclosures are typically made of heavy wood panels, which are able to absorb the vibrations without vibrating itself.

There are four primary types of speaker enclosures:

- Sealed enclosures
- Bass reflex enclosures
- Dipole and bipole enclosures
- Bandpass enclosures

PART III

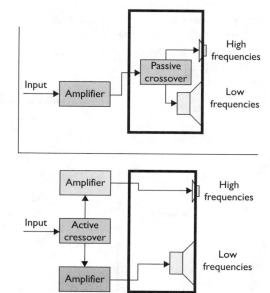

Figure 10-14
A single amplifier separates high and low frequencies in a passive speaker control.

Figure 10-15
Discrete amplifiers process the high and low frequencies in an active speaker control.

Sealed Speaker Enclosures   Sealed enclosures, which are also referred to as acoustic suspension enclosures, are the most commonly used type of speaker enclosures. A sealed enclosure is an air-tight box in which the air pressure inside the speaker box is used to assist in moving the speaker's driver to produce vibrations (sound waves). The speaker driver (or what most people call a speaker) is mounted to the enclosure and sealed so that no air can escape from inside. Figure 10-16 illustrates how a driver is mounted into a sealed enclosure.

Bass Reflex Speaker Enclosures   Where a sealed speaker enclosure uses its internal air pressure to push the driver back out when it moves inward, a bass reflex speaker enclosure allows the inward movement of the driver (as it moves in and out to create vibrations) to push the air in the enclosure out a port built into it. This type of enclosure is commonly used with woofers and subwoofers because the enclosure port allows the deepest sounds (lowest frequency sound waves) to escape. Higher frequencies are produced when the driver moves forward, and lower frequencies are produced when the driver moves backward. Figure 10-17 illustrates a bass reflex speaker with a port built into the enclosure.

Dipole and Bipole Enclosures   Dipole and bipole speaker enclosures are designed to allow sound to generate both forward and backward from the enclosure. While most dipole and bipole speaker enclosures are square or rectangular, some are trapezoidal and even triangular with three or more surfaces on which speaker drivers are mounted at right angles. Figure 10-18 illustrates a common configuration of these types of enclosures.

Both dipole and bipole speaker enclosures generate equal amounts of sound from at least two of their sides, which are commonly referenced as their fronts and backs, although the sides could be adjacent (as shown in Figure 10-18). The difference between a dipole and a bipole enclosure is whether or not the front and back sounds are in phase.

Phase refers to the timing of two or more sound waves in relation to one another. For example, to enjoy stereo sound, the two stereo channels should be in phase so that you hear them at the same time. To produce in phase sound from two or more speakers, the speaker drivers must be synchronized in their movement, meaning that they must be moving in and out at the same time.

Figure 10-16
A cross-section
of a sealed
speaker enclosure

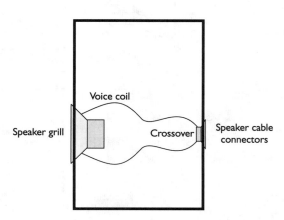

Figure 10-17
A bass reflex speaker enclosure has a port through which low-frequency sound travels.

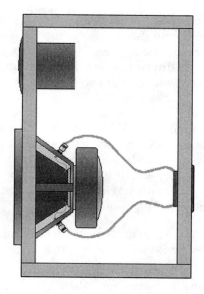

A dipole speaker produces equal amounts of sound forward and backward, but the two speaker drivers are not synchronized, making them *out of phase*. A bipole speaker produces sound just like a dipole speaker does, but the two sound streams are produced in phase. Bipole speakers, because they are in phase, are commonly used in surround sound systems.

There are passive and active versions of bipole and dipole enclosures. A passive enclosure is very similar to a bass reflex enclosure except that a passive speaker driver is placed in the port. A passive driver doesn't have a voice coil (an active speaker does) and uses sound waves produced by another driver passing through it to generate sound. So, in a passive enclosure, the sound pushed back into the enclosure is used to produce additional sound through the passive driver.

Figure 10-18
Speakers in bipole speaker enclosures

Photo courtesy of Mordaunt-Short.

Bandpass Enclosures A bandpass enclosure is designed to allow only a single band of frequencies to exit the enclosure, such as bass frequencies. Common types of bandpass enclosures are the single and dual reflex bandpass enclosures. A bandpass enclosure has a single driver mounted in a rear, interior sealed chamber and a front chamber that is ported with one or two (or more) passive reflex ports.

Types of Speakers

The characteristics of the speakers to be installed depend on a number of factors. Primary among these are the type and capacity of the amplifier that the speakers will be connected to and whether the system is to be a surround-audio system or a two-channel stereo system. In addition, the space they will be located in, the type of listening that will be done, and aesthetics are all important when selecting speaker types.

There are nine standard types of speakers:

- **Bookshelf** These are smaller speakers designed to sit on shelves, stands, or other surfaces. Bookshelf speakers provide the maximum flexibility when designing a room's audio system.

- **Floor-standing/freestanding** These are larger, cabinet-mounted speakers that usually include one or more tweeters (treble speakers) and woofers (bass speakers). Figure 10-19 shows a floor-standing speaker.

Figure 10-19
Floor-standing
speakers

Photo courtesy of Klipsch Audio Technologies.

Figure 10-20
An in-ceiling
speaker

Photo courtesy of SpeakerCraft.

PART III

- **In-ceiling** These speakers are engineered to be built into a ceiling, with most of the speaker hidden inside the ceiling cavity. In-ceiling speakers come in many sizes and shapes. However, the most commonly used in-ceiling speaker design is the round "can" speaker like the one shown in Figure 10-20.

- **In-wall** These speakers are designed to be built into a wall with most of the speaker hidden inside the wall. Like in-ceiling speakers, there are a variety of sizes and shapes available, but the most common are rectangular in shape. Figure 10-21 shows one example of an in-wall speaker.

- **Outdoor** These speakers come in a wide variety of shapes and sizes that range from standard wall-mount, all-weather speakers to shapes that include rocks (see Figure 10-22), blocks, and other shapes meant to blend into a garden or patio setting.

- **Animated** This type of speaker is designed to react to the sound it produces with either motion or light or both. The animated speaker can be a doll, person, animal, or any other jointed character that dances or moves in synch with the music being produced. An animated speaker can also be a device that produces various shades of light in sync with the sound it produces.

- **Surround** Surround sound systems are typically used in home theater setups and are usually a combination of special-purpose speakers, each supporting a different part of the audio signal.

- **Subwoofer** These speakers are designed to reproduce the lowest audio frequencies at a volume level that can be felt as well as heard. The "sound" of a subwoofer is made up of frequency waves so large that it is often perceived more through vibrations felt in one's spinal column and skull than the manipulation of the eardrum. For this reason, some home theaters actually supplement the subwoofer system with mechanical devices that cause the

Photo courtesy of Klipsch Audio Technologies.

listener's chair or floor to actually shake. Figure 10-23 shows a freestanding subwoofer with the grill cloth removed. Exact placement in the room is not critical, but subwoofers are usually freestanding on the floor or hidden in a cupboard or closet, and the sound disperses through cloth or vents.

Photo courtesy of Klipsch Audio Technologies.

Figure 10-23
A subwoofer
speaker with its
grill removed

Photo courtesy of Sonance.

- **Wireless**   There aren't really any wireless speakers, but there are wireless speaker systems. A wireless speaker system uses an audio out transmitter and a remote receiver where the speakers are connected. The audio signal is transmitted using radio frequency (RF) signals to the receiver and on to and out of the speakers. As more devices in the home emit RF interference, the reliability and performance of wireless speakers becomes more compromised and inconsistent. This is probably why they are less popular than when they were first introduced about 15 years ago. Wireless speakers are typically not recommended except as a last-ditch solution in a multiroom audio system.

- **Invisible**   Just as they're called, these speakers are not visible. They are located behind the drywall and use the wall cavity to resonate the sound. There are two types of invisible speakers. Transducers are mounted inside a wall or ceiling cavity between wall studs or ceiling joists and use the drywall to transmit the sound to the room. The other kind of invisible speakers with a mesh over them are mounted flush with the drywall or plaster wall (a hole is cut in the wall board of a wall or ceiling). A thin layer of plaster is then applied to make them blend into the drywall. Figure 10-24 shows how one such speaker is attached to the back of a wall.

Local Controls

Regardless of whether the distributed audio system is in one or multiple zones, the objective is to control the centrally located equipment from any remote listening location. Much of the benefit of a distributed audio system is lost if the home's occupants must physically go to a central location to change the source device or the station, track, disc, or channel.

Figure 10-24
A cut-away view of an invisible speaker assembly inside a wall

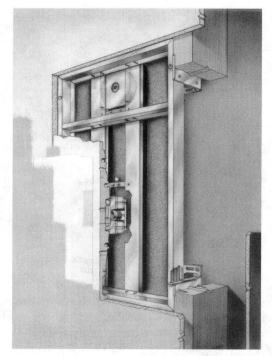

Photo courtesy of Sound Advance Systems, Inc.

The best approach to controlling a distributed audio system is using distributed remote controls that transmit control signals back to the central equipment and allow the user to control the unit just as if he or she were standing right in front of it.

The most popular ways of controlling a distributed audio system are

- Local volume controls
- Control keypads
- Remote controls

Volume Controls

Volume controls come in several styles, including rotary dial, keypads with rocker switches, and push buttons. The type of volume controls used in home audio systems depends on the homeowner's preference and the number of zones the system supports. In a single zone multiroom system, it is advisable to have a volume control located in each room where speakers are installed, to provide local volume control.

Sometimes designing subzones (individual rooms within a zone) makes sense. An example might be a kitchen and breakfast nook that shares an open air space. In this case, it might be desirable to have a zone keypad in the kitchen, with individual volume

Figure 10-25
A rotary
volume control

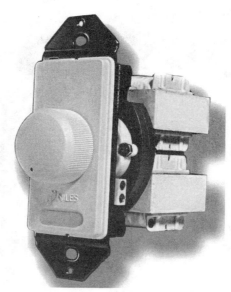

Photo courtesy of Niles Audio Corporation.

controls and speakers in both the kitchen and breakfast nook. It might make sense to play the speakers in one room area louder than the other, but it would never make sense to have two different music sources playing in the two rooms simultaneously.

Figure 10-25 shows a rotary volume control used to simply mute or turn up or down the volume of local speakers. Volume control can also be handled by standalone devices requiring manual operation, or they can include infrared (IR) receivers that allow them to be controlled by a remote control device.

Control Keypads

Control keypads are available in a variety of styles. They can be used to simply mute or turn up or down the volume of local speakers, or they can perform a full range of control functions, including controlling multiple source devices when wired to a zone splitter device, as well as controlling their volume in a room.

Keypads can be sold as part of a distributed audio system or be designed specifically to control the distributed audio system. They can also be of a generic nature and designed and programmed by the installer to control equipment (see Figure 10-26). Programming can be done at the keypad or on a computer and downloaded to the keypad. Follow the manufacturer's documentation for setup and programming procedures.

Remote Controls

IR is the most commonly used technology for the remote control of audio components, including centrally located source devices controlled from a room or zone. IR control is most reliable when its signals are received by an in-room receiver, such as a keypad volume control, and transmitted directly over homerun wires to the audio components using an IR repeater system.

Figure 10-26
A touch screen
audio system
keypad control

Photo courtesy of Niles Audio Corporation.

An IR repeater system typically includes in-room IR receivers (see Figure 10-27) and a main system unit where the IR receiver is wired. The IR receiver converts the signal for transmission over the wire to the master system unit, which converts the transmitted signal back to IR and "flashes" an IR beam to the audio source device or remote speakers.

If coaxial cable has been placed in multiple rooms or zones, it can be used to send IR commands from remote locations to the central video system. IR signals are received remotely and converted for transmission over the coaxial cable. Special products must be used to extract and isolate the IR signal from the video signal on the coaxial if it is also being used to send a TV signal to that room.

Figure 10-27
An in-room
IR receiver

Photo courtesy of Niles Audio Corporation.

NOTE A signal extension system is only needed in situations where the device being controlled is not in the same room. In a single zone setup, where the entire home is one large listening zone, an IR extender can be used to control a centralized audio source device.

Multiple Device Controllers

If the design goal of the audio system is to have the capability of supplying a completely discrete sound stream to any room in the home, using multiple device controllers (see Figure 10-28) that are hard-wired over Cat 5e/Cat 6 homerun cable back to the centralized audio source equipment is recommended.

A multiple device controller is able to receive signals from IR remote controls and serve as a replacement device that consolidates the separate remote controls of the source devices. In-room multiple device controllers can be wall-mounted, as shown in Figure 10-28, handheld, or tabletop (Figure 10-29).

Another type of multiple room/multiple device system controllers is a system built on the A-BUS technology that transmits audio, IR, and source status signals over Cat 5e/Cat 6 cable. The A-BUS input unit receives incoming audio signals, distributes them, and provides audio and source status signals to the system as well as receiving IR command signals through its enhanced keypad devices.

A-BUS is a multiple room system that is able to control audio in four rooms and can be expanded in increments of four rooms by adding additional zone distribution hubs. A-BUS also provides support for connecting local source devices, such as portable players, for playback on local speakers.

Figure 10-28
An in-room multiple device audio system keypad controller

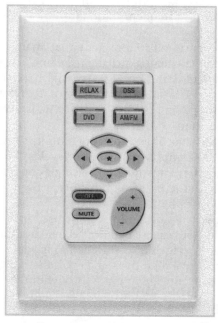

Photo courtesy of Niles Audio Corporation.

Figure 10-29
A touch screen universal remote control

Photo courtesy of Koninklijke Philips Electronics NV.

Chapter Review

Sound is produced when an object creates vibrations in air, liquid, or something solid. Different sounds have different vibration patterns and air pressure fluctuations, which translate into a sound's frequency and amplitude. A dB measures the intensity or the level of a sound.

Recorded or broadcasted sounds are either analog or digital. Analog sound is in its natural state. To convert analog into digital sound, a sound wave is sliced into a number of samples at different points on its wavelength. Each sample is then converted to a numeric value and stored as a binary number or digital value. Analog sound is converted for digital recording with an ADC, and a DAC is used to reconvert the digital values back into analog sound.

A line level audio signal has 1 to 2 V of amplitude and is used as the normal interface level between audio components. Speaker level audio is an amplified line level signal.

Unbalanced audio is transmitted on a single conductor cable that has a single shield. Balanced audio has at least two conductors, a live conductor and a return conductor, which are in opposite phase.

Two types of twisted-pair cabling can be used in a distributed audio system: Cat 5e/Cat 6 or XLR cable. Both carry a balanced signal, but Cat5e/Cat 6 cabling has two advantages over XLR cabling: the devices needed to modulate the audio signal onto the cable are much less expensive then the same equipment used with XLR cable, and category-rated cabling is likely already in place throughout the home. Cat 5e/Cat 6 cabling can carry analog audio signals as far as 5,000 feet and digital audio up to 1,400 feet.

Resistance measures the physical opposition of a conductor to the flow of an electrical current through it. Resistance is measured in ohms. Capacitance measures the capability of a circuit to store an electrical charge. Capacitance is measured in farads. Inductance measures the resistance of a conductor to changes in current. Inductance is measured in henrys. Impedance is the resistance force a conductor has to an AC flow. Reactance measures the cumulative effect of capacitance and inductance on an AC flow.

A true surround sound system incorporates several speakers that separate the sound by frequency, as well as physically literally surrounding the listener. A true surround sound system has five, six, or seven speakers. A LFE speaker is a subwoofer speaker that is used to reproduce the very lowest frequency sounds. The standard professional level surround sound is the 5.1 system.

RMS is the measurement for the maximum amount of amplified sound signals the speaker is designed to handle. Frequency response of an amplifier indicates the lowest and highest frequencies the amplifier is able to amplify and retransmit.

A distributed audio system provides an infrastructure that allows an entire house to share audio technologies. It is possible for each room to control the local volume and source devices as well. Centralization is key to distributed audio.

There are two types of audio amplifiers from which to choose: constant current amplifiers and constant voltage amplifiers. A constant current amplifier supports only one or two speakers because of low impedance. A constant current amplifier is typically used in small, distributed audio systems with small speakers. Constant voltage amplifiers have a higher impedance output than constant current amplifiers and can support cable runs up to several thousand feet.

There are two choices that can be made for amplifying audio signals: centralized amplification and distributed amplification.

There are two general approaches to the configuration of a whole house audio system: single zone and multiple zones. In a single zone approach, all of the speakers in a house play the same sound from a single source. In the multiple zone approach, each room can select and listen to the audio from multiple zones.

For most home audio systems, the audio source devices are generally among the following: AM/FM tuner, CD/DVD player, DMX cable music receiver, MiniDisc player, MP3 players, hard-drive based music servers, satellite radio tuners, and tape players.

Audio system speakers translate electrical signal representations of audio sounds back into the vibrations that create the sound waves we hear. A speaker consists of these major components: driver, cone or dome, suspension/surround, and voice coil. Some speakers have specially adapted drivers that produce sound for a specific frequency range. The primary three frequency range speakers are woofers, tweeters, and midrange.

A crossover is used to separate the sound produced by each speaker. There are two types of speaker crossovers: passive and active. Passive crossovers get their operating power from the audio signal passing through it. Active crossovers are electronic devices that separate the frequency ranges before the signal passes through an amplifier.

A speaker enclosure houses the drivers and the crossover. It absorbs the vibrations the driver produces. The primary types of speaker enclosures are sealed enclosures, bass reflex enclosures, dipole and bipole enclosures, and bandpass enclosures.

The standard types of speakers are bookshelf, floor-standing, in-ceiling, in-wall, in-visible, outdoor, surround, subwoofer, and wireless.

The ways available for controlling a distributed audio system are local volume controls, control keypads, and remote controls.

Questions

1. Which two of the following are types of audio amplifiers?

   A. Current volume amplifier

   B. Constant current amplifier

   C. Constant volume amplifier

   D. Constant voltage amplifier

2. Which two of the following are configuration types for speaker wiring?

   A. Series

   B. Parallel

   C. Inline

   D. Discrete

3. What type of configuration is in use in a house when all rooms hear the same audio playback?

   A. Single zone

   B. Multizone

   C. Composite

   D. Aggregate

4. The audio source device that increases the amplitude of reproduced sound is called a(n)

   A. Tuner

   B. Radio

   C. Amplifier

   D. Amplitude modulator

5. What speaker system has become popular in home theater installations?

   A. Sealed enclosure

   B. In-wall or in-ceiling

    C. Stereo

    D. Surround

6. What type of speaker is designed to reproduce the lowest audio frequencies at a volume that can be heard?

    A. Bookshelf

    B. Tweeter

    C. Monitor

    D. Subwoofer

7. Where should volume controls be located in a single-zone multiroom audio system?

    A. One central location only

    B. In each room where speakers are located

    C. For each speaker pair

    D. In all rooms of the home

8. Which of the following can be used to control a distributed audio system?

    A. Keypad

    B. Remote control

    C. Rotary volume control

    D. Multiple device control

    E. All of the above

9. What type of wiring is typically used to connect a multiple device controller to centrally located source equipment?

    A. Speaker wire

    B. Cat 5e cable

    C. Coaxial cable

    D. Quad wire

10. Which of the following is an audio control system that transmits audio, IR, and source status signals over Cat 5e cable?

    A. A-BUS

    B. CEBus

    C. MP3

    D. PLC

Answers

1. **B and D.** The other two choices were made up.

2. **A and B.** A third possibility is in series in parallel, which combines the two correct choices. The other two choices do not apply to speaker wiring.

3. **A.** A multizone configuration allows each zone to control the different audio sources being heard.

4. **C.** Yes, that's the job of the amplifier. Often the signal strength of reproduced sound is not strong enough to drive the cone on the speakers to produce sound.

5. **D.** A surround sound system enhances the experience of watching a video.

6. **D.** Woofer would also be an acceptable answer.

7. **B.** If the goal of the system is to provide enjoyable audio to every room, the occupants should be able to control the volume in any room with speakers. This goal is defeated if there is only one volume control in the home.

8. **E.** Any or all of these devices can be used to control a distributed audio system.

9. **B.** The multiple wire pairs provide flexibility for multiple devices in a room or zone.

10. **A.** B and D would not be acceptable audio control technologies, and MP3 is a digital audio file format.

Designing and Installing Distributed Audio Systems

In this chapter, you will learn about:
- Designing and planning a distributed audio system
- Performing a rough-in installation of audio system components
- Performing the trim-out phase for the audio system
- Setting up the components, system, and testing

In a recent survey conducted by a home automation industry group, homeowners and people looking to buy a home responded that a whole-house audio system was either something they were planning to install or regarded as a plus when considering a new house. We are no longer limited to playing a radio very loud so it can be heard throughout the house (and possibly the neighborhood). Whole-house audio systems can be as sophisticated as the legendary system in Bill Gates' home, where the music played in each room is individualized to the room's occupant automatically, or as simple as the same audio output being played by all speakers placed in the ceilings or walls of each room of a home.

Planning, designing, and installing a whole-house audio system isn't really all that complicated, but there are some design considerations, pitfalls, and compatibility issues that must be included in the planning and design phases.

Like a computer network or a distributed video system, a distributed audio system can be retrofitted into a home. However, in new construction situations, with proper planning and the use of a structured wiring infrastructure, all three types of systems can be easily integrated. As the various audio system topics in this chapter are discussed, keep in mind structured wiring and how the audio system can be combined into an integrated home system.

Planning for a Distributed Audio System

The very first consideration when planning for a distributed audio system is whether the system is a new construction or a retrofit, meaning if it is to be added to an existing structure. In many ways, a retrofit installation is more difficult than a new construction installation. It is certainly much easier to wire an audio system into a house while it is being built than it is to run wire through existing and closed up walls, ceilings, or floors.

In a retrofit situation, or what the electricians call "old work," the most important project considerations are first where to place the distributed devices, such as speakers and controls, and then where and how to run cable to them from the centralized source devices.

Planning for Distributed Audio

Typically, at the start of any distributed audio installation project, whether for an existing or new structure, no real plan exists for what exactly is to be done. The homeowners may have some idea of what they desire, but not necessarily any idea of actually how it is to be accomplished. During the planning phase of the project, a number of issues must be considered, including:

- Will there be one or multiple audio sources?
- Are one or multiple audio zones desired?
- Will there be a single or a number of distributed controllers?
- Are local source devices to be integrated into the distributed audio system?
- Will the system include both interior and exterior devices?
- Should the planning provide for devices to be installed now and in the future?
- Are the source devices and speakers new or do they exist?
- Does the house's floor plan present any limitations or constraints to the design?
- What is the budget?

The last question in this list may be the most important consideration of the entire project. How much the homeowners are willing to spend may influence some of the plan and design issues for you. You know how it goes: hi-tech tastes on a low-tech budget. Assuming that isn't the case, the planning phase for an audio system needs to address each of the issues listed and perhaps a few more. The simplest way to determine the answers to the remaining questions in the list is to ask the following two questions about each room in the home:

- Do you want to be able to listen to music in this room?
- Would you ever want to listen to something in this room that is different from what is playing in the rest of the house?

Laying Out the System

To a certain extent, the planning phase of a distributed audio project is the fact-gathering phase. It is virtually impossible to design a system for installation without collecting all of the facts about home use and the owners' desires that will impact the labor and materials required.

Start with a floor plan drawing and work with the customer to place the speakers, source equipment, and controllers in the rooms included in the system. For an existing house, the floor plan drawing may be something that must be created; in a new construction situation, a floor plan drawing is usually available. It is also very important that the length and width of the building and each of its rooms be obtained during this phase of the project. The floor plan should illustrate the layout of the building and include the dimensions and preliminary placement of the distribution panel and wall outlets. With the floor plan in hand and a concept of the customer's desires, you should be able to move on to the design phase of the project.

Designing a Distributed Audio System

During the design phase of the project, it's important to decide what components will be included in the system. For a residential distributed audio system, the following components must be considered:

- **Audio source units**   In most home situations, the common audio source device is a CD or DVD player or an AM/FM tuner. However, with the emergence of digital audio, MP3 files or Internet radio from a computer are becoming popular choices as well. The homeowner may also have legacy equipment, such as a cassette tape player, a reel-to-reel tape player, or even a phonograph or turntable.

- **Amplifier/Receiver**   Often combined into one device, the receiver portion receives AM/FM signals and the amplifier portion boosts the signal and distributes it to the speakers. In some cases, separate receiver and amplifier units provide for the best performance and flexibility in terms of adding additional source units and speakers to the system. In many cases, an existing amplifier/ receiver can be used only as an amplifier. In multiple zone applications, a multizone amplifier unit with multiple channels, equalization, and other features may provide the best results.

- **Distribution system**   The cabling and impedance matching the distributed audio system must be carefully considered. If multiple rooms in a single-zone system are planned, the impedance-matching capabilities of the distributed volume controls and speakers must be matched to the amplifier. The characteristics of the speaker wiring must also be considered.

- **Speakers**   The choices in speakers vary from in-wall, ceiling, wall and surface mounted, and camouflaged "natural" shape speakers. The primary considerations for speakers are

  - **Physical appearance**   The speakers should be consistent with a room's décor or style.

  - **Audio coverage (dispersion)**   The speakers should provide the maximum audio coverage for their zone, with consideration given to the room's shape, size, and major features, such as a large chandelier, table, or the like.

- **Acoustic sensitivity** Large rooms, such as family rooms, recreation rooms, or living rooms, can present an audio balance challenge, especially if the room's furniture, draperies, or carpeting absorbs sound, decreasing the volume that is heard. In smaller rooms, such as laundry rooms or bathrooms, the hard surfaces make the volume seem louder. Larger rooms may need additional or larger speakers, and smaller spaces may need fewer or smaller speakers. Most manufacturers supply specifications about the sensitivity of each model of speakers they make, which is normally expressed as a number of decibels (dB) at one watt when measured at one meter from the speaker. This specification helps determine the best speaker or speaker set for a room and the amplifier requirements needed to drive the speakers in a room.

- **Volume and keypad controls** The design of a distributed audio system must show the number and placements of the controls incorporated into the audio system, regardless of whether the controls are dedicated speaker volume controls or keypad controls that control the actions of several of a home's subsystems. Including the controls in the design will assure wire installation allows for these connections.

Fitting Sound to Rooms

In the design process, the speakers must be matched to the room size and the dB output desired for the room. The factors involved are the number of rooms and the number of speakers in each room. The power rating (in watts) of the amplifier must be sufficient to drive the speakers at the volume (in dB) desired for each space. The rule of thumb is that larger rooms need more power to produce acceptable sound levels. And for customers that like to play their music loud, even more power may be needed from the amplifier.

Speaker Sensitivity

Speaker or acoustic sensitivity ratings are available for nearly all quality speakers. Understand that a speaker sensitivity rating has almost nothing to do with sound quality, but everything to do with the amount of volume a speaker can produce from an input at a given power level.

The sensitivity rating of a speaker is stated as db/Wm, which translates to decibels per watt of power measured at one meter (about 3.3 feet) from the speaker. If a speaker has an acoustic sensitivity rating of 90 db/Wm, this means that the speaker produces 90 dB of sound from an input of one watt of power from the amplifier about 3 feet (1 meter) from the speaker.

NOTE 90 db/Wm is a fairly average sensitivity rating for most speakers. A speaker with a rating of 87 or below is considered low sensitivity, and a speaker with a 93 or higher rating is considered high sensitivity.

When designing the sound system for a particular room or zone using an average amplifier that produces only a few watts of output power, this means that speakers with higher sensitivity will be needed in areas where louder volumes are desired, such as in a home theater. The other way to address this issue is to drive low sensitivity speakers with more watts from the amplifier. However, be aware that the watts rating of amplifiers can also be a moving target. For example, on an inexpensive amplifier the potential watts-per-channel rating may coincide with the distortion level on each channel. Higher quality (and typically higher cost) amplifiers provide more accurate power ratings.

Acoustical Room Issues

Not every room is acoustically engineered—in fact, few rooms are. Sound produced by speakers in a room resonates around a room, and the room's width and length can impact its quality, loudness, and clarity. The dimensions of a room affect the sound coming from a speaker in the same way that the sound from a pipe organ is affected by the diameter and length of each pipe.

A typical room has three physical features (a ceiling, a floor, and the walls), each producing a different audio frequency as sound resonates (bounces) around the room. Depending on where the speakers are located in a room, the sound produced will seem louder or softer due to the architectural features the sound encounters between the speaker and the listener.

The placement of speakers in a room is typically the only method available to you to improve the acoustics of any space, assuming that the ceiling, walls, floors, locations, and coverings cannot be changed.

Acoustical Design Issues

To improve the acoustical quality of any room, there are a number of issues to consider in the design and placement of speakers in the room:

- The dimensions of a room
- The placement of doors, windows, and other architectural features in the room
- The location of heating, ventilation, air conditioning (HVAC) vents and ducts
- The materials used in the wall, ceiling, and floor construction

Each of these issues should be considered when determining the location of the speakers in a room. Any of these issues can affect the quality of the sound a speaker produces by blocking the sound, vibrating because a speaker is placed to close to it, or absorbing too much of the sound.

Locating Speakers and Controls

The location of an audio system's speakers and controls are largely determined by the homeowners' desires and the room's décor. The homeowners' desires should help determine where built-in or freestanding speakers are best for any given room. The homeowner should also help in the placement of controls, as they know how the room will be laid out and used.

PART III

Built-In Speakers

Built-in speakers come with their own set of limitations and problems. When designing the installation for built-in speakers, check the manufacturer's baffle specifications to avoid a situation where there are too many or too few wall studs, hangers, or other construction features near the speakers.

Built-in speakers produce a conical audio pattern, which means that the sound produced can be heard very well directly under the speaker. However, when stereo sound is separated to two speakers, unless the speakers are placed in an overlapping pattern, the listener may hear one stereo channel louder than the other. Figure 11-1 illustrates this point, although this illustration is somewhat exaggerated to make the point. In the shaded area the listener hears both stereo speakers equally. However, as the listener moves either left or right, the speaker on that side becomes dominant.

Built-in speakers are designed to be installed in walls or ceilings with the speaker grill flush with the wall or ceiling surface. They are designed to be installed in a wall or ceiling cavity, but it's a good idea to configure the cavity so the back of the speaker is covered to prevent insulation, dust, and other debris from getting inside the speaker. A simple solution is to fold a piece of cardboard from the speaker's carton and wedge it into the hole before installing the speaker. Some manufacturers now offer in-wall boxes (for new construction) or damping/isolation kits (for retrofit applications). Another consideration is to use weatherized speakers if the speakers will be exposed to a lot of humidity in the speaker cavity.

Freestanding Speakers

Freestanding speakers have finished surfaces such as wood boxes or laminate surfaces for display and aesthetics. They can be placed on a stand, pedestal, bookshelf, or in a speaker cabinet. They can be mounted to walls, ceiling, or overhangs. In fact, speakers are typically designed and manufactured for a specific type of mounting. An in-wall (built-in) speaker would look and sound terrible mounted on a pedestal.

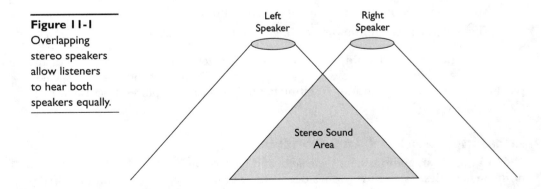

Figure 11-1
Overlapping
stereo speakers
allow listeners
to hear both
speakers equally.

Placing Speakers   Speakers should be placed in a room or zone where they produce the best stereo sound effects for the listener. The general guidelines for placing speakers in a room are

- **Separation**   The speakers should provide left and right stereo separation when the listener is facing the main feature of a room. If there is no main feature, then the speakers should be placed facing the primary seating area. A room's main feature may be a fireplace, large window, or a television set or monitor. Speakers should not be placed any closer than 24 inches to any room boundary, including walls, corners, ceilings, or floors.

- **Zoning**   A general practice used for speaker placement is to divide the room into three conceptual equal-sized listening zones. A speaker should be placed at the points where any two of the zones intersect, placing the speakers about the same distance from the room's corners and the main listening location. Speakers should not be placed too close to a room's corners to avoid what is called "doubling," which creates a booming sound in the audio. To avoid doubling, the speakers should be placed about one-quarter or one-third of the distance into the room away from a corner or wall.

- **Directionality**   The ideal placement for freestanding speakers is to have the tweeters at approximately the same height as the listener's ears, as high frequencies tend to be more directional. Since this placement option is rarely available when using in-wall or ceiling speakers, many manufacturers now offer tweeters or midtweet baffles that are designed to pivot, allowing the installer to adjust the speaker to direct the high frequencies toward the listening position.

Designing Equipment Configuration

Before beginning to actually install an audio system (or an audio/video system), you should carefully plan how the source, distribution, and end devices are to be laid out and connected to the distribution wiring, as well as to each other.

The best way to document the layout, connections, and equipment placements in an audio system is to create a line diagram of the system. Figures 11-2 and 11-3 are examples of simple line drawings and very detailed drawings, respectively, of an audio visual (AV) system. Normally, all that is needed more closely matches Figure 11-3 than Figure 11-2, but with a sufficient level of detail on the diagram, the drawing can be included in the system's documentation for future reference.

Pre-Wiring

The standard for the wiring systems in residential settings is Telecommunications Industry Association/Electronic Industries Alliance (TIA/EIA) 570A, which provides for both existing and most new technologies expected in the near future. This standard provides specification and standards for the primary cable runs of a distributed audio system.

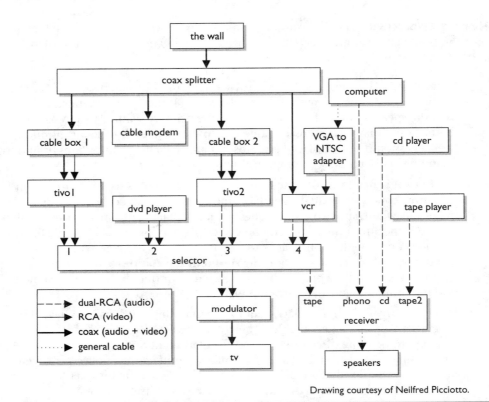

Drawing courtesy of Neilfred Picciotto.

Figure 11-2 A simple line diagram for an AV system showing the general connections between the components of the system

Figure 11-3
A complete
AV system line
diagram that
details each of
the connections,
wiring runs, and
components of
the system

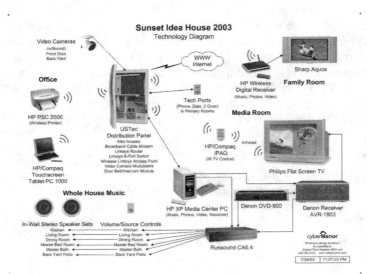

Drawing courtesy of cyberManor.

A wiring plan for the distributed audio system should be developed with each of the three types of basic wire runs indicated on the plan. Figure 11-4 illustrates a very basic pre-wiring plan for 1) amplifier to distribution device, 2) distribution device to volume controls, and 3) volume controls to speakers.

There are four basic types of cable runs in a distributed audio system:

- **Amplifier to distribution device**   The source equipment is connected locally to the amplifier, and it is then connected into the system's central distribution device. It is usually best to locate the distribution device as close to the amplifier as possible. The recommended cable support for the amplifier to distribution device is

  - **Three pairs (six conductors, usually 16- or 14-gauge) of speaker wire** Four of the speaker wires' conductors connect and carry the left and right speaker signals from the amplifier to the distribution device. The remaining two conductors can optionally be used to carry direct current (DC) voltage to the distribution device for control applications.

  - **One run of Cat 5e/Cat 6 cable** The four-pair Cat 5e cable provides support for such features as infrared (IR) extension, data communications, and video distribution.

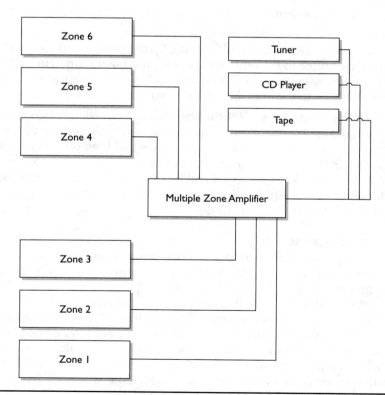

Figure 11-4   A pre-wiring plan for a distributed audio system showing the paths of the cable runs

NOTE   Multiple cable runs should be planned into a room or zone to support situations where multiple system components are to be installed.

- **Distribution device to volume controls**   The cables in these runs connect the distribution device to the volume controls in each zone. The cables that should be included are

  - **Two pairs (four conductors) of speaker wire**   These wires carry the audio signals to the volume controls that will pass the signals to the speakers.

  - **One run of Cat 5e cable**   This cable provides for future expansion or a multiuse faceplate that could provide for a possible control keypad or IR reception for a remote control extension system. The cable can be used to support keypads, displays, amplified speakers, or IR extension systems. Many in-wall and ceiling speakers have knockouts that allow a remote IR sensor to be placed behind the speaker grill.

- **Volume controls to speakers**   Wiring is required from the volume control to each speaker in a zone. The cabling in this run should include:

  - **One run of two-conductor speaker wire to each speaker**   These runs carry the audio signal from the volume control to each speaker.

  - **One run of four-conductor speaker wire to each speaker**   Leave a two-foot loop of wire at the location of the first speaker, and then run the four-conductor cable to the other speaker's location. Four different colored wires allow for easy hookup and wire-pair matching at each speaker. Be sure you pay attention to the impedance of the system.

- **Local source to speakers**   If the room has a CD, stereo, television, or another type of audio source component, the speaker wiring should loop from the volume control to the local source component and then on to the speaker. Both the four-conductor speaker wire and the Cat 5e cable should run from the volume control or keypad control and be connected to the outlet to be used by the local device. Figure 11-5 illustrates how a local source device is connected into a distributed audio system.

Cable Considerations

Typically, 16-gauge stranded twisted-pair (TP) wiring is used for an average length speaker run, with heavier wiring used for very long runs. The twist in the wire helps reduce the interference the cable could pick up.

There is a difference between real speaker cable and what is called interlink, or interconnect, cable. Speaker cable is designed to carry a powered signal, which means that it doesn't need much in the way of shielding to protect it from interference. For the most part, basic speaker cable is clear-jacketed. Audio interconnect cables carry a line-level, nonpowered signal between two audio system devices and are susceptible to interference; therefore, this type of audio cable requires shielding.

Figure 11-5
Local audio
source devices
designed into
a distributed
audio system

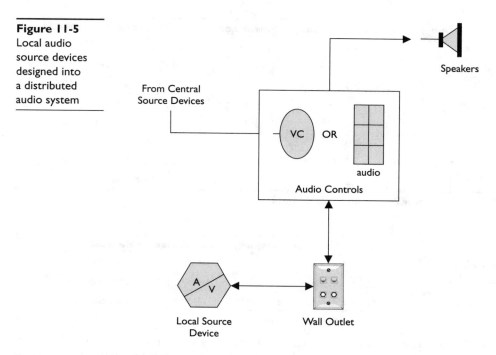

From Central
Source Devices

Speakers

VC OR

audio

Audio Controls

Local Source
Device

Wall Outlet

Choosing Speaker Wiring

There are several types of speaker wire on the market. The following terms are commonly used to describe speaker wire and its characteristics:

- **Cable ratings** The cable that meets the standards for a specific use is normally tested and rated for that use. For example, a cable designed for installation inside a wall, generally called plenum cable, carries a premise-wiring rating. Unfortunately, you can't assume that all speaker cable has a premise-wiring rating. Cable that has a premise-wiring rating complies with the National Electric Code (NEC) and National Fire Protection Agency (NFPA) standards, which provides you and your customer assurance that the cable meets the appropriate fire safety and electrical standards. Speaker cable that is installed inside a wall must meet all local and national electrical and fire safety standards as a high fire-retardant wire. Premise rated speaker cable and wire carries either an Underwriters Laboratory (UL) Class (CL) 3 or CL3R (riser) rating (see Figure 11-6). CL3 plenum cabling can be strung inside an HVAC duct if needed, but the cable should not be installed on or near a dust-collecting electrostatic wire inside the duct.

Figure 11-6
An illustration
of a CL3-rated
speaker cable.

Speaker Ohms	Percent of dB Loss	Power Loss	16 AWG Run	14 AWG Run
4	0.5	11	60 feet	100 feet
4	1.0	21	130 feet	210 feet
4	2.0	37	290 feet	460 feet
4	3.0	50	500 feet	790 feet
8	0.5	11	120 feet	190 feet
8	1.0	21	260 feet	410 feet
8	2.0	37	580 feet	930 feet
8	3.0	50	990 feet	1,580 feet

Table 11-1   Speaker Wire Power Loss Budget Table

Table 11-2 Speaker Wire Gauge to Run Length	Wire Length to Speaker	Wire Gauge to Be Used
	50 to 100 feet	16-4 or 16-2 AWG speaker wire
	100 to 150 feet	14-4 or 14-2 AWG speaker wire
	Over 150 feet	12-4 or 12-2 AWG speaker wire

- **Gauge**   The wire gauge selected for a home AV system should be chosen based on its properties and the distance of the wiring runs. Speakers have low impedance (4 to 8 ohms); therefore, the resistance in the wiring is key to determining how much of the audio signal will reach the speaker. For example, a 100-foot run of 16-gauge TP wiring has a round-trip resistance of 0.8 ohms. When this wire is used with a 4-ohm speaker, 17 percent of the signal is lost to the resistance on the wire, and only 83 percent of the sound signal actually reaches the speaker. The solution to this is to use heavier wire. The wire sizes typically used for home audio systems are 16 American Wire Gauge (AWG) or 14 AWG. They provide good compromises against signal loss, cost, and ease of installation. On top of that, the connectors on most audio devices are designed for these wiring sizes. Table 11-1 shows the power loss budget for 16 AWG and 14 AWG speaker wiring. Table 11-2 shows the gauge wire to be used based on the length of the run for virtually any home audio.

 NOTE   For virtually any home audio installation, 16 AWG or 14 AWG wire should work well for runs that are 100 feet or less. It is recommended that 12 AWG wire be used for runs in excess of 150 feet.

Design Issues

Here are some cable facts you should consider during the design phase:

- **Oxygen-free copper**   The best conductive copper for wiring and cabling is 99.99 percent oxygen free. Standard speaker wire cable is typically 99.90 percent oxygen free. If you wish to install the best cabling available, look for the code OFC (oxygen-free copper) printed on the cable's outer jacket.

- **Lower gauge/thicker cable**   A lot of speakers will work adequately with cable as small as 22-gauge wire. However, for longer cable runs, a thicker cable (with a lower gauge) extends the attenuation point of the wire. In terms of price and performance, at least 16-gauge wire should be used for the in-wall wiring for speakers.

- **High strand count/better performance**   When a higher number of strands are used in a wire, it creates a greater surface area. When a signal is transmitted across a wire, the electrons flow along the surface of the wire. So, more surface area means a better quality signal with less signal loss.

Audio System Rough-In

There are actually three different rough-in activities involved with a distributed audio system: wiring, installing speakers, and establishing local room controls. Each of these rough-in activities has its own particulars, but in the end they all come together to provide the infrastructure of the audio system.

Rough-in is performed after the electrical cabling, plumbing, and HVAC rough-in has been completed and before the finished wall surface, typically drywall, is installed. Waiting until after the other rough-in work is completed prevents any of the other in-wall systems, such as running electrical wiring through the same holes of the audio wire, from interfering with the audio system's cabling.

Figure 11-7 illustrates the general concepts of rough-in for an audio system. Although this illustration simplifies this part of the project, it does show the parts of an audio system that are installed during the rough-in phase of the project.

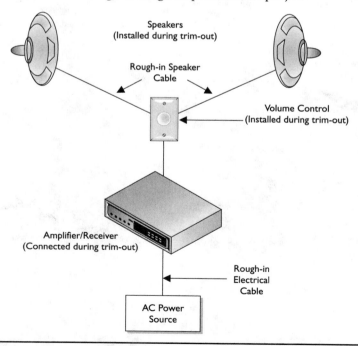

Figure 11-7   The primary components of a distributed audio system

Speaker Rough-in

During the design phase, either you or the customer (or both) have selected the size, shape, and brand of speakers and volume controls to be installed. When installing speakers and volume controls during a new construction project, you should install mounting brackets, if available, for any in-wall or in-ceiling, flush-mounted speakers and boxes for volume and keypad controls during the rough-in phase. Figure 11-8 shows the rough-in mounting bracket for a round in-ceiling speaker. Most speaker manufacturers sell rough-in kits separately for virtually all in-wall and surface mount audio speakers and controls.

Rough-in boxes for mounting volume controls or control keypads are available in a variety of types. These boxes and mounting brackets can be either single-gang or double-gang mountings, with open or backless boxes, to hold one or more control devices. Figure 11-9 shows two styles of rough-in mounting boxes for volume or keypad controls. The box on the left is a single-gang backless box and the box on the right is an electrical box with a low-voltage mounting bracket attached to its side.

Figure 11-8
A rough-in mounting bracket for a flush-mounted speaker

Photo courtesy of Crutchfield New Media, LLC.

Figure 11-9
Two systoles of low-voltage boxes that can be installed during rough-in for later use for volume controls or keypads

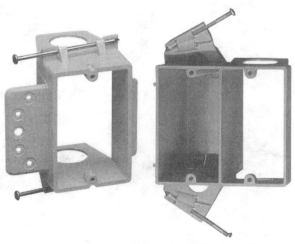

Photo courtesy of Lamson & Sessions.

There are pros and cons to using rough-in kits. The benefits of rough-in mounting brackets include the early placement of speakers, resolving speaker mounting support issues, the fit of recessed speakers, and more accurate hole cutting when the drywall is installed. The primary disadvantages of using rough-in kits are that they can lock in a device brand, size, and shape and the location of an audio system device, and the rough-in mounting's alignment is critical to the finished fit and alignment of a flush-mounted device.

In-wall and flush-mount speakers come in a variety of sizes and shapes. Typically, flush-mount ceiling speakers, like the one shown in Figure 11-10, require specific mountings to ensure fit and proper function, depending on their depth and circumference. If a mounting bracket isn't installed during rough-in, you have two choices: as illustrated in Figure 11-11, you can zigzag and loosely staple the wiring between a pair of studs that straddle the location of the speaker, or you can install a speaker that has mounting clips or clamps built in, like the speaker shown in Figure 11-12. If you choose to zigzag the wiring, you should photograph the wall prior to the drywall being installed over wiring so you later know where to make your cut in the drywall for installing the speaker.

Surface-mount or wall-mounted speakers require only that a standard J-box, mounting box, or mud ring, and of course the speaker cable, be installed so that the mounting bracket or foot on the speaker can be secured to the wall.

Whether or not a rough-in kit is used to locate a wall or ceiling speaker depends on the customer's wishes or your preferences. If the customer and you decide against using a rough-in mounting, remember that you will need to cut the drywall to accurately install the recessed speakers using the wiring installed during pre-wire in the locations documented by your pre-wire photographs.

Figure 11-10
A flush-mounted
ceiling speaker

Photo courtesy of Broan-NuTone, LLC.

Figure 11-11
Zigzag wiring between wall studs for future speaker installations

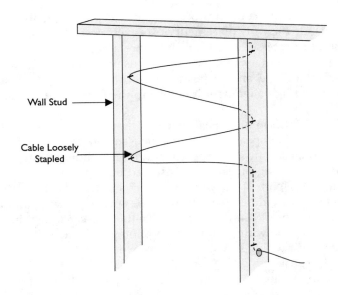

Wall Stud

Cable Loosely Stapled

Figure 11-12
A short depth recessed ceiling speaker

Photo courtesy of Niles Audio Corp.

Installing Audio Cable

In a new construction situation, the installation of audio cabling follows the general structured cable installation guidelines. However, installing in-wall cable in what is called an "old work," or retrofit situation, and rough-in is a bit trickier. The outlet boxes and cable must be installed behind existing walls without damaging the drywall surface.

NOTE As each cable is installed, it should be labeled according to the wiring diagram. Ensure that all of the cable that terminates at the central wiring distribution panel is labeled to ease the installation and connection of the distribution panel. The labels also help to facilitate wire testing and the trim-out and finish work yet to be accomplished.

Snaking in the Cable

Perhaps the hardest part of installing structured cabling in a retrofit situation is install-ing the cable inside the walls. Inside an existing wall there is likely electrical, telephone, and TV cabling, not to mention plumbing and perhaps wiring for other fixtures.

Depending on the home and its design, there are three options for installing audio cable (or any structured cable component):

- **Inside the walls** This method requires that the cable be routed through the existing studs while avoiding electrical, plumbing, and other previously installed systems.

- **Through an attic** Using this method, the audio cable can be run from the central distribution panel, which is referred to as an integrated service unit (ISU), to and through the top rail of the wall studs above the cavity in which the outlet box is or will be installed. Of course, using this method presumes a clear space exists above the main floor of the house in which to run the cable.

- **Under the floor** Provided the house has either a basement or a crawl space in which to run the cables, the cables can be pulled through the footing rail of the wall studs and into the cavity in which the outlet box is installed.

Installing Cable in the Walls

Perhaps the most important task of installing audio cable in an existing wall is to first locate the wall studs and any plumbing lines that lie behind the drywall or other sur-face covering, such as lath and plaster. Most quality stud-finders will locate wall studs as well as any metal behind the wall.

When all of the studs or pipes are located in the walls you plan to use to install the cable, you can plan the route for the audio cable. Always work with a whole-house diagram, rather than each room individually. Before you begin cutting access holes in the walls to run the cable, you should first check for obstructions or wiring in the space through which you plan on running cable. Once you have settled on the wire path, use either a drywall saw or a box cutter knife to cut away the drywall and expose the wall stud through which the cable will pass. Use a hand drill and a small drill bit to cut a hole in the wall in an out-of-the-way location that can be patched easily should the location prove unusable. A good practice is to use locations that are inconspicuous or can be hidden behind furniture or other objects.

 NOTE When you are working on a retrofit project, don't expect to have a whole house diagram from which to work. It is a rare day indeed when you get one. While it would be better to have this diagram, you should be prepared to go into most walls blind; not knowing just what is inside.

Push a straightened-out wire coat hanger bent at an angle into the hole and fish around gently (there could be electrical wiring in there!) for any wires or pipes in the space where you plan on installing the audio cable. If you find fixtures in that location, adjust your wire plan accordingly.

NOTE If your budget allows it, a wide assortment of bendable "snake" cameras are available. These tools are designed specifically for the purpose of seeing inside of a wall. The camera snake is inserted into the wall through a small hole and, using a small light on the end of the camera head, you can have a look around to see what is inside the wall. If you are doing a lot of retrofit work, one of these tools is a must-have.

Use a long-length drill bit to drill a wire path through the wall stud. A flexible shaft "flex-bit" is very handy in this application. Typically, the wire path should be at a slight downward slope because of the small opening in the wall through which the drill bit is inserted.

Push the cable through the wall opening and through the hole in the wall stud towards the next opening. Use the straightened coat hanger (with bent hook big enough to fit around the cable) to pull the wire to the wall opening. Drill the next hole, insert the cable, and pull it to the wall opening, repeating the steps until the cable is installed throughout the room or the house.

Special Installations

Not all walls have wood studs. In some newer construction, sheet metal studs may be used for a house's framing. In these cases, after drilling a hole for the cable, insert a plastic grommet before inserting the cable through the stud to protect the cable from the sharp edges of the metal.

When passing through a metal stud or ceiling joist, the NEC requires that the cable be no closer than 1.25 inches to the edge of the stud or joist and that a protective plate at least 1/16 of an inch thick be installed to protect the cable from nails or screws.

Remember that speaker wire should be installed separately from all other wire and should be at least one foot away from any other wiring, including other structured cable and electrical wire, and any light fixtures in the walls or ceilings.

Volume Control Rough-In

In both new construction and retrofit situations, outlet boxes of sufficient depth to mount the volume control units must be installed in the walls where the volume controls are to be located. Follow the guidelines described in Chapter 3 to place the boxes in the walls and pull cable to them.

The speaker wiring should run to the volume control and then to the speakers to be controlled with a loop at the volume control location. In a multiple zone application, the speaker wire is usually left in a continuous loop to the speakers since the audio signal comes directly from the distribution equipment. The Cat 5 cable is used to connect the local keypad to the system's zone control preamp at the main system location.

Although many brands specify specific cables for their zone control keypads, most brands now offer compatibility with Cat 5 cable.

Local Source Rough-In

If the customer wishes to use the speakers in a room or zone for local AV sources in addition to the whole house system, some switching method, either manual or automatic, must be designed into the system. If local sources are designed into the system, the design must reflect that the speaker wiring go to the source switch before going to the speakers. If a local volume control is also included, it is wired before the source switch.

Testing the Cable

After the cabling is installed, a cable verification test should be performed. This testing determines if nails, screws, or any other sharp items in the wall may have damaged the cable during installation. For any unterminated cable, such as speaker wire, the testing procedure should test for any opens or shorts in the speaker cable and the continuity of each conductor in the wire.

CROSS-REFERENCE   See Chapter 1 for more information on wire basics and wire testing procedures.

Audio System Trim-Out

As is the case in any trim-out operation, the cables are terminated and tested. In the trim-out phase of a distributed audio installation, each of the speakers, speaker jack wall plates, volume controls, and keypads are installed. Follow specific manufacturers' instructions for installation of these devices.

CROSS-REFERENCE   Chapter 2 details the audio connectors and when each is used.

In addition to the connectors detailed in Chapter 2, some speakers require spade-type connectors (illustrated in Figure 11-13). Spade connectors are crimp-on connectors that are easily installed.

Audio System Setup and Testing

After all devices are trimmed out, install the components and hook up all equipment per documentation. Be sure to follow the line diagram of equipment hookup developed during the design phase. If any changes are made on site, be sure to record them on the line diagram so that final documentation of the system hookup will be complete.

PART III

Figure 11-13
Spade connectors on an audio cable

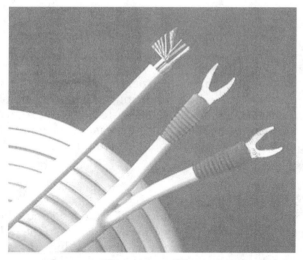

Photo courtesy of Monster Cable Products, Inc.

All control keypads need to be set up and programmed if necessary. This may include programming through setup software and learning the IR codes needed to control the equipment. Follow the manufacturers' documentation for setting up and programming.

Now test the system in every zone. Be sure to test each volume control in each location and make sure every speaker has output and sounds good. On the control keypads, test and verify that every button performs as set up and programmed.

Chapter Review

The first consideration when planning a distributed audio system is whether the system is a retrofit or new construction. During the planning phase of the project, a number of issues must be considered, including single or multiple audio sources, zones or controllers, local source devices, future devices, the limitations of the floor plan, and the budget.

Begin the design with a floor plan and work with the customer to place the speakers, source equipment, and controllers into the rooms. During the design phase of the project, the decisions on the components to be included are made.

Speakers must be matched to the room size and the dB output desired. The factors involved are the number of rooms and the number of speakers in each room. The rule of thumb is that larger rooms need more power to produce acceptable sound levels. An average amplifier produces only a few watts of output power and the speakers may need higher sensitivity where louder volumes are desired. The placement of speakers in a room is typically the only method available to you to improve the acoustics of any space, assuming that the ceiling, walls, floors, locations, and coverings cannot be changed.

To improve the acoustical quality of any room, a number of issues should be considered in the design and placement of speakers in the room, including the dimensions of a room; the placement of doors and windows; the location of HVAC features; and the wall, ceiling, and floor materials and construction. Speakers should be placed in a room or zone where they produce the best sound applying certain principles: separation, zoning, and directionality.

The standard for the wiring systems in residential settings is TIA/EIA 570A, which provides specification and standards for the primary cable runs of a distributed audio system. There are four basic cable run types in a distributed audio system: amplifier to distribution device, distribution device to volume controls, volume controls to speakers, and local source to speakers. Several types of speaker wire are available. Cable rating and gauge are the terms commonly used to describe speaker wire and its characteristics.

Three rough-in activities are involved when installing a distributed audio system: wiring, installing speakers, and establishing local room controls. In a new construction situation, the installation of audio cabling follows the general structured cable installation guidelines. After installing the cable, it should be tested to determine if nails, screws, or any other sharp items in the wall have damaged it during installation.

During the trim-out operation, cables are terminated and tested, and the speakers, wall plates, volume controls, and keypads are installed. After the connection devices are trimmed out, the components are installed and hooked up. Next, all controls are set up and programmed. Finally, the system is tested in every zone.

Questions

1. Which of the following is not a distributed audio system design consideration?

    A. Single or multiple audio sources

    B. Brand and model of source devices

    C. New or existing source units or speakers

    D. Budget

2. What is the purpose of an amplifier in a distributed audio system?

    A. Signal amplification

    B. Volume control

    C. Impedance matching

    D. Stereo sound balancing

3. What is the standard for residential structured wiring for audio?

    A. TIA/EIA 568A

    B. TIA/EIA 568B

    C. TIA/EIA 570A

    D. TIA/EIA 232

4. Which of the following is not a basic cable run in a distributed audio system?

   A. Amplifier to distribution device

   B. AC power wiring for source units

   C. Distribution device to volume controls

   D. Volume controls to speakers

5. By what factor should the amplifier's output be increased to effect a 10 dB increase in speaker output?

   A. Two

   B. Three

   C. Five

   D. Ten

6. During which phase of an audio installation project is the wiring installed?

   A. Planning

   B. Rough-in

   C. Trim-out

   D. Testing

7. What is the acoustic sensitivity rating of an average speaker?

   A. 80 dB/Wm

   B. 87 dB/Wm

   C. 90 dB/Wm

   D. 93 dB/Wm

8. What is the purpose of testing an audio cable at the end of the rough-in phase?

   A. To check for proper termination

   B. To check for shorts in the wire

   C. To check for wire continuity

   D. All of the above

9. What rating should an audio cable have to be installed in an HVAC duct?

   A. 22 AWG

   B. Premise wiring

   C. Plenum rating

   D. No specific rating required

10. Which of the following are included as rough-in activities when installing a distributed audio system?

    A. Wiring

    B. Installing speakers

    C. Establishing local room controls

    D. All of the above

Answers

1. **B.** During the planning phase, only the power requirements and impedance issues are important. The other choices are important, but perhaps budget is the most important consideration.

2. **A.** Most amplifiers don't perform the other actions listed.

3. **C.** TIA/EIA 568 standards cover Cat 5 wiring, and 232 is a serial connection standard.

4. **B.** AC wiring is not included in structured wiring systems.

5. **A.** The amplifier's output in watts must be increased by a factor of two to achieve an increase of 10 dB.

6. **B.** Wiring is pulled into the walls during the audio rough-in phase, along with the installation of speaker brackets and boxes. Planning and testing are self-explanatory, and during trim-out the wire is terminated.

7. **C.** A rating of 87 dB/Wm or below is considered low sensitivity and a rating of 93 dB/Wm or higher is considered high sensitivity.

8. **D.** These are the primary tests that should be performed on newly installed and terminated cabling.

9. **C.** This rating describes a cable that is fire-rated for use in ducts and commercial applications.

10. **D.** Each of the activities included in answers A, B, and C are performed as rough-in activities for a distributed audio system.

CHAPTER 12

Troubleshooting Audio Systems

In this chapter, you will learn about:

- Common audio cable and system problems
- Troubleshooting audio cable

There may be nothing worse for a homeowner than to fire up his or her distributed audio system to play a favorite recording of Mozart or the Rolling Stones and hear static, hum, or buzz drowning out their dulcet tones, or, even worse, nothing at all.

A distributed audio system typically involves more than source devices, cable, and speakers. In many systems, there can also be selectors, volume controls, and remote controls, and each can introduce problems into the system.

This chapter looks at the most common problems a distributed audio system can develop and the processes and devices used to diagnose and troubleshoot audio problems.

Diagnosing Audio System Problems

A distributed audio system is a series of audio devices that are connected to one another over structured wiring. The parts of the distributed audio system that can cause audio performance problems are all of the components (including the speakers) and the cabling that connects the speakers and controls to the source devices. So, when you get a call that there is a problem with the audio system, gather as much information as possible and be sure to listen and analyze what the homeowners are saying. For example, if they say there is no sound or an improperly functioning control device, the obvious place to start tracking down the problem is by checking the source devices. Start with checking the components, the connections, and the parts of the system related or connected to the structured wiring system—oh, and check the power too!

Review the audio system configuration and identify all equipment components and how they are connected. The line diagram completed earlier in the project (like the one included in Chapter 11) is an excellent reference for this information. Use a structured step-by-step troubleshooting process that includes at least these steps:

CROSS-REFERENCE   See Chapter 11 for information and examples of an audio system line diagram.

1. Identify the problem.
2. Start troubleshooting at the audio source.
3. Use a methodical approach.
4. Eliminate components one at a time as the source of the problem.
5. Refer to the manufacturer's documentation for troubleshooting suggestions specific to a particular component.

The detail steps performed within this framework should include most of these steps:

- Ruling out the obvious
- Checking all connecting cables
- Checking all control devices inline with the suspected components
- Checking that the connection is the correct type for the equipment in use

Rule Out the Obvious

As obvious as it may seem, make sure that all of the connections are secure and fit properly, including the alternating current (AC) connection on the amplifier and any other source devices related to the problem. Make sure all components have power, especially if they are powered through a surge protector.

Check the speakers to make sure that all of the connections are secure. See if only one or both of the stereo speakers are not working. If only one is not working, check the connections throughout the distributed audio system that deliver the signal to that channel. If both speakers are not working, check the connections on both channels throughout the system and look closely at the connections from the source equipment.

Also, check the volume controls, both at the source and in the affected room or zone. A room or zone volume control can't increase the volume if the source device's volume is set low. Another quick test of the audio is to plug a portable speaker directly into the source device. If the sound is available from the portable speaker, then the problem is likely in one or more of the distributed audio cables or speakers.

Check the Cable

As is the case with all distributed cabling systems, there is a short list of cable problem causes, including:

- A broken connector caused by someone tripping over a connector cable
- Corroded connections caused by too much moisture in a wall or room

- Stretched or broken conductors caused by too much pull tension during installation

- An audio cable that was damaged during installation

Your diagnostics should be organized to identify and isolate these common problems.

In most cases, the best way to test audio or video cables is to test the input or output levels of the cable with a signal from one of the system devices on the cable. For example, to check the cable connecting a CD player, play a CD and test the cable at the speaker terminations where it connects to a volume control or the speakers. By far the most common audio video cable problem is an open circuit, which most commonly occurs at the cable ends.

Cable Properties

The three properties that should be tested, usually with a good quality multimeter, on an audio cable (or any cable for that matter) are

- **Capacitance**   Cable capacitance is a common problem on audio lines that are more than 100 feet or 30 meters in length. If the capacitance is too high, it may interfere with systems that have high impedance. Use a handheld multimeter or a cable test device to determine the capacitance of the cable. If the capacitance is too high for the device to which it is connected, consider replacing the cable with one that is rated at less than 100 picofarads per foot (pF/ft).

- **Inductance**   High inductance can affect audio by changing the tone of the sound during transmission. Inductance can vary depending on the cables that are installed and whether they are coiled or looped. A coiled up cable will typically have higher inductance than an uncoiled cable. The best way to correct inductance is to ensure that the length of the cable between two devices is appropriate and without unnecessary loops or coils. Some systems also have inductor circuits built-in to block certain frequencies in an audio signal; for example, the crossover in a woofer may "roll-off" higher frequency sounds. If the audio is distorted in this situation, the problem may be in the crossover and not the cable.

- **Resistance (impedance)**   Depending on the needs of a specific audio system, if the resistance is too high, the audio signal may be decreased in quality, especially at the speakers. Impedance is how much a cable impacts the flow of current through the wire and is measured in ohms. Systems are either high impedance or low impedance, but low impedance systems are typically in the range of 150 ohms to 800 ohms and high impedance is generally in the range of a few kilo-ohms to tens of kilo-ohms. Residential systems are typically low impedance devices, and the rule of thumb is to assume output impedance at around 1 kilo-ohm (K-ohm). The speakers and other distributed components of an audio system should be matched for resistance and impedance.

To troubleshoot the audio visual (AV) system for resistance, perform these checks:

- Check all connectors and connections for improper installation, loose shielding, stray strands, or damage.
- Check the cable for continuity using a volt-ohm meter (VOM) or multimeter.
- Check any cables that terminate at the distribution panel from the end of the cable terminated at a wall outlet. The resistance of the cable should be close to that of the terminator or the device connecting to the outlet.
- If RG6 cable is installed, use a multimeter or VOM to check the resistance between the center conductor and the shielding in the cable. If the resistance is below 100 K-ohms, it is likely that the cable has a short in it at some point and should be replaced.

Cable Verification

If you suspect that a problem may exist in the distributed audio cabling, you should perform the same cable tests you performed to test and verify the cable during trim-out:

- Visually inspect the terminations at the distribution panel, at the source device, and at the outlets. Depending on the type of cable in use, check to see that the connector or jack is properly attached:
  - **Coaxial cabling**   Is the connector's wire mesh inserted around the outer channel of the connector body? Is the center conductor wire extending the proper distance (about ¼-inch) beyond the front of the connector? If the connector is a crimp-on type, is the connector tightly crimped to the cable? Is the screw-on collar (on an F-type connector) properly aligned and tightly connected?
  - **Speaker wire**   Are the wire conductors in contact when they connect to the outlet jack (a condition that may exist if too much insulation was stripped from the wire)? Are the jacks securely fastened to the conductors?
  - **Twisted-pair (TP)**   If RCA or miniplug jacks are in use, is the wire pair insulation preventing the two conductors from touching at the jack? If a balanced interface is in use, is the connection providing a ground line?
  - **Commercial audio cabling**   When using a manufactured audio cable set, are the connectors firmly attached to the cable without breaks, cracks, or splits between the connector plug or jack and the cable?
- If the connector jacks and plugs are good, next test the cable for its transmission properties:
  - **Digital versus analog**   Verify which interface format is in use. In most systems, the format will be either be analog or the more common standard digital signal formats used in residences, Audio Engineering Society/European Broadcast Union (AES/EBU), which recommends shielded TP cable. Verify that an analog device is not connected at the source or in a room or zone. AES/EBU does not convert digital signals back to analog.

- **Coaxial cable**   The cable should carry 75 ohms of impedance, which can be verified with a multimeter. Check the cable for continuity as well.

- **Speaker wire**   Most speaker wire (also called zip wire) fails to meet the requirements for in-wall cabling specified in the building and electrical codes. Distributed audio wire should have a Class 2 or 3 fire insulation rating, and clear insulation speaker wire doesn't. There are commercial audio cables that do meet the codes, but not many do. If standard two-conductor, clear-insulation speaker wire is installed in the walls of a home, your first recommendation is that it should be replaced. It must also carry 4 ohms to 8 ohms of impedance, which can be verified with a multimeter.

- **TP**   Shielded TP (STP) cable should carry from 100 ohms to 120 ohms of impedance if connected to a digital interface. TP cable used for analog audio transmission should carry 45 ohms to 70 ohms of impedance. Verify that an analog device isn't connected to a digital device. If it is, you may have found the problem. Verify continuity and impedance and perhaps even run a wire map test on the cable.

Ground Loops

Another common problem that is typically attributed to cabling is a ground loop that can create a humming noise in the audio playback. A ground loop is caused when two or more AC-powered devices that are connected to the electrical system on two different outlets in two different rooms are linked to one another with an audio cable and part of the AC power flows over the cable.

Solving ground loops is not an easy task because there are no absolute grounding systems. Solving this problem may require assistance from an electrician to balance the grounding of the outlets in use or, if an unbalanced line is in use, the installation of a balanced audio interface.

Check the Controls

Distributed volume controls and selector controls can and do go bad, but not often. In most cases, if a volume control is not properly responding to changes in its setting, the problem is either the connection or the volume control itself.

Remove the control from its outlet, assuming it is not a remote control, and check its connections carefully. Also check the wiring where it comes into the outlet box or structured wiring bracket. If the wire is bent or kinked, that could very well be the issue. If the connections appear to be proper, replace the control with a new one. If this solves the problem, then the control was bad. However, if the problem persists, you should check the cabling both before and after the control.

Balanced versus Unbalanced

Beyond the obvious, such as the source device being unplugged, AC power can cause audio problems, especially if the speaker interface is unbalanced. There are two types of audio interfaces used in audio systems: unbalanced and balanced.

Unbalanced Interface

An unbalanced interface is typically installed on a single conductor shielded wire, such as a solid core conductor cable like coaxial cable. The shielding around the wire serves to ground not only the cable, but also the two devices connected to it, typically an amplifier and a speaker, but could also include a microphone or other audio source device. Unbalanced cabling is typically terminated with RCA or miniplug connectors.

The problem with an unbalanced interface, especially one of some run length, is that it is very susceptible to picking up what is called ground loop interference that can add hum or buzz to the audio playback by a speaker.

Ground loop interference is a common characteristic of shielded copper wire. Removing the cause, the cable's shielding, isn't the way to solve it. However, it can be removed with an isolation transformer. While all systems that use an unbalanced interface are likely to have ground loop interference problems, on smaller systems it's typically not much of a problem. However, in a high-end system that includes some professional level audio or video equipment, either the cabling should be replaced or an isolation transformer installed.

Balanced Interface

Professional and better audio devices are connected using balanced cabling, constructed to minimize the amount of interference they pick up. A balanced cable has the built-in capability to pass along the audio signal and filter out interference.

A balanced cable includes two 24-gauge conductors to carry signals plus a grounding wire. Several manufacturers produce a variety of balanced cabling. Balanced cabling is typically terminated with an XLR connector. The balance in this type of audio cable is achieved by maintaining the impedance of the two signal lines equal to that of the ground. However, balanced audio also works on ungrounded cabling as well with the right equipment.

Chapter Review

The obvious place to begin diagnosing distributed audio problems is checking the source devices. Make sure that all of the connections are secure and fit properly, including the AC connection on the amplifier and any other source devices related to the problem. Check the volume controls, both at the source and in the affected room or zone. If sound is available from a portable speaker connected to the source device, the problem is likely in one or more of the distributed audio cables.

There is a short list of cable problem causes, including a broken connector, corroded connections, stretched or broken conductors, or damaged cable. Your diagnostics should be organized to identify and isolate these common problems.

The three properties that should be tested on an audio cable (or any cable for that matter) are capacitance, inductance, and resistance (impedance). To determine if a problem may exist in the distributed audio cabling, test and verify the cable using the same tests used during trim-out. Visually inspect the terminations at the distribution panel, at the source device, and at the outlets. Test the cable for its transmission properties.

A ground loop can create a humming noise in the audio playback. A ground loop is caused when two or more AC-powered devices that are connected to the electrical system on two different outlets in two different rooms are linked to one another with an audio cable and part of the AC power flows over the cable.

If a volume control is not properly responding, the problem is either the connection or the volume control itself. Remove the control from its outlet and check its connections carefully. Check the wiring where it enters the outlet box for bends and kinks. If the connections are proper, replace the control with a new one. If the problem persists, check the cabling both before and after the control.

There are two types of audio interfaces used in audio systems: unbalanced and balanced. An unbalanced interface is typically installed on a single conductor shielded wire, such as a solid core conductor cable like coaxial cable. An unbalanced interface is very susceptible to ground loop interference and can add hum or buzz to the audio playback by a speaker.

A balanced cable has the built-in capability to pass along the audio signal and filter out interference. A balanced cable includes two conductors and a grounding line.

Questions

1. When diagnosing an audio system problem, what should be the first area to check?

   A. Structured wiring

   B. Volume controls

   C. Connections

   D. Source devices

2. Which of the following is not a common cable problem?

   A. Broken connector

   B. Corroded connection

   C. Cable quality too high

   D. Stretched or broken conductors

3. Which of the following can impact the performance of an audio system?

   A. Capacitance

   B. Inductance

   C. Resistance

   D. Cable length

   E. All of the above

PART III

4. What is the rule of thumb for residential audio system impedance (resistance)?

    A. 4 ohms

    B. 20 ohms

    C. 1 kilo-ohm

    D. 20 kilo-ohms

5. Which of the following can cause audio cable problems at the connector?

    A. Insulation material

    B. Stranded versus solid wire conductors

    C. Conductor wires in contact

    D. Ground loop

6. Which of the following is a digital audio standard?

    A. AES/EBU

    B. IEEE

    C. NEC

    D. S/PDIF

7. What impedance should a coaxial cable used in a distributed audio system carry?

    A. 15 ohms

    B. 50 ohms

    C. 75 ohms

    D. 100 ohms

8. Which of the following cable types is least likely to meet the building and electrical codes for fire safety?

    A. STP

    B. Coaxial

    C. Speaker wire (zip wire)

    D. UTP

9. What audio system problem are two AC power devices that are connected to AC power in two different rooms and are linked by an audio cable likely to cause?

    A. Feedback

    B. White noise

    C. Ground loop

    D. Clipping

10. What type of cable is an unbalanced audio interface typically installed on?

    A. Solid core, single conductor cable

    B. Stranded speaker wire

    C. UTP

    D. STP

Answers

1. **D.** If a source device is not connected, powered, or has improper settings, it is likely the cause of at least one audio system problem.

2. **C.** I'm not sure if it is entirely possible to have too-high a quality cable, but about the only problem it can cause is cost. The other issues listed are all common cable problems.

3. **E.** Actually, just about anything at all relating to an audio system can, if only in a small way, cause some problem. But these choices are the causes, either alone or in combination, of many audio system problems.

4. **C.** Most systems will range a bit lower than 1 kilo-ohm, but that is the standard rule of thumb.

5. **C.** If the insulation has been stripped too far back on the conductors so that they make contact at the connector, the audio signals are being shorted out.

6. **A.** AES/EBU does not convert digital audio signals back to analog and, as a result, the standard is not compatible with standard analog audio devices.

7. **C.** Coaxial cabling is commonly used in unbalanced audio that has longer run lengths.

8. **C.** Commonly available speaker wire typically has transparent insulation, which doesn't carry the NEC/UL fire safety ratings for in-wall installation.

9. **C.** A ground loop condition can add buzz to the audio signal.

10. **A.** The lack of a grounding conductor is the key characteristic of an unbalanced cable.

Distributed Video Basics

In this chapter, you will learn about
- Video signal types and applications
- Video cable types and applications
- Satellite video services
- Media servers

One of the truly daunting parts of writing a book on technology, let alone an emerging technology such as home audio/video (AV), is that the technologies included are changing as fast as this book is being written. Okay, it may not be as bad as that, but home AV technologies are fast-moving targets. So, this chapter takes a look at some of the currently available and emerging video services and video recording, storage, and distribution devices.

Much of the material in this chapter is background information. However, that doesn't mean you don't need to know it. In fact, if you are new to distributed video, this chapter is a must-read.

Transmitting Video Signals

Video signals are broadcast in either an analog or a digital format. Analog signals are broadcast through the air and received by a home's TV antenna. However, analog signals can also be transmitted to a home over a cable system. Digital video signals are typically not broadcast, but transmitted over a cable system between a source device and a video display device. High-definition television (HDTV) is the closest an on-air analog broadcast system comes to reproducing the quality of a digital video signal because HDTV transmits a signal with more lines of resolution than a standard analog broadcast.

Analog video signals are radio frequency (RF) signals regardless of whether they are transmitted through the air or carried on a cable system. Broadcast, or "over the air," video signals are limited to licensed broadcasters, who are typically VHS broadcasters licensed by the Federal Communications Commission (FCC) to do so. Unlicensed, or "cable," operators transmit their video signals using dedicated broadcasting methods, such as microwave and cable transmissions.

Baseband versus Broadband

Just like data transmissions, two basic types of transmitted radio frequency (RF) signal formats are used to carry video signals: baseband and broadband.

Baseband

Baseband communications use the entire transmission medium to carry a single-frequency or composite signal in its original, unmodulated form. There are three types of baseband signals:

- **Composite**   This signal format transmits the complete video signal, including its picture (luminance), color (chrominance), and signal-blanking and synchronization pulses.

- **Component**   This signal format uses three conductors to carry five separate frequency bands (one each for red, green, and blue, also known as RGB, and one each for luminance and chrominance). Component baseband is rarely used, except in very high-end video systems.

- **S-Video**   This signal format, which is also known as Y/C video, super video, and separate video, transmits the luminance and chrominance signals separately, which improves the picture clarity. The Y (luminance) signal carries the brightness information, and the C (chrominance) signal carries the color information.

Two baseband cables are required to transmit the video and audio source signals in a television broadcast. Figure 13-1 illustrates how broadband RF signals are received by an antenna and passed to a TV receiver, which splits the audio and video into separate baseband signals for other devices.

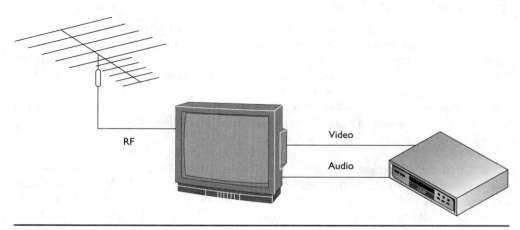

Figure 13-1   On-air baseband television reception

Broadband

Broadband communications transmit multiple signals using a separate frequency for each one. The most common broadband video system is the cable television system, which transmits its broadband RF signals over coaxial cable. Broadband coaxial cable, which is commonly referred to as Community Access Television (CATV), is capable of transmitting 130 analog (RF) channel transmissions, and in some cases even more.

Table 13-1 lists the standard channel allocations for broadband RF. Each channel carries both the audio and video signals of the transmission.

High-Definition Multimedia Interface (HDMI)

This is an audio/video interface used to transmit uncompressed digital signals. It is slowly replacing radio frequency (RF), direct cable, composite video, component video, and S-Video as the connection interface of choice in Blu-ray disc players, video game consoles, and digital audio/video receivers to digital audio, televisions, and computer monitors. Because HDMI is able to transmit any television or computer video format, including high-definition video, as well as up to eight channels digital audio on a single cable, it fits more into the broadband category, but not exactly.

Modulation

The video device used to convert baseband to RF (broadband) signals is a modulator, but not all video signals require modulation. The analog video signals received by a home antenna and those transmitted over cable television service are RF signals and don't require modulation for transmission or playback.

Two objectives must be designed into the cabling used to carry RF signals in a home's distributed video system (typically coaxial cabling): the signal strength must be sufficient to provide a quality signal to the display or playback device and radio and electrical interference must be minimized or eliminated. The best way to make these assurances in a video distribution signal is to use high-quality RG6 cable and connectors.

Band	Frequencies	Broadcast Channels	CATV (Cable) Channels
Very high frequency (VHF) low band	54–84 MHz	2–6	2–6
Frequency modulation (FM) radio	88–108 MHz		
CATV midband	120–170 MHz		14–22
VHF high band	174–212 MHz	7–13	7–13
CATV super band	216–296 MHz		23–36
CATV hyper band	300–468 MHz		37–64
CATV extended hyper band	468–820 MHz		65–121
Ultra high frequency (UHF) band	470–806 MHz	14–69	

Table 13-1 RF Broadcast and CATV Bands

Figure 13-2
A one-line to two-line RF splitter with a distribution box mounting

Photo courtesy of Channel Vision.

Video cabling only transmits RF signals from point A to point B. They can't be used in parallel to transmit signals in a one-to-many arrangement because the receiving end of the cable expects to receive only a single 75-ohm signal. In situations where a single RF video source is to be transmitted to more than one end device, a splitter (see Figure 13-2) must be used. A splitter is a device that takes in a single 75-ohm RF signal and outputs two or more separate 75-ohm signals. The most common type of splitter used is a passive splitter, which does nothing to enhance the strength of the split signals.

Another RF signal device that can be used in a distributed video system is a combiner, which is, in effect, the mirror opposite of a splitter. A combiner combines two (or more) incoming RF signals into a single combined broadband signal, as long as the two incoming signal lines don't share any common channels. A combiner can be used to combine cable television service with the signals from a digital satellite system passed through a modulator to change their channel modulations so there is no overlap with the cable channels.

Video Signal Loss

As the video signal is distributed throughout a home's video system, the signal strength suffers loss as it passes through splitters, combiners, and connectors. As a result, the signal strength that reaches the display device may not be sufficient to provide a quality picture or sound, especially on systems where the video signal is being distributed to multiple displays.

 NOTE Video signal strength is measured in decibels (dB), and most televisions operate on a signal between 0 dB and 12 dB, although most will operate with −4 dB to 15 dB.

To maximize signal strength, focus the antenna or satellite by using either a compass to point it in the appropriate direction of the broadcast source or the signal strength indicator that is sometimes built into the receiver. If you are not sure of the provider's transmission location, give them a telephone call.

For a strong enough signal where no amplifier is required, you must have 0 dB signal off of an off-air antenna (ultra high frequency, or UHF, and very high frequency, or VHF). The digital satellite signal (DSS) level should be between −55 dB and −35 dB.

Always use 75-ohm resistor terminators at any unused jack to prevent signals from traveling back up the line and causing ghosts. If direct current (DC) power or infrared (IR) signals are being sent over coaxial cable, use a DC blocking capacitor.

There are several places on a video line where signal loss can occur, but the most significant locations are

- **Connectors**   Signal is lost wherever a connection is made. This is where most signal strength is lost in a typical residence.

- **Wiring**   Signal is lost as it travels through the coaxial cable. This loss is dependent on the length of the wire (the average is 3 dB to 6 dB of signal loss per 100 feet), the type of wire, and the frequency of the signal being carried. Losses are greater at higher frequencies; the greatest loss occurs at channel 13 in a VHF system or channel 83 in a UHF/VHF system.

- **Splitters**   Line splitters split the signal into two, three, four, or eight separate lines. Splitters divide the input signal equally, providing the same amount of signal at each output of the splitter. When a splitter is inserted in the line, the signal in each branch leg will be less. The quality of the splitter used does have an impact on the amount of loss incurred with the splitter. The losses that occur with average quality splitters are

  - **Two-way splitter**   3.5 to 4 dB loss

  - **Three-way splitter**   3.5 dB loss

  - **Four-way splitter**   6.5 to 8 dB loss

  - **Eight-way splitter**   10 to 12 dB loss

The signal sent to each branch of the system is equal to the signal sent into the splitter minus the loss induced by the splitter. For example, an input of 30 dB into a three-way splitter delivers a signal of 26.5 dB to each branch of the system (30 dB minus a 3.5 dB loss).

Figure 13-3 illustrates this phenomenon. As illustrated, the incoming video line signal has signal strength of 15 dBmV (decibels per millivolt on a 75-ohm line). Each splitter or combiner device through which the signal passes causes signal loss in varying amounts (see Table 13-2). In Figure 13-3, an 8-way splitter causes a loss

Figure 13-3

Signal loss on a video distribution system

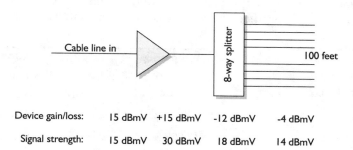

| Device gain/loss: | 15 dBmV | +15 dBmV | -12 dBmV | -4 dBmV |
| Signal strength: | 15 dBmV | 30 dBmV | 18 dBmV | 14 dBmV |

Table 13-2	Device	General Signal Loss
General Signal	2-way splitter/combiner	−4.0 dBmV
Loss of Video	3-way splitter/combiner	−6.5 dBmV
Distribution	4-way splitter/combiner	−8.0 dBmV
Devices	8-way splitter/combiner	−12.0 dBmV
	100 feet RG6 cable	−4.0 dBmV

of −12 dBmV, reducing the signal to only 3 dBmV. A cable run of 100 feet introduces additional loss of −4 dBmV, leaving the cable with a negative gain or virtually no signal strength.

Signal loss can also be caused by the length of the cable over which it is transmitted. Table 13-3 lists the common signal loss (measured in decibels per each 100 feet of cable length) on the two standard coaxial cable types used in residential video systems.

Amplification

To overcome the loss of signal on the distributed video line, an amplifier should be added to the system. The purpose of the amplifier is to add sufficient gain to the signal to compensate for the signal loss on the line. Amplifiers also stop signals from radiating outside the house. To properly size an amplifier, the amount of loss accumulated on the distributed line must be added up (per the specifications of each device).

When choosing an amplifier, the four main considerations are the frequencies and number of channels to be received; the total distribution system losses (the losses caused by cable, splitters, and connectors); available input signals (the signal levels fed to the distribution amplifier input); and the output capability of the distribution amplifier (the maximum signal the amplifier can deliver without overloading). An amplifier has three primary inputs and outputs:

- **Input level** The video signal coming in
- **Gain** The amplification of the video signal
- **Output level** The video signal going out

Remember that the amplification of the input signal plus any gain added to the signal equals the signal strength of the output signal. The "input plus gain" of a signal needs to be greater than the total loss the signal suffers on the distribution system.

Table 13-3	Frequency	RG59	RG6
Maximum	55 MHz	2.06 dB	1.60 dB
Attenuation	270 MHz	4.47 dB	3.50 dB
(dB Loss Per	400 MHz	5.48 dB	4.30 dB
100 Feet) for	750 MHz	7.62 dB	6 dB
Coaxial Cabling	1 GHz	8.87 dB	7 dB

However, the output level of the signal can never be greater than the output capability of the amplifier. Some amplifiers have a variable gain adjustment, which can be very useful in some applications. An attenuator/tilt compensator may need to be added to decrease the amplification of the lower frequency signals that are amplified much easier than the higher frequencies. Also, the FCC limits a signal to no more than 15.5 dBmV at any outlet.

In most installations, an isolation amplifier can be used to provide enough gain to compensate for the loss suffered by signals as they travel through the cabling and devices of a distributed audio system. As illustrated in Figure 13-4, an isolation amplifier (labeled "AMP") is installed on the primary antenna or cable input line. This amplifier increases the gain on the line sufficiently high enough to withstand the loss introduced by the devices between it and the terminal device. However, an isolation amplifier is rarely needed, though in situations where the incoming signal is too weak to withstand passes through the distribution devices without additional amplification, it is an easy solution to the problem.

Another approach, and a more common solution, is the inclusion of a main system amplifier in the video distribution system. An amplifier with a variable output level (gain) is best, but a fixed output amplifier can be used if it is able to provide sufficient gain to offset any loss in incoming signals. The amount of gain required from an amplifier is calculated by adding up the signal loss on the input side (before the amplifier) to the loss on the output side (after the amplifier).

An amplifier only converts an incoming signal, regardless of its source, into a signal that has increased amplitude, or signal strength, to ensure delivery and quality playback on any connected devices. Most common amplifiers have the capability to increase the gain (volume) potential of a signal from 0 MHz to 400 MHz, with somewhere around 100 MHz as typical.

Gain refers to the percentage of signal strength or performance when the input signal is compared to an amplifier's output signal. There are actually two types of gain associated with video systems. The first is the amplification of the audio signal that accompanies a video signal, which increases the volume potential for the playback. The second type of video gain refers to how much light (projected image) is reflected by a projection screen. As a screen is able to reflect more light, it produces a better quality image.

Figure 13-4

An amplifier is added to the video circuit to overcome signal loss.

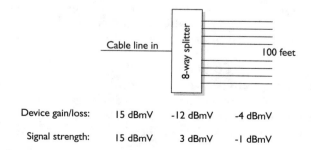

Device gain/loss: 15 dBmV   -12 dBmV   -4 dBmV

Signal strength: 15 dBmV   3 dBmV   -1 dBmV

Receivers

Many systems combine the functions of an amplifier and a receiver, but these two devices perform completely separate functions. Most video receivers have an amplifier built-in. Very high-end systems may choose to use a separate amplifier, claiming that the receiver's circuitry can add noise in the form of a buzzing sound to the audio. However, this is true only on the very low-end units. Good quality receivers, not necessarily the most expensive ones, don't have this problem.

A receiver is an AV device that receives signals that are broadcast through the air and converts them to a form for viewing or listening presentation. There are receivers designed to receive and convert radio, satellite, cable, or microwave transmissions. A video receiver in its most common form is an ordinary television set and includes a complete AV system with a receiver, an amplifier, speakers, a display screen, an antenna, a tuning control, and volume controls.

An AV receiver is essentially an audio device that is included in a system to receive, convert, and coordinate the audio part of video playback. However, it should include support for all of the audio and video inputs that are planned to be used (and then some) and have the capability to pass video signals directly to a video display device.

Signal Converters

In order to use a source video signal that may be analog or digital with a distribution device that uses a different signal format, a signal conversion device may be necessary in a video distribution system. A variety of signal converters are available that either convert a specific signal format to another or include the circuitry to convert multiple input signal formats to a variety of output signal formats.

The primary signal conversion devices available are

- Analog to digital converters
- Digital to analog converters
- Specialized video converters

Analog to Digital Video Converters

An analog to digital converter (ADC) converts a continuous analog signal into a digital binary sequence. This action involves sampling the analog voltage and representing it as a digital numeric value.

The ADC devices most commonly used with video signal conversion are direct conversion (flash ADC) devices. Direct conversion devices are fast, but can limit output resolution to only an 8-bit resolution scheme.

Digital to Analog Converters

Digital to analog conversion (DAC) devices tend to be more specialized because of the number of different digital formats that can be used to transmit a digital signal. Video signals from a computer, DVD player, or PVR (personal video recorder) must be converted to analog signals so they can be displayed on an analog television or monitor.

As digital-format flat screen televisions and Digital Visual Interface (DVI) and High-Definition Multimedia Interface (HDMI) devices become more popular, the need for DAC devices should lessen. However, depending on the equipment the homeowner wishes to use in her or his distributed video system, a DAC may be needed. Many of the modern source devices, such as CD, DVD, and PVR players, have built-in DAC components that convert the source digital signal into a line-level analog signal that can be fed into the video distribution system.

Specialized Video Converters

One specialized type of video conversion used in home technology systems is a video over IP (VIP) device. A VIP device converts and compresses an analog video signal into a digital format and then inserts it into a series of IP frames or wrappers for transmission over an Ethernet network. If the transmitted IP frames are to be displayed on an analog video device, a receiver VIP unit is used to reconvert and decompress the signal into an analog format. Because the transmitting VIP converts the video into network-transmittable frames, the video signals can be transmitted over both a local area network as well as across the Internet.

Video signals can also be transmitted over a wireless network. Several manufacturers now have available a variety of video signal transcoders that have the capability to transmit video over 802.11 wireless networks. For example, the Matrix II system from ViXS Systems is capable of transmitting video at 40 Mbps over a range of 100 feet.

Systems are also available to convert either to or from analog or digital video and common computer interfaces, such as USB, IEEE 1394, and serial connections. For the most part, these products involve a hardware interface and the use of specialized software.

Satellite Video Systems

In addition to cable and over-the-air broadcasting, a third source system for television reception is direct broadcast satellite (DBS) services. These services transmit audio/video streams using direct video broadcasting satellite (DVB-S2) format that is able to transmit one or more MPEG-2 streams.

Most pay-to-view, or subscription service DBSes, require the use of a conditional access module (CAM), which is in effect a smart card in the main receiver unit. The CAM provides the key to decrypt the encrypted transmission stream that ensures that only paying customers are able to view the received signals.

Besides the disk itself and the proprietary receiver unit of a home-based DBS system, there are three devices in the satellite system you should know about:

- Low-noise block (LNB) converter
- Diplexer
- Multiswitch

Low-Noise Block Converter

One or more low-noise block (LNB) converters are installed on the satellite dish as either a single or dual LNB unit (see Figure 13-5). Because microwave satellite signals are transmitted on fairly high frequencies, they don't typically pass through the walls,

Figure 13-5
A satellite disk with a dual LNB unit

roof, or windows of a house. And since satellite receivers must be outdoors, the received signal must be converted for transmission over a cable. An LNB converts and amplifies the high frequency band received to an intermediate frequency (IF) and transmits it over a coaxial cable to the satellite receiver unit.

Diplexer

A diplexer combines two received signals (TV and FM-stereo) in a piggy-back fashion for transmission over a single coaxial cable (typically an RG6 cable is required). At the receiver unit, a second diplexer separates the two signals, sending one to the television receiver and the other to an integrated receiver/decoder (IRD) in the satellite receiver unit or set-top box.

Multiswitch

In installations where dual LNBs are installed on the satellite dish or antenna, a multi-switch is used to direct the reception of the LNB units. Typically, the multiswitch directs one of the LNB units to receive signals from even numbered satellite transponders and the other LNB to lock onto odd numbered transponders. When the viewed channel is changed on the receiving unit, the multiswitch determines which of the LNB units it needs to access to receive the requested signal stream.

For example, in the U.S. there are 32 transponders numbered 1 to 32. Each of the transponders transmits a unique set of channels and, because an LNB can only see either even or odd-numbered transponders at one time, the purpose of the multiswitch is to access the LNB corresponding to the requested signal and transmit it to the receiving unit. In a satellite system with only a single LNB, the LNB must switch from even to odd transponders, depending on the channel requested.

Video Signal Formats

There are a variety of video signal formats in use in video distribution systems as well as on computers. Video signals are either optical or electronic. Optical signals originate from a camera or a scanner, and electronic signals originate from a computer's graphics card. Regardless of how a video signal originates, it is made up of electric impulses that represent the intensity of each of three primary colors—red, green, and blue (RGB)—and the vertical and horizontal synchronization of each picture frame. The primary video signal formats are RGB, component, S-Video, and composite.

The RGB encoding tells the display mechanism at the receiving end how to re-create each picture element (pixel) of the original image. It is assumed that the final image has red, green, or blue colors in it. The video signal indicates how much, or the intensity, of each color used in each pixel. The intensity of each of these three colors, when combined by the human eye, determines the final color displayed.

If you look at the display of your television set, assuming it has a cathode ray tube (CRT) (more on this later in the section "Video Screen Formats"), using a magnifying glass, you should see either a dot pattern or a pattern of lines. In either of these display methods, an electron beam is used to energize colored phosphor, which coats the glass on the face of the CRT's tube either in patterns of dots or stripes.

Processing Video Signals

Regardless of the method used to create the display on the CRT, how the signal is processed, stored, or transmitted can have more to do with the quality of the displayed picture than the capability of the display device itself.

Table 13-4 lists the most common of the video signal formats in use.

 NOTE You may have noticed that plain red/green/blue (RGB) is not listed in Table 13-4. RGB is not a video standard. It is a standard for computer monitors.

Signal Format	Description
RGBHV	RGB with horizontal and vertical sync.
RGBS (RGB)	RGB with composite sync.
RGsB (SoG)	Aka Sync on Green, RGB with a sync signal sent on the green single, like composite video.
YCrCb	Component video, a black and white composite video signal that includes luminance (Y) brightness information and composite sync, and two signals that carry matrixed color information (chrominance) for red and blue (Cr and Cb) that can be removed from the Y signal to yield the green information.
S-Video (Y-C)	Black and white composite video that contains Y brightness and composite sync information. The composite C (chrominance) contains all of the color information. S-Video is also referred to as SVHS.
Composite video	The one composite video signal contains all of the information on brightness, color, and synchronization.
TV/CATV	Composite video and audio modulated to allow multiple signals to share a common transmission medium, such as terrestrial aerial, cable TV, or satellite.

Table 13-4 Video Signal Formats

To combine the color information and the brightness and synchronization (timing) information, both must be coded. There are three primary coding schemes, also referred to as broadcast standards, in use:

- **National Television System Committee (NTSC)**   The NTSC developed the first color television coding system in 1953. It uses a fixed resolution of 525 horizontal lines and a variable number of vertical lines, depending on the electronics or format in use. NTSC displays 30 frames per second. NTSC is also a type of television signal that can be recorded by various tape recording formats, including VHS, 3/4-inch, and U-matic.

- **Phase Alternation by Line (PAL)**   This European improvement over NTSC was released in 1967. PAL uses 625 horizontal lines, which also make up its vertical resolution. It produces a more consistent tint, but at 25 frames per second.

- **Systeme Electronique Couleur Avec Memoire (SECAM)**   This encoding method was introduced in France in 1967 and, like PAL, uses 625 lines of resolution and displays 25 frames per second.

These three-color encoding standards are incompatible with one another. However, most modern television sets are multistandard and can decode a video signal encoded with any of these schemes. Table 13-5 provides a sampling of the countries using these three-color standards.

The most common of the video signal formats in use is S-Video. Virtually all AV amplifiers support S-Video, but only a few include higher-level formats such as component or RGBHV. If higher-level signal formats are all that is available, the signal can be converted to a lower-level signal for one or more devices. For example, an incoming RGB signal can be converted to S-Video for distribution throughout a home.

Table 13-5

Video Color Encoding Methods used in Countries Around the World

Country	Encoding Standard
Canada	NTSC
Chile	NTSC
China	PAL
Egypt	SECAM
France	SECAM
Japan	NTSC
Mexico	NTSC
Russia	SECAM
United Kingdom	PAL
USA	NTSC

Remember that there is no advantage or picture quality improvements gained by converting a signal to a higher-level format such as S-Video to RGB.

Television Video Formats

When the primary video types and broadcast standards are applied to the primary television formats, a variety of speeds, resolutions, and tape and disc record times result. Table 13-6 lists the various television, tape, and disc formats available.

Common Video Signals

For a home theater installation, the video receiver should support the three primary video signal formats: component video, S-Video, and composite video. However, it is not common for an audio receiver to include jacks for all three input types. Sometimes there is a problem in that a receiver that does support these three signals may not include support for HDTV or progressive scan digital versatile disc or digital video disc (DVD) signals.

HDTV and Digital TV   HDTV is one of the digital television standards defined by the ATSC. Digital TV (DTV) transmits using binary data (using positive and negative electrical impulses to represent ones and zeros, just like a computer uses) to encode its images and audio. Standard analog TV signals use waveforms, frequencies, and amplitudes to transmit images and audio. In addition to the actual images and audio, the digital data of the DTV signal includes information that defines the resolution, aspect ratio, refresh rate (how often the image is scanned), and the type of scanning in use (interface versus progressive).

Format	Broadcast Standard	Max Time (Minutes)	Media
VHS	NTSC	480	T-160
	PAL	600	E-300
	SECAM	600	E-300
SuperVHS	NTSC	480	ST-160
	PAL	480	SE-240
Digital VHS (D-VHS) and Digital Video Computing (DVC)	NTSC	60	MiniDV cassette
	PAL	180	DVC
Video 8	NTSC	240	P6-120
	PAL	180	P5-90
Hi-8	SECAM	180	P5-90
	NTSC	240	P6-120ME
	PAL	180	P5-90ME
LaserDisc	NTSC	60	Constant Linear Velocity (CLV)
	PAL	72	CLV
DVD	NTSC	Varies	Dual Layer (8.6 GB)

Table 13-6   Common Video Formats

HDTV can be delivered to a home using one of the following four methods:

- **Broadcast digital satellite**   Companies like the DISH Network and DIRECTV offer HDTV to customers that have upgraded their satellite dishes and receivers for DTV signals. The satellite dish needs to be a dual low noise block feedhorn (LNBF) to receive both HDTV and standard programming. Remember that standard digital satellite signals are not necessarily the same as DTV.

- **Over the air (OTA) broadcasting**   A DTV antenna and a DTV receiver are required to receive OTA broadcast DTV signals. OTA DTV uses 8-VSB (vestigial sideband), modulation.

- **Recorded media**   HDTV programming that can be recorded on Digital VHS videotapes, DVDs, or high-definition PVRs. Playing back DTV from either a VHS or DVD source device may require replacing or upgrading the device.

- **Terrestrial cable**   Cable television companies now offer HDTV channels that typically require a quadrature amplitude modulation (QAM) set-top box to decode the DTV signals. QAM is the modulation method used to transmit DTV signals over a cable.

Video Bandwidth   When choosing a video receiver, it is very important to consider its bandwidth (MHz). Table 13-7 lists the bandwidth required by the common home video system components.

Audio and Video Standards

Up to now, this book has discussed the separate and distinct standards that have been brought together to create a home AV system. Largely, a home AV system that meets or exceeds a customer's requirements is the result of the designer and the installer acting together as system integrators.

Home AV Interoperability (HAVi)

Several leading consumer electronics and computer manufacturers are seeing the potential of integrating a variety of technologies in the home and as a result have developed the Home Audio/Visual Interoperability (HAVi) standard. The HAVi standard

Table 13-7	Device	Bandwidth Required
Bandwidth Requirements of Video System Devices	Standard DVD	7 MHz
	Progressive scan DVD	14 MHz
	Progressive scan to 4:3 compression devices	18 MHz
	720p HDTV	22 MHz or 37 MHz
	1080i HDTV	37 MHz

Video Modes

There are a lot of numbers being tossed around when HDTV video modes are discussed, especially 1080i, 1080p, and, to a lesser extent, 720p. The numbers (1080 and 720) refer to the number of vertical lines of resolution each video mode produces, and the letters ("i" and "p") refer to interlaced and progressive, respectively. Currently, HDTV uses 1080i, which has an aspect ratio of 16:9 and horizontal resolution of 1920 pixels.

What differentiates 1080i, as it's used in various countries, is the frame rate. Two frame rates are commonly used, 25 Hz and 30 Hz. The frame rate is designated as a suffix after the "i," such as 1080i25 or 1080i30. Those countries that use PAL or SECAM signal encoding (see Table 13-5) use 1080i25, and those using NTSC, like the U.S., Canada, and Japan, use 1080i30.

In the future, it's likely 1080p50 or 1080p60 will become the broadcasting standard for HDTV in most countries.

defines how home entertainment and communication devices interface and interact, including home PCs and single controller devices, such as TV sets, home appliances, radios, stereos, and more.

The primary difference between the HAVi standard and the general networking and interoperability guidelines now used is that HAVi uses the IEEE 1394 (FireWire or i.Link) standard as its interconnecting medium. Another big difference is that a HAVi network doesn't require a computer to interact.

For example, consider a home where the TV and telephone system have been integrated using a HAVi 1394 connection. When the telephone rings, the TV is programmed to automatically mute itself and switch to pick up the incoming video-telephone signal. Or, on another occasion, when a television show uses a word you don't recognize, you speak the word into a nearby microphone, which feeds the sound to an Internet browser-based audio to text dictionary lookup program that searches for the word and displays its meaning in the corner of the TV screen. You may even rig up the TV to serve first as a monitor to display the image captured by a security camera and then as a communication device between you and someone at the front door. At least these examples are within the goals of the HAVi initiative. The HAVi standard promises brand independence and interoperability, hot Plug-and-Play, and the ability to use some legacy devices that can be easily upgraded as required.

The HAVi specification is made up of a set of application programming interfaces (APIs) and interface software ("middleware") that can automatically detect entering or leaving devices on the network, manage their networking functions, and ensure their interoperability.

HAVi relies on other home networking standards, such as Jini and Universal Plug and Play (UPnP), for its platform neutrality.

Jini

Unlike many Internet standards or products, the letters in the name Jini don't stand for anything. Jini is not an acronym; it is derived from the Arabic word for magician and pronounced "DJEE-nee."

Jini was developed by Sun Microsystems as an architecture to help users create what Sun calls "spontaneous networking." It enables peripheral devices, such as printers, storage devices, speakers, and even computers, to be added to a network and become instantly available to everyone on the network. When a device is added to a network, every user is notified of its availability.

Jini is an extension of the Java programming language and is intended to provide the extension that allows a network to appear as one large computer, in application. Where HAVi has a consumer electronics focus, Jini is not limited to only consumer electronics and extends to the computer and digital worlds, as well.

Versatile Home Network (VHN)

The Video Electronics Standards Association (VESA) establishes and supports industry-wide interface standards for personal computers, workstations, and other computing environments with an emphasis on interoperability and the display of information. In the late 1990s, VESA began working on a standard for home AV device interoperability, which they called the VESA Home Network (VHN) standard. VESA later combined with the Consumer Electronics Association (CEA) and renamed the standard the Versatile Home Network (VHN).

The VHN standard also uses IEEE 1394 as its backbone architecture on Cat 5 UTP cabling. Actually, it specifies the IEEE 1394b standard, a longer distance version of IEEE 1394. VHN uses the networking concept of IP subnetting to create its "zones." Because it uses the standard Internet Protocol (IP) technologies, non-IEEE 1394 devices can be used to create subnets for other home automation technologies, such as X10, CEBus, and others. Another benefit of an IP-based network is that it interfaces to the Internet very easily.

The idea behind the VHN standard is that the creation of a home network will become even more of a Plug and Play affair than it already is. Figure 13-6 illustrates the concept of a VHN.

Universal Plug and Play (UPnP)

The underlying standard for most home networking architectures, including HAVi and VHN, is UPnP, a Microsoft tool that provides discovery functions to dynamic network environments, like those we've been discussing. UPnP uses a series of IP-compatible protocols to provide services that discover and configure new devices added or removed from a network.

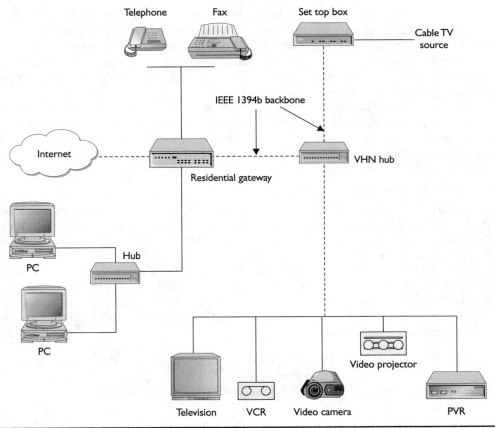

Figure 13-6 An example of a VHN that integrates both IEEE 1394b and IP networking

Internet Media

More and more the Internet is becoming a source of digital media. In the recent past, we've seen the tussles of Napster and KaZaA with the recording industry and copyright issues. However, with the emergence of pay-per-download sites, such as Apple's iTunes.com (www.apple.com/music/store) and BuyMusic.com (www.buymusic.com), and free-to-listen sites, such as Lycos Rhapsody (http://music.lycos.com/rhapsody) and Yahoo! Launch (launch.yahoo.com), you can download and enjoy music and video without risking heavy fines, being hauled into court, or going to jail.

On some "jukebox" sites, you can create a playlist and listen to your favorite music via a streaming audio feed in much the same way you would listen to the radio, which is something else you can do online. The Internet is a very broad range receiver and allows you to listen to radio stations around the globe or those created especially for the Internet.

The number of video sources on the Internet is also growing. Sites such as MovieFlix (www.movieflix.com) and InternetMovies (www.internetmovies.com) allow you to open a streaming download of a movie and watch it on your desktop. Of course, the problem with watching a streaming download is that you can't save it to disk. If you want to watch the movie again or stop it and finish watching it later, you'll have to pay and download the movie again.

This problem is being solved by websites such as MovieLink (www.movielink .com) that will sell or rent a (24-hour) license for a movie and allow you to download and store it on your computer for later viewing. It can't be that long before you'll be able to direct the stream to your PVR.

Streaming Media Types

To play back an A/V file back in 1995, before streaming technologies had come along, the entire file had to be downloaded and stored before the playback could begin. At the data transfer speeds available at that time, a ten-minute video clip could take anywhere from two minutes to two hours to download.

With the advent of streaming media technologies, the content in an AV file can begin its playback as it is being downloaded and before the entire file is downloaded. Of course, heavy traffic on the Internet or an interruption in the connection can cause the sound or picture to break up or hesitate, but that's the price we pay for convenience.

There are two types of media streaming:

- **True streaming**   This is the type of streaming just described. Playback of the AV content begins after only a portion of the file is received, and it is continuous while the remainder of the file is received. True streaming is commonly used for longer AV files.

- **Progressive streaming**   Before the playback of a file begins, a significant portion of its contents must be received. This streaming method is common for short media pieces of 15 seconds or less and allows users to save the file to their hard drives for later viewing.

If you were to download a movie file from a pay-per-view site on the Internet, most likely the movie would be streamed to you using true streaming. However, if you were renting the movie for a period of time, the file would be streamed to you progressively so you could save it to disk.

Streaming media can include virtually any AV content that can be recorded, including text, recorded video or audio, still images, and live radio or television broadcasts. All of these media types can be consolidated into a single streaming file, provided the originator and the receiver each have the sufficient bandwidth to support it.

There are three major proprietary and distinct streaming technologies in use on the Internet: RealNetworks (RealMedia), Apple QuickTime, and Windows Media Player. At one time, to play back a file created for a particular media player, you needed to use that specific player. This is not the case anymore; for the most part, these players now play back a wide range of audio and video formats.

Streaming Media File Formats

The most common streaming media file formats in use on the Internet are those that match up with the three most common streaming media players:

- **RealMedia** The two primary file types used are RAM and RPM.
  - RA RealAudio clip
  - RAM   RealMedia file
  - RM   RealVideo and RealFlash clips
  - RPM   RealMedia plug-in file
- **QuickTime**
  - MOV   QuickTime movie file
  - QT, QTL, and QTM   QuickTime AV files
  - QTV and QTVR   QuickTime virtual reality movie files
- **Windows Media**
  - ASF   Windows Media Advanced Streaming Format file
  - AVI   Windows Media AV Interleaved file
  - WMA   Windows Media audio file
  - WMV   Windows Media AV file
  - WMX   Windows Media playlist file

There are a few other open standard media file formats in use, with likely more to come, but for now the more popular ones are

- **MPEG-2**   This media type is used commonly in digital TV, interactive graphics, and interactive multimedia. Don't confuse MP3 files with MPEG-2. MP3 files are actually MPEG-2 Layer 3 files.
- **MPEG-7**   This is an emerging standard that will allow users to search for audio and video files by their content.
- **Multipurpose Internet Mail Extension (MIME)**   There are several MIME file types, but only two AV file types: audio and video.

Digital Rights Management

Digital rights management (DRM) is a group of technologies that attempts to protect digital media from being copied, converted, or in some cases accessed by end users, by the media producers, such as Apple, Microsoft, and Sony. DRM doesn't include access technologies, such as passwords or keys, and may not be applied to all of the contents of a digital media. DRM is common on software release, movie, and some audio DVDs and CD-ROMs and can prevent a DVD or CD from begin capability with some playback devices.

DRM technology is also used with downloadable music and video from the Internet. A downloaded file that contains a DRM may be able to be played only with certain playback software or may have the number of views or plays restricted. For example, any audio content downloaded from the WalMart.com music store can only be played by software that is compatible with Microsoft's PlaysForSure system. Music or video downloaded from the iTunes store (Apple) may carry DRM that restricts it to systems with the Apple FairPlay DRM.

Video Receivers, Televisions, and Monitors

If the customer wishes to configure and install a home theater or just merely connect her television set to the audio/video/computer-integrated network, there's more to it than just plugging the TV into the network.

Along with any decisions to be made about the wiring, speaker placement, seating arrangements, and the like, there are a number of video system issues that must be considered, including screen formats, amplifiers and receivers, sound formats, DVD or CD capabilities, and the display device itself. Once you have a clear understanding of the customer's vision, you can work through these issues to design and implement the customer's dream system.

Video Screen Formats

One of the primary considerations when choosing a video display device is aspect ratio. Occasionally when you watch a movie on television or a rented DVD or video, the image is centered vertically on the screen and the top and bottom portions of the screen are black boxes. The black areas are called letterboxes and are the result of a video signal that is set for a different aspect ratio than your television or monitor supports. In this case, the video is playing back in widescreen and not full screen.

Distributed Video Terminology

The following list includes the more important video system terms you should know when specifying, selecting, and interfacing with video systems:

- **Interface scan**   A display format where the displayed image is separated into two passes: the first pass scans the odd-numbered horizontal lines (1, 3, 5, and so on) and the second pass scans the even-numbered lines.

- **Progressive scan**   A display format that displays each horizontal lines of an image in a single pass at typically 24, 30, or 60 frames per second (fps).

- **National Television Standards Committee (NTSC)**   The signal format used to broadcast standard (non-HDTV) television.

- **Standard Definition Television (SDTV)**   The standard interlace scan TV display using 460 by 480 pixels. Also referred to as 480i.

- **Advanced Television Standards Committee (ATSC)**   The signal format used to broadcast HDTV.

- **Enhanced Definition Television (EDTV)**   A progressive scan format that supports 460 by 480 pixels (standard TV) and 720 by 480 pixels (widescreen). Also referred to as 480p (480 vertical lines using progressive scan) and 720p.

- **High Definition Television (HDTV)**   A display format that supports either 1280 by 720 pixels for progressive scan or 1920 by 1080 pixels for interlace scan. Also referred to as 1080i and 8-level Vestigial Sideband (8-VSB), which is the radio frequency broadcasting format used for HDTV.

- **Advanced Television Standards Committee (ATSC)**   The signal format used to broadcast HDTV.

Aspect Ratio

The aspect ratio of any display device, including televisions and monitors, states the number of picture elements (pixels) used horizontally and vertically to form the displayed image. For example, most display devices are set for an aspect ratio of 4:3, or four to three. This means that for every four horizontal pixels used in the display, three vertical pixels are used. Another way to think about this is that the image is displayed about 1.33 times wider than it is tall. Widescreen video is set for a 16:9 aspect ratio, which is why it doesn't always exactly fit on a home television screen. The 4:3 aspect ratio has the early standard for the movie industry.

When television became popular in the 1950s, it, too, adopted the 4:3 aspect ration ratio, so it could show movies in their standard form. To compete with television, the movie industry began creating different screen formats, especially those that provided a wider or larger image display, such as CinemaScope and Panavision. Today the recognized standards of the movie industry are 1.85:1, which is called Academy Flat, and 2.35:1, which is called Anamorphic Scope. These standards are often translated into a standard aspect ratio of 16:9, or 16 units of width for each 9 units of height.

Three methods are used to fit the motion picture's 16:9 aspect ratio onto the television's 4:3:

- **Letterbox**   When a 16:9 picture is fitted onto a 4:3 television frame, the result is black bars at the top and bottom of the displayed picture. This reduces the displayed image to what can be likened to a mail slot or a letterbox. This is a common effect from DVDs.

- **Pan and scan**   This method produces a full-screen display at the cost of picture quality. The image is created by panning and scanning left to right in order to fit the entire picture on the display. This method is common with VHS tapes and movies shown on broadcast television.

- **Movie compression**   This method forces the 16:9 image into the 4:3 display and produces images that are taller and thinner in appearance than intended.

Of course, the solution to the incompatibility between 16:9 and 4:3 is to display the image on a display device that can handle the widescreen aspect ratio of the movie.

Resolution

A display characteristic closely related to the aspect ratio is resolution that defines the number of pixels used to produce the displayed image. As more pixels are used to display an image, the image quality improves.

The resolution of the displayed image on a television or monitor can be the result of any one, two, or all of the following factors:

- **Transmission quality**   The extent to which the resolution of the original picture when it is broadcasted or stored (like on a DVD) is retained has a direct bearing on the resolution of the displayed image.

- **Recording quality**   The resolution used to capture live or art-based images can impact the resolution that can be produced by the display device during playback.

- **Displayed resolution**   The resolution that a display device is capable of producing is the final link in the picture quality of a displayed image.

Nearly all display devices produce an image by electrifying clusters of RGB dots. Just like the images in a black and white newspaper are made up of dots of black printed on a white background, where the number and separation of the dots causes the human eye and brain to form a picture using shades of black and gray, a television uses illuminated RGB dots that the human eye and brain can make into images.

Most conventional television sets and computer monitors use a picture tube that is a cathode ray tube (CRT). A CRT produces an image by illuminating color dots with an electron beam. The intensity used to illuminate a pixel and its proximity to other pixels causes the human eye to assign a color or shade to that area of the screen. It is the number of pixels horizontally and vertically used to create the displayed image that defines a display's resolution.

 NOTE   Although the CRT is used to explain the concepts of displaying an image, these characteristics also apply to other display types, including liquid crystal display (LCD) and plasma. Display types are discussed later in the section "Video Display Devices."

The CRT and virtually all other display types must refresh the display constantly to keep each pixel illuminated (the brightness of an illuminated pixel begins to fade almost immediately) and to accommodate changes in the image, like the motion in a motion picture. To refresh the screen, the electron gun sweeps (scans) the screen in a left to right, top to bottom pattern, sometimes in multiple zones of the screen simultaneously. Figure 13-7 illustrates a common scan pattern for a CRT display device.

The common resolutions for television, recorded, or broadcast images use 525 horizontal scan lines (top to bottom) on the display screen. The resolution of the display is stated as the number of pixels available on each horizontal scan line. The most common

Figure 13-7
The scan pattern used by a conventional CRT display

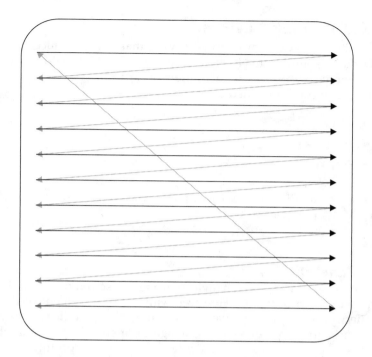

advertised horizontal resolutions for television sets are 240, 425, 500, with some even higher. The number of scan lines on the display establishes the vertical resolution for the display, typically 525 scan lines. So, for an average television set, the resolution could be 500 by 525, or 500 horizontal pixels and 525 vertical pixel rows (scan lines).

Of course, the size of the display and the size of each pixel has a direct bearing on the number of pixels that will fit on each horizontal line and the number of scan lines that can be fit onto the screen. The higher number of pixels, the better the display can deal with diagonal or circular lines.

It is important to note that a display doesn't use all of its scan lines in the NTSC standard—the standard used for broadcast television—to produce an image. There, pictures use only 480 of the 525 scan lines, and each line has only 440 pixels visible, to create a 480 by 440 picture grid.

Dot Pitch

Another factor of resolution is the dot pitch, or the proximity of the pixels (see Figure 13-8), on the display. This factor applies to virtually all displays, including rear projection units.

Figure 13-8
Dot pitch measures the space between pixels.

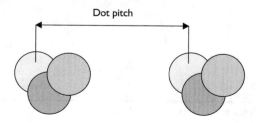

Dot pitch

Video Display Devices

Video display devices, or terminal devices that can reproduce video images and, typically, audio sound from either an amplified digital or analog signal, are available in a variety of types and sizes, with a variety of capabilities.

The most common video display device types are

- CRT
- Flat panel
- Projection

NOTE CRT displays, actually standard television sets, are discussed in the preceding section.

Flat Panel Displays

It wasn't that long ago that hanging a television screen on a wall like a piece of art was considered science fiction. However, with the development of flat panel technology, a variety of displays are available that can be hung on the wall or placed on a narrow table. It is no longer necessary to assign floor space solely to a television. Flat panel screens, like the one shown in Figure 13-9 can be set on furniture, hung on the wall, ceiling, or placed just about anywhere.

Flat panel display devices are currently available using two primary display technologies: advanced liquid crystal display (LCD) and plasma.

Photo courtesy of Sony Electronics, Inc.

Figure 13-9 A flat panel television display

LCD Displays LCD screens use positive and negative voltage to rotate the polarization of the crystals to either pass or block light through the crystal. The crystals form the pixels used to produce the displayed image. LCD televisions are backlit, and the crystals reflect and manipulate the light. LCD displays are available in sizes that range from 6 inches, measured diagonally, to 108 inches (and soon larger, I'm sure).

Plasma Displays Plasma displays have been in use for a number of years in point-of-sale monochrome displays and other similar uses. However, using a plasma display as a television monitor is a relatively new use of this technology.

The technology of a color plasma display is very similar to that used in a conventional CRT. The display consists of an array of RGB cells (pixels). An electrical current reacts with the cells that contain xenon and neon gas in a plasma state that is conductive to produce light in an RGB color. Unlike LCDs, plasma displays produce their own light source and are not backlit. Plasma screens are mostly used for screens sizes above 30 inches and currently are available up to more than 60 inches.

The advantages of a plasma television display are

- **Higher resolution** Compared to standard, and even some DTV sets, a plasma display uses 1024 by 1024 pixels to display its images.
- **Wide aspect ratio** Plasma displays have a 16:9 aspect ratio.
- **Flat screen** A CRT screen is curved and can distort an image along the side edges and in the corners. This is eliminated on a flat screen and the picture can also be viewed from wide angles as well.

Laser Displays A laser television display isn't actually a new type of television; it's a newly developed technology for producing images on a display screen. In place of a DLP, liquid crystals, or an electron gun, a laser beam is used to project images onto a screen. Because this technology is relatively new, it may not be available for purchase until late 2008.

Video Projection Systems

One of the options available for a home theater system, meaning beyond a standard television set or an LCD or plasma television, is a video projection system (see Figure 13-10). These devices project the images transmitted to them on a screen or virtually any flat surface.

The most common types of video projectors use one of two technologies:

- **Digital light processing (DLP)** A DLP projector directs light through a rotating RGB filter onto a digital micro-mirror device (DMD) chip that reflects the colored light out of the projector's lens and onto a screen. The DMD chip is covered with more than 900,000 micro-mirrors, each producing one pixel of the displayed image.
- **LCD technology** An LCD projector uses three LCD glass panels, one each for red, green, and blue, to project the image transmitted to the projector. The light that is passing through the color glass panels is controlled using LCD technology and the opening and closing of the liquid crystals.

Figure 13-10
A video projector can be used to project images onto a screen.

Photo courtesy of Fujitsu Siemens Computers.

DLP and LCD projectors are typically front or forward projectors, and both are commonly used as ceiling-mounted projection systems. The major difference between LCD and DLP projectors is color adjustment. Because an LCD project uses separate controls for RGB, its brightness, color, and contrast can be adjusted at the color channel level. This adjustment process can take quite a bit of time: four hours or so. An LCD projector typically produces a brighter display. On the other hand, the color settings on a DLP projector are essentially fixed in place and require minimal or no adjustment.

Personal Video Recorders (PVR)

For most downloaded AV files, once you have them stored on a computer hard drive, it is a simple matter of opening them to play them again. However, what about storing live television or radio for later playback? There are two ways to go: use a PVR or convert a personal computer (PC) into a digital video recording device.

In order to pass an AV file intact between one device and another, the AV content has to have been recorded in a digital format. This can take place on a computer, digital video camera, or a digital video recorder (DVR).

Adding a PVR device to a home network allows a homeowner to expand the capabilities of a traditional video system. Products are now available that incorporate live Internet streaming, video archiving, and format translation directly into the network (see Figure 13-11). In other words, having an integrated PVR function on the network is like having an AV studio with an IP address.

PVR devices can record up to 80 hours of television in digital format. PVRs can be standalone devices or they can be built into set-top devices, such as those included in a digital broadcast satellite (DBS) receiver.

Some other features of PVRs are

- **Sharing recorded programs** Shares recorded content of two PVRs room to room as a streaming file, a file transfer, or a unicast file transfer over the Internet.

- **Digital audio output** Connects the PVR sound output into a sound system.

- **Instant replay** Jumps back in seven-second intervals to replay a missed segment.

PART III

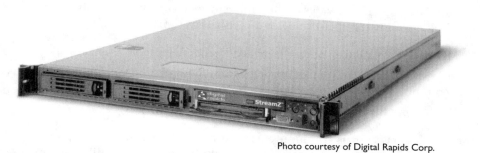

Photo courtesy of Digital Rapids Corp.

Figure 13-11 An IP-addressable PVR (DVR) can be added to a distributed video system.

PC-Based PVR

A home computer can also be used as a PVR by installing a PVR expansion card into the computer. Products like the one shown in Figure 13-12 enable a user to watch TV on a PC and to record from a cable or antenna television feed or stereo FM radio, as well as other digital video sources.

Media Servers

In the context of home automation, a media server refers to any network computer or network device that uses UPnP to recognize and connect to any consumer electronic (CE) device and supports any AV content produced by the CE device. In the UPnP world, devices like VCRs, CD players, DVD players, audiotape players, digital cameras, digital camcorders, radios, PVRs, televisions, set-top boxes, and, of course, a computer can all be a media server.

Figure 13-12
A PVR computer expansion card converts a PC into a video recorder.

A media server acts as a go-between to mitigate the various file formats used by the different AV devices and provides a compatible format to each device wishing to access media files. The functions performed by a media server include:

- Identifying the media content provided to clients on the home network
- Processing requests for media content from networked devices and negotiating a common transfer protocol and file format
- Controlling the transfer of media content to target devices

The term *media server* is commonly used in connection with Voice over IP (VoIP) functions, and in instances where a customer wishes to install VoIP functions on a home network, a media server function must be present on the network. VoIP media servers are normally created with the installation of the VoIP control software.

A multiroom audio video (MRAV) system is one that allows a variety of centrally located video (and audio) source devices to be distributed throughout a home under the control of a single system controller, which acts as the system media server. The use of an MRAV system allows any (and all) video sources to be made available throughout a home to any room so that two rooms can be watching the output of the same video source or choose to view different source streams.

Chapter Review

Video signals are broadcast in either an analog or a digital format. Analog signals are RF signals that are broadcasted through the air and received by a home TV antenna or transmitted over a cable system. Digital video signals are transmitted over a cable system.

Broadband coaxial cable is capable of transmitting 130 analog channels; baseband video cable is capable of carrying only a single video or an audio transmission. The video device used to convert baseband to broadband signals is a modulator.

In situations where a single RF video source is to be transmitted to more than one end device, a splitter is used. Another RF signal device used in a distributed video system is a combiner, which combines two (or more) incoming RF signals into a single broadband signal.

Splitters, combiners, and even connectors can impact the video signal's strength. An amplifier is used to compensate for the signal loss on the line. An isolation amplifier can be installed on the incoming line to provide sufficiently high enough gain. A main system amplifier with a variable output level may also be used. An amplifier increases the gain of the incoming signal.

A receiver is an AV device that receives broadcasted signals and converts them for viewing or listening. The most common video receiver is a television set.

There are a variety of video signal formats in use in video distribution systems as well as on computers. The primary video signal formats are RGB, component, S-Video, and composite. The three primary coding schemes or broadcast standards are NTSC, PAL, and SECAM. The most common video signal format is S-Video, which is supported by virtually all AV amplifiers.

HDTV is one of the digital television standards defined by the ATSC. Digital TV transmits using binary data (using positive and negative electrical impulses to represent ones and zeros, just like a computer uses) to encode its images and audio. HDTV can be delivered to a home using one of the following four methods: broadcast digital satellite, over the air broadcasting, recorded media, and terrestrial cable.

Several new AV standards are emerging, including HAVi, IEEE 1394, Jini, VHN, and UPnP. In addition, Internet-ready devices can support two types of media streaming: true streaming and progressive streaming. The primary streaming media formats are RealMedia, QuickTime, and Windows Media. Other open standard file formats also used for Internet media are MPEG-2, MPEG-7, and MIME.

The primary considerations when choosing a video display device are aspect ratio, resolution, and dot pitch. Different methods are used to display incompatible aspect ratios: letterbox, pan and scan, and movie compression. Resolution is the number of pixels used to produce a displayed image and is the result of three factors: transmission quality, recording quality, and display resolution. Dot pitch is the proximity of the pixels on a display. The most common video display device types are CRT, flat panel, and projection.

Storing live television or radio for later playback can be accomplished using a PVR. A media server refers to any networked computer that connects to any consumer electronic device.

Questions

1. Which of the following standards makes a network appear to be a single computer?

   A. VHN

   B. HAVi

   C. Jini

   D. UPnP

2. What is the backbone architecture used with the VHN standard?

   A. IEEE 1284

   B. IEEE 802.3

   C. IEEE 1394b

   D. IEEE 802.15

3. What is the underlying discovery function in HAVi and VHN?

   A. UPnP

   B. IEEE 1394

   C. True streaming

   D. IP

PART III

4. What type of file is an AV file where playback can begin prior to the entire file being received?

   A. Digital

   B. Streaming

   C. Analog

   D. Progressive

5. What differentiates a progressive streaming file from a true streaming file?

   A. A significant portion of the file must be received before playback begins.

   B. Only a small portion of the file must be received before playback begins.

   C. All of the file must be received before playback can begin.

   D. There is no substantial difference between a progressive and a true streaming file.

6. Which two of the following are technologies used with flat panel displays?

   A. CRT

   B. DLT

   C. Plasma

   D. LCD

7. Which of the following aspect ratios produces the widest displayed image?

   A. 4:3

   B. 1.33:1

   C. 16:9

   D. The aspect ratio doesn't affect the width of the display.

8. What video display characteristic most affects the clarity of the displayed image?

   A. Aspect ratio

   B. RGB

   C. Resolution

   D. Refresh rate

9. What is the common name for a device that records from a digital television feed preset by a user?

   A. Digital object recorder

   B. Video cassette recorder

   C. Personal video recorder

   D. Personal object recorder

10. What is the device or service that coordinates and supports the AV content produced by UPnP CE devices on a home network?

    A. VoIP server

    B. Media server

    C. Media client

    D. UPnP server

Answers

1. **C.** This Sun Microsystems protocol creates seamlessness for the network for all devices. VHN and HAVi are home AV network standards, and UPnP is a device discovery and configuration protocol commonly used with CE.

2. **C.** Remember that the "b" version of IEEE 1394 is a faster, more robust version. The other choices are printer and Ethernet networking standards.

3. **A.** UPnP is commonly used in most home AV standards.

4. **B.** Of course it may be digital, but that has nothing to do with its playback format. It could be progressive, but it must first be streaming. Analog files aren't streamed.

5. **A.** As opposed to a streaming video file, more of a progressive streaming file must be buffered (received) before its playback can begin.

6. **C, D.** CRT is the picture tube in a conventional television and DLP is the technology used in one type of a projection television.

7. **C.** The standard aspect ratio for widescreen displays is 16.9; 4:3 and 1.33:1 are equivalent aspect ratios. Choice D is absolutely false.

8. **C.** The higher the resolution capability on a display, the better the picture quality is likely to be, subject to the resolution of the original image. None of the other choices have much to do with the clarity of the displayed image.

9. **C.** PVRs are also called digital video recorders (DVRs).

10. **B.** A media server is also a central component of a VoIP network.

CHAPTER 14

Designing and Installing Distributed Video Systems

In this chapter, you will learn about
- Designing and planning a distributed video system
- Installing a distributed video system
- Configuring and connecting the components of a distributed video system

A distributed video system is a network of video source and display devices that are interconnected through a house's structured wiring and a centralized service panel or facility. What a distributed video system can do is allow the output signals produced by a DVD, video cassette recorder (VCR), personal video recorder (PVR), satellite or cable TV, or any other video playback device to be viewed in any room of the house that is connected to the system. No longer will each room need its own VCR, DVD, or receiver in order for multiple viewers in multiple rooms to view the same programs.

Often, a key element of a complete distributed home video system is one or more security surveillance cameras and the associated video monitors. However, that part of a video system is covered in Chapter 31.

Designing a Distributed Video System

The design of a distributed video system should be developed using a systematic approach intended to identify the customers' objectives and the equipment, cabling, and controls needed to achieve their goals.

Your role in this process, besides that of the designer, is to guide your customers through the maze of choices in equipment, layout, function, and installation to create a distributed video system that meets or exceeds their wishes, while remaining within or below their budget.

Performing the design steps in a certain sequence is the best way to complete the design phase to everyone's satisfaction. The major steps of the design phase should be

1. Identifying and designating the distribution points
2. Planning the layout of each room or zone

3. Deciding on the control system to be used in each room or zone

4. Planning for the centralization of the source equipment

Each of these design phase activities is outlined in the sections that follow.

Designate the Distribution Points

The decision of whether or not any particular room in a house is wired into a whole house distributed video system is strictly that of the homeowner. If the customer wishes to have the bathrooms, laundry rooms, or storage rooms, in addition to the living room, family room, bedrooms, and other living spaces, included in the system, then so be it. However, you should point out that each room should be considered on a cost-benefit basis. In most situations, only the living room, family room, den, one or more bedrooms, and perhaps a home theater or home office are included in a distributed video system, but the choice is up to the customer.

In a structured wiring environment, the potential distribution points are based on the wiring and where the video system is or will be installed. Where the video system is able to connect to the wiring can, in many situations, predetermine its design and potential distribution among separate rooms or zones.

Essentially, each area of a house that shares a common video signal belongs to the same video zone as any other area also receiving that signal. If the video distribution system is to provide the capability for each room to select its own source device or signal, then each room is potentially a separate zone. Whether a distributed video system is to support one, two, or multiple zones is a key decision that must be made early on in the design phase of the project.

Lay Out Each Room

Unlike a distributed audio system, which should complement the video system, the primary choices for each room are where the video cable will terminate at a wall jack and if a control system or extender is to be installed, what kind is to be installed and, if applicable, where it is to be located. In most situations, these issues are usually considered during the planning of the structured wiring.

The ideal situation is to place the video connection in proximity to the video display device. For example, if a standard television in a bedroom is to be connected to the system, then the video connector should be on the wall, behind, or close to the side of the TV set.

Decide on the Control System

One of the most important decisions to be made with designing a distributed video system is the type of controls to be installed in each zone. If all zones are to receive the same video signal, then perhaps only on/off and volume controls are needed in each room for the audio. However, if the intent is that each room can choose its audio source device or video signal, then more sophisticated controls are necessary.

On most zone video display devices, the volume control is part of the same device, like it is on a television set or a computer. However, if a standalone video monitor or display device that lacks volume controls is used and the audio portion is to be fed to speakers in the room, the audio portion of the signal must be controlled separately. Video system controls that can be mounted on a wall or other room surface range from relatively simple volume controls to sophisticated LCD touch screen panels and multiple device controllers.

Local Control

The on/off function on any video display device physically located in a zone can be easily controlled from a local handheld remote control or on the device itself. This allows for local control of the display device (on/off/source/channel). It also allows for control of the audio if the audio comes directly from a display device such as speakers built into the television. When the audio of the local video display device has been integrated into an audio system, it can be controlled manually with a volume control.

Volume controls are typically rheostat controls that look very much like the dimmer dials used with lighting systems (see Figure 14-1). The idea is simple: turn the dial to turn up or turn down the volume. Most rotary dial volume controls have 8 to 12 volume level settings and an on/off position as well.

CROSS-REFERENCE   See Chapter 13 for more information on audio control.

Figure 14-1
A wall-mounted
rotary volume
control

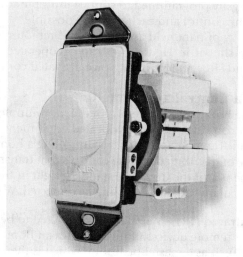

Photo courtesy of Niles Audio.

PART III

Figure 14-2
An all-in-one
remote control
unit

Photo courtesy of Intrigue Technologies, Inc.

Multiple Device Control

If the customer wishes to be able to control a centralized source device from a zone, some form of remote controller is necessary. Multifunction controllers, on the low-end, are all-in-one handheld remote controls like the one shown in Figure 14-2. These devices can be easily programmed to control multiple source devices, provided line-of-sight between the control and each device is possible.

The technology of handheld and hands-free remotes is evolving quickly. For example, the remote shown in Figure 14-3 can be operated as either a handheld remote control or a hands-free remote using voice-activated commands.

Controlling a Centralized System

Regardless if the home video system is in one or multiple zones, the key to ease-of-use is the ability to control the centrally located equipment from any remote listening or viewing location. The best approach to controlling a home audio visual (AV) system is through the use of distributed remote controls that transmit control signals back to the central equipment as if the user were standing right in front of it.

The most popular ways of controlling a connected AV system from a zone are

- **Wired infrared (IR)**   Wired IR is considered to be the most foolproof way to control remote devices. It incorporates an IR receiver placed in a remote location, such as a master bedroom, which is then wired to an IR emitter that has line-of-sight to the equipment being controlled, such as a CD player in the family room.

Figure 14-3
A remote control
unit that can be
used as either
a handheld or
hands-free device

Photo courtesy of Brookstone Company, Inc.

- **Wireless infrared (IR) or radio frequency (RF)** Wireless is generally considered a single zone solution, but this method is the easiest and least expensive to implement and use. With this approach, the IR beam or radio frequency (RF) signal produced by the wireless remote control is received by a receiver located either in the same room (in the case of IR, it requires line-of-sight) or within a 100-foot range and then converted into either a RF signal or a powerline control (PLC) signal that is transmitted to a base station attached to the device being controlled. An example of this system is shown in Figure 14-4. This device converts IR signals from a handheld remote control into RF signals that are transmitted to the receiver, where the signals are converted back into IR and "flashed" to operate the electronic equipment. IR and RF extender systems are also available that translate the control signal for transmission over a PLC system to a receiver connected to the central equipment.

 NOTE A signal extension system is only needed when you are not in the same room as the equipment being controlled. In a single zone setup, where the entire home is one large listening zone, an IR or RF signal may need assistance reaching your single set of AV equipment.

- **IR over coaxial cable** If coaxial cable has been placed in multiple rooms or zones, it can be used to send IR commands to the central video system. The coaxial cable must be home run back to the AV equipment for this to work.

Figure 14-4
An IR extender system converts IR to RF for transmission to a base station.

Photo courtesy of X-10 Wireless Technology, Inc.

- **Discrete controllers in multiple zones** If the design goal of the AV system is to supply a completely discrete set of sight and sound streams to every room in the home, a controller can be set up to communicate with and control the centralized AV equipment. This discrete controller can be hard-wired back to the equipment or communicate by RF to a base unit back at the equipment location that communicates with the AV equipment (see Figure 14-5), using one of two basic methods:
  - Direct homerun wiring from the controller to the central AV equipment using Cat 5e/Cat 6 wiring.
  - IR controllers communicating to a base station device connected via home-run wiring or RF to the central AV equipment.

In either case, the discrete room controller must either be able to receive the signals from original equipment remote controls or be a replacement device that consolidates as many of the separate remote controls as possible. These devices can be handheld (see Figure 14-5), wall-mounted, or tabletop (see Figure 14-6).

Centralizing the Sources

For new construction or remodel projects where it's easier to run cable from each zone back to the centralized AV equipment, the use of direct and dedicated cable runs is definitely preferred over other signal-transmission schemes. IR or RF signals can be converted by in-zone receivers and transmitted over the wire back to the centralized equipment.

Figure 14-5
A handheld
remote control
that can control
up to nine devices

Photo courtesy of Philex Electronic, Ltd.

Select the location of the central equipment and the wiring panel associated with it. All of the cables from the different rooms or zones should terminate here along with the wiring from all external sources (cable, telephone, satellite, antenna, and the like) that provide the video signals that are to be distributed throughout the house.

NOTE Since most locations will include structured wiring and a structured wiring distribution panel, the video or audio cabling should eventually terminate at the distribution panel, where it can be connected to the cabling that distributes it throughout the house.

Figure 14-6
A table-top touch
screen audio/
video controller

Photo courtesy of AMX Corp.

The location of the equipment should meet the homeowners' design, accessibility, and usage needs. Many homeowners wish to display their equipment in a nice rack arrangement in a prominent location. Others may place this equipment in a closet, utility room, or another out-of-view location. Of course, the homeowner could also hide some from view and display the really cool pieces, kind of like electronic artwork.

Depending on your customer's desires and budget, the equipment found in the central hub location may include the following:

- AV controller
- Cable TV converter
- CD player/burner
- Digital satellite system (DSS) receiver
- DVD player/burner
- Internet gateway
- PVR
- VCR
- Digital media storage device
- Video distribution panel

Installing Video Cable

Video distribution transmits RF signals over physical cable, which is typically shielded coaxial cable. A coaxial cable is able to carry more than 130 standard channel frequencies, and a major part of delivering a quality signal to produce a quality image is keeping the video signal in the cable and other signals that might interfere outside the cable. Each channel transmitted on the coaxial cable has both video and audio components, and with MPEG Transport Streams (MTS) encoding in use, each channel can also carry stereo sound.

A coaxial cable is able to carry many channels and their signals at the same time. However, baseband signals, like those produced on a VCR or DVD player, require an entire cable for each channel. So, transmitting the entire baseband AV output from a VCR player requires two coaxial cables or a coaxial cable and separate audio cables.

For the best results, use quality RG6 coaxial cable (or a wireless RF system) to distribute video signals throughout a home. Depending on the design of the system, each room included in the distributed video system should have at least one cable connection jack. In rooms where there may be one or more video sources, additional jacks should be installed.

Another design consideration is the load on the video cabling. Remember that 6 dBs of signal is lost for each 100 feet of RG6 cable. If the number of devices and the cable run lengths add up to too much attenuation, you may want to consider designing in a video amplifier. Also remember that if you use splitters or combiners (typically a hybrid single device), as shown in Figure 14-7, there is loss when the signal passes through that device as well.

Figure 14-7

A video signal splitter/combiner

Photo courtesy of Channel Vision.

CROSS-REFERENCE See Chapter 13 for more information on video signal loss and calculation.

The cables that work best with different video applications are

- **Coaxial** This cable is the standard used for cable television connections. It is typically terminated with a barrel Bayonet Neill Concellman (BNC) connector, but it can also be terminated with an RCA connector. Although other applications are in development, coaxial cable is used primarily for antenna and cable inputs.

- **Component (also called digital component)** The newest of the cable and connector types that provides the best picture quality. The video signal is separated into three separate signals (Y, R-Y, B-Y, where Y represents black and white luminance, R represents red, and B represents blue) and results in better color and clarity. The connection for a component cable has three plugs, one for each color component. Make sure the colors are matched to the device jack colors.

- **Composite** A standard video signal format that contains the color, brightness, and synchronization information. Virtually all VCRs and other legacy video equipment have composite video input or output. The jacks and plugs used for composite video are RCA connectors. This signaling and connection format is distinctive in that it uses three wires for connections: a yellow jack for video, a white jack for left-side audio, and a red jack for right-side audio.

- **S-Video** The signal is split into two color groups: chrominance and luminance. Chrominance carries color information, and luminance carries brightness and lighting information. S-Video is used primarily to transmit video signals to a television from a VCR or game device. The pin configuration on the jack and plug on an S-Video connection prevents the connection from being made incorrectly.

- **Video Port (VPort)**   This connector is primarily used to connect video game devices that have an RCA VPort connector that carries a composite video signal. It was originally designed to host the Microsoft Xbox video gaming device on RCA televisions.

- **Digital Video Interface (DVI)**   This interface connector provides connections for both analog and digital monitors on a single cable. Each of the three DVI configurations is designed to accommodate either analog (DVI-A), digital (DVI-D), or integrated (DVI-I) signals. When a DVI connector and port are used, a digital signal sent to an analog monitor is converted to an analog signal. If the monitor is a digital monitor, like a flat panel display, no conversion is performed.

- **High-Definition Multimedia Interface (HDMI)**   An improvement over the DVI interface, HDMI supports either RGB or YCbCr digital video at rates well above the 2.2 Gbps required by high-definition television (HDTV). HDMI also supports up to eight channels of digital audio.

Rough-In Cable Installation

During the rough-in phase of construction, the outlet boxes are mounted, and cabling is installed in the walls while the walls are still open. From the outlet boxes, the video and audio cables are run to the location of the central panel. It isn't absolutely necessary to install the central distribution panel during rough-in, but it can be a good idea, especially if the panel is to be flush-mounted on a wall. Of course, this presumes that a floor plan and wire layout has been created and approved by the customer before you begin the installation of the rough-in items.

Rough-in work is generally done right after the electricians, plumbers, and heating, ventilation, air conditioning (HVAC) technicians complete their rough-in work and before the wallboard (drywall) is installed. Working after the electricians, plumbers, and other technicians allows you to install the cable so that it has the minimum distance and clearance from electrical wiring and any other objects inside the walls. Table 14-1 lists the minimum distances that AV cabling should be from the other fixtures in the house.

 NOTE   Remember that if the video cable must cross an electrical cable, it should do so at a 90-degree angle.

Table 14-1
Minimum Cable
Placement
Distances

Fixture	Minimum Distance
AC electrical cable	6 inches
Motors and motor wiring	12 inches
Fluorescent lighting and wiring	24 inches

Passing through Studs

The structured wiring being installed, which includes the video and audio cabling, can be an inch or more in diameter. To pass the cable through the wall studs, a hole at least 1/8-inch larger should be drilled through each stud along the cable path. Remember the general cable installation guidelines (see Chapter 1) and keep the structured wire bundle the proper distances from the electrical and other wiring that should already be installed. The same process applies even if only a single cable is being installed. Generally, the path for the AV cable can follow the path used by the electricians for the electrical cabling, keeping the proper distances, of course.

Outlet Boxes

A wide variety of low voltage mounting brackets and outlet boxes are available for use, as illustrated in Figure 14-8. The primary issue when selecting outlet boxes for structured wiring, including video and audio cables, is the bend radius of the cable. Coaxial and Cat 5 cable cannot be bent sharply, which may create a problem for inserting the cable into a standard electrical outlet box. For this reason, open back outlet boxes and mud rings, like those shown in Figures 14-8 and 14-9, or standard electrical outlet boxes, commonly called J-boxes, with the backs removed should be used. The common practice for home wiring systems is the use of blue or metallic boxes for electrical systems and orange nonmetallic boxes for structured wiring.

It may be necessary to adjust the locations of the structured wiring outlet boxes from the original plans in order to avoid the electrical wiring and other in-wall systems. However, new dual voltage outlet boxes and add-on single and dual gang boxes that accommodate both electrical and low voltage cabling are available. These boxes allow for a common placement of both electrical and structured wiring outlets.

Figure 14-8

A sampling of different outlet boxes available for use in a distributed audio system

Photo courtesy of Lamson & Sessions.

Figure 14-9
An open-back
outlet box
protects cabling
from sharp bends.

Photo courtesy of Lamson & Sessions.

Install the outlet box so that the front edge of it will be inside the hole the drywall installers will cut around the box. The box shouldn't extend so far out from the stud that it extends beyond the drywall, but it shouldn't be so far back that it ends up behind the drywall either. Check with the drywall installers or the contractor, if possible, to determine the correct distance the box should extend beyond the stud. Typically this measurement should be either 1/4- or 3/8-inch. The box should be placed at the same height from the floor as the electrical outlet boxes, if for no other reason than aesthetics.

Most outlet boxes can be nailed or screwed to an adjacent stud using either the nails already on the box, like those in Figure 14-10, or through the holes provided on the box.

Trim-Out Installation

The trim-out phase of a distributed video system installation project is when the system begins to take shape. Trim-out is when the finish work of the project is done, which includes terminating, testing, and making the connections. This phase of the project has three primary steps:

- Terminating the cable and installing the face plates on the outlet boxes or mud rings
- Testing the cable system
- Configuring and connecting the central video distribution panel and the distributed video sources

Figure 14-10
An outlet box
attached to a
wall stud

Photo courtesy of Lamson & Sessions.

Terminating the Video Cable

Terminating the video cable at the outlet box or mud ring involves attaching the cable to the connectors on the back of the wall outlet jack. If coaxial cable is used, then the raw cable must be terminated with a male F connector and then connected to the female connector on the back of the wall outlet. If twisted-pair (TP) cable is in use, the back of the wall outlet will have a 110 punchdown block.

CROSS REFERENCE   See Chapter 2 for more information on coaxial and twisted-pair cable connectors.

The wall outlet used should reflect the systems in its vicinity. For example, if only a television set is in the room, the wall outlet needs to support only an F connector for video distribution. However, if the room also has one or more computer, speakers, and other end devices, a multiple-jack outlet, like the one shown in Figure 14-11, would support the existing requirements and possibly help to future-proof the room.

Trim Out the Central Distribution Panel

The central distribution panel is the key component of a structured wiring scheme. Each of the video cable runs should terminate and interconnect to the cables connecting to the source devices at the distribution panel.

The procedure for connecting the cable runs to the distribution panel is much the same as that for connecting each of the jacks in the wall outlets and uses the same tools.

Figure 14-11
A multiuse modular outlet with two twisted-pair jacks, an S-Video jack, a BNC barrel connector, and two F connector jacks

Photo courtesy of SmartHome, Inc.

TP cabling is attached to a 110 block on the panel, and coaxial cabling is attached using F connectors. It is usually possible for the distribution panel itself to be purchased separately from its enclosure.

A structured wiring or structured media distribution panel interconnects the cabling that runs to rooms with the cabling running from the source devices. The panel shown in Figure 14-12 includes interconnects for TP and coaxial cable as well as room for line support devices, like an impedance amplifier or line converter.

Testing the System

The first part of testing the system is performing a thorough visual inspection of the wall outlets and the connections at the distribution panel. If anything looks wrong—even slightly wrong—it should be examined very closely and when in doubt, either repaired or replaced.

To test the video cabling system, you should use a cable tester to check the unshielded twisted-pair (UTP) and coaxial cables for bad connections and cable continuity. The next level of testing involves dynamic testing of the cabling using a structured wiring test device, like the one shown in Figure 14-13, to perform the Telecommunications Industry Association/Electronic Industries Alliance (TIA/EIA) TSB-67 tests on TP cabling and the TIA/EIA 570 tests for coaxial cabling.

CROSS-REFERENCE See Chapter 1 for more information on wire basics and wire testing procedures.

Figure 14-12
A media
distribution panel

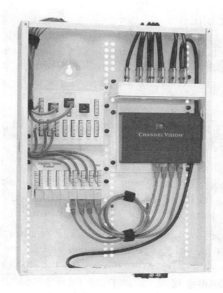

Photo courtesy of Channel Vision.

Figure 14-13
A structured
cable tester

Photo courtesy of Megger/Avo Multi-AMP Corp.

Equipment Hookup

In general, the steps to connect the video source equipment together and into the distribution system should be performed in a specific sequence. Although the steps in the following list are fairly general (and a particular video system may require some additional or specialized steps), the steps you should perform are

1. Remove the components from their boxes in the order you wish to install them. Set aside the product warranty, user guides, and other documents, along with the original remote control, for later use.

2. Set the component in the location it will occupy permanently.

3. Study the component's owner's manual. Make a note of any special hookup instructions required for the device (unplanned connectors, equipment cords, and the like), but don't hook up the equipment just yet.

   • If the video components (cable receiver, digital broadcast satellite receiver, DVD-player, videotape player, and so on) are from a single manufacturer, which is somewhat unusual, follow the instructions in the manufacturer's documentation very closely, using the specified cables and connectors as prescribed.

   • If the equipment is from several different manufacturers, verify the connector jacks on the backs of the devices and that the devices have common connections between them before beginning to cable the devices together. It is a good idea to "dry run" the system before actually beginning to connect the components together with their cables, just to verify that you have the correct cables and connectors required.

4. Connect the video components together and install a small television set on each of the output lines (one at a time) that will supply distributed video throughout the home. Check the video picture and correct any problems at the device, following the troubleshooting guides in the device documentation.

5. If the video devices are performing as they should, connect the video output or source lines into the distribution panel and connect to the video splitter or amplifier.

6. Retest the system using the small television set at each of the distribution outlets that terminate the video distribution cabling. Once it is verified that the outlets are working, hook up the video devices in each room, working with one device and one room at a time. If there are any problems in the distributed video signal received at the outlets, the problem is likely in the outlet or the cabling it terminates. The cable should be tested using the appropriate equipment and in accordance to the specification of the splitter, amplifier, or end device to which it connects.

 CROSS-REFERENCE See Chapter 13 for more information on testing distributed audio/video cabling.

Figure 14-14 illustrates the connections typically made in a distributed video system.

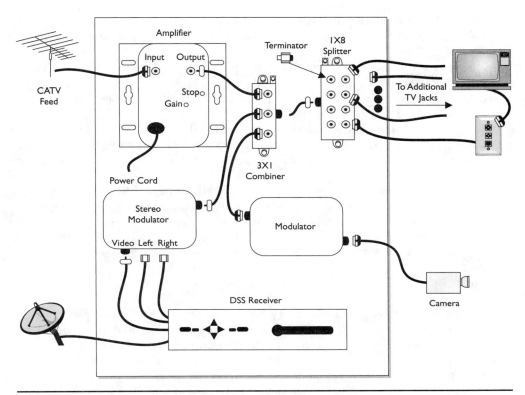

Figure 14-14 The connections made in a distributed video system

Chapter Review

The design phase for a distributed video system involves designating the rooms to be included, laying out the locations for the wall outlets, and deciding on the type of controller for each room or zone.

Each area that shares a common video signal is in the same video zone. Whether a distributed video system is to support one, two, or multiple zones is a key decision that must be made early on in the design phase of the project. The video wall connector should be placed in proximity to the video display device. Video controls range from relatively simple volume controls to LCD touch screen panels and multiple device controllers.

The common controller types are wireless IR or RF, dedicated device controllers, extended IR or RF controllers, and IR over coaxial cable.

Video distribution transmits RF signals over physical cable, which is typically shielded coaxial cable. A coaxial cable is able to carry more than 130 standard channel frequencies, and a major part of delivering a quality signal to produce a quality image is keeping the video signal in the cable and other signals outside the cable. Baseband signals, like those produced on a VCR or DVD player, require an entire cable for each channel. So, transmitting the entire baseband AV output from a VCR player requires two coaxial cables.

RG6 coaxial cable is the best choice for distributing video signals throughout a home, but other cable media can be used, including coaxial, component, composite, DVI, HDMI, S-Video, and TP.

In the rough-in phase of construction, the outlet boxes and cabling are installed in the walls after the electricians, plumbers, and HVAC technicians complete their rough-in work and before the wallboard (drywall) is installed. The structured wiring is installed to pass through the wall studs.

A wide variety of low voltage mounting brackets and outlet boxes are available for use with structured video cabling. The common practice for home wiring systems is the use of blue or metallic boxes for electrical systems and orange nonmetallic boxes for structured wiring.

Install the outlet box so that the front edge of it will be inside the hole the drywall installers will cut around the box. The box should be placed at the same height from the floor as the electrical outlet boxes, if for no other reason than aesthetics.

During the trim-out phase of a distributed video system installation, the finish work of the project is done, which includes termination, testing, and making the connections. If a room has one or more computer, speakers, and other end devices, a multiple-jack outlet should be used to support the existing requirements and to help future-proof the room.

A key component of a structured wiring scheme is the central distribution panel, which is where each of the zone cable runs terminate and connect into the source devices. The procedure for connecting the cable runs to the distribution panel is much the same as that for connecting each of the jacks in the wall outlets and uses the same tools.

The first part of the testing system is a thorough visual inspection of the wall outlets and the connections at the distribution panel. To test the video cabling system, a cable tester should be used to check the UTP and coaxial cables for bad connection and cable continuity.

Questions

1. Which of the following is not typically a step performed in the design phase of a video system project?

   A. Planning the layout of each room or zone

   B. Planning the centralization of the source equipment

   C. Identifying and designating the distribution points

   D. Getting quotes from materials and equipment suppliers

2. Which of the following is not generally considered for the centralized location of a distributed video system?

   A. Cable TV converter/receiver

   B. DVD player

   C. Speakers

   D. Video distribution panel

3. What is the term applied to an area in a house where everyone receives the same video signal?

   A. Room

   B. Video area

   C. Zone

   D. Theater

4. If a homeowner desires to control a centralized source unit using an IR remote control from a remote area of the house, what device should be considered?

   A. RF remote control

   B. IR extender

   C. RF extender

   D. Voice controlled remote

5. What is the number of AV channels a coaxial cable is capable of carrying?

   A. 1

   B. 16

   C. 130

   D. 256

6. What is the dB signal loss per 100 feet from RG6 coaxial cable?

   A. 1

   B. 2

   C. 4

   D. 6

7. Which of the standard video formats splits the image coding into two groups, one for luminance and one for chrominance?

   A. S-Video

   B. Composite

   C. Component

   D. DVI-D

8. When is the rough-in phase of a structured wiring project performed?

   A. Before the electrical, HVAC, and plumbing is installed

   B. Before the wall studs are erected

   C. Before the drywall is installed

   D. After the drywall is installed

9. What is the minimum distance away from an AC cable that a structured media cable should be installed?

   A. 3 inches

   B. 6 inches

   C. 12 inches

   D. 24 inches

10. During which of the following phases of a structured wiring project should the cable be terminated and tested?

   A. Prewire

   B. Rough-in

   C. Trim-out

   D. Finish

Answers

1. **D.** Until the design phase has completed, you really won't know what materials and equipment are needed or desired to complete the installation.

2. **C.** Unless the homeowner plans to sit in the central distribution point to listen to audio, it's fairly unusual to include speakers in the centralized distribution hub.

3. **C.** A home can have one or multiple zones. It can have multiple and overlapping audio and video zones.

4. **B.** Another choice would be IR over coaxial cable using wall outlet mounted IR receivers that are cabled back to the source unit.

5. **C.** This is why coaxial cable is a common choice for video systems.

6. **D.** Additional signal loss occurs if splitters or combiners are used.

7. **A.** Most of the other video standards use a single channel to transmit color and brightness information.

8. **C.** It's best to wait until after the electrical wiring is installed so you can avoid installing structured media cable too close to other wiring.

9. **B.** More is always better, but in a wall that may be difficult. Also remember that if the media cable must cross the electrical wiring, it should do so at a 90-degree angle.

10. **C.** Prior to this phase the surfaces of the walls are not finished, and the connectors and plates would be exposed to possible damage. However, continuity testing should be performed in the rough-in phase and then again in the trim-out.

Troubleshooting Video Systems

In this chapter, you will learn about
- Common cable-related distributed video problems
- Troubleshooting video cabling and distribution systems

Regardless of the actual source of a problem, a homeowner who can't watch the big game, the latest episode of *24*, his favorite talk show, or whatever show he wants is experiencing a video system problem. With all of the connection and distribution points involved in a distributed video system, tracking down the source of the problem can be daunting.

In a structured wiring environment, tracking down the cause of a problem (assuming that the problem is cable- and distribution-related) is eased a bit because access points to all of the cable homeruns are available for testing, as are all of the distribution and interconnection points.

This chapter focuses on the cabling and connection problems that can affect the performance of a distributed video system and the troubleshooting steps that can be used to identify a problem source.

Diagnosing Distributed Video Problems

As is the case with other distributed media systems, most distributed video problems can be traced to cabling. How the cable was installed, how it was terminated, and how it's connected into the source and distribution equipment can have an effect on the quality of the video seen on that big, expense high-definition TV (HDTV) plasma display.

As with all problems reported by a customer, you should listen, look, and analyze the situation before beginning your diagnostics. Once you have a clear understanding of what the customer sees as the problem, you can begin your diagnostics to isolate the cause and apply a remedy.

Rule Out the Obvious

As I've said a few times already in this book, before you begin performing cable tests, check out all possible systems that are related to the problem, and even those that aren't. Check for things such as unplugged electrical cords, poorly mounted connections, and the like. In a majority of cases, especially in those where the system has been in place for more than 30 to 90 days, it is likely that the cause is external to the cabling and its termination and is something fairly simple.

Check the Cable

Video systems are generally installed over coaxial cabling, either RG59 or RG6. However, video systems can be installed on twisted-pair cabling as well. In any of these cases, how the cable was installed and terminated should be the first check in your diagnostics.

Coaxial Cable

As illustrated in Figure 15-1, coaxial cable actually has two conductors: the center, solid-core copper conductor and the shield placed around the dielectric insulating material and the inner conductor. The center conductor is the primary signal carrier of the cable, and the mesh shield provides a return path for the signal ground. When a coaxial cable is terminated, if attention isn't paid to both conductors, the quality of the transmitted signal can be affected.

Cable Shielding   The shielding on a shielded cable can be one of several materials, but typically it is wire mesh, foil, or both (including two of one or both). Each of these different shield types is designed to resist certain kinds of radio frequency interference (RFI) and electromagnetic interference (EMI). A foil shield is primarily used to deflect RFI from the cable. Foil shields have a thin drain wire that allows the foil to be connected to the outer channel of an F-type or BNC connector. A wire-mesh or braid shield, which is usually made of tinned copper, is used to ward off EMI from the center conductor. In high-quality cables, both shields may be installed. In either case, the shield must be in contact with the metal body of the connectors to perform its task.

Center Conductor   The center conductor can also be a source of cable performance issues. If the center conductor extends too far from the connector, it can easily be bent or pushed to the side when the connector jack is attached to the connector plug.

Figure 15-1

A cut-away view of a coaxial cable

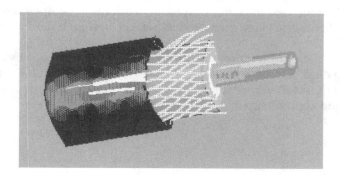

A too-long center conductor could also start to act like an antenna and pick up electrical noise from other nearby sources. This situation can occur at any termination, such as the wall plate, the splitter, or the terminated cable end that connects to a source or playback device. To avoid these issues, the center conductor should be cut to the proper length. However, if the center conductor isn't extended far enough out from the connector, the conductor may not meet the conductor on the other half of the connector. Notice the center conductor extending beyond the connector body in Figure 15-2.

Cable Properties   The performance of a coaxial cable in a video system is determined by the properties of the cabling installed. The primary properties that can affect the performance of a coaxial video cable are

- **Frequency**   As the frequency of the signal transmitted over coaxial cable increases, the greater the effect the cable's capacitance and conductive resistance have on the signal.

- **Interference**   RFI and EMI can distort the signal if the cable is not properly shielded against them. Crosstalk is a type of interference that occurs when cables that are run adjacent aren't properly shielded and pick up signals from one another, which can distort the signal on either or both cables.

- **Length**   The longer a signal travels through a cable, the more its quality decreases. All copper cabling is susceptible to attenuation, which is caused by an electrical signal being affected by the materials of the cable as the signal travels through the cable. Each series of coaxial cable has a specific maximum cable segment length. For example, RG6 coaxial cabling has a rating to about 200 meters.

- **Specifications**   The four primary properties included in a manufacturer's cable specifications are

  - **Attenuation**   This is perhaps the most important specification for a coaxial cable and is stated in the number of decibels (dB) of signal loss that occurs beyond a fixed length (typically around 30 meters or 100 feet) for different signal frequencies. An example of an attenuation specification is –2.2dB/100 feet @ 100 MHz, which means that a transmitted signal will lose 2.2 decibels per 100 feet of run length. In addition, the attenuation rating of a cable also changes as the run length of the cable increases. In effect, attenuation gradually decreases the quality of the signal as the signal travels over the line, which can impact the display produced by a signal transmitted over an extended length run.

PART III

Figure 15-2
The center conductor of a coaxial cable extending out from the connector

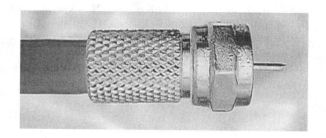

- **Capacitance** Capacitance measures a cable's capability to take an electrical charge, hold the charge, and then discharge. In a coaxial cable, capacitance indicates how well a cable can hold a change in its dielectric insulator to offset the potential difference between the conductors, which on a coaxial cable is the center conductor wire and its shielding. One video condition that can be affected by a cable with an improper capacitance is the black-to-white transition of the video signal, which might be displayed with a gray transition between the black and white. The capacitance of a coaxial cable is measured in picofarads per foot (pF/ft), or one-trillionth of a farad.

- **Impendence** This rating determines the amount of signal flow the cable supports. A possible source for system performance issues is unmatched impedance, which can cause the signal to be reflected back up the cable instead of on to its destination. Reflection signals can also be caused by improper termination. Coaxial cable typically has 75-ohm impedance.

- **Resistance** A cable's resistance rating defines how resistive the cable is to signal flow. A cable with a very high resistance impairs the amplitude of a signal and converts the lost voltage to heat. The materials used in the cable and their dimensions, as well as the temperature of the area in which the cable is installed, determine a cable's resistance. A cable's resistance is stated in ohms per 1,000 feet (305 meters).

- **Temperature** Heat can affect the performance of a cable, which can also make troubleshooting difficult. In areas such as walls, ceilings, and equipment racks that may not be properly ventilated to prevent heat buildup, cables can be subject to higher heat. Special cabling types are available for installation in locations where heat may be a problem.

Terminations The different types of connectors used with coaxial cabling can impact the quality of the signal transmitted because they may create an impedance mismatch on the line. For example, a BNC connector has 75-ohm impedance, which matches that of the typical coaxial cable. However, an RCA connector typically has between 35- and 55-ohm impedance. This doesn't mean that an RCA connector should not be used with coaxial cable, it just depends on the system being supported. Some systems include a 25-ohm resistor on the incoming cable jack.

Not all video connectors use crimp-style attachments. Many styles of connectors must be soldered into place, which creates another failure point for the cable. Improperly applied soldering can create problems with continuity, impedance, and resistance of a cable.

Another potential problem area that actually extends beyond the scope of structured cabling is the patch cords used with coaxial distribution cables, which should also be coaxial cable that matches the specification of the main distribution cable.

Figure 15-3
A video cable
terminated with
RCA connectors

Photo courtesy of Canare Corporation of America.

The equipment cords provided with video devices by the manufacturer are good for use only directly between devices and aren't designed or provided for use as patch cords between the distribution cable and the device.

The difference between a patch cord and an equipment cord boils down to connectors. BNC and F-type connectors are used with coaxial cabling on both distribution and patch cords. Equipment cords commonly have RCA connectors, like the cord shown in Figure 15-3 and are used for line-level audio and composite or component video interfaces.

Twisted-Pair Audio Cables

Unshielded twisted-pair (UTP) cable can be a less expensive alternative to coaxial cable for a distributed video system. Cat 5e or better (meaning Cat 6 or Cat 7) can be used to distribute video signals if it's properly installed and terminated.

The SCART Connector

In European countries, the connector used to connect televisions, VCRs, and set-top boxes is the SCART (Syndicat des Constructeurs d'Appareils Radiorécepteurs et Téléviseurs) connector, which is illustrated in Figure 15-4. This connector, which is also called a Peritel connector, is used to terminate input lines, output lines, and lines that do both. The SCART connector is a 21-pin block crimp on connector type.

Many brands of television sets and most of the sets manufactured for sale in the United States and Europe have a SCART connector on them.

Figure 15-4
A SCART
connector

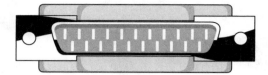

Using UTP cable for a video system requires that one pair of wires is used for each signal. Or in other words, up to four video system signals can be transmitted on a UTP cable, one signal per wire pair.

Attenuation   One specification of UTP cabling that can be an issue for a video system is attenuation. If a system is performing poorly, and UTP cabling is in use for distributing the video signal, attenuation could be the problem. Table 15-1 compares the dB/100 feet loss of coaxial and UTP cabling.

To offset the dramatic attenuation differences shown in Table 15-1, video baluns (transformers) should be placed between BNC connectors (coaxial cable) and RJ-45 connectors (UTP cable). A video balun, besides providing an interface between the two termination types, converts the UTP line from unbalanced to balanced.

CROSS-REFERENCE   See Chapter 13 for more on video baluns and their use with UTP cable.

Common UTP Video Problems   Perhaps the most common problem for video systems installed on UTP cable is color separation. For example, light-colored lines or the edges of light-colored objects appear to have a red or purple tinge to them. This is caused by the number of twists per inch of the wire pairs inside the Cat 5e/Cat 6 cable. If the twists per inch of one wire pair, carrying one part of the video signal, is tighter than on another wire pair, the signals arrive at slightly different times, especially on long cable runs. This problem is more noticeable on high-resolution systems.

If the customer is complaining of this problem from a video system installed on UTP cable, you may need to install a video graphics array (VGA) to UTP adapter to correct the RGB conversion and signal timing. This device uses a potentiometer to adjust the skew of the signal timing.

Table 15-1
Decibel Loss
per 100 Feet of
Common Video
Cabling

MHz	RG6	RG59	Cat 5
1	0.2	0.4	1.8
10	0.6	1.4`	5.8
50	1.4	3.3	11.0
100	2.0	4.9	19.3
400	4.3	11.2	42.0

Cable Testing

The cable tests recommended in Chapter 3 are the same procedures used when performing diagnostics on coaxial or UTP cabling in a video distribution system. However, the following few sections provide a brief overview of these tests and their use in diagnosing and troubleshooting a distributed video system.

Coaxial Cable Tests

The primary tests that should be performed on coaxial cabling as part of your diagnostics are

- Test the cable for 75-ohm impedance
- Test for continuity on both the center conductor and the shield
- Test for attenuation
- Test for cable length

If there are other tests that are required by your company, city, county, state, or federal regulations, you may want to repeat them at this time just to verify that none of the cable's characteristics have been changed.

Testing Guidelines

When testing coaxial cabling, follow these guidelines:

1. Perform a visual inspection and verify the correct cabling is installed, the connectors are the appropriate type, the terminations are correct, the patch or equipment cords are appropriate, and that you don't see any visible cable damage.

2. Start your tests at the central distribution panel or the demarcation point of the video system, such as the cable television network interface device (NID).

3. If you suspect that the problem may be attenuation on a very long run of cable, add a repeater to the link as near to the middle of the cable as you can. If the problem continues, the repeater may not be necessary.

4. If you suspect a particular device or system is causing the problem, after eliminating the cable as the source of the problem, remove that device from the system, if possible, and retest.

5. Connect each modulator or video hub directly to a television set to verify the device is working properly.

Coaxial Cable Test Tools

When testing coaxial cabling as a part of your diagnostics, certain tests are used to answer certain questions. Table 15-2 lists the troubleshooting questions and the test tools you can use to provide answers.

Question	Test Tools
Which cable is this?	Documentation, tone generator/probe
Is the cable run wired correctly?	Multimeter
Is the cable too long?	Multimeter, time domain reflectometer (TDR)
Is the impedance correct?	Multimeter, certification test set
Is there too much interference on the line?	Certification test set

Table 15-2 Coaxial Cable Diagnostic Testing Tools

Troubleshooting Video Problems

Many video system performance problems are less directly related to the cable than they are to the overall system configuration. Table 15-3 lists several common video system problems, their causes, and what you should consider to resolve each problem.

Problem	Cause	Possible Solution
Dark bars on video display	AC power interference	Move cable at least 18 inches from AC power lines.
Modulated signals not displaying on monitor	Cable TV box may not pass modulated signals	Add splitter in front of cable box and install high-pass filter to modulated line.
Modulated signals ghosting	Inadequate shielding on coaxial cable	Replace existing cable with cable that has appropriate shielding.
No picture on TV	Coaxial cable problem	Perform a signal strength test on each cable segment.
		Test before and after each cable run, including testing before and after the cable demarc, splitter, amplifier, distribution panel, and the patch cord to the TV.
No picture on some channels	Insufficient cable bandwidth	Replace RG59 cabling with RG6 and verify capacity of video splitters, if any.
		Also the problem may be that the TV set's tuner is not capable of displaying certain channels.
Rolling lines or patterns on many television channels	Signal strength is too high	Add a line attenuator to reduce signal amplitude.
Static or snow on some channels	Problem coaxial cable run	Damaged cable or broken connector.
Snowy (static) picture on all channels	Signal interruption between TV and modulator	Check connection at each end of cable.
		Verify modulator settings.

Table 15-3 Common Video and Power Issues

Chapter Review

How the cabling is installed, terminated, and connected can affect the quality of the video display.

Before you start testing, check out all possible systems that may be related to the problem, such as unplugged AC cords, poorly mounted connections, and the like. If the system has been in place for more than 30 to 90 days, the problem is likely caused by external devices.

Video systems are generally installed over coaxial cabling, either RG59 or RG6, but distributed video systems are installed on TP cabling. How the cable was installed and terminated should be the first check in your diagnostics.

·Coaxial cable actually has two conductors: the center solid-core copper conductor and the shield placed around the dielectric insulating material and the inner conductor. The center conductor is the primary signal carrier of the cable, and the shield provides a return path for the signal ground. When a coaxial cable is terminated, if attention isn't paid to both conductors, the quality of the transmitted signal can be affected.

The performance of a coaxial cable in a video system is determined by the properties of the cabling installed. The primary properties that can affect the performance of a coaxial video cable are frequency, interference, length, specifications (which includes attenuation, capacitance, and impendence), resistance, and temperature.

The different types of connectors used with coaxial cabling can impact the quality of the signal transmitted because they may create an impedance mismatch on the line. Many styles of connectors must be soldered into place. Improperly applied soldering can create problems with continuity, impedance, and resistance of a cable.

UTP cable can be a less expensive alternative to coaxial cable for a distributed video system. Cat 5 or better (meaning Cat 5e, Cat 6, or Cat 7) can be used to distribute video signals if it's properly installed and terminated. One specification of UTP cabling that can be an issue for a video system is attenuation. If a system is performing poorly, and UTP cabling is in use for distributing the video signal, attenuation could be the problem. A video balun, besides providing an interface between the two termination types, converts the UTP line from unbalanced to balanced.

The cable tests used during trim-out should be used when performing diagnostics on video cabling. The primary tests that should be performed on coaxial cabling as a part of your diagnostics are testing the cable for 75-ohm impedance, testing for continuity on both the center conductor and the shield, testing for attenuation, and testing for cable length.

Questions

1. Which of the following is not recommended for distributing video signals in a structured wiring environment?

   A. RG59

   B. RG6

PART III

    C. Speaker wire

    D. UTP

2. In a coaxial cable, which layer carries the signal to ground current?

    A. Center conductor

    B. Dielectric insulation

    C. Shielding

    D. Outer jacket

3. Which type of coaxial cable shielding is used to resist RFI?

    A. Foil

    B. Dielectric

    C. Wire mesh

    D. Wire braid

4. Which of the following coaxial cable problems could create a continuity problem on a video distribution run?

    A. Cable pierced by a staple

    B. Center conductor not extended far enough

    C. Center conductor extended too far

    D. Wire mesh not in contract with the connector body

    E. All of the above

5. Which of a cable's properties limits the distance a cable is able to successfully carry a transmitted signal?

    A. Attenuation

    B. Capacitance

    C. Frequency

    D. Resistance

6. What is the normal impedance level of a coaxial cable terminated with a BNC connector?

    A. 35 ohms

    B. 55 ohms

    C. 75 ohms

    D. 120 ohms

7. When UTP cabling is used for distributing video signals, which of the following is true about the cable configuration?

   A. One signal per single wire

   B. One signal per wire pair

   C. One signal per cable (four pairs)

   D. Two signals per wire pair

8. True or False: The dB loss per 100 feet of UTP cable is typically less than that with either RG6 or RG59 coaxial cable.

   A. True

   B. False

9. Which of the following is a test that may not be performed on coaxial cabling during troubleshooting?

   A. Attenuation

   B. Crosstalk

   C. Impedance

   D. Continuity

10. When troubleshooting a coaxial cable for length, what testing tool should be utilized?

    A. Cable certification set

    B. Time domain reflectometer

    C. Tone generator/probe

    D. Wiremap tester

Answers

1. **C.** Speaker wire is not rated for in-wall installation, nor is it robust enough to carry the frequencies required for video transmissions. The other choices are used for video systems.

2. **C.** Whether the shielding is foil or wire mesh or braid, it is used to provide a return for the signal to ground current.

3. **A.** The foil shield resists RFI and the wire mesh or braid shield resists EMI. The dielectric insulator is used to provide capacitance.

4. **E.** Any one of these conditions could cause continuity problems on a coaxial cable.

5. **A.** On every copper cable, including UTP, there is a distance point at which the signal strength begins losing power.

6. **C.** UTP cable is typically in the range of 35 to 55 ohms.

7. **B.** Up to four signal paths can be provided by a single run of Cat 5 or better UTP cable.

8. **B.** The attenuation on a UTP cable can be on the order of two or more times greater.

9. **B.** Unless you believe that there are two coaxial cables carrying high frequencies that are placed too close together, this would not typically be a problem with coaxial cable.

10. **B.** TDR is the most commonly used test for testing copper (and fiber optic) cabling length.

PART IV

Telecommunications

357

Home Communication System Basics

In this chapter, you will learn about
- Home telecommunication system characteristics
- Telephone operations and fundamentals
- Intercom operations and fundamentals
- Telephone and network integration
- Telecommunication system service options

For those of us old enough to remember rotary dial telephones and dialing without an area code (to really date ourselves), the telephone and telephone service has drastically changed over the past couple of decades. This chapter discusses telecommunications systems for the home, including telephone and intercom systems, their functions, operations, and characteristics. We also discuss the possibilities of integrating a home telecommunications system into its control and data networks.

Telecommunications Basics

In most cases, a home telephone and telecommunications system is limited to RJ-11 outlet jacks (Figure 16-1) in one or two rooms of a home that is more than seven to ten years in age or in just about every room of a newer home. The telephone outlet jack can be used for local and long distance calling, to support a fax machine, as a part of a cable or direct satellite TV system, to support a dial-up modem connection, or a digital subscriber line (DSL) connection (through a signal splitter) for either a single computer or a computer network. Actually, when you think about it, that little telephone jack really has quite a bit of capability, which is generally underutilized in most homes.

The Telephone System

Most people take the telephone system for granted and get very used to the idea that, for the most part, it always works. Before you can begin designing a home telecommunications system, you should have some understanding of how this system works and its various components.

Figure 16-1
An RJ-11 jack
faceplate

Photo courtesy of Belkin Corporation.

The telephone network consists of two network layers: the plain old telephone system (POTS) and the Public Switched Telephone Network (PSTN). POTS service consists of the wiring and cabling that connects a house to the local telephone company switching system at the telephone company's network interface device (NID) on the side of the house. PSTN includes the switching system and all of the equipment and transmission lines used to carry the voice signals to the house by the phone company.

The Connection to the Central Office

The line that runs back to the telephone company or the telephone service provider (aka the Telco) terminates at a house in what is called the *demarc*. The demarc (short for *demarcation point*) is a terminating device that connects the wires in the Telco bundle to the home. In many respects, the demarc is very much like a network's patch panel in that it interconnects the telephone wiring in the home to the Telco's cabling and switching systems.

Demarcation Point   The demarc is typically located on an outside wall of a home or in an easily accessed location, such as inside a garage or basement. The official name for the telephone demarc is a network interface device (NID), and it is commonly a gray plastic or metal box with a snap-tight cover (see Figure 16-2).

As shown in Figure 16-2, an NID has two sections, the panel of connections on the right side of the box are accessible by the homeowner or their contractors for testing and connection purposes and the panel of connections on the left has an inside cover and is accessible only by Telco personnel. The owner-accessible panel (Figure 16-3 shows a zoomed-in view) has four to six screw connectors that connect the Telco's incoming lines (the connections made in the Telco-accessible panel) to the short piece of telephone cables that are plugged into the RJ-11 jacks. When the RJ-11 plug is removed from the jack, the line (and service) from the Telco is disconnected. However, if a phone

Figure 16-2

A Network interface device (NID) showing both the Telco-only side (left panel) and the owner-access side (right panel) connections

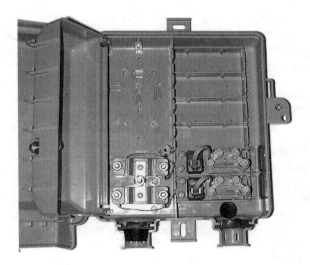

is plugged into this jack and works during a service test, any problem with the phone system in the house is being caused by the inside wiring, not by the Telco service.

The demarc is where the Telco's lines and system meet the telephone lines of a home. The Telco owns and is responsible for the lines up to the demarc (and typically the demarc itself), but no further. Beyond the demarc, everything belongs to and is the responsibility of the homeowner. However, especially on new homes, some homeowners are choosing to install their own NIDs, which aren't expensive. Installing and owning the demarc allows for more flexibility for expanding the telephone system inside the home, better quality connections at the demarc, the ability to complete the inside wiring (to the demarc) even before the telephone service is installed, and perhaps the best reason, the homeowner can put the demarc wherever they wish. However, the Telco's responsibility ends at the terminator on their cable, which may be a good reason to let them install their NID.

Figure 16-3

A close-up of the owner-accessible panel in an NID

The Central Office   The wiring that connects a house to the telephone network connects the NID to the wiring and intermediate devices that lead back to the nearest switching center for the Telco, called a central office (CO). Figure 16-4 illustrates the basics of the connections that link a house to the CO.

The Telco's CO is a switching station that routes calls (including signals on DSL and ISDN services) to the location of the number being called. A CO handles all of the telephone traffic in a particular area. In smaller towns, the CO handles all calls; in larger areas, the CO handles a certain area of a city, county, or a specific area code.

Cabling and Entrance Bridges   If we look at the cabling used to provide a telephone service connection to a residence and start at the CO, in older situations, copper cabling with tens or even hundreds of wire pairs; in newer lines, fiber optic cabling is used to distribute "dial-tone" (analog telephone services) to every home. In areas where the telephone cabling is installed underground, a device called either an entrance bridge or a buried distribution pedestal is located in the yards of each or every two, three, or more houses. This device is about 2 to 3 feet tall and about 8 inches square (see Figure 16-5) and is where 50 pairs of wiring come up from underground to be interconnected into houses. On occasion, larger boxes that are about 4 or 5 feet tall and 2 feet wide are also located in neighborhoods that serve as intermediary bridges that distribute wiring to the entrance bridges.

Analog Lines   Analog telephone systems operate using voice and sound signals. Analog phone equipment is designed to interpret audible signals (of the number dialed) and route each call to its destination, building (or "nailing up") a temporary virtual circuit along the way on which the caller and the called can speak or transmit. This circuit is then "torn down" after the call is disconnected.

Digital Lines   Digital telephone circuits convert sound waves into digital (binary) signals for transmission to the other end of the connection where another telephone, modem, or even a television, converts the digital signals back to audible tones. The primary difference to the telephone user is clarity, because the digital system is able to remove any distortion in the signal. In addition, more features can be carried over the digital line than over an analog line.

By installing the proper switching and bridging equipment, existing telephone wiring can also be used to transmit digital data, such as with digital subscriber lines (DSL),

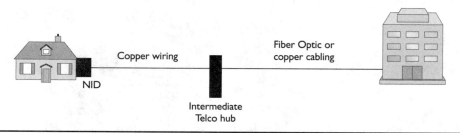

Figure 16-4   Telco lines connect a house to the central office (CO) for telephone service.

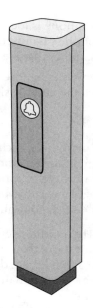

Figure 16-5
An entrance bridge is used to distribute telephone system wiring to individual houses.

Integrated Systems Digital Network (ISDN), and frame relay services. Digital services use the existing copper and fiber optic cabling to transmit digital (binary) data rather than analog (audible) signals.

Dialing Systems

Placing a local or a long-distance call requires a number of elements to be available:

- A telephone key set
- A dial-tone sound
- Telephone bandwidth
- A telephone number

Telephone Key Sets   A telephone, or what is also commonly called a key set, has four primary parts:

- **Hook switch**   This is the part of the phone that opens and closes the circuit loop that tells the phone's circuitry whether the phone is on hook (circuit open) or off hook (circuit closed). When the phone's handset is lifted (or the speaker phone button is depressed), the circuitry of the phone detects that the loop is closed and plays the dial tone sound or passes sound through it.

- **Keypad or rotary dial**   On older phones, a rotary dial was used to emit pulses, with 0 to 9 pulses representing the numbers 0 to 9. Newer phones are touch-tone that emit a recorded sound at a certain frequency for each number pressed on the keypad. For example, as you dial the numbers in a phone number, the phone emits a stream of combined frequency tones; the combination represents each number on the keypad.

- **Microphone**   A microphone is located in what is most commonly called the mouthpiece of a telephone's handset. The microphone converts the sound it picks up into sound samples that are transmitted to the telephone system.

- **Speaker**   The speaker in the handset of a telephone key set is a small 8-ohm speaker that plays back the audible signals transmitted to or played by the phone circuitry.

Dial Tone   The dial tone, as well as the tones representing the numbers dialed and several other common dialing sounds, such as busy, off-hook, and others, are recorded sounds embedded on a chip on the telephone's circuitry.

All of the tones produced by a telephone are a combination of two frequencies. For example, combining a 350 Hz tone with a 440 Hz tone creates the dial tone, and the busy signal is a combination of a 480 Hz tone and a 620 Hz tone that is cycled on and off.

System Bandwidth   The public telephone system limits transmitted sounds to not less than 400 Hz and not more than around 3,000 Hz. Any sounds with frequencies below 400 Hz or above 3,000 Hz are discarded, which is why a person may sound completely different over the phone than in person, where you can receive the full range of their voice's frequencies.

The telephone key set also limits the bandwidth requirement of voice communications by transmitting sound samples rather than the entire sound it receives. A concentrator circuit works with the telephone's microphone to create 8,000 samples per second of the sound it hears and transmits the sound samples across the public telephone system for playback by the speaker at the other end's handset.

Telephone Number Digits   Like the physical address of a networked computer or the address of a home, a telephone number is a unique address for a destination circuit. Each part of a telephone number has meaning, from a country code used to dial an international call, the area code, the prefix, and the line number. For example, in the number 509-555-1212, the 509 is the area code, the 555 is the prefix, and the 1212 is the line number.

- **Area code**   Area codes in the United States are regulated and assigned by the Federal Communications Commission (FCC) to designate a specific geographic region that could be a part of a city or state. For example, 509 is the area code for Eastern Washington State. Each area code can address 7,920,000 prefix and line number combinations. In the United States, around 400 area codes are in use out of the 680 possibilities.

- **Prefix**   At one time, the prefix represented a specific switch (at the CO) where a particular telephone was connected. However, since automated switches came into use, phone numbers, including the prefix have been portable under a method called local number portability (LNP), which means that a prefix and line number can connect to either a land line or cellular telephone.

- **Line number**   The CO switch identifies a specific line using the last four digits of a telephone number.

Caller Identity   Most new telephone key sets are able to display the identity (the phone number and the name the phone number is registered to) of the calling party either on the phone itself or on a satellite caller ID box.

The technology used to provide caller ID isn't new; in fact, it is the same used by modems to set up a connection—frequency shift keying (FSK). This technology uses certain tone frequencies to represent binary digits, such as 1,200 Hz for a one and 2,200 Hz for a zero, and the telephone or caller ID box converts these to ASCII characters for display.

Wireless Telephones

To this point, we have been discussing telephones in general, so most of this information applies to the standard wire-connected telephone and key sets. However, it is common for today's homes to include one or many cordless or wireless telephones, either in addition to or in replacement of standard telephones.

Cordless Telephones

A cordless telephone, like the one shown in Figure 16-6, allows a user to talk through the telephone's handset without being tethered to the telephone's base unit. As far as functionality goes, cordless phones have essentially the same features offered by a standard or corded telephone.

RF Functions   Cordless telephones combine the functions of a standard telephone with those of radio frequency (RF) transmitter/receiver. The base of a common cordless phone is wired into the telephone system just like a standard telephone. However, the base communicates to the handset using RF communications and a frequency modulation (FM) signal. The handset receives the FM radio signal and converts it back to

Figure 16-6

A cordless
telephone

Photo courtesy of Siemens Information and Communication Mobile, LLC.

an audio signal and is sent to the handset's speaker. The microphone on the handset performs an opposite action, translating the audio signals into FM radio signals for transmission to the base unit that converts the RF signals to voice signals for transmission through the telephone wiring.

The handset and base of a cordless telephone use a pair of different frequencies, one for incoming signals and one for outgoing signals. A frequency pair that is used this way is referred to as a duplex frequency. For example, the base unit may use 44 MHz to transmit and 49 MHz to receive, which is reversed on the handset where 49 MHz is used to transmit and 44 MHz is used for the receiver.

Operational Issues   A cordless telephone does have a few operational issues that a standard telephone doesn't have:

- **Interference issues**   One of the drawbacks to cordless phones that operate in the 2 and 5 GHz frequency bands is that they can pick up interference from household appliances, such as a microwave, and they can interfere with wireless networks or security systems in the home. In 2006, the Digital Enhanced Cordless Telecommunications (DECT) 6.0 standard was released that defines a cordless telephone system that transmits in the 1.9 GHz range for voice-only communications. Unlike the 2 and 5 GHz cordless phone, DECT 6.0 phones are hyped to be "interference-free communications" and won't interfere with other wireless systems in a home.

- **Range limitations**   The operating frequency (RF band) of a cordless telephone has a direct impact on the operating range of the handset or the distance the handset can be from the base and continue to work properly. For the most part, unless the phone is poorly made, nearly all cordless phones have a minimum range of 100 meters, and most have much more.

- **Sound reproduction**   The sound quality of a cordless phone's handset is affected by a variety of things, including distance and interference created by obstructions, such as walls or electrical appliances.

- **Security issues**   Because a cordless phone transmits using RF signals on common radio frequency bands, the transmitted signals can be intercepted by other RF devices, including other cordless phones that operate on the same band, baby monitors, radio scanners, and the like.

The performance issues of a cordless phone are the result of the phone's design and features, primarily the phone's RF band, whether the phone is analog or digital, and the number of channels it has available.

Inexpensive cordless phones are commonly analog devices that are generally electrically noisier, susceptible to interference, and more easily intercepted by other RF devices. Digital cordless phones provide a better sound quality and, because they also use digital spread spectrum (DSS) signaling, they are generally more secure than an analog phone. DSS uses several frequencies to transmit signals between the base and the handset, which makes it very hard for another device to intercept an entire conversation.

RF frequency bands can be divided into several channels; the more channels available, the better chance the base unit is able to find a channel pair that is relatively free from interference. Typically, a low-end 900 MHz phone has from 20 to 60 channels; higher-end 900 MHz, 1.9 GHz, 2.4 GHz, and 5.8 GHz phones have as many as 100 channels.

Residential Telephone Systems

If the homeowner desires only a single telephone line with multiple extensions without any added features beyond those provided by the Telco, chances are that the house has everything it needs to fulfill this requirement once the wiring and the phone jack outlets are installed during pre-wire.

However, if the homeowner wishes to have multiple phone lines accessible throughout the house, careful consideration must be given to exactly what features the homeowner is looking for and if a telephone system will meet their needs.

There are several advantages to a telephone system over the standard telephone service found in most homes. These advantages include:

- **Call routing**   An automatic call distribution (ACD) allows callers to select the direct line to a member of the household or leave a voice message for a specific user.

- **Multiple phone line accessibility**   All phones have access to the phone lines connected to the phone system and allow for the automatic selection of the next available line—no current conversations can be interrupted by someone else in the home picking up the phone on the same line.

- **Intercom capabilities**   All phones, and even a doorbell station, can be intercom stations and can be called from other phones in the house. Also, phones can be put on "private mode" so the room is not interrupted with the telephone ringing.

- **Expandability**   Phone systems are typically based on an expandable base unit to which additional features or telephones can be added or upgraded as the homeowners' needs change.

- **Fax/modem connections**   A phone system can provide connections for a fax or modem without tying up a voice line.

- **Voice and data integration**   Many phone systems include the ability to integrate high-speed voice and data communications using computer telephony integration (CTI).

- **Voice messaging**   Phone systems commonly have the ability to record outgoing announcements for each household member and record incoming voice messages in separate voice message boxes.

KSU-Based Systems

A KSU (key service unit) is a central device that provides the switching and control services for the entire network of key sets on a telephone system. In some cases, the KSU may also be referred to as a public branch exchange (PBX) or a computerized PBX (C-PBX).

Regardless, a KSU provides additional or advanced features to standard telephone sets, including such features as call forwarding, extension dialing, voice mail, music on hold, and more. The fact that a KSU must be configured in a star topology is considered a drawback, but structured wiring provides this sort of topology, and a phone system can easily be installed on structured wiring. Most KSU-based systems may require proprietary or specially configured key sets that add to the overall cost of the system.

KSU systems provide many business functions as well, including an auto-attendant that answers the phone with a recording and allows the caller to select an extension from a recorded menu, such as "For Ron, press 1; for Connie, press 2," and so on.

KSU-based systems also offer a wide range of optional features as well, including:

- Automatic routing for fax calls to a fax machine
- Toll restriction that prevents certain users from placing certain outgoing toll or long-distance calls
- PC-accessible call and activity reporting
- Call waiting
- Music on hold from an external music source
- Three-party teleconferencing
- A do-not-disturb function that blocks incoming calls (internal and external) from ringing on a blocked extension
- Call pickup that allows calls on one extension to be picked up on another extension when put on hold
- The ability to connect a door phone or an intercom station to talk with visitors on any extension phone
- An interface to relay devices or AC outlets that allow home lights, appliances, and other devices to be turned on and off through the telephone

KSU-less Systems

Another type of KSU system, at least in terms of functionality, is the KSU-less system. KSU-less systems are relatively low-cost options for residential phone systems with two to seven telephone lines. The primary attractiveness to a KSU-less telephone system, beyond its features, is that it can work with nearly any ordinary phone, including both rotary dial and touchtone. However, to utilize all of the features of the system, a central unit or specialized telephone stations may be required. KSU-less systems typically provide all, or at least the majority, of the features of a KSU-based system, but commonly at a much lower cost.

Digital Systems

Digital telephone systems are key systems like KSU-based systems and rely on a central processor for many of their functions. Digital key systems, also like a KSU system, allow the telephone system to share multiple CO lines across a number of key stations.

Figure 16-7
A digital
telephone
system with
a digital PBX,
key station, and
cordless phone

Photo courtesy of Panasonic USA.

Figure 16-7 shows the central unit and samples of the digital key stations for one residential and small business system.

Because they have what amounts to a computer at their core, digital telephone systems are programmable, typically through a graphical user interface that can be accessed either by attaching a monitor to the central unit or connecting the central unit to a data network.

One of the downsides to a digital telephone system is that it requires the use of special digital telephone key sets, and any existing fax machines and modems must continue to use separate analog phone lines. On the other hand, however, digital phones include such features as:

- **Automatic Call Distribution (ACD)**   Callers can use a hierarchy of voice prompts and menu choices to route themselves to the proper phone.

- **Computer Telephony Integration (CTI)**   This feature supports the integration of some telephone functions with those of a computer network. A common CTI feature is the routing of voice mail into a user's e-mail mailbox.

- **Incoming and outgoing call logs**   Digital systems have the ability to store calling line identification (CLID) information and prepare listings reporting call, time, and date information.

- **Intercom**   Most digital systems provide intercom functions for station-to-station communications.

- **Integrated Voice Response (IVR)**   This feature is less important for residential use but can come in handy for home offices. IVR allows the voice response of information retrieved from a computer file or database. If you've ever called a credit card company for your balance, you were likely using IVR.

PART IV

- **Programmable key set buttons**   Each key station on the system can be customized to the needs of the user.

- **Speakerphone**   Digital phones provide high-quality audio, which facilitates hands-free conversations, teleconferencing, and background music playback, all with volume control.

- **Speech recognition**   This feature allows callers to use voice commands to navigate through ACD menu choices.

IP-Based Telephones

A relatively recent development in home telephony systems is the availability of telephone systems that transmit over network bandwidth using Voice over Internet Protocol (VoIP), which is a bundle of networking protocols specifically designed to package analog voice for transmission across a digital packet–switched network. VoIP is commonly used as a generic term to cover all IP-based telephony, which has also been called IP telephony, voice over broadband, or broadband phone systems.

VoIP is implemented in one of two ways: Direct Inward Dialing (DID) or the use of an access number. DID works much like a POTS line with the sender (caller) dialing the phone number of the receiver (person being called), and the call is directly connected when answered. An access number system typically uses only a few main telephone numbers with each subscriber assigned an extension number off of a main number. Using a postal mail analogy, DID is like direct home delivery and access numbers are more like a post office box.

There are several large providers of regional or international VoIP services, with Skype and Vonage probably the largest operators in terms of subscribers. Systems like Skype are free, but require calls to any mobile or PSTN number to be originated from a computer using free software. Systems like Vonage require the purchase of a proprietary phone adapter to which any touch-tone phone can be connected, including cordless or corded phones. The benefits to the homeowner for either type of VoIP system is that the calls are either totally free or an unlimited amount of calls can be made for a fixed-amount service fee.

Quality of Service (QoS)   One of the major considerations that must be made when contemplating the use of VoIP in a home is the quality of service (QoS) offered by the supporting provider. Because broadband networks can and do lose packets and audio sampling rates of VoIP systems are something less than high-quality audio, there can be drop-offs in the service, especially in congested, high-volume areas or over extremely long distances. However, as VoIP technology continues to advance, the QoS of a VoIP system will improve over time.

Not all VoIP systems include QoS (which is used to indicate that some Internet traffic, such as voice transmissions), have a higher priority over others. Table 16-1 lists the QoS priorities for IP-based traffic. VoIP packets have a QoS priority of 5, which is a fairly high priority, but should the network become congested, packets can still be discarded. In comparison, e-mail, which is transmitted with a QoS of 0 on those systems that apply QoS to e-mail traffic, is transmitted only when the network is fairly idle.

	QoS Priority	Traffic Type
Table 16-1 Quality of Service (QoS) Priority Levels	0	Best effort transmissions
	1	Background transmissions
	2	Standard transmissions
	3	Business critical transmissions
	4	Streaming multimedia transmissions
	5	Voice and video transmissions
	6	Layer 3 network control transmissions
	7	Layer 2 network control transmissions

Events like packet loss, the packet discard rate, network delay, end system delay, signal-to-noise ratio, echo, and jitter (anomalies or variations in the signal's amplitude, frequency, or phase) typically occur in peak usage periods on a network. QoS can be applied to ensure a certain level of performance, but at the cost of additional overhead on the transmission system. Although QoS, as defined under the telephone industry's X.902 standard, is an actual measuring and error-capturing suite of protocols, it cannot overcome hardware-based errors. The result is that QoS, in common application, has come to describe a subjective user experience relating to the reliability, clarity, and continuity of the service.

Ring Equivalence Number (REN) An issue that also can affect the performance of a standard analog telephone system, but which becomes somewhat complicated on a VoIP system, is the ring equivalence number (REN). The REN is a measurement of the amount of power a telephone connection (jack) pulls from the telephone line to ring the phone for an incoming call. For example, if a phone outlet box is rated with a REN of 4 and three phone sets, each with a REN of 2, are connected to the outlet, the REN draw of 6 (from the three phone sets) being larger than the outlet's REN of 4 will likely cause the three phone sets to not work properly, especially if they have caller-ID or call-waiting services, because there is not enough power available to them.

On a VoIP system, especially one that uses an analog telephone adapter (ATA) or integrated access device (IAD), the foreign exchange subscriber (FXS) jacks (all connections to a phone system are FXS connections) each have a REN limit, typically between 3.0 and 5.0 for about 200 feet. If the devices attached to the FXS port have a combined REN total higher than that of the FXS port, all of the devices attached to the VoIP interface device may not work. Newer analog and digital telephones typically have a REN of less than or equal to 1.0. However, some VoIP-compatible devices take all of their power from the phone line and can have a REN higher than 1, which means the number of devices attached to the FXS port is limited.

Session Initiation Protocol (SIP) The Session Initiation Protocol (SIP) allows one VoIP caller to place a call to another VoIP user. When a caller "dials" the phone number of a VoIP-based user, SIP converts the telephone number into the IP address of the destination phone and then sends an "invitation" to the destination address, which causes the phone to ring.

Another protocol, the Simple Traversal of UDP through NATs (STUN), allows a SIP device that is on a local network behind a Network Address Translation (NAT) router to work with the NAT device to allow VoIP phones to be called by other VoIP phones, regardless of where they are on the network.

VoIP Paging Paging over a VoIP network is an emerging technology that may remain somewhat expensive in comparison to an analog paging or intercom system for at least the near-term future. However, where it can be afforded, it provides a fairly future-proof way to expand or extend a paging system should another home be added or if more parts of the home are added to the system at a later date.

To add paging to a VoIP system requires the installation of a VoIP gateway that supports paging, something not typically included in the standard VoIP ATA devices initially installed with the system. A VoIP gateway that includes a paging system can cost more than $400, where the standard VoIP gateway or ATA devices are commonly less than $100.

Another consideration for planning to install a VoIP system with paging support is the cost of the IP-capable speakers. These specialty speakers can cost as much as ten times the cost of an analog speaker and can require a Power over Ethernet (PoE) hub to power them.

Intercom Systems

There are two general categories of intercom systems that can be installed in a home: wired and wireless. There are two ways to implement an intercom system in a home: through the telephone system or through the installation of an independent, stand-alone wall-mounted intercom system.

Telephone-Based Intercom Newer key stations and analog telephones feature intercom and speaker-phone capabilities that allow the telephone to be used to call room to room, typically with the press of a single button, and talk with someone in another location in the house with a totally hands-free conversation.

Standalone Intercom Systems We refer to these systems as independent only to differentiate them from telephone-based intercom systems. This type of intercom system consists of master units, remote controls, speakers, and now even displays that are typically wall-mounted devices placed at the mouth-level of the average person.

There are a variety of standalone intercom systems available:

- **Doorbell intercom** This type of intercom system includes a doorbell for visitors to ring the standard phones in the house with a unique ring-ring to identify it is the doorbell intercom and not an incoming phone call. When a phone is answered in the house, the connection becomes a two-way voice intercom that allows the homeowner to speak with the visitor. Some systems also include the ability to remotely open or unlock a door.

- **Voice-only intercom**   This is the type of intercom system that is implemented on a telephone system and on low-end intercom systems. Low-end voice intercom systems typically only support half-duplex (two-way communication, but only one way at a time) conversations where the user must push a button to speak or announce. Voice-only intercom systems implemented on KSU, KSU-less, or digital telephone systems generally support full duplex (two-way communications, two ways at the same time) conversations.

- **Voice/radio intercom**   These systems represent the midrange in cost and capability in intercom systems. Many limit voice communications to half-duplex, but more full-duplex systems are now available. The master unit of a voice/radio intercom includes an AM/FM radio that can be played throughout the system. Some newer models also include playback units for audiocassettes or CDs.

- **Video intercom systems**   Video intercom systems are primarily used to identify someone at a doorway or other secured areas. These systems incorporate a voice intercom and video capture and display and are available with a single built-in, wide-angle camera or have the ability to connect to multiple external cameras. The video image can be one-way, where only the master unit inside the house has a video screen, or two-way, where both the inside and outside devices have displays.

Chapter Review

The telephone network consists of two network layers: the plain old telephone system (POTS) and the Public Switched Telephone Network (PSTN). POTS refers to the wiring and cabling connecting a house or building to the local CO. The PSTN includes CO and the equipment and transmission lines that carry voice signals to a destination.

The Telco's POTS line, which terminates at a house at the demarcation point (demarc) or network interface device (NID), is a terminating device that interconnects Telco wiring to a home's telephone wiring. The demarc is commonly located on an outside wall of the house. The Telco owns the lines up to the demarc (and most times the demarc itself), but all internal telephone wiring is the responsibility of the homeowner. The POTS lines connect a house to the Telco's central office (CO) or switching facility. The CO routes calls to the CO and switching associated with the number being called.

Analog telephone systems transmit voice and audio signals. Analog telephone lines also provide support for modem connections made by computers. Digital services use the existing copper and fiber optic cabling to transmit digital (binary) data rather than analog (voice) signals. Digital services include DSL and ISDN.

A telephone set has four primary parts: hook switch, keypad or rotary dial, microphone, and speaker. Combining two audible frequencies creates the tones produced by a telephone. For example, combining a 350 Hz tone with a 440 Hz tone creates the dial tone.

The telephone system transmits sounds between 400 Hz and 3,000 Hz. Sounds below or above this range are discarded, which is why people sound different on the phone than in person. Telephone key sets transmit sound by creating 8,000 sound samples per second.

Each part of a telephone number has meaning. A telephone number typically consists of an area code, a prefix, and a line number. Caller ID uses frequency shift keying (FSK) to transmit ASCII caller identification information.

A cordless telephone includes a stationary base unit and a portable (unwired) handset. Cordless telephones combine a standard telephone with a radio frequency (RF) transmitter/receiver. The cordless phone base communicates to the handset using RF communications and a frequency modulation (FM) signal.

There are three primary types of residential home telephone systems: KSU-based systems, KSU-less systems, and digital key systems. A KSU is a central device that provides the switching and control services for the entire telephone system. KSU-less systems are relatively low-cost options for residential phone systems with two to seven telephone lines and work with standard telephones. Digital key systems rely on a central processor for their functions and provide advanced features.

Common features for residential telephone systems are automatic call distribution (ACD), computer telephony integration (CTI), intercom capability, programmable key set buttons, speaker-phone compatibility, and speech recognition.

Three general types of intercom system can be used in a home setting: doorbell intercoms, standalone voice intercom systems, and intercoms integrated into phone systems.

Questions

1. What connecting jack and plug standard is used for telephone system wall outlets and key sets?

    A. RJ-232

    B. RJ-45

    C. RJ-32

    D. RJ-11

2. What is the name applied to the cabling used to connect a house to its local CO?

    A. PTSN

    B. POTS

    C. PSTN

    D. ISDN

3. What is the common name for the device used to terminate the CO line to a house?

    A. POTS

    B. PSTN

    C. Telco

    D. Demarc

4. What Telco device is used to distribute CO line wiring to individual houses or buildings?

   A. Multiplexer

   B. Entrance bridge

   C. Line splitter

   D. NID

5. Which type of telephone system transmits a telephone call as audible signals?

   A. Analog

   B. Digital

   C. KSU

   D. KSU-less

6. What is a high-speed broadband service that transmits over existing POTS lines?

   A. POTS

   B. PSTN

   C. DSL

   D. H.323

7. What are the frequency ranges transmitted by telephone systems?

   A. 0 to 10,000 Hz

   B. 400 to 3,000 Hz

   C. 1,000 to 8,000 Hz

   D. 2,000 to 10,000 Hz

8. What is the technology used to transmit caller identification information?

   A. PSTN

   B. DSL

   C. H.323

   D. FSK

9. What technology do cordless phones use to transmit between the handset and the base unit?

   A. IR

   B. RF

   C. IVR

   D. DSL

10. What digital key system feature allows for the integration of voice and data features and functions?

   A. ACD

   B. CLID

   C. CTI

   D. IVR

Answers

1. **D.** An RJ-45 jack is used to connect twisted-pair wiring; the other choices don't exist.

2. **B.** The plain old telephone system (POTS) describes the analog wiring and service used to connect a CO to the demarc of a house. PSTN is the Public Switch Telephone Network that includes the switching systems of a Telco; ISDN is the Integrated Services Digital Network, which is a digital data system; and PTSN is not a Telco abbreviation.

3. **D.** Demarc is short for demarcation point, which is also called a network interface device (NID). POTS and PSTN are the different network layers of the telephone network, and Telco is a short form of telephone company.

4. **B.** An entrance bridge is a 2- to 3-foot tall device where the underground cable is distributed to individual buildings.

5. **A.** Analog systems transmit signals in their native form without converting them into digital format. KSU and KSU-less systems are types of facility-based telephone systems.

6. **C.** Digital subscriber line (DSL) service uses existing POTS lines to carry digital broadband signals. H.323 is an IP telephony standard.

7. **B.** This relatively small range is the reason people sound different over the telephone than in person.

8. **D.** Frequency shift keying uses different frequencies to transmit binary-encoded ASCII data to a telephone set.

9. **B.** Radio frequency technology is used to connect the handset to the base of a cordless phone. IR (infrared) is not used for this purpose; IVR is a key system feature; and DSL is a POTS broadband technology.

10. **C.** Computer Telephony Integration provides the ability for voice mail messages to be saved as e-mail messages. ACD, CLID, and IVR are other key system features.

Designing and Installing a Home Telephony System

In this chapter, you will learn about
- Residential telephone design considerations
- Standard phone line installation hardware and termination points
- Telephone system installation hardware and termination points
- Intercom installation

The primary considerations when designing a residential telephone and telecommunications system are meeting the client's needs and integrating the telephone system and its wiring into the structured wiring, data network, control system, and other whole house systems.

In this chapter, we discuss design considerations and installation activities for the structured wiring installation for both standard phone lines and an automated phone system.

Residential Telephone Systems Design

The design process for a residential telephone system using structured wiring must address the inclusion and placement of the telecommunication wiring schemes, outlet boxes, wire termination, jacks, punch-down blocks, patch panels, wire identification and labeling, and of course, the telephone key sets (specialized phones designed to work with the key system unit).

Wiring Schemes

Telephone system wiring is typically installed using one of two schemes: series wiring or star (also known as homerun) wiring. The star wiring scheme is the basis of a structured wiring approach and is always recommended for new construction or complete retrofit installations. Unfortunately, series wiring is very common in older homes.

Series Wiring

Before 1980, series wiring was the standard wiring scheme used by telephone companies to install residential telephone service. The series wiring scheme is also referred to as daisy chain wiring because the wiring is installed by running wires from one contact to the next. However, in situations where the telephone wiring must be reconfigured to accommodate more central office (CO) lines or more than three or four extension telephones, series wiring can become very restrictive.

Perhaps the best way to plan for a new telephone system around series wiring is to insert a punch-down block or patch panel and pull separate runs to each room or zone of the house. Figure 17-1 shows a simplified drawing of series wiring in a house. In this case, the telephones (perhaps more than would be normally found in a home, but included to make the point) are wired in a daisy chain from the single connection in the network interface device (NID). Figure 17-2 shows a possible rework for the telephone system incorporating a Key Service Unit (KSU) phone system.

CROSS-REFERENCE   See Chapter 23 for more information on KSU systems.

Star Wiring

A star wiring approach (see Figure 17-3) for a residential telecommunications system runs telephone wiring from each phone jack in the rooms of a house to a central point that is usually located near the demarc (demarcation point) or NID where the line or lines from the Telco's CO arrive at the house.

Running a separate run of four-pair Cat 5e/Cat 6 unshielded twisted-pair (UTP) wire to each telephone outlet jack provides flexibility in terms of which incoming CO lines are linked to which phones. In situations where only a single CO line comes into

Figure 17-1

A telephone system using serial wiring

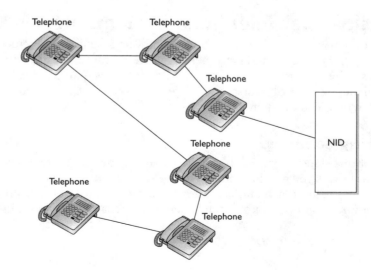

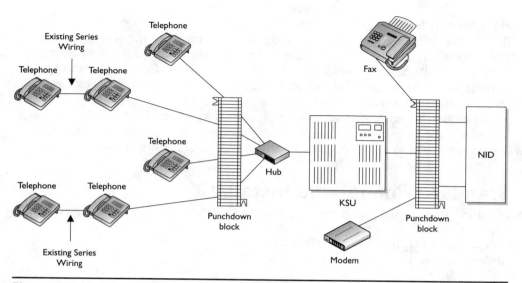

Figure 17-2 A series wiring system reconfigured into a star wiring approach

a house, the choices may be to make some outlets only intercom stations and give access to the CO line to others. However, should more CO lines be added to the system at some point, using a punch-down block or a central telephone system control device, such as a KSU or digital control unit, makes it easy to configure which outlets have access to which CO lines.

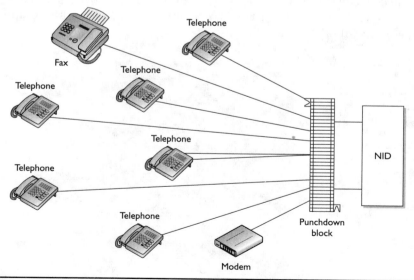

Figure 17-3 A telephone system installed on a star wiring approach

Horizontal Wiring

Because the telephone wiring inside a house, meaning all of the wiring beyond the demarc, is the responsibility of the homeowner, it is important to use only wiring that is category verified and carries a Underwriters Laboratories, Inc. (UL) marking on its outer jacket. Category verified wiring meets or exceeds industry fire, electrical, and materials specifications and also meets local building codes.

The current industry standards and recommendations specify a minimum of UTP Category 3 wiring for residential voice applications, although many new construction installations use Cat 5e or Cat 6 (and perhaps even Cat 7) wiring in its place.

Standard Phone Line Installation

Installing a residential telephone system in a new construction situation requires that you first identify the wiring installed by the telephone company and then how to install structured wiring to support a standard telephone system. Each of these areas is discussed in the sections that follow.

Telephone Wiring

When working with the wiring installed by the telephone company, you may find one or more of the following wire and cable types:

- **25-pair cable** This is a gray-, beige-, or pink-jacketed cable that contains 25 pairs of twisted wire, as shown in Figure 17-4. Although this large of a cable is unusual in residential situations, some older large homes have been known to have a 25-pair cable connected to the demarc using an RJ-21 50-pin connector, commonly called an Amp (short for Amphenol) Champ. RJ-21 connectors are used to connect this size cable to punch-down blocks and other types of distribution panels.

Figure 17-4
A 25-pair UTP cable cut away to show the internal wire pairs

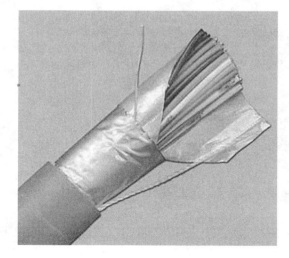

Figure 17-5
A satin cord terminated with an RJ-11 plug

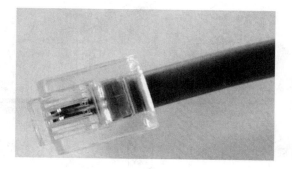

- **Satin cord**   So called for its silver coating, this flat cable has four untwisted 26-gauge wires, has either RJ-11 (shown in Figure 17-5) or RJ-45 jacks, and is used to connect a wall outlet to a telephone set.

- **Station wire**   Many existing residential telephone systems use station wire, which consists of four 24-gauge solid-core wires (see Figure 17-6) that are twisted together into two wire pairs—one consisting of red and green wires and one consisting of yellow and black wires. This type of wire is also called plain old telephone service (POTS) wire. Newer types of station wire are made up of blue and orange wires banded with white in which one pair is blue/white and orange/white and the other pair is white/orange and white/blue.

Structured Wiring for Standard Telephone System

Chapter 3 discusses the requirements for installing structured wiring. However, there are product specifications and handling issues that should be considered.

Standard Phone Outlet Wiring

Four-pair UTP Cat 3 minimum wiring (Cat 6e recommended for future-proofing) should be installed between a location near where the demarc can be easily reached and the main telephone system distribution point inside the home. The wire pairs provide the capability to connect up to a combination of four phone, digital subscriber line (DSL), fax, or modem lines to inline locations in the house, as illustrated in Figure 17-7.

Figure 17-6
Station wire has four solid-core wires.

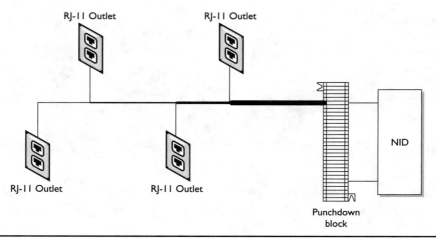

Figure 17-7   Cat 5e wiring installed for a telephone system

Cable

If a structured wiring installation is to support only a telephone system, only a four-conductor cable, such as station wire, is required and category-rated cabling isn't needed. However, installing Cat 5e cable to each outlet of the telephone system helps to future-proof the system. If structured wiring is being installed to support audio, control, video, and other whole-house applications, it may be better to install composite cable that includes all of the various wire types needed to support each of a home's subsystems and also provides for future cable requirements.

The wire elements included in common composite cables are typically two or more runs of either Cat 5e or Cat 3 UTP and one or more runs of coaxial cable. Figure 17-8 illustrates the makeup of one type of residential structured wiring cable. In most instances, installers use Cat 5e cabling in a composite cable for both voice and data networking.

Punch-down/Distribution Blocks

Structured wiring concepts involve a central distribution point that serves as both the center of the star topology and a single testing, maintenance, and configuration location.

Figure 17-8
Composite
structured wiring
cable with two
runs each of Cat
5e and coaxial
cable

A cable interface, patch panel, or punch-down block, also called a cross-connect block, is typically used as the distribution point in structured telephone wiring installations. If a structured pre-wiring system is in use in the home, then the telephone lines will terminate in the central service unit of that system.

Distribution Panels   There are several models of telephone system distribution panels made especially for, and incorporated into, residential telephone systems. Residential phone distribution modules simplify the wiring for a home telephone system because they include features such as already in-place bridging for up to 4 CO lines to 12 or as many as 48 telephone outlets, 110-style punch-down or RJ-style connectors in and out, and wall-mount kits. Most of these systems also satisfy the requirements for home distribution devices as required by the Electronic Industries Alliance/Telecommunications Industry Association (EIA/TIA) 568 and 570 wiring standards.

For many residential installations, an RJ-11 patch panel makes more sense than using a punch-down patch panel to create the cross-connect between the CO line entrance cables and the Cat 3 or Cat 5e cable runs to the RJ-11 outlets. Most homeowners are not technical and, should the need arise to talk a customer through a line change for testing purposes, it is much easier to explain how to move an RJ-11 jack than a punch-down or pole and screw connection.

A patch panel, such as the one shown in Figure 17-9, incorporates 110-type punch-down connectors that link a CO line to distributed RJ-style connectors, which are connected to the cabling that runs to the outlets. There are also patch panels available that have RJ-style connectors for both incoming and outgoing connections.

Figure 17-9

Front and rear views of a patch panel

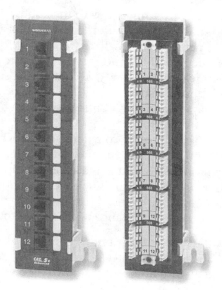

Photo courtesy of Signamax Connectivity Systems.

Connecting to the Demarc

Once the pre-wire stage is completed and the horizontal wiring is pulled into where the central distribution panel is located, the next step in completing the telephone system wiring is to bridge the demarcation point to the outlet wiring runs. This bridge is created using either a distribution panel or a patch panel.

Demarc to Patch Panel   The simplest way to connect the demarc point or the NID into the distribution point is to terminate a single run of Cat 5e or Cat 6 wire with an RJ-11 jack and plug it into the customer access side of the NID. A single run of Cat 3, Cat5e, or Cat 6 wire accommodates up to four incoming CO lines. The four pairs of wire in the Cat 3/5e/6 wire are then terminated into the distribution panel, which for this discussion is an RJ-11 patch panel with 110-type punch-down blocks.

For testing purposes, it is always best to terminate the wiring from the demarc/NID at standard phone jacks at the phone system location. This allows for testing of each phone line inside of the house before the phone system itself is installed. If there is a problem with one or more phone lines, this rules out the phone system as the cause of the problem.

NOTE   It is always advisable, especially if there is a phone system or security system, to run the cable of each phone line from the NID through a surge suppressor before connecting it into the distribution panel. Many structured wiring panels have built-in surge suppressors to protect alternating current (AC) electrical outlets, coaxial cable outlets, and RJ-11 outlets.

Distribution Panel to Outlets   The cable installed during pre-wire for the telephone outlets should be terminated with the appropriate RJ-style outlets in the rooms of the house and into the distribution panel so that each outlet is bridged to the appropriate CO line, per the homeowner's wishes.

Depending on the type of telephone system you are installing, the outlet jacks can be a standard telephone (RJ-11) or an RJ-45 outlet that supports a KSU/telephone system or an IP-based telephone system. Since RJ-11 jacks fit in both RJ-11 and RJ-45 outlets, it is advisable to always install RJ-45 outlets to accommodate both standard phone and future phone systems.

Outlet jacks are typically color-coded and are either a 66- or a 110-punch-down. The 66-type is more common with telephone equipment and the 110-type is more common with networking devices. If the outlet is a standard phone jack, the red and green pins are used to enable line one; if a second line is being connected to the jack, line two is connected to the yellow and black pins. If you are using a data jack (RJ-45), the blue pins are connected for line one and the orange pins are used for line two, if needed.

Telephone to Outlet   If the phone cords aren't already terminated or you decide not to purchase already terminated cords, you may need to terminate the cords with RJ-11 plugs. A variety of manufacturers now make self-terminating jacks for RJ-11 and RJ-45 outlets that eliminate the need for wire stripping, untwisting wires, and a punch-down tool.

Table 17-1 RJ-11 and RJ-11/12 Pinouts for Station Wiring Connectors	Signal	Cat 3/5 Wire Color	RJ-11/12 6-Pin	RJ-11 4-Pin
	Line three (tip)	White/green	1	
	Line two (tip)	White/orange	2	1
	Line one (tip)	White/blue	3	2
	Line one (ring)	Blue/white	4	3
	Line two (ring)	Orange/white	5	4
	Line three (ring)	Green/white	6	

Table 17-1 lists the pinouts for RJ-style plugs typically used to terminate Cat 3 or Cat 5e cable. Figure 17-10 compares 4-pin RJ-11 and 6-pin RJ-11/12 jacks.

NOTE The terms *tip* and *ring* are used in telephony to indicate the pins and wires that carry positive and negative voltage. These terms come from the old switchboard plug-in where the positive voltage was connected to the tip of the plug and the negative voltage was connected to a slip ring that was around the plug.

Telephone Outlets

Communications outlets are placed at the same height as the electrical outlets in a room, but no closer than one foot from an electrical outlet horizontally. If a room has a wall phone, its outlet should be mounted at about eye level, between 48 and 52 inches, on a wall. Wall phones require special outlet wall plates to support the physical phone on the wall.

Modular Jacks   Modular jacks are common in older and most existing homes. This type of jack is surface mounted and provides connections for up to two communication lines on a single jack. Figure 17-11 shows the common modular jack design.

Figure 17-10
4-pin (left) and
6-pin (right)
versions of an
RJ-11 plug

 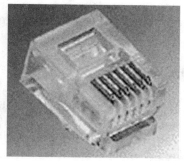

Figure 17-11
A modular
RJ-11 jack

Outlet Wall Plates and Jacks   Flush-mounted wall outlet jacks are more common in today's newer homes than in homes built before the 1960s. Wall jacks are available with up to six jack configurations. Typically, each of the individual jacks in a wall jack has either a 110-type connector or a RJ-11/12 style connector to receive and terminate the incoming telephone wiring.

Installing a KSU Telephone System

Installing a KSU (Key Service Unit) system is an alternative to installing a standard telephone system in which many services, such as voicemail, caller ID, and call-waiting are provided as subscribed services by the telephone company (Telco). A KSU-based telephone system has its own separate controller (the KSU itself) that can independently provide many of the same Telco subscriber services to specialized and/or standard telephones in the home.

The features typically provided by a residential KSU system include the capability to connect to standard telephones (and not proprietary key stations like many business KSU systems), voice-messaging (voicemail), station-to-station intercom support, auto-attendant, music-on-hold, caller ID, and in many cases, support for a door intercom.

Not every home needs or can afford a KSU telephone system, but in those homes with several phone lines and multiple extensions that desire these features and perhaps a few more, a KSU may be a very good value.

Installing the KSU

The KSU or controller of a KSU system should be treated like any central control unit and placed in a central location within the home, very near where the telephone line wire runs terminate. The commonly used method for connecting the KSU to the cable homeruns that are linked to the telephone outlets throughout a home is to terminate the cable runs into a 66-type punch-down block that bridges the cable runs to patch cords (also called pigtails) to the KSU using 25- or 50-pin Telco-type connectors (see Figure 17-12).

Figure 17-12
A 25-pin Telco connector is used to connect the internal phone wiring to a KSU.

The KSU should also be located fairly close to the connection for the Telco lines entering the home. In most cases, KSUs have RJ-11 jacks to connect to as many as eight incoming phone lines. The KSU should have a clean AC power source, preferably with a surge suppressor installed inline between the KSU's power supply and the AC outlet.

Programming

In most cases, a KSU telephone system is preprogrammed for most of its basic functions for a certain number of stations. However, some adjustments may be required to set the clock, program speed dials, or add additional phones or features. Depending on the changes required, the programming manuals for the system should detail the process used to effect these changes. Some KSUs can be programmed through a system phone, or they can provide an interface for connecting to a computer system or a terminal; in this case, changes are entered through software on the KSU. In other cases, some form of user interface, such as a liquid crystal display (LCD) and a keyboard, may be included on the KSU itself.

Planning for KSU Programming

The homeowners decide which features should be configured on the KSU system. Prior to beginning any programming changes or station configuration, you should summarize the system's features on a worksheet that details the number of telephones to be installed and the features available to each telephone. Table 17-2 shows a portion of a sample worksheet that could be used to record the KSU system's features your customer desires.

Programming Key Sets

If proprietary key sets (telephones) are installed along with the KSU, you will likely need to do some programming to set up each key set. In these instances, do this programming on each key set, following the procedures outlined in the system documentation.

Unit	Feature	Yes	Comments
Master Unit (KSU)			
	Auto-attendant		
	Automatic Call Distributor (ACD)		
	Caller ID		
	Direct Inward Dialing (DID)		
	Hunt group (rollover)		
	Unified messaging		
Station 1			
	Do Not Disturb (DND)		
	Intercom		
	One-number dialing (speed-dialing)		
	Speakerphone		
Station 2			
	Do Not Disturb (DND)		

Table 17-2　An Example of a KSU Features Worksheet

If standard telephones are to be connected to the KSU, you may need to do some programming on the KSU unit as well as through the telephone, using the specialized buttons and the standard touchtone buttons of the telephone.

Labeling Key Sets

KSU systems that require proprietary key sets (telephones) typically have a preprinted faceplate with labeling for the features supported by the system. On standard telephones connected to a KSU, some labeling will be required to mark the keys that activate certain functions. If multiple key presses are required to activate or deactivate a feature, a phone card or an instruction sheet should be made up for each station. Labeling the functions on the telephone or key set helps minimize the training required for the homeowner and extend its effectiveness.

Installing an Intercom

An intercom can provide a home's occupants with the convenience of being able to speak to each another without having to share the same space or shout at each other. Intercom systems are fairly common in new upscale homes and are a feature homeowners generally like.

There are three basic types of intercom systems:

- **Independent intercoms** These types of intercom systems are not interconnected into another system, although they may use existing wiring in a home to communicate. Independent intercoms can be installed using three forms of communications:

- **HomePNA intercoms** These types of independent intercoms communicate through a home's existing telephone wires and the users speak through standard telephone handsets. The intercom action is started by pressing a certain sequence of keys or the number of a special station number on a standard telephone. These systems allow a person arriving at a home's doorway to place a telephone call into the home and ring the phones with a unique ring. This provides both security and convenience to homeowners.

- **PLC intercoms** These types of intercoms communicate over AC electrical lines and operate in a similar fashion to HomePNA intercoms. However, PLC intercoms can cause potential problems with other PLC systems, such as lighting controls and PLC-based computer networks. For this reason, this type of intercom system isn't recommended if other PLC systems are in use.

- **Wireless intercoms** Wireless independent intercom systems are essentially room-to-room systems, such as baby monitors and tabletop or wall-mounted units. These units use ultra high frequency (UHF) or very high frequency (VHF) radio frequency (RF) signaling and work on the same principles as a walkie-talkie. Some wireless intercoms also offer the capability to encrypt transmission to prevent exterior interception. Keep in mind that many intercoms advertised as "wireless" are, in fact, PLC systems.

- **Standalone intercoms** Standalone intercoms are self-contained systems that communicate over their own dedicated wiring. These types of systems have been, and still are, somewhat popular in homes. In addition to allowing a home's occupants to communicate room-to-room, they can also include doorway units and master unit options that can include a radio receiver and a tape or a CD player that plays music throughout the intercom system stations. Figure 17-13 shows a fully featured standalone intercom master unit.

Figure 17-13
A standalone intercom master unit

Photo courtesy of Broan-Nutone.

NOTE Some homeowners prefer to use standard telephones throughout their home and install a standalone intercom system.

- **Telephone-based intercoms** Using the existing or standard telephone wiring and standard phones in a home, a doorbell intercom unit can be installed to enable the doorbell unit to ring a unique ring throughout the home on standard telephones and provide intercom service between the door and the telephones.

Chapter Review

The design process for residential telephone systems includes telecommunication wiring schemes, outlet boxes, wire termination, jacks, punch-down blocks, patch panels, wire identification and labeling, and telephone key sets. Telephone wiring is installed using either series wiring or star/homerun wiring, but star/homerun wiring is preferred.

The telephone wiring inside a home is the responsibility of the homeowner. It is important to use only category-verified wiring that meets or exceeds industry, fire, electrical, and materials specifications, and standards and local building codes. Current industry standards specify a minimum of UTP Cat 3 wiring. However, most new construction installs Cat 5e wiring.

There are four basic elements to a home telephone system: structured wiring, outlet jacks, punch-down or distribution blocks, and phone devices. Wiring installed by the telephone company can include 25-pair cable, satin cord, or four-conductor station wire.

Structured wiring support for a telephone system must address standard phone outlet wiring, structured wiring cable, punch-down/distribution blocks, and connections to the demarc.

Modular jacks are common in most existing homes. This type of jack is surface mounted and provides connection for up to two communication lines on a single jack. Flush-mounted wall outlet jacks are more common in newer homes.

A KSU-based telephone system has its own separate controller that provides many of the same Telco subscriber services to the telephones in the home. The features provided by a residential KSU system include the capability to connect to standard telephones, voice-messaging (voicemail), station-to-station intercom support, auto-attendant, music-on-hold, caller ID, and, in many cases, support for a door intercom. A KSU telephone system is preprogrammed with its basic functions. To add additional phones or features, some adjustments to the KSU's programming may be required. Prior to beginning any programming or station configuration changes, you should summarize the system's features on a worksheet that documents the number of telephones to be installed and the features available to each telephone. A worksheet should be used to record the KSU system's features desired by the homeowners.

There are three basic types of intercom systems: independent intercoms, standalone, and telephone-based intercoms. The most common types of independent intercoms are HomePNA intercoms, PLC intercoms, and wireless intercoms. Standalone intercoms are self-contained systems that communicate over dedicated wiring. Telephone-based intercoms allow for intercom service between the doorbell and the house telephones.

Questions

1. Under a structured wiring approach, telephone systems should be installed using what wiring scheme?

   A. Series

   B. Bus

   C. Ring

   D. Star

2. What device is placed at the center of the structured wiring for a telephone system?

   A. RJ-11 outlet

   B. Distribution panel

   C. Demarc

   D. Telephone key set

3. Virtually all household wiring standards require the use of what type of wiring?

   A. Cat 3

   B. UL Category verified

   C. Riser

   D. Plenum

4. A type of telephone system that is implemented on a central control unit that supports standard telephones or proprietary phones is a/an:

   A. Intercom

   B. KSU

   C. Telco

   D. Wireless

5. Which of the following is not a type of intercom system?

   A. Standalone

   B. Independent

   C. Telephone-based

   D. KSU

6. Which of the following should be done before making any programming changes to a KSU system? (There may be more than one answer.)

A. Complete features worksheet

B. Interview homeowners

C. Program telephone

D. Remove default programming

7. What cable is typically used to connect a telephone key set to a wall outlet?

A. Station wire

B. Coaxial cable

C. Satin cord

D. Zip wire

8. Which of the following is not a type of outlet jack commonly associated with telephone connections?

A. F-type

B. Modular

C. Face plate

D. Inline

9. What do the terms *tip* and *ring* refer to?

A. Incoming signal and bell

B. Positive and negative

C. Ring and busy tones

D. Dial and busy tones

10. How many phone lines can be supported by a single run of Cat 3 or Cat 5e cable?

A. Two

B. Three

C. Four

D. Six

Answers

1. **D.** Structured wiring is installed using a star topology. The other choices listed can be used for data networks but aren't recommended for residential wiring.

2. **B.** The other choices listed should be configured as satellites from the distribution panel.

3. **B.** Category verified cable has been tested and certified to meet residential cable standards. The other choices listed represent residential cable types or characteristics.

4. **B.** A KSU is a central controller device that supports the functions of the telephone units connected to it.

5. **D.** A KSU is a type of telephone system. The other choices are all types of intercoms.

6. **A and B.** Prior to making any programming changes to a KSU, you should interview the homeowners and record their desires on a KSU system worksheet that includes the features of the master unit and each of the telephones.

7. **C.** This flexible preconfigured wire is the common standard for outlet-to-station connections. Station wire, if used, is used for horizontal cabling; coaxial cable is rarely used in voice applications (although it could be); and zip wire is absolutely not voice system wiring.

8. **A.** F-type connectors are associated with coaxial cabling. Inline, though not mentioned in the chapter, is used to connect two RJ-11 connectors together.

9. **B.** At one time, these terms may have had other purposes, but today they represent only positive and negative voltage.

10. **C.** A four-pair UTP cable is able to support as many as four phone lines.

CHAPTER 18

Troubleshooting and Maintaining Home Communication Systems

In this chapter, you will learn about
- Common voice communication system problems
- Troubleshooting telephone system problems
- Communication system troubleshooting tools
- Testing communications cabling

Of all of the various systems in a home, the one that people can't seem to live without is the telephone system. So when problems develop, even minor problems can seem like an emergency. Your ability to diagnose, troubleshoot, isolate, and resolve a problem on a home's communication system becomes extremely important to restoring the home's ability to communicate with the outside world.

This chapter is focused on identifying the problems common to home communication systems and the methods and tools used to resolve these problems quickly and efficiently. The good news is that in a structured wiring environment, many of the processes are the same used to troubleshoot wiring and connection problems for most of the other systems in a home. As a home technology integration professional, you must know which troubleshooting process is used to identify and isolate each type of problem.

Wiring Issues

The telephone company's responsibility for problems on a home telephony system ends at the demarcation point or network interface device (NID), which is where the telephone company's lines terminate at the home. Beyond the NID, the wiring that provides telephone service throughout a home is considered to be customer premise inside wiring (CPIW) by the phone company. The homeowner is responsible for any problems that occur with the CPIW, unless the homeowner purchases wire maintenance services from the telephone company—but even then there are limits to what the telephone company will service.

Figure 18-1

The wires in a four-wire telephone line (quad wire)

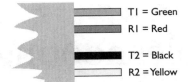

T1 = Green
R1 = Red
T2 = Black
R2 = Yellow

NID Wiring

Basic telephone wiring is a four-wire cable that actually consists of two pairs of wire: green and red wires that are treated as one pair and black and yellow wires that are treated as another pair. Each pair of wires carries the tip and ring signals used by a telephone to connect and communicate. As shown in Figure 18-1, the green wire is the tip wire in pair one, and the black wire is the tip wire in pair two. The red and yellow wires provide the ring link in each pair, respectively. On occasion, the phone company uses six-wire cable, which adds white and blue wires to those in the quad wire cable.

The NID is usually located on an outside wall of the house. At the NID (see Figure 18-2), each incoming line uses one of the two pairs in the telephone cable. If only a single line is entering the home, by telephone company standards, the red and green wires are connected to the point where the CPIW attaches to the NID. If a second line is provided, then the yellow and black wires are also connected. However, when connecting a second line, the black wire is treated as if it were green and the yellow wire as if it were red. If more than two lines are entering the home, the incoming wiring is likely to be Cat 3 cable with its four-wire pairs. See Table 18-1 for color-coding of wiring.

Figure 18-2

In the NID, each incoming telephone line is connected in its own connection segment.

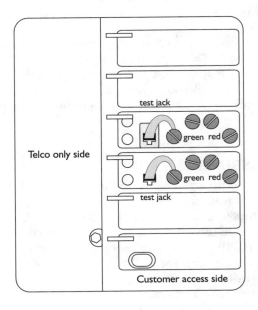

Table 18-1

Quad Wire to Cat 5e Conversion Conventions

Cat 5e Wire Color	Quad Wire Color	Function
White-Blue	Green	Line 1 tip
Blue	Red	Line 1 ring
White-Orange	Black	Line 2 tip
Orange	Yellow	Line 2 ring
White-Green	N/A	Line 3 tip
Green	N/A	Line 3 ring
White-Brown	N/A	Line 4 tip
Brown	N/A	Line 4 ring

One wiring problem you might run into inside the NID is that in situations where the red or the green wires have become damaged, the black and yellow wires may have been used to replace them instead of installing a new run of quad wire back to the distribution point. If you encounter this, and a second line is being installed, the phone company will need to replace their service line with a good four-wire cable.

Cat 5e/6 and the NID

When Cat 5e or Cat 6 wiring is connected to an NID, there are no red, green, yellow, and black wires to use, only blue, orange, green, and brown. If one or more lines in a home are having connection problems, the problem may be wiring inconsistencies at the NID.

Each of the four-wire pairs in a Cat 5e or Cat 6 cable can be used to replace the green and red (tip and ring) wires required for the connection. Table 18-1 lists the wire color replacement convention when using Cat 5e or Cat 6 in place of quad wire. As you can see, the white striped wire in each pair replaces the "green" wire (tip) in the telephone convention and the solid color wire in the pair replaces the "red" wire (ring).

 NOTE A good way to remember the order that the Cat 5e colors should be used for multiple telephone lines is to remember that the colors go from sky to earth: blue sky, then orange sunset, green trees, and brown dirt.

The order and assignment of the Cat 5e or Cat 6 wire pairs listed in Table 18-1 should be used throughout the home communications system. It is very important to use the same wiring scheme throughout a system to ensure conformity and consistency, since this can eliminate at least one potential problem when you have to troubleshoot the system.

Troubleshooting the NID

If a telephone line is dead on all inside telephones as well as at the structured wiring distribution panel, the problem could very well be with the incoming telephone line. To troubleshoot the connections in the NID, follow these steps:

   1. Locate the test jack (Figure 18-3) for the incoming line in question inside the NID.

Figure 18-3
Each incoming phone line connection in the NID has a test jack.

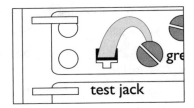

test jack

2. Ensure the RJ-11 plug connected to the green wire's setscrew is inserted into the jack securely.

3. You should remove and reinsert the plug into the test jack and recheck the problem telephone line to see if the problem wasn't just a problem with the connection at the test jack.

4. If the problem persists, remove the plug and connect a good telephone handset directly into the test jack. Removing the plug disconnects that line from the CPIW. When you insert a plug connected to the handset, the line is now connected directly to the telephone company's distribution system. If the line is still dead (no dial tone) then the problem is on the telephone company's lines and they should be notified of the problem.

5. However, if plugging directly into the test jack yields a dial tone, try calling a working telephone number to make sure there are no other problems on the telephone line.

6. If the line is working normally, then the problem is with the CPIW and you need to troubleshoot the structured wiring connected to the communications system.

Inside Wiring Issues

If a telephone line is working at the NID but not inside the home, the problem is most likely a wiring problem somewhere between the NID and the structured wiring panel or the telephone outlets (assuming you've already checked the handset and the telephone patch cord connecting it to the outlet).

The best way to troubleshoot exactly where the problem may be is to connect a handset to each connection point along the cable path. When you find the point where there is no dial tone on the phone, you can then begin to determine why that link is not working. Some common problems on the faulty link to look for are

- **Loose setscrew**   Check any terminal strips or setscrew connections to ensure they are tightened down. You should check the NID for this condition as well.

- **Reversed wires**   The wires in a wire pair may be reversed, two pairs may be reversed, or a split pair condition may exist.

- **Faulty termination**   Verify that the plug and jacks are securely attached to the cable. Check the wire pinout used in an RJ-11 or RJ-45 jack and plug. Replace the termination with the correct pinout, if needed.

- **Wire damage**   If some telephone jacks have phone service but others don't, the problem may be a damaged cable where only one or two wire pairs are shorting to each other because the cable has been cut or pierced. To verify this condition, you should run length, TDR, and wire map tests.

Interference and Noise

If a homeowner is complaining about a hum, static, or that conversations on one of a home's telephone lines can be heard on another, the issue is likely in the wiring somewhere.

Here are some common wire issues that can create noise on a telephone line:

- If the outer jacket of a cable is cut and even a small hole is opened, static or crackling may be heard on the phone lines attached to that cable. If even a small amount of moisture enters the cable, it can create a low-level short between two or more pairs, which may be heard on the line as static, snapping, or crackling.

- If there are any loose or poorly done splices (heaven forbid!), taps, or loose connections between the distribution panel and an outlet, users may hear static, buzzing, or a hum on the line. If there are any splices or taps in the line, they should be removed and any loose connections repaired or replaced.

- If the users complain of a loud hum on a line, the problem is likely a connection made to a grounded line. The connection should be redone avoiding the ground. You will need to retrace the wiring back to the main electrical panel to identify the circuits connected to the main's ground then reconnect the telephone wiring to avoid a connection to these circuits.

- If the outlet has a line splitter installed and a fax machine, answering machine, or even another telephone is sharing the line, it can add noise to the line when they are in use. If the other equipment has permanent needs, additional lines should be installed to service them.

- The telephone patch cords that come with telephone sets are also called line cords, but they aren't always the best quality. A faulty or poor quality line cord can create noise on the line at the handset.

- EMI and RFI can be a problem for communication systems that are installed on UTP. If all other troubleshooting tests fail to identify the source of noise on a line, verify the placement of the UTP cable and ensure that it is installed per the EIA/TIA guidelines regarding other electrical equipment and AC power lines.

Connector Issues

When a second phone line is added to an existing telephone system, the outlet jacks and wiring blocks are commonly overlooked. If the original installation didn't provide wiring blocks and jacks that were pre-wired for two or more lines, the wiring connecting the second line to the outlet is virtually dead-ended. Whenever installing new wiring, be sure to terminate all wires and connections.

PART IV

If a phone line isn't working for only a single outlet or handset, check the termination of the homerun cable at the wiring block or structured wiring panel and into the jack. An RJ-11 plug will connect into an RJ-45 jack, so verify that the RJ-45 jack has been terminated for a telephone connection and not a data network connection. Use Table 18-1 earlier in the chapter and the information in Chapter 10 to differentiate these connections.

HomePNA Issues

If a Home Phoneline Networking Alliance (HomePNA) networking system is installed on telephone circuits that are still in use for voice communications, problems with line noise on the circuit can greatly affect the performance of both the data network and the telephone system.

In addition to correcting the interference and noise issues listed earlier in the chapter, you may also need to install a low-pass filter, such as a DSL filter (see Figure 18-4), between the computers and their HomePNA connections.

Cable Testing

The cable conditions that can impact the performance of a home communications system are the same as those that can affect all other systems connected to the structured wiring system.

Common Wire Faults

The more common cable faults that can affect the telephone system are

- **Crossed pair** This condition occurs when a wire pair is connected to different pins on each end of a cable run; for example, if wire pair 2 is connected to pins 4 and 5 on one end of the cable and pins 7 and 8 on the other end.

Figure 18-4
An inline ADSL filter removes interference from a telephone line.

Photo courtesy of NetComm Limited.

CROSS-REFERENCE   Chapter 2 also discusses cable faults and includes illustrations of the conditions described here.

- **Improper impedance**   Although a connector terminating a Cat 5e cable might appear to be attached correctly, the connector may not measure at 100 ohms, which is the normal impedance for Cat 5e cable. If the connector and the cable have different impedance, signal reflections can occur. Another problem that can affect the impedance of a cable is a very sharp bend or kink in the cable causing the cable to not test out at 100 ohms.

- **Open circuit**   This condition is caused when a cable pair doesn't have continuity between the ends of a cable. An open circuit condition could be caused by a broken wire strand, a kinked wire, or an improperly terminated wire. This is the most common problem with copper cabling.

- **Reversed pair**   This condition occurs when the tip and ring wires of a telephone line are reversed at the termination of one end of the cable. For example, if one of the wires in pair 2 is connected to pin 1 on one end of the cable and pin 2 on the other end, and the other wire in the wire pair is connected between pins 2 on one end and pin 1 on the other end, the telephone signals will be transmitted or received improperly.

- **Short circuit**   If two of more conductors in a cable are in contact (metal to metal), it creates a short circuit, which is like a roadblock for signals traveling on the cable pairs affected.

Working Safe

A telephone circuit carries electrical currents in various voltages that are also present in any connectors and terminal screws. If the phone line you are working on is connected through to the NID and a call comes in on that line, you could get an electrical shock.

Here are some tips for working safely on a telephone circuit:

- Ensure that the cable you are working on is not connected directly or indirectly to the NID. If you cannot disconnect the cable from the NID, on a standard corded connected phone set the handset portion of the telephone so it is not in its cradle, or on a cordless phone press the on or talk button, which busies out the phone.

- Use screwdrivers that have insulated handles.

- Don't touch bare conductor wires or screw terminals with your hands or body.

- I hope this one is obvious, but don't work on a telephone circuit during a lightning storm.

Wire Testing Tools

When testing UTP cabling used for a communications system, the tools used are essentially the same used for testing UTP in a data network (see Chapter 14). The following list provides an overview of the testing tools most often used to troubleshoot the cables in a communications system:

- **Butt set (Buttinsky)**   Also known as a lineman's handset, this is one of the primary testing and troubleshooting test tools used by telephone technicians for testing a variety of telephone functions, including dialing, sending, receiving, and testing for a dial tone. Originally called a Buttinsky, after the inventor, a butt set typically has either a touchtone or a rotary dial (or both), punch-down block clips, a butt set clip, polarity test components, and a few other features common to analog telephone sets. Figure 18-5 shows a basic butt set device.

- **Cable certification testers**   This tool can be used to verify that a cable meets the performance standards specified in EIA/TIA TSB-67, the test standard for network cable. The tests performed by a certification tester are impedance, length, attenuation, wire map, and near-end crosstalk (NEXT).

- **Multimeter**   Whether analog or digital, a multimeter measures voltage, current (amps), and resistance (ohms) on copper wiring. If used with a shorting device, a multimeter can also test for continuity. Performing an ohms test with a multimeter is one way to identify an open circuit on a cable.

- **Telephone test set**   This tool is used to simulate the functions of a telephone system and to perform circuit diagnostics and perform standard telephone cable testing.

- **Time Domain Reflectometry (TDR) testers**   A TDR test is performed to identify any problems or defects on a cable and its termination, but TDR tests are most commonly used to measure cable length or pinpoint the location of a problem on a cable.

- **Wire map tester**   This tool, also called a pair scanner, is used to test for opens, shorts, crossed pairs, split pairs, and reversed pairs on a UTP cable.

Figure 18-5

A butt set can be a valuable multifunction telephone line testing tool.

Photo courtesy of Harris Corporation.

CROSS-REFERENCE The chapters in Part I of this book cover wiring and data network cable testing in more detail.

Chapter Review

The telephone company's responsibility for problems on a home communication system ends at the demarcation point or network interface device (NID) of a home. Beyond the NID, the telephone wiring is customer premise inside wiring (CPIW) and is the responsibility of the homeowner.

Basic telephone wiring is a four-wire cable (also called quad wire) that has green, red, black, and yellow wires. The green and red wires are treated as one pair, and the black and yellow wires are treated as another pair. Each pair of wires carries the tip and ring signals used by a telephone to connect and communicate. The four wire pairs of a Cat 5e cable can be used for the tip and ring wires of the telephone connection.

If a telephone line is dead on all inside telephones as well as at the structured wiring distribution panel, the problem could very well be with the incoming telephone line. If a telephone line is working at the NID but not inside the home, the problem is most likely a wiring problem somewhere between the NID and the structured wiring panel and telephone outlets. Some common problems on the faulty link you may want to look for include a loose setscrew, reversed wires, faulty termination, and wire damage. Many common wire faults can create noise on a telephone line.

The common cable faults that can affect the telephone system include crossed pair, improper impedance, open circuit, reversed pair, and short circuit.

The testing tools that should be used to troubleshoot the cabling of a communications system include cable certification tester, multimeter, telephone test set, TDR tester, and wire map tester.

Questions

1. At what point do the telephone company's responsibilities end for the telephone wiring of a home?

   A. Distribution panel

   B. Network interface device

   C. Telephone handset

   D. Telephone outlet

2. What are the two functions associated with the wires of a telephone circuit?

   A. Dial tone

   B. Ring

   C. Caller ID

   D. Tip

3. If Cat 5e wiring is used to distribute telephone service throughout a home, what is the basic color of the wire pair used to replace the wires used for Line 1?

    A. Blue

    B. Orange

    C. Green

    D. Brown

4. After determining that a telephone line is dead on all circuits inside a home, what should be checked to determine if there is a problem with the incoming telephone line?

    A. Distribution panel

    B. NID

    C. Inside cable

    D. None of the above; only the telephone company can make this determination.

5. Which of the following would be the prime suspect when no interior handsets are able to get a dial tone?

    A. Damaged wiring

    B. Faulty termination

    C. Loose test jack or connection in the NID

    D. Reversed wires

6. Which of the following can be a cause of static or other noise on a telephone line?

    A. Cat 5e cabling

    B. Spliced cabling

    C. RJ-45 connectors

    D. Low-pass filters

7. What is the condition created when the conductors of a wire pair are connected to different pins of a terminator at each end of a cable?

    A. Crossed pair

    B. Open circuit

    C. Reversed pair

    D. Short circuit

8. Cat 5e cabling should have 100 ohms of impedance. When used in a communications system, how much impedance should the terminations of a Cat 5e cable have?

    A. 50 ohms

    B. 75 ohms

C. 100 ohms

D. 150 ohms

9. What testing device is most commonly used to measure voltage, current, and resistance?

A. Cable certification tester

B. Multimeter

C. TDR

D. Wire map

10. Which testing device is commonly used to test for opens, shorts, crossed pairs, split pairs, and reversed pairs on a UTP cable?

A. Cable certification tester

B. Multimeter

C. TDR

D. Wire map

Answers

1. **B.** This device is also called the demarcation point, or demarc for short. The other devices listed are all interior devices, which are the responsibility of the homeowner.

2. **B and D.** These functions are used to complete the circuit on a telephone line.

3. **A.** The order of the wires used for lines 1 through 4 of a telephone system is blue, orange, green, and brown.

4. **B.** The incoming line can be checked using the test jack inside the NID.

5. **C.** If the plug in the test jack isn't properly seated or wires aren't secure on the connection terminals, the line may be interrupted before it can enter the home.

6. **B.** In a structured wiring system, there are no spliced wires, but if in an existing system the wire is spliced or tapped, a bad connection can cause noise on the line.

7. **A.** The signals on the telephone line would not be properly received or transmitted.

8. **C.** The impedance must match on the cable and its terminations.

9. **B.** The other devices listed are used for higher-level and more complicated testing procedures.

10. **D.** A wire map tester is used to test wire pairs on category UTP cable.

PART V

Security System Basics

CHAPTER 19

Security System Basics

In this chapter, you will learn about
- Residential security systems types
- Security system devices
- External security services

Numerous studies have shown consistently that the homes with the most risk of crime typically have the least protection. And in a significant percentage of these homes, there is no protection or warning systems installed beyond door locks and fencing. Those homes that do have some type of protective system commonly have some form of burglar alarm, but even this is only common in more expensive homes.

Of course, protection is the main purpose of a security system. However, the primary benefit of a residential security system is not necessarily protection, but rather the peace of mind that comes from having a security system installed.

The type and technology of a residential security system should be fitted to the home, lifestyles, and level of protection desired by the homeowners. In this chapter, we look at security system basics, including the various types of systems available, their components, the communications technologies they employ, and a few of the external services that can be used for monitoring.

Residential Security Systems

A home security system provides protection at two levels: interior and perimeter. Interior protection includes the detection of, and an alarm for, events inside the home, including:

- Someone moving about inside
- Someone breaking into a cabinet, cupboard, or the like
- Smoke, fire, or carbon monoxide gases
- Environment sensors

Perimeter protection provides detection of, and an alarm for, events such as:

- A door opening
- A window breaking
- Someone in the yard
- Unauthorized access to the property

Reactive versus Proactive Security

Traditional security systems are *reactive* in that they react to an intruder and sound an alarm. This alarm usually scares the intruders away, warning them that they have been detected and that the local authorities are probably already on the way. But the alarm is in response to the intruder already being in the home and jeopardizes the safety of the occupants.

By integrating a security system with home control, the system can be *proactive* in that it will increase the safety of the occupants by lighting the way outside when the smoke alarm goes off or lighting the walkway when they arrive home late at night. It can deter the potential intruder from selecting the home to break into by giving the home the "lived-in look" when the homeowners are away.

Interior Protection

The function of interior detection is to keep safe and protect a home's occupants and contents from intruders. The primary features of interior security include:

- **Access control** A process that allows or denies access, or entry, to the home itself or to a particular area. Typically, access control systems require the entry of codes, the use of a key, an access card, a proximity card, or a physiological characteristic of a person, such as hand or thumb print. Access control can be as simple as a mechanical lock and key or as sophisticated as biometrics, which is an access control method that uses fingerprints, retinal scans, and the like.

- **Intrusion detection** The opening of a door, a window breaking, a shock or vibration on a surface, or even a motion in a secured area can create a notification or an event that triggers an alarm to sound, or sends an intrusion alert message to an external security monitoring service that then contacts the local police and fire departments.

- **Smoke, fire, and dangerous gas detection** Independent or integrated sensors can detect smoke, the heat from a smokeless fire, and even carbon monoxide or radon gases and sound a built-in alarm, send an alarm signal to a central security system controller, or relay a message to an external security monitoring service.

- **Panic buttons** Though they are not found in all security systems, a panic or emergency alert feature can be a desired feature for some customers. Typically, a centrally or conveniently placed button or a special sequence of digits on the telephone or alarm keypad can be used to sound an alarm or to transmit an emergency request to the monitoring service to dispatch the local emergency services or the police department.

- **Environment sensors**   Optional temperature and humidity sensors can be installed to monitor the environment. Low temperature sensors can detect when the heat goes too low and notify the monitoring service or indicated parties prior to the pipes freezing and bursting. Humidity and temperature sensors help maintain the correct environment for wine cellars and cigar rooms. Flood or water sensors can detect when water is at a level it shouldn't be, such as when a sump pump fails or a pipe breaks in the basement.

Perimeter Protection and Detection

The primary purpose of perimeter protection is detecting intruders in the area around a home before they attempt to enter it. In addition, exterior detection can make it a safer place for the homeowners and their guests when it is interfaced with the outside lighting. The primary features of perimeter protection and detection are

- **Access control**   Gates or an entryway onto the property can be secured and entry granted to only those people the homeowners allow to enter through a remote control or remote switch or those people who know the security code or have an access card.

- **Intruder detection**   If intruders enter the secured space around a house, the system should detect their presence and perform a variety of optional security functions, such as signaling the lighting system to turn on the exterior lighting after dark, sounding an alarm, alerting the homeowner, or contacting a monitoring service after hours.

- **Glass breakage detection**   Because double-paned glass is common on most new homes, sensors should also be placed on the exterior windowpane to detect an intruder attempting to enter the home by breaking through a window.

- **Screen breakage detection**   By placing a sensor on the screen frame or using special screen woven for security detection, an alarm signal can be sent to the security system if the frame is removed or the screening cut.

Security System Components

Many residential security systems come with a certain number of features and components, such as hard-wired systems with a control panel, an RJ-31x interface, multiple zone inputs, and a keypad controller and wireless systems that include a control panel, sounder (alarm), keypad, window or door contacts, and a remote control. Different manufacturers offer different systems, packaged with what they believe to be the most commonly used features, components, and devices. However, it is virtually impossible for a manufacturer or reseller to know exactly which features and devices a specific house requires for its security system installation. This is why most of the components needed are offered as options.

Regardless of whether or not a system is a wireless or hard-wired system (and most of the newest systems can be adapted to include both), the most commonly used components are available for use with either type of system. The most commonly used security system components and features include:

- **Security control panel**   Commonly the security control panel is incorporated into a comprehensive home automation control panel, such as the one shown in Figure 19-1. Standalone security control panels are also available, but if other systems in the home are to be automated or included in the home control system, an integrated system provides for overall control and is typically more cost effective than separate controls for the various systems. In any case, the central security control panel serves as both a command center and a distribution point for the devices and features connected to or managed by the system. Whatever control panel is chosen, it should have the capacity to support the number and type of devices in the system and provide a feature set that's both desired by the homeowner and required by the security system.

- **Keypads**   Virtually every residential security system includes a keypad (see Figure 19-2), which is the homeowner's primary interface and input device for entering setup parameters and setting security system features on or off. Many hard-wired systems also provide a computer connection and control software that allows these functions to be performed from a PC terminal. Many keypad models also provide wireless remote access through a PLC relay, a handheld remote control, or a key fob control.

Figure 19-1
A touchscreen home control panel that includes security controls

Photo courtesy of Embedded Automation, Inc.

Figure 19-2
A security
system keypad

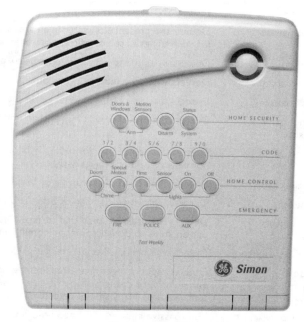

Photo courtesy of General Electric Company.

- **Sensors**   There are a variety of sensors that can be installed as a part of a home security system, each designed to detect a different event. Table 19-1 lists the more common sensors used in home systems and their functions.

- **Alarms, sirens, and sounders**   Nearly all security systems include some means to alert a home's occupants of an intruder, smoke, or other security event. In most cases, this is an internal siren, alarm, or sounder circuit that activates an external sounding device. Table 19-2 includes the most commonly used terminology regarding security systems and alarms.

- **RJ-31x interface**   Most of the better residential security systems include an RJ-31x jack that facilitates a specialized feature on a standard telephone line called line seizure. The RJ-31x interface is used when a security event triggers a call to be placed to a homeowner's remote telephone number, cell phone, or pager, or to a security monitoring service. By seizing the phone line, the security system is able to disconnect any calls on the line and use the phone line to make its security notification call.

- **Hard-wired sensor converter**   This device is used to adapt existing sensors, such as a door or window contact into a wireless device.

- **Cameras and monitors**   Security cameras and monitors can be part of a security surveillance system.

Sensor Type	Function
Water/flood sensor	Detects the presence of water in an area where it shouldn't be. Used for such things as spa overflow, pipes breaking, and sump pumps failing.
Low temperature sensor	Detects when the temperature goes below a preset temperature.
Humidity sensor	Detects when the humidity goes outside of a preset range.
Natural gas sensor	Detects the presence of natural gas in the air.
Carbon monoxide (CO) sensor	Detects the presence of a higher than normal level of CO in the air.
Contact sensor	Detects the opening or closing of a window or door in opposition to its normal state, either Normally Open (NO) or Normally Closed (NC).
Glass-break sensor	Detects the sound of shattering or breaking glass.
IR beam sensor	Detects when the line of an IR beam is broken.
Floor mat sensor	Detects the pressure on a thin surface. Often placed below the carpet on steps to detect someone coming upstairs.
Shock/vibration sensor	Detects the presence of natural gas in the air.
Heat sensor	Detects rapid changes in an area's temperature using a metal strip that either melts or changes shape when exposed to higher than normal temperatures. Many smoke detectors have heat sensors built in.
Motion sensor	Uses passive infrared (PIR) technology to detect movement in an area. Sensitivity can be adjusted to detect only objects over a certain size and weight, or the lens can be masked out to not see pets below a certain sight line.
Smoke detector	Uses an ionization chamber or a photoelectric cell to detect the presence of smoke in the air. Smoke detectors typically have an internal alarm as well as a relay to send an alarm signal to the central unit (see Figure 19-3).

Table 19-1　Residential Security System Sensors and Their Functions

Figure 19-3
A cutaway view
of the internal
components of a
smoke detector
and alarm device

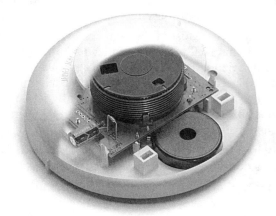

Photo courtesy of General Electric Company.

Security System Feature	Devices Used to Implement the Feature
Perimeter detection	Sensors, such as contact sensors, placed on exterior doors and windows that activate an alarm.
Interior detection	Sensors, such as motion detectors and smoke detectors, placed in the interior of a home excluding windows and doors.
Silent alarm	An alarm that notifies a monitoring service that an alarm event has occurred without sounding an alarm in the home to alert the intruder.
Local alarm	A siren or bell that is sounded in or outside of a home with no other notification made.
Silent/audible alarm	A switching feature on security systems that allows the alarm to be silent when a home is unoccupied but sounds a siren or bell when occupants are in the home.
Digital dialer	An electronic device that uses an RJ-31x connection to grab the phone line to place a telephone call to a monitoring service and then verify the connection and send an alarm activation message.
Line seizure	An RJ-31x connection is used to capture and hold a telephone line until an alarm call can be made and completed. When it seizes the line, it hangs up any phone connection already in progress.

Table 19-2 Common Security Devices, Features, and Options

 CROSS-REFERENCE Surveillance systems, including cameras and monitors, are covered in Chapter 24.

Security System Connections

Residential security systems use two means to link their sensors, detectors, and alarms to the control unit: radio frequency (RF) signals and wire or cable runs. Wireless RF-based systems don't require unit-to-unit wiring and typically provide the most flexibility during installation, but do require ongoing maintenance because the detection devices operate on batteries. Hard-wired systems must be preplanned so that the appropriate cabling can be installed during the pre-wire phase of a new construction or a remodeling project.

Hard-wired systems generally offer a better quality signal than a wireless system, provided the cabling used is installed to specification. However, as wireless technology continues to improve—for example, as a larger number of communication channels are added—wireless systems are proving to be much more reliable.

Another difference between wireless and hard-wired systems is the initial cost factors. Wired system components are generally less expensive than the wireless versions, but part of the cost savings realized with a hard-wired system is eaten up with the cost of the cabling and its installation. Over time, the wired system usually lasts longer because the components do not include the advanced technology that is present in wireless systems.

Hard-Wired Security Systems

In many residential situations, a hard-wired security system has some advantage over a wireless one. A hard-wired system directly and physically connects the components of the system—the contacts, sensors, and so forth—to the main unit with a cable or wire. The primary benefit of the hard-wired approach is that unlike a wireless system, the hard-wired system is significantly less sensitive to electromagnetic and radio frequency interferences, especially if the system's wiring was properly installed.

Hard-wired systems are made up of a main security control panel, like the one shown in Figure 19-4, which is connected to the system's contacts, sensors, alarms, keypads, and other devices with homerun wires. (The illustration in Figure 19-4 is highly simplified; the controller unit is typically centrally located with the devices wired into it attached to homerun wiring and located throughout a home.)

Hard-wired systems are certainly easier to install during a new construction project, but they can also be retrofitted to a home provided there is open wire run space in an attic, basement, or crawl space.

Wiring a Hard-Wired Security System

In general, hard-wired security systems recommend the use of 2-conductor or 4-conductor cabling that should be planned along with the structured wiring plan

Figure 19-4

An illustration of the control panel and wiring leads of a hard-wired security system

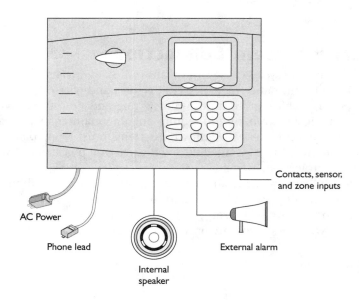

Security System Component	Wire Recommendation
Keypads	Standard: 22 AWG 4-conductor stranded
	Advanced (with voice pickup and playback): 2 runs of 18 AWG 2-conductor shielded stranded
Internal and external alarms, speakers, and sound devices	18 AWG 2-conductor copper wire
AC power connections	18 AWG 2-conductor copper wire
Motion sensors, glass break detectors	22 AWG 4-conductor copper wire
Door and window contact sensors	22 AWG 2-conductor copper wire
Fire alarm connections, smoke detectors, and heat detectors	FPLP (fire power limited plenum) cable or FPL (fire power limited) cable: 18 AWG 4-conductor
Ground connection	14 AWG 1-conductor copper wire
RJ-31x console	22 AWG 4-conductor copper wire minimum, CAT 5e or CAT 6 preferred
Wireless sensors	Any of the above sensors, but with RF communications and batteries to power them; no wiring is required
Video monitors and video capture devices	RG-6 coaxial cable

Table 19-3 Wire and Cable Guidelines for Hard-Wired Security Systems

during the design phase and installed during the pre-wire phase of the project. However, there are wiring guidelines (minimum cable recommendations) for use with different security system components. Table 19-3 lists the more commonly used components and the recommended wiring or cabling to connect them into a hard-wired security system.

Wireless Security Systems

Depending on how technically you define the term *wireless*, wireless security systems can be either completely wireless RF-based systems or powerline control (such as X-10 or the newer A-10) systems, or both.

Wireless security systems typically provide the same functions as hard-wired systems, especially with the expanded RF range (around 600 feet) of some newer products. Essentially, a wireless system requires only that a main control unit, like the one shown in Figure 19-1 earlier in the chapter, be connected to an AC power source, and the system is ready to use. Of course, sensors, detectors, and other devices need to be installed where appropriate, but these operate on self-contained batteries. The main benefit of a wireless system is that no wiring is required.

Wireless systems allow for flexibility when defining multiple wireless security zones and some systems can also be connected into an existing wired security system to extend the original system or replace the wired system control unit.

CROSS-REFERENCE See Chapter 21 for more information on designing security zones.

IP-Based Security Systems

IP-based security systems are typically centered on surveillance systems using IP-capable video cameras. The benefit of this type of system is that special monitoring equipment is not required; the output of the video cameras can be viewed in a web browser on virtually any computer from virtually any location.

In most situations, monitoring software manages the video feeds transmitted from the cameras and stores them on a computer, an external hard disk drive, or a DVD. The downside to an IP-based security system can be the amount of storage space required to store the captured video streams and the additional cost of IP-capable surveillance cameras.

 NOTE One consideration of using wireless devices is that the detectors and sensors are typically battery operated, which means that although these devices normally have a long battery life, the batteries do need to be replaced on a regular schedule, such as every six months.

Security Reporting Formats

Regardless of the media type in use for a security system, the security detection devices must be able to communicate a security event to the security system controller in a way that identifies not only where the event is occurring, but also what type of event is being reported. In the past, the number of security system reporting formats was just a few less than the number of manufacturers.

As the reporting formats continue to evolve to take advantage of technology advances, a group of standards have emerged, such as those issued by the Security Industry Association (SIA). However, the newer alarm and detection devices continue to support the older formats, including some that are essentially obsolete at this point. The more common of the reporting formats that are standards for communications between detection devices and system controllers are listed in Table 19-4.

Format	Description
3/1	A legacy tone burst format; transmits a 3-digit account (location) number and a 1-digit alarm code at either 1400 Hz or 2300 Hz.
4/2	A legacy tone burst format; transmits a 4-digit account code and a 2-digit alarm code at 1400 Hz; also known as SK (Silent Knight) 4/2. A tone burst signal transmits a single audio tone of 0.5 to 1.5 seconds at the start of a transmission.
Dual-tone multifrequency (DTMF)	A signal used in newer versions of tone burst systems that is essentially the same as the format used with touchtone telephones. DTMF format systems typically support a wide range of reporting standards.

Table 19-4 Alarm Reporting Codes

Format	Description
Frequency-shifting key (FSK)	A frequency modulation method that transmits digital data using the frequency changes of a carrier wave. Binary FSK (BFSK), which uses only two frequencies, is a popular variation of this format. FSK transmits a 3-digit account number followed by the event information.
SIA	A standardized reporting format that reports eight (SIA8) or twenty (SIA20) events per transmission using a 6-digit account number and a two-character event code, such as BA for burglary alarm and DF for door forced (open).

Table 19-4 Alarm Reporting Codes (continued)

External Security Services

Some security systems can be programmed to call a phone number (residence, friend, cell phone) when the system goes into alarm, but this does not notify or dispatch the police. This system depends upon someone answering the call at the time it is received, listening to the message, and responding immediately.

Some homeowners prefer to have someone outside the home monitoring their home security system because it gives them the assurance that there is always somebody to summon help when there is a break-in or an emergency. This involves a recurring monthly fee. For these homeowners, there are two basic types of external security services available:

- Alarm monitoring
- Remote viewing monitoring

Alarm Monitoring Services

Alarm monitoring services are usually connected to a home through an RJ-31x connection that places a call to the service's monitoring system and communicates digitally whenever the security system is breached and an alarm event is triggered, regardless if an alarm sounds in the home or not. The connection to the monitoring company can also be through a cell phone or long-range radio. Some security systems allow for the monitoring service staff to "listen in" through the security keypads in the home. The security system may even provide two-way voice communication between the monitoring service staff and the occupants of the home.

Some companies will work with the installer and the homeowner to design a security system that best provides the security level desired and then contract for the alarm monitoring services for that system. Most, if not all, city and county police and sheriff departments no longer provide alarm monitoring and security review services and only respond to calls from security monitoring services. Many municipalities also have a policy of charging the homeowner for repeat false security alarm calls.

PART V

The upside to alarm monitoring services is that they are always there—24/7—and are able to respond immediately. The downside is that because they are off-site, they can dispatch the police or fire department to investigate the cause of an alarm, especially in cases when the homeowner is away from home. Should the problem be caused by something other than an intruder, such as a branch blown through a window or an alarm caused by an electrical fault, the homeowner can be charged a fine for a false alarm.

Remote Viewing Monitoring Services

Another type of residential security services is remote access monitoring services, which use surveillance cameras and microphones to monitor a home's interior and exterior for unauthorized access or presence.

 CROSS-REFERENCE See Chapter 22 for more information about the types of service provide by monitoring services.

Chapter Review

A home security system can be either *reactive* or be interfaced to a home control system and be *proactive*. A security system provides protection on two levels: interior and perimeter. Interior protection systems include detecting and sounding alarms in response to events inside and outside a home. The function of interior detection is to protect a home's occupants and contents from intruders. The purpose of exterior or perimeter protection is detecting intruders in the area around a home before they attempt to enter the house.

A residential security system links to its sensors, detectors, alarms, and control units using either radio frequency (RF) signals or wire or cable runs. Wireless RF-based systems don't require unit-to-unit wiring. Wireless security systems can be completely wireless RF-based systems or interfaced to wired systems. Hard-wired systems must be preplanned so that the appropriate cabling can be installed during the pre-wire phase of a new construction or a remodeling project.

A hard-wired system directly and physically connects the components of the system— the contacts, sensors, and so forth—to the main unit with a cable or wire. The primary benefit of the hard-wired approach is, unlike a wireless system, a hard-wired system is significantly less sensitive to electromagnetic and RF interferences, especially if the system's wiring is properly installed to avoid interference sources.

Common devices and features of a residential security system include a control panel, an RJ-31x interface, multiple zone inputs, alarms, window or door contacts, a remote control, and a keypad controller. An important feature on systems that support alarm monitoring is an RJ-31x interface.

Two basic types of external security services are available: alarm monitoring and remote video monitoring.

Questions

1. Which of the following is not a common feature of a residential interior security system?

   A. Access control

   B. Intrusion detection

   C. Perimeter intrusion detection

   D. Smoke or fire detection

2. What communications technology is used by a truly wireless system?

   A. PLC

   B. HomePNA

   C. Cat 5e

   D. RF

3. A security system integrated into a home system controller is said to be

   A. Intrusive

   B. Preventive

   C. Proactive

   D. Reactive

4. What type of alarm only notifies a monitoring service that an alarm event has occurred?

   A. Silent alarm

   B. Local alarm

   C. Digital alarm

   D. Zone alarm

5. What device is used as the homeowner's primary interface to a security system?

   A. Control panel

   B. Keypad

   C. Remote control

   D. Personal computer

6. What is the specialized connection used in security systems to seize a telephone line for purposes of notifying an alarm monitoring service of a security breach?

   A. RJ-11

   B. RJ-12

   C. RJ-31x

   D. RG-6

7. What type of sensor is used to detect the opening or closing of a door or window?

   A. CO sensor

   B. Glass-break sensor

   C. Contact sensor

   D. PIR sensor

8. If a homeowner wishes to have an outside party take action on security and alarm events that are triggered, the type of firm contracted would be a

   A. Remote monitoring service

   B. Alarm monitoring service

   C. Remote alarm management service

   D. Alarm security service

9. Which of the following is not a form of a protection provided by a security system?

   A. Someone moving about inside a home

   B. Someone breaking into a cabinet, cupboard, or the like

   C. Smoke, fire, or carbon monoxide gases

   D. A door opening

10. Which of the following is not a protection provided in a perimeter security system?

   A. Access control detection

   B. Smoke, fire, or carbon monoxide gases detection

   C. Glass breakage detection

   D. Screen breakage detection

Answers

1. **C.** Interior systems, which should be obvious from its name, include all security measures placed inside a home. The other choices are all typically included in an interior security system.

2. **D.** Radio frequency (RF) signals are used by wireless systems to communicate. X-10, which is a form of wireless system, uses existing electrical power lines to communicate; Cat 5e is a networking cable standard; and HomePNA (Home Phoneline Networking Alliance) is a standard for communications over interior telephone lines.

3. **C.** Security systems that are integrated into a home automation control system provide proactive security.

4. **A.** This alarm doesn't sound an alarm locally, but notifies the monitoring services. An audible alarm can also notify services although it also sounds an alarm that the intruder can hear. A local alarm sounds a siren or bell without notification action. The term digital alarm is erroneous; a digital dialer is the mechanism used to notify the monitoring service.

5. **B.** Regardless of the system type, hard-wired or wireless, the homeowner's interface to a security system is primarily through a keypad. However, a PC can be used with most hard-wired control panels and a remote control can be used to activate or deactivate the alarm system.

6. **C.** Actually, the connection is an RJ-31x. RJ-11 and RJ-12 are one- and two-line telephone line connectors and RG-6 is a coaxial cabling standard.

7. **C.** This sensor detects that it has been either opened or closed, depending on whether it is set to Normally Open (NO) or Normally Closed (NC). A CO sensor detects carbon monoxide gas; a glass-break sensor detects the sound of breaking glass; and a PIR (passive infrared) sensor is a motion detector.

8. **B.** A remote monitoring service performs video surveillance on a property; the other choices are just plays on words.

9. **D.** Detecting an exterior door opening is a part of a perimeter security system.

10. **B.** Smoke, fire, and CO detectors and alarm systems are classified as components of an interior security system.

CHAPTER 20

Home Security Devices

In this chapter, you will learn about
- Access control devices and protocols
- Security peripherals and accessories
- Integrating security devices into a security system

All security systems, even you and your trusty, loyal watchdog involve some sort of a detection and alarm devices. You and your dog can both see an intruder and can sound an alarm by shouting or barking, respectively. However, in those times when you are not looking, not awake, or not at home, you may need some type of electronic device and system to detect an intruder or a risky situation and set off some sort of an alert, whether it be an alarm or just an indicator.

This chapter continues the discussion on security devices started in Chapter 19 and covers devices that can be included in a home security system, the purpose of each, and a brief description of how they are installed or integrated into a comprehensive security system.

 CROSS-REFERENCE The security devices discussed in Chapter 19 and in this chapter are discussed further in Chapter 21.

Access Control Devices

A home access control system can be very simple and involve only such things as standard door locks. It can also be very complex and include the latest biometric devices straight out of the James Bond world. The level of complexity required for any home depends on two issues: the level of security required by the homeowners and their budget.

An access control system is any combination of devices that secure a home and prevent or detect an unauthorized entry through a door, window, or other exterior feature that can be used to gain access to a home. For the majority of homeowners, the access control system in use is limited only to a key-locking door handle and perhaps a deadbolt lock on the front and maybe the rear doors of the home. Often, sliding glass doors and the like are secured only with a toggle lock that is really not all that burglarproof. Adding additional access control security to any home can only make it safer.

Residential access control systems consist of a variety of devices that can be used to gain access to a secured home. The devices that are most commonly considered for a home's access control system are

- Card readers
- Proximity card scanners
- Keypads
- Electronic door locks and keys
- Driveway loops

Card Reader Systems

Card reader systems scan coding on a credit card– or smaller-sized plastic or laminated card to unlock or open a door. While this technology is fairly commonplace in the business world, only a few types of card reader systems have been adapted for residential use. While newer card reader systems support the use of keychain cards in place of the credit card–sized cards, the plastic card is still the most common form of key card in use.

Most basic card readers only read a number from each card and transfer it to the card reader's control unit or to the security system controller for processing by either the standard software or custom programming, respectively. More sophisticated systems offer the capability to create customized software, using C-language programming or a Windows-based interface on the card reader controller.

Depending on the type of card system in use, the need and the complexity of the actions that can be programmed into the system vary from very simple read-only features to Smart Card systems that can be used to activate a wide range of home security and automation actions. As the capabilities of the system increase, the level of programming required to customize the system also increases. Some manufacturers of the more sophisticated systems offer a variety of preprogrammed modules and templates that can be downloaded from the Internet or obtained on a disk as a means to simplifying this process.

The most common card reader systems used in residential applications are

- Barcode readers
- Magnetic stripe readers
- Proximity card readers
- Wiegand proximity card readers

Card Reader Wiring

Depending on the type of card the card reader is designed to scan, the wiring or connectors will vary. Card readers that are designed to interface with computer equipment directly will have either a 9-pin DB connector (DB-9) or an RF-45 plug. Some include a six or more–position screw terminal strip to which the ground, power, and relay wires are connected. Powerline communications (PLC)–compatible card readers must

Figure 20-1
The wiring configuration of a PLC card reader connected to an electric door strike

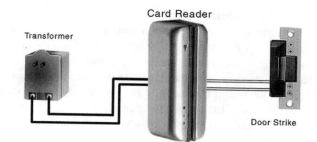

Photo courtesy of Smarthome, Inc.

be wired to a transformer that provides both the electrical power and the connection to the alternating current (AC) power lines. Figure 20-1 illustrates the wiring required for a PLC card reader.

Barcode Readers

The technology of a barcode reader is quite similar to the readers used in the check-out stands at most supermarkets and chain stores. The primary difference between the home security barcode reader and the ones at the store is that in home systems, the barcode is swiped through a reader and not scanned.

The barcode-encoded information, which is typically either a card number or a personal identification number (PIN), is printed on a plastic credit card–sized card or on a paper card that has been laminated to prevent wear.

Actually, the reader reads the white (or dark gray) spaces of the barcode and not the black stripes (see Figure 20-2). The thickness of the white area represents a number or an alphabetic character that is then transmitted to a control unit and either verified (and the door is unlocked) or rejected. Some systems do include the capability to signal an erroneous read as well.

PART V

Figure 20-2
An example of barcode, similar to what is found on barcode reader access control system cards

Magnetic Stripe Readers

On the back of virtually all credit and automatic teller machine (ATM) cards is a black or reddish-brown stripe that is permanently magnetized with information, and in the case of home access security cards, it is a card number or PIN. When the card is passed through a magnetic stripe card reader, the reader picks up the electromagnetic fields of the stored information and translates it to digital data for processing.

There are two types of magnetic stripe cards: low coercivity and high coercivity. Low coercivity cards are easily damaged by a wide variety of magnetic sources, including other types of magnetic stripe cards that they may come into contact with in a wallet or purse. High coercivity cards are less easily damaged and are able to hold their information even when in contact with low-grade magnetic sources.

NOTE Coercivity is the strength of a magnetic field required to reverse the polarity on a magnetic medium.

High coercivity cards are more reliable because they are more resistant to common magnetic forces. However, the reliability of any magnetic stripe card depends on the magnetic film tape used on the card. The magnetic force that can erase a magnetic stripe card is coercive force, which is measured in Oersteds. A standard bankcard has a coercivity of around 300 Oersteds, which is low coercivity. At this level, a magnetic stripe card can be damaged by other cards in the same wallet or by the magnetic clasp on a purse. Card systems using magnetic materials with coercivity ratings of 2,100 to 4,000 Oersteds are less susceptible to being erased or damaged.

When the card is swiped through the reader (see Figure 20-3), the magnetic stripe reader scans the magnetic stripe on the back of a card, translates the information, and then either transmits the information to a control unit that issues a signal to one of its relays, or processes the information and sends a signal out one of its onboard relays. The relay where the approved signal is sent is attached to an electronic lock that releases, and the door can then be opened. Unauthorized or damaged cards are rejected by a signal sent back to the card reader.

Magnetic stripe readers are not a good option in areas where dust, dirt, heavy rains, or fog are a problem. Dust and moisture can cause the stripe reader to misread or fail altogether.

Figure 20-3
A magnetic stripe reader can be a standalone device like this one or built into another device.

Photo courtesy of Scan Technology, Inc.

Proximity Card Readers

Unlike magnetic stripe card readers or barcode card readers, a proximity card reader doesn't require a card to be inserted into the reader. When a proximity card is held near or in the proximity of the card reader (from two inches to six feet), the reader is able to detect the information on the card and capture it for processing.

Proximity cards and readers use low-frequency radio signals to communicate. A proximity card has a passive radio frequency (RF) transmitter embedded in it that continuously transmits its information. When the card is within range of the card reader, the information is received, processed, and verified, and signals are passed to the appropriate relay to open or unlock a door or gate. Passive devices do not require a battery to operate.

Many proximity card reader models also include a keypad like the one shown in Figure 20-4. On systems that require two levels of security, the keypad is used to enter a PIN after the card is scanned. On other systems, the keypad can be used in lieu of the card reader.

The primary benefit of a proximity card reader is convenience to the user. Another benefit is that they are also good for either indoor or outdoor use. The downside is that metal objects nearby can create interference, and the scanner in the reader can be damaged if the card is bent or flexed when it's being scanned. However, the convenience of the system and its longevity—typically longer than contact readers like the magnetic stripe or barcode readers—outweighs the potential problems.

Wiegand cards have special electromagnetic wires embedded in them in a specific pattern that is unique to each card. Like a standard proximity card reader, the cards and readers communicate using low-frequency radio waves. Because of this, they are virtually impossible to counterfeit. Another benefit to this type of card and reader is that they operate in extreme weather and environmental conditions, something not all other card reader types can do.

Figure 20-4

A proximity card reader with a built-in keypad

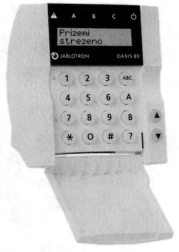

Photo courtesy of Jablotron s.r.o.

PART V

Figure 20-5
A Wiegand key fob proximity credential

Photo courtesy of HID Global.

The Wiegand technology permits the "card" (also called a credential) to be reduced to the size of a coin, key fob, small card, and other convenient sizes, like the key fob shown in Figure 20-5.

NOTE Every access card, regardless of the type, is manufactured with a unique facility or site code. This code differentiates one user's cards from another's and prevents one user's card from working with another user's reader.

Keypads

Keypad access control systems require a user to enter a multiple-digit code to gain access. Keypad units (see Figure 20-6) typically have a 10-digit number pad where the user can punch in his or her pass-code.

Figure 20-6
A keypad access control unit

Photo courtesy of Kenny International.

Keypad systems are a good low-cost option in low-risk situations. This system is safe as long as the code stays secret. However, resetting the numerical code is simple using access directly on the keypad through an administrative number code.

Keypad Wiring

The wiring requirements for a keypad access control device depend on the devices the keypad will control, such as an electric door strike or the other systems the keypad is to be connected to. If the keypad and a door strike are from the same manufacturer, it is likely that documentation details the wiring requirements of the two devices. However, if the keypad is to be used as a standalone key entry device that reports to a security system controller, the wiring, while fairly standard, may be a bit involved.

In every case, study the manufacturer's documentation before beginning the installation of the keypad, which should normally happen during the trim-out phase. Some keypad devices may include a user interface connection on the internal circuit board that accepts a strip connector with up to 12 wire positions. Study the wiring diagrams if this is the wiring approach to be used to connect the keypad for remote trigger, panic, or other relay outputs or inputs.

On basic keypad devices, electrical wiring no larger than 16 AWG should be used to connect the keypad to its power source and a door strike, if used. Either unshielded twisted-pair (UTP) or shielded twisted-pair (STP) wiring is used to connect the keypad to the home security system controller for relay signals out or in.

Keypad Programming

Keypad systems can be programmed for several features, including settings that allow entry only during certain hours of the day, eliminating unauthorized access during set periods of the day or night. Programming a keypad system can be done a number of ways. The most common method to program the functions of a keypad system is to press the keys in certain sequences, according to the manufacturer's documentation. Uploading a keypad's program from the system controller or downloading the program from the system controller is another common way to program some keypads. In many cases, a computer-based programming interface is used to create keypad programming on the system control unit and then uploaded to each keypad.

Electronic Key Systems

There are a fairly wide variety of electronic key systems available, ranging from those that work essentially like a regular lock and key to those that include proximity readers, keypads, and card access. Although we are talking about residential locks here, this technology has become common on automobiles as well.

For a home, the system includes an electronic key that can be used simply by inserting the key into a reader to either permit or deny access through a door, as well as allowing the door to be unlocked manually in case of a power failure (like the one shown in Figure 20-7). A reader can be set up to allow certain keys entry into some areas and other readers can be set up to not allow access to others.

Figure 20-7
An electronic
door key that can
be used either
electronically or
mechanically

Photo courtesy of EVVA-WERK GmbH & Co.

The advantage of an electronic key system is that a home's locks do not have to be re-keyed should a key be lost or stolen. Instead, the system can be easily reprogrammed to make the lost key inoperable.

Spare or new keys are typically assigned a pass-code number using a separate device called a *key programming unit*. The electronic cylinder or door lock unit can be programmed for additional key numbers or pass-codes using a lock programming unit that attaches to a personal computer. New programming is loaded to the cylinder unit through a special key attached to a cord on the lock programming unit.

Electric Door Lock Systems

Electric door lock systems are typically used in conjunction with an authorization device, such as a card reader, electronic key, or keypad. This type of access control device can be used to limit both entry and exit through a door. A card reader and other authorization systems send signals to an access control panel or directly to a connected device, such as an electric door lock. These signals, if received on the appropriate relay, instruct the lock to release the door.

Electric door locks consist of a number of components, including electric strike plates, magnetic locks, drop bolts, and electric locksets. However, not every door will work with an electric door lock, and the door lock system needs to be fitted to the door, doorknob, and latch in each case.

A wide variety of products fall within the general category of electric locks, including remote control deadbolts, push-button and keypad door locks, and electric door strikes that can be used to upgrade an existing mechanical door lock.

Remote Control Deadbolts

A remote control deadbolt (see Figure 20-8) works essentially the same way a manually operated deadbolt does. The difference is that remote control deadbolts can be locked or unlocked using a multiple-function infrared (IR) remote control in addition to allow for manual operations.

Push-button/Keypad Door Locks

Push-button and keypad door lock systems are keyless locks that can be unlocked by entering a code number sequence by pressing buttons or keys on the face of the door lock.

Figure 20-8
An IR-remote
control deadbolt

Photo courtesy of Videx, Inc.

As shown in Figure 20-9, the face of this type of lock system has a keypad. The keypad is used to both operate the door lock and enter programming commands. There are mechanical and electronic versions of this type of door lock system. A mechanical (non-electric) push-button lock requires its buttons to be pressed in a certain sequence.

One or more AA batteries are typically used to power an electronic keypad door lock. These devices electrically retract the locking mechanism in the door latch when the correct sequence of keys is pressed. Programming, which typically means entering or changing the number set and sequence, is accomplished through the keypad.

Figure 20-9
A keypad entry
door lock system

Photo courtesy of Ingersoll-Rand Co.

Electric Door Strikes

Electric door strikes are available in a variety of styles to fit a variety of door materials and should be chosen based on the type of door in use. All electric door strikes, like the one shown in Figure 20-10, work essentially the same way: when an electrical charge is sent to the door strike, the locking mechanism releases to unlock the door. The door strike can be operated from a central security control unit acting on a command from a keypad to send a charge to the strike through a relay or a simple push-button release, like those used in many apartment houses and secured entries.

Several door lock system manufacturers also offer electric door strikes that are compatible with their standard door locks. Electric strikes operate on either 12- or 24-volt direct current (DC) or AC power. Most electric strikes include a fail-secure feature that keeps the door locked should the power source fail.

The installation of an electric door strike is performed much like the installation of a standard nonelectrical door strike in that the strike is installed into the door frame or on a wall in line with the door's latching mechanism. The primary difference between an electrical strike and a nonelectrical strike is cabling.

The wire size installed to carry electrical signals to the strike varies by manufacturer, but one thing nearly all manufacturers agree upon is that the wiring must be plenum rated. In most cases, the connector used is a two- or three-position snap-fit jack and plug that terminates the wiring of the strike's electronic module and the plenum cable.

Biometric Access Control Systems

Biometric access control systems use a feature of the users' bodies to verify their identities, such as fingerprints, facial features, or even retinal patterns. For residential systems, the most commonly used biometric system uses fingerprints to control access.

Figure 20-10

An electronic
door strike

Photo courtesy of Rutherford Controls International Corp.

Figure 20-11

A biometric fingerprint reader access control

Photo courtesy of Precise Biometrics.

These systems, like the one shown in Figure 20-11, typically have a finger well or touchpad in which the user places his or her finger. The reader then scans the fingerprint and matches the pattern entered during setup.

The advantage of biometric access control systems should be obvious. There are no keys, cards, or codes to lose or forget. The homeowners carry their security devices with them at all times—right on the tips of their fingers, on their faces, or in their eyes.

The wiring required for a biometric access control system depends on the application. Biometric units produce a low-voltage charge to signal a pass condition, meaning the biometric scan produced a valid match. If the unit is to operate an electric door strike or other electric locking system, a relay module is required. However, if the signal is to be transmitted to a home security system controller, typically no additional modules are required for the biometric unit.

Wiring for biometric units can vary, but for the most part, four to six conductors of UTP wiring is required. Many units feature either RJ-45 or RJ-12 jacks for connecting to a network or a communications system. Electrical power is most commonly provided through a power-converting transformer plugged into an AC outlet near the device.

Programming a biometric unit, which is typically done through its keypad or interface, involves training the unit to record and recognize the hands, fingers, eyes, or other anatomical features of authorized users. Some additional programming may be required if the unit is to take more than a single output function. As the programming methods vary by model, follow the unit's documentation for the programming process used.

Some high-end biometric units also record an exportable log file that can be accessed through a network or serial interface. The log file records all successful and, perhaps more importantly, unsuccessful attempts to gain access through the lock controlled by the unit. Whether or not the unit records a log file is a programming option.

PART V

Driveway Entry Detection Systems

If a home has a gated driveway, all of the access control systems so far discussed can be used to control access through the gate. However, for homes without gated driveways but with a long driveway, the homeowners may wish to install a system that detects and reports a pedestrian, cyclist, or car entering the driveway. Driveway detectors can also be used to activate lighting systems along the driveway after dark. The signal from the driveway detector can be used to turn on entry and interior lighting.

There are a variety of driveway detection and monitoring systems available:

- Induction loop systems
- Metal detection systems
- Motion detection systems
- Entrance beam detection systems

Induction Loop Systems

This type of system is installed with loops of special cable placed under the driveway and uses a very similar technology to that used to detect cars on a street to trigger the traffic lights. As illustrated in Figure 20-12, the buried cable is induction cable that emits an electromagnetic field that has a fixed frequency. As a vehicle enters the induction cable's field, the vehicle's electromagnetic field interacts with that of the cable and changes the frequency of the inductive field. The control unit detects this frequency change and a relay is activated. Most driveway loop systems allow the sensitivity of the system to be set between high and low sensitivity, but it should not be set higher than necessary to detect vehicles entering the driveway so that vehicles passing by on the road do not trigger the control unit.

Typically, the induction cable is installed under the concrete or paving material of a driveway in a rectangular or quadratic shape. Depending on the area and length of the driveway, multiple runs of the inductive cabling may need to be placed in the loop slot where the cable is laid. More cable is needed for smaller circumference loops than for larger loops. The cable should be laid far enough away from the street so it doesn't false trip when a car on the road drives by the driveway.

Figure 20-12
A car entering the electromagnetic field of a buried induction cable of a driveway loop system causes an alarm event.

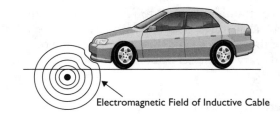

Electromagnetic Field of Inductive Cable

Figure 20-13
The components of a driveway metal detection system

Photo courtesy of Absolute Automation, Inc.

Metal Detection Systems

This type of system uses sensors that detect large metallic objects moving past, which can include steel-toed boots or other metallic objects such as an automobile that passes close to the sensor. These systems are typically installed as a wired system, with one or more sensors (see Figure 20-12) buried or placed on the ground's surface along the side of the driveway and then hardwired into a control unit that can then be connected to a home system. The control unit is then wired into the home system controller or home security system controller through its screw post connections, which are shown in Figure 20-13.

Motion and Entrance Detection Systems

Exterior motion detectors and IR-beam detectors use passive infrared (PIR) to detect when an object enters a driveway or another exterior space. These systems are intended to provide a homeowner with early intruder detection.

Exterior Motion Detectors

Exterior motion detectors use the same basic technology as interior motion detectors. A PIR beam or sweep constantly scans a fixed area and signals a security event should the beam be interrupted. Some systems can be adjusted to detect only larger moving objects and can be configured with "pet alleys" to avoid signaling an alarm for pets and wild animals. Although several types of exterior motion detectors are available, many are wireless systems with ranges of up to 1,000 feet. Many exterior motion detector devices are incorporated into exterior security lighting fixtures, like the one illustrated in Figure 20-14.

Figure 20-14
An exterior security lighting fixture with a built-in motion detection illuminator

Photo courtesy of RAB Lighting.

Beam Entrance Detectors

A beam detector transmits a continuous IR beam, referred to as an IR laser beam in some models, between two stations, across a driveway, a garage entrance, a walkway, or whatever exterior feature the homeowner wishes to monitor. As illustrated in Figure 20-15, an IR beam detector requires two IR transceivers to be placed in direct line of sight of each other across a monitored pathway or driveway. When an object, meaning a person, animal, or vehicle, breaks the IR beam, a signal is generated from the controlling transceiver. This signal travels to a controller device that then communicates it on to the subsystem control to which it's connected.

Each transceiver requires its own power source. Typically, transceivers are powered through a 12V DC current from an AC power transformer. One or both of the IR transceivers are wired into a device controller. The controller is then connected to a PLC control module or, with UTP cable and either an RJ-12 or RJ-45 connector, to the home control system.

Other Detection and Security Devices

There are a couple of additional security devices that don't really fit into any other category: motorized security gates and environmental (weather) detection devices.

Motorized Security Gates

In a home that is set back from a street and has a lengthy driveway, a barrier that prevents access to the driveway can provide both security and, in many cases, aesthetics as well. A remote control motorized security gate provides security by allowing only users with the proper remote access control device or keypad code to open the gate for entry.

A motorized gate is equipped with a two-directional motor system that is used to open and close the gate upon receiving a signal. When the device controller receives a signal, it activates the gate motor, which performs the action opposite of the action last performed. This means that if the last action the gate performed was to open the gate, the next action will be to close the gate, much in the same way a garage door opener operates. Motorized gate systems are available as swing gate, slider gate, and lift gate systems.

Figure 20-15
An IR beam detects someone entering an area or crossing a boundary.

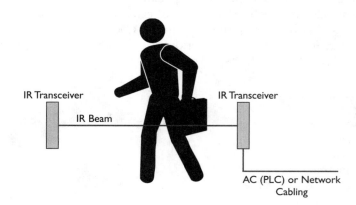

IR Transceiver

IR Transceiver

IR Beam

AC (PLC) or Network Cabling

Figure 20-16
A rain sensor
can be used to
prevent over-
watering.

Photo courtesy of Rain Bird Corporation.

Access through a motorized security gate is gained commonly through a remote control device, much like a garage door remote control, or through a keypad or card reader located on the side of the driveway. Although the gate can be closed using a remote control or other access control device, including telephone-based systems, most systems can be configured to automatically close after a preset period of time, typically 30 to 60 seconds.

In a typical scenario, as a vehicle approaches the security gate, the driver uses an access control device to send a signal to the gate control device that activates the motor to open the gate. On a high-end system, inductor loops can be embedded under the driveway as outer and inner loops. As the vehicle moves through the gate, it passes from the outer loop to the inner loop, which creates a signal to keep the gate open. After both loops are cleared, a timer in the control unit controls when the motor is activated to close the gate. When a vehicle approaches the gate to exit the property, the inner loop signals the controller to open the gate and the gate is held open until the vehicle clears the outer loop.

Environmental Detection Devices

Several home management systems can be configured to use signals to control watering schedules, zone watering, run-on protection, and the integration of weather or rain sensors that can detect wind, freezing temperatures, or rain (like the one shown in Figure 20-16), to cancel or temporarily suspend watering.

Access Control System Installation Considerations

The primary installation issues for an access control system are wiring and the effective placement of the detection and control devices. The manufacturer's recommendations for the type of wire to be used, placement of the sensors, inductive cables, and so on, should be followed to ensure an effective and functional installation.

PART V

Access Control Panels

The central point of most access control systems is a control panel. The reader, scanners, card slots, driveway systems, and other access control devices connect to the control panel as input devices, and the door locks and door releases connect as output devices. In addition, the output can be wired as an input to a security system. Sometimes detection devices such as an exterior motion detector are wired directly to a security panel. The security system can sound an alarm or trigger an output such as notifying the lighting system to turn on the driveway and entry lights if it is dark.

In some preconfigured access control systems, the control panel (see Figure 20-17) performs the authentication process and in others, the control panel serves as a bridging device that redirects signals through relays to activate preset actions, such as through the lighting system, security system, door locks, and so on.

Access Control System Wiring

The most commonly recommended wiring standard for access control systems is RS-485, which requires 2- to 6-conductor 24 AWG twisted-pair cable. However, the cable properties specified in RS-485 are more than satisfied by Cat 5e cable.

When planning the structured wiring for a home that is to include an access control system, be sure to include homeruns of additional Cat 5e cabling to connect the system's detection and locking devices to the access control panel and to the home control unit.

 NOTE Wiring for access control systems varies by manufacturer and, in some cases, even between models. Be sure to follow the manufacturer's documentation and recommendations when wiring an access control device. Remember, no matter what, you should always follow the standard electrical and low-voltage wiring guidelines and codes applicable to a home's location.

Figure 20-17
A security system control panel

Photo courtesy of Amtel Security Systems, Inc.

Chapter Review

An access control system is any combination of devices that secure a home and prevent or detect an unauthorized entry through a door, window, or other exterior feature that can be used to gain access to a home.

Residential access control systems consist of a variety of devices used to gain access to a home, including card readers, door locks, driveway loops, keypads, proximity card scanners, and motorized gates.

Card reader systems read coding on a credit card– or smaller-sized plastic or laminated card to unlock or open a door to a home. A basic card reader reads a number from the card and transfers it to a control unit or security system controller.

A barcode reader is similar to the devices used in the checkout stands at supermarkets. Barcode-encoded information is printed on a plastic or paper card.

A magnetic stripe reader reads the information stored on a black or reddish-brown magnetic stripe placed on a plastic card. There are two types of magnetic stripe cards: low coercivity and high coercivity.

Proximity systems read information from a card held near the card reader using low-frequency radio signals. Wiegand cards are a type of proximity readers that have special electromagnetic wires embedded in them in a specific pattern, unique to each card.

Keypad access control systems require the entry of a multiple-digit code sequence.

An electronic key system works much like a regular lock and key, except that electronic keys are inserted into an electronic reader.

Electric door lock systems are typically used in conjunction with an authorization device, such as a card reader, electronic key, or keypad. This type of access control device can be used to limit both entry and exit through a door. A wide variety of products fall in the general category of electric locks, including remote control deadbolts, push-button and keypad door locks, and electric door strikes that can be used to upgrade existing mechanical door locks.

A remote control deadbolt works much like a manually operated deadbolt, except that a remote control deadbolt can be locked or unlocked through an IR remote control.

Push-button and keypad door lock systems are keyless locks that can be unlocked by entering a code number sequence by pressing buttons or keys on the face of the door lock.

Electric door strikes lock or unlock a door acting on a command from a charge sent to the strike through a relay or a simple push-button release.

Biometric access control systems use features of the users' bodies to verify their identities, such as fingerprints, facial features, and even retinal patterns. For residential systems, the most commonly used biometric system uses fingerprints to control access.

There are a variety of driveway detection and monitoring systems available: induction loop systems, metal detection systems, and motion detection systems.

An induction loop system installs loops of special cable under a driveway. The induction cable emits an electromagnetic field that interacts with anything that changes the frequency of the inductive field.

Metal detectors use sensors to detect large metallic objects moving past.

Exterior motion detectors emit a PIR beam or sweep that constantly scans a fixed area and signals a security event should the beam be interrupted. Beam detectors transmit a continuous IR beam between two stations; when an object breaks the IR beam, a signal is generated from the controlling transceiver.

A motorized gate is equipped with a two-directional motor system that is used to open and close the gate upon receiving a signal. Motorized gate systems are available as swing gate, slider gate, and lift gate systems.

The primary installation issues for an access control system are wiring and the effective placement of the detection and control devices. The manufacturer's recommendations for the placement of the sensors, inductive cables, and so on, should be followed to ensure an effective and functional installation.

The central point of most access control systems is a control panel. The reader, scanners, card slots, driveway systems, and other access control devices connect to the control panel as input devices and the door locks and door releases connect as output devices.

The most commonly recommended wiring standard for an access control system is RS-485, which specifies 4- to 6-conductor 24 AWG twisted-pair cable. The cable properties specified for RS-485 cabling are more than satisfied by Cat 5e cable.

Questions

1. What purpose are access control systems primarily used for?
    A. Intrusion detection and alarm
    B. Remote monitoring services
    C. Preventing unauthorized entry
    D. Securing windows

2. Which of the following is not typically part of a home's access control system?
    A. Card reader
    B. Interior motion detector
    C. Electric door lock
    D. Keypad

3. Which of the following types of readers does not require a card or key be inserted or swiped?
    A. Barcode
    B. Magnetic stripe
    C. Proximity cards
    D. Electronic key

4. What type of card system uses embedded wires arranged in a unique pattern?

    A. Proximity

    B. Magnetic stripe

    C. Barcode

    D. Wiegand

5. What technology is used with proximity card systems?

    A. Barcode

    B. Magnetic stripe

    C. RF

    D. IR

6. What is the drawback to using keypad access control systems?

    A. Length of the numerical code

    B. Limited number of codes

    C. Unauthorized person learning code

    D. Weather

7. Which of the following is the physical feature most commonly used for residential biometric access control systems?

    A. Facial features

    B. Fingerprint

    C. Retinal scan

    D. Ear scan

8. What type of system uses cables installed under the driveway to detect a car entering the driveway?

    A. Induction loop systems

    B. Metal detection system

    C. Motion detection systems

    D. Visual detection systems

9. What cable type can be used in place of the recommended RS-485 cabling for an access control system?

    A. Cat 3

    B. Cat 5e

    C. Coaxial cable

    D. Quad wire

PART V

10. What device is used to bridge and control the sensors and detection systems of an access control system to door locks and other entry security devices?

    A. Bridge

    B. Central switch

    C. Control panel

    D. Hub

Answers

1. **C.** Interior and exterior security systems incorporate the other choices, but an access control system is used to control the entry into a home.

2. **B.** Access control systems focus solely on alerting the homeowner to a visitor's presence and the control of access to the home.

3. **C.** These systems use RF signals that can be detected from a short distance of the reader. The other choices require that a card or key be inserted or swiped through a reader.

4. **D.** Because the pattern of wires in a card is essentially manufactured into the card, they are virtually impossible to counterfeit.

5. **C.** Proximity cards use passive low-frequency radio frequency technology to communicate.

6. **C.** As long as the code number to be entered on the keypad is secret, the system remains secure. None of the other choices are typically much of a problem.

7. **B.** Although the other choices—perhaps with the exception of an ear scan—can be used, the equipment is prohibitively expensive for residential applications. As far as I know, there are no ear scan systems.

8. **A.** As a car drives over the induction loop, the frequency of the electromagnetic field changes, which is detected by the system's controller. The other choices listed are generally above-ground systems.

9. **B.** Cat 5e wiring, which is typically used for structured wiring anyway, can be used to connect access control sensors and detection systems to the access control panel.

10. **C.** In most access control systems, the microprocessor and processing capabilities exist in the control panel, which performs authentication and authorization functions.

Designing and Installing a Home Security System

In this chapter, you will learn about

- Design issues for a home security system
- Planning the structured wiring for a home security system
- Interfacing lighting to the security system
- Wiring and installing home security sensors, contacts, and keypads
- Configuring the security system control panel
- Testing a home security system

The basic idea behind the inclusion of a home security system is to protect the home's occupants and their belongings. The design of a home security system must secure any possible point of entry into a home, detect any breach in that security, and notify and alarm the home's occupants and any desired outsiders (such as monitoring services or family and friends) should there be a breach of security. When the security system interfaces with a home control system, it adds safety and gives the homeowners and occupants peace of mind. The residential security system technology must fit the requirements of the homeowners, as well as their budget.

The activities involved with the installation of a home security system are about the sensors and contacts. In order for the home security system to perform and protect the residence and its occupants, they must be carefully placed to do their job properly. If a window contact doesn't contact correctly or an opened door blocks a motion sensor, the security system won't be able to perform as it should and detect an intruder, which defeats the purpose of the entire system.

This chapter focuses on the issues to be considered when designing a home security system and some options that can make the system more effective, as well as the steps used to install and test the security system. The focus is on installing hard-wired systems, but some information about the installation of a wireless system is included as well.

 CROSS-REFERENCE Video surveillance systems are covered in Part VIII of the book.

Design Considerations for a Home Security System

The first consideration when designing a home security system is whether the home is a new construction or an existing house. The options in a new construction situation are numerous since you have more flexibility in planning and installing a structured wiring environment. In an existing home, the choices are more challenging and may be more limited.

Deciding What Should Be Secured

In many cases, homeowners aren't sure exactly what they wish to have included in a home security system; they just want their home secured and to feel safe. Considering that most customers also have a limited budget for this type of project, it is important to identify the minimum protections they should consider installing as well as options to further enhance the system.

Based on the recommendations of the security services industry and several police and fire department checklists, the questions listed in Table 21-1 should provide the information you need to determine the must-haves and the could-haves of a home security system.

Interview the homeowners to identify how much interior and exterior detection and protection they desire. Review the floor plans and be sure to discuss the following items:

- Doors—all entry doors as well as and doors to separate areas of the house
- Windows and/or screens to be protected
- Interior motion sensor locations
- Fire protection—has an electrician installed it? Is it interfaced to security system? Be sure to follow local codes
- Environment considerations—wine cellar, pool, spa, basement, low temperature areas
- Keypads at main entry points, plus the master bedroom
- Exterior motion detection and actions
- Their desire to interface with home control of lighting and heating, ventilating, air conditioning (HVAC)

In addition, be sure to discuss how many security access codes the homeowners would like and if they want to be able to secure a portion of the house while using the rest of it (this is called *partitioning* in security jargon). The results of this interview will help determine the security panel and components you will use.

Security System Technologies

In new construction situations, wired security systems are the first choice. They are easy to install during the pre-wire stage and are cost-effective over wireless technology components. However, wireless systems can be easily retrofitted into an existing home, though wiring is an option if the attic, crawlspace, and basement allow for retrofit wiring.

Other technologies, such as infrared (IR), ultrasonic, electromagnetic induction, and digital signal processors (DSP) are used in the sensors and detectors that can be incorporated into the system. However, the most important consideration when designing a security system is the technology that is to be used to interconnect the components of the system, wired or wireless.

Security Zones

An important element in the design of a security system is the planning of the security zones and how the security system's components are to be placed in each zone. A security system zone includes the adjacent areas of a home that will be reported together when an alarm occurs. Each zone in a home can have a different number of doors and windows and can include different contents of the room or rooms. A security zone may be a single room, multiple rooms, open areas, or the exterior of the home.

The zoning of a home should be based on the floor plan or layout of the home, the requirements of the homeowners, and the capabilities of the selected security system. For example, the zoning plan illustrated in Figure 21-1 creates five zones, each of which has different needs and requirements. Table 21-2 lists these five zones and their security needs.

Situation	Possible Solutions
Do all the exterior doors have deadbolt locks?	Automatic door locks and (NC) contacts
Are all the exterior doors lighted?	Security lighting
Are all the exterior doors visible to the street or sidewalk?	Security lighting
Is the main entrance to the home convenient to the main activity areas or bedrooms in the home?	Door intercom and keypad, remote control of automatic door locks, camera at the main entrance
Does the garage door have an automatic door opener?	NC contacts and automatic door opener
Do all windows have locks?	Window locks and NC contacts
Are all windows in plain sight and not hidden by shrubbery or trees?	Window locks, contact sensors, security screen wiring, security lighting
Is exterior lighting installed to illuminate all sides of the home?	Security lighting
Are motion detectors installed to control the exterior lighting?	Motion detectors and security lighting
Are smoke detectors installed in the hallways, bedrooms, stairways, basement, and garage?	Smoke detectors
Is a carbon monoxide detector installed in or near the bedrooms and near the furnace?	Carbon monoxide detectors
Are the smoke or carbon monoxide detectors hard-wired or battery powered?	Hard-wired detectors
Is at least one telephone available on every floor of the house for emergency use?	Installation of additional telephone outlets
Are keys to the house hidden near the main or secondary entrances?	Doorway keypads

Table 21-1   Security Issues and Solutions

PART V

Zone	Rooms	Outside Doors	Windows	Contents
1	Master bedroom	1	4	TV, jewelry, art
2	Bedrooms	0	6	TVs, collectibles
3	Office, baths	0	1	Computer, office equipment
4	Kitchen, family room	2	4	Microwave, appliances, home entertainment center
5	Entry	1	2	Art

Table 21-2 The Zone Plan for the Layout Shown in Figure 21-1

Beyond the planning shown in Figure 21-1 and Table 21-2, additional information must be included, such as:

- Local fire safety laws and building codes require smoke detectors in all sleeping areas, hallways, kitchens, and on each level of a home
- Four of the bedroom windows are located on the street side of the home
- The two doors leading to the patio and the family room door leading to the porch are sliding glass doors

Security Component Planning

The owners of the home illustrated in Figure 21-1 have expressed a desire for the security system, when it's enabled, to detect doors and windows being opened, glass breaking on street-side windows and sliding doors, a person entering through the main doorway or the home office, and a vehicle on the driveway. In addition, they are considering

Figure 21-1
An example of a zone layout plan diagram

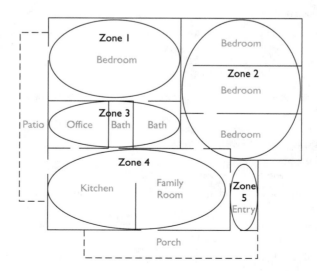

	Zone						
Component	1	2	3	4	5	Exterior	Total
	Master Bedroom	Bedrooms	Office & Baths	Kitchen & Family Room	Entry		
Cameras	0	0	0	0	0	2	2
Door contacts	1	0	0	2	1	0	4
Glass break detectors	1	0	0	1	0	0	2
Driveway sensor	0	0	0	0	0	1	1
Motion sensors	0	0	1	0	1	0	2
Smoke detectors	1	3	1	1	0	0	6
Window contacts	4	6	1	4	2	0	17

Table 21-3   Security System Component Planning

installing security cameras on the exterior of the home and security lighting on the front and street sides of the home. Table 21-3 summarizes the components required to provide this level of security by zone.

Defining the zones and sensors to be included helps you outline the specifications for selecting the security control panel. Most panels come with a standard number of zones, such as eight, and the panel can be expanded to add more zones. When designing which devices will be on what zones it is important to look at each of the device's power requirements and the maximum power that can be supplied by the security panel. It may be necessary to add additional power sources to feed all of the powered devices. Consult the manufacturer's documentation for details.

If the security system design includes either interior or exterior surveillance cameras or motion detectors, consider their placement carefully to ensure they can "see" the areas they are intended to view.

CROSS-REFERENCE   See Chapter 19 for more on the functions and use of security system components and devices, and see Chapter 24 for more on video surveillance systems.

Security Systems and Structured Wiring

The next step in the design of the security system is to plan the cable requirements for the system. If the plan is to install homerun wiring to each of the security system components, the structured wiring plan must be adapted to include these cable runs.

Security System Wiring

In a structured wiring environment, wiring is terminated at the security system's master unit, or panel, from each sensor, keypad, contact, smoke or heat detector, or alarm sounding device. The wiring, like all structured wiring, is installed in a star topology with a homerun between the security system control panel and each device. Be sure to include the security wiring on the structured wiring chart or make a separate chart for it.

Hard-Wired Systems

The wiring installed to connect each component to the security system control unit should be homeruns between the security panel and each of the security devices. Looping, that is, installing several devices such as window or screen contacts on a single loop of wire in series, should be minimized, if possible. Any security device that will be used to trigger the action of another home system device, such as a door contact or motion detector signaling a room's lights be powered on, must be wired separately and individually.

Table 21-4 lists the more commonly used security system components and the wire type recommended for each device.

Security System Component	Wire Recommendation
Keypads	Standard: 22 AWG 4-conductor stranded
	Advanced, with voice pickup and playback: 2 runs of 18 AWG 2-conductor shielded stranded
Internal and external alarms, speakers, and sound devices	18 AWG 2-conductor copper wire
AC power connections	18 AWG 2-conductor copper wire
Motion sensors, glass-break detectors	22 AWG 4-conductor copper wire
Door and window contact sensors	22 AWG 2-conductor copper wire
Fire alarm connections, smoke detectors, and heat detectors	Fire power limited plenum (FPLP) cable or fire power limited (FPL) cable: 18 AWG 4-conductor copper wire
Ground connection	14 AWG 1-conductor copper wire
RJ-31x console	22 AWG 4-conductor copper wire minimum, Cat 5e preferred
Wireless sensors	Any of the sensors listed in this table but with radio frequency (RF) communications and batteries to power them so no wiring is required
Video monitors and video capture devices	RG59 coaxial cable

Table 21-4 Wire Recommendation for Various Security Devices

Wireless Systems

Wireless security systems communicate with RF signaling that is typically in the range of 300 to 900 MHz. In many situations, a combination of wireless and wired devices may prove to be a more reliable design, depending on the distance from the wireless device to the base unit (range) or the necessity to install wireless devices to eliminate the need to pull wiring into the walls of a home. To ensure good performance, be sure to read and follow the specifications of the manufacturer's products when installing wireless devices. Also be sure to note battery replacement is recommended annually.

RJ-31x Connections

If the security system is to include a telephone link, such as to the homeowner's cell phone or a security monitoring service, for calling out when an alarm condition occurs, the design should consider whether a single phone line connection or multiple line connections are best for the home.

In the event of a security event (break-in, fire, and so on), the system can call out on a standard phone line or, by using an RJ-31x phone jack, it can seize the telephone line and hang up any phone call in progress, preventing any disruption from interfering with the automated telephone alert process.

Lighting Interfaced to the Security System

Security lighting has been proven to prevent intrusions, deter malicious activity, and enhance the aesthetics of a home. By interfacing with a home control system the lights can be programmed to go on when an alarm sounds, blink when a fire alarm sounds, and even turn on and off while the homeowners are away to make the house look occupied. All of these events can be linked to the time of day so they only occur when it is dark. Many security systems today have some form of lighting control built into them for just these reasons and act as the home control system.

The design goal for a security lighting system should be to light the areas of a home's exterior, especially those close to the home that would, without lighting, be shadowed or dark. Motion detectors can be used to turn on lighting around the home should movement be detected. These same outdoor motion sensors can also be set up to sound a simple chime inside the home to alert the occupants that someone is outside.

When designing lighting control for security purposes, consider the following:

- **Accent lighting**   Down lights, coach lights, landscape lighting
- **Security lighting**   Flood lights
- **Interior lighting**   Kitchen lights, living room lights, bedroom lights for a "lived-in" look

Make a list of the lighting loads to be controlled and be sure to communicate with the electrician that these loads will be controlled by the security/home control system, so no timers or daylight sensors are needed.

PART V

The best way to provide good lighting and vision in exterior areas is to install medium intensity, nonglare lighting fixtures that are aimed downward or shielded. For exterior lighting, three types of lamps can be used:

- **Halogen** These are commonly used as floodlights or landscaping lights because they provide a bright white or near-white light. Halogen lamps can be used to brightly light an area in connection with a motion detector sensing movement in its monitoring area.

- **High-Intensity Discharge (HID)** These lamps include mercury vapor, metal halide, high-pressure sodium, and fluorescent lamps. With the exception of fluorescent lamps, HID lamps require a warm-up period before reaching their full brightness. For this reason, HID lamps should not be used in situations where the security system requires instant-on lighting. HID lamps are better used as general lighting to constantly light an area, such as landscape or accent lighting.

- **Incandescent** These high wattage lamps can be used in just about any security lighting situation. However, because of their relatively limited life, they can be prone to burn out and defeat the purpose of the security lighting system if they are not properly maintained with a regular group replacement scheme.

If security lighting is being included in the security system design solely to provide lighting for exterior surveillance cameras, consider using cameras that include IR lighting capabilities that allow the camera to virtually see in the dark.

Installing a Home Security System

A hard-wired security system requires very little after-installation maintenance. This type of security system provides the assurance that if a sensor or contact trips, the system master or control panel will receive a signal, which may not always be true of a wireless system. However, a wireless security system is easier to install in a retrofit situation, although it also has some placement and operational issues that are discussed later in the chapter.

Component Wiring and Installation

Installing security system components as part of a new construction project allows the cabling required for the sensors, contacts, and keypads to be placed in a room or zone to be installed along with the structured wiring system. However, if the system is being installed in an existing home, wiring must be pulled through the existing walls, floor, or ceiling. Remember, the right wire type needs to be installed for each specific type of device.

The minimum wiring requirements for each of the more common security system components are detailed in the following sections.

Security System Control Panel

The system control panel, also referred to as an alarm system or a master unit, is where all the wiring of a security system's sensors and contacts terminates. The system control panel should be placed in the same area as the structured wiring distribution panel or, if that is not possible, in a centrally located and convenient location that is not easily accessible from the outside (do not place it in the garage). A closet and the mechanical room are good locations.

The only specific electrical wiring required for the system control panel itself is access to an electrical outlet for the AC power transformer. The wire used should be 4-conductor 22-gauge copper cable from the control panel to the transformer.

Keypads

Security system keypads, like the one shown in Figure 21-2, can be wall-mounted or recessed units that provide a user interface to the security system to control a single zone or the whole-house system.

Security system keypads require a 4-conductor 22-gauge copper cable. Two of the wires carry power from the control panel to the keypad, and the other two wires are used to transmit signals between the keypad and the control panel.

Door and Window Contacts

Door and window contacts are passive switches and don't require separate power from the system control panel. To connect a door or window contact to the control panel, use 2-conductor 22-gauge unshielded copper cable. Door and window contacts can be wired in series in a loop, with the wiring from the last contact looping back to the first contact. In this configuration, a signal from any of the contacts in the loop will be transmitted back to the control panel from the first unit in the loop. Figure 21-3 illustrates how window contacts can be wired in series on a single loop of wire.

Door and window contacts are available in a variety of styles. The most commonly used styles include roller-ball styles, which operate by compressing and releasing a

Figure 21-2

A security system keypad is used to control the security settings of a zone.

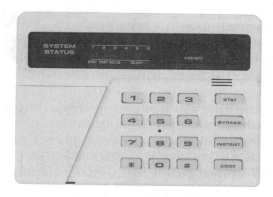

Photo courtesy of Honeywell International, Inc.

Figure 21-3
Window and glass-break sensors wired in a series loop

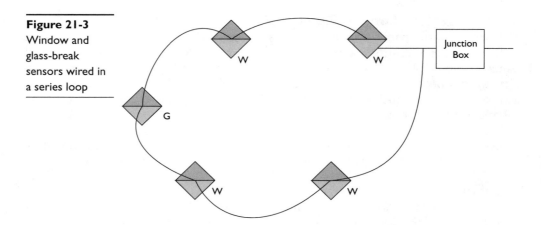

roller-ball (as shown in Figure 21-4); recessed switches, which are inserted in holes drilled in the door or window and its framing (see Figure 21-5); surface-mount switches (see Figure 21-6).

Figure 21-6 shows how a surface-mount window contact works. When the window is closed, a magnet in the part mounted on the window closes the switch into its normally closed (NC) position. When the window is opened, the magnet moves away from the spring-loaded switch inside the frame-mounted part and a trip signal is generated. A door contact operates in the same way; the only difference being that the magnet part moves away from the switch part when the door is opened.

To allow for a window to be open and still provide security protection, a second magnet can be mounted in the window frame to detect contact while the window is in the open position. This allows for the window to be in two positions, closed and open to this distance, and either location provides a NC contact.

Figure 21-4
A roller-ball door and window contact switch

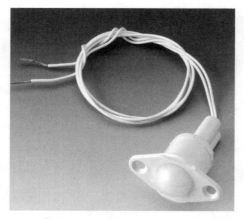

Photo courtesy of Honeywell International, Inc.

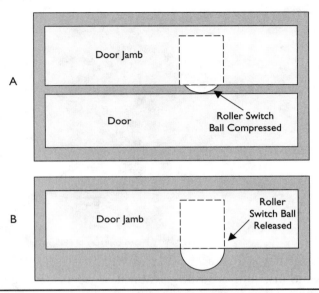

Figure 21-5 Part A of this illustration shows a recessed roller-ball contact sensor compressed when the door is closed. Part B shows that when the door is opened, the ball is released and an alarm event is triggered.

Glass-Break Sensors

The two common types of glass-break sensors are acoustic (sound) and vibration (shock). Which type is better for a particular installation depends on the type of glass (plate glass, tempered glass, or laminated glass) in the window, door, or relight pane.

Acoustic Glass-Break Detectors Acoustic detectors, also called active sensors, are tuned to pick up only the sound of breaking glass. This prevents them from generating a trip signal for any other sounds. Acoustic glass-break detectors are placed on a wall or ceiling near the windows to be monitored. Typically, a single acoustic sensor (see Figure 21-7) is able to monitor all the windows of a medium-sized room.

Figure 21-6

The operation of surface-mounted window contact switch

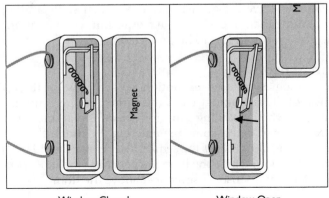

Window Closed   Window Open

Figure 21-7

An acoustic glass-break detector "hears" the sound of breaking glass and triggers an alarm event.

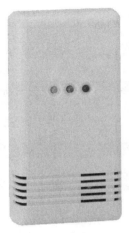

Photo courtesy of FBII.

One challenge to installing acoustic glass-break sensors is testing them. Instead of actually breaking a window to see if the sensor is working, several sensor manufacturers also sell glass-break detector testers that make the sound of glass breaking—a much better way to test these units.

Acoustic sensors require power from the control panel plus two conductors for signaling; so 4-conductor 22-gauge copper wiring is required. If the sensor has a tampering relay and the homeowner wishes to connect it to the control panel, six conductors are needed.

Vibration Glass-Break Detectors   Vibration glass-break detectors, also called passive detectors, are place directly on the glass or on the window frame very close to the window. If an intruder knocks or taps on the glass or breaks it, the vibration is sensed and a trip signal is generated.

Vibration detectors (see Figure 21-8) are passive devices that don't require power from the control panel. Two-conductor 22-gauge wire is used to connect the detector to the control panel.

When deciding the type of glass-break detector to install, be sure to consider if power is available to drive the acoustic sensors. When strategically placed, acoustic sensors can cover more than one window at a time, but with vibration detectors one should be installed on every window to be protected.

Motion Sensors

Two technologies are used in motion sensors: passive IR (PIR) or active ultrasound. Regardless of the technology used, the wiring requirements are the same. The most important issue when installing a motion sensor is placement in the room. If the purpose of the sensor is to detect someone entering the room, the sensor cannot be placed so that an opening door blocks the sensor. The sensor should be placed so that it monitors the areas of a room where the homeowners have the most concern. The recommended height of a motion sensor is seven feet above the floor.

PART V

Figure 21-8
A vibration glass-break detector is mounted on a windowpane to sense vibrations from knocks, taps, or hits on a window.

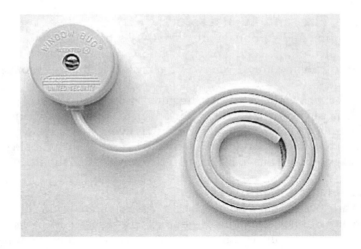

A common cause of standard PIR motion detectors signaling false alarms is small children or household pets entering a room. Many PIR units are available with horizontal scan "pet alleys" that prevent movement by short or small children or pets from triggering an alarm. Adaptive units such as PIR/microwave sensors self-adjust to the room and its environment. Other sensors are designed to be pet-smart, with horizontal bands of the scan range set aside for pets and small children. Some units even attempt to estimate the weight of a scanned object and suppress the alarm for moving objects that are estimated to weigh less than 80 pounds.

Motion sensors, like the one shown in Figure 21-9, require a minimum of four conductors between the control panel and the sensor: two to carry 12V DC power from the control panel and two to carry the trip (motion-detected) signal. Some motion detectors also have additional contacts to detect attempts to tamper with the sensor and to report self-diagnostics to a control panel. Although these additional tamper monitoring terminals are generally not connected in home systems, if the homeowner wishes to include these functions in the security system, add two additional conductors in the cable to connect the sensor to the control panel.

Figure 21-9
A motion sensor detects movement in a space and creates an alarm event.

Photo courtesy of Honeywell International Inc.

Smoke, Fire, and CO Detectors

Smoke, fire, and carbon monoxide (CO) sensors are surface-mount devices that are installed on the ceiling or above doorways in hallways near bedrooms, kitchens (close to cooking areas), stairways, garages, mechanical rooms, and near furnaces and boilers.

Smoke, fire, and CO detectors require a 4-conductor 18-gauge unshielded fire-rated cable and can be wired in series (daisy-chained) with the wire terminating at the control panel connected to the first sensor, which is then wired to the second sensor, and so on. If more than five sensors are to be installed in series, they should be split up into separate series of four units to make troubleshooting easier, should it be necessary later.

Photoelectric Beam Devices

There are locations in a home where a passive infrared (PIR) device just isn't practical. For many of these situations, a photoelectric device may be used instead. This technology is commonly used in smoke detectors, where a beam of light is used to detect smoke entering its testing chamber. If smoke interrupts the light beam, an alarm event is generated (typically sounding a shrill screeching sound). However, a photoelectric device can also be used inside windows, doors, and skylights (including outdoors) using the same basic principle of PIR and the photoelectric beam in the smoke alarm. If the light beam is interrupted, an alarm is generated. Newer developments in photoelectric detection devices employ two, four, and even six beams across a space as wide as 44 inches.

Sirens

Most residential security systems use what are called speaker sirens. The siren (sounding) unit is a module located in the security system control panel that is connected to the siren speaker using 2-conductor 18-gauge copper cable. The siren speaker is a passive device that doesn't require power, much like a standard audio speaker. However, it does require a heavier gauge cable than the sensors so that the sound signal is not lost as it travels over the cable.

Speaker sirens are available in two general styles: horn or surface-mount. Horn-style speaker sirens are typically used for exterior applications or placed in an out-of-the-way location, like an attic or a garage. Surface-mount speakers (see Figure 21-10) are like small audio speakers that can be mounted in a room or another interior location.

Low Temperature Sensors

There are two types of low-temperature sensors: those that have a mechanical switch, also called a *freezestat*, and those that use a length of tubing that acts as an averaging sensor. In either case, when the temperature falls below a certain level, for example 39 degrees Fahrenheit or 41 degrees Fahrenheit (both common settings), the sensor sounds an audible signal if desired and transmits a signal to a security system controller. Some devices are hardwired and send signals through a relay, and others connect using an RJ-12 connection to structured wiring.

Figure 21-10
A surface-
mounted
speaker siren

Photo courtesy of Ademco.

Water Detectors

These types of sensors or detectors are also called *leak detectors* because they detect water leaks. They do this by monitoring for water pooling in a certain area or any detectable change in the water pressure in a pipe or tube. Nearly all water detector sensors can be connected to a home security network through either an interface module or via a relay connection on the sensor.

Humidity Sensors

Humidity sensors monitor the moisture content of the air inside a home or enclosed area. Most of the better humidity sensors have both a high and low setting that signal when the humidity gets too low or too high. Other humidity sensors have only a single set point and either signals when the humidity is too low or too high, but not both. Those humidity sensors that can be interfaced to a home security control system are able to connect to any system that recognizes relay signals or dry contact switches, such as power line communication (PLC) and other power line technologies.

Telephone Interface Connections

Most security control panels have a relay connection that is used to seize a telephone line to transmit an alarm signal, message, or voice recording to a home security monitoring service or telephone numbers programmed in the system.

The security system control panel should be the first device on the telephone wiring in the home. This means that the RJ-31x jack on the control panel or an add-on telephone module (see Figure 21-11) should be connected directly from the network interface device (NID) and before the telephone distribution module of the structured wiring system. The wiring from the NID to the security control panel and between the security control panel and the telephone system panel should be Cat 5e cable.

Figure 21-11
A telephone
interface module
with RJ-31x jacks

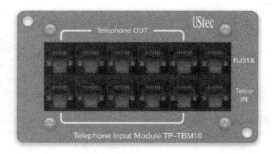

Photo courtesy of UStec.

Configuring the Security System Control Panel

The detailed steps used to configure the security system control panel for a home security system vary by manufacturer. Most systems have a proprietary configuration process that is tied to the particular modules that are included in the standard configuration of the control panel. When installing and configuring a home security system control panel, follow the manufacturer's documentation to set up and configure the system.

Perform an interview with the homeowner about the security system to get the information necessary for system setup and user codes. Using the worksheets usually provided by the manufacturer, identify any further information required. You can complete much of this information prior to the interview, so just get the homeowner's approval and a few more details to help speed the process along.

When setting up an alarm system, the modules and functions that usually must be configured to ensure the proper operation of the security system are

- Hardware and devices
  - Control panel install and power up
  - Telephone connection
  - Keypad hookups
  - Sensor interfaces
  - Fire alarm interfaces
  - Sounder outputs
- Programming and configuration (where applicable)
  - Zone type setups
  - User codes and setups
  - Entry/exit delays
  - Panic modes
  - Digital communicator setup

- Alarm verification process setup
- Home control setups
- Remote telephone control

Again, be sure to follow the specifics for setup outlined in the manufacturer's documentation.

Home Security System Testing

The installation of a home security system isn't finished until the entire system has been completely tested and any necessary adjustments are made and retested. The testing process essentially boils down to triggering trip alerts on each installed component of the system. This means that every sensor, contact, and detector must be tested by forcing the condition it was installed to monitor: opening windows and doors and entering rooms or areas outside the home monitored by motion detectors. The complete security system should be tested, including any video surveillance (Chapter 24) or home access (Chapter 20) systems that are installed and attached to the security system control panel.

The testing should start with the testing of the components in each of the rooms in a single zone. After one zone is completely tested, proceed to the next zone. It is recommended that the first room and zone tested should be the one nearest the security system control panel. Be sure to use a zone list or wire chart to check off every device tested.

Cable Tests

During pre-wire or prior to device installation be sure to conduct cable or wire testing. You should perform the standard structured wiring cable tests, including continuity and impedance. This should be done at pre-wire so as to catch any problems that can easily be remedied while the walls are open. Testing can also be done at trim-out prior to the installation of devices to confirm all the wiring is good and if a problem exists, it would be with the devices being installed.

 CROSS-REFERENCE Chapter 3 covers testing procedures for wiring.

Detector Tests

After installation, hookup, and setup programming of all devices, perform the following testing steps in each room:

1. Set the exit timer to its lowest setting. Security systems usually have at least two settings that allow a variable amount of time before the system arms or disarms to give the homeowners time to enter the home and disarm the system or exit the home after arming the system.

2. Centrally arm the system as it will be when the homeowners leave the home.

3. Allow the exit delay time to lapse.

4. Open each protected door and window or enter a space monitored by a motion sensor to cause a trip signal and verify the alarm is triggered.

5. Also test each smoke and CO sensor located in each room or zone by pressing the test button on each. If the expected alarm isn't activated, continue to troubleshoot and test the sensor, control panel, and the alarm until all three are working properly, then move onto the next sensor.

6. On most systems, you'll need to reset the system after testing each contact, sensor, or zone.

7. After completing the testing in all zones, repeat the testing, with the customer observing, on at least one sensor in each zone.

8. Remember to reset the exit time setting to the desired time before leaving.

After completing the detector testing, test all of the user codes and any other unique system setup areas. Finally, orient the customer to the system and train the customer on the system's normal operations.

Documentation on how to use the security system should be given to the homeowners for reference. Documentation of the security wiring and zones should be kept in the security control panel. Documentation of the system setup should also be given to the homeowner for safekeeping away from the panel and not readily accessible to others. Finally, in your project folder, be sure to keep documentation of the security system setup, programming, testing, digital communicator, and ongoing maintenance and service of the system.

Security and Fire Alarm Testing Regulations

In addition to the home security industry's guidelines, many countries, states and provinces, counties, and cities have regulations or guidelines on how frequently a home security system must be tested. Ensure the customer is aware of the regulations and guidelines. Testing guidelines for home security systems are developed and published by the National Fire Protection Agency (NFPA), Security Industry Association (SIA), Underwriters Laboratories (UL), American National Standards Institute (ANSI), Canadian Standards Association (CSA), and the National Burglar and Fire Alarms Association (NBFAA), as well as standards organizations, and police and fire associations around the world.

Table 21-5 lists testing frequencies of monitored and unmonitored control panel components. A monitored component is one that the control panel has circuitry to monitor and display an alert should the component begin to fail, even intermittently. Unmonitored components are those for which a failure is not alerted. For example, a security keypad near a back door of a home may be an unmonitored component of a security system. If the keypad malfunctions, the homeowner knows the device should be repaired or replaced, but the security system may not display a notice or signal the component failure. However, the security system should alert the homeowner if a monitored component such as a door contact or a motion sensor fails to respond to monitoring signals.

Table 21-5	System Component	Testing Frequency
Recommended Security System Testing Frequencies	Monitored control panel components	Annually
	Unmonitored control panel components	Semiannually
	Control panel diagnostic services	Annually
	Control panel/telephone interface	Annually
	Smoke and CO detectors	Annually
	Door and window sensors	Annually
	Sirens, sounding devices, and strobe lights	Annually

Also explain to the homeowners that they should review the alarm ordinance in effect in their city, county, or state or province, and that they may be required to get a permit or license for their home security system before it will be recognized as a legal system by that authority. As a billable service to your clients, you may identify this information and process the necessary paperwork for them.

Chapter Review

An important element in the design of a security system is planning the security zones and how the security system's components are to be placed in each zone. A security zone may be a single room, multiple rooms, open areas, or the exterior of the home. The zoning of a home should be based on the floor plan or layout of the home and the requirements of the homeowners.

The design of the security system should include a plan for the system's cable requirements. Structured wiring is installed in a star topology with a homerun from the security system master unit to each device. Wireless security systems communicate with RF signaling. A combination of wireless and wired devices may prove to be more reliable.

If the security system is to include an RJ-31x jack to provide the system with a telephone link, the system will have the capability to seize a telephone line to place an automated telephone alert.

Security lighting has been proven to prevent intrusions, to deter malicious activity, and to enhance the aesthetics of a home. The design goal should be to light areas along a home's exterior that are in the shadows or dark. Motion detectors can be used to turn on lighting around the home should movement be detected. In addition, lighting should be identified and controlled to give the home the "lived-in" look.

Installing security system components as part of a new construction project allows the cabling required for the sensors, contacts, and keypads to be placed in a room or zone to be installed along with, or as part of, the structured wiring system. If the system is installed in an existing home, wiring must be pulled through the existing walls, floor, or ceiling.

The system control panel terminates the wiring from all sensors or contacts. The system control panel should be placed in the same area as the structured wiring distribution panel or a protected area; not in the garage. The system control panel usually requires electrical wiring to an AC outlet for the plug-in power transformer.

PART V

Door and window contacts are passive switches and don't require separate power from the system control panel. Door and window contacts are available in a variety of styles, including recessed switches, surface-mount switches, and roller-ball styles.

The two common types of glass-break sensors are acoustic and vibration. The type that should be used for a particular installation depends on the type of glass used. Acoustic detectors are tuned to pick up only the sound of breaking glass in a medium-sized room. Vibration glass-break detectors are placed directly on the glass or the window frame of every window being protected.

Security system keypads are wall-mounted or recessed units that provide user interface to the security system to control a single zone or the whole-house system.

Motion sensors are either passive IR (PIR) or active ultrasound. The recommended height of a motion sensor is seven feet above the floor.

Most residential security systems use speaker sirens that are activated by the control panel sending audio signals. Speaker sirens have two styles, horn or surface-mount.

Smoke, fire, and carbon monoxide (CO) sensors are surface-mount devices installed on ceilings or above doorways in hallways near bedrooms, kitchens (close to cooking areas), stairways, garages, and near furnaces and boilers. Smoke and fire detectors must be installed with fire-rated wiring.

Environmental monitoring sensors, which include low temperature sensors, water or moisture detectors, photoelectric and humidity sensors, can be integrated into a security system to prevent conditions from harming the home or its contents.

Security control panels use a relay connection inside an RJ-31x telephone jack to seize a telephone line and transmit an alarm signal, message, or voice recording to a home security monitoring service or programmed phone numbers. The security system control panel should be the first device on the telephone system.

The process and detailed steps used to configure the security system control panel for a home security system varies by manufacturer, and a proprietary configuration process is used to configure the control panel. When installing and configuring a home security system control panel, follow the manufacturer's documentation to set up and configure the system.

The installation of a home security system can be considered finished when the entire system has been completely tested and any necessary adjustments are made and retested. The testing process involves triggering trip alerts on each installed component of the system. Testing should begin with cable or wire testing and continue by testing the sensors and contacts in each room or zone. Documentation should be done of wiring and zones and kept inside the security panel. Documentation of setup should be given to the homeowner for safekeeping, and all documentation should be kept in the installation company's project folder.

Many countries, states and provinces, counties, and cities have regulations or guidelines concerning the frequency for home security system testing. Homeowners should be made aware of any alarm ordinances in effect in their city, county, or state or province.

Questions

1. In a home security system, where do homeruns to zone sensors and contacts terminate?

   A. Security system control panel

   B. Home automation controller

   C. Keypad

   D. Wiring distribution panel

2. Which type of glass-break sensor is typically mounted directly to the glass of a window or door?

   A. Acoustic

   B. Vibration

   C. PIR

   D. All of the above

3. At what height should a wall-mounted motion detector be installed?

   A. Four feet

   B. Five feet

   C. Seven feet

   D. It should be even with light switches and keypads.

4. On some sensors, there are tamper sensors and self-diagnostic relays. When these options are wired, what wire/cable should be used to completely wire a motion sensor?

   A. 4-conductor 22-gauge unshielded copper wire

   B. Two runs of 4-conductor 22-gauge unshielded copper wire

   C. Cat 5e

   D. None of the above; motion sensors are passive devices.

5. Which of the following is not a recommended location for a smoke detector?

   A. Bedrooms

   B. Hallways near bedrooms

   C. Kitchen

   D. Bathroom

6. What connector type is used to connect a security system control panel to a telephone interface?

   A. RJ-11

   B. RJ-21x

   C. RJ-31x

   D. RJ-45

7. Which of the following security system elements should be checked and tested at least semiannually?

   A. Monitored control panel components

   B. Unmonitored control panel components

   C. Smoke and CO detectors

   D. Door and window sensors

8. Which type of security system sensors or contacts can be wired in series on a loop?

   A. Door contacts

   B. Window or screen contacts

   C. Cameras

   D. Motion sensors

9. In general, what is the recommended cabling for window and door contacts and sensors in a home security system?

   A. 14 AWG 1-conductor copper wire

   B. 22 AWG 2-conductor copper wire

   C. Cat 5e

   D. RG6

10. Which of the following lamp types is/are commonly used for brightly illuminating the exterior area in a security lighting system?

    A. Halogen

    B. HID

    C. Incandescent

    D. IR

    E. All of the above

Answers

1. **A.** The homerun wiring of the security system could be routed through the structured wiring distribution panel or the home automation controller, but this approach would complicate the home's wiring unnecessarily. Keypads only serve as user interfaces and zone controls in a security system.

2. **B.** PIR is not a type of glass-break sensor, and acoustic sensors are typically mounted where they can listen to and monitor all of the windows in a room.

3. **C.** This height allows the sensor to scan the full-height of any person entering or occupying a room.

4. **B.** Six conductors are required to complete the wiring of a sensor with tamper detection.

5. **D.** It is not necessary to install a smoke detector here. The other choices are locations where a smoke detector should be installed.

6. **C.** A telephone interface module with an RJ-31x jack facilitates line seizure and the ability to place a security alert on a telephone line.

7. **B.** The other security system components should be tested annually.

8. **B.** Window or screen sensors can be wired in a series-connected loop. All other security system devices should be wired in parallel with individual homeruns.

9. **B.** These devices require only 2-conductor wire.

10. **A, B,** and **C.** IR lighting is used to allow security cameras to see in the dark, but it won't work to light up the exterior area of a home.

CHAPTER 22

Monitoring and Troubleshooting a Home Security System

In this chapter, you will learn about
- Preventing false alarms
- Troubleshooting home security systems
- Maintaining a home security system

Unfortunately, for a home security system to be truly effective, it cannot be just a "set it and forget it" type of thing. Home security systems should be monitored regularly for attempted intrusions, other security events, and proper functioning. To continue to function properly, a home security system must be regularly checked, maintained, and when necessary, troubleshooting must be done.

Even more than most other home systems, a security system is one that the homeowner must be able to depend upon. For the most part, a security system is rarely activated, and most homeowners hope it is never needed. However, if or when an intruder attempts to gain access to a home, the security system must function properly.

The key to a reliable security system is regular preventive maintenance and testing, and these procedures are the focus of this chapter.

False Alarms

The single most important issue for a homeowner and a home security system is false alarms and preventing them. However, on some systems, there can be a fine balance between a system that provides immediate detection and activation in the event of a home security breach and one that sets off frequent and costly false alarms. In many cities and counties, false alarms are not only embarrassing for the homeowner, but they can also be expensive.

In an effort to deter false alarms, especially for alarms systems monitored where emergency services are called, many communities have passed ordinances that levy escalating fines for multiple false alarm offenders to offset the cost to the community for providing these response services. The solution is to prevent false alarms with a well-defined and regularly performed maintenance and testing program.

There are many causes for false alarms, including:

- User errors
- Power or battery problems
- Ill-fitted, misaligned, or improperly placed sensors and contacts
- Malfunctioning detection devices
- Sensors not configured for pets or children
- Heating, ventilating, air conditioning (HVAC) vents or air drafts that cause light objects to move

User Errors

More than two-thirds of all false alarms are caused by user errors that can include operating the system improperly and forgetting the access codes. Another major reason for a sudden rash of false alarms from a system can be changes to the home, such as guests visiting, the addition of a new family member or pet, or remodeling doors, floors, windows, or ceilings.

The homeowner should train new family members or houseguests on the use of the security system. In addition, the homeowner may contact his or her security system provider whenever these or other changes occur to the home. He or she should also contact the security system provider and request that a "visitor" user code be set up when keys are given to outsiders or should the house be put up for sale.

Some municipalities require a home security system be inspected and tested by a certified (licensed) technician no less than once a year, with some requiring semiannual inspections and testing. During the annual or semiannual inspection, maintenance, and testing, the homeowner should be given a fresh orientation to the system, with emphasis placed on any user error–caused false alarms since the last visit.

The user should also be advised on how to prevent future false alarms. This includes what to check before activating the alarm system, such as locking all protected doors and windows and keeping pets, plants, balloons, holiday decorations, and the like out of the scanning field of a motion detector or sensor.

Power or Battery Issues

A security sensor or contact that is intermittently reporting false alarms (also called false positives) may have power or continuity issues caused by cable or wire problems. Passive security devices receive power through their primary wiring from the security control panel. Active security devices require an independent power source that is typically supplied through a power supply or battery. A device with faulty wiring, or an active device with the wrong type of battery installed, may cause false positive signals to be transmitted to the security system controller.

Misaligned Sensors or Contacts

A window or door contact that is even slightly misaligned may generate a false alarm even if the window or door is closed and locked. A window or door that is not completely closed and locked in the position where its contact was aligned can create this situation. This problem can also be caused by a window or door warping or otherwise changing its fit. All doors and windows should be closed completely and locked before the alarm system is activated.

Motion sensors can generate false alarms if they are in view of outdoor activities that could trigger them. Be sure the line-of-sight of a motion sensor is clear of any unwanted motion.

Sensors and detectors can also generate false alarms if they are placed too closely to some normal activities in a home. For example, if a smoke detector is located directly above a stove after a kitchen remodeling, it can generate false smoke alarms.

Malfunctioning Detection Devices

Detection devices have been known to fail over time. When they do fail, they can stop functioning completely or function intermittently and cause random false alarms. Hopefully these are caught during routine maintenance checking. Replacing the device in question should rectify the false alarm problem. It is a good rule to replace carbon monoxide detectors every three to four years as their performance deteriorates over time.

Pets and Children

Motion sensors can be configured to avoid signaling an alarm event for small children and pets. If this setting is overlooked during installation, incorrectly set originally, or reset by the homeowner, the sensor can generate a false alarm. When installing motion sensors with adjustable viewing, be sure to set these up per the manufacturer's instructions and test extensively from all angles of view of the motion sensor.

Moving Objects

If the placement of motion sensors does not take into consideration the location of HVAC vents or ceiling or room fans, the movement of an object, such as a houseplant or curtain, may set off an alarm from a motion detector. Or perhaps the motion detector was not properly aligned to avoid these objects during its installation. In either case, the motion sensor could be generating false alarms that may not be easily resolved if the cause isn't happening during an investigation. Watch out for balloons filled with helium (especially the Mylar type that seemingly hang around forever), such as those given to say "Happy Birthday" or "Get Well Soon," which can rise and fall with a change in room temperature and become an unwanted target of a motion sensor.

Lost Setup on the Security System Controller

The security system panel is programmed to know the types and names of the security zones. In addition, it is programmed to know all of the user codes and other system setup variables. If any of this information is lost in the memory of the system, false alarms can easily occur as zone types and setups usually default to factory settings.

Should this happen, any programmed names or descriptors no longer appear and the default value are displayed. This can occur after a prolonged loss of power or when the battery is exhausted. To correct this situation, restore power to the system and re-program it or, if supported by the system, download a saved setup of the programming. Many systems now have remote access capabilities, and the security system provider can phone the home and download this information.

Troubleshooting a Home Security System

When troubleshooting a home security system, you must first determine whether the problem is being caused by one of the four major areas of a security system:

- Contacts, sensors, or detectors
- The security system controller
- The wiring
- The interface to the telephone system

One of the better ways to pinpoint a fault on a home security system is to completely retest the system using the same procedure used during the trim out of the system (see Chapter 21). Once you have isolated the room or zone where the problem is occurring, you can then begin to focus on the security devices in that area.

Troubleshooting Contacts, Sensors, and Detectors

If you suspect that a home security system problem is being caused by a contact or sensor, you should check the alignment, fit, cleanliness, and wiring of the device to ensure that they haven't changed since installation.

NOTE A quick way to check the wiring connecting any contact, sensor, or detector device to a control panel or system controller is to replace it with a known-good device. If the known-good device fails, the problem is likely in the wiring; otherwise, if the known-good device works as it should, the problem is the failure of the original device.

Door and Window Contacts

The alignment of the two halves of a door or window contact sensor is crucial to its proper operation. If the contacts do not line up properly, the electromagnetic functions of the sensor are either defeated or can give false positives intermittently. The misalignment of door and window contacts can be caused by the door or window becoming warped or sagging on its hinges or frame, most commonly from extreme hot or cold temperatures or sudden temperature changes. The contacts may have been bent, moved, or knocked off by a hit or struck with some force, such as when furniture or other large objects are moved through a doorway. A regular visual inspection is the best way to spot these conditions. The remedies are to realign, reinstall, or replace the contact to its correct position.

As a part of a visual inspection, check the contacts for corrosion and cleanliness. If the contact has been subjected to moisture, it is possible the contact face has become corroded or perhaps even shorted out. The contacts should be cleaned using denatured alcohol (isopropyl alcohol) and a lint-free cloth in any case and retested.

If you or your company didn't install the security system, you should also check that the contacts are wired properly. Normally Closed (NC) contacts are typically wired in series, and Normally Open (NO) contacts are typically wired in parallel. Also verify that the wiring to each contact is correctly attached using proper wiring methods and that the appropriate wire types were installed.

To test NC contacts wired in series, the contacts should be tested in sequence, starting with all but the first contact disconnected from the wiring. After each contact is tested (and all is well), the next contact in line should be added back to the system and tested, until all contacts are reconnected, tested, and any defective contacts have been replaced.

Motion Sensors

The first step in troubleshooting a motion sensor is to verify its line-of-sight or scanning field. Objects such as curtains, draperies, art, or plants may be moving because of air-flow in the room. The airflow may be from a window that is regularly open or even an HVAC system vent. Perhaps the swing of a door into the room was overlooked during installation and is blocking the view of the sensor, or the sensor is set too high or too low to properly detect unusual motion in its room.

If the scanning field of the sensor is unobstructed and properly set, the next thing to check is the power. If the sensor is an active device, verify that its power light-emitting diode (LED) is on. If the power indicator is not on, check the device's power source, especially if the device uses an alternating current/direct current (AC/DC) converter, to ensure it is snugly plugged into an AC outlet. (Some AC/DC converters are too heavy for the AC connectors and can fall out of the socket.)

If the device is a passive device and gets its power from its wiring, check the wiring and verify that it conforms to the device's documentation. If the wiring is correct, check the accessory connections on the system controller using a multimeter to verify a connection of 12 to 18 volts to match the power requirements of the device.

If the wiring checks out, it is likely the device has failed, regardless of whether it is passive or active, and should be replaced.

Smoke, Fire, and CO Detectors

The first step in troubleshooting a smoke, fire, or carbon monoxide (CO) detector or alarm is to determine how the device is powered. If the detector is battery powered, change the battery and test the device; if it works, the battery was dead. However, if the detector fails to work regardless of its power source (assuming the power source is good), it may be that the photoelectric circuits (the detectors) have failed or have been damaged. In either case, this means the detector should be replaced.

If a smoke, fire, or CO detector is giving false alarms, the activities in its room or area may be the cause rather than the device itself having a problem. For example, CO detectors can generate an alarm from some common household products, such as hairspray, spray air deodorizers, bleach, paint, glue, nail polish and nail polish remover, dirty baby diapers, cigarette smoke, or even the nitroglycerin in heart medication—any product that may give off a vapor or contains CO gas. Carbon dioxide (CO_2) detectors also deteriorate over time and should be replaced every three to four years. A smoke detector placed too close to a normal activity that could produce some smoke, such as cooking, can also generate an alarm.

In these cases, the location of the detector may be the problem. However, if this is not the case, check the device wiring, and if all is well, replace the device.

Troubleshooting Keypad Controls and Wiring

If a security system fails to respond to the commands made through a keypad controller, the first suspect should be the wiring connecting the keypad to the system controller. The wiring should be tested for continuity, and the wire terminations on the keypad and at the control panel should be checked and verified.

If the wiring proves to be okay, the problem could be that the control panel or keypad has failed, but it may also be in the configuration or programming of the security system. If the keypad can be replaced successfully with a known-good device, then the keypad was the problem. However, if this is not the case, the system should be reprogrammed for that keypad or reprogrammed by restoring a backup of the controller, or by reentering the original (and tested) configuration.

Troubleshooting RJ-31x Connections

If a security system fails to connect to a telephone line to place an outbound call to a security monitoring system or to emergency services in a security event, the RJ-31x connections of the system should be tested and diagnosed.

To troubleshoot a system's RJ-31x interface, follow these steps:

1. Verify the installation and validity of the wiring to the security system controller and the telephone system to the RJ-31x jack, as well as the cabling and termination to the jack.

2. Check the continuity of telephone line wiring. If an open circuit or damaged contact exists, track it down, repair it, and retest the RJ-31x interface.

3. If the RJ-31x interface still has problems, check the RJ-31x jack and plug carefully. An RJ-31x jack has shorting bars that cross terminals 1 to 4 and 5 to 8. When the plug is inserted in the RJ-31x jack, the contact wires are lifted away from the shorting bars and make contact with the tip and ring circuits leading to the security system. Should the jack or plug become damaged, it is possible that the contact wires are not making the proper contacts to the security system or the phone. Visually inspect the jack and plug for damage and replace either or both if necessary.

4. To completely test the RJ-31x interface, cause a security event on the control panel and verify that the security system has seized the line and the interior lines cannot access the phone line.

Preventive Maintenance

A regular periodic program of preventive maintenance can assure the homeowners that their security system is properly functioning and reliable. The frequency of the preventive maintenance program should never be less than at least once annually, with quarterly or semiannual programs at the discretion of the homeowners. The frequency also depends on the complexity of the system—as the complexity of the system increases, so should the frequency with which it is checked.

While there aren't any disadvantages to frequent preventive maintenance checks to a homeowner, other than perhaps the cost, the advantages are

- Preventing false alarms
- Causing fewer service or problem calls
- Having desired changes implemented when needed
- Increased reliability of the system
- Having the manufacturer's upgrades applied regularly
- Developing or potentials problems being corrected before they cause the system to fail

Periodic Testing

To be in compliance with National Fire Protection Association (NFPA) 72 guidelines (and possibly the homeowner's insurance company), a home security system must be tested at least once per year. A certified system tester must perform the annual test, but the homeowner should know how to test the system and perform a test every 30 days (which is the requirement of some local security system ordinances).

Homeowner Testing

The testing procedure performed by the homeowner should include the following tests:

- **Arm and disarm the system** Every person with a key to the home should perform this test.
- **Fail all exterior ingress points** Test each window and outside door contacts and motion sensors. The homeowner should alert the monitoring service before the testing begins and when it is complete.
- **Test smoke and CO detectors** Press the test buttons on all of these devices.

Preventive Maintenance Testing

The testing performed as a part of a preventive maintenance check should approximate the testing performed during the original acceptance tests (see Chapter 21). If a local emergency services authority such as the police department monitors the system, they may require the system to be recertified each year and that a Certificate of Completion, which is a NFPA form prescribed in NFPA 72, be issued (although this is primarily for fire alarm systems, some communities also use it for security systems in general). Figure 22-1 shows the first page of the NFPA 72 Certificate of Completion.

In some communities, the local fire or police service may be required to reinspect the system. In these cases, a Certificate of Completion must have been completed, issued, and recorded by the installing or recertifying contractor.

Fire alarm Certificate of Completion

Business Name _____   Installation Company _____
Business Address _____   Company Address _____
telephone Number_____   Telephone Number _____
Supplier_____   Business License Number _____

1. Type(s) of System or Service

NFPA 72, Chapter 3 - Local
If alarm is transmitted to location(s) off premises, list where signal is received:
Address: _____
Telephone: _____

NFPA 72, Chapter 3 - Emergency Voice/ Alarm Service
Quantity of voice/ alarm channels: _____ Single _____ Multiple _____
Quantity of speakers installed: _____ Quantity of speaker zones_____
Quantity of telephones or telephone jacks included in system: _____

NFPA 72, chapter 5 - Auxiliary
Indicate type of connection:
    Local energy   Shunt   Parallel telephone
Location of telephone numbers for receipt of signals: _____

NFPA 72, chapter 5 - Remote Station
Alarm: _____
Supervisory: _____

NFPA 72, chapter 5 - Proprietary
If alarms are transmitted to a public fire service communications center or other, indicate and telephone numbers of the organization receiving alarm:
Address: _____ Telephone _____
Indicate how alarm is retransmitted: _____

NFPA 72, chapter 5 - Central Station
Prime Contractor: _____ Central station location _____

Means of transmission of signals from the protected premises to the central station:
    McCulloh   Multiplex   One-way radio
    Digital alarm communicator   Two-way radio   other
Means of transmission of alarms to the public fire service communications center:
(a) _____

Figure 22-1 An example of the certificate of completion prescribed by NFPA 72

Chapter Review

The prevention of false positives or false alarms should be one of the primary purposes of a regular maintenance and testing procedure. There are many causes for false alarms, including user errors, power or battery problems, misaligned or improperly placed sensors and contacts, sensors not configured for pets or children, malfunctioning detection devices, HVAC vents or air drafts that cause light objects to move, and setup configurations lost in the security panel. Most false alarms are caused by user errors and changes made to the home. Some municipalities require a home security system to be inspected and tested by a certified (licensed) technician no less than once a year, with some requiring semiannual inspections and testing.

A security sensor or contact that is intermittently reporting false alarms may have power or continuity issues caused by cable or wire problems. A window or door contact that is even slightly misaligned may generate a false alarm even if the window or door is closed and locked. All doors and windows should be closed completely and locked before the alarm system is activated. Sensors and detectors incorrectly placed can also cause false alarms. Motion sensors should be configured to avoid alarm signals for small children and pets. The placement of objects in a secured room should take into consideration the location of HVAC vents or room fans.

When troubleshooting a home security system, you must first determine whether the problem is being caused by one of the four major areas of a security system: contacts, sensors, or detectors; the security system controller; wiring; or the interface to the telephone system.

A regular periodic program of preventive maintenance can assure the homeowners that their security system is properly functioning and reliable. The frequency of the preventive maintenance program should never be less than at least once annually, with quarterly or semiannual programs at the discretion of the homeowner.

The advantages of periodic preventive maintenance on a home security system are preventing false alarms, causing fewer service or problem calls, having desired changes implemented when needed, increased reliability of the system, having the manufacturer's upgrades applied regularly, and potential problems being corrected before they cause the system to fail.

In compliance with NFPA 72 guidelines, a home security system must be tested at least once per year. If a local emergency services authority, such as the police or fire department, monitors the system, they may require the system to be recertified each year and have a Certificate of Completion issued.

Questions

1. What is the primary performance and maintenance issue with a home security system?

   A. Corroding window contacts

   B. False alarms

    C. Dead batteries

    D. System programming

2. What is the cause of more than two-thirds of home security system false alarms?

    A. Faulty wiring

    B. Misaligned contacts

    C. System programming

    D. User error

3. Which of the following could be the cause of window or door contact generating false positives?

    A. Misalignment

    B. Corrosion

    C. Change in the shape or fit of the door or window

    D. Damage to the contact

    E. All of the above

4. Which one of the following is most likely the problem when a motion detector that is otherwise functioning properly does not sense someone entering the room where it is located?

    A. The lighting level is too low

    B. The opening door blocks the scanning field

    C. The sensor is set too high or too low

    D. Too many objects are in the room

5. Which of the following should be included in the troubleshooting process for a security system controller?

    A. Reload the controller's backup

    B. Apply all manufacturer's upgrades

    C. Test the system

    D. Disconnect all zone devices before troubleshooting the system controller

6. When troubleshooting NC contacts wired in series, what procedure should be used?

    A. Test all contacts in the series

    B. Disconnect all but the first contact and add the contacts back to the system one at a time

    C. Disconnect all but the last contact and add the contacts back to the system one at a time

    D. NC contacts should be wired in parallel

7. Which of the following is a good troubleshooting technique for a suspected faulty contact or sensor?

   A. Disconnect the suspected device and retest the system

   B. Disconnect all but the suspected device and retest the system

   C. Replace the suspected device with a known-good device and retest

   D. Replace the suspected device immediately

8. When performing a visual inspection of contacts and sensors, for which of the following should you look?

   A. Corrosion

   B. Cleanliness

   C. Alignment

   D. Wiring

   E. All of the above

9. What is the national standard that governs the installation and testing of fire alarm systems?

   A. NEC 72

   B. IEEE 72

   C. NFPA 72

   D. EIA/TIA 72

10. When troubleshooting an RJ-31x connection, which of the following steps should be performed?

    A. Check jack and plug for damage

    B. Check continuity of wiring to security system controller

    C. Check continuity of wiring to telephone system

    D. Cause a security event from the control panel and verify the interior line has been seized by the system

    E. All of the above

    F. None of the above

Answers

1. **B.** False alarms can be embarrassing and costly for a homeowner.

2. **D.** Improper training is likely the underlying reason behind the number of user errors resulting in false alarms.

3. **E.** All of these are possible causes for any security device to generate a false positive.

4. **B.** The opening door blocks the scanning field. Improper placement of a motion sensor can defeat its function.

5. **C.** Before any other action is taken, the system should be retested completely to ensure that the reported problem is not caused by another underlying problem.

6. **B.** Disconnect all but the first contact and add the contacts back to the system one at a time. However, if the devices are wired in parallel, they can be tested individually.

7. **C.** Replace the suspected device with a known-good device and retest. Replacing a suspected device with a known-good device is a quick way of identifying or eliminating a device as a problem.

8. **E.** All of these choices should be included when visually inspecting security devices.

9. **C.** Many communities use this standard as the local standard as well.

10. **E.** All of these steps should be included when troubleshooting an RJ-31x connection.

PART VI

Home Surveillance Systems

Surveillance Camera Basics

In this chapter, you will learn about
- Surveillance camera basics and design considerations
- Surveillance systems video formats and standards

In the past, security surveillance systems were typically added as an extension of a home security alarm system. Now, in most installations, they are the centerpiece of a home security system. A surveillance camera system provides homeowners, or their surveillance monitoring service, the capability to visually monitor their home's exterior and interior spaces. When used in conjunction with a security alarm system, the homeowner is able to visually scan an area where an alarm has sounded to determine if the problem is in fact a threat or if it is a false alarm. Surveillance systems can also be used in less threatening situations, such as seeing who is at the door, how the kids are getting along, or how the baby is doing in the nursery.

In the world of home technology integration, surveillance systems are comprised of cabling, cameras, mounts, monitors, and control systems. In this chapter, we look at each of these devices as well as their standards.

Video Surveillance Devices

The primary components of a video surveillance system are

- Video camera
- Video monitor
- Video switchers
- Cabling and connectors

Video surveillance equipment is a natural extension of home security. However, it isn't necessary to have a home security system to install video surveillance cameras and equipment.

CROSS-REFERENCE This chapter focuses on video cameras. The remaining components of a video surveillance system (monitors, switchers, and cabling) are discussed in Chapter 24.

A video surveillance system uses the same technology used to distribute video images throughout a house, where modulators send video signals from a source such as a VCR or DVD player to any number of televisions. The primary difference between a video surveillance system and a cable or satellite television system is merely the source of the video images. In a security surveillance system, the image source is one or more cameras placed around the interior or exterior of a home.

The general technology that is used in video surveillance systems is referred to as closed-circuit television, or CCTV systems. Because the links in a residential video surveillance system run only between a local camera to a monitor or recording device, the loop is considered a closed loop, or a closed circuit.

Video Cameras

A video surveillance system can include a wide variety of camera types, including cameras that range in style, focal length, interior versus exterior use, and certainly price, which we won't be discussing here.

Camera Styles

The type or style of camera used in a home security system depends on its location and the range of view desired. There are five basic camera styles to choose from:

- **Board camera** Board cameras are designed to be used as hidden cameras and to be placed inside household objects, such as walls, books, or other objects where they can be camouflaged. Board cameras are not typically protected for exterior use. Figure 23-1 shows an example of a board camera, also known as a pinhole camera.

- **Box camera** This camera type gets its name from its shape (see Figure 23-2). The box casing is weatherproof and allows the camera to be mounted on exterior surfaces. Some box models include zoom capabilities.

- **Bullet camera** This type of camera gets it name from its elongated shape. Bullet cameras come in a wide range of sizes and capabilities, ranging from large (see Figure 23-3) indoor-outdoor cameras to ultra-small concealable "spy" cameras. The standard (large) size is commonly used on building exteriors in both home and commercial security systems.

- **Dome camera** Dome cameras are common in stores, casinos, and other commercial installations. Dome cameras are typically capable of pivoting to provide a 360-degree pan view of an area. Dome cameras can be retrofitted into an existing home but are easier to install during new construction. Figure 23-4 shows an example of a dome camera.

Figure 23-1
A board camera is typically is typically hidden away from view.

Photo courtesy of Sony Electronics, Inc.

- **PTZ (pan, tilt, and zoom) camera** Pan means moving side to side, tilt means moving up and down, and zoom means moving the focal point closer to or farther from a point and magnifying the image. PTZ refers more to the ability to control a camera than an actual camera type, because dome, box, and bullet cameras can all have a built-in PTZ control or be mounted to a pan and tilt base (the zoom is a camera function). A PTZ camera, like the one shown in Figure 23-5, can be controlled through a manual control, such as a joystick controller, or automatically through software or IR systems.

Figure 23-2
A box security camera gets its name from its shape.

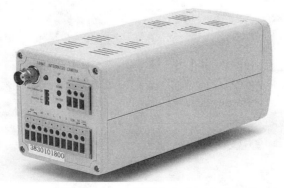

Photo courtesy of JVC Professional Products Company.

Figure 23-3
A bullet security
camera

Photo courtesy of Hwan Ming Enterprise Co., Ltd.

Although they're only an adaptation of board cameras, another category of cameras you commonly see listed is hidden cameras. These devices are built into such objects as smoke alarms, motion detectors, clocks, exit signs, and the like. Some hidden cameras are also referred to as "nanny cams" because of their capability to observe household workers and occupants.

Choosing a Security Camera   Once the types of cameras to be used inside and outside a home are selected, the characteristics of these particular cameras must be considered. The four primary features that should be considered for a home surveillance system include the camera's focal length, light sensitivity rating, lines of resolution, and if it's color or black and white.

Figure 23-4
A dome camera
is able to view
an area with
a 360-degree
sweep.

Photo courtesy of JVC Professional Products Company.

Figure 23-5
An outdoor
scanning camera
on a pan and tilt
mount

Photo courtesy of Pelco.

- **Focal length**   The focal length of a camera is the distance (in millimeters) from the lens to the point where the image is in focus. The most common focal range on security cameras is 3.6 millimeters (mm), which typically provides a full view of a room if the camera is mounted in a corner near the ceiling. A longer focal length, such as 6.0 mm, provides a greater magnification of images, such as faces, hands, and the like, at a distance.

- **Light sensitivity**   The light sensitivity of a camera is measured in lux (lumens). One lux is the equivalent of the amount of light produced by one candle measured at a distance of one meter. The lux rating on a camera indicates the minimum amount of light the camera needs to capture images clearly. Those cameras that have a lux rating of less than 1.0 are capable of capturing images in very dim light. While there are some 0 lux cameras, most security cameras are in the range of 0.1 to 0.8, able to capture photo in low light.

- **Lines of resolution**   This characteristic measures the number of horizontal lines used to represent the images a camera captures. For example, a standard television set typically has 300 lines of resolution, but video monitors often support many more (800 lines is common). Higher resolution on a camera means that images at a distance are more easily recognizable. A camera that produces a higher number of lines of resolution translates to a better image on the monitor (providing the monitor is capable of reproducing the resolution of the camera). The normal range available is between 300 and 600 lines. However, the better the resolution, the more expensive the camera.

- **Color**   Another consideration for choosing a camera is if it's black and white or color. For most installations, black and white is probably adequate, but some homeowners may wish to install (and pay for) color cameras.

How to Calculate Focal Length

If you wish to have more detail through the lens of a security camera and wish to look for something beyond a 3.6 mm focal length, here's how to go about it (remember, you're insisting on this!):

1. Measure the viewing width, the distance between the points you wish to be the left and right extremes of the image viewed. This means measure how wide a field of view you wish to capture. Figure 23-6 illustrates how this is done.

2. From the center of the line between the right and left edges of view, measure the point where the camera lens will be mounted. Figure 23-6 illustrates how the viewing distance is measured.

3. Depending on the camera and its format—it should be 1/3-inch, 1/2-inch, or 2/3-inch (also referred to as 1/3 chip, 1/2 chip, and 2/3 chip)—a factor that corresponds to the format is used to adjust for either the horizontal range or the vertical range of the lens. Table 23-1 lists the various horizontal and vertical factors for the common security camera formats.

4. The formula used for calculating focal length is one of the following, depending on whether you wish to use vertical or horizontal adjustment:

   ```
   Focal length (f) = v * (Viewing distance / Viewing width)
   ```

   or

   ```
   Focal length (f) = h * (Viewing distance / Viewing width)
   ```

   So, assuming you wish to emphasize the horizontal view of a 1/3-inch format camera and your measurements (in millimeters) are a 380 mm viewing width and an 1800 mm viewing distance, the calculation for the focal length is:

   ```
   f = 3.6 * (1800 / 380) = 3.6 * (4.8) = 17.3 mm
   ```

5. The result of 17.3 mm is the focal length desired. Security camera lenses are available with focal lengths that typically range from 1.9 mm to 25 mm. The closest lens size to the desired focal length is a 16 mm (f16) lens, but you can move up to an f25 if you wish to improve the viewing range.

Image Capture Formats

Not all cameras are alike. What separates cameras and their capabilities more than any other characteristic is how they capture an image (or in this case video images). The most common camera types used for surveillance purposes are black and white analog

Factor	1/3-Inch Format	1/2-Inch Format	2/3-Inch Format
Horizontal (h)	3.6	4.8	6.6
Vertical (v)	4.8	6.4	8.8

Table 23-1 Focal Length Calculation—Horizontal and Vertical Multipliers

Figure 23-6
Measuring the
viewing distance
and viewing depth

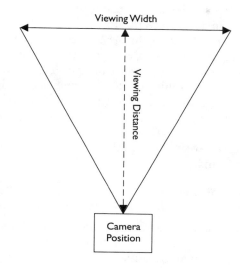

cameras, primarily because of their relatively low cost. However, black and white and even color digital cameras are becoming popular for surveillance use as well.

The most common types of cameras used for security surveillance purposes are

- Analog cameras
- Digital cameras
- Infrared cameras

Analog Cameras Analog cameras use the RS-170 television standard to capture and transmit images as analog signals. In the transmitted video signal each new video line is synchronized by a horizontal synchronization pulse and the intervals between video blocks are indicated by vertical synchronization pulses. The synchronization pulses in the video signal are supplied by the video camera. The transmitted image is created through a sampling process that captures a set number of frames per second (fps), and the position of each feature in a particular frame is determined by the timing between its signal and the synchronizing pulse. A feature called a frame grabber interprets the analog signals and resamples the video images into pixels that are transmitted to the video display device. Analog cameras produce 8-bit resolution, which is able to represent only 256 grayscale shades.

Although commonly referred to as a digital device, another analog image capture device is a CCD (charge coupled device) chip. A CCD chip is light sensitive and captures images in grayscale. Color CCDs uses a RGBG (red, green, blue, and green) mask to provide color images to the display device (the second green is used to create contrast on the image). CCDs are typically connected directly to an analog-to-digital converter (ADC), which provides a digital representation of the captured images.

Digital Cameras A digital camera is really an analog camera that has an ADC built in. Because the analog image is converted to digital pixel coding inside the camera, the quality of the signal is improved, and the image accuracy is better than on an analog camera.

Digital cameras use a progressive-scan mode to capture images that produce larger image sizes, higher frame rates, and better resolution. Digital cameras are able to produce higher than 8-bit resolutions; 10-bit cameras can produce 1024 grayscale shades; and 12-bit cameras can produce 4096 grayscale shades of resolution. Digital color cameras use 24-bit resolution or the combination of 8 bits each for red, green, and blue color channels.

The connection between the digital camera and the display devices is commonly one of the following formats:

- **IEEE 1394** Also known as FireWire and iLINK, this link competes with USB (Universal Serial Bus) for ease of use and data transfer speed.

- **Parallel interface** The most common parallel formats used with digital video cameras are TTL (transistor-to-transistor logic), EIA/TIA (RS) 422, or LVDS (EIA/ TIA [RS] 644) signaling formats.

  - Parallel TTL (through-the-lens) can only be used with very short cable runs (less than 15 feet) and works best with a TTL-capable monitor and requires a TTL-to-TTL cable.

NOTE Don't confuse TTL (through-the-lens) focusing and light metering capabilities on a camera with TTL (transistor-to-transistor logic) signaling.

  - EIA/TIA-422 is a differential serial interface that provides greater distances and faster data speeds than the more common EIA/TIA-232 serial interface.

  - LVDS (low-voltage differential signaling) is a gigabit high-speed low-voltage, low-amplitude signaling format for copper wiring.

  - USB (Universal Serial Bus) A high-speed serial interface.

Table 23-2 lists the specifications for each of these cable standards.

Table 23-2	Interface	Conductors	Cable Requirement
Camera Interface Cabling Standards	IEEE 1394	4, 6, or 9	Double Shielded 20–28 AWG
	Parallel	16 or 18	Shielded 22–30 AWG
	USB	4	Shielded 20–28 AWG

Infrared (IR) Cameras Infrared (IR) cameras use IR light to illuminate the field of view and an analog CCD chip for image capture. In dim or dark lighting conditions, the IR illuminators enhance low-light visibility and allow the CCD to capture images in black and white at low resolution.

Day/Night Cameras A day/night camera is essentially what its name suggests: a camera that is able to "see" in both daylight and the dark of night. Some day/night cameras have built-in IR capability to help them see in the dark and others have only a sensitive imaging chip that allows them to see in low light, such as a street light or bright moonlight. Obviously, day/night cameras are designed for exterior uses primarily, but there are some specifically designed for interior use that include IR illuminators, which allow them to see in the dark.

IP Cameras Although not technically a type of image capture, IP (Internet Protocol) cameras use any image capture technology and have the built-in capability to connect to and communicate over a network running the TCP/IP protocols. Figure 23-7 shows a rear view of an IP-compatible surveillance camera and its RJ-45 connector.

IP cameras have a built-in network adapter, network connectors, and circuitry to support network communications. Connecting an IP camera to a home network allows captured images to be transferred across the data network and be displayed on computer monitors or stored as digital files on networked storage devices.

Wireless Cameras There are several types of wireless cameras that can be connected into a home surveillance system:

- **IP wireless cameras** These types of wireless cameras are designed to connect into wireless Ethernet data networks using the 802.11 wireless networking standards.

- **ISM (industry, science, and medical) wireless cameras** ISM cameras transmit images using the 2.4 GHz radio frequency (RF) band, which is the same band used by many home wireless products, such as cordless telephones.

- **PLC "wireless" cameras** PLC (powerline carrier) cameras are wireless only in the sense that they require no new wiring. They operate over the existing electrical lines.

Figure 23-7
A rear view of an IP camera showing its RJ-45 connection

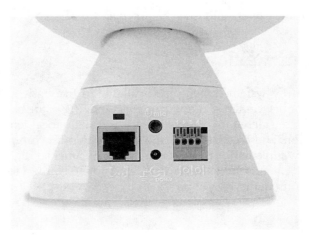

Wireless cameras require a compatible receiver or base unit connected to a computer or a television monitor. In terms of reliability, wired camera systems continue to be more reliable due to potential interference problems with wireless transmitted video signals.

Truly wireless systems either have a wireless transmitter built into the camera itself or connect to a wireless transmission unit or use a wireless balun-style transmitter. A wireless receiver must be connected to a switcher or monitor. The downside of this type of wireless system is that it typically uses the 2.4 GHz RF band, the same band used by many other wireless systems in a home, including cordless telephones, baby monitors, and the like.

Audio-Capable Cameras Several surveillance camera models include built-in microphones to pick up sounds from the immediate surrounding areas. Adding audio to the video images captured by the surveillance camera can provide input on activities that may be out of the camera's range, such as directly beneath the camera. Cameras that include audio capabilities use triple RCA composite audio/video cabling and connectors.

 CROSS-REFERENCE See Chapter 10 for more information about audio cabling and connectors.

Camera Power Sources

Virtually all CCTV video cameras use either 120V AC or 24V AC power sources.

- **120V AC** Common household AC power is a common power source for video cameras. 120V AC cameras typically come with a 6- to 10-foot power cord, so the camera must have an AC power outlet within that distance.

- **24V AC** Most commercial security systems use this voltage, which is usually provided through an external plug-in low-voltage power adapter or power supply that can be some distance from the camera. The power source can be connected to the camera using 18- or 20-gauge speaker wire or using what is called Siamese wire. Siamese wire has a power cable and a coaxial cable inside a single outer jacket. Using a central power source, all wiring can be run up to 350 feet to a central location. However, typically a 24V AC power supply is not provided with the camera and must be purchased separately.

Chapter Review

Home security system cameras are available in five basic styles: board cameras, box cameras, bullet cameras, dome cameras, and PTZ cameras. The characteristics that should be considered for a surveillance camera are focal length, light sensitivity, lines of resolution, and color or black and white. The most common types of cameras used for security surveillance purposes are analog cameras, digital cameras, and infrared cameras. IP cameras have the built-in capability to connect to and communicate over a network running the TCP/IP protocols.

Several types of wireless cameras can be connected into a home surveillance system: IP wireless cameras, ISM wireless cameras, and PLC cameras. Several surveillance camera models include a built-in microphone to pick up sounds from the immediate area around the camera. Virtually all CCTV video cameras use either 120V AC or 24V AC power sources. TV monitors are commonly used with video surveillance systems: security system monitors, video-in TVs, and computer monitors.

Questions

1. What is the general technology used in residential video surveillance systems?

   A. CATV

   B. HDTV

   C. CCTV

   D. FM

2. Which of the following is not a primary component of a video surveillance system?

   A. Cameras

   B. Monitors

   C. Sound systems

   D. Switchers

3. Which of the following surveillance camera types is able to pivot, move up and down, and in and out under remote control?

   A. Board camera

   B. Box camera

   C. Bullet camera

   D. PTZ camera

4. Which of the following is not a primary consideration when choosing a video camera for a surveillance system?

   A. Mounting style

   B. Focal length

   C. Light sensitivity

   D. Lines of resolution

5. Which of the following surveillance camera types is able to provide illumination in darkened areas?

   A. Analog

   B. Digital

    C. IR

    D. RF

6. Analog cameras, such as CCDs, convert analog signals to digital signals using which device?

    A. DAC

    B. DSP

    C. CCD

    D. ADC

7. Which of the following is not a common connection type supported by a digital surveillance camera?

    A. IEEE 1394

    B. EIA/TIA-422

    C. USB

    D. RJ-45

8. What is the voltage requirement of most residential security surveillance systems?

    A. 5V

    B. 12V

    C. 120V

    D. 240V

9. What is the distance from the lens to the point where the image is in focus called?

    A. Focal length

    B. Resolution

    C. Effective range

    D. Sensitivity

10. What is the unit used to measure the light sensitivity of a camera?

    A. Lines

    B. Lux

    C. Feet

    D. Microfarads

Answers

1. **C.** Closed-circuit television (CCTV) is used primarily for security purposes. CATV is cable television; HDTV is high-definition television; and FM modulation is used with some wireless systems, but typically still within the CCTV system.

2. **C.** Not that sound systems couldn't be included in a surveillance system, but our focus here is video surveillance. The other choices are all components of a video surveillance system.

3. **D.** Pan, tilt, and zoom cameras are able to be repositioned under remote control. The other choices are typically stationary cameras, unless they are mounted on a PTZ mounting.

4. **A.** If all other features of a camera are desired, the mounting style can be adapted to. However, if the camera application (dome, PTZ, and so on) is not appropriate for the intended use, the other features hardly matter.

5. **C.** Infrared illumination cameras can use IR light to illuminate an area so that the camera can "see" in the dark.

6. **D.** Analog-to-digital converters do just what their name says they do. The other devices are a digital-to-analog converter (DAC), a digital sound processor (DSP), and a charge-coupled device (CCD), which is an image capture device used in video cameras.

7. **D.** By using a balun, a coaxial BNC adapter can be converted to an RJ-45 to send signals over twisted-pair wiring. The other choices are all fairly common camera connector types.

8. **C.** Residential surveillance systems require common household currents and voltage. Commercial systems typically use 240V.

9. **A.** The point at which a camera lens focuses is its focal length.

10. **B.** Lux or lumens are used to measure the light sensitivity of a camera. Lines of resolution, focal length in feet, and power usage account for the other answers, respectively.

CHAPTER 24

Designing and Installing a Home Surveillance System

In this chapter, you will learn about
- Analog versus digital video systems
- Video surveillance system design and installation considerations

A video surveillance system in a home, especially a home that includes integrated control and access technologies, provides an added measure of security, safety, and peace of mind to the home's environment. However, there's more to installing a video surveillance system than just mounting a camera on a wall, running cable, and watching the captured images on some form of a display.

If the decision has been made to include video surveillance as a part of a home's security system, there are some design considerations you must address. While the basic considerations may seem obvious, where to point the camera and where and how to monitor the captured images, there is a bit more to it. In order for the video surveillance system to provide value, it must be carefully thought out, and its design and installation must directly support the homeowners' reasons for including the surveillance system in the first place. Then on top of that you also need to make the decision between an analog or a digital camera, each of which has its benefits and its issues, which we'll discuss.

Analog versus Digital Video

Perhaps the second most important consideration in the design of a video surveillance system after deciding to have one in the first place, is whether the system is to be based on analog or digital video capture and playback.

Analog Video Considerations

If the homeowner wishes to install an analog video system, the design and installation issues primarily involve cabling, and most of its operational issues involve its use after installation. Analog video systems involve the use of videotape recorders and analog monitors.

While the cameras, recorders, and monitors are very important components of an analog video system, so are videotapes or cassettes and their handing, storage, and reliability. In a situation where the homeowners wish to keep a video record over a period of time, say a week at a time, an analog video system, especially one that is set to run constantly, can fill up a high number of videotapes in a relatively short time. In addition, tapes must be rewound, labeled, and stored. Even if there is no requirement to keep a video image beyond its immediate availability for playback, videotapes on most systems must be manually rewound and the system reset to record. Not to mention that analog systems must be viewed from the beginning as the recorded images are placed serially on the medium.

Analog video systems can be configured to record using a lower frames-per-second rate, which can reduce the usability of the recorded information as a trade-off against the amount of recorded images a videotape can hold. Using slower frames-per-second rates also reduces the playback time required to review the recorded images.

However, the true downside to using analog video surveillance systems is its impending doom. Analog systems are rapidly becoming extinct, which means parts, supplies, and even repair shops may be harder and harder to come by. The upside, at least for the near-term, is that analog video is homeowner-friendly, easy-to-operate, and comparatively less expensive than a digital system (discussed in the next section). In those situations where a homeowner is considering the installation of a video surveillance system, an analog video system can be an effective first step that can be replaced at a later date with a digital system.

Digital Video Considerations

Digital video surveillance systems have largely replaced analog systems in the marketplace. A wide variety of digital video systems are available that provide a range of features, functions, capabilities, and prices.

In addition to the capabilities inherent with digital video system controls typically being on a computer, the primary advantage digital systems have over analog systems is their image quality. Digital video recording captures an image in a higher resolution than an affordable analog camera. To obtain the clarity needed for a particular camera location, an analog camera may lose the effectiveness of some of its focus range should it have to remain zoomed-in to capture a clear image.

Surveillance System Design Considerations

The design of a video surveillance system must specifically address the desires and vision of the homeowners and definitely be able to view, record, and monitor the areas of the home, internally and externally, that the homeowners wish to included.

Table 24-1 shows a sample of a planning worksheet used to organize, designate, and locate the cameras of the video surveillance system. As indicated by the headings in Table 24-1, the design process must address the location, type of mount (often dictated by the location), any special requirements of each device (such as the type of camera or lens to be used), and the wiring that must be pulled to the location, if it hasn't already

Location	Mount	Type	Lens	Wiring
Front Door	Wall	Weatherproof	3.6 mm	Cat 5e
Rear Door	Wall	Weatherproof	3.6 mm	Cat 5e
Entry	Ceiling	Dome	Standard	Cat 5e
Office	None	Modulator—4 channel	N/A	Coaxial
Office	None	Splitter—4 channel	N/A	Composite
Office	None	Monitor—15-inch	N/A	Composite

Table 24-1   A Sample Video Surveillance System Planning Worksheet

been installed. In addition to the cameras, the planning worksheet should also include the monitors and support equipment, such as switchers, multiplexers, and modulators, if applicable.

The planning and design of a home video surveillance system should also address the various types of sensors to be used in the home. Sensors can detect sound, motion, entryway (doors and windows) openings or closings, air movement, temperature to determine if an intruder is present (there are a few other types of sensors as well). Because there are people who live in the home, the design should address the means to train or "aim" the system so that false positives are either eliminated or, in the worse case, highly minimized.

Viewing Zones

Since it is unlikely that the design objectives for a video surveillance system include surveillance of the entire home (all areas—all the time), the home's layout (inside and out) should be divided into viewing zones—also known as security zones, detection zones, and privacy zones.

The viewing zones are the areas to be viewed by the video camera lenses. In essence, each camera and what it views in a stationary position or motion sweep sets up a separate viewing zone (see Figure 24-1). However, you'll need to decide if the cameras are to be stationary or pan-tilt-zoom (PTZ), if any of the viewing zones need to overlap, or if there are locations for a future camera placement to be included in the plan. It's these types of considerations that must be addressed when laying out the surveillance system.

Typically, the viewing zones for a video surveillance system include all of the gates, doors, windows, and entry points into the home. If vandalism is a problem, then those areas of the property that are most accessible to vandals should be included. Another consideration is the direction that people (invited or uninvited) face when entering a certain space.

Interior cameras are typically placed either in a ceiling corner of a room or on the ceiling of a passageway. In any case, be sure to include the main entrances and exits from a room or areas in the camera's view.

Exterior cameras should be weatherproof and, if placed in unlighted areas, also include an IR illumination source.

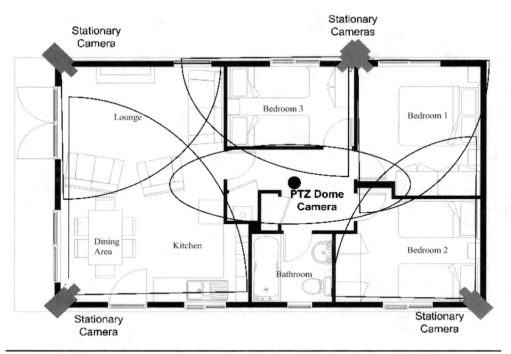

Figure 24-1 An example of a home layout with video surveillance viewing zones overlaid

Camera Locations

Surveillance cameras are available for indoor, outdoor, hazardous, or just about any situation. In a home system, only indoor and outdoor cameras are needed (I hope!). Beyond their image capture characteristics, their location has as much, if not more, to do with their effectiveness than their features or cost.

Essentially, a surveillance camera should be placed in those locations where people frequently, with or without permission, enter a home: the front door, the back door, the driveway, and perhaps the perimeter of the property. Cameras need to be placed where there are no obstructions or blind spots in the viewing plane, especially if PTZ cameras are to be used.

The presence of adequate lighting is another important consideration for the location of a camera. Unless the homeowner wishes to include more expensive security cameras that can operate in relatively low lighting or with infrared lighting, the area to be viewed must be adequately lighted at all times, including the avoidance of shadows during the day.

 NOTE Remember that many municipalities, counties, and states have regulations and laws limiting, prohibiting, or controlling the use of video cameras in a home or business. Common sense should also tell you that there are certain locations in a home where a video camera is not appropriate.

Figure 24-2
Surveillance video monitors are essentially specially designed television sets.

Photo courtesy of Pelco.

Video Monitors

Essentially, standalone video monitors used with video surveillance systems are television sets (see Figure 24-2) that are designed specifically for use as a security system monitor or have a video-in jack to connect directly to a camera or a modulation unit.

- **Security system monitors**   These monitors are sold as a part of a complete security system or as an option or extra to a brand-name line of security products designed to work together. These monitors typically have their controls on a front panel and multiple input and output jacks on the back. They typically range in size from 5.5 inches to 13 inches diagonally measured. Some security system monitors also have the capability to display two to four different camera inputs simultaneously using split-screen technologies.

- **Video-in TVs**   Any television that has a video-in jack compatible with the cabling and connectors of a particular video camera can be used as a video surveillance monitor. In cases where the TV is unable to connect directly to a video camera (because of signaling differences primarily), a video signal modulator can be used to convert the signal to a standard TV format (a TV channel) that can be displayed on the monitor.

- **Computer monitors**   Video camera signals can also be displayed on a computer monitor if the computer is equipped with the proper interface device or expansion card. IP cameras transmit video images in a format that can be immediately displayed on a computer monitor using video display software. Other signal formats, such as CCTV, CATV (community antenna TV), or NTSC (National Television Standards Committee) must be modulated before they can be displayed on a computer monitor using either an external or a video capture card inserted into an available PCI slot on the motherboard.

PART VI

Modulators

Modulators are devices that convert a video signal from one format to another. In the context of a home video surveillance system, a modulator converts the baseband video signal from the camera into one that is compatible with one or more VHF (very high frequency) or UHF (ultra high frequency) television channels and broadcasts the video image on that channel. If the homeowner wishes to display the video from a security camera on a specific channel of a television set, a modulator is needed between the camera and the TV to modulate the signal accordingly.

To display a video image, a display device must receive a video signal formatted for the particular signal configuration it displays. Devices with the capability to display a selection of multiple video signal channels (such as a TV) separate the incoming signals based on their modulation. Transmitted video signals are modulated (converted) for a particular channel. When you change the channel on a TV set, you are telling the receiver to display those signals modulated for the channel you want to see.

In a home system, especially one with multiple video source devices, each device must be modulated to a particular channel so it can be displayed on a TV monitor or a computer monitor. For a home system, a range of different modulators is available:

- **Single channel modulators**   This type of modulator converts the incoming video signal (from one or more selectable sources) to the format of a single TV channel, typically channel 3 or 4. A good example is a VCR or DVD player.

- **Multiple channel modulators**   This type of modulator accepts multiple input sources and modulates each video input to unique selectable output channels. This type of modulator, shown in Figure 24-3, allows you to select which source device is displayed on which TV channel.

- **Micro modulators**   This type of modulator is typically embedded on a digital video capture card to allow incoming analog video signals to be displayed on computer monitors or digital TVs.

Video Switchers and Multiplexers

If a home's video surveillance system requires more than one camera, whether the cameras are interior or exterior, some form of switching is typically required. A video switcher sequences between multiple cameras to permit viewing or recording from the full-screen display from each camera, one at a time.

Figure 24-3
A multiple input video modulator in a distribution center rack mounting

Photo courtesy of Channel Vision Technology.

Switchers

There are several types of switchers to choose from for a surveillance system, depending on the number of cameras and the needs of the homeowner:

- **Alarming switcher**   This type of switcher can be connected to a motion detector or an alarm device. When an alarm signal is detected on that channel, the switcher stops any sequencing and locks onto the camera associated with the alarm. The switcher can also automatically connect the selected camera to a recording device when the alarm signal is detected.

- **Bridging sequential switcher**   This type of switcher supports two outputs, but typically has multiple inputs. A bridging switcher is able to display two cameras on separate monitors, and on some models they can even sequence multiple cameras on either monitor.

- **Homing switcher**   This type of switcher has only one output connection, but can support multiple inputs. This switcher can display or record one camera or multiple cameras in a rotating sequence.

- **Sequential switcher**   This type of switcher automatically switches between multiple cameras or video recorders and has the capability to record a variable amount of delay between the switching from one unit to the next.

Quadrant Switchers

Another type of specialized video switcher is a quadrant switcher (quad switcher) that allows the viewing or recording of up to four cameras on the same screen at one time. If the video signal is recorded, the recorded image is also in quadrant format. Figure 24-4 illustrates the connections made with a quadrant switcher.

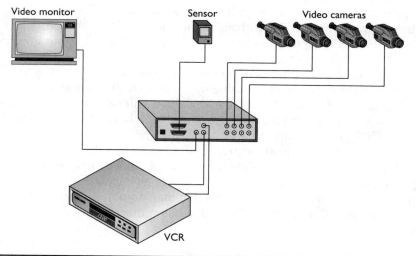

Figure 24-4   The connections used with a quadrant switching system

Multiplexers

There are two types of multiplexers used in video surveillance systems: simplex and duplex. A multiplexer is able to mix and match devices together for display, recording, or playback. It can display one camera on a monitor while another camera is being recorded on a video recorder.

A simplex multiplexer can display one camera while recording all other cameras, and a duplex multiplexer is able to display one or more live cameras while recording all other cameras and even displaying playback from a second video recorder.

Hybrid Surveillance Systems

A hybrid surveillance system is one that is able to receive and record video streams from virtually any type of video camera, including analog, digital, and IP-based cameras (both wired and wireless). Hybrid video systems commonly include a recording capability either through a hybrid capture card or a hybrid digital video recorder (DVR) specifically designed for security systems. The benefit of a hybrid video surveillance system is that most can be accessed remotely through any Internet-capable device, including a computer, a personal digital assistant (PDA), and some cell phone devices, which effectively eliminates the need for video monitors on the system.

Cabling and Connectors

Most surveillance systems available on the market are wired systems that use the same standard cabling used in structured wiring schemes. However, there are wireless systems where the camera sends its video signals to a base station using RF signaling. This base station then displays the image or transmits the video signal over wire to the monitor.

For most of the connections needed in a video surveillance system, such as from a camera to a monitor, RG6 coaxial cable can be used, provided none of the individual cable runs are more than 200 feet. For distances longer than 200 feet, RG59 coaxial cable should be used. Home video systems typically use RG6 cable, but in certain situations RG59 may be a better choice.

Twisted-pair cabling can be used, provided a video balun is used. A video balun must be installed at each end of the cable run to convert the coaxial cable-compatible signal video signal into one compatible with twisted-pair cabling. Figure 24-5 shows a sample of a video balun. Note that one end of the balun has an RJ-45 jack and the other end has a push-on F-type connector.

Most security camera kits come with a length of cable for installation, but in a structured cabling environment the cabling for the surveillance system should be installed during the pre-wire process. If coaxial cable is used, an adapter cable may be required to connect F-type connectors to the camera that may support only an RCA, parallel, or S-video connector. If Cat 5e cabling is used, a balun must be installed at each end of the cable.

Figure 24-5
A video balun
interfaces
coaxial cabling
to twisted-pair
cabling.

Photo courtesy of Almex Ltd.

 NOTE Some video security systems use proprietary or special cabling that provides both video transmission from and electrical power to the camera. On these types of systems, the cabling is connected to a single system distribution box that connects into the house electrical system.

Chapter Review

A video surveillance system uses modulators to transmit and convert video signals from source devices to the system's monitors. The technology used in video surveillance systems is CCTV systems.

The primary components of a video surveillance system are video cameras, video monitors, video modulators and switchers, and cabling and connectors. For most video surveillance connections, RG6 coaxial cable is used, and RG59 can also be used. UTP cabling can be used with a video balun.

The first design consideration of a video surveillance system is the layout of the viewing zones. The next consideration is where to place the cameras. What features of the home or exterior should be watched? Gates, doors, windows, and other entry points into the home are the primary targets. If vandalism is a problem, then those areas of the property that are most accessible to vandals should be included. Another consideration is the direction that people (invited or uninvited) face when entering a certain space.

Interior cameras are typically placed either in a ceiling corner of a room or on the ceiling of a passageway. Exterior cameras should be weatherproof and, if placed in unlighted areas, should also include an IR illumination source.

PART VI

Questions

1. What device is typically required in order to display multiple cameras on a single monitor?

   A. Switcher

   B. Modulator

   C. Multiplexer

   D. Hub

2. What is the cabling type most commonly used with video surveillance systems?

   A. RG6

   B. RG59

   C. UTP

   D. Fiber optic

3. The use of videotapes is an inherent feature of which type of video system?

   A. Transmitted

   B. Digital

   C. Analog

   D. All video systems

4. Which type of video camera typically captures images with a higher resolution?

   A. Analog

   B. Digital

   C. Hybrid analog

   D. CCTV

5. What is the term used to describe an area in or around a home that can be viewed through a video camera's lens?

   A. Focal range

   B. Grid

   C. Viewing zone

   D. Sweep

6. What video system device is used to convert the image signal from one format to another?

   A. Codec

   B. Modulator

    C. Multiplexer

    D. Switcher

7. What type of video switcher automatically switches between multiple cameras or video recorders and has the capability to record a variable amount of delay between the switching from one unit to the next?

    A. Alarming switcher

    B. Homing switcher

    C. Sequential switcher

    D. Modulator

8. Which type of video switcher enables the system to display or record up to four video camera sources at a time?

    A. Alarming switcher

    B. Homing switcher

    C. Sequential switcher

    D. Quad switcher

9. What type of coaxial cabling is recommended for use for cable runs longer than 200 feet?

    A. RG6

    B. RG8

    C. RG58

    D. RG59

10. What device is required to transmit video signals across twisted-pair wiring?

    A. Balun

    B. Modulator

    C. Switcher

    D. Multiplexer

Answers

1. **A.** Switchers, well, switch. They switch between cameras, monitors, and video recorders either manually or automatically.

2. **A.** RG6 coaxial cabling is the same coaxial cable used in structured wiring.

3. **C.** Digital video data can be recorded on a computer hard disk or some form of removable media.

4. **B.** Digital cameras typically have a much higher resolution than an analog camera, except for very high-end analog devices.

5. **C.** Also called the security zone, this is an area that is to be recorded by the video system.

6. **B.** A modulator adjusts the frequency and other characteristics of a transmitted signal to those compatible with a receiver.

7. **C.** Switchers switch between input feeds and, depending on their purpose and functions, allow the system to display or record on different devices.

8. **D.** A quad switcher supports up to four display or recording devices.

9. **D.** RG6 is the common coaxial cabling for home systems, but RG59 is recommended for longer runs.

10. **A.** A video balun is used to adapt video signals on a coaxial cable to those compatible with twisted-pair cabling.

CHAPTER 25

Troubleshooting a Home Surveillance System

In this chapter, you will learn about

- Identifying common video camera problems
- Troubleshooting cabling and termination issues
- Troubleshooting bandwidth issues
- Resolving surveillance system design issues

There are two major problems that can occur with a home video surveillance system: no video at all and bad video reception. The first indicates a possible complete system failure, and the latter indicates possible connection issues. The process to troubleshoot a system failure is obviously more intensive than that used to find a connection problem, which is generally the same process used to track down all network connection problems.

The video security industry sees home video and its related problems as stemming from two primary areas: communications and cabling. Communications refers to the ability of the technical professional to communicate with the end user on the requirements, components, and operation of a video system installed in a home. Cabling is a large problem in IP-based video systems, in that the physical media of a home network must be properly designed and installed to support both data and video—and possibly voice as well.

This chapter lists the most common problems that can occur in a surveillance system and the steps used to identify, isolate, and resolve each problem.

Identifying the Problem

The first step in all problem solving processes is to identify the problem as best you can. If you are coming into a home on a service call, your first (but not necessarily your best) source of information is the homeowner. The explanation and description of the problem as he or she sees it provides insight into the result of the problem.

Rarely will the homeowner be able to provide a detailed analysis of the cause or contributing factors of the problem. So this is where your knowledge of the system, its installation, its maintenance, and, hopefully, its operation provide you the information needed to devise a troubleshooting plan. Where did you get all of this information? From the system maintenance logs that were initiated during installation and meticulously maintained since then, right?

Using your knowledge and the information in the maintenance log, you should be able to answer the following questions:

1. Has the current problem or a related problem been worked on before this?

2. What was the resolution, and is that resolution still pending (waiting on parts, etc.)?

3. What type of cabling is in use?

4. What is the configuration of the video system?

5. Has a change been made to the configuration of the video system or new equipment installed at or before the time the problem started?

6. Has the user been properly trained on the operation of the system?

The information gathered from a review of the maintenance log and listening to the user should provide you with a good place to start to identify the problem.

Solving Common Problems

The most common problems that can occur with a home video surveillance system, other than improper alignment of cameras and perhaps power issues, typically involve either cabling and termination issues or bandwidth issues

Troubleshooting Cabling and Termination Issues

More than half of all video performance problems on an IP network are caused by the cabling and terminations that connect the camera to the network. If a camera is connected to improper cabling or if the cabling installed isn't terminated properly, the result is poor video quality or no video at all.

Cabling Issues

Digital and IP cameras are configured for connection to Cat 5e or better cabling. The same care and installation procedures that ensure network cabling is properly installed must be used with security cameras, just as with any network device. To troubleshoot cabling issue as the suspected cause of a video malfunction, follow the same procedures discussed in Chapter 4 for Cat 5e or better cabling.

Termination Issues

If coaxial cabling is used to connect a video camera to a video integration or encoding device or to the network through a video balun, 75 ohms is the magic number. Video cabling must be configured to 75 ohms of impedance and termination. Impedance and termination are separate characteristics of a cable.

Impedance consists of resistance and reactance on the cable, which should be 75 ohms on coaxial cabling. Termination absorbs the 75-ohm signals at the terminal device to prevent signal overload. Most baseband video systems, such as television, have built-in termination. If two or more terminations are included on a video cabling link, the signal strength is reduced by half for each terminator on the link. For example, if there are two terminations on a link, the signal received at the monitor is reduced to 50 percent. If there are no terminations on the video link, the monitor or recording device is overloaded by the incoming signal.

There are two ways to configure termination on most video devices: setting a manual switch or using an on-screen menu. To set termination on a device manually, most video devices, including monitors, switchers, integrators, encoders, and even some cameras, include a toggle or slide switch that sets the termination for the device. This switch is commonly labeled 75-ohm (on or off) or HiZ, which means high impedance. If the device is the terminal device in a video loop, this switch should be set to on. Otherwise, it is set to off.

Many monitors and other types of display devices include the capability to display a menu through which the device can be configured. Typically, one of the menu choices is termination, which can be set on or off. However, it is also common that when the device is powered off and then on, this setting resets to the faculty default, which is typically to turn on termination.

 TIP Some new video devices include circuits to automatically detect where the device is in a video loop and set the termination accordingly.

Troubleshooting Bandwidth Problems

Adding support for video cameras on an IP network can create operation problems for not only the video portion of the system, but the entire network as well. Bandwidth on an internal network is a function of the cabling and the devices connected to the primary cabling. For example, a video camera that transmits 16-bit color images using a configuration of 8 channels, 15 frames per second (fps), M-JPEG compression, and 16 kilobits (Kb) frame size requires 15 megabits (Mb) of bandwidth, which is 15 percent of a 100 Mbps network's bandwidth just for the video camera.

If a video capture device, such as an IP video camera, is unable to access the amount of bandwidth it needs, the result may be images not acceptable for viewing or recording. If you suspect that a video system problem is related to the bandwidth available on the network, it could be in the configuration of the camera or video server's video bandwidth settings.

The bandwidth usage for a security camera (or any image capture device) is calculated as:

```
Bandwidth Usage = (Scaling * Compression Rate) * Frames Per Second
```

Adjusting any one of these three settings will directly affect the bandwidth usage of a video camera, up or down. To reduce the bandwidth usage of a camera, you must find a balance of these settings.

Compression Technology

Most IP cameras offer only one video compression technology, but some high-end cameras offer a choice of compression techniques. Depending on the type of camera in use, the compression method in use is likely to be MPEG-2, MPEG-4, MJPEG, H.264, or ACC (Active Content Compression). MPEG stands for Moving Pictures Experts Group; MPEG standards are change-only compression techniques. JPEG stands for Joint Photographic Experts Group, and JMPEG compression is a frame-by-frame compression method. Frame-based compression generally requires more bandwidth and storage space than a change-only compression method. However, in order to produce fairly detailed images, a change-only method needs to operate at a higher fps, which essentially negates any bandwidth or storage savings.

Analog cameras use the Common Intermediate Format (CIF) compression technique. CIF devices offer compression rates between Quarter CIF (QCIF), which produces 176 × 144 resolution and 16CIF with resolution of 1408 × 1152. Typically an analog security camera is set to either 4CIF (704 × 576) or 2CIF (704 × 240).

Each compression technology requires a different bit rate, which can be either a constant bit rate (cbr) or a variable bit rate (vbr), and works best with a certain fps. If the camera is configured to produce the highest possible video images, which requires high bit and fps rates, the camera could be flooding the network, resulting in transmission losses.

Another concern with the compression method in use is the amount of disk storage it requires, assuming the homeowner wishes to store, at least for a short time, captured video streams for later review. For example, an 80GB disk drive can hold from 30 minutes to 12 days of video, depending on the compression technique in use.

Regardless of the compression technique in use, most offer the capability to decrease or increase the percentage of compression applied to the images produced. Setting the compression technique to a higher percentage can reduce the amount of bandwidth required.

Frames per Second

Of course everyone wants the highest possible image quality possible, but when a camera that is able to produce a higher fps rate than there is available bandwidth to support is installed on the network, the result is just the opposite. Most IP cameras have fps settings that can be configured to fit the bandwidth available.

The typical security camera produces images at 7.5 fps, but on some models the image rate can range up to 30 fps, which is a television-quality image. A higher fps produces better quality images but also requires higher bandwidth. The simplest way to reduce the bandwidth requirements of a security camera is to reduce its fps setting. However, depending upon the desires of the homeowner, the storage requirements of the image stream, and the devices in use, an fps setting between 7.5 on the low end and 15 fps on the high end should satisfy all of these requirements.

Scaling

Scaling is often referred to as resolution, in that it configures how many lines of pixels are to be compressed and transmitted on the network. The best image quality for digital security cameras is produced at 640 × 480, which means that 480 rows of 640 pixels are included in the image. However, because the bandwidth requirement increases with the number of pixels in the image, lower scaling settings (such as 320 × 240) may be a better fit for the system.

One interesting and somewhat contradictory fact about scaling is that the higher the scaling setting, the lower the impact on the network bandwidth will be, in terms of frames transmitted per second. For example, a scaling of 320 × 240 produces a file size between 65Kb and 100Kb and produces eight to ten frames per second in additional network traffic. In contrast, a scaling of 640 × 480 produces a file size between 320 to 480Kb but produces frames at a much slower pace, resulting in virtually no impact on the network.

System Design Solutions

If bandwidth issues continue to be an issue in a particular installation with two or more security cameras, there are additional design remedies that may help to solve the problem:

- Increase network bandwidth
- Use detected motion recording
- Use edge recording

Increase Network Bandwidth

If the home network was installed on a 10 Mbps system, it may be time to upgrade the network to a 100 Mbps or 1 Gbps (or higher) system. This is an obvious choice that addresses future needs as well as current issues. However, because a home network integrates many of the systems, this change must be carefully analyzed for its impact on the devices (and cabling) installed in the home.

Use Detected Motion Recording

If the security cameras are currently recording 24/7, you may want to add an accessory to each camera that starts video capture and transmission only when a motion detector issues an alarm event (meaning that something in the view of the detector moved). In a worst-case scenario, you may need to replace the existing cameras with models that include motion detection built-in. This reduces the need for constant bandwidth, reduces the amount of storage space to save the captured images, and eliminates possible hours of "nothing happening" on the system.

Use Edge Recording

Some new cameras or video integration devices include USB ports to which an external hard disk drive can be connected. This allows the captured video stream to be stored at the source and downloaded only when it needs to be viewed. Because the video stream is not being transmitted across the network, the bandwidth requirement is greatly reduced.

Chapter Summary

The first step in all problem-solving processes is to identify the problem as best you can. However, rarely will the homeowner be able to provide a detailed analysis of the cause or contributing factors of the problem. Your knowledge of the system and its system maintenance logs provide the information needed to devise a troubleshooting plan.

The most common problems with a home video system involve either cabling and termination issues or bandwidth issues. More than half of all video performance problems on an IP network are caused by the cabling and terminations resulting in poor video quality or no video at all. To troubleshoot a cabling issue as the suspected cause of a video malfunction, follow the same procedures to troubleshoot network cabling connections.

If coaxial cabling is used to connect a video camera to a video integration or encoding device or to the network through a video balun, 75 ohms is the magic number. Video cabling must be configured to 75 ohms of impedance and termination. Impedance and termination are separate characteristics of a cable: impedance consists of resistance and reactance on the cable, which should be 75 ohms on coaxial cabling, and termination absorbs the 75-ohm signals at the terminal device to prevent signal overload. There are two ways to configure termination on most video devices: setting a manual switch or using an on-screen menu.

Bandwidth on an internal network is a function of the cabling and the devices connected to the primary cabling. If a video capture device is unable to access the amount of bandwidth it needs, the result may be images not acceptable for viewing or recording. If you suspect that a video system problem is related to the bandwidth available on the network, it could be in the configuration of the camera or video server's video bandwidth settings.

Depending on the type of camera in use, the compression method in use is likely to be MPEG-2, MPEG-4, MJPEG, H.264, or ACC. Analog cameras use CIF compression technique. Each compression technology requires a different bit rate. A camera configured to produce the highest-quality video images requires high bit and fps rates. Setting the compression technique to a higher percentage can reduce the amount of bandwidth required.

Scaling is often referred to as resolution, in that it configures how many lines of pixels are to be compressed and transmitted on the network. The best image quality for digital security cameras is produced at 640×480; however, because the bandwidth requirement increases with the number of pixels in the image, lower scaling settings may be a better fit for the system.

Questions

1. What is the first step that should be performed in the troubleshooting process?
   A. Recreate the problem
   B. Test the system termination points
   C. Identify the problem
   D. Replace the suspected device

2. Which of the following is not a common cause of video system problems?
   A. Cabling
   B. Termination
   C. Bandwidth
   D. Faulty camera

3. When troubleshooting video issues on a Cat 5e network, the procedure is unique and much different from that used to troubleshoot data network cabling issues.
   A. True
   B. False

4. What is the ohms level required on a video system for impedance and termination?
   A. 110 ohms
   B. 75 amps
   C. 110 volts
   D. 75 ohms

5. What characteristic of a video cabling loop absorbs the signal?
   A. Resistance
   B. Impedance
   C. Termination
   D. Reactance

6. If two terminations are present on a video loop, what percentage of the signal will arrive at a display device?
   A. 100 percent
   B. 75 percent
   C. 50 percent
   D. 0 percent

PART VI

7. Which of the following is not included in the bandwidth usage calculation for a video system?

A. Compression rate

B. Frames per second

C. Color level

D. Scaling

8. Which of the following is not a commonly used compression method used for video images?

A. ACC

B. MJPEG

C. VGA

D. MPEG-2

9. Scaling sets what characteristic of a video image?

A. Bandwidth

B. Color

C. Resolution

D. Speed

10. Analog cameras commonly use what compression technique?

A. MPEG

B. CIF

C. ACC

D. JPEG

Answers

1. **C.** Before you do anything else, identify and isolate the problem.

2. **D.** Cameras and other video equipment don't "go bad," typically, so the problem is most common in its connections and configuration.

3. **B.** The process used for troubleshooting any particular type of cable is the same regardless of application.

4. **D.** Both impedance and termination should be 75 ohms.

5. **C.** Termination absorbs the signal on the media.

6. **C.** The signal is reduced by half for each termination on the loop.

7. **C.** The bandwidth usage of a video device is a function of its compression rate, frames per second, and scaling.

8. **C.** VGA is a signaling format and not a compression scheme.

9. **C.** Scaling adjusts the number of pixels horizontally and vertically in the image.

10. **B.** CIF is a commonly used analog compression technique.

PART VII

Home Lighting Systems

CHAPTER 26

Home Lighting Basics

In this chapter, you will learn about
- Light and lighting terminology
- Lighting loads and types
- Lighting fixtures

In a typical home, to turn a light fixture either on or off, you must be in the same room and access either a wall or lamp switch. However, through a home lighting control system, it's possible to turn lights on or off from another room, or perhaps even another town.

When designing a lighting system for a home, you have more to deal with than just how to turn light fixtures on or off. To properly design a lighting system, you must consider a number of issues, including the following:

- Where to place the lights
- What kind of lights should be used and how many
- Where to put the switches, what type of switches should be used, and what lights are controlled by what switches
- What lights are to be controlled remotely

Lighting systems have some very basic operational components: light, light sources, light fixtures, and lighting controls. These basic components, when used in the right combinations and programmed well, can provide a system of lighting that serves the needs of a home's occupants.

This chapter covers lighting basics and fixture types. Although I mention a few of the devices typically included in a lighting system, Chapter 27 covers that area in more detail.

Light

Perhaps the first topic we should discuss is *light*, which is obviously a central part of a lighting system. The word *light* has over 30 different meanings in an English dictionary, but in the context of a home's lighting system, *light* takes on only a few meanings:

- The illumination that enables us to see
- A device that produces illumination
- The illumination from the sun

In the daylight hours, we depend on the sun and its light rays to provide illumination. However, after sundown, artificial light sources must be used. In designing a home's lighting system, the trick is to place the light sources and the correct level of illumination in the right places.

What Is Light?

Visible light, which means the light that you can see, is only one band in the electromagnetic spectrum that has radio waves at one extreme and gamma rays at the other extreme. Visible light is about in the middle of the electromagnetic spectrum—right between infrared (IR) waves and ultraviolet (UV) waves.

Although it may sound like a contradiction, we can't actually *see* visible light; we can see only reflections of light waves from objects, not the actual light source. What this means is that you can't see light before it hits an object and is reflected back into your eye. Without going into the astrophysics of lighting and luminescence and the history and evolution of modern lighting devices, let's just agree that the design of a lighting system must take into consideration how light is reflected to achieve desired results.

Light Waves

Light reflects from objects in waves of energy that can travel through virtually any space, including a vacuum. A light wave has the same properties of any electromagnetic wave, including wavelength and frequency. Visible light has a wavelength between 400 nanometers (nano means one-billionth) and 700 nanometers (nm). The full spectrum of electromagnetic light (see Figure 26-1) ranges from gamma rays (at 1 nm) to radio

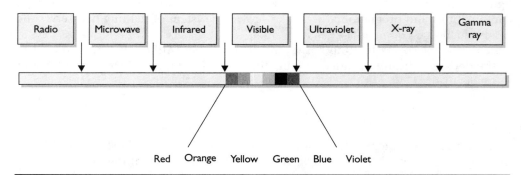

Figure 26-1 The electromagnetic spectrum showing the colors (frequencies) of visible light

waves (in meters and centimeters). The frequency, or the number of waves per second, is measured as hertz (Hz). It is the frequency of visible light that we see as color. For example, the light we see as red has a frequency of 430 trillion hertz (teraHz), and the light we see as violet has a frequency of 750 teraHz. Between these two frequencies exists the other primary colors (orange, yellow, green, and blue), each at a different frequency.

Generating Light

Producing light involves applying a charge to the atoms of a material to energize their electrons. The energized electronics emit photons, which are the particles that produce the light we see. The photons produced from different materials, which means different types of atoms, have a particular frequency. The frequency of the photon determines the color of its light. For example, the sodium atoms in a sodium vapor light produce photons of a frequency that falls in the yellow light spectrum.

The most common way to energize atoms to produce light is with heat, which is the action behind incandescence, as in an incandescent lamp. Applying enough heat to a material creates photons in every color spectrum that merge together to create what is called white light, or colorless light. For example, in an ordinary 100-watt lamp, an inner metallic strip is heated using electricity to generate light.

 NOTE White light, or colorless light, is the light produced by the sun. With just our naked eye, we can't see the colors that combine to create its colorlessness, but if the light shines through a glass of water or a prism, we can see its various color frequencies.

Light and Color

To create colored light, you have two choices: color by addition and color by subtraction. Here's how they work:

- **Color by addition**   If you pass white light through a colored filter, such as a colored glass or piece of cellophane, the resulting light becomes the color of the filter. This works on the same principles we learned in grade school about mixing different paint or crayon colors together—red and blue make violet, blue and green make cyan, and green and red make yellow (see Figure 26-2). This is the same principle used by computer monitors to create colors on their screens.

- **Color by subtraction**   Absorbing certain frequencies of a light beam—in other words, removing one or more colors—is another way to create light of a particular color. The resulting light will have only the frequencies of the light that weren't removed. Again, without getting too scientific here, this is how paint and ink work. Paint and ink are engineered to absorb all or part of some light frequencies and reflect back only the remaining light, which results in the colors we see. When you look at a wall and see green, the paint on the wall has absorbed the red and blue frequencies, so all you see is green. Figure 26-3 illustrates that when color is removed from a visible color, another color is produced, including black (the effect of removing all color frequencies).

Figure 26-2
Red, green, and blue colors can be combined to create other colors, including white.

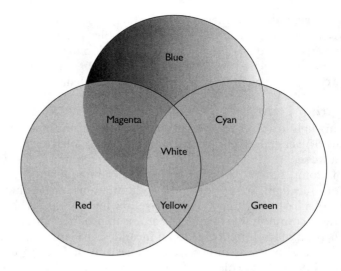

Figure 26-3
Colors change when paint or other colors are designed to absorb one or more colors.

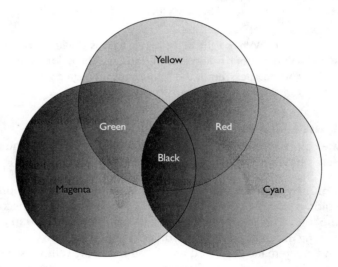

The bottom line on light and color is that an object can create light by emitting the frequency of a certain color or it can absorb light frequencies to reflect a certain color.

Light and Objects

When light shines on any object, the light interacting with the object's surface will do one of four things:

- **Absorption** The object absorbs the light or certain frequencies of the light, such as from a painted wall or a color photograph.

- **Transparency** The light passes through the object without changing, such as light through a windowpane.

- **Refraction** The light passes through the object, but is divided into its separate frequencies.

- **Reflection** The light bounces back or is scattered by the object.

More than one of these actions can occur when light strikes an object.

Lighting Characteristics

Light is measured in a variety of standard measurements. The light produced by lighting fixtures is measured using the following:

- **Foot-candles** This is the measurement of the amount of light that reaches a particular object. Foot-candles are commonly used to measure the amount of light hitting a video screen. A foot-candle is the equivalent of one lumen per square foot. For example, most rooms and areas of a home, such as the bathrooms, kitchen, hall, and living spaces, should have 35 foot-candles of light for general lighting. In areas where task lighting is needed, 70 foot-candles of lighting should be available.

- **Lumens** The amount of visible light produced by a light source. The exact definition of a lumen is very technical but, in general, the more lumens a light source produces, the better.

- **Wattage** In the context of lighting, wattage (or watts) measures the amount of electricity a lighting source uses and not the amount of light it produces. In most cases, a higher wattage lamp produces more light because it uses more power to produce light, but not always.

Light Sources

The primary light sources in home lighting, besides the sun, are incandescent lamps, fluorescent tubes and lamps, and halogen and Xenon lamps. The type of lighting source (lamp or tube) used in a lighting fixture can make a huge difference in the lighting level and color in a room or zone.

For example, in a screw base lighting fixture, such as a table or floor lamp, the light produced by a 100-watt incandescent lamp is much different than the light produced by a 75-watt compact fluorescent lamp, besides the obvious difference in wattage.

Incandescent Lamps

Incandescent lamps, or what are commonly called light bulbs, are not complex devices. The primary components of a lamp are its two metal contacts, which are attached to two wires and a thin metal (commonly tungsten) filament. The whole assembly is enclosed inside a glass bulb that is filled with an inert gas, such as argon. When the bulb is screwed into a socket and the power is switched on, electrical current flows through the wires and the filament, which heats up to about 4,000 degrees Fahrenheit (or about 2,200 degrees Centigrade) and emits light. Incandescent lamps emit what is called *warm light*.

Lamps are rated by the amount of light (measured in watts) they produce in a certain period of time. Lamps with more power have larger filaments and, in turn, a higher watt rating. A three-way bulb actually has two different filaments on two separate circuits, each producing a different wattage. The socket for a three-way lamp has three positions to select each of the two circuits, or both at the same time.

Fluorescent Lights

A fluorescent light has a low-pressure mercury vapor inside, and when ionized, emits ultraviolet (UV) light. UV light can be harmful to humans, so the inside of the light's glass tube is coated with phosphor, which converts the UV light into visible light. Inside the fluorescent tube are electrodes at each end that excite the mercury in the tube into a vapor that emits UV light. The legacy fluorescent tube emits what is called *cold light.*

Fluorescent Tube Markings

If fluorescent lighting is included in a lighting design, it's important to use the right fluorescent tubes or bulbs for the job. To know you have the correct lights, you should be able to decode the markings on the tube (see Figure 26-4).

If you find a fluorescent tube marked with something like F40T12CW/IS or F30T8 RS, here's how to decode it:

- The "F" indicates a fluorescent lamp, which you probably already knew.
- The next two digits (40 or 30 in this case) indicate the wattage.
- The "T" indicates a tube type lamp.
- The next number represents the tube's diameter in eighths of an inch. For example, 12 means 12/8 (twelve-eighths) or 1.5 inches, and 8 means 8/8 (eight-eighths) or 1 inch in diameter.
- The remaining letters represent the characteristics of the lamp. Some of the more common markings are
  - **CW** Cool-White, the type of light emitted by the lamp

Figure 26-4
Standard
fluorescent
light tubes

Photo courtesy of General Electric Lighting.

- **IS** Instant Start, the type of fixture ballast for which the lamp is designed

- **RS** Rapid Start, another type of ballast

- A fluorescent lamp may also have HO (High Output) or VHO (Very High Output) either before or after its coding to indicate its ballast type. A VHO lamp requires a special fixture with a specific connector set.

Compact Fluorescent Bulbs

The latest development in fluorescent bulbs is the compact fluorescent (CF) bulb (see Figure 26-5) that is a screw-in replacement for an incandescent bulb and fits in most standard light fixtures. In comparison to an ordinary lamp, the compact fluorescent bulb has a longer life (as many as 10,000 hours), uses less energy, produces less heat, and emits a warmer light. As you have undoubtedly heard or seen, CF bulbs are one of the latest "hot" products in energy-saving devices.

For all of their energy-saving abilities, fluorescent or CF lights may not be the best lighting choice in every situation. Table 26-1 compares the characteristics of incandescent and fluorescent lights. However, in terms of pure efficiency, meaning the number of lumens produced per watt required (see Table 26-2), fluorescent lighting is far superior.

Halogen Lamps

Incandescent lamps aren't very efficient, and they only last up to about 1,000 hours of normal use. On top of that, most of the energy produced by an ordinary lamp is heat. The tungsten filament of a halogen lamp is encased inside a quartz enclosure filled with halogen gas, which enables it to produce a brighter light. However, like the incandescent bulb, the halogen lamp also produces a lot of heat. Because of its design and elements, a halogen lamp (see Figure 26-6) can outlast a regular lamp. Some halogen-type lamps are filled with Xenon gas, which produces a brighter and whiter light.

Figure 26-5
A compact fluorescent bulb

Photo courtesy of General Electric Lighting.

PART VII

Table 26-1

Comparison of Incandescent and Fluorescent Lighting

Lighting Characteristic	Incandescent Light	Fluorescent Light
Lumens per watt	10–30	20–100
Lamp life (in hours)	750–4,000	7,500–20,000
Color rendition	Good to excellent	Fair to excellent
Optical control	Good to excellent	Fair
Dimming	Excellent	Fair to excellent
Cost of lamp	Low to moderate	Moderate
Cost of operation	High	Low to moderate

Minimum Lumens Produced	Incandescent Bulb (Watts)	Efficiency (Lumens per Watt)	Compact Fluorescent Bulb (Watts)	Efficiency (Lumens per Watt)
450	40	1.3	15	3.0
800	60	13.3	20	40.0
1,100	75	14.7	25	44.0
1,600	100	16.0	30	53.3
2,600	150	17.3	50	52.0

Table 26-2 Efficiency of Incandescent and Fluorescent Bulbs

Figure 26-6
A halogen lamp can be a good choice for task or showcase lighting.

Lighting Load

There are actually two types of lighting load that can be calculated: circuit lighting load and lighting load. A circuit lighting load is the total electrical draw placed on an electrical circuit breaker in the central electrical panel. A circuit lighting load typically includes the multiple lighting loads in one or more rooms. For example, in the electrical panel, circuit breaker #4 could be connected to the kitchen ceiling, kitchen sink area, and the kitchen island area lighting loads.

A lighting load, as opposed to a circuit lighting load, is the total electrical draw from all of the fixtures controlled by a single lighting switch or control. For example, a kitchen wall switch may control the six ceiling fixtures in the kitchen. One of the more important outcomes of a lighting design is the determination of the lighting loads. The lighting load of a room or zone is the total wattage requirement (energy consumption) of all of the fixtures in that area. For example, if a kitchen has four ceiling-mounted recessed light fixtures, each with a 100-watt lamp, the total potential lighting load for that room is 400 watts. If a dimmer control (see Chapter 27) is installed, when the dimmer is set to 50 percent (one-half brightness), the lighting load for the room is reduced to 200 watts. The total or maximum lighting load of a room is a key consideration when deciding on the best lighting control to use.

NOTE   A standard rule of thumb to follow to estimate the lighting load of any space is to multiply the square footage by three watts.

CROSS-REFERENCE   Chapter 28 covers the importance of lighting load on the lighting control in detail.

An important part of designing a home lighting system is to reduce or minimize the amount of energy and the peak energy consumption, in the form of electricity, of the lighting fixtures and their lamps and bulbs.

Lighting Types

There are essentially three types of lighting used in most homes:

- General or ambient lighting
- Task lighting
- Accent lighting

General and Ambient Lighting

General lighting is used to replace sunlight in open living areas. It is the lighting type that provides illumination to enable occupants of a room or space to see the objects in

Estimating Lighting Loads

To estimate the energy consumption or wattage requirements for a room, use these two guidelines:

- For general lighting requirements, multiply the total square footage of the space by 3 watts of lighting load per square foot. For example, in a room with 120 square feet of space, the general lighting load is estimated at 360 watts of light.

- If fluorescent lighting is being considered, the lighting load estimation factor is reduced to 2.5 watts per square foot for general lighting and 1.5 watts per square foot for ambient lighting. For task lighting, the estimation factor should be 4 watts per square foot.

a room and walk about safely. General lighting, which is also called ambient or mood lighting (see Figure 26-7), can also be used to show a room and its contents in their "best light."

The types of lamps or light fixtures typically used to provide general lighting are chandeliers, wall and ceiling-mounted fixtures, recessed or track lighting for indoor spaces, and exterior lamps and other light fixtures for outside walkways and patios.

Task Lighting

Task lighting is what it sounds like—lighting specifically designed for close work, such as reading, cooking, hobbies, games, sewing, and the like (see Figure 26-8). The objective for task lighting is to provide the proper amount of light to illuminate the task area, reduce glare and shadow, and relieve eyestrain.

Figure 26-7
An example of general or ambient lighting in a room

Photo courtesy of LiteTouch, Inc.

Figure 26-8
Task lighting is used to reduce glare and shadows in a specific workspace.

Photo courtesy of LiteTouch, Inc.

Task lighting is typically provided using recessed or track lighting, pendant lamps, or portable (table or adjustable arm) lamps.

Accent Lighting

In most instances, accent lighting is used as a part of a room's overall décor to spotlight interior artwork, plants, draperies, or other room features (see Figure 26-9). Accent lighting can also be used outdoors to highlight exterior landscaping features. To provide the proper level of light and to draw interest to the lighted feature, the lighting level should be at least three times higher than any of the general lighting in that area.

Typically, recessed, track, floor, ground, or wall-mounted fixtures are used as accent lighting.

Figure 26-9
Accent lighting can be used to spotlight specific room or landscaping features.

Photo courtesy of American Fluorescent.

PART VII

Lighting Fixtures

A wide variety of lighting fixture types can be used to provide the type of lighting desired: ceiling-mounted, wall-mounted, chandelier, pendant, portable, recessed, track, and under-counter. Here's a description of each of these fixtures types:

- **Ceiling-mounted fixtures**   Ceiling fixtures, like those in Figure 26-10, provide general or ambient lighting in spaces such as hallways, bedrooms, kitchens, bathrooms, laundry rooms, and the like.

- **Wall-mounted fixtures**   These fixtures are mounted to walls and include light-bars and sconces (shown in Figure 26-11). Wall-mounted fixtures are used to provide general lighting, but can also be used to provide task lighting in some areas, such as above a bathroom mirror.

- **Chandeliers**   Although a chandelier is actually a ceiling-mounted fixture, I list it separately because, in most cases, it is much more expensive than other lighting fixtures in a house and is chosen as much for its appearance as its ability to provide general or task lighting. Chandeliers, like the one shown in Figure 26-12, come in a wide variety of sizes, shapes, and designs and are commonly used in foyers, living rooms, and dining rooms with higher ceilings. Chandeliers can provide ambient lighting or, through pendant-style elements, task lighting over tables, pianos, and the like. If a chandelier is to be a part of the lighting control system, its typically high wattage should be taken into account.

Figure 26-10
Ceiling-mounted lighting fixtures provide ambient lighting.

Photo courtesy of LiteTouch, Inc.

Figure 26-11
Wall-mounted fixtures provide general or ambient lighting.

Photo courtesy of LiteTouch, Inc.

Figure 26-12
A chandelier
light fixture

Photo courtesy of LiteTouch, Inc.

- **Pendant fixtures** This is another ceiling-mounted fixture that can be used for either task or general lighting or both. Pendant fixtures, like the one shown in Figure 26-13, can be used over cooking areas, tables, and work areas or, if fitted with a globe or shade, as a part of a room's general lighting.

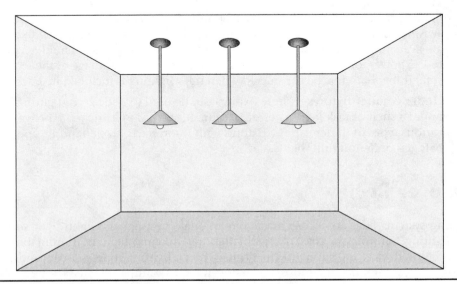

Figure 26-13 Pendant fixtures are used to provide task lighting.

PART VII

Figure 26-14
Track lighting
fixture

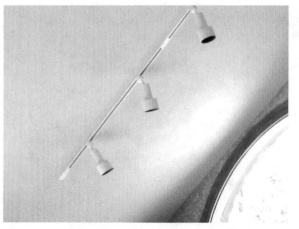

Photo courtesy of Connie J. Price.

- **Portable fixtures**   Table lamps, floor lamps, torchieres (a type of floor lamp that directs its light upward from an inverted cone shade or reflective bowl), adjustable task lighting, and special-purpose lamps, such as art or piano lamps, are all considered to be portable lighting fixtures. Portable fixtures are used to provide general, task, and accent lighting.

- **Recessed lighting**   Recessed lighting utilizes ceiling-mounted fixtures to provide general, accent, and task lighting inconspicuously. Recessed lighting can be used virtually anywhere inside a home, but it is common in areas with low ceilings.

- **Track lighting**   This fixture type allows flexibility by providing adjustable lighting scenes in a room. Most track lighting fixtures (see Figure 26-14) can be swiveled or rotated to adjust the areas being illuminated. Track lighting fixtures are available with built-in or external converters (to convert household AC power to DC power for the lamp), which impacts the shape and wattage of the fixture, something that must be considered when track lighting is included in a design.

- **Under-counter fixtures**   These fixtures can be used to add accent lighting under a shelf or task lighting under a cabinet, such as in a kitchen. There are various types of under-cabinet fixtures with fluorescent, track lighting, and halogen or Xenon mini-lights.

Chapter Review

Lighting systems have some very basic operational components: light, light sources, and lighting controls. In the context of lighting systems, light is illumination, an illumination device, and sunlight. The primary home lighting sources are incandescent lamps, fluorescent tubes and bulbs, and halogen lamps. Lamps are rated by the amount of watts they produce in a certain period of time. A fluorescent light has a low-pressure mercury vapor inside and when ionized, emits ultraviolet (UV) light that is filtered through phosphor. The fluorescent tube emits cold light. The tungsten filament of a halogen lamp is encased inside a quartz enclosure filled with halogen gas. This enables it to produce a brighter light.

Light is measured in a variety of standard measurements, including foot-candles, lumens, and wattage. The lighting system must be designed to provide the minimum light needed.

The lighting load for each room or zone must be determined before selecting the lighting controls. To estimate the energy consumption (lighting load) of a room or zone, multiply the total square footage by three watts to yield the lighting load per square foot for the space. There are essentially three types of lighting used in most homes: general or ambient lighting, task lighting, and accent lighting. General lighting replaces sunlight in open living areas. Task lighting provides the proper amount of light to illuminate the task area, reduce glare and shadow, and relieve eyestrain. Accent lighting is used as a part of a room's overall décor to spotlight interior artwork, plants, draperies, or other room features.

A wide variety of lighting fixtures can be used to provide the type of lighting desired: ceiling-mounted, wall-mounted, chandelier, pendant, portable, recessed, track, and under-counter.

Questions

1. Which of the following is not a commonly used lighting source for home lighting systems?

   A. Incandescent bulbs

   B. Fluorescent tubes

   C. Mercury vapor lamps

   D. Halogen lamps

2. What is the meaning of the "T12" in the fluorescent tube marking of F40T12CW?

   A. A tube 12 inches long

   B. A tube 1.5 inches in diameter

   C. The tube requires a terminated ballast of 12V AC

   D. It is a manufacturer's identity code

3. What is the life expectancy for a compact fluorescent lamp?

   A. 200 hours

   B. 2,500 hours

   C. 1,000 hours

   D. Unlimited

PART VII

4. What is the measurement used to measure the amount of light that reaches an illuminated object?

   A. Foot-candle

   B. Lumen

   C. Watt

   D. Voltage

5. What is the measurement used to measure the amount of electricity used by a lighting source?

   A. Foot-candle

   B. Lumen

   C. Watt

   D. Voltage

6. What is the factor used to estimate general lighting loads?

   A. 1.5 watts per square foot

   B. 2 watts per square foot

   C. 3 watts per square foot

   D. 4 watts per square foot

7. Which of the following is not a type of residential lighting?

   A. Spotlight

   B. Ambient

   C. Task

   D. Accent

8. What ceiling or wall-mounted lighting fixture type is used to provide adjustable lighting scenes in a room?

   A. Track

   B. Pendant

   C. Vanity

   D. Chandelier

9. Calculating the lighting load for a particular space is important for choosing which of the following?

   A. Lighting fixtures

   B. Lighting sources

   C. Lighting controls

   D. Sky lights

10. What material is used to filter UV light to create visible light on a fluorescent lamp?

   A. Halogen

   B. Mercury

   C. Phosphor

   D. Tungsten

Answers

   1. **C.** Mercury vapor lamps are commonly used for exterior lighting, but virtually never as an interior lamp as the other choices are.

   2. **B.** The number, which is typically either 8 or 12, represents the number of eighths of an inch in the tube's diameter. The "T" indicates tubes.

   3. **C.** The standard incandescent bulb has a life as long as 1,000 hours.

   4. **A.** Lumens measure the amount of visible light produced by a lighting source. Watts measure the amount of power used by a lighting source. Voltage is not a lighting measurement.

   5. **C.** Foot-candle refers to the luminance on a one-square foot surface from a one lumen source. Lumens measure the amount of visible light produced by a lighting source. Voltage is not a lighting measurement.

   6. **C.** The other factors are used for fluorescent as well as task and accent lighting.

   7. **A.** A spotlight is a type of accent lighting; ambient lighting is the general lighting in a room; and task lighting is used in work areas.

   8. **A.** Track lighting can be repositioned, rotated, or swiveled to create a new lighting scene when desired.

   9. **C.** Lighting fixtures and lighting sources contribute to the lighting load and determine the energy consumption specified by the lighting load. A skylight should be considered when determining the lighting level in a space, but isn't a part of the lighting load calculation. Lighting loads are very important to the selection of the appropriate lighting controls.

   10. **C.** The color of the phosphor provides the color of the light produced by the lamp.

Home Lighting Devices

In this chapter, you will learn about
- Lighting fixtures and devices
- Lighting controls
- Wire run and wireless lighting control
- Powerline controls

A lighting system in a home is created from the combination of lighting fixtures chosen to provide the desired amounts of light in each room or area of the home. The previous chapter provided an overview of the basics of lighting and lighting system elements. This chapter takes the next step and details the fixtures and luminaries that can be incorporated into a residential lighting system.

Lighting Fixtures

Lighting fixtures are known by a variety of names, including lamps, chandeliers, pendants, tracks, luminaires, and others. Each of these fixtures is designed to produce visible light, each with its own specific use and purpose. A light fixture, such as a lamp, is first and foremost an electrical device that produces visible light. Secondarily, a light fixture can also be considered a piece of furniture or part of a room's décor that holds light bulbs or other light source devices.

You will often see some light fixtures referred to as a luminaire. The term luminaire refers to all of the components of a light fixture, including its light source and the features used to distribute or diffuse the light, mount the light fixture to a surface, and protect the light source.

In Chapter 26, I listed the most common of the lighting fixture types, and now we'll discuss the components that make up each type of fixture and where and how each is best applied.

Architectural Luminaires

Built-in lighting systems are referred to as architectural luminaires. In most cases, a luminaire is a constructed feature that encloses a fluorescent fixture with one or more linear (meaning tube type) lamps. Architectural luminaires are most commonly attached to a wall or ceiling with a shielding board or structural feature used to hide the fixture.

Architecture Luminaire Types

Architectural luminaires are used to add ambient lighting accents to rooms with light-colored walls and ceilings and to provide task lighting in kitchens and baths. Here are some common examples of architectural luminaires:

- **Coves** The light from a cove luminaire is directed up. Cove luminaires, as shown in Figure 27-1, are commonly used in rooms with high ceilings or above the cabinets in a kitchen.

- **Soffits** A soffit luminaire directs its light down. Soffits are commonly used to provide ambient lighting in rooms with low ceilings or to provide task lighting for a counter or work area table.

- **Valances** A valance luminaire directs its light both up and down. Valances are used to provide ambient lighting, but can also be used for washing a wall with light. Typically, valance lighting is used above windows and doors.

Luminaire Lighting

The lighting effect and the direction of the light produced by a luminaire can be controlled through the use of baffles, louvers, and diffusers.

- **Baffles** Baffles are either parallel slats or a crosshatched grid placed over the light source to block direct views of the lighting source. Figure 27-2 shows a fluorescent fixture with baffles installed. Baffles are available in a variety of sizes and spacing.

- **Diffusers** A diffuser serves two purposes: to completely block views of the light source and to spread or scatter the light in an even pattern in all directions. Figure 27-3 shows a compact fluorescent light fixture covered with a plastic diffuser.

- **Louvers** Louvers, also called egg crates, are a cross-hatched grid work of cells (see Figure 27-4) that block direct views of the lighting source and concentrate the light into a narrower pattern in the direction the fixture is pointed.

Figure 27-1
Cove lighting creates lighting effects and provides ambient lighting.

Photo courtesy of Connie J. Price.

Figure 27-2
A fluorescent fixture with a grid of baffles installed

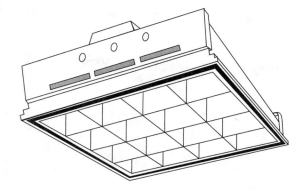

Figure 27-3
A compact fluorescent fixture with diffuser

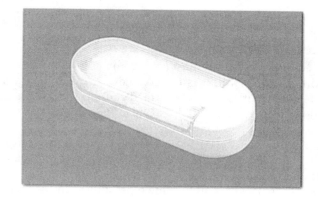

Figure 27-4
A louvered cover on a fluorescent light fixture

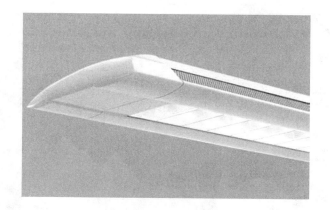

Figure 27-5
An adjustable round recessed downlight

Photo courtesy of Electric Lighting, Inc.

Recessed Downlight Fixtures

The recessed lighting fixtures most commonly used in homes are primarily downlights installed in ceilings. Two types of recessed downlights are available: round recessed downlights (see Figure 27-5), also called *cans* and *high-hats*, and square or rectangle recessed downlights (see Figure 27-6), also known as *troffers*. However, there are also troffer styles that can be surface-mounted.

Round downlights can be incandescent, halogen, or compact fluorescent. Square downlights, typically larger than round downlights, are usually linear (tube) fluorescent or halogen lamps.

Downlights are used for all lighting types, but are most typically used for wall-wash and ambient lighting applications. If positioned properly, a downlight or group of downlights can also create task lighting.

 NOTE When installing a recessed downlight in an insulated ceiling, the lighting fixture must be approved for this type of installation. The IC (insulated ceiling) marking should be on the lighting fixture in plain sight.

Figure 27-6
A recessed troffer style downlight

Photo courtesy of Amerillum Corporation.

Ceiling and Wall-Mounted Fixtures

Many of the same fixtures that can be used in architectural or recessed installations will also work for surface mounting on a ceiling or wall. Ceiling-mounted lighting fixtures, like the one shown in Figure 27-7, are available in a wide variety of shapes and sizes to fulfill not only the lighting requirements of a space, but also to add to the room's décor.

Ceiling fixtures can be classified as chandelier, flush-mounted, close to ceiling, pendant, and spotlight, each with its own purpose and best use. Linear or circline fluorescent fixtures, incandescent fixtures (even with compact fluorescent lamps), pendant fixtures, and track lighting provide for ambient lighting, and in some instances, task lighting in a room. Linear fluorescent fixtures can provide good light levels for laundry rooms, bathrooms, garages, kitchens, and the like that require ambient lighting that nears the level of task lighting. Incandescent fixtures are commonly used for general lighting in all areas of a home. Pendant and track lighting fixtures are more commonly used to provide task lighting to a specific area.

Wall-Mounted Fixtures

The name of this type of lighting fixture basically explains the application and placement of these fixtures. Wall-mounted fixtures include wall sconces, vanity lighting, track lighting, and spotlights.

- **Wall sconces** These fixtures are designed to use either incandescent or compact fluorescent lamps. Sconces are used in hallways, living rooms, bedrooms, and rooms with low ceilings to provide accent and ambient lighting.

Figure 27-7
A spotlight ceiling-mounted light fixture provides task lighting.

Photo courtesy of Access Lighting, Inc.

Figure 27-8
Vanity lighting
above and to
the sides of a
bathroom mirror

Photo courtesy of Connie J. Price.

- **Vanity lighting**   Vanity lighting is applied in bathrooms and occasionally bedrooms to provide task lighting. Typically, vanity lighting is placed either on the sides or above a bathroom mirror. Figure 27-8 depicts a bathroom that uses both overhead and side-mounted vanity lighting.

- **Track lighting**   In wall-mounted placements, track lighting can use either incandescent or halogen lamps to provide flexible accent and task lighting. Figure 27-9 shows track lighting installed in a hallway.

- **Spotlights**   Spotlights can be used to provide wall-wash, general, and task lighting. The light should be positioned to prevent direct view of the light source, as this type of lighting is typically high-output. Figure 27-9 illustrates a spot lighting fixture.

Figure 27-9
Track lighting
placed to
spotlight wall
locations for
future art pieces

Photo courtesy of Connie J. Price.

Daylight Considerations

One lighting source that should not be overlooked when considering the lighting sources for a room or zone is daylight—the natural sunlight that comes in through any windows, skylights, or the like. There are a variety of ways to control the amount of daylight entering a room, which, in some rooms, such as home theaters and home offices, can be a desired feature.

Daylighting

Daylighting is a lighting design technique that uses artificial light and natural daylight to maintain a certain level of lighting in a room or zone. Daylighting requires the use of photocell and timer controls; both are discussed later in the chapter. However, in summary, photocell controls sense the amount of light present in a certain area and turn on artificial light fixtures to bring the lighting to a certain level or turn off artificial lighting when the daylight entering the area is sufficient to supply the lighting level desired. Timers can be used in conjunction with photocells to either turn on or turn off the artificial lighting on a preset schedule when the daylight levels in a room are predictable, such as a room that only gets morning light or afternoon light.

Window Treatments

An often-overlooked way to control the lighting in a room is window coverings and UV filters. Window coverings include draperies, blinds, shades, and the like. UV (ultraviolet) filters are typically films that are placed on the interior of the windows to block UV rays and reduce the temperature of the energy generated by sunlight passing through the window glass.

Window Coverings   In the context of home technology integration, the focus should be on the automation of window coverings, which can be integrated into the lighting controls as a part of a lighting scene. For example, if the homeowners wish to be able to darken a room so they can show their digital vacation pictures or video using a digital projector, it is conceivable that they will want a ceiling-mounted screen to descend, the room lights to automatically dim, and the light-blocking window shades or draperies to automatically close. All of this should happen at the touch of a button on a local control station or on a remote control.

There are a variety of motorized and controllable window shades (including UV filtering shades), draperies rods, and horizontal and vertical blinds that can be controlled as a stand-alone system or integrated into either a lighting control system or a home automation control system.

UV Filters   UV window filters are available as either window shades, special drapery materials, or a glued-on window film. Window films are typically dyed, polyester opaque film that is installed either permanently or temporarily on a window's interior surface using a low-tack adhesive. Window films filter out high temperature and UV rays, and its color controls the amount of sunlight entering a room.

UV Light

Ultraviolet (UV) radiation is one of the parts of the sun's light spectrum. UV light is invisible, but it can have a damaging effect on people, fabric, and even plants. Overexposure to UV light can cause sunburn, and if the exposure is over a long period, it can even cause skin cancer, eye cataracts, and damage to the human immune system. In a home, the UV light coming through a window can fade or damage fabric, carpets, furniture, and artwork.

Exterior Lighting

Lighting installed on the exterior of a home serves a variety of purposes, perhaps the four most important being:

- **Illuminating leisure areas**   Exterior leisure spaces, such as patios, sports courts, and play yards can be lighted to make them usable at night.
- **Highlighting landscaping**   Lighting that highlights the décor of a home's landscaping can add to the visual attractiveness of the home during dark hours. Trees, large bushes, and yard art can be illuminated to make them visible at night.
- **Providing security**   Security lighting illuminates the exterior of a home to create a visual deterrent to crime, or it can take the form of detection devices, such as passive infrared or other motion detection systems that turn on exterior lighting when someone enters a certain area.
- **Providing safety**   Pathways and driveways can be lighted to provide for safe passage of people in and around a property and to illuminate a pathway or a doorway to show its direction or location. In rural areas, safety lighting can also include roadway lighting in front or near a home.

The type of exterior lighting fixture used in each of these external lighting situations depends primarily on the application and the size of the area to be illuminated. These applications could include any of the following:

- **Large area lighting**   The most effective lighting for large areas is PAR (parabolic aluminized reflector) lamps, which can be incandescent, halogen, or high-intensity discharge (HID) tubes. To conserve energy, motion detectors or photocells that turn on the lights only when someone enters the area or during nighttime hours should be used.
- **Porch and entry lighting**   Because these areas are small and the lighting is used primarily as general lighting, a wall-mounted, post-top, or architectural luminaire will supply the illumination needed.

- **Landscape and walkway lighting**   The choices for walkway and landscape lighting include both wired and no-wire solutions. Solar-powered lighting doesn't require wiring and usually includes photocells to turn the lamps on or off depending on sunlight or the lack thereof. Floodlights can also be installed to wash a walkway to highlight landscaping features.

- **Leisure area lighting**   Wall-mounted fixtures designed for exterior use can be used to provide both general and task lighting for exterior settings.

Lighting Fixture Components

The primary components of a lighting fixture are its electrical wiring, its light source receptacle, and its diffuser. The components of a light fixture are designed together for use in a particular application and to produce a specific range of light.

Light Fixture Wiring

In order to produce light, a lighting fixture must have an electrical source. The electrical power required by the fixture to produce light can come through a direct interconnection into a home's electrical wiring, from a plug-in connection to an electrical outlet, or from a battery. For use as a part of a home lighting system, we will consider only the first two of these power sources, as battery-powered lighting fixtures are not typically included as part of an integrated lighting system.

Hard-Wired Lighting Fixtures   Nearly all lighting fixtures, and especially those that are ceiling or wall-mounted fixtures, are hard-wired into the electrical system (see Figure 27-10), meaning that they are directly connected to the household electrical system using the wires provided by the fixture's manufacturer.

Figure 27-10

The hard-wire installation of a ceiling-mounted light fixture

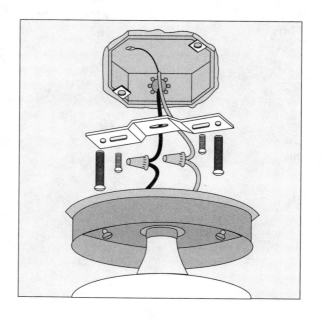

Outlet Plugs   Freestanding lamps and those fixtures designed to be portable are generally not constructed for hard-wiring installation and use a two- or three-prong plug that is inserted in a standard AC receptacle. Table and floor lamps, some under-counter fluorescent or halogen lights, and portable task lighting are generally outlet plug type fixtures.

Light Socket or Receptacle

Regardless of the type of lighting to be used, each has a built-in receptacle, socket, or a pair of sockets (like in a fluorescent fixture) where the bulb, tube, or light source is installed. Incandescent light fixtures have a threaded socket that the light bulb is screwed into. Fluorescent fixtures have a pair of sockets where a fluorescent tube is installed by placing the pins on the ends of the tube into the slots on the socket and twisting the tube to lock it into place. Halogen and other high-intensity fixtures have a two-contact socket into which the lamp is pushed.

Diffusers and Shades

Nearly all light fixtures include a cover or what is called a diffuser. A diffuser, like the globe on the light fixture shown in Figure 27-11, is an opaque or translucent glass, plastic, acrylic, or perhaps alabaster piece that performs two functions: to shield the light source and to spread or scatter the light in an even pattern in all directions.

Diffused lighting produces less shadowing than direct lighting because the light doesn't come from any definite direction. In addition to a diffuser that is a part of a light fixture, a white or light colored wall could also produce diffused light.

A lampshade may seem like it could be a diffuser as well, but the purpose for a lampshade on a table or floor lamp or perhaps a wall or ceiling-mounted fixture is to shade the light source and protect your eyes from a direct view of the light source. In most cases, lampshades are used to direct light either down or up and, although some light may be diffused through the cloth, plastic, or glass of the shade, its purpose is not the same as a diffuser.

Figure 27-11
The globe on this light fixture diffuses the light produced by the fixture's light source.

Diffuser

Lighting Controls

Lighting controls, depending on the type in use, are used to lower a room's light levels to conserve energy and extend the life of a light source, change the ambient lighting in a room, set the light level of task lighting, and create a variety of lighting scenes at the touch of one button for each space.

As briefly discussed in Chapter 26, there are a variety of lighting controls that can be used in a home that range from the common toggle on/off switch to new wireless in-room and whole-house controls.

In-Room Controls

The most common in-room lighting control is still the two-position on-off switch, but technology no longer limits the choice to this basic light control. A variety of new controls are available that not only control room lighting, but also provide flexibility and in many cases, reduce energy costs. The most common of the in-room lighting controls are

- **Dimmers**   This type of switch is used to reduce the voltage flowing to a lighting fixture that in turn reduces the light produced by the fixture. Dimmers are usually associated with incandescent lighting, but with a dimming ballast installed, fluorescent lighting can also be controlled using a dimmer. Dimmer switches are available in a variety of control types: rotary (shown in Figure 27-12), slide (shown in Figure 27-13), or touch styles.

- **Motor Speed Controllers**   Another form of dimmer control is an AC motor speed controller, which is a circuit specifically designed to control the amount of electrical power flowing to a device. Depending on the circuit's design, the output power to an electrical device, such as a lamp or light fixture, can be controlled either manually or electronically.

Figure 27-12

A rotary-style dimmer control

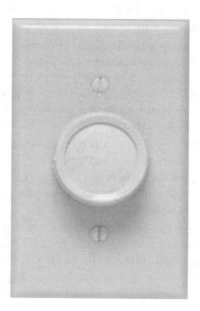

Figure 27-13
A slide switch
dimmer control

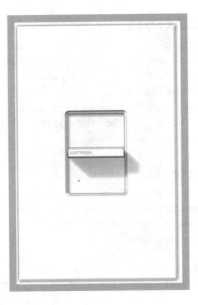

- **Motion and occupancy detectors**   Not only do motion detector controls provide convenience for a person entering a room, but they also help save energy by turning off lighting in unoccupied rooms. Different types of motion detector controllers are available, including fully automatic and manual on/automatic off. Motion and occupancy sensors use two different technologies: passive infrared (PIR) and ultrasonic. PIR sensors detect changes in energy generated by occupants entering or moving about in a space. Ultrasonic sensors send out high-frequency sound waves that bounce off objects in the space. Moving objects in the space change the frequency of the wave, which is interpreted as somebody being in the room, and the lights are turned on or stay on for a preset amount of time.

- **Photocells**   Photocells, also called photoelectric cells and electric eyes, are small devices that can be mounted on a ceiling (see Figure 27-14), wall, along a driveway, or just about anywhere. A photocell senses changes in lighting levels and sends a signal to a central controller that interprets the signal as a need for turning on lighting fixtures in a room or zone. Some photocells also include the signal processing and can be used to directly control a lighting fixture directly wired to it.

- **Switches**   The everyday on-off light switch is convenient and still preferred by some homeowners for home resale purposes. Beyond the two-position up or down toggle switch, there are variations that replace the toggle with a two-position rocker or a push-button and some that include an indicator light that glows when the lighting is on.

- **Timers**   Timers can be electronic interval timers or some form of a rotary control. Timers are best applied in rooms that are infrequently occupied or with lighting that is used only for short periods, such as the lighting in bathrooms, closets, and pantries.

Figure 27-14
A photocell can be mounted on a ceiling or a wall.

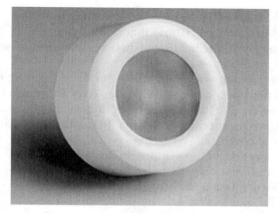

Photo courtesy of Leviton Manufacturing Company, Inc.

Automated Lighting Controls

The primary component of a centralized whole-house automated lighting control system is the keypad interfaces placed throughout the home. With keypads the walls are cleaned up, because a single-gang keypad can control up to nine different lights or scenes. Keypads, like the one shown in Figure 27-15, allow a room's lighting to be controlled by the touch of a button to create preferred lighting in a room. Each preset lighting variation or combination in a room or area is called a lighting scene.

Lighting control keypads can be in-wall devices, handheld devices, or tabletop touch-screen units.

Figure 27-15
A multifunction keypad lighting control

Photo courtesy of Smarthome, Inc.

Wireless Lighting Controls

Wireless lighting controls (those that don't require new wire to be installed) provide the ability to control the lighting of an occupied room, as well as in other rooms, to set or change lighting scenes easily.

The most popular wireless lighting control systems use either radio frequency (RF) signaling or powerline carrier (PLC) technology. RF signals require radio wave transmitters and receivers. PLC actually does work on wires, but we list it here under wireless since it requires no special/new wiring. PLC transmits and receives its signals over the AC wiring in a home.

Wireless control systems require the installation of "smart" switches. With RF control, if wall-mounted keypads are to be used, the wiring for keypads must be done during the pre-wire phase of construction or retrofitted.

Powerline Lighting Controls

PLC systems use the AC wiring of a home to communicate signals to a lighting control system. PLC system remote controls use RF technology to communicate to a PLC receiver device, such as a light switch, lamp module, or appliance module. Some PLC systems also offer a portable keypad that can be plugged into any AC outlet and send signals to control the lights connected to the PLC system. PLC systems can be configured to control dimmers, light switches, and even ceiling fan switches.

The primary components of a PLC system are

- **Light switches** PLC light switches look just like a standard light switch and are wired into the electrical system using nearly the same procedure. The difference between a PLC light switch and an ordinary light switch is that the wiring is used for signal transmission rather than opening and closing the circuit to the lighting fixture.

- **Lamp controls** Lamp control modules either plug directly into an AC outlet (plug-in lamp controls) or can be inserted into the lamp to control a lamp (screw-in or bayonet lamp controls). There are two types of plug-in modules: dimmer and screw-in. Lamp controls are used to reduce or raise the AC power to a lamp, which dims or brightens the lamp. Dimmer modules are controlled using an RF dimmer or keypad.

  - **Plug-in lamp controls** This type of PLC lamp control is plugged into an AC outlet and the lamp to be controlled is then plugged into an AC outlet on the face of the control module (see Figure 27-16).

  - **Screw-in or bayonet lamp controls** This type of PLC lamp control (see Figure 27-17) is either screwed or inserted and twist-locked into the lamp socket of the light fixture. The light bulb or lamp is then screwed or inserted into the control. The control is operated using a remote control to dim and turn off the lamp.

- **Appliance controls** These modules plug directly into an AC outlet. They control like a relay and can only turn the device plugged into them on or off. They cannot dim like a lamp module. They come either with a two-prong plug or a three-prong plug with a ground.

Figure 27-16
A PLC plug-in
lamp control
module

Photo courtesy of Smarthome, Inc.

- **Room keypads**   PLC room controls commonly have buttons that allow for individual device control and preset lighting scenes.

- **Whole house controllers**   This type of controller allows for programming of devices by time and situation and also allows for setup of scenes. When combined with keypad buttons, it gives remote and scene control throughout the house. It is a larger and smarter version of a PLC room keypad that is capable of controlling the lighting throughout a house from any room.

Figure 27-17
A PLC screw-in
lamp control
module

Photo courtesy of Smarthome, Inc.

PLC System Mapping   In a PLC lighting control system, a combination of codes is used to address the individual remote controls, transceivers, and modules. The addressing scheme uses a combination of codes, a house code and a unit code, to address as many as 256 devices on a system. An alphabetic letter from A to P commonly represents the house code; the unit code is a number, usually from 1 to 16.

The house and unit codes are typically set on a device by turning the house and unit code wheels with a small screwdriver. Only devices with the same house code will communicate with one another, so if you are installing a PLC lighting control system, be sure to set the house and unit codes, which can be assigned sequentially, before installing the devices.

NOTE   The default house code on most systems is "A." It is recommended that "A" not be used to avoid any possibility of the next-door neighbor turning on or off the lights.

Wireless RF Controls

In addition to PLC wireless controls, there are also RF lighting control transceivers that interpret the RF signal for transmission over twisted-pair wire and some that transmit directly to an RF receiver connected to the lighting system controller. One such system is the Lutron RadioRA system that includes the following RF devices in its basic package, as illustrated in Figure 27-18:

- **Wall-mounted master control**   This control allows for preset lighting scenes or the control of individual lamps. Wall-mounted controls in one room can be used to turn on lighting in other rooms or throughout the house.

- **Dimmer controls**   Dimmers are controlled by a master control module that directs the dimmer to turn on, dim, brighten, or turn off one or more lights in a room or area.

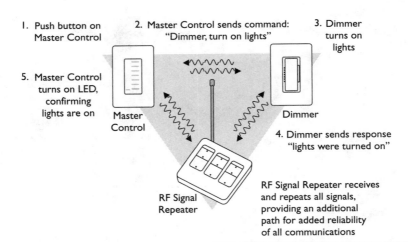

Figure 27-18   The Lutron RadioRA system; its components interact via wireless RF signals.

- **RF signal repeater**   In large homes or in systems that wish to have a larger RF range, an RF repeater receives and retransmits the signals of the lighting control system. A signal repeater enables such optional features as car controls (to turn on the lights from within a car pulling into the driveway) or exterior lighting controls.

- **Tabletop controls**   Remote control devices can be used to activate room or area lighting scenes or to turn on or off lighting throughout a home.

- **Entry master controls**   Allows the lighting system to be controlled from outside at an entryway into the home.

Wired Lighting Controls

Wired lighting control systems are essentially what they sound like—lighting controls connected to lighting fixtures or controllers by electrical wiring or networking cable.

Standard Lighting Controls

Perhaps the most basic of wired lighting controls is the standard on/off toggle switch or dimmer controls found in virtually every home. The switch or dimmer is wired directly in line with the lamp or fixture it controls. The most common controls found in standard lighting control systems are

- **On/off switches**   The traditional type of lighting control used in virtually all homes. This control is simply a two-position or toggle switch that either turns on or turns off the electricity flowing to a light fixture.

- **Rotary dimmer controls**   The most common type of dimmer control found in homes, this control uses a push-on/push-off switch that can be rotated to change the lighting level of a room.

- **Slider dimmer controls**   A variation on the rotary dimmer; these controls have a slider switch that allows the lighting level of a room to be set manually.

- **Timer controls**   These controls incorporate a clock or timer to complete or break the electrical circuit to any light fixtures attached to the device. These controls can be either separate or built-in devices.

- **Touch dimmer controls**   Using either a one-button control or a keypad, the lighting level in a room can be changed.

Automated Lighting Controls

A more advanced approach to wired lighting control systems are those that connect room controllers and modules using low-voltage cabling, such as coaxial or twisted-pair cable. Basically, this type of system consists of room control stations that are connected over structured wiring to a central lighting system controller that receives and transmits signals to carry out the commands requested by the control stations to and from the controllers connected to light fixtures. The central controller device in a digital lighting control system is either a proprietary microprocessor-based controller or a networked PC running specialized lighting control software.

Automated lighting controls can either be centralized or distributed. *Centralized* means that all the lighting loads controlled are wired to a central control panel for control. In a *distributed* system, the control switch or device is located locally in the area of the lighting being controlled, such as the wall switch. In some spaces, such as a home theater, having the master control unit local simplifies the cabling.

CROSS-REFERENCE Chapter 28 covers lighting system design and installation.

Chapter Review

Lighting fixtures are known by a variety of names, including lamps, chandeliers, pendants, tracks, luminaires, and others, with each designed for a specific use and purpose. A light fixture is an electrical device that produces visible light.

Built-in lighting systems are referred to as architectural luminaires, which are constructed features that enclose a lighting fixture. Architectural luminaires are most commonly attached to a wall or ceiling with a shielding board or structural feature used to hide the fixture. Common examples of architectural luminaires are coves, soffits, and valances. The lighting effect of a luminaire can be controlled through the use of baffles, louvers, and diffusers.

Recessed lighting fixtures are primarily installed in ceilings. Two types of recessed lights are available: round recessed downlights and square or rectangle recessed downlights. Round downlights can be incandescent, halogen, or compact fluorescent. Square downlights are usually linear fluorescent or halogen lamps.

Ceiling fixtures can be classified as chandelier, flush-mounted, close to ceiling, pendant, and spotlight. Linear or circline fluorescent fixtures, incandescent fixtures, pendant fixtures, and track lighting provide for ambient and task lighting. Linear fluorescent fixtures provide light for laundry rooms, bathrooms, garages, and kitchens. Incandescent fixtures are used for general lighting. Pendant and track lighting fixtures are used to provide task lighting. Wall-mounted fixtures include wall sconces, vanity lighting, track lighting, and spotlights.

Daylighting is a lighting design technique that uses artificial light and natural daylight to maintain a certain level of lighting in a room or zone. Daylighting requires the use of photocell and timer controls. Window coverings and UV filters can be used to control the amount of sunlight that enters a room.

Lighting installed on the exterior of a home serves a variety of purposes, including illuminating leisure areas, highlighting landscaping, providing security, and providing safety. The exterior lighting fixture types used for these types of lighting are large area lighting; entry lighting, landscape lighting, walkway lighting, and leisure area lighting.

Lighting controls are used to lower a room's light levels to conserve energy and extend the life of a light source, change the ambient lighting in a room, set the light level of task lighting, and create a variety of lighting scenes. A variety of lighting controls are used to control room lighting: dimmers, motion and occupancy detectors, photocells, switches, and timers.

The primary components of a centralized whole-house automated lighting control system are keypad interfaces placed throughout the home. Keypads allow a room's lighting to be controlled by the touch of a button. Lighting control keypads can be in-wall devices, handheld, or tabletop units.

Wireless lighting controls provide the ability to control the lighting of an occupied room, as well as in other rooms, to set or change lighting scenes easily. Wireless lighting control systems use RF or PLC technology. PLC systems use AC wiring to communicate signals to a lighting control system. PLC systems can be configured to control dimmers, light switches, and even ceiling fan switches. The primary components of a PLC system are lamp controls, room keypads, and whole house controllers.

RF lighting control transceivers interpret signals and transmit them over twisted-pair wire or directly to an RF receiver at the lighting system controller.

The most common controls found in standard lighting control systems are on/off switches, dimmer controls, and timer controls.

An advanced approach to lighting control systems connects room controllers and modules over low-voltage cabling. The central controller device is a proprietary microprocessor-based controller or a networked PC running specialized lighting control software. Automated lighting controls can either be centralized or distributed.

Questions

1. What lighting system technique uses artificial light to augment natural light levels in a room or area called?

   A. Downlighting

   B. Daylighting

   C. Skylighting

   D. Sunlighting

2. In order to block sunlight from a room with windows, which of the following lighting control features could be used as a part of an automated lighting control system?

   A. Motorized draperies or shades

   B. Block-out window inserts

   C. Photo-sensitive glass

   D. UV filters

3. Which of the following is not a purpose for exterior lighting?

   A. Landscaping

   B. Growth lighting for exterior plants

   C. Safety

   D. Security

4. Which of the following is not a type of dimming control?

   A. On/off

   B. Rotary

   C. Slide

   D. Touch

5. What technology is commonly used to detect when someone enters a room?

   A. Photocell

   B. PIR

   C. RF

   D. Time clock

6. PLC systems are applications of which communications technology?

   A. RS-232

   B. RS-422

   C. HomePNA

   D. X-10

7. What are the two types of PLC lamp controls?

   A. Automatic

   B. Bayonet

   C. Dimmer

   D. Relay

8. Up to how many devices can a PLC system address using a combination of home codes and unit codes?

   A. 8

   B. 64

   C. 128

   D. 256

9. What type of cable are wired lighting control system keypads typically installed on?

   A. High-voltage wiring

   B. Low-voltage wiring

   C. HVAC wiring

   D. Telephone wiring

10. A lighting control system where the devices in a room are controlled by devices located in that room is said to be

   A. Centralized

   B. Decentralized

   C. Distributed

   D. Isolated

Answers

1. **B.** Downlighting is a type of lighting installation where the lamps are ceiling mounted or luminaires; skylighting is a window treatment; and sunlighting is neither.

2. **A and D.** Block-out window inserts and photo-sensitive glass are not part of an automated lighting control system—one requires manual installation and the other is a chemical reaction to sunlight.

3. **B.** Okay, so it was a bit obvious, but I wanted you to remember the purposes for exterior lighting and to reflect on how exterior lighting can be included in a lighting control system. Of course the purposes for the exterior lighting are security, safety, and to show off the landscaping, but I think that, for the most part, the sun takes care of the growth light issue.

4. **A.** Rotary, slide, and touch controls are all types of dimming controls. An on/off switch can only turn a lamp on or off.

5. **B.** Passive infrared technology (PIR) is the most commonly used technology in motion and occupancy detectors. Ultrasonic sensors is another technology that is used in this type of device.

6. **D.** X-10 is a communications technology that transmits signals over AC power lines. CEBus is another AC powerline technology, though most systems available are based on the X-10 technology. RS-232 and 422 are types of serial data communications, and HomePNA is used primarily for data networking.

7. **C and D.** In order for a PLC system to be automatic, some type of sensor must be used. Bayonet is one of the types of screw-in dimming controls, but the general types of PLC lamp controls are dimmers and relays.

8. **D.** Given that each home code can typically address up to 16 unit codes, only 16 home codes are required to address up to 256 devices from a central lighting controller.

9. **B.** LV wiring, meaning the type of cabling used in a structured wiring system (coaxial and UTP), are typically used for wiring automated centralized lighting control systems.

10. **B.** A centralized system is controlled through a single system controller in which local controllers are distributed. A decentralized system controls the lighting from within a room or zone. Isolated is not a lighting control system term.

PART VII

CHAPTER 28

Designing and Installing a Home Lighting System

In this chapter, you will learn about
- Designing interior lighting scenes and zones
- Designing exterior lighting
- Installing interior lighting control systems
- NEC compliance in lighting systems

Designing a whole house lighting system involves more than selecting the lighting for each individual room. Each room of a house can have several levels of lighting requirements. At different times a room's occupants may desire a room to have ambient lighting or task lighting, and the lighting system must be able to accommodate either lighting type easily. You must also consider how the lighting is to be provided and the type of light to be used.

A residential lighting control system provides a homeowner with the ability to control the lighting in a room or zone and to set a variety of lighting scenes in each area. Whenever home technology integration or home automation is discussed, lighting control is almost always included in the conversation. Lighting controls not only provide for better task lighting, they also can be used to "set the scene" through their ability to control the lighting levels in a given area or an entire house. On top of these benefits, a lighting control system can also save homeowners money by reducing energy costs and increasing lamp life.

This chapter covers both the design and installation of lighting systems, including the different types of lighting controls, the devices used in setting them up, and National Electric Code (NEC) compliance.

Designing a Home Lighting System

Like the design process used for all systems in a home technology integration project, a systematic approach is necessary when designing a home lighting system. The use of a step-by-step approach will ensure that the system is complete and addresses the needs and requirements of the homeowners.

The steps that should be used to design a home lighting system are as follows:

1. Identify the lighting loads to be controlled by each lighting control station.
2. Identify the lighting type associated with each load.
3. Calculate wattage requirements of each lighting circuit.
4. Determine the type of control devices to be used.
5. Determine the locations of the lighting controls and lay out their wiring loops.
6. Determine the lighting scenes to be programmed into each room or zone.
7. Plan and program the layout of the control switches.

Lighting Loads

As is discussed in Chapter 26, a lighting load is the amount of energy consumed to provide a certain level of illumination in a space. Knowing the lighting load of a house and its rooms and ensuring that the load doesn't exceed the electrical power available to each space are essential parts of any lighting system design.

Types of Loads

On the electrical side of lighting, there are two types of loads that must be considered: inductive loads and resistive loads.

- **Inductive load**   An inductive load is created by electrical devices that have moving parts, from devices with motors like power drills, fans, and vacuum cleaners to devices that include transformers, such as a fluorescent light fixture.

- **Resistive load**   A resistive load provides resistance to the flow of electrical current. Devices that create resistive loads include electric heaters, electric stoves, and even irons, but in the context of lighting loads, incandescent and halogen lamps create resistive loads.

The primary reason you should know the type of load a lighting device produces is that it allows you to match lighting controls to the type of load created by the fixture being controlled. Inductive load devices should not be controlled with resistive load controllers, and vice versa. Table 28-1 lists the common lighting types, their load type, and the type of controller typically matched to them.

Calculating Lighting Load

Prior to the pre-wire phase of a home's construction, the lighting loads must be determined based on your understanding of the customer's lighting requirements and desires. The number of lighting fixtures on each of the lighting loads is used to determine the number of electrical circuits required to support the lighting requirements of a space.

Lighting Type	Load Type	Controller Type
Incandescent	Resistive	Incandescent dimmer.
Fluorescent	Inductive	Relay or special fluorescent dimmer; lighting fixture may require dimmable ballast.
High intensity discharge (HID)	Inductive	Relay or special HID dimmer; fixture may require dimmable ballast.
Low voltage	Inductive	Low voltage dimmer.
Quartz halogen	Resistive	Incandescent dimmer.

Table 28-1 Lighting Types, Loads, and Controllers

Some estimate must be made as to the type and number of lighting fixtures to be used to accomplish the lighting requirements. Once this has been decided, it is possible to estimate the total lighting load for each circuit, room, and the entire house. For example, an incandescent load with three fixtures, each with 75-watt lamps, equals a total load of 225 watts. This information is needed when designing the control requirements and layout of the total lighting system.

The lighting loads are calculated slightly different from incandescent and fluorescent and high-intensity discharge (HID) lighting. Incandescent lighting loads are calculated as the wattage of all of the lamps connected to a single control, such as a switch, dimmer, or keypad.

When calculating the lighting load for a control connected to fluorescent or HID lamps, the power required by the ballasts may need to be factored in. Magnetic ballasts, whether for fluorescent or HID fixtures, use an additional 15 percent of power over and above the power requirements of the lamps, which means that the total wattage requirement for a lighting circuit needs to be multiplied by a factor of 1.15. However, if electronic ballasts are used, no additional wattage needs to be included.

Table 28-2 shows the lighting loads in a kitchen that has three incandescent fixtures of 100 watts each, two fluorescent fixtures with 40-watt lamps, and three under-counter fixtures with HID lamps of 60 watts each. Assume here that each lighting type is connected to a dedicated control.

Volt-Amps, Watts, Lumens

The measurements used when designing a lighting system are volts, amperes, watts, and lumens. However, which of these measurements is used depends on what is being measured. These electrical and lighting measurements are discussed in the following sections.

Lighting Type	Watts/Lamp	Number of Lamps	Lighting Load
Incandescent	100	3	300 watts
Fluorescent	40	2	80 watts
HID	60	3	180 watts
Total lighting load			560 watts

Table 28-2 A Lighting Load Calculation Example

Volt-Amps

Volt-amps, or voltage-amperes (VA), are commonly stated as kilo (1,000) volt-amps (KVA). VA represents the value of an AC circuit's current (A) times its voltage (V). VA is just one way to define the electrical power requirements of a lighting fixture and its lamp. On resistive circuits, such as a circuit with incandescent lighting fixtures, the VA requirement can also be referred to as the apparent power requirement and stated as watts.

Watts

Watts are calculated using Ohm's law, which computes watts as equal to the voltage times the amps on a circuit. All lamps use electricity to produce light, and the amount of electricity required is stated in watts (W). One watt is the equivalent of 1 volt-amp.

Lighting lamps are all rated in watts, especially incandescent lamps. The wattage rating on a lamp indicates the amount of power the lamp uses to operate efficiently. On fluorescent fixtures, the lamps or tubes use electrical power, but because the fluorescent lights require a ballast to start up, its wattage (typically rated in amps) must be included in the power requirements of the fixture.

Lumens

Different lamps produce differing amounts of light. However, as the amount of light produced increases, so does the amount of power consumed to do so. For example, a 100-watt incandescent light bulb produces more light than a 60-watt bulb and requires 40 more watts of power to do so. Because of this, many people believe that the wattage rating on the bulb is a statement of how much light the bulb produces. To a certain extent this is comparatively true, but not exactly.

The amount of light produced by a lamp is measured in lumens. Lumens are typically stated as lumens per watt (LPW) on the packaging of a lamp. LPW indicates the number of lumens produced for each watt of power used and is, in effect, a measure of the lamp's efficiency in converting power to light. Because some lamp types are more efficient than others, the LPW varies by lamp type. Incandescent lamps are generally rated in the 17–20 LPW range, and fluorescent and high-output lamps can produce as much as 90 LPW.

Designing Room Lighting

Many countries around the world have standards for recommended levels of light for different types and uses of spaces. Of course there are a number of factors that must be considered when determining the level of light for any particular space. Rooms can require different light for a variety of activities. For example, a room that needs task lighting for detailed activities requires more light than a room that needs only ambient lighting. Other criteria for the amount of light a room requires are the preferences of the occupants and if the lighting levels are to be incorporated into a room's décor.

In new construction situations, the lighting designer may need to work closely with the architect to achieve a balance between the basic lighting requirements of an area and any artistic uses of lighting.

Fitting the Light to the Room

When designing the lighting levels for a space, you must consider the color of the light, the shape of a room and its contents, and the size and dimensions of the room.

Light Color

Light produced by lighting fixtures has color, which can be used to accent the décor and design of a room and its contents. In a lighted room, the color on any surface is produced as a combination of the color of the surface and the color of the light hitting that surface.

The light produced by a lamp in a light fixture can literally change the perceived color of the walls and objects of a room. Color can also affect the mood of a room's occupants. Bright and varied color in a room can create a mood of happiness, but monotone and dark colors and gloomy light can cause the opposite effect. Different room and lighting colors produce different effects—red is warm and blue or green is cool.

Objects in a Room

The angle at which light strikes an object can alter the perception of its size or shape by creating glares or shadows. Of course, this issue is difficult to predict for a home that may not be built or furnished yet, but if these issues are important to the homeowners, adjustable lighting should be considered.

Room Size and Dimensions

Light can be used to change the perception of a room's size or volume or to highlight a room's design elements to make them more attention grabbing.

Different lighting levels and styles can be included in a room's lighting plan to enhance a room's features. For example, illuminating a ceiling can create the illusion of a high ceiling, and low lighting on a structural feature can make it appear smaller or closer. Lighting can also be used to create a virtual pathway through a room or between rooms. For example, when the rear of a pathway is more brightly lit than its entrance, visitors are drawn to the rear by the lighting.

Identifying Lighting Needs

Lighting is easily the least expensive decorating option available to homeowners, at least compared to the cost of remodeling and home decorating. This is a good reason for the lighting design to focus on complementing the lifestyle of the homeowners.

One very important consideration when identifying lighting needs and loads is the amount of sunlight available to light a room during the day. If a room doesn't directly receive much sunlight, it may require day lighting as well as nighttime lighting.

Identify Room Lighting Needs

The lighting design for a room should take into account how a room is to be used, the mood or atmosphere desired, and any room décor or contents that are to be highlighted. Another consideration is the color of the walls, ceiling, and floor coverings. Dark colors absorb light and light colors reflect light, and the lighting design should reflect this.

Rooms planned for multiple uses or activities may require multipurpose, adjustable, or perhaps multiple lighting types to provide the desired and recommended lighting for each activity. The recommendations for the common rooms of a house are as follows:

- **Bathroom** The lighting in a bathroom should be evenly distributed and as shadow-free as possible. Vanity lighting and recessed wall-mounted or ceiling-mounted fixtures are most commonly used in this space.

- **Bedrooms** Bedrooms typically require adjustable lighting along with task lighting. Ceiling-mounted or wall-mounted fixtures, controlled with a dimmer control, can be used for general lighting and task lighting supplied through table lamps or wall sconces can provide the task lighting.

- **Dining room** Depending on the homeowners' plans for how a dining room will be used, the lighting can include general, accent, and task lighting to provide the appropriate lighting levels for entertaining, family gatherings, and perhaps homework, hobbies, or games.

- **Hallways and entrances** Entrances typically use a single, large ceiling-mounted lighting fixture, such as a chandelier, to provide general lighting. Hallways should be lighted every 8 to 10 feet for safety reasons, typically using recessed ceiling-mounted or wall-mounted sconces. Track lighting can also be used, especially if art or other objects are to be accent lighted.

- **Living or family rooms** These rooms typically are multipurpose rooms. General lighting should be included for entertainment or watching TV; task lighting should be provided for reading and other close or detailed activities; and, if desired, accent lighting should be included to accent or highlight plants, art, or architectural features of the room.

- **Kitchen** Kitchens are work areas but can also be gathering places, so both general and task lighting is commonly installed in this area. Under-counter and ceiling-mounted task lighting are also commonly used in kitchens. If desired, cove or soffit luminaires can also be included to provide room accent lighting.

Lighting Scenes

A lighting scene is the preset combination of lighting levels for load(s) configured to provide the lighting appropriate for a particular activity or purpose. Lighting scenes can be manually adjusted using one or more dimmers or lighting controls. However, lighting scenes are typically associated with automatic controls and are one of the key benefits of lighting control.

Multiple lighting scenes can be defined for a single room or area. Different combinations of lighting level settings on the lighting fixtures in a room can be defined to create one or more ambient lighting levels, one or more task lighting patterns, and one or more accent lighting patterns. Selecting the desired lighting scene is then as easy as pressing a button on a keypad or a touch screen controller. For example, the keypad controller shown in Figure 28-1 has been programmed with four lighting scene selections.

Figure 28-1
A four-function lighting control keypad

Photo courtesy of Smarthome, Inc.

Lighting Zones

A lighting zone can include one room, multiple rooms, open floor areas, hallways, stairways, exterior areas, and any combination of these areas. A lighting zone is an area of a house for which a lighting scene is established. When selected, a lighting scene illuminates a lighting zone. Likewise, a lighting zone can have many possible lighting scenes defined for it, but only one can be in use at a time.

When designing lighting scenes in lighting zones, the dimensions, shape, contents, and colors of the zone must be considered. If any part of a lighting zone prevents the desired lighting effect from being achieved, it may be necessary to divide the zone into multiple lighting zones.

Lighting Controls

There are essentially two types of lighting controls that can be installed in a home: dimming and switching. Each of these control types can achieve the goal of controlling the lighting level in a room, zone, or home, but they do it in slightly different ways.

Dimming Controls

Dimming controls change the amount of light emitted by a lamp from none to the lamp's full capability. Dimming controls are typically more expensive than switching controls, but they provide more cost saving and a less abrupt transition from one light level to another. Another advantage to a dimming controls is that they are more easily readjusted should the lighting requirements of a room, zone, or home change.

A variety of dimming control types is available, including rotary, slide, and touch controls. Manual rotary dimmers are available for either incandescent or fluorescent lamps, although a fluorescent lamp also requires dimmable ballast (more on this in the sidebar "Controlling Fluorescent Lamps").

Switching Controls

A basic single-lamp switching control has two settings: the lamp is either on or off. More lamps, such as in a typical two-lamp fixture, can have both lamps on or both lamps off, and there are no intermediate settings between on and off for any of the lamps. Two-position light switches are the most common lighting control used in a home.

Controlling Electrical Flow

One of the basic principles underlying a lighting control system is that what is actually being controlled is the electricity flowing to light fixtures. Dimming controls reduce or increase the amount of voltage flowing to a fixture, thereby decreasing or increasing the amount of light the fixture's lamp produces. Switching controls either turn on or turn off the power flowing to the fixture, turning the lamp on or off.

Exterior Lighting

Lighting zones and lighting scenes aren't just interior lighting areas. The exterior of a home and its landscaping, leisure areas, work spaces, and play areas can be designated as lighting zones in which safety, security, ambient, and accent lighting scenes can be defined.

Standard and specialized lighting fixtures can be used to create a variety of lighting effects for a home's exterior, especially with landscaping and gardens. Lighting can be used to create general moonlighting effects, focal points, uplights on trees, and spotlights on sculpture or other objects. The basic types of landscape lighting are as follows:

- **Backlighting** Creates a backdrop of light that creates a visual depth in the dark.
- **Downlighting** Replaces the sun and natural lighting on fixtures, walls, or gardens. The lighting fixtures can be mounted to walls, in taller trees, or mounted on elevated ground.
- **Moonlighting** A form of downlighting that uses lighting fixtures suspended in trees or mounted on higher objects to create a soft, diffused light that emulates the effects of moonlight.
- **Uplighting** Produces large shadows and illuminates a tree, statue, or other object. The typical placement for an uplighting fixture is on or near the ground.

- **Safety lighting**   A very important reason to include exterior lighting in a lighting design; safety lighting provides a lighted pathway on steps, sidewalks, walkways, and around potentially hazardous landscaping or objects. Safety lighting is down-pointing and positioned so that it is glare-free to avoid shining into anyone's eyes.

- **Security lighting**   Lighting spread evenly around buildings and their immediate surroundings, especially doorways and ground floor access points, can serve as a deterrent to prowlers or other intruders. Eliminating shadows is the primary objective of security lighting. Photocells and motion detectors can add to the effectiveness of security lighting.

Power Line Control (PLC) Devices

A PLC lighting control system can be a very simple affair, consisting of few plug-in modules and a handheld remote control, or it can be a very complex whole-house system controlled by a home automation controller or PC-based home control software. A PLC system works by sending control commands over the electrical wiring; the appropriate control switches or devices respond and execute the command received.

X-10 technology uses coding, where each of the controlled devices is given a code that consists of a letter (A–P) and a number (1–16). For example, the kitchen sink light could be coded D-4 and the kitchen counter lights D-5. The command "D-4 ON" would turn on the kitchen sink light. The command "D ALL OFF" would turn off both the kitchen sink light and the kitchen counter lights. The following sections describe the various devices that may be used in a PLC lighting control system:

- **Switches**   A PLC light switch replaces a standard light switch and is used to stop, start, reduce, or increase the amount of electrical power flowing to a lamp. There are essentially two types of PLC switches:

  - **Dimmer**   A PLC dimmer works virtually the same as a manually operated dimmer, except that the dim/bright setting is activated through a signal transmitted over the PLC lines. Some models of dimmer switches allow for dim/bright control to happen at the switch. A common form of a PLC dimmer switch is a rocker switch, where pressing the rocker down dims the lamp.

  - **Relay**   A PLC relay is essentially an on-off switch that is used to complete or interrupt a power circuit to a device and turns on or turn off a lamp.

- **Plug-in modules**   This type of PLC module connects to the electrical wiring of a home through a room outlet by plugging into the electrical system like any other electrical appliance. The device you wish to control, such as a lamp or fan, is then plugged into the PLC module.

  - **Dimmer**   PLC lamp modules that plug into an electrical outlet are used to provide dimmer control of table lamps and other lamps that can be plugged into an AC outlet on the module.

  - **Relay**   PLC appliance modules can be used to control the on/off functions of lamps and other electrical devices. They do not allow for dim/bright control. Figure 28-2 shows a PLC plug-in relay module.

Figure 28-2
A PLC plug-in
relay module

Photo courtesy of Smarthome, Inc.

- **Hard-wired modules**   This type of PLC lighting control module is directly installed and connected to the AC wiring of a home.

  - **Dimmer**   Hard-wired PLC dimmers are switches that offer remote control of dim/bright/on/off functions of lighting. Figure 28-3 shows a hard-wired PLC control module.

  - **Relay**   Hard-wired PLC relay modules can be used to control the on/off functions of lamps and other electrical devices. They do not allow for dim/bright control.

Figure 28-3
A PLC hard-wired lighting module

Photo courtesy of Smarthome, Inc.

- **Controlled outlet**   Hard-wired electrical receptacles offer either one or two PLC-enabled and remotely controlled AC outlets in a duplex device. Relay devices are also available that are installed directly into the AC system without the need to replace existing light switches.

- **Control devices**

  - **Plug-in controller**   PLC plug-in interfaces and controllers can be used to control any device controlled by PLC such as switches, plug-in modules, hard-wired modules, and controlled outlets.

  - **Wireless handheld remote**   PLC wireless remote controls use radio frequency (RF) signals to control both plug-in and hard-wired PLC modules. A handheld remote control communicates to a remote control transceiver module that is connected to the home's AC lines by plugging into an outlet. It receives the RF signal, converts it to a PLC signal, and sends the desired control command out over the electrical wiring.

  - **Wired remote control switch**   PLC control signals can be sent from hard-wired control switches that transmit PLC control commands.

  - **Wireless remote switch**   Many PLC devices are remote control–enabled to allow the on/off and dimmer functions to be controlled remotely through a handheld or tabletop remote control.

  - **System controller**   PLC controllers are available that provide the capability to program control of the lighting in a single room, zone, or a whole house. Programming can usually be done to control several lighting loads at a time, by time of day, day of week, sunrise/sunset, or an input to the system.

Wired Lighting Control System Devices

A wired lighting control system can be a very simple affair, consisting of a local wall-mounted controller, or it can be a very complex whole-house system that is integrated into a programmable controller. A wired lighting control system works by wiring each lighting load back to a control module that regulates the electrical power to the load. The following sections describe the various devices that may be used in a wired lighting control system, but the emphasis is on a more robust system.

The devices that can be used in a wired lighting control system are

- System controller
- System enclosure
- Modules, such as the following
  - Relay module
  - Dimmer module
  - Circuit breaker module
  - Relay input/output module
- Control station
- Sensors

Lighting System Controller

Also referred to as the master unit or CPU, the lighting system controller includes the microprocessor, clock, and operating memory of the lighting control system. A particular brand of lighting control system may require multiple controllers—one for each zone—or the system controller may be capable of controlling multiple zones. The system controller, like the one shown in Figure 28-4, typically has a user interface that consists of a keypad (or keyboard) and display (a small window or full size monitor) through which the controller is programmed, controlled, and diagnosed. Or, the controller has the option for connection from a computer for downloading and uploading of programming.

Many lighting control systems are available with a complete control panel. These systems typically include all of the features required by an average-sized home, but in larger homes the fully integrated control system may need to be assembled from a robust controller and optional modules and components to get the correct mix of device controllers, breakers, and power.

System Enclosure

Depending on the system, the enclosure cabinet will accommodate a varying number of control modules. The size of the enclosures and the quantity needed should be chosen based on the number of control modules to be placed inside the enclosures. The number of control modules is determined by the number and type of lighting loads to be controlled. Many models of enclosures are available to accommodate anywhere from one to six different lighting control or power modules and up to 48 relays or 30 dimmers, with some even larger. Common features of lighting control enclosures are locking doors, internal venting fans, internal power supply, and optional flush-mounting kits.

Figure 28-4

A lighting system controller

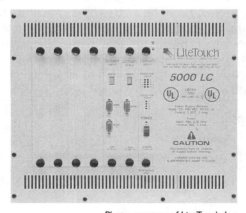

Photo courtesy of LiteTouch, Inc.

Controlling Fluorescent Lamps

In many situations, switching controls are used to regulate fluorescent lamps. However, dimmable electronic fluorescent ballasts are available that allow the illumination produced by a fluorescent lamp to range from as low as 2 percent of its capability to a full 100 percent illumination.

Dimmable fluorescent ballasts vary in how much they are able to dim a fluorescent lamp. Ballasts are available with dimming ranges that range from 100 percent to less than 20 percent, less than 10 percent, less than 5 percent, and less than 1 percent. How much dimming is required by the lighting design will determine which dimmable ballast should be installed. Note, though: as the dimming range increases, so does the cost of the ballast.

Modules

Modules are installed inside the enclosures, and lighting loads controller are connected to the appropriate type of module. Power is fed to the enclosure, then to each of the modules, and then on to the individual lighting loads. The type of lighting load determines the type of module needed.

Relay Modules

Relay modules control the on/off controls of a variety of loads including light fixtures, fans, proprietary two-wire, and virtually all three-wire devices such as fluorescent, incandescent, and other types of low-voltage lighting.

Dimmer Modules

Dimmer modules (see Figure 28-5) control the on/off/dimming controls of incandescent light fixtures. Some dimmer modules can handle certain types of low-voltage lighting.

Figure 28-5
A dimmer
control module

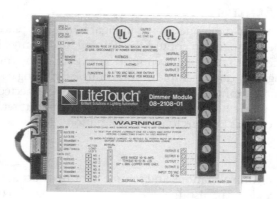

Photo courtesy of LiteTouch, Inc.

PART VII

Figure 28-6
A relay module is mounted in the central lighting control unit.

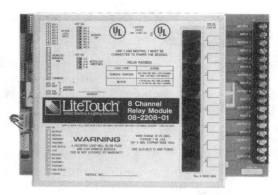

Photo courtesy of LiteTouch, Inc.

Circuit Breaker Modules

Some lighting control systems offer controllable circuit breaker modules or panels that can be preset to provide circuit-level lighting control, such as security lighting, landscape or pool lighting, or other large lighting groups. In some systems, the breaker modules and panels can be networked to provide for additional zones under a common controller.

Relay Input/Output Modules

Relay I/O modules (see Figure 28-6) are used in lighting control systems for low voltage input and output signals to and from the system controller. Examples of what might be on a relay input module include security system or a driveway probe. Examples of what might be on a relay output module include a motorized shade or garage door opener. Typically, the relay modules of a lighting control system can be interconnected on a common high-speed data link that allows them to share input and output among themselves and with the controller unit. In some systems, the relay modules have independent processors that allow them to function with or without the controller online.

Control Stations

Control stations, like the one shown in Figure 28-7, are placed in the individual rooms and allow the occupants to control the lighting loads/lamps in the room or around the house, individually and by scene control. Since each of the control buttons is designed in programming, they can do simple on/off control, dimming control, scene control, or they can even be programmed to control outside systems connected to the lighting control system such as a whole-house music system. Many manufacturers offer custom engraving on the lighting control's buttons to mark each button with the scene or zone it controls.

Sensors

In addition to control stations and remote controls placed in a room or zone, the lighting control system can also include sensors that detect occupancy and daylight levels. The sensors used for this purpose are

Figure 28-7
A multifunction remote station lighting control unit

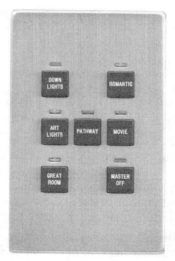

Photo courtesy of LiteTouch, Inc.

- **Motion or occupancy detector** This type of detector senses when someone enters a room or when there is movement or activity within its scanning range. The two types of motion or occupancy detectors are

  - **Passive IR (PIR)** PIR sensors detect changes in the energy radiating from occupants in a room. Like all IR sensors, PIR sensors require a line of sight to work properly. Typically, one or more sensors are placed in a room to encompass its doorway and the primary activity areas.

  - **Active ultrasonic** Ultrasonic sensors work something like sound wave radar. The sensor emits a high-frequency sound wave that is reflected off an object in the room. Movement in the room changes the frequency of the reflected sound wave, which is interpreted as somebody entering the monitored space. A signal is transmitted to the controller, which then turns on the lights.

    There are sensors available that incorporate both PIR and ultrasonic technologies to detect occupancy or movement in a space. Most have settings that can be adjusted to ignore pets or vibrations produced by the HVAC system.

- **Photo sensors** This type of sensor detects the level of natural light in a room or zone. Typically, a photo sensor is used to detect the need for additional artificial light to augment natural daylight to maintain a certain level of lighting in a space.

Wireless Lighting Control System Devices

A wireless lighting control system can be a very simple affair, consisting of a small wall-mounted controller, or it can be a very complex whole-house system that integrates remote wireless switches and control devices into a programmable controller.

PART VII

The following sections describe the various devices that may be used in a wireless lighting control system.

The devices that can be used in a wireless lighting control system are

- **System controller**   The system control unit is essentially the same type of unit as is used in a hard-wired system with the exception of wireless RF communications that allow the system to receive and send signals for control anywhere inside or nearby the exterior of the home.

- **Wireless switches**   Wireless lighting system switches are hard-wired to the electrical and can be operated either locally or remotely using RF signals. They transmit and receive signals via RF to/from a base station or the system controller. They should not be confused with PLC wireless remote control switches. Wireless lighting system switches, like those of a hard-wired or PLC system, are either dimmers or relay-type controls.

  - **Dimmer switches**   Wireless dimmer controls are either a part of a whole-house wireless lighting system or they can be stand-alone devices that control only one or two individual lamps. Stand-alone wireless dimmers require a receiver unit be installed in the lamps to be controlled by the dimmer; when the dimmer is operated manually, it transmits an RF signal to the lamp receiver that dims or brightens the lamp.

  - **Relay switches**   Like other relay light switches, a wireless relay switch (see Figure 28-8) controls the on/off functions of a lighting load/lamp. Like wireless dimmer switches, there are devices that are intended for use as a part of a whole-house system and stand-alone devices, which require a receiver to be installed on the lamp.

Figure 28-8
A wireless relay switch and lamp receiver

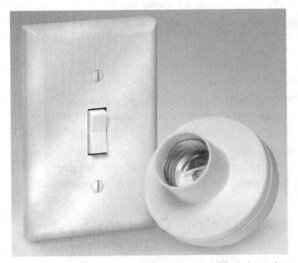

Photo courtesy of Smarthome, Inc.

- **Remote control station**   Typically, a wireless lighting system station, which provides the same functions as hard-wired control stations, also serves as a signal extender to ensure the signal strength throughout a home.

- **Sensors**   Wireless occupancy sensors or motion detectors transmit their event or alarm signals using RF transmission rather than requiring hard-wired connections.

Lighting Controller Security Interface

Regardless of the type of system used to control the lighting in and around a home, the importance of including the lighting system in the security system should not be over-looked. Most dedicated security system controllers have the capability for including the lighting system as a part of the security scheme through a network (IP) interface, a PLC interface, a UPB (Universal Powerline Bus) interface, and in some systems, even a wireless (RF or Z-Wave) interface. PC-based software controller systems typically have modules for controlling the lighting system as an extension of the security system, but may require an add-on lighting control interface device.

Adding the lighting system as an extension of the home security system allows some or all of the lights in a home to be used to illuminate all or part of a home. The security controller interface to the lighting control system (which may actually be parts of the same control system) is used to communicate a command event to the lighting system when a security event is triggered.

Programming Control Options

The most powerful benefit of a lighting control system is the extensive automated or logical control that can be programmed, including scheduling, scenes, and what-if situations. Programming can enhance the simple control, safety, security, and energy savings of a home.

Scheduling Programming

A scheduling program turns lighting on, off, down, or up based on a preset daily time schedule or day of the week or calendar date. This approach to lighting control is intended to avoid lighting areas during daylight hours or periods when a home is not occupied. In many systems, each zone can be programmed with a different lighting schedule according to the lighting needs of the homeowners. The program can often be set up to know the latitude and longitude of the location and, so, figure out sunrise and sunset. Schedules can then be made based on this information, such as turning landscape lights on at sunset.

Scenes

Virtually all lighting control systems have the ability to control a number of different lighting scenes, often in more than one lighting zone. Creating a preset lighting scene, with the press of a single button on a local control station, involves first and foremost some detail planning.

Depending on the lighting control system in use, a lighting scene is created with either a top-down or a bottom-up approach. In the top-down approach, the lighting scene function, such as "movie," is created first. Then the lighting devices to be controlled in the scene are added, and finally the dimmer level of each lighting fixture included in the scene is set, typically as a percentage of its maximum lighting level. In a bottom-up approach, the various lighting levels for each lighting device are created and given some form of an identity, such as "ceiling lights—50%," "sconces—25%," or "lamps—10%." This creates a sort of menu from which the lighting events desired for a particular scene can be added together to create the scene.

What-If Situations

Based on input, lighting control commands are executed in what-if situations. The input can be from known information such as "Security system in Nighttime mode." An example would be "If security armed in Nighttime, landscape lights off." What-if questions can be combined to have complex decisions made regarding lighting control. These compound what-if questions are a form of Boolean logic. An example would be "If dark AND security armed in Away mode THEN turn on living room lights." You would repeat this command with the same what-if question to have them turned off at 10:15 PM, or if it is Friday or Saturday, turn them off at 11:20 PM.

Occupancy Sensor Input for Lighting Control

When a sensor placed in a room or zone detects that someone has entered a room, a signal is sent to the lighting system controller, and it takes the necessary action to turn the lighting on in that space. Occupancy control systems are more energy efficient because lighting is provided only when a room is occupied. If the sensor determines the room is not occupied, or that there hasn't been any activity in the room for a certain time, the controller can then turn off the lights. The type and placement of the sensor used is the key to how well this type of lighting control approach works.

Daylighting Sensor Input for Lighting Control

Daylighting sensors attempt to use the natural daylight in a room to determine the amount of artificial light that should be added to produce a certain preset amount of lighting in the room. Daylighting systems, which are also called daylight harvesting systems, can be used with either dimming or switching controls. However, the availability of dimming controls for fluorescent lamps has made this type of system very popular in commercial settings and more recently in homes.

Daylighting systems use photoelectric sensors to detect the lighting level in a room or space. When the lighting is too high, the controller dims or turns off light fixtures to lower the ambient light. When the lighting is too low, the controller turns on or up the lighting in the room to bring the light up to the desired level. In a large area, more than one sensor may be required to prevent uneven lighting.

Boolean Logic

In the 1800s, a mathematician by the name of George Boole developed a correlation between mathematics and logic called Boolean algebra, which is based on combinations of true and false or on or off conditions.

Boolean algebra, more commonly referred to as *Boolean logic* these days, is the mathematical principle used in computer logic. Boolean logic creates logical relationships between entities using three primary comparison operators (OR, AND, and NOT) to determine if a logical comparison is true or false.

The OR operator returns true if any entity in a set meets the conditions of the logical comparison. For example, if the conditional test of "Is a Girl" is applied to a set of children made up of two boys and one girl, the result is true because one entity in the set actually is a girl. The fact that two of the children are boys is irrelevant: because the girl is a girl the set satisfies the test, which is applied as "if this one is a girl, or that one is a girl, or the other one is a girl, then 'Is a Girl' is true." In a lighting situation, the test might actually be something like, "If Night OR Morning, then …" This test would return true if either of the preset values Night or Morning were true themselves.

The Boolean AND operator tests for all entities of a set meeting a logical condition. If you were to apply the test of "Is a Girl" to the same group of children (two boys and one girl) using the AND operator, the result would be false. In order to satisfy the conditions of the test, all three of the children would have to be girls. This test is applied as "if this one is a girl, and that one is a girl, and the other one is a girl, then Is a Girl is true, otherwise Is a Girl is false." An example of how the AND operator is used in a lighting control program might be something like, "if Daylight AND < 1700, then …" In this case, if the variable Daylight is true and it's earlier than 5:00 PM, then the test returns a true and performs whatever action is indicated by the "then" statement.

The Boolean NOT operator reverses the test by being true only if the result is false. If you test for "Is NOT a Girl" on each of the children, you would get two trues and one false. As convoluted as it may sound, when this test is applied to the children, you are actually testing for "Is a Boy," because the NOT operator reverses the test. So, when we test "Is NOT a Girl" on a boy, the result is true because he is not a girl. An example of how this could be used in a lighting program is "If NOT Activated, then …," which would return true only when the system is not activated.

Without becoming too complicated, Boolean NOT logic also can be used to reverse OR and AND comparisons as well. For example, "NOT Girl OR Boy" would return a true only if all of the children were girls or boys, which is effectively the same as testing "Girl AND Boy." In the same way, "NOT Girl AND Boy" returns a true if the set includes both girls and boys—or the equivalent of "Girl OR Boy." As you can see, NOT logic is probably best used when testing a single value.

Lighting System Standards and Guidelines

A licensed electrician must perform electrical work. You need to work with the project electrician on the layout and installation of the lighting control system. Remember to plan for electrical power for the controller and discuss if a generator will be in the home and if so, what lighting loads (and the system controller) should be on it. The wiring for the remote control stations is usually low voltage wiring and in most areas does not need to be done by a licensed electrician.

In any case, you should be aware of the national, state, and local electrical codes and regulations that apply to the installation of a lighting control system and any wiring supporting it.

NEC

The National Electric Code (NEC) is the generally accepted basis for almost all state and local electrical codes. However, some areas may exceed the requirements of the NEC and require higher quality materials or more stringent cable management requirements. Be sure to know what is practiced in your area.

The general requirement by the NEC is for a minimum of 14 American Wire Gauge (AWG) circuit wiring protected by a 15-amp circuit breaker or fuse. There are some exceptions to this requirement, such as the wiring for doorbells and a few other low-voltage systems, but by and large, 14-gauge wiring is the standard. However, there is a trend in home construction to install 12-gauge wiring on 20-amp circuits, which has become a standard in some locales.

If given a choice, you should use the heavier 12-gauge wiring and the 20-amp circuit breaker. This larger wiring will provide the lighting system with brighter lights, better energy efficiency, and far fewer tripped circuit breakers or blown fuses.

Some other areas where the NEC has requirements that impact a lighting system are in the areas of the height (from the floor) for wall switches, outlets, and connectors and its specifications for acceptable light fixtures and switches.

 CROSS-REFERENCE See Chapter 27 for more information on fixture placements.

Chapters 4 and 5 of the NEC detail the requirements for low-voltage lighting systems (including lighting control systems), particularly Article 411 of the NEC. Residential lighting and lighting control systems come under the requirements specified in Article 411 and UL (Underwriters Laboratories) 2108, and the components installed in these systems must comply with the requirements of these regulations.

The primary issues to consider when installing a lighting control system to comply with the NEC regulations are that the lighting control panel must not be placed in close proximity of the home's main electrical panel, and any relays installed in the lighting control panel must be protected by a circuit breaker or fuse. Be sure that all components of the lighting control system conform to NEC Section 110-10 and Article 411 regulations and any applicable UL, CSA, or other fire safety testing authority guidelines.

All elements of the total control system must be considered and matched to the circuit and its over-current protection devices (circuit breakers or fuses). The NEC refers to this rating as a component short-circuit current rating (SCCR). Remember that if any one component in the entire system doesn't comply with the applicable regulations, the entire system is not in compliance.

Installation Safety

Your safety and that of your customer are the intent of the NEC and the other electrical and fire safety regulations that govern the components and installation of lighting control systems. To ensure a safe and effective installation, here are some guidelines you should follow:

1. Ensure that all devices to be installed are matched to the voltage level of the circuit to which they are to be attached.

2. Turn off the power supply of the control system and turn off the electrical supply on its circuit and the main electrical panel before you begin installation.

3. Test all newly installed wiring for continuity prior to connecting it into the lighting control panel.

Completing the Installation

The following steps should be used to complete the installation of a lighting control system:

1. Power up the system control panel following the manufacturer's instructions.

2. Install all local control devices and test them locally, room by room.

3. Test the remote control devices.

4. Program the preset lighting scenes and set local station functions. Test all scene settings to ensure they are properly set.

5. If scheduling and what-if situations programming are in use, test and observe these functions during complete cycles.

Chapter Review

PLC lighting control uses the electrical wiring to send command signals to control switches and devices. In X-10 technology, each device is coded by a letter (A–P) and a number (1–16). The PLC devices typically used are switches, plug-in modules, hard-wired modules, and control devices.

A hard-wired lighting control system can consist of local wall-mounted controllers, or it can be a whole-house system integrated into a programmable controller. The devices that can be included in hard-wired lighting system are a system controller, several types of special purpose modules, remote stations, and sensors.

The lighting system controller includes the microprocessor, clock, and operating memory. Multi-zone systems may have a single controller or require multiple controllers. The system controller typically has a user interface that consists of a keypad or keyboard and a display.

Control stations in the individual rooms allow occupants to control the lighting loads/lamps in the room, or around the house, individually and by scene control. In addition to simple on/off and dimming control, some control stations can be programmed to control outside systems.

Sensors can be used to detect occupancy and daylight levels. The sensors used for this purpose are motion or occupancy detectors and photo sensors.

A wireless lighting control system provides the same functionality as PLC and hard-wired systems, with the exception that the control of the lighting control switches and devices is by RF communications. The devices used in a wireless lighting control system, include system controllers, wireless control switches, relay modules, remote stations, and sensors.

The most powerful benefit of a lighting control system is automated or logical control that can be programmed to provide scheduling, lighting scenes, and what-if situations. Programmed lighting control commands are executed in what-if situations, where time, day, and sensor inputs are tested to determine the activation of certain lighting scenes.

A lighting load is the amount of energy consumed to provide a certain level of illumination in a space. The two types of loads that must be considered are inductive loads and resistive loads. Electrical devices with moving parts create an inductive load. A resistive load provides resistance to the flow of electrical current. Lighting load is determined by the amount of wattage used by the lamps connected to a single control. Volt-amps, or voltage-amperes (VA), measure the value of an AC circuit's current (A) times its voltage (V).

Lighting scenes are preset combinations of lighting levels that provide lighting for a variety of activities. Lighting scenes are typically associated with automatic controls.

A lighting zone is an area where a lighting scene is established. If any part of a lighting zone prevents the desired lighting effect from being achieved, it may be necessary to divide the zone into multiple lighting zones.

The various types of exterior lighting scenes that can be created are landscape lighting, safety lighting, and security lighting.

The National Electric Code (NEC) is the generally accepted basis for almost all state and local electrical codes. The general requirement by the NEC is for a minimum of 14 AWG circuit wiring protected by a 15-amp circuit breaker or fuse. Residential lighting and lighting control systems are specified in NEC Article 411 and UL (Underwriters Laboratories) 2108.

Questions

1. What two types of lighting controls are generally used in most residential lighting control systems?

   A. Dimming

   B. Inductive

   C. Photocell

   D. Switching

2. What is the type of lighting control that has the ability to range the amount of light emitted by a lamp from off to the lamp's full capability?

   A. Dimming

   B. Inductive

   C. Photocell

   D. Switching

3. True or False: A switching control has the ability to lower a lamp to 50 percent of its lighting capability.

   A. True

   B. False

4. What type of lighting control sensor involves the use of IR sensors?

   A. Daylighting

   B. Occupant-sensing

   C. Scheduling

   D. Preset

5. What type of technology uses AC power lines to transmit lighting control system signals?

   A. Bus

   B. Data networking

   C. Wireless

   D. PLC

6. What device is the primary unit of a lighting control system?

   A. Remote station

   B. Relay module

   C. Breaker module

   D. System controller

7. Which part of the NEC specifies the requirements for lighting control systems?

   A. Article 411

   B. Section 110-10

   C. UL 2108

   D. SCCR

8. A watt is equivalent to a

   A. Foot-candle

   B. Volt-amp

   C. Lumen

   D. KVA

9. Which of the following is not a design consideration for lighting scenes?

   A. Light color

   B. Color of the lighting fixture

   C. Room objects

   D. Room size

10. Which of the following best describes a lighting scene?

   A. A preset combination of lighting levels each designed for a certain activity

   B. The area covered by a preset lighting set

   C. One or more rooms for which lighting is defined

   D. Multiple lighting zones

Answers

1. **A and D.** Lighting control systems have the option of either dimming the lamp of a fixture or switching it on or off.

2. **A.** The only other choice available that makes any sense at all is switching, and it has only on or off settings.

3. **B** (False). Switching controls are all or nothing devices.

4. **B.** Motion or occupancy detectors are used to turn on the lighting of a room when a room is occupied or someone enters the room.

5. **D.** PLC technology is most commonly implemented as X-10. The other choices do not apply in this case.

6. **D.** The other choices are optional devices in any lighting control system, but the system needs a controller unit.

7. **A.** NEC Chapters 4 and 5 are the general references, but Article 411 is specific to lighting controls.

8. **B.** Foot-candles measure the amount of light needed to illuminate a 1-square foot that is 1 foot from a light source, and a lumen measures the intensity of that light. KVA refers to kilo-volt-amp.

9. **B.** The customer may have a preference, but it hardly matters to the lighting scene.

10. **A.** Lighting scenes for a room are used to preset certain lighting patterns, typically matched to certain activities.

CHAPTER 29

Troubleshooting and Maintaining a Home Lighting System

In this chapter, you will learn about
- Maintenance activities for a lighting control system
- Diagnostic and troubleshooting procedures for a lighting control system
- Troubleshooting power line control (PLC) control devices in a lighting control system

Unfortunately, lighting control systems are rarely "set-'em-and-forget-'em" affairs. There are certain services and tasks required to maintain the system, including its lamps, remote controls, and programming.

This chapter focuses on the maintenance tasks and services you should perform on a customer's lighting control system to keep a home's lighting system working as designed. It also covers the procedures used to troubleshoot and diagnose a lighting control system, with an emphasis on systems installed on PLC technology.

Maintaining a Lighting Control System

The maintenance activities for a lighting control system primarily involve ensuring the lighting levels and controls desired by the homeowner are maintained. The purpose of the lighting control system is to provide the type, mix, and level of lighting the system was designed to produce, all controlled easily. However, there are a number of factors that can contribute to a lighting system failing to perform as expected.

In the context of home technology integration and home automation certifications, the maintenance activities for a lighting control system are

- Preventive maintenance
- Control changes
- Manufacturer upgrades

Preventive Maintenance

A preventive maintenance plan should be developed and regularly executed for all control systems in an automated home, including the lighting control system. The purpose of a preventive maintenance plan is to maintain the system in proper working order and to prevent or detect problems early on.

At minimum, preventive maintenance should be performed on the lighting control system once a year. Every task in the maintenance plan must be completed and a written record indicating what was done and who did it produced.

The maintenance plan should include, at minimum, the following activities:

- Checking all connections and visible wiring
- Cleaning the control panels and keypad controls
- Cleaning any fans and motors in the control panel
- Verifying the lighting load of each circuit
- Applying any control changes or lighting adjustments desired by the homeowner
- Creating a backup of the control panel programming
- Updating the system's maintenance log

Check Connections

The connections at the lighting system control panel should be checked and verified for proper contact. This check should include both a visual check and an electrical check using a multimeter to ensure electrical continuity and voltage for each line in the system.

You should also visually inspect the condition of the exposed wiring for deterioration of the insulation or conductors. If a problem is found, the problem and your recommended solution should be brought to the attention of the homeowner.

Cleaning

The interior of the control panel should be cleaned to remove any dust or other debris that may have accumulated. Avoid using a standard vacuum cleaner to prevent the introduction of high levels of static electricity to the controller's circuits. Use either a special-purpose vacuum cleaner (the type recommended for cleaning the inside of computers works best) or a can of compressed air to clean the inside of the control panel.

The exterior of the control panel should also be cleaned. First, use a nonstatic cloth (such as the 3M Electronics cleaning cloth) to remove any dust on the exterior of the controller and the keypad, if one is present. Use a nonsudsing cleaner to clean the exterior of the controller. In most cases, the manufacturer's documentation should indicate the acceptable cleaning solutions that can be used. These same procedures should be used to clean the keypad, dimming, and switch controls throughout the home.

Check Fans

If the lighting control system has a cooling fan, verify that the fan is working properly. The fan should be cleaned regularly to ensure proper airflow to the circuits inside the controller. Use compressed air to blow away any dust collected on the fan's blades. Avoid using any liquids to clean the fan. Also clean the exterior and interior grills, if any, of the fan assembly.

Check Lighting Loads

It is possible that the homeowner may have replaced an original lamp with one that is outside the designed operating limits of a lighting circuit and inadvertently increased the lighting load of the circuit. If the current lighting load of a circuit is outside the operating tolerances, this situation should be explained to the homeowner, and the lamp should be replaced with one that brings the circuit into its designed load.

Check with the homeowners to see if they wish to have any or all of the lamps in the home replaced. If they so desire, replace the lamps, retaining any good lamps as spares for the homeowner.

Control Changes

The homeowner may wish to change one or more lighting scene or control level of the lighting system. If so, make the necessary programming changes and thoroughly test the system to the homeowner's satisfaction.

Also check with the manufacturer for any controller or system upgrades that can be applied. You should understand the effects of any upgrades to the system and make a recommendation to the homeowner on whether or not the upgrade should be applied. Some manufacturers issue accumulative upgrades that allow some upgrade levels to be skipped, and others issue incremental upgrades that must be applied in every case. After applying any system upgrades, retest the system thoroughly to ensure it's functioning properly.

NOTE Many manufacturers issue maintenance bulletins with recommended upgrades. Another good place to find information about upgrades to the system is the manufacturer's website.

Back Up the Controller

Regardless of whether programming changes are made or not, a backup of the controller's programming should be created. In some cases, this may be only a print out of the programming statements or commands. In other cases, it may be possible to create a backup to a removable media (such as a USB drive or a CD-RW disc), especially if the controller is programmed from a PC.

A copy of the backup should be kept at the home and another copy should be stored in the project folder off premises.

Maintaining Maintenance Logs

The importance of maintaining a maintenance log that records all maintenance activities is not often realized until a problem arises that can be traced back to a maintenance action performed in the past. The most common types of troubleshooting problems are those caused when another problem is fixed. Maintaining a maintenance log that records every action, repair, upgrade, and even preventive maintenance provides another technician with a history of the types of actions a system has required.

Table 29-1 illustrates an example of a simple maintenance log form and the types of information that should be recorded.

Date	Activity	Technician	Comments
1/5	Clean controller interior	HH	Dust heavy; should clean more frequently
1/5	Clean controller exterior	HH	Dusty; clean more frequently
1/5	Check wire contracts	HH	Normal
1/5	Continuity check	HH	Normal
1/5	Backup controller	HH	Copy to HO; copy to office

Table 29-1 Sample Preventive Maintenance Log

Manufacturer Upgrades

Most control system manufacturers continue to upgrade and improve their systems and upgrade packages, or perhaps just software, is released periodically. Not every system requires every upgrade. However, those installed systems that are actively using the features affected by the upgrade or modification should be alerted to its availability for possible application. The choice remains the homeowner's as to whether this type of maintenance is performed or not, but the homeowner can't make an informed choice unless they are made aware of the benefits and risks of applying the upgrade.

Newer releases of software and hardware may also improve the operation of a system or correct an issue that had to be omitted completely from an installation or used in a limited way. Again, it is the homeowner's decision whether to upgrade, but communication of all possible improvements provide her or him with the information needed to make that decision.

Troubleshooting Lighting Control Systems

Before beginning any other diagnostic or troubleshooting activities, your first action should be to debrief the homeowner on the nature of the problem he or she is experiencing with the lighting system. Especially in an integrated system environment, a problem may be showing up as a lighting issue when, in fact, it could be a problem with another subsystem or the structured wiring. After gaining a full understanding of the problem from the homeowner, you can begin your activities to isolate the problem and repair it.

Debriefing the Homeowner

Feedback from the homeowner is maybe the best way to learn about performance problems on a newly installed lighting control system. Debrief the homeowner to learn if the lighting scenes are still effective; if scheduled lighting scene changes occur when they should; if there are problems with lighting levels in any room, zone, or on a particular fixture; and if the lamp life on a particular fixture or lighting group is less than it should be.

Troubleshooting Lighting Controls

When a problem is identified with a distributed or stand-alone relay or dimmer switch, the best place to start your investigation is at the switch in question. You'll use a different repair approach on hard-wired switches, stand-alone switches, or PLC switches.

Troubleshooting Hard-Wired Switches

Hard-wired lighting controls generally have one of two problems if they aren't working correctly: the switch itself is faulty or a problem has developed with its wiring. If the switch is bad, it should be replaced, but never assume that is the only problem. The switch failing could very well be caused by a problem on the alternating current (AC) wiring, such as a short or open circuit. So, check the switch for scorch marks or other causes for its failure, and also verify the characteristics of the AC connections using a multimeter.

Relay switching controls, like those controlling an incandescent lamp, have relatively simple problems and are generally easy to troubleshoot—for example, problems such as a broken toggle switch, no power, or bad wiring. However, dimmer controls can be a bit harder to troubleshoot.

One reason dimmer controls can be harder to troubleshoot is that there are several different types. Further, they have more internal parts to go bad. Table 29-2 lists some of the more common problems that dimming controls may have.

Problem	Diagnostic	Troubleshooting
Lamp remains off	Is power available to the dimmer?	Verify the AC connection before checking the dimmer control.
	Is the circuit breaker tripped or the fuse blown in the electrical panel?	
	Is a rotary dimmer or push-button control connected to AC power?	
	Is only one dimmer in a room not working?	If shorting around the dimmer powers the lamp, change out the dimmer control.
Lamp remains on	Does the lamp remain on after disconnecting the neutral wire?	The dimmer's thyristor is likely bad. Replace the dimmer control.
Lamps flicker	Are the incandescent lamps flickering and the lighting cannot be controlled up or down?	The dimmer is bad and should be replaced.
Lamps flicker at some adjustment levels	Is there an electronic transformer on the circuit?	A dimmer for incandescent lamps cannot be connected to a leading-edge transformer. The dimmable ballast cannot be connected to a failing-edge transformer.
Dimmer range is limited	Does the dial turn the full distance without adjusting the lamp to its full range?	Change the Min or Max setting on dimmer.
Other dimmer performance problems	Is the impedance on the lighting cable 25 kilo-ohms?	Test the impedance on the lines linking the dimmer to the fixtures.

Table 29-2 Troubleshooting Dimmer Controls

Troubleshooting Stand-Alone Lighting Controls

Stand-alone controls that control only a single lamp or multiple lamps connected to a common lighting circuit are much like hard-wired controls in terms of what areas should be diagnosed for a problem. There are three major areas you should investigate, and all three should be checked each time, even if you think the problem is obvious: the control, the wiring, and the lamp or lamps being controlled.

Troubleshooting PLC Lighting Controls

A common problem with X-10 and other PLC controls is that the device coding for one or more control modules is incorrect. Each X-10 device is identified to the system with a unique combination of a house code and a unit code that is typically set using two dials located on the device (see Figure 29-1). In larger homes, each zone can be coded to a different house code, with each unit within the zone numbered serially.

Another common problem with PLC systems can be the phase of the electrical current on the AC lines. The electrical phase, especially if different electrical phases are present on a home's wiring, can cause problems for lighting control systems that use PLC to communicate with controlled switches/devices. If some devices in a powerline lighting control system work and others don't, the nonworking devices could be on a different phase of the house wiring from those connected to the control unit that serves the signal.

Another common problem with powerline systems is that voltage spikes on the AC lines can independently trigger modules. If this is a common occurrence in a home, a spike suppressor or phase filter should be installed on each phase at the main electrical panel.

Figure 29-1

The house code/ unit code dials on an X-10 device

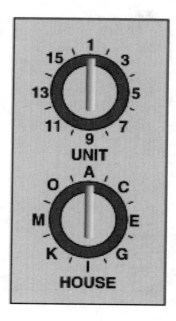

The problem of modules operating independently can also be caused by power dips (short sags in the voltage) or brownouts (longer sags in the voltage). Many powerline lamp modules include a local control feature that allows the module to be turned on or off using the switch on the lamp or device connected to it. The local control feature operates by sensing changes in the voltage level, either up or down, and a sag or spike can cause the module to turn on or off. If this problem occurs frequently, the local control option should be defeated or the modules replaced with modules that don't have this feature. Of course, another option is to provide backup power at the main electrical panel.

Powerline systems are also susceptible to line noise on the AC circuits. Many TV sets generate electrical noise and dump it onto the AC lines. If you suspect that a television or other appliance is affecting the power line control, plug the problem device into a line filter to isolate it from the AC circuits.

Hard-wired intercom systems that transmit over house wiring can block powerline signals if they are left in transmit or talk mode. If this problem exists in a home, there are limited possibilities for resolving the issue. Try changing the lighting control system to a different phase of the electrical system or install phase couplers on the electrical panel. However, these changes may not solve the problem. Unfortunately, installing a wireless intercom is not an answer either. For some reason, PLC controllers and wireless intercoms cannot both work in the same house.

Here is a list of things to avoid when using powerline-controlled switches and control modules:

- **Lamp modules**   Don't use a lamp module to control appliances, fans, fluorescent lamps, any incandescent lamp greater than 300 watts, or any lamp that has a built-in dimmer.

- **Grounded modules**   Always use a grounded module when controlling a grounded device.

- **Wall switch modules**   Don't use a dimmer wall switch module to control fans, appliances, fluorescent lamps, and any lamp less than 60 watts or incandescent lamp with more than 500 watts. Don't use a dimmer wall switch module to control an outlet into which somebody may plug an appliance, fan, or vacuum cleaner. Relay wall switches are available for controlling these types of loads.

Troubleshooting System Controllers

If a problem develops with the system controller of a lighting control system, in most cases the problem is related to power: the AC power to the enclosure is interrupted, the AC power to the controller is interrupted, or the controller's internal power supply has failed.

NOTE   Of course, a problem with a system controller could be related to programming, but every make and model of lighting control systems has fairly unique command sets. There is no way I can really address those issues here. If you suspect a controller problem may lie in its configuration, check the manufacturer's documentation and your programming setup.

PART VII

AC Power and Phase Shifts

When the AC power in a home produces two different currents from its main electrical panel, the different currents are said to be in different phases. Several factors can cause phase shifts, such as inductance, reactance, resistance, and so on, but at some point the electrical system is carrying electrical power waves that are identical in every respect, except for their timing.

Figure 29-2 illustrates two electrical currents that are in different phases. Current A and Current B are identical, but Current A peaks and troughs at different times from Current B. If powerline devices are on different phases, the receiving station may not properly interpret the command signals transmitted across the AC wiring. The effect is very similar to attenuation on a copper data cable when the signal attempts to move between phases.

A cure for phase shifts is the installation of a phase coupler at the electrical panel.

Troubleshooting Load Control Modules

If a relay or dimmer module is failing or performing erratically, check the power source to the module or replace the module itself. However, if you suspect the module is a malfunctioning zone control, check the data line connections and check for continuity and impedance to ensure they conform to the manufacturer's specifications. Also, verify the ground connection for the main power supply to the enclosure.

Verify the connecting cables between the modules mounted in the lighting control system's enclosure. If the ambient room temperature where the enclosure is located is warm, make sure the enclosure's exhaust fan is properly functioning and clean. The modules may be overheating, which may cause them to fail or function intermittently.

Common Lamp Problems

Some problems are common to all lamps. Table 29-3 lists a few of the most common of these problems.

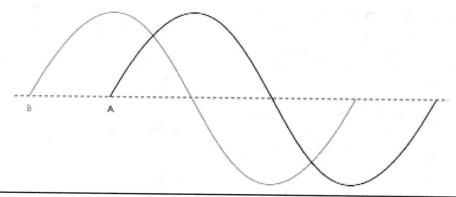

Figure 29-2 Two AC currents that are out of phase

Problem	Diagnostic	Resolution
Lamps flickering	How long have the lamps been installed?	A lamp must burn in for around 100 hours before it will produce initial lumens (full light). This includes fluorescent lamps, which should be burned in before dimming.
	Is the line voltage constant?	Test the line voltage to the lamp and to the lighting control for constant current.
	Is the HVAC blowing air across the lamp?	Change the direction of airflow away from the lamp, so that the temperature of the lamp remains constant.

Table 29-3   Common Problems with Lighting System Lamps

Incandescent Lamps

Incandescent lamps are fairly easy to troubleshoot because the problem is typically one of only a few possibilities: the lamp is burned out, the glass bulb of the lamp is cracked or broken, or the lamp is not getting electricity. Table 29-4 lists common problems with incandescent lamps that you should eliminate when troubleshooting a lighting system with this type of lamp.

The most common problem with incandescent lamps is burnout. While every bulb has an average life rating, all this means is that half of a batch of lamps last longer than the average and half do not. Table 29-5 lists the average life ratings for common incandescent lamp bulbs.

Problem	Diagnostic	Resolution
No light from lamp	Is the lamp burned out or defective?	Replace lamp.
	Is the lamp properly seated in its socket?	Remove the lamp and check the socket for good metal-to-metal contact; reseat the lamp.
Short lamp life	Is the voltage supply too high?	Check circuit to correct over voltage situation.
	Is the lamp subject to vibrations or sudden jarring?	Replace with compact fluorescent or rough-duty lamp.
Lamp bulb has deposits	Is the lamp cracked?	Check for moisture around the lamp and correct; replace lamp with silicone-coated lamp.
Lamp bulb blistering or bulging	Is the operating temperature too high?	Check the wattage of the lamp and match it to the fixture; replace the lamp.
Lamp in recessed fixture burns out too quickly	Does the lamp conform to manufacturer's recommendations?	Recessed fixtures build up heat; too high a wattage or the wrong type of lamp may cause failure sooner than expected.
Lamps brighten or dim when other fixtures are turned on or off	Is the AC power neutral connection properly wired?	Check the neutral connection in the main electrical panel or any subpanels.

Table 29-4   Troubleshooting Incandescent Lamps

	Wattage	Average Life (Hours)	Minimum Lumen Output
Table 29-5 Incandescent Lamp Average Life and Lumen Output Ratings	100	750	1670
	75	750	1150
	60	1000	840
	40	1500	440

Fluorescent Lamps

Fluorescent lamps and fixtures have more components that can fail. Troubleshooting a fluorescent lamp or fixture is a bit more complicated than it is with an incandescent lamp, as evidenced by the length of Table 29-6. The good news is that there are several common failures, and they are the easiest to resolve. Table 29-6 lists common problems with fluorescent lighting systems.

Problem	Diagnostic	Resolution
Lamps do not start or start slowly	Are the lamps properly aligned in their sockets?	Reseat the lamps in their sockets.
	Are the sockets cracked or broken?	Replace the fixture.
	Is the fixture defective?	Install a good lamp to determine if problem is the lamp or fixture.
	Is the ballast defective?	Replace the ballast.
Good lamps are not lighting	Is the manual reset on starter pressed?	Press reset button on the starter.
	Is the starter defective?	Replace the starter.
	Is the ballast defective?	Replace the ballast.
	Are the lamp and ballast compatible?	Check the labels of the lamp and ballast and replace the lamp with a compatible lamp.
	Is the lamp dirty?	Clean the lamps and ballasts.
	Is the line voltage correct?	Check the line voltage and make necessary repairs.
	Is the fixture wiring correct?	Compare the wiring against the wiring diagram on the ballast's label and correct as needed.
	Is the ballast working properly?	Replace the ballast.
Lamp has short life	Is the lamp burned out?	Replace the lamp; some lamps fail earlier than others. If problem continues, check the line voltage.
	Are the ballast and lamp compatible?	High-output (HO) lamps and very high-output (VHO) ballasts (or vice versa) are not compatible; replace lamp with correct type.

Table 29-6 Troubleshooting Fluorescent Lamps

Problem	Diagnostic	Resolution
Ballast cycles continuously	Is the line voltage correct?	Check the line voltage.
	Are the lamps good?	Replace lamps to isolate the problem as a ballast problem.
	Is insulation covering part or the entire fixture?	Make sure that the ceiling or wall insulation isn't covering part of the fixture, especially the ballast. Too much heat causes the ballast's thermal protector to cycle.
	Are fixtures mounted to the ceiling designed for that use?	Some fixtures require air space for cooling purposes. Replace the fixture with one designed for ceiling mounting.
Lamp starts too slowly	Is the ballast a rapid-start or instant-start type?	Replace rapid-start ballast with a compatible instant-start ballast.
Lamp will not start	Is the ambient temperature below 50 degrees Fahrenheit?	Many ballast require a minimum starting temperature of 50 degrees Fahrenheit or higher.
Lamps are noisy	Is the ballast securely mounted?	Check the ballast mounting and other loose fixture components that may be vibrating.
	Is the sound rating of the ballast appropriate?	Check the sound rating of the ballast and either replace it or mount it remotely to the fixture.

Table 29-7   Troubleshooting Fluorescent Lamp Ballast Problems

The ballast can often be the cause of a problem in a fluorescent fixture, especially in dimmable fixtures. If the lamps in a problem fixture work in another fixture, then the problem is likely either the ballast or starter, or it's power-related. If the problem is the ballast, it should be replaced. Table 29-7 lists a few problems specific to a failing ballast.

Troubleshooting HID Lighting

High-intensity discharge (HID) lighting is a general term used to describe any lamp that uses a gas-filled arc tube which operates at much higher vacuum conditions than those used in fluorescent lamps. HID lamps are named by the type of gas contained in their arc tube, such as metal halide, mercury vapor, and high-pressure sodium lamps.

Troubleshooting an HID lamp is very much like troubleshooting fluorescent lamps. Most of the problems, beyond burned out lamps or failed ballasts, are related to power and grounding issues. HID lamps must be matched to the ballast in use to prevent lamp or ballast failure. Another common problem is the use of the wrong lamp in a fixture. For example, metal halide and high-pressure sodium lamps are physically interchangeable, but cannot be interchanged electrically.

If an HID lamp fails immediately after being installed, check the impedance on the AC line. HID lamps are negative impedance devices and require a current-limiting ballast.

PART VII

HID ballasts provide an HID lamp with three functions: the proper starting voltage, the proper operating voltage, and conditioning the current for a particular type of HID lamp. If an HID lamp is not working properly, the problem is either the lamp or the ballast, or both.

Lighting Control System Maintenance Plans

In order to maintain a lighting control system in top working order, there are certain activities that should be performed as a part of a regular periodic preventive maintenance program. Whether the person performing these activities is you or the customer isn't as relevant as the fact that they are performed, and performed regularly.

Lamp Disposal

State and federal regulations govern the methods that can be used to dispose of lamps and ballasts removed from a lighting system. Fluorescent and HID lamps contain mercury, and ballasts contain polychlorinated biphenyls (PCBs), two potentially hazardous waste materials.

The U.S. Environmental Protection Agency (EPA) controls the disposal of fluorescent and HID lamps under the Resource Conversation and Recovery Act (RCRA), which treats these lamps as hazardous waste. As such, these lamps must be disposed of in hazardous waste landfills or recycled. Under the RCRA, they cannot be dumped in a general solid waste landfill or burned. However, recently some newer (and more expensive) lamps have been designed to meet the requirements of the EPA and can be disposed of as general trash.

Prior to 1979 magnetic ballasts contained PCBs, which are also considered hazardous material. A magnetic ballast has a service life of around 25 years, so many are still in service. Many newer magnetic ballasts are now manufactured without PCBs and are labeled as "No PCBs." However, without that marking, you must assume the ballast contains PCB and must be handled according to the EPA regulations.

Chapter Review

Feedback from the homeowner may be the best way to learn about performance problems on a newly installed lighting control system. Debrief the homeowner to learn if the lighting scenes are still effective; if scheduled lighting scene changes occur when they should; if there is a problem with lighting levels in any room, zone, or on a particular fixture; and if the lamp life on a particular fixture or lighting group is less than it should be.

The maintenance activities of a lighting control system primarily involve ensuring the lighting levels and control desired by the homeowner are maintained. The maintenance activities are performing preventive maintenance, applying control changes, and applying manufacturer upgrades. Troubleshooting and diagnostics of reported problems can also be an integral part of a sound maintenance program.

A preventive maintenance plan should be developed and regularly executed for the lighting control system. The purpose of a preventive maintenance plan is to maintain the system in proper working order and to prevent or detect problems before they become major. At minimum, preventive maintenance should be performed on the lighting control system once a year.

A backup should be made of the lighting system controller's programming each time preventive maintenance is performed. One copy of the backup should be kept at the home and another copy should be stored in the project folder off premises.

The importance of maintaining a maintenance log that records all maintenance activities is not often realized until some point in the future when a problem arises that can be traced back to a maintenance action performed in the past.

Hard-wired lighting controls generally have one of two problems: the switch itself is faulty or a problem has developed with its wiring. Relay switching controls, like those controlling an incandescent lamp, have relatively simple problems (broken toggle switch, no power, or bad wiring) and are generally easy to troubleshoot.

A common problem with PLC controls is that the device coding for one or more control modules is incorrect. Each PLC device is identified to the system with a unique unit code that is typically set using one or two dials located on the device. Another common problem with PLC systems can be the phase of the electrical current on the AC lines.

If a problem develops with the system controller of a lighting control system, in most cases, it's related to power: the AC power to the enclosure is interrupted, the AC power to the controller is interrupted, or the controller's internal power supply has failed. If a relay or dimmer module is failing or performing erratically, check the power source to the module or replace the module itself.

In order to maintain a lighting control system in top working order, certain activities need to be performed as a part of a regular periodic preventive maintenance program.

Questions

1. When you are troubleshooting a power line lighting control system, the modules on one electrical circuit are working properly, but the modules on a second electrical circuit work intermittently, if at all. What electrical issue may be causing this problem?

    A. Faulty wall outlet modules

    B. Line noise on all circuits

    C. Different electrical phases on separate circuits

    D. Faulty lamp modules

2. What record should be maintained for an installed home system?

    A. A detail of installation activities

    B. A log that lists repair actions only

    C. A log that lists maintenance activities only

    D. A log that lists all maintenance and repair activities

3. Which of the following steps should be included in a comprehensive preventive maintenance program for a lighting control system?

   A. Clean fans

   B. Apply manufacturer upgrades

   C. Verify lighting loads

   D. Identify new or replacement systems now available that could be installed

4. What action should be taken before beginning any diagnostic or troubleshooting activities?

   A. Retesting the system

   B. Disconnecting all controls

   C. Debriefing homeowner

   D. Applying all manufacturer upgrades

5. What should be verified or reset when a single X-10 control module is not functioning properly?

   A. House code

   B. Unit code

   C. PLC device model number

   D. PLC device serial code

   E. A and B

   F. A and D

6. What electrical activities on AC lines can independently cause modules to activate on a PLC lighting control system?

   A. Voltage spikes

   B. Voltage sags

   C. Brownouts

   D. Electrical noise

   E. All of the above

7. If you suspect a zone load control module or zone control is failing, which of the following should you troubleshoot?

   A. The AC power connections to the control

   B. The connections to devices and controls connected to the control module

   C. The data line connections before and after the zone control

   D. Replace the control unit

8. What is likely the problem when a dimmable fluorescent lamp is exhibiting intermittent problems?

   A. Lamp

   B. Fixture

   C. AC power

   D. Ballast

   E. A or D

   F. A or C

9. If a problem is isolated to a lighting system controller, what are likely the primary issues?

   A. Power

   B. Data connections

   C. Programming

   D. Revision level

· 10. What is the best source of information regarding upgrades and revisions to a lighting system controller?

   A. Trade magazines

   B. Product bulletins

   C. Troubleshooting logs

   D. Manufacturer's website

Answers

1. **C.** PLC signals can suffer attenuation when attempting to bridge electrical phases.

2. **D.** Maintaining a maintenance and repair record of all actions performed on a system can reduce the guesswork when troubleshooting a system.

3. **A, B, and C.** When performing maintenance, it may not be the appropriate time to up-sell a customer on newer models or systems.

4. **C.** If some time has passed since the last maintenance or repair activity, the information the homeowner has about the system's performance and any needed repairs, corrections, or upgrades can be critical to tracking down any reported problems.

5. **E.** X-10 PLC devices have both a house code and a unit code. Even if the X-10 device has only a unit code, it must be assigned uniquely within the system or house.

6. **E.** Any abnormal electrical events can cause PLC devices to activate independently or cause PLC command signals to be lost due to attenuation.

PART VII

7. **A.** The first troubleshooting step should be to check the AC power connections and, if a DC transformer is in use, the DC power connections.

8. **E.** Problems with fluorescent lamps are typically either the lamp or the ballast. However, when the problem is with a dimmable fluorescent lamp, the first place to begin your troubleshooting is with the ballast.

9. **A.** Power is often the contributing factor to a system controller problem.

10. **D.** The manufacturer's website can provide troubleshooting and upgrade information about a device.

PART VIII

Home Control and Management

601

CHAPTER 30

User Interfaces

In this chapter, you will learn about
- Types of user interfaces
- Handheld, wall-mount, tabletop, and remote control technologies
- User interface issues

Our love of remote controls is evidenced by our viewing and listening activities. In fact, it is not unusual for someone to spend several minutes searching for a misplaced remote control, rather than taking a few seconds to just walk over to the TV, DVD player, VCR, or stereo to change the program, station, disc, or track.

Despite what this may say about us, when you're working with a distributed audio or video system or a whole-house control system, managing the source or control devices can mean walking to a room that may be on the opposite side of a home. One of the primary justifications for installing an integrated home control system is convenience. And handheld remotes, keypads, and other local controls are some of the most important conveniences the system provides.

In this chapter, we take a look at the various types of controls that can be used with automated home systems, including how they work and what the issues are with different types of user interfaces.

Types of User Interfaces

Nearly all consumer electronics these days come with some type of remote control. This includes stereo equipment, televisions, DVD and VCR players, and even video cameras. In addition, home systems, such as lighting, audio, video, and computer systems can also be operated from some form of a remote control. Types of remote control devices range from simple to complex (and expensive), including:

- Handheld remotes and key fobs
- Keypads
- Touch screens
- Voice-activated controls
- Telephone

- Computer
- PDAs and web pads
- Remote access devices
- Hands-free controls

Handheld Remote Controls and Key Fobs

There are a wide variety of remote controls in many sizes and shapes and with many functions. Essentially, any small remote control that will fit into a normal-sized person's hand can be considered a handheld remote control. However, some of the remote controls that could be included in the handheld category are larger in size and are better categorized into the user interfaces that I describe below.

Handheld remote controls are usually infrared (IR) or radio frequency (RF) devices that are 1.5 to 3 inches wide and from 4 to 10 inches in length. Some models control a single device, and some have the capability to control multiple devices, although only one at a time.

Remote controls that are small enough to attach to a key ring are categorized as key fob remote controls. These types of remote controls are typically single-device remote controls that are used to open doors, turn on lights, control appliances, and similar type functions in a home.

Most key fob remote control devices transmit RF signals to an RF receiver built into the device or devices they control. However, because this type of control typically has a fairly narrow broadcast range, they are considered to be line-of-sight devices.

Some key fob remotes are programmed to a single device, but replacement models are available that can be programmed to control any compatible device. Some can be set to control two separate devices, such as the garage door and the lighting system, and, as we discuss later in the chapter, perhaps even at the same time.

Power line carrier (PLC) key fob controls have the capability to control as few as one to as many as eight receivers and transceivers. They can directly control a device plugged into the receiver or use a transceiver to communicate with a home automation controller using PLC signaling.

Keypad Controls

Although keypads have been covered in several places in this book, they have not been discussed in the context of their function as user interfaces. Keypad controls are typically wall-mounted devices that allow for a single control function, such as raising or lowering the volume of the speakers in a room or zone or controlling multiple devices such as lights in a single zone or throughout the house.

Another type of handheld remote control is an IR device that communicates with base units that are inserted into an AC outlet and sends a PLC signal over the electrical lines to turn electrical devices, such as appliances, lamps, and the like, on or off.

Like remote controls, keypads can have hard keys and soft keys, a single light-emitting diode (LED), or a liquid crystal display, and they can be single function or multiple function controllers. Figures 30-1 and 30-2 show examples of the different levels and

Figure 30-1
A wall-mounted keypad control can be used to control one or more devices.

Photo courtesy of Vantage/Legrand.

Figure 30-2
A multiple zone security controller

Photo courtesy of Home Automation, Inc.

configurations of keypad controllers. Some keypad-style remote controls are full-color touch screen displays that are made to mount in or on the wall, or sit on a tabletop.

Touch Screen Controls

When a user touches a touch screen with a finger, the resulting action is similar to pressing a button or clicking a mouse. A touch screen device is a video display screen, typically an LCD screen, which serves as an input and interface device.

Figure 30-3
A touch screen controller can be wall-mounted or used on a table top.

Photo courtesy of Elan Home Systems, LLC.

There are two touch technologies that can be used, light pen (an external device) or touch overlay (an internal device), both of which output an XY coordinate signal. Of the two touch screen technologies, the touch overlay is by far the most commonly used touch screen system for residential systems. Touch screen controllers, like the one shown in Figure 30-3, can be hard-wired to a centralized home system controller or interfaced to multiple control devices using RF or IR signals.

Touch screen devices are available as wall-mount and tabletop devices or as stand-alone devices that communicate with a base unit using IR or RF signals. The base unit can be self-contained or be connected to a home system controller using PLC or hardwire connections. Examples of these devices are

- **Wall-mount touch screen devices** Wall-mounted devices can be small, with only a few touch screen "soft keys," or they can be large, with a multifunction, multilayer touch screen program.
- **Tabletop or handheld touch screen devices** Figure 30-4 shows an example of a tabletop touch screen controller that can also be a handheld controller. This type of touch screen device is commonly used to control a whole-house system.

Voice-Activated Remote Controls

If changing the channel on the television or controlling the volume of the stereo without getting up from your chair still involves too much physical effort, new remote control devices are entering the market that allow users to control a variety of devices using only spoken words. While these products seem perfect for the hopelessly lazy, the original intent was to assist disabled or infirmed consumers who are unable to operate a conventional remote control.

Voice-activated remote controls are voice-recognition devices that digitize and store the sound wave pattern of spoken command words.

Figure 30-4
A multiple
device table top
controller

Photo courtesy of Marantz America, Inc.

NOTE Before most voice-activated systems can be used, the user must "train" the device or its controller by recording a list of command sounds or words. On most devices, just about any spoken sound can be recorded to control one of the remote's functions, although most come with a list of as many as 60 suggested voice commands that can be recorded by as many as four family members. After the controller has been trained, whenever it receives sound, it searches through its database of recorded sound prints. When it finds a match, it performs the action associated with that sound, just as if a button had been pressed on a keypad.

Voice-activated remote controls typically operate either through recognized voice commands or through their keypad. Voice-activated controls continuously receive sounds from their immediate vicinity. Each sound it receives is then converted to a digital pattern and matched to stored digital images of prerecorded sounds. Should the digital image of a received sound match a digital image of a recorded sound, the function or action associated with the recorded sound is activated. For example, if the sound recorded to control turning on a TV set is "picture," whenever the person who recorded this command speaks the word "picture," the voice-activated remote transmits an IR signal to the TV to turn it on. The words used to designate the remotely controlled actions should be chosen carefully so that normal conversation doesn't create a series of random electronic device events.

Telephone Controls

If you are away from home and you want to arm your security system, you can turn on a few lights or interact with any of the other automated functions in your home, if the home automation control system is configured for it. These functions can all be done by the homeowner simply placing a telephone call to the home and pressing a few phone number pad keys.

Figure 30-5

A mobile telephone that can also be used as a media remote control.

Photo courtesy of AwoX.

Many home automation controllers have either built-in or optional phone control modules that allow a homeowner to access the controller and enter commands using a telephone number pad on a phone either inside or outside the home after entering a security code.

Another approach to using a telephone as a remote control is a group of newer devices that combine a cordless or wireless telephone with a universal remote control. The handset of these devices doubles as both a telephone handset and a multiple-device IR or RF remote control. Figure 30-5 shows a touch screen version of a mobile telephone that can also be used as a remote control.

Computer Controls

Home systems can be controlled through a personal computer through the installation of specialized software and a few peripheral devices added to the computer, such as IR or RF transmitters, Electronic Industries Alliance/ Telecommunications Industry Association (EIA/TIA) 232 or parallel ports, PLC interfaces, Universal Serial Bus (USB) or Institute of Electrical and Electronic Engineers (IEEE) 1394 ports, and the like. A PC can be used to control a home system through a variety of interfaces:

- **Automation** Home automation control software can convert a PC into a home automation controller that can be connected into the home automation network in very much the same way as a stand-alone home system controller. By definition, a PC can be connected into the UTP and coaxial wiring of a home's structured wiring and used to control the home system by transmitting control commands over the cabling. However, a PC can also be interconnected into a PLC network to transmit control commands across the AC wiring of the home to PLC controllers and modules throughout the home. The type of network system installed will dictate the type of software system used on the PC.

- **External control and communication** A PC connected to the Internet provides the option for a homeowner to access the home automation system running on the PC from outside the home using the Internet. This allows the homeowners to check the system status and to make changes to the security, lighting, or other systems or to be alerted to certain events while they are away from home. Some of the home automation control software systems include features to send an e-mail, or to dial a pager or cell phone in the event of an alert.

- **PC control**   The computer user can use specialized software to directly control the lighting, appliances, and other PLC devices throughout the home by indicating the desired result to the software that then generates the appropriate commands to carry out the user's wishes.

- **Remote control**   With the appropriate transmitters (IR or RF) attached, a PC can also be used as a remote control device to control the on/off switch and other functions of devices within its line of sight (IR) or broadcasting range (RF). Specialized software is required to facilitate this control, along with an IR or RF transmitter.

In general, the software used for home automation or device control is designed to run on one or more specific operating systems. However, in nearly every case, the software uses a graphical user interface (GUI, pronounced "gooey") that allows functions to be selected using a mouse.

PDAs and Web Pads

Personal digital assistants (PDAs), those handheld appointment books, notepads, phone directories, and personal information manager devices, can also be used as a remote control for several consumer electronic devices, such as a TV, VCR, CD, DVD, and even home control systems. By adding special software (and perhaps a hardware chip) such as the Nevo software from Universal Electronics and proprietary offerings from Sony and Palm, a PDA can be used as a full-featured, customizable universal remote control. PDA remote control systems display stylus-selectable soft-keys on the PDA display that can be programmed to virtually any device. Communication from the PDA can be via IR or wireless RF that transmits using the IEEE 802.11b wireless communications standard, also called wireless fidelity (Wi-Fi). The benefit of using 802.11b communications in place of IR or other short-range RF technologies is that the device then has a range of about 330 feet (100 meters). To complete the wireless remote control system, the central home automation controller needs to be connected to an 802.11b network access point (AP) that supports Ethernet networking.

Web pad is a generic term used for tablet PCs and other wireless, self-contained, handheld computers. Web pads are generally full-featured PCs that allow users to surf the Internet, receive and send e-mail, and perform most PC-based functions, including data entry. By loading software on the web pad, the computer can become a control device and touch screen.

Web pads are wireless RF devices that transmit using the IEEE 802.11b wireless communications standard, Wi-Fi. Just like the PDA with wireless control, web pad devices, or the central home automation controller it is controlling, need to be connected to an 802.11b AP that supports Ethernet networking.

Remote Access Control

It is also possible to control an automated home system remotely, in this case from outside the home, using the Internet or a connection from one PC to another. However, this does require some special software, in most cases.

If the home automation system is controlled by software running on the home computer network, then all that is required is PC remote control software, such as pcAnywhere from Symantec or GoToMyPC from Expertcity. This allows you to either dial up using a modem-to-modem connection or a broadband connection. You then access the home network either directly or over the Internet. Once the remote PC is connected to the home network, the home automation controller can be managed and the settings changed on any of the subsystems linked to the controller.

Special telephone modem interfaces are also manufactured for specific home automation subsystems. For example, Honeywell offers a product called the Telephone Access Module (see Figure 30-6) that allows remote computer access to control the heating, ventilating, and air conditioning (HVAC) subsystem of a home.

Hands-Free Controls

When you hear the term *hands-free*, you may wonder how the control works if you don't use your hands in some way, like touching a handheld remote button, keypad, or touch screen. Hands-free means the control is triggered by motion sensors located throughout the house. They sense the presence of someone within their scan pattern and act

Figure 30-6
The Honeywell
Telephone Access
Module provides
remote dialup
access to control
an HVAC system.

Photo courtesy of Honeywell, Inc.

according to a preset plan initiated by the earlier input of a command through traditional user interfaces. For example, you could turn on the music in the kitchen on the wall keypad so that when you walk down the hall from the kitchen and into the living room, the lights and music come on as you enter the room and go off in the kitchen because no one is there. Later, when you leave the living room and head back to the kitchen, the reverse occurs: lights and music go off in the living room and on in the kitchen.

Control Characteristics

There are some characteristics that are common to all types of remote controls, regardless of their size, their shape, or the device or devices they control. The most common of these characteristics are

- **Hard key** A key or button on the remote control activates a fixed function and is linked to a single command code. The term *hard key* is derived from "hard-wired." Hard keys are permanently labeled on the face of the remote or on the key itself for the function it performs; they are the buttons that have been printed or silk-screened with their associated function.

- **Soft key** On some remote controls, especially multiple device controls, the buttons on the side of the display screen are not typically preassigned as hard keys. These buttons are *soft keys*, and their functions are assigned logically, depending on the device selected for control. The soft key's function is displayed adjacent to the button on the screen. When a soft key is pressed, it performs different functions for the device currently selected depending on the settings displayed on the remote's user interface.

- **User feedback** On many remote controls, the user feedback is only an LED that lights when a button is pressed and a command code is activated. On other remote controls, an LCD is used to give visual feedback and can display status messages, command functions, show the device menu, and on some remote devices, assign the functions of soft keys. Some models have auditory feedback, such as a click or sound when the button is engaged. On some models, the user interface is both hard keys and a touch screen offering a full array of soft keys.

The operating characteristics that all forms of remote control devices use to determine if a particular type of remote control is appropriate in a given situation are

- **Display** Depending on the type and size of a remote control device, its user feedback display could be as simple as a single LED or an LCD display, or as advanced as a full-color touch screen display.

- **Ease-of-use** A remote control should be easy to use and intuitive, and its keypad should be logically laid out, including its hard keys and soft keys. Related keys should be grouped together and clearly labeled. Consistent placement of the same keys on every keypad or screen (LCD or touch screen) is critical for ease of use. The graphics should be easy to read, even for those who might be "small font-size challenged," and pleasing to the eye.

- **Two-way versus one-way communications**   Many higher-end remote controls (wall-mounted keypads and tabletop controls) are two-way devices that are able to display system feedback and status information. Most handheld remote control devices are capable of only one-way communications. The benefit of two-way communication is obvious: you know if the command you sent was received and gave the desired result. With one-way communication, you will often hear the saying "Send and pray" because you have no idea if the command sent was received and executed.

Remote Control Technologies

Handheld remotes come in a wide variety of shapes and sizes, but only two types of signal transmission technologies are used:

- Infrared (IR)
- Radio frequency (RF)

The basic difference between an IR remote control and an RF remote control is line-of-sight and operating range. An IR remote control uses a light beam to communicate with the device being controlled and must have a direct line-of-sight to operate within a fairly limited area. On the other hand, an RF remote control broadcasts radio waves and doesn't require a line-of-sight. In fact, many RF remotes don't even need to be in the same room as the devices they control, because they have a much larger operating range.

IR Controls

The core technology of an IR device is, of course, IR signaling. Infrared light is invisible light that is just below the red band of the visible light spectrum. On virtually all IR devices, a red glass or plastic lens or filter is placed over an LED to produce the red color most people associate with IR devices.

IR Command Codes

Each button on an IR remote control's keypad is associated with a command code. When a button is pressed, the circuitry inside the remote modulates the frequency of the light beam to send the number associated with its command function for that button in a binary-encoded format. For example, if the number one is pressed on the keypad, the remote modulates the light beam to send the command value of one as a binary number.

Command Code Sets   The Infrared Data Association (IrDA) has developed a standard coding scheme for computers and peripheral devices, but in the home entertainment market, unfortunately, no standard command code set exists, and many manufacturers use a proprietary code set to control their devices. Table 30-1 lists a sample of IR command codes used by Sony for its television systems.

Command Code	TV	DVD
0	I	I
3	4	4
11	Enter	Enter
14	Channel guide	Return
16	Channel up	Search reverse
18	Volume up	Search forward
19	Volume down	Channel up
21	Power	Power
30	Brightness up	Program
43	Clock, time	Play mode
59	Jump, last	Step forward
66	Video 3 select	Disc 3
78	Cable select	Mega control
96	Menu, guide	Slow reverse
107	Auto program	AV center

Table 30-1 Sony IR Command Codes

Notice in Table 30-1 that the codes for a television and the codes for a DVD have only a few basic commands in common, demonstrating that even within the products of a single manufacturer, the IR command codes can vary for different devices.

Command Code Modulation The most common method of modulating an IR signal combines amplitude key shifting and turning the carrier on and off. When a button on the keypad is pressed, the command value associated with it is generated by the circuitry inside the remote. Then, a modulated signal where the frequency is raised and lowered to represent the binary digits (see Figure 30-7) is sent to the light producing circuitry. The light-emitting part of the remote then transmits the command code values by turning the carrier frequency on and off in a pattern that represents a one, zero, or the short spaces between the digits and the long spaces separating the commands.

Figure 30-7 Remote control command codes are represented as a modulated signal.

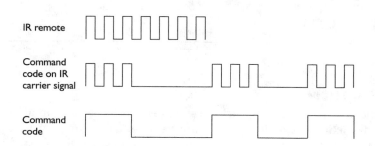

IR remote

Command code on IR carrier signal

Command code

Binary Number System

The binary number system represents values using ones (1) and zeros (0) to indicate whether a position, which has a value of two to a certain exponential power, is included in the number being represented or not.

For example, the binary number 101 indicates that 2 to the power of 0 and 2 to the power of 2 are included in the value it represents, which in this case is the decimal number 4. The positional values of a binary number are listed in Table 30-2.

In an 8-bit binary number, the positional values of each bit are as follows:

2^7	2^6	2^5	2^4	2^3	2^2	2^1	2^0
128	64	32	16	8	4	2	1

When a 1 is present in a position, it indicates that the positional value of the position is included in the number represented. For example, in the number 00010010, the values included are

2^7	2^6	2^5	2^4	2^3	2^2	2^1	2^0	– Powers of two
128	64	32	16	8	4	2	1	– Positional values
0	0	0	1	0	0	1	0	– Binary digits
0	0	0	16	0	0	2	0	– Included values

Table 30-2 Binary Positional Values	Position in Binary Number (Right to Left)	Power of Two	Decimal Value
	8	2^7	128
	7	2^6	64
	6	2^5	32
	5	2^4	16
	4	2^3	8
	3	2^2	4
	2	2^1	2
	1	2^0	1

So, in this example, 00010010 represents 16 plus 2, or 18.

Using the information in Table 30-1, the IR command code of 18, which is volume up on a Sony system, would be modulated and transmitted as the binary value of 10010.

RF Controls

Radio frequency devices, including remote controls, emit an alternating current electromagnetic field (radio wave) using a wide range of frequencies and wavelengths. RF devices, such as cordless and cellular telephones, televisions, radios, baby monitors, and most garage door openers, are found in most homes.

A garage door opener is a commonly used example of an RF remote control. When the button on the handheld device is pressed, the unit transmits a radio wave signal in a fixed frequency. The receiving device is searching for signals in just that frequency, and when it detects the right radio waves, it closes the contact, which opens or closes the door. Of course, this type of system isn't foolproof because the garage door opener's receiver has no way to sense the identity of the source of the signal, only that it was in the proper frequency.

RF remote control devices include a transmitter with an encoder circuit, and the controlled device includes a receiver and a decoder circuit. The operation of an RF remote control is very similar to an IR remote control (discussed in the last section). Pressing a button on the remote activates the encoding circuit, and the transmitter sends out radio waves. The receiving device decodes the transmitted signal and applies the command transmitted.

Most handheld RF remote control systems, especially the all-in-one and universal models, replicate the IR command signals associated with each device controlled after receiving the RF command. Because so many consumer electronic devices are equipped with IR receivers for use with IR remote controls, to use an RF remote control with any IR device, the RF signal must be converted into an IR signal, as illustrated previously in Figure 30-7.

An RF remote control is typically a universal or an all-in-one device with the capability to control up to ten different source devices from anywhere in a home. The remote control unit communicates by beaming RF signals to a base unit that is in a line-of-sight orientation to the source devices to be controlled. The RF base then issues IR control signals to the source device selected on the remote control.

RF remote controls can also be integrated with PLC systems to control centrally located devices such as those that change the media (music or video) being delivered to a room or zone. These systems work much the same way as the universal remote control described in the preceding paragraph. RF receivers are either base stations or built into wall-mounted keypads, switches, or they are just receivers that convert the RF signals into IR signals that are PLC-based. These signals transmit over the AC lines in a home to another PLC device that converts the PLC-based signal into an IR signal that is "flashed" to the equipment to be controlled.

Chapter Review

Nearly all consumer electronics and most home control systems include some form of a remote control. Types of remote controls include handheld remotes and key fobs, keypads, touch screens, voice-activated, telephone, computers, and PDAs and web pads.

A small remote control that fits a normal-sized person's hand is considered a handheld remote control. Handheld remote controls are usually IR or RF devices that range from 1.5 to 3 inches in width and from 4 to 10 inches in length. Some models control a single device and some control multiple devices one at a time.

Keypad controls are wall-mounted devices that allow for a single control function or the ability to control multiple devices. Keypads have hard keys, soft keys, or both as well as one or more LED indicators, and some have LCD displays.

A touch screen device is a video display screen engineered to also serve as an input or interface device. Most home touch screen devices use resistive LCD screens. Other touch screen technologies are acoustic wave, capacitive, NFI, and IR.

Voice-activated remote controls are voice-recognition devices that digitize and store the sound wave pattern of spoken command words. After a voice-activated control is "trained," it searches through its database of recorded sound images for any sound it receives. If it finds a match, the action associated with that sound is activated.

Many home automation controllers have either built-in or optional phone control modules that can be used to access the home system controller and enter commands over a telephone.

Home systems can also be controlled through a PC with specialized software and the appropriate peripheral devices used to execute the desired commands. PCs can be used to control in four ways: automation, external control, PC control, and remote control.

Several characteristics are common to all remote controls: hard keys, soft keys, and user interfaces. Remote controls use two types of signal transmission technologies: IR and RF. The difference between an IR remote control and an RF remote control is the line-of-sight and operating range. The core technology of an IR device is infrared light. Each button on an IR remote control's keypad is associated with a command code. RF devices emit an alternating current electromagnetic field (radio wave) using a wide range of frequencies and wavelengths. RF remote control devices include a transmitter with an encoder circuit, and the controlled device includes a receiver and a decoder circuit. Pressing a button on the remote activates the encoding circuit and the transmitter sends out radio waves. The receiving device decodes the transmitted signal and applies the command transmitted.

Questions

1. What are the two communications technologies generally used by handheld remote controls?

   A. IR

   B. PLC

   C. RF

   D. Bluetooth

2. Which of the following communications technologies can be used together in a remote control system?

   A. IR

   B. PLC

   C. RF

   D. HomePNA

3. What type of remote control key has a fixed function and is linked to a single command code?

   A. Hard key

   B. Soft key

   C. Touch screen key

   D. Virtual key

4. What action must be taken before a voice-activated remote control is fully operational?

   A. IR range test

   B. RF range test

   C. It must be trained.

   D. None of the above; voice-activated controls are ready for use out of the box.

5. Which of the following can be considered to be remote control devices?

   A. PDAs

   B. Touch screens

   C. Key fobs

   D. All of the above

6. Which of the following devices could be used to control a home automation system?

   A. PDA

   B. Notebook PC

   C. Laptop PC

   D. Web pad

7. What are the two ways that a PC outside the home can access a home automation controller?

   A. By modem

   B. Hard-wired

   C. Over the home network

   D. Via the Internet

8. What is the operating range of a wireless 802.11b system?

   A. 3 meters

   B. 30 meters

   C. 50 meters

   D. 100 meters

9. Which of the following is not a commonly used display type on keyboard controls?

   A. LCD

   B. CRT

   C. LED

   D. Plasma

10. A PC can be used as a system controller with which of the following system types?

   A. PLC

   B. EIA/TIA 232

   C. RF

   D. IR

   E. All of the above

Answers

1. **A and C.** PLC communicates over household AC wiring, but is not directly used in remote controls, and Bluetooth is a type of RF technology used to create a PAN.

2. **A, B, and C.** IR and PLC can be used together to access centralized devices from anywhere in a home. RF has the operating range to provide remote access throughout a home. HomePNA is not used for remote control.

3. **A.** A hard key is, in effect, hard-wired to a specific function. Soft keys and touch screen keys are virtually the same, can be programmed by the user to a desired function, and are typically aligned with a display that indicates their function.

4. **C.** Training a voice-activated device involves recording the user's spoken voice for a series of command words.

5. **D.** Any device that has some control over another device's operations, configuration, or function can be considered a remote control.

6. **D.** Actually, all of the devices listed could be used as remote controls with a home automation system and commonly are.

7. **A and D.** Once a connection is made to the system controller or to a home's data network, the effect is the same as if the remote unit were directly connected to the controller or network from within the home.

8. **D.** This is the technology used with PDAs and web pads.

9. **D.** Plasma screens are being used in television monitors, but they have not yet made their way into user interfaces on keypad controls.

10. **E.** All of the choices can be interfaced to a PC equipped with system control software and the appropriate interface ports.

CHAPTER 31

Home Control Systems

In this chapter, you will learn about
- Features of home system controllers
- Communications technologies used by controllers
- Configuring a controller

At the heart of an integrated home control system is the controller. It is like a conductor of an orchestra, directing when each instrumental section plays, how loud or soft they play, and so on. In a similar manner, the controller of a home system directs when each subsystem is activated and provides its settings, such as the volume, operating patterns, and the like. The home controller creates the total experience for the occupants of the home, just as the orchestra creates the total experience.

A home system controller is the integrator of the independent systems in the home. It pulls the home's subsystems into a single integrated system and through its control settings and programming manages a home's total environment.

This chapter focuses on the different types of home system controllers and their components, functions, and configuration. Essentially, all home system controllers perform the same basic tasks. However, this chapter covers how they go about performing these tasks.

Controller Features and Characteristics

The primary feature of any home system controller is control. More specifically, this means the controller's capability to interface, interact, and communicate with the different subsystems in an automated home.

The true benefit of installing a controller in a home system is that it consolidates the functions of the separate subsystem controllers into a single interface for the homeowner. In home subsystems, each system, such as the lighting control; the heating, ventilating, air conditioning (HVAC); the security, and the distributed audio/video, has its own separate controller and unique user interface. Often, the convenience gained from each subsystem is lost in the complexities, and possible overlapping, of the controls.

Integrating the subsystem controls into a single home control system means there is only one user interface for the homeowner to learn and manage. For example, a single button on a room controller might dim the room lights, turn on the audio, turn up the room heat, and turn on the outside lighting. Or a button labeled "Outta Here" could turn down the heat, lower the house lighting, and arm the security system. With independently controlled subsystems, each of these actions would require the homeowner to take several steps instead of using a single button, leaving nothing forgotten. The capability to set whole house environmental scenes through the push of a single button is perhaps the biggest advantage a controller-based home system provides.

Hardware- and Software-Based Controllers

Home system controllers can be either hardware-based or software-based. However, in either case, the system controller involves a computer microprocessor. A home system controller doesn't have to be a separate device installed in a control box or central panel. The controller can be a PC running home system control software from anywhere in the home.

Hardware-Based Controllers

Hardware-based controllers are specialized devices with a microprocessor for processing inputs and providing control. They are equipped with relays, input and output jacks, and a variety of optional communication ports, and they have embedded processors to provide stand-alone functionality for the home control system.

Hardware system controllers provide a variety of features, including:

- **Communications** A home control system controller typically has relay or contact closures; infrared (IR) ports; a radio frequency (RF) port; and serial RS-232 and RS-485, Universal Serial Bus (USB), Universal Powerline Bus (UPB), or RJ-45 connections for Ethernet that are used to communicate with local controls, devices, and subsystems directly.

- **Macros, modes, and scenes** Better controllers have the capability to set the operating levels and functions of different combinations of local devices to create a local scene, also called a mode or a macro.

 NOTE A macro is a setting on a controller that can be enacted with the press of a single button to send numerous commands and settings to several different devices as a part of a single control sequence.

- **Multiple-zone control** System control units have the capability to control devices in more than one room or zone of a home.

- **Reliability** Many types of hardware-based system control units have the capability to modulate the signal strength to overcome interference on the communications lines.

- **Remote access** Quality home system control units also provide the capability to access the control system remotely, using the phone line, remote portable computer, modem, or the Internet via TCP/IP.

- **User interface** A home control system is typically operated through either local keypad control, touch screens, or through software running on a web-enabled device such as a PDA or PC.

Software-Based Controllers

Several types of home control system software are available that can be installed on a PC and connected to the home network, be it the power line carrier (PLC) type or Ethernet home network.

Many of the home system control software products available are designed to work with Ethernet networking, regardless of the transmission media or technology in use. Some are specific to certain media, such as PLC, but the better systems are designed to work over any hard-wired home network operating on Ethernet protocol.

PLC software products interface to the AC power lines using Electronic Industries Alliance/Telecommunications Industry Association, or EIA/TIA (RS) 232 or 485 serial interfaces and typically use a DB-9 connector or a USB interface. Using one of these serial connections, the PC is connected to a PLC interface that provides the link to the AC electrical lines and any other PLC devices connected to the AC system. Some software control systems provide an IR interface to allow the PC to control devices with a line-of-sight connection.

Communications

A home system controller, as shown in Figure 31-1, can be connected directly to the devices it controls or it can be connected for communication with the subsystems it is sending control commands to. There are four possible ways the controller can be connected to the devices or subsystems that it must communicate with:

- Hard-wired
- IP-connected
- PLC
- Wireless

Controllers communicate with devices and subsystems and their control modules in either a one-way or a two-way direction. A home system controller may communicate with the lighting system using a one-way direction, but it may communicate with the room control requesting a lighting scene change using a two-way direction. When the room control requests the scene change, the controller signals the lighting control module to activate a preset lighting configuration (one-way) and then notifies the room control (two-way) to confirm the change has been made.

Figure 31-1

A rear view of a home control system controller

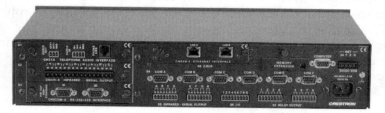

Photo courtesy of Crestron Electronics, Inc.

One-way communications are used to transmit control signals to devices or subsystem controllers or to receive signals from subsystem controllers. The home system controller may have only one-way communications with a subsystem controller, which then has two-way communications with the devices under its control.

Two-way communications are used to send or receive command requests to and from subsystem controllers and room control devices and then to transmit command signals and status information to these same devices.

When the controller issues commands to a subsystem controller, it must use the signal format and coding scheme understood by the subsystem. Most robust control systems are able to communicate in a variety of ways including relay/contact closure, IR, RF, RS-232, RS-485, and TCP/IP. So, in some ways, a home system controller also acts as a translator and interpreter between the various components and subsystems connected to it.

Hard-Wired Controllers

Some subsystems, such as telephone, security, and surveillance systems, have their own unique signal formats that require a direct connection to the controller and to a subsystem module. The subsystem module can either be integrated into the controller or act as a stand-alone controller connected to the home system controller. It receives, interprets, and transmits signals in the proper format. The subsystem module can also communicate with the controller's main circuitry, often a microprocessor, to hand off signals with a system-wide impact. For example, a disarm signal could be received by the security system control module, this signal could be passed to the home system controller, which could then first communicate with the lighting module to turn up the house lighting and then tell the music system to play jazz.

Hard-wired control systems are the most reliable type of communications links that can be used to connect a system controller to subsystems and room controls. However, they usually work on proprietary communications protocol. In addition, they are usually the most expensive of the available options.

Most hard-wired systems communicate over the Cat 5e cabling installed as a part of a structured wiring system or over a proprietary cabling system. The controller can be connected to the network cabling using two primary methods: using a network adapter that is either built into the device or available as an add-on module (see Figure 31-2) to the controller, or through a connection made in the distribution panel. Although Figure 31-2 shows an Ethernet interface card, most systems also have interface modules for IR, PLC, and other communications protocols.

Another advantage of a hard-wired control system is that it is able to perform multiple tasks at one time. Because of the data speeds supported by unshielded twisted-pair (UTP) cabling, a hard-wired system is able to communicate at a faster data transfer speed and still maintain its reliability. Hard-wired systems are best installed during new home construction, as they are difficult to install with the necessary wiring as part of a retrofit or remodel project.

Photo courtesy of Crestron Electronics, Inc.

Figure 31-2 A controller network interface add-on module

IP-Connected Controllers

A variation on the hard-wired approach to communications in a home control system is an Internet Protocol (IP) control system. IP control systems interconnect the home system controller and the room controls into the home computer network to create what amounts to a home intranet that is called a controller-attached network (CAN). An intranet is a network contained within a home, as opposed to an Internet, which extends way beyond a single home.

On an IP control system, the communication protocol is Ethernet-based TCP/IP. Each device connected to the network is assigned an IP address and the network communicates with it using that address.

PDC Controllers

Perhaps the most affordable type of home control system is Powerline control (PLC) systems, which are more commonly known as X-10 or CEBus. PLC uses a home's existing AC power lines to communicate.

The heart of a PLC home control system is its network control unit, which serves to integrate and control the various PLC units and modules. A variety of PLC system controllers are available, ranging from software for PC to stand-alone controllers. PLC systems are easy to install because the network media is already installed in the walls of a home (the electrical wiring). Here's an overview of the advantages of PLC communications:

- They use existing AC power lines for communications media.
- Access is available to the PLC network through any AC outlet.
- They are compatible with data transmission and control signal transmissions.
- They are capable of transmitting audio signals (although not typically very well).
- The system can be added to and expanded over time; it is not necessary to install everything at the time of new construction.

However, there are some disadvantages to PLC communications as well:

- PLC signals are very susceptible to interference and electric noise on a circuit from electric motors, thermostats, dimmer controls, television signals, and radio signals picked up by the wiring.
- Electrical noise on the AC lines can lower the transmission speeds of PLC signals.
- PLC systems do not provide a high-level of security because they transmit over insecure media.
- Attenuation can be an issue because of line noise and interference.
- PLC-enabled devices can be more expensive than their standard networking counterparts.
- PLC-enabled devices are only capable of transmitting one signal at a time, which is transmitted sequentially, since the signal requires time to travel over the electrical lines.
- No standard has been established for PLC communications.
- Windows computer operating systems do not include drivers for PLC products.

In spite of its disadvantages, PLC can be used in certain situations fairly effectively, such as controlling light fixtures and electric devices in a single room or smaller-size home (less than 2200 square feet).

PLC/UPB Controllers

Perhaps the most affordable type of home control system are *powerline communications* (PLC) systems, which are more commonly known as X-10 or CEBus. Another similar and interoperable standard for powerline communications is Universal Powerline Bus (UPB). Both PLC and UPB use a home's existing AC power lines to communicate.

PLC   The heart of a PLC home control system is its network control unit, which serves to integrate and control the various PLC units and modules. A variety of PLC system controllers are available, ranging from software for PC to standalone controllers. PLC systems are easy to install because the network media is already installed in the walls of a home (the electrical wiring). Here's an overview of the advantages of PLC communications:

- They use existing AC power lines for communications media.
- Access is available to the PLC network through any AC outlet.
- They are compatible with data transmission and control signal transmissions.
- They are capable of transmitting audio signals (although typically not very well).
- The system can be added to and expanded over time; it is not necessary to install everything at the time of new construction.

However, there are some disadvantages to PLC communications:

- PLC signals are very susceptible to interference and electric noise on a circuit from electric motors, thermostats, dimmer controls, television signals, and radio signals picked up by the wiring.
- Electrical noise on the AC lines can lower the transmission speeds of PLC signals.
- PLC systems do not provide a high-level of security because they transmit over insecure media.
- Attenuation can be an issue because of line noise and interference.
- PLC-enabled devices can be more expensive than their standard networking counterparts.
- PLC-enabled devices are only capable of transmitting one signal at a time, which is transmitted sequentially, since the signal requires time to travel over the electrical lines.
- No industry-wide standard has been established for PLC communications.
- Windows operating systems don't include drivers for PLC and additional software is required.

In spite of its disadvantages, PLC can be used in certain situations fairly effectively, such as controlling light fixtures and electric devices in a single room or smaller-size home (less than 2200 square feet).

UPB   Universal Powerline Bus (UPB) is an emerging industry standard for the communications over electrical wiring between controlled devices in a home automation system. UPB, which was introduced in 1999 by PCS Powerline Systems, is based on the X-10 PLC protocol, but dramatically improves the reliability and speed over other PLC standards.

Compared to the PLC protocols, especially the X-10 protocol, UPB has some advantages:

- UPB is compatible with the PLC protocols.
- UPB is capable of transmitting audio systems, although at the present time the quality is still suffering.
- UPB has a transmission reliability of over 99 percent.
- UPB uses a 40-volt transmission versus the 4-volt transmission of PLC.
- UPB is as much as 30 times faster than PLC.
- Electrical noise interference issues are greatly reduced and filtering is not required.
- UPB supports up to 64,000 addresses.
- Windows Vista includes UPB support.

Wireless Controllers

Wireless control systems can communicate using IR, RF, or IEEE 802.11b standards. Most often, wireless control systems, room, zone, and whole house remote controls transmit command and control signals to the central home system controller through the air using radio waves.

The IEEE 802.11b standard, also known as wireless fidelity (Wi-Fi), is a wireless communications standard that operates in the 2.4 GHz RF band. The 802.11b offers up to 11 Mbps of bandwidth in a range of around 150 feet indoors. At the present time, 802.11b is the most commonly used wireless networking standard. Table 31-1 lists the characteristics of the wireless networking standards on the market.

The advantages of wireless networking include the elimination of cabling between a remote control device and the system controller, as well as the portability provided by the lack of wiring. Another advantage is that the system is fast enough to provide bandwidth to overcome most interference problems, which are highly probable.

The disadvantage of wireless networking is its operating frequency. All of the 802.11 standards and the Bluetooth standard operate at 2.4 GHz, the same frequency used by many cordless phones, some garage door openers, baby monitors, and other wireless products commonly found in a home. In addition, wireless digital subscriber lines (DSL), or wireless Internet access to a home, also operates on this frequency. However, although the possibility for interference is real, as mentioned earlier, the bandwidth and data speeds are high enough that in most cases, interference can be overcome.

In its best application, the use of wireless communications should be limited to transmissions between room and zone controls and the system controller only. This is for two reasons. First, there aren't many wireless subsystem interface modules available; and second, the traffic stream between the system controller and the subsystem control unit needs to be reliable. In this case, wiring is the best option. In a home that has structured wiring installed, the best approach is to interconnect the home system controller into the hard-wired environment for communications between the system controller and the subsystem controls over the structured wiring.

Standard	RF Band	Maximum Bandwidth	Indoor Range
802.11a	5 GHz	54 Mbps	25 to 75 feet
802.11b	2.4 GHz	11 Mbps	150 feet
802.11g	2.4 GHz	54 Mbps	150 feet
802.11n	5 GHz or 2.4 GHz	248 Mbps	230 feet
Bluetooth	2.4 GHz	720 Kbps	33 feet
ZigBee	2.4 GHz	250 Kbps	246 feet

Table 31-1   Home Network Wireless Communications Standards

Controller Setup

When installing a home system controller, there are some basic steps you should follow to ensure the control system meets the needs of the homeowners and that the installation goes efficiently. On all systems, you should work on much of the system configuration prior to visiting the site for installation and setup. The programming needs to be done very carefully. It is much more effective to find the problems and resolve them at the workbench then out in the field. Troubleshooting on site is inevitable, but you want to keep it to a minimum.

The steps you should use to set up and configure a home system controller are

1. **Interview the homeowners**   To be sure that the controller will best serve the needs of the homeowners, you should discuss the lifestyles and desires of the homeowners to help define the setup of the system. Also discuss system options and capabilities in detail to gain an understanding of the homeowners' expectations of how the system will perform once it is in place.

2. **Set up control devices and programs**   Here is where you layout the devices to be controlled and the desired programming. Be sure to follow the basic configuration of the controller according to the manufacturer's specifications and guidelines. Documentation is critical at this point because you will probably need to refer to it in the field. Remember, it is much easier to preprogram the controller in advance off site and then just install it on site and upload the programming as necessary.

3. **Program macros and scenes**   During this step of the process, you should program and document any scenes or macros into the controller for testing on site. Some systems include interactive macro creation software, but for most, the process involves opening a new macro and recording the keypad buttons using a logical order of operations, as if the user were pressing the buttons to request the sequence of actions included in the macro. Again, follow the programming documentation supplied by the manufacturer.

4. **Design and create user interfaces**   Most home system controls and many touch screen and keypad controls allow you to customize the placement and the function of hard keys and soft keys to meet the needs and wishes of the users. Using the information gained during your interview with the homeowners, design and set up the user interfaces on the control devices to meet the homeowners' requirements. Again, remember that documentation is critical. It is often beneficial to share the physical layout of the buttons on keypads and touch screens (an actual drawing of the control device with buttons labeled) with the homeowner prior to programming them, as they may have changes they would like and it is easy to make them initially.

5. **Install the controller**   Now is the time to visit the site and physically install the controller unit or the control software on a local PC. Load the setup and programming you've done previously, and you're ready for the next step.

6. **Connect communications links and test local controls**   You should now connect and test the communications links with the control functions for both the local controls and the system controller, at least at a basic operational level. For example, does the request to dim the lights in a room result in the lights actually being dimmed? The settings may not be exactly right at this time, but the objective is to ensure the controller and the local controls are able to communicate and function together. Also check that any status messages that should be returned to a local control with a user interface display are displaying properly. You should test all controls thoroughly and correct any problems you encounter before proceeding to the next step.

7. **Acceptance testing**   When the system is completely set up and configured properly, perform a complete test of the system to ensure none of the homeowners' requirements have been overlooked or aren't working properly. Once you are satisfied that the system is working as specified, assist the homeowners in a complete run-through of all of the system's functions and actions. If the homeowner requests adjustments or changes, make the modifications and perform this step again completely.

8. **System maintenance**   Chances are that the homeowner will want some changes to the system or the user interfaces within the first 30 days of the system's operation. In anticipation of this, you should make some arrangement, with an appropriate fee schedule, with the homeowner for a warranty, system changes, and ongoing system support.

On many systems, modifications can be made without the need for a house call, or what the communications people call a "truck roll." On systems that provide remote access, most problems or minor changes can be done by accessing the system through a modem or over the Internet and gaining access via a security code (which should be kept top secret at all times). A house call should be necessary only for major reconfigurations of the system or hardware problems, and if the system has been properly installed to the homeowner's wishes, it shouldn't be a common occurrence.

Chapter Review

A home system controller consolidates the functions of the separate subsystem controllers into a single user interface for the homeowner. Home system controllers can be hardware-based or software-based.

Hardware-based controllers are specialized devices with a microprocessor for processing inputs and control. They are equipped with relays, input and output jacks, and a variety of optional communication ports, and they have embedded processors to provide stand-alone functionality for the home control system. Many home system control software products work with Ethernet networking, regardless of the media in use, although some are specific to certain media.

Home system controllers can be connected directly or can use communications media to transmit signals to the devices controlled. Four methods used to connect a controller to the devices or subsystems it controls are hard-wired, IP-connected, PLC, and wireless. Home system controllers use either one-way or two-way communications.

Hard-wired control systems are the most reliable of the communications links that can be used to connect a system controller to subsystems and room controls. However, they usually operate on proprietary communications protocol and are usually the most expensive of the available options. IP control systems interconnect the home system controller and the room controls into the home computer network. On an IP control system, each device connected to the network is assigned an IP address and is communicated to across the network with that address. The most affordable home control system is PLC, which uses a home's existing AC power lines to communicate. Wireless control systems communicate using IR, RF, or IEEE 802.11b standards.

When installing a home system controller, some basic steps should be followed to ensure the control system meets the needs of the homeowners and the installation goes efficiently. The steps that should be used to set up and configure a home system controller are interview the homeowners, set up control devices and programs, program macros and scenes, design and create user interfaces, install the controller, connect communications links and test local controls, perform acceptance testing, and provide system maintenance.

Questions

1. Which of the following best describes the basic function of a home system controller?

   A. Centralized maintenance

   B. Centralized interface

   C. Consolidation of separate subsystem controller functions into a single user interface

   D. Remote access for system maintenance

2. Of the following, which is not a commonly used communications technology or protocol for home system control systems?

   A. Hard-wired

   B. IP-connected

   C. PLC

   D. HomePNA

3. Of the media configurations common to home control systems, which is considered to be the most reliable?

   A. Hard-wired

   B. IP-connected

   C. PLC

   D. HomePNA

4. On what cable media are hard-wired home control systems typically installed?

   A. AC power lines

   B. Coaxial cable

   C. UTP cable

   D. 2-conductor 22 AWG wiring

5. What technology does the popular home system protocol X-10 operate on?

   A. Ethernet

   B. IEEE 802.11b

   C. PLC

   D. Wi-Fi

6. What is the indoor range of an 802.11b network access point?

   A. 25 to 75 feet

   B. 50 to 100 feet

   C. 300 to 500 feet

   D. 330 meters

7. What is the primary disadvantage of using IEEE 802.11 networking?

   A. Interference with other 2.4 GHz devices

   B. Limited system controller offerings

   C. Line-of-sight

   D. Operating range

8. Which of the following are not typically features of a hardware-based home system controller? (Choose all that apply)

   A. Communications with standard protocols

   B. Local access only for security reasons

   C. Macros

   D. Multiple-zone control

9. What should be the first step performed when preparing to install a home systems controller?

   A. Perform acceptance testing

   B. Install controller

   C. Interview homeowners

   D. Connect communications links and test local controls

10. A command sequence of several actions that can be enacted through a single button is called a(n)

    A. Automated local control

    B. Macro

    C. System interface

    D. Program

Answers

1. **C.** The other choices listed are features of a home system controller, but the home system controller's primary purpose is to consolidate the control of the subsystems.

2. **D.** HomePNA is primarily used for data networking, although some advancements are being made to apply this technology to home control systems.

3. **A.** Hard-wired systems are the least susceptible to interference.

4. **C.** UTP cable is installed as part of a home's structured wiring system.

5. **C.** Power line control (PLC) protocols include X-10 and CEBus.

6. **B.** The range of this technology depends on the construction of the home and its furnishings.

7. **A.** None of the other choices are factors with 802.11 wireless communications.

8. **A and B.** Although local access for security may sound right, most of the better home control systems offer remote access that is gained only after a security code is entered and nearly all systems are compatible to standard communications standards.

9. **C.** It's hard to know exactly what the homeowners' vision or expectations are for the control system without first discussing their lifestyles and the system and its functions in detail with them.

10. **B.** Also called a mode or a scene, macros group a sequence of commands together so they can be executed as a single command stream.

HVAC Controls

In this chapter, you will learn about
- Residential HVAC equipment
- HVAC system controls
- Designing and configuring HVAC zones

Heating, ventilation, air conditioning (HVAC) includes the equipment, ducting, and vents that either collectively or separately provide heat, ventilation, or cooling to a home. As indicated by its name, an HVAC system provides the basic environmental services: heating, cooling, and air handling, ventilation, and air quality. Home automation can extend to include controlling a home's HVAC system. This includes automating the function of the thermostat either on a whole-house or zone basis.

HVAC systems with thermostat control use standardized electrical signals to communicate with external thermostats. It's that part of HVAC systems this chapter addresses.

Residential HVAC Systems

There are several types of heating and air conditioning systems found in homes, but the primary types are forced air, baseboard and convection, hydronic, central heating, and evaporative cooling systems.

Forced Air Systems

Forced air systems use a circulating blower to move heated or cooled air into the rooms of a house (see Figure 32-1). There are two very general types of forced air systems: constant air volume (CAV) and variable air volume (VAV).

CAV Systems

CAV systems supply a constant flow of air to the whole house. The central terminal-reheat unit heats or cools its flow of air to heat or cool the coldest or warmest zone in the house. Each zone, an area of a house equipped with a zone terminal-reheat unit and controlled by a zone thermostat, then adjusts the temperature of the central forced airflow to meet its specific heating or cooling needs. These types of CAV systems are also referred to as single-duct systems and are the most common type of HVAC found in existing homes.

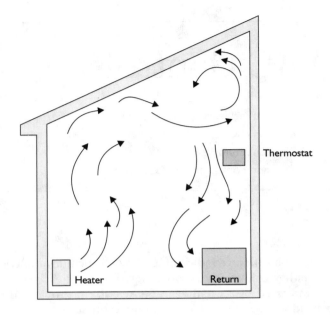

Figure 32-1
A forced air system circulates warm or cooled air to change a room's temperature.

Thermostat

Heater

Return

NOTE A terminal-reheat unit maintains a comfortable temperature in a zone by reheating or cooling the airflow to the temperature set on a zone thermostat.

In most cases, the airflow into the zone has been partially cooled or heated to a general setting by the central air-handling device. Dual-duct CAV systems supply both cool and warm air, each in its own ducting, to a mixing chamber in each zone. The zone thermostat controls the temperature of the air leaving the mixing chamber by managing the amount of warm and cold air allowed to enter the mixing chamber. This type of CAV system eliminates the need for terminal-reheat units in each zone.

VAV Systems

VAV systems supply air that is heated or cooled to a constant temperature to each HVAC zone. Each VAV zone is controlled by a thermostat that uses a damper to regulate the temperature in each room by controlling the amount of cool or warm air allowed to flow into the zone. Typically, the damper is not closed all the way, which allows some fresh airflow into each zone.

VAV systems offer a number of advantages over CAV systems, including that they cost less to purchase and install, their operating costs are typically lower, and because only those areas requiring heating or cooling receive air, they are more energy-efficient than CAV systems. However, on the downside, VAV systems don't provide much variability and flexibility when heating or cooling selected zones in a house, because there is only a single air supply and no local zone equipment.

VAV systems also do very little to balance both ventilation and temperature control, and because they generally reduce the volume of heated or cooled air flowing into any particular zone, air quality can be compromised.

Baseboard and Convection Systems

Baseboard devices installed along the baseboards of a wall, typically under a window, can provide heat by either using an internal electric heating element or the flow of air or water to a baseboard or freestanding register from a central gas or oil-fired furnace.

These units can be controlled using several methods. The most common are

- An on/off switch on the unit

- A thermostat controlling one or more local units

- A thermostat controlling the central heating device

Figure 32-2 shows an example of an electric baseboard heating unit.

Although some baseboard and most in-wall heating units include air blowers, most baseboard units use convection to heat a room. Convection heating uses the natural phenomenon of heated air rising: when the rising heated air comes into contact with the cooler temperatures of the window surface, the heat is forced outward from the window into the room.

Convection system electric baseboard units or water-flow registers are placed on the floor against the bottom edge of a wall centered under a window in the outside wall of a room. Most convection devices use either an internal electric heating element or a gas-flame heating chamber to heat a room until the room air temperature matches that of an in-room thermostat or a thermostat built into the convection unit itself.

Another type of local heating device is an in-wall electric heating unit, like the one shown in Figure 32-3. These units are either self-contained devices that include an electric heating element, a blower, and a built-in thermostat, or gas-fired heating chambers that reheat the airflow from a central heating system.

Figure 32-2
An electric baseboard heating unit

Photo courtesy of Cadet Manufacturing.

Figure 32-3
An in-wall electric heating unit

Photo courtesy of Cadet Manufacturing.

Those electric baseboard or heating chamber devices that are locally controlled using an in-room or in-zone on/off switch can be connected into a home control system and centrally controlled using relay switches. In those units that are controlled using a room thermostat, the thermostat is typically limited to turning the unit on or off according to its temperature settings. The units that are connected to a centralized control system through a thermostat interface can be controlled remotely.

Hydronic Systems

The term *hydronic* has recently replaced the term hot water when describing heating systems that use boiler-heated water to provide convection and radiant heating in rooms, floors, ceilings, and even walkways, patios, and driveways.

Hydronic baseboard heating is commonly found in houses built over the past 30 years or so, especially in those areas with colder winters. Well known for its efficiency and low-operating cost, hot-water heating is also making a comeback largely because of improved and more efficient oil- and gas-fired boiler systems.

Hydronic Baseboard Heating

Hydronic heat uses hot water that is heated in a boiler or some form of a water heater to transfer heat into a room or zone. For room hydronic systems, hot water is circulated through heating elements that have long, thin aluminum-finned radiators; these radiators have largely replaced the tall cast-iron radiators of the past.

The length of the radiator in a particular room is determined by how quickly heat dissipates from a room and the amount of heat required maintaining a comfortable range in that room. The room radiators are incorporated into a continuous loop of copper pipe that loops from room to room. Like other convection heating systems, hydronic baseboard units are placed beneath windows.

Hydronic systems offer several advantages: they are quiet, provide constant warmth, and are fuel-efficient. However, controlling individual zones requires a separate piping and pumping system for each zone. Even with a separate hydronic system for each zone, hydronic systems are either on or off.

In hydronic systems, a boiler heats the water, which circulates through the piping throughout a zone or the entire house. A separate pipe returns the cooling water back to the boiler or water heater. The water is circulated through the system by a circulating pump.

Hydronic Radiant Heating

Another form of hydronic heating gaining in popularity is radiant heating that is embedded or installed inside room floors, patios, driveways, walkways, and other exterior areas where the heat can be used to melt snow or ice.

To install radiant floor heating, the hydronic piping system is either attached to the underside of a floor or embedded in a concrete slab, as illustrated in Figure 32-4. Hot water or some other type of liquid running through the piping heats the flooring or concrete surface, providing warm floors and clear and frost-free exterior passageways.

Radiant heating can be zoned to separate rooms or hallways. Using multiple boilers provides more specific settings and control. How the boilers are fueled can vary from

Figure 32-4
Radiant heating
coils installed in
a room's floor

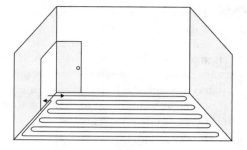

natural gas to fuel oil to electricity and even to solar energy to either directly or indirectly heat the water.

Radiant floor heating takes a long time to heat up, so it is not a likely candidate for automated control by temperature. A simple on/off remote control makes sense in situations where the home is a vacation home and not always occupied. One benefit to radiant floor heating is it removes the decorative limitations of radiators, vents, outlets, and return vents of other types of room heating.

Central Heating Units

Heating systems are typically defined by their central units, which are typically referred to as furnaces. The common central heating units are

- **Electric furnace** Inside an electric furnace are resistance wires that heat up when a current passes through them. A circulating fan passes cooler air from inside the house over the heated wires to heat the air and return it into the rooms of the house. Because no exhaust gases are produced, electric heating systems don't require venting or chimneys.

- **Electric heat pump** Many people confuse a heat pump, shown in Figure 32-5, with an air conditioning system because both are exterior devices and their appearances are very similar. Heat pumps use a specific piping system to extract heat from outdoor air, even at very cold temperatures. The heat is then transferred to a coil located inside the house. A blower then blows air over the coil, which warms the air before it is circulated into the heating zones.

Figure 32-5
An electric
heat pump

- **Gas furnace**   This type of heating unit is actually a heat exchanger that transfers heat into a home. Natural or propane gas is mixed with air brought in from outside and fired inside a heat exchanger. The exhaust gases travel through the heat exchanger and exit the home through a vent pipe or chimney. A fan circulates cooler air from inside the home over the heat exchanger. The heated air is then circulated through the home's ductwork into the rooms. Some newer gas furnace models have multiple heat exchangers that improve the heat exchange efficiency and heat the circulating air faster.

- **Oil furnace**   The operating principle of an oil furnace is very much like that of a gas furnace. The obvious difference is that fuel oil is used instead of gas vapor. Because the oil is liquid, it must first be converted into a vapor-like mist and mixed with air before it can be burned.

Evaporative Cooling

An older, but still effective, cooling system is evaporative cooling, which is also called swamp cooling by some HVAC people. Evaporative cooling works on the two principles of water evaporation and the relative humidity of the air. The first principle is that when moisture is added to air that has less than 100 percent relative humidity, the temperature of the air is lowered. The second principle is that the lower the relative humidity of the air, the greater the temperature drop will be when moisture is added to the air.

In the western United States and other dry-climate areas around the world, evaporative cooling can provide an energy-efficient alternative; it uses one-fourth less energy than compressor-based air conditioning systems.

There are three basic types of evaporative cooling systems:

- **Direct evaporative cooling**   Direct evaporative cooling devices are commonly referred to as swamp coolers because they provide the same cooling effect as a breeze blowing across a swamp, lake, or another body of water. This type of evaporative cooling simply adds moisture to a moving airflow to increase its humidity and thereby lower the temperature of the airflow. However, direct evaporative cooling requires a moving air source with air that is drier than the space being cooled. Commonly, outside air is forced through a constantly wet fiber or corrugated pad by an inner air turbine that also pushes the moistened air into a space displacing drier indoor air. To ensure that the pad stays wet, a recirculating pump pours more water onto the pad than it can evaporate. The excess water flows into a sump to be recirculated. The system replaces any water that evaporates using an automatic valve to refill the sump to a preset depth. Direct evaporative cooling systems are either on/off systems that can be controlled directly or by using a relay switch on a central home system controller.

- **Indirect evaporative cooling**   Indirect evaporative cooling systems are commonly used in larger commercial applications, but there is no reason this type of system can't be installed in a large home. Like a direct evaporative system, indirect systems use water evaporation to cool air. However, an indirect system does not increase the humidity of the inside air. Rather, it separates the wet side of the process from the dry air used to cool a space. A direct evaporative process is used to cool air or water on one side of a heat-exchanging surface, such as plastic plates or tubes.

The heat exchanger transfers the cooling to an air stream that is used to cool a space. Indirect evaporative cooling systems are used either as complete cooling systems or to supplement a compressor-based air conditioning system. These systems are essentially on/off systems and, as a result, can be controlled directly or by using a relay switch on a home system controller.

- **Two-stage evaporative cooling**   This type of evaporative cooling system uses both direct and indirect evaporative cooling to cool an airflow. In effect, the air flowing into the two-stage unit is cooled using the direct evaporative method. The cooled air is then passed through an indirect cooling system before flowing into a space.

HVAC Controls

The primary control in a HVAC system is typically a room thermostat. Some homes may have only a single thermostat for the entire house, but most newer homes have a separate thermostat in each room or zone. If you wish to include the control of the HVAC system in a home automation and control system, the HVAC control device (thermostat) must also be compatible with the type of home control media you are using.

Thermostats

When selecting a thermostat for a home HVAC system, the first rule is that it must be compatible with the HVAC system. That may sound obvious, but not all thermostats are compatible with all systems.

The more common types of thermostats are

- **220V baseboard thermostat**   This type of thermostat is different than nearly all other types because it has to be mounted to an in-wall high-voltage (220V) outlet box. It is not commonly installed in new homes and is typically being replaced.

- **Digital thermostats**   Also known as electronic thermostats, this type of thermostat features a digital temperature and set point (the point at which the HVAC system is activated) display. At the low-end price range, digital thermostats are typically mechanical thermostats with a digital display. A digital thermostat draws its operating power (for the display) from one or more batteries or from the 24V HVAC line. Other common features are the auto-changeover switch in the HVAC system between heating and cooling, capability to work with heat pump systems, and capability to be wired to an external control device, such as a motion sensor, timer, or computer-based control system.

- **Mechanical thermostat**   Mechanical thermostats are available for heating-only control as well as heating and cooling control. Some models include setback timers, but they typically don't include an auto-changeover feature. In general, mechanical thermostats are not compatible with heat pump systems.

- **Programmable thermostat**   This type of digital thermostat allows users to preset heating and cooling changes with a built-in clock (time and day of the week) using a keypad. When the conditions programmed into the thermostat are met, such as either the temperature or clock time, the thermostat activates the HVAC system.

- **Remote control thermostat** Remote control thermostats are digital thermostats that can be adjusted, programmed, or activated remotely. These thermostats allow the user to change the current set point or heating/cooling mode using a remote control device. The commands sent to the thermostat can be transferred over dedicated wiring from the controller to the thermostat or over the home's existing AC power lines using power line technology.

Other features that are available on some thermostat models are

- **Heating/cooling anticipator** Because thermostats, both mechanical and electronic, aren't always located in the same room as that receiving heat, the room can actually be overheated by the time the temperature at the thermostat reaches the set point. A heating or cooling anticipator is an adjustable setting inside the thermostat that turns off the HVAC system at a point that anticipates the desired condition, turning off the heating or cooling system early. A heat anticipator is one way to compensate for a less-than-perfect thermostat location.

- **Remote temperature sensor** In many houses, the thermostat is not placed in the best possible location, but in an adequate location where it can be easily accessed. By placing a temperature sensor in a location where it can sense the desired room or zone temperature readings accurately, the thermostat may better serve the heating and cooling needs of the homeowner, so its placement isn't as critical. A remote temperature sensor can be used to trigger the set point on a thermostat; this way, the homeowners don't have to rely on the thermostat's built-in thermometer. Remote sensors can be connected to the thermostat directly using thermostat wire or using power line technology.

Control Thermostats

Power line control (PLC) thermostats are remote control thermostats that allow the user to change the current set point or heating/cooling mode using a remote control device. The commands sent to the thermostat are transferred over the home's existing alternating current (AC) power lines using PLC technology.

There are two basic types of PLC-compatible thermostats:

- **One-way** This type of remote control thermostat carries commands to the thermostat, but doesn't have the capability to carry any feedback back to an X-10 remote control device. Some one-way control thermostats are compatible with telephone responder units that also allow the thermostat to be controlled remotely through a telephone, though they are only one-way with no feedback.

- **Two-way** This type of remote control thermostat has the same capabilities as a one-way device, but it is also able to transmit information, including the temperature, set point settings, and current mode, back to the controlling device.

Other types of remote control thermostats are currently available, including Electronic Industries Alliance (EIA)-232 and EIA-485 devices. These devices use serial interfaces to provide a reliable high-speed connection that is directly compatible with computers (EIA-232) or can be networked with other sensor and control devices (EIA-485).

HVAC Zones

Creating HVAC zones in a house can save energy as well as better serve the heating and cooling needs of different areas of the house. Many people confuse zones with independent systems where each area has a separate HVAC system. Zoning a house involves the design and installation of a series of airflow dampers that control the ambient temperature separately from other zones or areas of the house using a single HVAC system.

A single-zone system or, in other words, a single HVAC system doesn't require damper systems; the whole house is a single zone with one ambient heating and cooling environment. A multizone HVAC system has at least two airflow dampers, with each damper managing the airflow into one specific zone and being independently controlled by a thermostat.

Zoning is recommended in homes that have any of the following characteristics:

- Multiple levels or floors
- A widespread design, such as homes with separate building wings or large ranch-style layouts
- Rooms with large window surfaces
- Large open architecture areas with vaulted or cathedral ceilings, an atrium, or a solarium
- Living space in a finished basement or attic
- Rooms with exposed concrete flooring (such as in a basement)
- An indoor swimming pool or spa
- Earth-shelter houses that have only one or two exterior walls

HVAC Zone Controllers

A standard HVAC system typically has a single thermostat that controls the heating and cooling for an entire house. A zone control system connects two or more thermostats to a single HVAC system. The thermostats aren't the zone controllers; rather, there is a master zone control device that is connected to the thermostats in each zone, the HVAC system, and each airflow damper.

The master zone controller reacts to the set points of the zone thermostats and opens or closes the dampers, which are located inside the source HVAC ducts leading to each zone. In their normal state, the dampers are open, but the controller can shut them to close off the flow of heating or cooling to a zone.

The zone thermostat operates normally to call for heating or cooling according to its set points. However, the zone thermostat signals actually go to the master zone controller that controls the HVAC system and adjust the dampers according to the zone settings.

The criteria for selecting a zone controller, such as the unit shown in Figure 32-6, are the number of zones, the type of HVAC system in use, and the size of the house. The size of the house is especially important, as is if the house has more than one story or levels, such as a two-story, three-story, or a tri-level house. In these situations, the master zone control unit should include a thermal equalization capability that balances the ambient temperature of the different levels.

Figure 32-6
An HVAC zone
control unit

Photo courtesy of Residential Control Systems, Inc.

HVAC Zone Design

HVAC zoning is very difficult to add to an existing HVAC system, so for the most part, zoning is a new construction application. Not many home automation firms take on the job of designing the actual HVAC system, the ductwork, or the location of the airflow registers, so leave this part of the job to the HVAC and mechanical engineering people.

Once the HVAC system is designed, the design of the HVAC zoning can be done using the following steps:

1. **Establish the number of zones.**   Typically, a two- (or more) story house has at least two zones, but the goal is to establish HVAC zones that are roughly the same size in area. The zones shouldn't be too small, because they will be difficult to control, or too large, because they may be subject to cold or hot spots. A zone should be created for each separate climatic environment the homeowner desires, typically defined by the activities of the area. For example, a family room where the occupants may be more active can be slightly cooler than a living room where the occupants are less active.

2. **Adjust the HVAC duct plan to fit the zone design.**   Ductwork must be designed so that each zone is a separate branch of the main HVAC duct system. The damper for each zone will be installed just after a zone's ducts branch from the main duct. The volume of the ductwork branches may need to be increased to handle an increased airflow volume. Work with the HVAC specialists to design the volume of the ductwork for a system that is open all the time. Each duct in the system should be able to handle the entire airflow volume of the HVAC system. This allows the system to function normally, even when a damper is closed, without putting too much back pressure on the HVAC system and possibly damaging it. The general rule-of-thumb for increasing the size of the ductwork is to add an additional 25 percent of volume for every two zones on the system. For example, a two-zone system should be increased 25 percent; a four-zone system should be increased 50 percent; and so on.

3. **Establish the location of the dampers and thermostats.**   During the prewire stage, run two-conductor thermostat wire to the damper locations and five to seven conductor thermostat wire to the thermostat locations. If you are using remote temperature sensors with the system, that wiring must be installed as well.

Zoning Hydronic Systems

Hydronic systems are generally zoned by default, but if you wish to be able to turn the heat on or off in different areas of a home, control valves must be installed in the hydronic piping in the same way dampers are installed in the air ducts of a forced air system.

Hydronic valves (see Figure 32-7) are motorized to open and close according to the commands of the master zone controller. They open and close the flow of water through the hydronic system.

Locating a Thermostat

For the best results, a thermostat should be located on an inside wall in an area that is frequently occupied. The thermostat should be at least 18 inches from any outside walls and at least five feet above the floor. It should also be placed in an area with freely circulating average temperature air. A thermostat should not be located in any of the following areas:

- On an outside wall
- In direct sunlight or near any heat produced by any closely placed appliances
- Near or in line with a heating or air conditioner vent, a stairwell, or an outside door
- Near any device that produces electrical interference

NOTE Some thermostats are "power-stealing" units. This type of thermostat takes power from the "W" (see Table 32-1 later in the chapter) heat connection running from the HVAC system. If multiple zone control units are also being installed, don't connect a power stealing unit or an older style mechanical or anticipator type thermostat to the controller. Neither of these thermostats will work properly with an HVAC control unit.

Figure 32-7
A hydronic
motorized valve

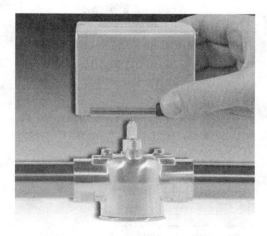

Photo courtesy of Invensys Building Systems, PLC.

Wiring a Thermostat

The wiring used to connect a thermostat to the HVAC systems must be no less than 20-gauge wire, and for wire runs longer than 100 feet, 18-gauge wire is highly recommended. Thermostat wiring is different from other wire, such as Cat 3 or 5, audio/video, or speaker wiring. Thermostat wiring has two to seven conductors of solid core wiring with the color-coding for a seven-wire cable consisting of white, red, green, blue, yellow, brown, and orange. Most HVAC central unit controls, which the thermostat wire connects to, use from five to seven conductors. However, in new construction situations, installing seven-conductor thermostat wire adds to the future proofing of the house.

Standard HVAC Thermostat   Typically, the HVAC technicians install the wiring for a central-system thermostat at the time the HVAC systems are installed. The wiring for the thermostat normally is either two- or four-conductor wiring to support either 24V or 120V systems, depending on the needs of the HVAC system and the thermostat planned into the HVAC system. If the plan is for the home system technician to install a standard thermostat, you will need to follow the thermostat manufacturer's wiring diagram. Figure 32-8 shows an example of a wiring diagram for a typical nonautomated, or noncommunicating, thermostat.

When connecting the thermostat wire to the thermostat terminals (see Figure 32-9), strip about a quarter-inch of the insulation at the end of each conductor. On most standard thermostats, the terminals are marked with either stickers or embossed letters in the thermostat's plastic that indicate which wire color should be connected to which terminal. Wrap the exposed end of the conductor wire clockwise around the terminal screw. The manufacturer's wiring diagram and documentation should also have these details.

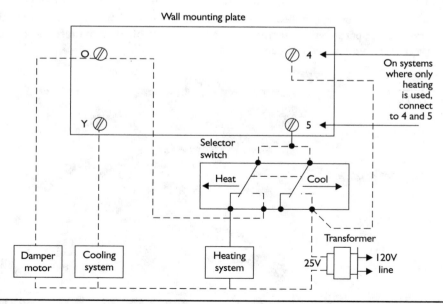

Figure 32-8   A sample wiring diagram for a standard thermostat

Figure 32-9
The wiring
on a standard
thermostat

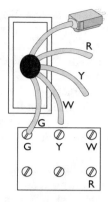

NOTE   Regardless of the type of wiring in use for the thermostat, you should turn off the power at the AC circuit breaker panel before beginning to attach the wire to the thermostat.

Remote Controlled Communicating Thermostat   It is more likely that if the system installation plans for a home include the home technology technicians installing a thermostat, the thermostat is one that can be remotely controlled by some form of remote control unit and is able to communicate with a central home system control unit either with radio frequency (RF) or PLC signals.

The basic wiring for a remotely controlled thermostat is typically very similar to that of a standard thermostat. However, additional installation steps are usually required to accommodate its communications functions.

If the thermostat uses RF signals to communicate to a receiver module located near the HVAC equipment or a home system controller, follow the manufacturer's guidelines for range and placement in a room. For example, most manufacturers recommend that an RF thermostat be placed at least five feet from the floor and not behind a door or other large object in a room.

If the thermostat uses PLC signals to communicate to a home system control unit, at least two devices must be installed and possibly three. This includes one or more wall display units and a control module that serves as an interface between the display units and either the HVAC system or the home system control unit, and possibly a separate communications module for remote control access.

Rough-In   If the HVAC wiring is going in before the HVAC system, meaning the central HVAC system, first identify the location of the HVAC system. In most houses, the HVAC system is either in a basement, garage, or utility closet. To help with interfacing to the HVAC system, install a low-voltage box on a stud near where the HVAC system will sit. Locate the outlet box so that it is accessible for wiring and hookup. One idea is to place it one foot above the floor (measured to the center of the box). You should leave eight to ten feet of thermostat wire available to later wire the thermostat to the HVAC control.

At the spot where each thermostat will be installed during trim out, leave about one foot of wire slack to connect to the thermostat. During trim out and before the thermostat is attached to the wall and connected to the wire, be sure to seal around the hole the wire is passed through to avoid cold or warm air from the wall affecting the performance of the thermostat.

When pre-wiring for the HVAC control, run the wire from the thermostat and route it by the HVAC system unit (in an outlet box with an eight to ten foot loop) and on to the home control unit. It is a good idea to always pre-wire for HVAC control, even if not desired initially by the homeowner. By installing the wiring now, it is easy to add HVAC control in the future.

HVAC systems have two levels of wiring: line voltage and low voltage. Line voltage wiring supplies power to the components of the HVAC system, including its condenser, fan, furnace, or boiler. An electrician typically installs line voltage lines. Low voltage wiring for an HVAC system includes the thermostats, zone controls, any relay or control modules, and the control wiring for the system.

Typically, the wire installed for the HVAC control links should be a shielded wire with conductors of not less than American Wire Gauge (AWG) 14. Many local electrical codes require that control wiring be twisted as pairs and referenced to a particular wire type and manufacturer, such as Belden 8760 (single shielded twisted pair) or 8770 (three-conductor shielded twisted resistance temperature devices [RTD] cable). In addition to the shielding on the cable, control wiring should be installed at least a distance of 12 inches from power lines.

At the location of the thermostat, label each wire with the letter code assigned to the terminals of the HVAC system and the thermostat using cable marking tape or masking tape. Label both ends of the cable to ensure conformity. Table 32-1 lists the terminal codes most commonly used in the more popular heating systems. Not every system will have every one of the codes included in Table 32-1 and, in some cases, they

Terminal Designation	Wire Color	Application
B	Blue or orange	Switch reversing valve on heat pump to heat
C	Blue, brown, or black	Transformer common
E	Blue, pink, gray, or tan	Heat pump emergency heat relay (not commonly used)
G	Green	Furnace fan
L	Blue, brown, tan, or gray	Service indicator light
O	Orange	Switch reversing valve on heat pump to cool
R	Red	Transformer hot lead
T	Tan (or gray)	Outdoor anticipator reset
W	White	Heat
X	Blue, brown, or black	Transformer common
Y	Yellow	Cooling compressor

Table 32-1 Commonly Used HVAC Terminal Codes

may substitute or reassign a wire color or terminal code to another function. Be sure to review the system wiring documentation before labeling the wires to ensure the wires are properly labeled at each end.

NOTE   Heat pumps have two stages of heating and cooling, while standard gas or electric HVAC systems have only a single stage of heating or cooling.

Chapter Review

The primary types of air systems are forced air, baseboard and convection, hydronic, and evaporative cooling systems. Forced air systems use a circulating blower to move heated or cooled air into the rooms of a house. The two types of forced air systems are CAV and VAV. CAV systems supply a constant flow of air. VAV systems supply heated or cooled air at a constant temperature.

Baseboard heating devices provide heat using an internal electric heating element or the flow of air or water to a baseboard element. Baseboard units use convection heating.

In-wall electric heating units are either self-contained devices that include an electric heating element, a blower, and a built-in thermostat, or gas-fired heating chambers that reheat an airflow from a central heating system. Electric baseboard or heating chamber devices are either locally controlled or connected to a home control system.

Hydronic heat uses hot water that is heated in a boiler or some form of a water heater to transfer heat into a room or zone. The advantage of a hydronic system is it is fuel efficient. Another form of hydronic heating gaining popularity is radiant heating embedded in floors, patios, and other areas.

The common central heating units are electric furnaces, electric heat pumps, gas furnaces, and oil furnaces.

Evaporative cooling works on the principles of water evaporation and relative humidity: Adding moisture to drier air lowers the air temperature. The three types of evaporative cooling systems are direct evaporative cooling, indirect evaporative cooling, and two-stage evaporative cooling.

The common types of thermostats are baseboard thermostats, digital thermostats, mechanical thermostats, programmable thermostats, remote control thermostats, heating/cooling anticipators, and remote temperature sensors.

Power line thermostats allow the current set point or heating/cooling mode to be changed through a remote control device. The two basic types of PLC-compatible thermostats are one-way and two-way devices.

HVAC zones save energy and better serve the heating and cooling needs of a home's residents. Zoning a house involves the design and installation of a series of airflow dampers that control the ambient temperature separately from other zones, or areas, of the house using a single HVAC system. A single-zone HVAC system doesn't require damper systems. A multizone HVAC system has at least two airflow dampers where each damper is independently controlled by a thermostat. A zone thermostat communicates with the HVAC system and adjusts the dampers according to the zone settings.

A thermostat should be located on an inside wall at least 18 inches from any outside walls and at least five feet above the floor in an area that is frequently occupied. The wiring of an HVAC system should be no less than 20 AWG for runs less than 100 feet; 18 AWG wire is recommended for runs longer than 100 feet. Thermostat wiring has two to seven conductors of solid core wiring and the color coding of a seven-wire cable is white, red, green, blue, yellow, brown, and orange.

The wiring for a remotely controlled thermostat is very similar to that of a standard thermostat. However, additional installation steps are required to accommodate its communications functions.

HVAC systems have two levels of wiring: line voltage and low voltage. An electrician typically installs line voltage lines. Low voltage wiring includes the thermostats, zone controls, any relay or control modules, and the control wiring for the system.

Questions

1. Which of the following is not a type of HVAC system discussed in this chapter?

    A. Forced air

    B. Forced hot water

    C. Hydronic

    D. Convection

2. What are the two types of forced air HVAC systems?

    A. CAV

    B. Hydronic

    C. VAV

    D. CAT

3. A CAV forced air system is also known as a

    A. Multizone system

    B. Single-zone system

    C. Single-duct system

    D. Multiduct system

4. A heating system that takes advantage of the natural phenomenon that heated air rises and reacts to cooler surfaces to circulate is called

    A. Forced air

    B. Induction

    C. Convection

    D. Zoning

5. Which type of system uses heated water circulating through pipes to heat a room?

    A. Forced air

    B. Heat pump

    C. Hydronic

    D. Convection

6. Which of the following is not a common type of fuel used with central HVAC units?

    A. Electricity

    B. Fuel oil

    C. Heat pump

    D. Natural gas

7. What type of thermostat includes digital displays and the capability to be preset with user-created HVAC settings?

    A. Mechanical

    B. Programmable

    C. Remote control

    D. Digital

8. What is the maximum number of conductors typically available in thermostat wiring?

    A. Two

    B. Four

    C. Five

    D. Seven

9. What type of wire should be used for HVAC controls?

    A. Shielded AWG 14 single conductor wire

    B. Shielded AWG 12 2 or more conductor wire

    C. Unshielded AWG 14 single conductor wire

    D. Shielded AWG 14 2 or more twisted conductor wire

10. What do you call the areas of an HVAC system that have been separated by a series of airflow dampers that control the ambient temperature of each area separately from the other areas?

    A. HVAC zones

    B. HVAC hot spots

    C. HVAC controls

    D. HVAC subsystems

Answers

1. **B.** Nor will you find this system discussed in any HVAC book. All of the other choices are common types of HVAC systems.

2. **A and C.** Constant air volume (CAV) and variable air volume (VAV) are the two types of forced air systems.

3. **C.** There are multiduct CAV systems, but they are most commonly called single-duct.

4. **C.** The heated air from any HVAC system rises—a natural physical phenomenon—and convection heating is built around that principle.

5. **C.** True, some convection systems are hot water systems. However, all hydronic systems use hot water.

6. **C.** The "fuel" of a heat pump system is actually electricity, even though its heating process is a heat transfer.

7. **B.** A digital thermostat does have a digital display, but not all digital thermostats are programmable and not all remote control thermostats are digital. Mechanical thermostats are neither.

8. **D.** Although many HVAC systems use five-conductor wire, using seven-conductor wire provides future proofing for the system.

9. **D.** National and local electrical codes recommend shielded twisted conductor wiring of at least 14 AWG.

10. **A.** None of the other answers apply to this definition.

CHAPTER 33

Configuring a Home Control System

In this chapter you will learn about:

- Programming a home control system
- Documentation and preventative maintenance of a home control system
- Interfacing a home control system

Each separate control system in home, such as a lighting control system, a central HVAC control system, an access control system, and others, provide specific control over its distinct functions. However, a centralized home control system that integrates these controls can provide not only convenience, but often the synchronized performance of multiple systems as well.

To properly operate and provide the lighting, heating, cooling, security, and general ambiance desired by the homeowners, a home control system must be correctly configured and interfaced to the subsystems it is to control. This chapter discusses the configuration issues that must be addressed when configuring and interfacing a home control system.

 NOTE Chapter 31 provides additional information on home control systems, their makeup, and installation.

Programming a Home Control Unit

When you configure and set up a home control system controller, it commonly involves programming. This doesn't mean programming in the sense of computer programming necessarily, but it does mean you need to specify the hardware connected to the controller, set system parameters, identify scheduled events, and create any desired macros.

Programming Methods

Programming or setting up a home control system is first and foremost an exercise in organization. First, you need to identify what the system is supposed to do and what you need to organize in terms of sequence and hierarchy before actually beginning to program.

Planning Ahead

Before beginning the actual programming, draw a sketch of how the functions should flow logically in a flowchart form to help you to organize the logical steps. In the sketch shown in Figure 33-1, a Home key is planned for a keypad control placed near the front door of a home. The sketch shows a simplified version of what should happen in the controller when it receives a signal from the keypad that the Home key has been pressed. As illustrated, a Home macro is to be activated, and the controller issues command signals to the lighting, heating, ventilating, air conditioning (HVAC), and music systems to take certain actions.

The sketch provides you with a road map to follow when completing the programming. Planning out the process in this way helps you to avoid overlooking any of the required actions in a particular series of events. The sketch also helps you to identify any actions that repeat or reuse a part of other actions; these actions can be turned into macros or subroutines and linked to different controls.

When setting up and programming a home controller, you usually follow these steps. By always following this procedure, you will minimize programming time and ensure that most, if not all, items are completed the first time around.

1. Set up controller parameters and user information.

2. Define and set up all devices to be controlled (this should already be done in previous documentation).

3. Identify and enter all programmed events.

4. Define and enter all macros.

5. Test, test, test.

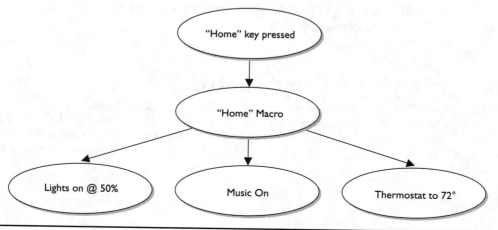

Figure 33-1 A sketch of the actions to be performed by the home control system when a key is pressed on the keypad

Programming a Home Control System

There are essentially four ways to program a home control system:

- Standard code programming
- Proprietary code programming
- Wizards
- Application driven programming

Standard code programming requires the knowledge of standard programming languages such as C++ or PERL. Few systems exist today that use standard programming languages; almost all have been simplified with either proprietary code programming or wizards, or they have applications already set up.

Most of the higher-end home control systems have built-in proprietary software interfaces for programming and configuring of the controller. These interfaces and their utilities are typically menu-driven or structured as a function or device hierarchy, as illustrated in Figure 33-2.

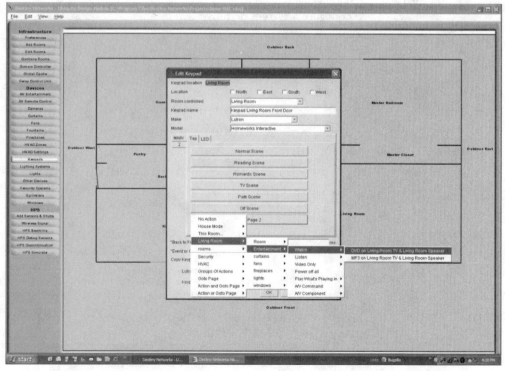

Image courtesy of Destiny Networks, Inc.

Figure 33-2 A sample configuration menu for a home control system's user interface

Whenever working with propriety programming software, it is strongly recommended, and often required, to participate in the manufacturer's training courses before selling, installing, and programming a home control system.

The manufacturers of the most popular systems, which are also typically the most expensive, have designed their systems with the end user and installer in mind. This effort is reflected in their programming interface, which is either embedded in the system control unit as firmware or is software that is installed on a PC with a hard-wired or wireless interface for uploading and downloading to the control unit.

If the controller's programming software is PC-based, it usually incorporates several features to simplify the configuration process and to aid in the navigation in the programming software. For example, menu bars, drop-down menu options, utilities, and wizards (see Figure 33-3) guide the programmer through the process of setting up devices and programming controls (see Figure 33-4). On these systems, if the programmer is familiar with the interfaces on a Microsoft Windows, Macintosh OS, or a UNIX/Linux X-Windows system, he or she should have little trouble navigating the programming software that includes wizard setup and application programming.

NOTE A wizard is a software routine that guides you through a process, such as programming lighting controls or setting up audio zones. A wizard allows you to configure a system or subsystem by answering questions or choosing options.

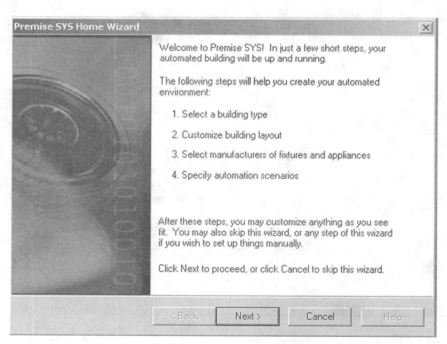

Image courtesy of Lantronix Corporation.

Figure 33-3 An example of a configuration wizard in the setup software of a home control system

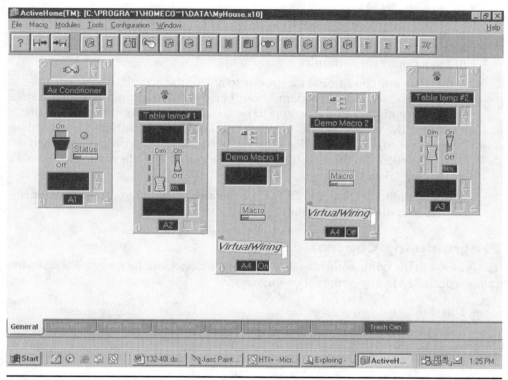

Figure 33-4   The configuration interface of a home control system's setup software

Application programming uses drop-down menus, making inputting information easy, and the software can automatically generate control programming and user interfaces. It is also much easier to make edits and changes, which is good for the programmer and the end user. This can allow the homeowner to make changes without always having to rely on the installation company to make them.

A Programming Example

Here is a brief example of how to program a device control, including the general steps used in a sample home control software system.

To create a command set to control the powered curtains in a home theater room, you could configure the following using the home control system's configuration interface:

1. Create a new device, class, or group for the curtains, or add this control to an existing device grouping, such as a group of lighting fixtures.

2. Set the timer control for this device or for the entire group. Separate events may be necessary for morning, evening, and on-demand timing events. A timer control is used to activate or deactivate events based on the time of day or a time duration, such as minutes, hours, or days.

PART VIII

3. Select the action or activity script to be linked to each timing event. If an action script doesn't exist, you will need to modify an existing script or create a new one. A script is a series of command instructions that are executed one at a time in sequence by the controller.

4. If there are any conditional exceptions to any of the actions, a logic stream, or in some cases a logic diagram, should be created to indicate the logic test for the exceptions and the actions to be taken when the conditions meet the logic test. The test for a logical exception is known as an if-then-else condition. If the test is true (for example, if the day is Tuesday), then the action linked to the test is taken (in this case, don't open the curtains). Otherwise, the normal actions are taken.

5. Save and name the new macro. Macros can also be exported on some systems for use with other installations.

Programming Control

The purpose of the home controller is to control the devices in the system. These devices can be controlled in any of the following ways:

- Direct device control
- Scheduled events
- Conditional control

As illustrated in Figures 33-2 and 33-4 earlier in the chapter, the programming interfaces on home system control configuration and programming modules typically include a menu, dialog box, or tree format for selecting specific devices for configuration, timing, and functions.

Provided that little or no scripting has been included in the system, the device interfaces are where most debugging and later modifications are typically made. How intuitive a user interface or menu system is should be key criteria when selecting a system for a homeowner or yourself.

Direct Device Control

The simple on/off control of a device can happen directly through programming or remote keypads, or touch screens can be set up to always control if a device is on or off. The key word here is *always*; this means that whenever the button is touched, it *always* controls the device it is defined to control. An example is the top center button on the keypad in the kitchen that controls (turns on or off) the kitchen ceiling lights every time it is pushed.

Scheduled Events

Timer routines are at the heart of any home control system. Once the cable, wire, devices, and interfaces are installed and working properly, much of the remaining programming involves setting timer events (what comes on or goes off at what time of the day) or grouping devices into scenes.

The system timer continuously scans its list of configured timer events (also called scheduled events on some systems) looking for a match. Items it checks for a match include the current time, day, date, sunrise or sunset, and the scheduled event times. This kind of programming is often referred to as *when statements* because when the timer detects a match for a scheduled event, it passes control of the event to the system's processor and the commands, scripts, and actions defined in the event are then performed. For example, if the outside lights of a home are to come on at 6:30 P.M., a scheduled event is predefined to execute this action: "When 6:30 P.M. turn on outside lights." At 6:30 P.M., the timer detects that the time criteria is met, this event is to be executed, and notifies the system processor, which then executes the event's commands to turn on the outside lights. The same sequence of actions takes place to execute another timed event that turns off the lights the next morning at the designated time.

Conditional Control

Conditional control is just what it sounds like it is: the control of the device depends on one or more conditions being met. The conditions are tested and if all are met, the command is executed. This type of control is often referred to as *if-then* programming because the statement reads, "If <condition is true> then <perform command>." For example: "If security system is Away, then turn on sink light at 6:30 P.M." Conditional statements can be nested and combined with *AND* and *OR* statements. For example: "If security is Away AND temperature in living room is greater than 80 degrees, then close drapes." This protects the house from heating up from direct sun and fading the furniture fabric. Remember that with an AND statement, both conditions must be met for the command to be executed. With an OR statement, only one of the conditions must be met for the command to be performed.

Documentation and Preventive Action

The complete documentation of the entire configuration and programming of a home control system is required. The procedures used to back up and restore the controller after modifications are made or in case of a system failure need also to be documented. These are the final pieces of any programming and setup job.

Documentation

No matter how well executed a manufacturer's documentation is, this documentation is general in nature and cannot possibly cover each specific installation. Every home control system must be treated as if it is a completely unique and custom installation, and the documentation you make should record everything about the system. Documentation should exist in two places: in your office and on site at the home with the installed control system.

The documentation you provide to the homeowner should address any concerns the customer may have after the system is installed and operating. This doesn't mean you can't include documentation supplied by the manufacturer as well, but the final documentation of the system should include all of the information the homeowner needs.

A full copy of the documentation should be stored on site for reference by a technician applying upgrades or making modifications to the system. Another full copy of the documentation should be stored in your company's files for future reference. Storing copies of the documentation at both the home and your office ensures that it is available when it's needed, in either location.

The documentation for the programming, configuration, and setup of the system controller should include at least the following:

- A narrative description of the system, including details on the devices controlled and any special features supported. In effect, this is a summary of the information gained from the customer during the preconfiguration interview.

- A diagram of the hardware components of the home control system, including all controlled or monitored devices, including their connections.

- A list of the locations of each of the software modules used to create and maintain the system's programming, meaning the PCs or the controller(s) where any copies of the configuration files are located. If the software is located only on the original programmer's PC, a note should be included to this effect. However, if this is the case, a backup should absolutely be created and its location noted as well. If the configuration software is embedded as firmware in the controller itself, this should be indicated, along with the commands used to access and start the configuration routines. Any passwords required should also be documented.

- An overview logic diagram of the control system and its relationships to controls or events defined for each major subsystem.

- A logic diagram of all timer and conditional events that have been configured or scripted.

- A maintenance and version log that tracks the date and technician for all installation, troubleshooting, upgrade, additions, and modifications made to the system, beginning with its initial installation.

- A hard copy of the system configuration, setup, and programming should be created, if at all possible. In many cases, these files can be saved to a text file and printed. A copy of the hard copy should be stored at the office in the customer file and another kept on site for a maintenance and debug reference.

- A hard media (zip disk, CD, or USB drive) backup that contains copies of all programming and configuration files specific to the system.

Preventive Action

Throughout the programming or configuration process of a system controller, the critical system information should be copied electronically to create a backup. A backup should also be created periodically and especially right after any changes or updates are applied to the system. The purpose of the backup is to provide a recovery image of the system at a specific configuration or development point. You can't make too many backups; the relatively small amount of time it takes to perform them is an investment in your ability to recover the system in the event of a catastrophe that causes the system and its programming or configuration settings to fail or become corrupt.

Backups

Any number of things can happen to wipe out the programming: power failure, somebody tripping over the power cord, the press of the wrong button, or even bad controller hardware or software.

The control systems that run on a PC typically include backup, restore, and reset functions that are used to copy the system configuration to a removable medium, restore the configuration should the PC where the controller is running fail, and remove any configuration changes made to the standard or default configuration, respectively.

The backup function should be used after each major event or device is programmed, at the end of each day of programming activities, and finally, when all programming is completed. The final backup of a system should be created even before the system is tested. If any changes are made during testing, additional backups should be created. Creating these electronic backups ensures that should the system fail, the programming is not lost or, if you simply wish to start over, the fallback point is not too far in the past.

If the homeowner will also have the ability to make changes to the system, the documentation should include instructions on how to create and restore backups. Of course, the best scenario is that you or your company is contracted to make all future programming changes, which ensures that all changes have been tested and the system backup has been created.

Backup Media

A backup of the system controller should be captured on some form of removable media. It doesn't do you or the customer any good to back up the system to a storage medium that remains in or on the system. Should something unforeseen happen, such as lightning striking the building, anything installed or inserted on the controller will likely be destroyed right along with the controller itself.

Virtually all standalone hardware home automation controllers have an interface to a PC that allows you to perform a variety of functions from the computer, including backup and restore of the controller's configuration or programming. For the most part, the critical system information that should be copied to a backup is relatively small in volume and may only involve a single file. This allows you to use such easy to use devices like CDs, DVDs, flash drives, or external hard disks, which can be easily removed and stored either offsite or at least external to the system controller.

Upgrades

Periodically, manufacturers release upgraded or improved versions of their software and hardware products. There are two schools of thought on upgrades: the first believes that "if it ain't broke, don't fix it," and the second believes that all upgrades should be installed regardless of need or the customer's configuration. The best approach to upgrades falls somewhere in the middle of these two philosophies. You should analyze the upgrade's documentation carefully to determine if a new feature or function will improve a customer's system or provide better performance with regard to the homeowner's expectations of the system. If the answer is yes, the upgrade will improve the customer's system, the upgrade should be applied. However, if the upgrade has no effect on the current configuration or performance of a customer's system, it is probably better not to install this particular upgrade at this time. Don't worry about losing track of which customer has which version; if the maintenance log part of the documentation is steadfastly maintained, there should be no mysteries.

Interfacing a Home Control System

Just because a device provides an interface to another device or a cable connecting to another device, it doesn't mean the devices are integrated. When two devices are connected using common cable or wire, the devices are interfaced. However, to be integrated, the devices must have onboard functions that support a specific communication between the devices using a common coding system or protocol. In a typical home control system, the home control system provides integration support, but it can be distributed to local controllers and, in some cases, to specific devices themselves.

A home PC and some specialized software can be used together to control and command a distributed home control system. On these systems, software running on a PC allows the user to set up zones and areas for controlling audio, video, lighting, and other home systems. The PC communicates to these types of systems typically through a serial, Universal Serial Bus (USB), or IEEE 1394 interface to a signal converter device that provides transceiver services to the distributed controls and modules of the system. For example, a PC running software to control an X-10 lighting control system transmits its signals through either a serial or USB port to an X-10 interface module that transmits and receives signals to and from the electrical wiring of the home.

The home control software typically runs on a single PC, which may or may not be connected into the home data network. Even if the PC is connected to the home network in a peer-to-peer network arrangement that is common to home networks, the control software is not likely to be accessible from other network computers.

Interconnecting the Networks

The first step involved with connecting the data network to the home control network is, of course, connecting the cabling or media of each system. After the physical connection is made, the signal format of the two systems must be converted in either direction to allow the systems to communicate. Typically, the home data network is installed on structured Cat 5e or Cat 6 unshielded twisted-pair (UTP) cabling or on one of the wireless media standards (IEEE 802.11a, 802.11b, 802.11g, or 802.11n), and it operates on the Ethernet protocol. To connect the home control system to the home network, the controller must have a compatible jack or transceiver to operate on an Ethernet network.

Not all home control controllers are designed for or equipped with a connection to an Ethernet data network. Some have optional third-party modules that can be installed to provide an Ethernet connection directly to the data network distribution panel. In any case, the arrangement used to connect a home data network to a home control system varies with the type of network media in use (wired or wireless).

To achieve a true integration of a home control system into a home network, the two systems must speak the same language. Just like two people who don't speak each other's language typically have trouble communicating, integrating an Ethernet data network to a proprietary home control controller can prove troublesome.

In some cases, this may mean that a signal converter or bridge must be used between the two systems, such as an Ethernet to serial bridge, an Ethernet to RS-485 converter, or an Ethernet to PLC module. However, where the home control system is able to connect directly to the Ethernet link, an external bridge is not needed.

Newer and developmental home control systems include microprocessors that are able to control home systems over Ethernet and Internet networks. These systems overcome the limitations that have prevented the easy interface for data networks and home control systems in the past.

 NOTE EIA/TIA (RS) 485 is a serial communications standard that, like Ethernet, requires dedicated media but, unlike Ethernet which uses eight wires, requires only two wires (one wire pair). This standard, with a bandwidth of about 10 megabits per second (Mbps), is also topology free and so can be easily installed in homeruns.

Another interface technology that can be used to integrate a computer network and home control system is the controller area network (CAN) protocols. CAN is a serial bus system designed to interconnect smart devices into smart systems and networks.

Why integrate a data network to the home control system? Good question. Even though the homeowners may not wish to control or monitor their home control systems from any networked PC in the home, the capability exists. Having a link to the home control controller from any networked PC in a home provides the possibility for monitoring, programming, troubleshooting, and controlling the home control controller and the distributed devices it controls.

In addition, if the Home Automation Telephone Interface (HATi) protocols are in use, a link to the home control controller can also allow the telephone system to be controlled from a PC, including placing and receiving telephone calls to any line in the home.

Chapter Review

A link to a home control system controller from a networked PC provides an additional access resource for monitoring, programming, troubleshooting, and controlling the home control controller and the distributed devices it controls.

Programming a home control system is an exercise in organization. Planning out the process helps to prevent any of the required actions planned for the system from being overlooked. Most higher-end home automaton control systems have built-in graphical user interfaces (GUIs) that are typically menu-driven or displayed as a function or device hierarchy. User interfaces on home system control configuration and programming modules typically include a menu, dialog box, or tree format for selecting specific devices for configuration, timing, and functions.

The documentation of the completed programming and the procedures used to back up and restore the controller a system failure are key pieces of a programming and setup job. A manufacturer's documentation is general and cannot cover each specific installation. It can be included, but the final documentation for a system should include the information needed by the homeowner and the next technician to work on the system.

Questions

1. What type of device is required to interface an Ethernet device to an EIA/TIA 232 device?

   A. Bridge

   B. PLC module

   C. Network adapter

   D. TCP/IP converter

2. What home system protocol can be used to integrate a computer network with home control controllers?

   A. CAN

   B. HAN

   C. LAN

   D. WAN

3. Which of the following is not an advantage of integrating a home data network into the home control system?

   A. Emergency backup

   B. Monitoring

   C. Programming

   D. Troubleshooting

4. What should be completed prior to programming a home control system?

   A. Backup of system software

   B. User wish list

   C. Sketch or outline of system controller functions to be created

   D. Programming language training

5. Which of the following is typically not included in the system documentation?

   A. Description of the system

   B. Diagram of hardware components

    C. Price list of system components and software modules

    D. Logic diagram of the control system and the relationships to controls

6. Which of the following is not a feature commonly provided by a hardware-based system controller?

    A. Communications

    B. Multiple-zone control

    C. Automatic backups

    D. User interface

7. A software routine that guides you through a process step-by-step to configure a system by answering questions or choosing options is called a

    A. Subroutine

    B. Setup interface

    C. Centralized interface

    D. Wizard

8. A full copy of the home control system documentation should be kept at which of the following locations? (Choose all that apply)

    A. On site

    B. Installer's office or shop

    C. Third-party storage

    D. Documentation not required after installation acceptance

9. Making a periodic system backup is a part of what maintenance activity?

    A. System security

    B. Preventive maintenance

    C. Upgrade installation

    D. System shutdown

10. What essential characteristic must be present in both a home automation system and a home control system for an interconnection of the two systems to be made?

    A. Wire standards

    B. Power supply

    C. Communication protocols

    D. Network standard

Answers

1. **A.** An Ethernet to serial bridge converts the communication signal into the formats required by each of the communication protocols in use.

2. **A.** A controller area network (CAN) interconnects home system control devices, as opposed to a home area network (HAN), which is a form of a local area network (LAN). A WAN is a wide area network and extends outside the home.

3. **A.** A PC may be configured to automatically provide a backup to a home control system. However, this is not typically done and is therefore not a likely advantage of the integration.

4. **C.** You don't really need to sketch out the system functions, but some form of a sequenced outline should be created. Any of the other choices could be done before you begin programming, but some form of an outline or sketch should absolutely be created.

5. **C.** Not only is this type of information likely to be out-of-date even before the system is completely installed, it is not valuable to the ongoing support of the system.

6. **C.** If backups are taken of the system software or configuration files, it is almost always a manual operation.

7. **D.** A wizard is generally a single-purpose software module that can be used to perform a task in a logical series of tasks.

8. **A and B.** Having a full copy of a home control system's documentation at both sites insures that this essential information is available in either location when it's needed.

9. **B.** Backups are an essential component of preventative maintenance. However, that doesn't mean that a backup shouldn't be taken in any of the other situations listed; backups are first and foremost preventive maintenance.

10. **C.** All of the above would be a great answer, but the more important characteristic listed is communication standards, which includes network standards. However, it really isn't all that essential that the power supplies are compatible.

Troubleshooting and Maintaining a Home Control System

In this chapter you learn about:

- Applying the troubleshooting process to an integrated home control system
- Identifying the subsystem that is the source of the problem
- Documenting the maintenance of a home control system

An integrated home control system may be a very efficient system to operate and experience, but when something goes wrong, it can also be very difficult to troubleshoot, diagnose, and isolate the subsystem or element causing the issue.

This chapter covers the basic troubleshooting procedure to troubleshoot a home control system and identify the source of a performance issue. Also discussed in the chapter are the information that should be recorded and its importance when documenting troubleshooting and maintenance on a home control system.

Troubleshooting a Home Control System

It is very important to gain some idea as to the nature of the problem being reported. Typically, this information comes from the system owner and can be somewhat cryptic or misleading. However, if you listen openly and restrain yourself from jumping to conclusions, you may actually hear a clue or two about just what is going wrong.

 CROSS-REFERENCE See Chapter 4 for more information on troubleshooting basics and how they are performed on various types of systems or components in a home system.

Many home control system issues relate to dead batteries in a remote control unit or wireless control panel, a misunderstanding by a user of the features of a subsystem, or perhaps even a configuration error made during installation. These common problems are easily diagnosed and corrected. However, there are other problems that can require troubleshooting and patience to determine their cause.

You should approach every problem report with a troubleshooting approach. A simple problem may not be as simple as you think at first. The customer may be either overstating or understating the symptoms, especially customers who believe they are more knowledgeable than is actually the case. Most homeowners are not technicians and cannot give a technical description of a problem beyond that something isn't working the way they believe it should.

Once you believe you have a clear understanding of the nature or symptoms of the problem, you should next attempt to reproduce the problem. If you are able to reproduce the problem, you are most likely well on your way to identifying its source and fixing the cause. However, in some cases, reproducing the problem or symptoms may serve only to identify that additional troubleshooting is required.

NOTE Remember that most system problems occur as the result of a change made to some part of the system.

The following sections detail some of the more common problems you may encounter with a home control system.

Troubleshooting a Hard-Wired Control System

If the nature of the problem being reported is that two hard-wired devices are not communicating or that a device is not responding to the home control system unit, or vice versa, it is very likely that the problem is wiring. Of course, wiring covers a lot, including connections, the wire core, terminations, and more.

Cable or wire terminations are the most common cause of devices in a hard-wired system not communicating. Your troubleshooting procedure should start by verifying with a multimeter that the signal is being placed on the cable or wire by the sending device. If the signal is present, but the receiving device is not responding, you should next check the wire termination (connector) on the receiving device end of the cable.

Chances are that the connector was improperly installed. Attempt to verify this diagnosis with a known good cable between the two devices. If the known good cable resolves the situation, remove the existing connector and install a new connector appropriate for the device on the cable.

However, if the problem is something other than the terminations, but the known good cable solves the problem, the problem may be the wire inside the walls. Ask if anything has been recently done to the walls in which the cabling is installed. Something as minor as hanging a picture on too large of a nail could have pierced a data cable and caused the performance issue. At this point you need to replace the cable. If you pulled an extra run of cable into the walls, you have a fallback point and a backup cable to use. Otherwise, you'll need to pull through another cable.

There is the possibility of another type of problem, which depends on if the system control unit is software-based and running on a personal computer. Windows systems, such as Windows XP, Windows 2003 Server, or Windows Vista, each have a Networks icon on their Control Panels (on Windows Vista, it's the Networks and Sharing icon).

The diagnostics available in the network configuration area can also let you know if the problem may be caused by the network configuration on the computer.

Troubleshooting a PLC System

If the control system is connected to the remote interface devices using a power line carrier (PLC) system, the problem is typically with the communications between the control unit and the remote interface module. To troubleshoot a PLC problem that didn't exist at the time of installation when the system was thoroughly tested and verified, there is a sequence of steps you should use:

1. Verify that no electrical circuit changes have been made near or in line with the PLC device suspected of causing the problem. PLC devices work best when they don't share a power circuit with a power strip, extension cords, a surge suppressor, or an uninterruptible power supply (UPS).

2. Confirm that all of the interface modules are working correctly by isolating them or plugging them into another outlet in another part of the house.

3. Many PLC devices have both a network and a device password. The device password for each interface module cannot be changed (it is printed on the PLC device's label). However, many manufacturers base their network password on the device passwords. Verify that a new PLC interface module hasn't been installed and changed the configuration of the password between devices.

4. If the problem is intermittent, the source of the problem could be one of two things:

   • The owners are plugging and unplugging existing or new PLC devices onto the network. The causes the entire system to reset, which usually takes five minutes or more to complete.

   • There is some device being placed on the electrical circuit that is causing electrical line noise that the failing devices cannot overcome. Such a device could be a vacuum cleaner, a blender, a freezer, or any other electrically noisy device. The best way to perform this test is to unplug any home appliances and reattempt the suspected circuit or devices.

5. Although the following items should have been checked during installation, you may want to check for old fuse boxes (the fuse type, not the circuit breaker type) or old wiring that is less than the current or recent electrical wiring codes.

To thoroughly test a PLC line noise problem, you should use a PLC troubleshooting key that includes a test transmitter and test receiver pair, so you are sure to get the proper signal strength to verify each outlet.

Troubleshooting a Wireless System

To troubleshoot any performance issues in a radio frequency (RF) wireless system, the process is the same as defined in Chapters 8 and 9. The issues causing a wireless system to malfunction are typically range, metal box, or standard-based. As is the case with all system problems on a system that was originally tested and verified, check for any new additions or changes to the system or the house.

Troubleshooting Configuration Issues

Performance problems not based on a communications list, but rather on a configuration problem or miscoding, are typically identified by the fact that all else is working but a certain event is not taking place at the proper time, if at all. This doesn't eliminate a communications problem, but if the porch light isn't coming on at 6:00 P.M., then you should first check the configuration of the home control unit to verify that this event is properly coded.

The problem could also be that the homeowner didn't fully explain this as a requirement and the system isn't configured to do it. So, the configuration documentation should be reviewed before you get too far into debugging the controller.

Documenting the Maintenance Activity

When the home automation system was installed, a maintenance log was created that benchmarked the system's configuration, layout, and performance. All troubleshooting, diagnostics, repair, or upgrade actions that have been performed on the system since installation are documented in the maintenance log. The maintenance log provides a running dialogue for whoever is the next technician to work on the system, is a source of information on any existing or ongoing issues, and is the basis from which to determine the cause of a new issue.

Chapter Review

Typically, the information regarding a home control system problem comes from the system owner. You should listen openly and avoid jumping to conclusions. Many home control system issues relate to dead batteries, a misunderstanding of the features of a subsystem, or a configuration error. However, other problems require troubleshooting to determine their cause.

Once you have a clear understanding of the problem, you should attempt to reproduce the problem. If you are able to reproduce the problem, you should be able to identify its source and what is needed to fix the cause. However, reproducing the problem can serve only to identify that additional troubleshooting is required.

If the nature of the problem is that two hard-wired devices are not communicating, the problem is likely in the wiring. Cable or wire terminations are the most common cause of devices not communicating. You should verify that the signal is being placed on the cable by the sending device and that the receiving device is able to receive the signal.

If the control system is connected to a PLC system, the problem is typically in the communications between the control unit and the remote interface module.

To troubleshoot a PLC problem, you should verify that no changes have been made and that the interface module in question is working correctly. In addition, you should confirm the device and network passwords and that line noise is not the issue. Some problems may be caused by a configuration issue.

A maintenance log should be maintained and updated each time troubleshooting, diagnostics, repair, or upgrade actions are made on the system.

Questions

1. You receive a technical support call from a homeowner who has an integrated home automation system that was installed by your firm. The customer reports that a battery-operated motion detector in one room of the house suddenly fails to cause an alarm to sound under control of the central control unit. Which of the following would you check first when troubleshooting this problem?

    A. The control system configuration

    B. The connector at the motion detection device

    C. The batteries in motion detector device

    D. The cabling between control system and motion detector.

2. A customer reports that the PLC home automation system in her home is intermittently turning on and off all of the lights in one room of the house. This situation has continued for about a week. When interviewing the customer, what information should you attempt to obtain first?

    A. Have any new electrical devices been plugged into the electrical circuits in the room in question?

    B. Are the light bulbs in the room securely installed?

    C. Has the PLC lighting modules in use been removed or replaced?

    D. Have any new electrical devices been put in service in the home?

3. When testing a new installation for an integrated home automation system that uses coaxial cable as a part of the security system, one camera is intermittently sending its video signal to the security video monitor and at times no signal is transmitted at all. The last six feet of the cable connecting the cable to the system is loose and sagging beneath the eaves of the home. While your first thought is that the problem is the camera itself, what other element of the system should be diagnosed as the potential problem?

    A. The connector to the camera

    B. The coaxial cable run to the camera

    C. The compatibility between the camera and the video monitor

    D. The camera itself

4. A homeowner who has recently had an integrated home automation control system installed in his home calls to report that the network jack in his office is no longer working. He has verified this by moving his notebook computer to a different room and connecting to the network without problem. The only change he can identify being made to the room in question is that a small shelf has been hung in the vicinity of the network jack, but he can't understand how that would impact the network connection. What do you suspect is causing the network jack to fail?

A. A bad RJ-45 connection at the outlet box

B. The customer is plugging into the wrong outlet jack.

C. The screws anchoring the shelf to the wall have penetrated the network cable.

D. The cable run between the outlet box and the central distribution panel has become stretched and has compromised the connections.

5. The best way to determine the nature of the problem is to first listen carefully to the customer and then to do what?

A. Determine what the problem is and start the repair.

B. Attempt to reproduce the problem.

C. Read the maintenance log to see if there have been any prior reports of this type of problem.

D. Reset the entire system.

6. The most common type of communications failure in a hard-wired system is

A. Cable failure

B. Line noise

C. Connector failure

D. Crosstalk

7. What are common causes of PLC system failures?

A. Line noise added to a circuit by a new electrical device

B. A PLC device sharing a circuit with a UPS

C. Electrical wiring below current building codes

D. New and old PLC devices mixed on a circuit

E. A, B, and C

F. A and B only

8. If an RF wireless home automation system ceases to operate properly, what should you suspect has happened in the home?

   A. New furniture or obstructions have been placed in the problem room.

   B. A new network device (hub, interface, or access point) has been installed that is not configured or consistent with the current network devices.

   C. Additional or new outside interference is causing the system to fail.

   D. A or B

   E. B and C

   F. B only

9. If a planned system event fails to occur at a preset time, where should you first investigate to find the problem?

   A. The fixture being controlled by the event

   B. The system clock

   C. Configuration or programming of the central control unit

   D. The AC power system

10. The importance of maintaining a maintenance activity log is

    A. History

    B. Chronology

    C. Responsibility

    D. Troubleshooting/diagnostics results

    E. B and D only

    F. All of the above

Answers

1. **C.** It always helps to eliminate the most obvious causes first, rather than to waste time on less common causes only to discover the problem was very obvious.

2. **A.** While answer D is very close to this, you should start at the source of the problem and work out. An electrical device put into service in the same room will usually have a more immediate impact on the system than one in another part of the house, but not always.

3. **A.** If there is a length of coaxial cable left free between the cable and the wall, a breeze could be causing it to sway, which would cause a bad connection to be intermittent. After that possibility is eliminated, you may check the remaining choices as you wish.

4. **C.** As stated before, eliminate the most obvious first—if removing the shelf's screws restores service, problem solved. However, should that not solve the problem, choice A is likely the next thing you should check.

5. **B.** Even before you check the maintenance activity log for any recent reports of a similar nature, you should first attempt to reproduce the problem.

6. **C.** Connectors, because they can receive frequent and not-so-gentle use, can be the weak spot of a network.

7. **E.** Choices A, B, and C can each contribute to a PLC communications failure. Only when mixing some manufacturers would choice D be problem.

8. **D.** If either choice A or B has happened in or near a home, the home RF network could cease to perform in one or more parts of the home. It would be very difficult for a homeowner not to know or notice should something like a radio transmission tower be built near the home.

9. **A.** Arguably, the choice between A and C is perhaps a toss-up, but without any history or other information, you may want to make sure the controlled fixture is powered and installed properly.

10. **F.** The maintenance activity log is your source of information about all that has come before on a home control system.

CHAPTER 35

Power Protection

In this chapter, you will learn about
- Identifying power protection options
- Installing power protection options
- Alternative power sources

When the control of an entire home depends on the availability and reliability of electrical power, regardless of the control method or protocols in use, the inclusion of certain power protection devices can help ensure that the system will remain powered and operational at all times. It doesn't do much good to have a home control system in a home when there are electrical problems, interruptions, or failures.

This chapter looks at the device that can be included in a home control system to make sure that the electrical power it needs provides both protection and availability.

Planning for Electrical Protection

The good news is that a home control system is powered by electricity, something you should be able to take for granted, provided the electricians do their jobs. However, the bad news is that the home system is powered by electricity, and you need to protect the system from that very same electrical power.

A home's electrical power supply experiences random spikes, surges, and lulls almost every day and, in some cases, every hour. Exactly why these events happen isn't really the issue. The issue is that protection must be designed into the system to prevent these events from damaging the system and its devices.

Electrical Events

External AC power sources can pass on a variety of power-related problems, including the following:

- **Line noise**   Consists of small variations in the voltage of the power line. A small amount of line noise is normal in just about every system and all but the very low-end devices can handle it. An electrical device connected to its own circuit (an unshared power line) should have little trouble with line noise.

However, for a device that shares a circuit with a refrigerator or a megaton air conditioner, line noise is not only a certainty, but it's likely that the line noise will cause problems. For example, if a transformer is connected to an AC power source with high levels of line noise, it may eventually have its power-regulating circuits burn out, after which time the line noise would pass through to the devices connected to the transformer.

- **Power surge**   A power surge or spike, which is also called an over-voltage event, occurs when electrical disturbances, such as distant lightning strikes or other anomalies in the electrical supply grid, create a sharp rise in the voltage level that is passed onto the power supply lines. In most situations, a spike or surge lasts only a few thousandths of a second, but depending on the amount of the rise in the line voltage, that is plenty of time for the voltage to increase to double, triple, or spike even higher. High voltage spikes and surges, if frequent enough, can degrade the electrical circuits of a home's electrical devices. In fact, multiple surges occurring frequently enough can eventually destroy some electrical devices, such as a computer's power supply.

- **Brownouts**   Called an under-voltage event, a brownout is the opposite of a power surge (over-voltage event) and occurs when there is a sudden dip in the power line voltage. In most cases, the power level drops below normal levels for a time and then returns to normal. Brownouts are extremely common during periods of heavy load on the electrical system, such as hot afternoons or cold mornings. The reduced voltage level causes many devices to run slower than normal or malfunction in other ways. Low voltage for an extended time can do just as much damage as spikes. A brownout doesn't typically last too long, but it can.

- **Blackouts**   A blackout occurs when the power fails completely. The problems caused by a blackout are usually more frustrating than damaging, but the fluctuation of power surrounding a blackout can cause harm. Typically, any damage associated with a blackout occurs when the power returns suddenly, usually in the form of a huge spike.

- **Lightning strikes**   This is the big spike, and it can deliver a million volts or more. I don't need to tell you what would happen if one were to hit a home directly. However, a strike even in the vicinity can result in a very high voltage spike.

 NOTE   Electrical events can cause two types of damage to an electrical device: catastrophic damage, which means a device is destroyed all at once by a single event, and degradation, which means a device is damaged slowly over a period of instances and has intermittent problems before failing altogether.

Surge Suppression

The most common electrical system event is a power surge or spike, which is a temporary increase in the voltage supplied on the electrical lines. For the most part, any power surge

Figure 35-1

A surge
suppression plug
strip

Photo courtesy of American Power Conversion Corporation.

to a home is passed on through the electrical distribution panel to the circuits in the home. The installation of surge suppression devices is the best and most economical way to prevent damage to any of the devices on the structured wiring system.

The least expensive and perhaps the least protective way to protect against electrical surges is a power strip surge suppressor, like the one shown in Figure 35-1. Surge suppressors are generally available and the most commonly used protection device. The device shown provides protection not only for electrical devices, but also provides surge suppression to telephone and data network links.

The primary component of a surge suppressor is a metal oxide varistor (MOV), which, in effect, takes the hit from voltage spikes. However, an MOV can be defeated by one big spike or an accumulation of small surges over time, which is why some surge suppressors have an LED to indicate that the MOV is still intact. A surge suppressor absorbs spikes and surges and smoothes out line noise, which is called line conditioning. The rule of thumb for selecting a surge suppressor is that you get what you pay for.

The two main features for choosing a surge suppressor are

- **Clamping voltage**   The voltage at which the suppressor begins to protect the circuit.

- **Clamping speed**   The amount of time that elapses between detection and protection.

Here are some other characteristics to consider when selecting a surge suppressor for a home system:

- **Energy absorption**   Surge suppressors are rated in joules, which is a measure of their capability to absorb energy. The higher the joules rating, the better the protection. Basic protection is 200 joules; 400 joules represents good protection; and 600 joules is better protection.

- **Line conditioning** The line conditioning capability of a surge suppressor is measured in decibels. The more decibels of noise reduction, the better the line conditioning.
- **Protection level** Surge suppressors have three levels of protection indicated as the maximum number of watts a suppressor allows to pass through. The standard ratings are (better to good) 330, 400, and 500.

 NOTE Underwriters Laboratories (UL) standard 1449 covers the construction and performance of surge suppressors. A suppressor with a UL approval has met this standard and will provide protection to its rated capacities.

A variety of surge protectors and suppressors are available for virtually all parts of a home automation network, including units designed specifically for wiring carrying electrical signals, including audio/video and network components (see Figure 35-2).

Power Conditioning

A power conditioner is an electrical device that is designed to remove electrical noise and crosstalk from an electrical line. Power conditioners come in all sizes, but common units for use with a single system or subsystem, such as a home theater, can have from 1 to 12 or more receptacles and outlets, each of which is isolated from the others. Many home system power conditioners, like the one shown in Figure 35-3, condition not only the electrical power, but also the electrical impulse transmissions for video and audio.

In some situations, depending on the design of the wiring and the systems attached, it may be a better choice to install a whole home power conditioner (see Figure 35-4). Models of whole home power conditioners are available in a variety of power load ratings and abilities.

Figure 35-2
A data network cable surge suppressor

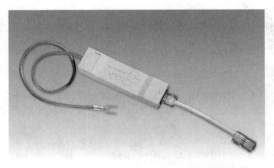

Photo courtesy of Tripp Lite.

Figure 35-3
A power conditioner designed for home theater systems

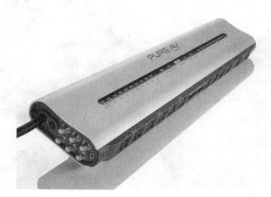

Photo courtesy of Belkin International, Inc.

Figure 35-4
A whole home surge suppressor and power conditioner

Photo courtesy of New Frontier Electronics, Inc.

Inverters

In some rare instances, it may be necessary to invert direct current (DC) to alternating current (AC) power for a particular device. This requirement most likely occurs when a home AC device is to be used in a DC-powered environment, such as a car or a recreational vehicle. It is possible that a homeowner may wish to use a device purchased specifically for a DC-powered environment in their home. Power inverters convert DC power into 120 V AC power. Figure 35-5 shows a power inverter.

Figure 35-5
Front and rear views of a power inverter, which is used to convert DC power into an AC current

Photo courtesy of Tripp Lite.

Applying Protection to Cable

While the protection method used to protect the different cabling types used in a home system is essentially the same, each cable has one or two unique characteristics. The following sections describe the unique protection methods used for each cable type.

Protecting Telephone Lines

In the event of an electrical storm or lightning strike, power can surge up the telephone lines just as fast as it can on power lines. Surge protectors should also be installed to protect any distributed phone lines between the network interface device (NID) and the distribution panel. In addition, add surge protection to any door intercoms before they connect to the house phone system, as they are located outside and susceptible to lightning hits.

Protecting Coaxial Cable

Surge suppression should also be added to coaxial cable lines that connect exterior sources to interior systems, such as the lines that provide cable television, an exterior antenna, or the lines connecting a digital satellite receiver to its dish outside the home.

The best devices for this purpose include a silicon avalanche diode (SAD) as their primary level of protection from over-voltage surges that may enter and be carried on a coaxial cable into a home. SAD devices provide fast and nondegrading surge protection for coaxial data and video source lines.

Protecting Twisted-Pair (Network) Cable

Like telephone lines, unshielded twisted-pair (UTP) cable, and more importantly, the devices it interconnects, should be protected from line noise and especially electrical surge. Devices like the one shown earlier in Figure 35-2 should be installed at each network termination and grounded to grounding lugs on the terminating device.

Alternative Power Sources

An uninterruptible power supply (UPS) provides a constant (uninterrupted) power stream to the electrical devices connected to it. Under normal operating conditions, most surge suppressors can handle short brownout conditions. However, when the AC voltage drops below a certain level or is disrupted completely, a UPS is designed to provide power for a certain amount of time.

All UPS units have two sets of circuits. One side is an AC circuit that provides surge suppression. The other side is a battery and a DC to AC converter. The batteries inside a UPS store a DC charge that must be converted to AC when needed to replace lost voltage.

There are two types of UPS units available, which differ in the following ways:

- **Standby**   Operates normally from its AC side. When the power drops, it switches over to its battery backup side.

- **In-line UPS**   Operates normally from its DC or battery backup side. The AC side is used only to maintain the power stored in the batteries or in the event of a problem with the battery-powered circuits.

NOTE   UPS units are often confused with a standby power supply (SPS), or battery backup, which supplies power only when none is available and has no power-conditioning capabilities.

The use of a UPS unit with home automation systems is optional, but in the case of electrically powered telephones and security systems, having power for even a short period of time after a power failure may be a necessity in some home situations.

Chapter Review

There are some basic electrical issues that need to be addressed during the planning phase for a structured wiring project, especially electrical event protection.

External AC power sources can pass on a variety of power-related problems, including line noise, power surges, brownouts, blackouts, and lightning strikes. Surge suppressors are generally available and the most commonly used protection device. Surge protectors should also be installed to protect any distributed phone lines between the NID and the distribution panel and any coaxial cable lines such as cable service, antenna or satellite. An uninterruptible power supply (UPS) provides a constant (uninterrupted) power stream to the electrical devices connected to it.

Power conditioning can serve to insulate a home from electrical events, but at the least surge suppression should be used to minimize any potential damage from electrical surges, spikes, and brownouts.

Questions

1. What is perhaps the single largest external danger to an electrical system?

   A. ESD

   B. Improper grounding

   C. Electrical events

   D. Number of electrical outlets in home

2. Which of the following is a low voltage electrical event against which power protection should be installed in a home system?

   A. ESD

   B. Surge

   C. Electrical noise

   D. Brownouts

3. What electrical event consists of small variations in the voltage of a power line?

   A. Brownout

   B. Blackout

   C. Line noise

   D. Power surge

4. What electrical event is also known as an over-voltage event?

   A. Brownout

   B. Blackout

   C. Line noise

   D. Power surge

5. What electrical event can cause devices to run slower than normal or malfunction?

   A. Brownout

   B. Blackout

   C. Line noise

   D. Power surge

6. What electrical event occurs when the power fails completely?

   A. Brownout

   B. Blackout

   C. Line noise

   D. Power surge

7. Which two of the following are the types of damage that can occur as the result of an electrical event?

   A. Asynchronous

   B. Catastrophic

   C. Degradation

   D. Synchronous

8. What device should be installed to protect against power spikes?

   A. Power conditioner

   B. Inverter

   C. Surge suppressor

   D. Uninterruptible power supply

9. What unit is used to measure the energy absorption capability of a surge suppressor?

   A. Amps

   B. Ohms

   C. Joules

   D. Volts

10. An electrical current inverter is most commonly used to convert _____ current to _____ current.

    A. Out of phase; in-phase

    B. 220; 110

    C. AC; DC

    D. DC; AC

Answers

1. **D.** The number of outlets in a home has no bearing on the design and planning of a structured wiring system, beyond their use as a guideline to the placement of structured wiring outlet boxes.

2. **D.** A brownout is a low-voltage current that can damage electrical systems over time. In many ways, it can be more damaging to power supplies than intermittent surges or spikes.

3. **C.** Line noise or electrical noise on an electrical line can raise and lower its voltage, causing damage to connected devices over time as well as disrupting any communications signals transmitted over the electrical system.

4. **D.** A power surge raises the voltage of the electricity on the line for short periods of time.

5. **A.** A brownout occurs when the line voltage is reduced for relatively extended periods of time.

6. **B.** A blackout is essentially what it sounds like. The damage from a blackout typically occurs from a surge when the power comes back on.

7. **B and C.** Some electrical events can destroy equipment and others cause small amounts of damage that can cause intermittent failures before the equipment is destroyed.

8. **C.** A surge suppressor can help to mitigate power surges and spikes. However, a surge suppressor should be checked after an electrical event to insure it is still effective.

9. **C.** Joules measure the capacity of a device to absorb electrical voltage.

10. **D.** Inverters are most commonly used to allow AC devices to be powered on a DC line.

PART IX

Appendices

About the CD

The CD-ROM included with this book comes complete with MasterExam and the electronic version of the book. The software is easy to install on any Windows 2000/XP/Vista computer and must be installed to access the MasterExam feature. You may, however, browse the electronic book directly from the CD without installation. To register for a second bonus MasterExam, simply click the Online Training link on the Main Page and follow the directions to the free online registration.

System Requirements

Software requires Windows 2000 or higher and Internet Explorer 6.0 or above and 20 MB of hard disk space for full installation. The Electronic book requires Adobe Acrobat Reader.

Installing and Running MasterExam

If your computer CD-ROM drive is configured to auto run, the CD-ROM will automatically start up upon inserting the disk. From the opening screen you may install MasterExam by pressing the MasterExam button. This will begin the installation process and create a program group named LearnKey. To run MasterExam use Start | All Programs | LearnKey | MasterExam. If the auto run feature did not launch your CD, browse to the CD and Click on the LaunchTraining.exe icon.

MasterExam

MasterExam provides you with a simulation of the actual exam. The number of questions, the type of questions, and the time allowed are intended to be an accurate representation of the exam environment. You have the option to take an open book exam, including hints, references and answers; a closed book exam; or the timed MasterExam simulation.

When you launch MasterExam, a digital clock display will appear in the bottom right-hand corner of your screen. The clock will continue to count down to zero unless you choose to end the exam before the time expires.

Electronic Book

The entire contents of the Study Guide are provided in PDF. Adobe's Acrobat Reader has been included on the CD.

Help

A help file is provided through the help button on the main page in the lower left-hand corner. An individual help feature is also available through MasterExam.

Removing Installation(s)

MasterExam is installed to your hard drive. For best results removing programs use the Start | All Programs | LearnKey| Uninstall option to remove MasterExam.

Technical Support

For questions regarding the technical content of the electronic book or MasterExam, please visit www.mhprofessional.com or email customer.service@mcgraw-hill.com. For customers outside the 50 United States, email international_cs@mcgraw-hill.com.

LearnKey Technical Support

For technical problems with the software (installation, operation, removing installations), please visit www.learnkey.com, email techsupport@learnkey.com, or call toll free at 1-800-482-8244.

Digital Home Technology Integration Glossary

This glossary includes the terminology, phrases, and most of the major standards publishers you will probably encounter or should know for working as a home technology integrator or an installer.

10Base2 (data networking)   The IEEE 802.3 standard for 10 Mbps thick coaxial cable Ethernet networks that have a maximum segment length of 185 meters. Also called *thinnet* or *cheapnet*.

10Base5 (data networking)   The IEEE 802.3 standard for 10 Mbps thick coaxial cable Ethernet networks that have a maximum segment length of 500 meters. Also called *thicknet* or *yellow wire*.

10BaseT (data networking)   The IEEE 802.3 standard for 10 Mbps Ethernet baseband networking over unshielded twisted-pair cable.

100BaseFX (data networking)   The IEEE 802.3 standard for fiber optic Ethernet networks with 100 Mbps bandwidth.

100BaseT (data networking)   The IEEE 802.3 standard for Fast Ethernet or 100 Mbps Ethernet baseband networking over unshielded twisted-pair cable.

100BaseT4 (data networking)   See *100BaseTX*.

100BaseTX (data networking)   The IEEE 802.3 standard for UTP Ethernet networks with 100 Mbps of bandwidth. Also called *100BaseT4*.

1000BaseTX (data networking)   The IEEE 802.3 standard for UTP Ethernet networks with 1000 Mbps of bandwidth. Also called *Gigabit Ethernet*.

110 block (data networking/structured wiring)   An IDC system used to terminate telephone and data cables. Also called *110 connector* or *110 punch-down*.

110 punch-down tool (data networking/structured wiring)   A special tool that is used to press wires into the IDC terminals on a 110 block.

11801 (data networking/structured wiring) The ISO/IEC international cabling standard that is based on the EIA/TIA 568 standards. Also called the *Generic Customer Premises Cabling standard*.

568A (data networking/structured wiring) The EIA/TIA standard defining RJ-45 jack pin-to-wire attachment for telecommunications wiring in commercial buildings.

568B (data networking/structured wiring) The EIA/TIA standard defining RJ-45 jack pin-to-wire attachment for data communications wiring in commercial buildings.

570 (data networking/structured wiring) The EIA/TIA standard defining standard telecommunications wiring in residential buildings.

802.3 (data networking) The IEEE reference standard that defines media access, cabling standards, and connectivity for Ethernet networks.

802.11a (data networking) An IEEE standard for wireless networking.

802.11b (data networking) An IEEE standard for wireless networking.

802.11g (data networking) An IEEE standard for wireless networking.

A

A-line lamp (lighting) A standard incandescent lamp used in indoor residential lighting.

AC (alternating current) (electricity) An electric current in which the flow of the current is alternatively reversed. The frequency of AC electricity in the U.S. is 60 Hz, and in many parts of the world it is 50 Hz.

accent lighting (lighting) Lighting used to highlight a particular object or room feature.

accumulator air coil (HVAC) A coil on some heat pump types that can be used as either an evaporator or condenser.

ADSL (Asymmetric Digital Subscriber Line) (data networking) A broadband DSL-telephone line technology that transmits voice, video, and data over existing copper telephone wires at very high speeds. ADSL provides faster data transfer speeds for download and slower data transfer rates for upload.

air change (HVAC) The amount of air needed to completely replace the air in a room, zone, or building.

air diffuser (HVAC) An outlet through which airflow is directed into a desired direction.

air handler (HVAC)   The fan, blower, filter, and housing of an HVAC system.

air infiltration (HVAC)   Air that leaks into a room or building through cracks, windows, doors, and other openings.

air terminal (HVAC)   An air distribution outlet or diffuser.

airflow (HVAC)   The distribution or movement of air.

AM (amplitude modulation) (audio, video, data networking)   The transmission method that merges a transmitted signal into a carrier signal by modulating the amplitude of the carrier.

ambient lighting (lighting)   The general lighting of an entire area or room made up of natural and artificial light.

ampere (electricity)   A standard unit measure of the rate of electron flow or electrical current in a conductor.

amplifier (audio, video)   A device that increases the amplitude of a signal retaining the same waveform pattern of the original signal. Amplifiers are analog devices.

amplitude (audio, video, data networking)   The wavelength of a transmitted signal that represents the strength or volume of the signal measured in decibels.

analog/analogue (audio)   The electrical representation of a signal that retains the properties of the original data.

ANSI (American National Standards Institute) (standards)   A standards organization that administers standards for the United States and represents the United States at the International Standards Organization (ISO).

Appletalk (data networking)   The network protocol suite used on proprietary Apple Computer networks.

armored cable (electricity)   An electrical cable assembly in which two or more insulated conductors are protected by a flexible metal conduit.

artifacts (audio, video)   Image or sound distortion that can occur when an audio or a video signal is compressed to a low bit rate. Also called *noise*.

ASCII (American Standard Code for Information Interchange) (data networking)   The 8-bit character encoding scheme that is the standard for computer data interchange.

ATSC (Advanced Television Systems Committee) (video)   An international standards organization that establishes voluntary technical standards for advanced television systems.

attenuation (data networking)   The decibel loss of signal that occurs when a signal is transmitted through a medium.

attenuator (audio, video) A passive transmission device used to reduce signal strength.

AWG (American Wire Gauge) (standards) A standard guideline used to measure wire diameter. Lower AWG values represent larger wire diameters.

B

backbone (data networking) The primary media of a data network that runs the length of the network and interconnects all network segments.

backmount (structured wiring) The mounting method used for attaching add-in modules inside a structured wiring distribution panel.

balance point (HVAC) The lowest outdoor temperature at which a heat pump is able to meet the heating demands of a home without using a supplementary heat source.

balanced line (electricity) A cable with two conductors with identical properties that provide common symmetry to ground.

ballast (lighting) An electrical device used in fluorescent or HID fixtures to supply sufficient voltage to start and operate a lamp. A ballast also limits the electrical current during lamp operation.

balun (balanced to unbalanced) (electricity) A device that is used to convert an unbalanced electrical line into a balanced line.

bandwidth (Data networking) The amount of data that can be transmitted over a medium in a specific period. The standard bandwidth measurement is megabits per second (Mbps).

bare wire (lighting) An electrical conductor wire that has no covering or insulation. Commonly ground wires in pre-wired lighting fixtures are bare wires.

baseband (video, data networking) A transmission mode that transmits digital data using time division multiplexing (TDM). Baseband transmissions use the entire capacity of the transmission media.

baseband video (video) Video signals that are unmodulated, such as NTSC, PAL, SECAM, and others, and carry no audio component.

battery backup (electricity) A rechargeable battery that is maintained in standby mode to supply power when an interruption in the normal power supply occurs.

bend radius (structured wiring) The angle to which a cable can be bent without damaging the cable or affecting its electrical properties.

bit (binary digit) (data networking)   The representation of a binary one or zero using positive and nonpositive electrical values, respectively.

bit rate (data networking)   The transmission speed of a network media expressed in bits. Bit rate is equivalent to bandwidth.

blocking (structured wiring)   A horizontally placed wooden or metal brace set between two wall studs.

Bluetooth (data networking)   A wireless RF communications technology used to link mobile devices into ad hoc networks.

BNC (Bayonet Neill Concellman) (Audio, Data Networking)   A standard coaxial cable connector that uses barrel and T connectors to join coaxial cables or connect to a networking or source device.

BPS (bits per second) (data networking)   A measurement of the number of bits transmitted over a medium in one second.

branch circuit (electricity)   A household electrical circuit that branches from the main electrical panel to an outlet box or a device.

breaker (electricity)   A toggle switch device that is used to connect and disconnect the power to an electrical circuit by nonautomatic means. Also used to pen a circuit by automatic means when a predetermined level of current passes through it. Circuit breakers can be reset.

bridle ring (structured wiring)   A cable management device that is used to loosely hold cabling in a loop, or plastic, wire, or other flexible materials.

broadband (audio, video)   The high-speed transmission media that transmits data at speeds of 1.544 Mbps or faster.

broadband (data networking)   The transmission mode for data, voice, and video using frequency division multiplexing (FDM) such as is used with cable television systems. Broadband transmissions use a single medium to carry several channels at once.

BTU (British thermal unit) (HVAC)   A heating system measurement that measures the amount of heat required to raise the temperature of one pound of water one degree Fahrenheit.

BX Cable (structured wiring)   A legacy cable type that is now illegal for use in homes.

byte (data networking)   A grouping of eight bits that is used to store or represent numeric values or ASCII characters in computer storage. Byte is a shortened form of binary digit eight.

C

cable (structured wiring)   A bundle of separated insulated wires wrapped with a single protective outer jacket.

cable clamps (structured wiring)   Metal clips inside a distribution panel, outlet box, or other electrical box that are clamped down on a cable using screws to hold the cable in place.

cable tie (structured wiring)   See *tie-wrap*.

capacitance (electricity)   The capability of a material to store an electric charge. Capacitance is measured in farads.

Cat (Category) 3 cable (structured wiring)   A four-pair TP cable once used for telecommunications and data networking that is now replaced by Cat 5 or Cat 5e cabling in the standards. Cat 3 cable is the minimum cable requirement for 10BaseT Ethernet networking.

Cat 5 cable (structured wiring)   A four-pair TP cable that provides a higher standard than Cat 3 cable because of an increased number of twists on the wire pairs and better resistance to interference. Cat 5 cable is the minimum cable requirement for 100BaseT and below Ethernet networking.

Cat 5e (expanded) cable (structured wiring)   The currently recommended category TP cable for use in residential cabling systems. Cat 5e cable is compatible with 1000BaseT and below Ethernet standards.

Cat 6 cable (structured wiring)   The cable standard for Gigabit Ethernet that is backward compatible with the Cat 5/5e and Cat 3 cable standards.

Cat 7 cable   An Ethernet cable standard that is backward compatible with Cat 5/5e and Cat 6 cable. Also referred to as Class F cable. The standards for Cat 7 cabling are still pending.

category cable (structured wiring)   TP cabling is rated into several numbered categories, ranging from Category 1 (Cat 1) to Category 7 (Cat 7), as specified by the EIA/TIA 568 cabling standard. The higher the category number, the higher the information capacity of the circuit.

cathode (lighting)   An electrode in a fluorescent lamp that emits or discharges electrons to the cathode at the opposite end of the lamp.

CATV (cable access television) (video)   An RF distribution system that distributes television broadcast programs, original programs, premium programming, and other services using a network of coaxial cable.

CCD (video)   Light detecting circuit arrays used in video cameras, scanners, and digital still cameras. Advantages include good sensitivity in low light and the absence of the burn-in and phosphor lag found in CRTs.

CCTV (video)   A closed circuit television distribution system that limits the reception of an image to those receivers directly connected to the origination point by co-axial cable or microwave link.

central monitoring station (security)   A facility of a privately owned protection service company that receives remote alarm signals and acts based on customers requests.

central monitoring station (security)   A central location in a home where surveillance images captured by video cameras are viewed and monitored.

CEDIA (Custom Electronic Design and Installation Association) (general)   A global trade association of companies that specialize in planning and installing integrated electronic systems in the home.

CFM (cubic feet per minute) (HVAC)   A standard measurement for airflow that measures the amount of air passing a stationary point.

chandelier (lighting)   A hanging light fixture that is often used as the focal point in a room or area.

channel (general)   A single path for communications. Channels may be one- or two-dimensional.

channel (video)   A defined band within the 6 MHz RF spectrum that transmits the audio and video carriers of a television signal.

circuit (electricity)   A continuous loop of electrical current.

circuit breaker (electricity)   See *breaker*.

cladding (general)   A low refractive index material that surrounds the core of an optical fiber causing the transmitted light to travel down the core and protects against surface contaminant scattering.

Class F cable (data networking)   The equivalent of Cat 7 cable that is defined in the ISO/IEC 11801 cabling standards.

CO (carbon monoxide) (security)   An odorless and colorless gas that is often called the "silent killer." Faulty furnaces can emit CO gas, which can poison the occupants of a home and can be lethal after extended exposure.

CO (central office) (communications)   The local telephone system's switching center. The nearest CO to a home is also called an *end office* (EO) or a *local exchange* (LE). The telephone lines that enter a home at the NID are terminated at the CO.

CO detector (security)   A sensor that can detect the presence of CO gas in a home and alert the occupants of the hazard.

coaxial cable (communications/video)   A two-conductor copper cable made up of a solid central conductor, a dielectric layer, and a second conductive layer that is usually a metal braid or mesh, all of which are inside an insulating jacket.

CODEC (compress/decompress) (video) An algorithmic video service that encodes and decodes video files for transmission over network media.

color temperature (lighting) A measure of the appearance of the light produced by a lamp that categorizes the light as either warm or cool.

compact fluorescent lamp (CFL) (lighting) A small, single-end fluorescent lamp that can be installed into an incandescent lamp socket.

composite video (video) The complete video signal including the brightness (luminance) signal, the blanking and sync pulses, and the color (chrominance).

compressor (HVAC) A pump used to increase the pressure of a refrigerant or gas between low-pressure and high-pressure cycles.

concealed wiring (structured wiring) Cable installed in a wall, between floors, in attics, or in crawlspaces to prevent the cable from being tampered with and to improve the aesthetics of the home.

condenser (HVAC) A pump that receives vaporized refrigerant from an evaporator and compresses it into a liquid state for return to the refrigerant control unit.

conductor (general) A material that offers little resistance to the flow of electrical current.

conduit (structured wiring) A metal or plastic tube that is used to protect the cabling running through it.

connecting block (communications) A plastic block containing metal wiring terminals used to establish connections from one group of wire to another with insulation displacement connections (IDC). Also called a *terminal block*, a *punch-down block*, a *quick-connect block*, or a *cross-connect block*. Used in residential wiring for terminating CPIW and provides a means for a telephone set to connect to the CPIW through a modular jack.

contacts (security, general) Electrically conductive points, or sets of points, that open and/or close circuits that ultimately control electrical loads.

contrast (video) The range of dark and light values in a picture or the ratio between minimum and maximum brightness.

control (general) A multiposition mechanical device, usually wall mounted, that allows for adjustment (attenuation or amplification) of the signal from the source or distribution device to an end device.

control panel (security) A device that arms, disarms, and supervises an alarm system at the user's premises.

controller (general) A device or group of devices that serve to govern, in some predetermined manner, the electric power delivered to the apparatus it is connect to.

convergence (video)   The alignment of the red, green, and blue video on a projected display such that the lines produced by the three "guns" appear to form one clearly focused white line and the perceived single image is clearly focused.

cove lighting (lighting)   A type of architectural lighting that uses light sources shielded by a ledge or recess to distribute light across a ceiling or wall.

CPIW (customer premise inside wiring) (communications)   Any and all telephone wiring inside a home and beyond the NID.

cross-connect (structured wiring)   A physical connection made between patch panels or punch-down blocks that interconnects cable runs from source devices and end devices.

crossed pair (structured wiring)   A wiring termination error on TP cabling in which the two conductors of a wire pair are attached incorrectly exchanged with the conductors of a different wire pair at one end of a cable.

crosstalk (structured wiring)   Interference on a cable caused by electrical energy being absorbed into adjacent conductors of a cable that may cause signal loss.

current (general)   The flow of electricity in a circuit, measured in amperes.

D

daisy chain (structured wiring)   A wiring technique in which multiple terminations are made on a cable or wiring branch that interconnects one device on the branch to the next.

damper (HVAC)   A device located inside a duct that is used to adjust the airflow.

data rate (data networking)   The number of bits of information that can be transmitted per second.

dB (decibel) (Electricity, Audio)   A measurement for the loudness or strength of a signal. One decibel is considered to be the smallest amount of difference between two sound levels that a human ear can detect. One bel indicates that an input signal is 10 times quieter or weaker than the output signal. A decibel is one-tenth of a bel.

DC (direct current) (electricity)   An electrical current that has no alternations or reversals.

definition (video)   The fidelity of a video picture reproduction. The clearer the picture, the higher the definition.

demarc (demarcation point) (communications)   The point at which a telephone company's lines terminate and are interconnected into a home's CPIW. Typically, the demarc of a home is the NID.

device (general)   Any electrical or mechanical equipment attached to a cable or wire.

DHCP (Dynamic Host Configuration Protocol) (data networking)   A networking protocol that allows network nodes to self-configure for IP address, subnet masks, default gateways, and more.

digital communicator (security)   A device that can be triggered automatically to electronically dial one or more preprogrammed telephone numbers using digital codes and report alarm or supervisory information to a receiver.

dimmer control (lighting)   An electrical device that controls the brightness of one or more lamps by varying the electrical current flowing to the lamps.

DIP (dual inline package) switch (data networking)   A set of toggle switches, rockers, or slides that are used to select settings on a modem or electronic circuit board.

distortion (video)   An undersized change in a wave form or signal.

distribution panel (structured wiring)   A centrally located panel that organizes and interconnects cable-based technologies, including data, voice, audio, and video signals throughout a home.

Dolby Pro Logic (audio)   Advanced surround sound system for the home using two front speakers, two rear-channel speakers for ambiance reproduction, and a front center channel speaker for dialog and "logic steering."

door contact (security)   A two-part magnetic sensor that detects when a door is opened and generates a trip signal.

downlight (lighting)   A light fixture that is typically recessed into a ceiling or an architectural feature that concentrates its light in a downward direction. Also called *can* or *recessed can*.

drop wire (communications)   A cable used to connect a home to telephone services that may either be underground or above ground and terminates at the home's NID.

drywall (general)   Also called *Sheetrock* (a brand name) or *wallboard*, drywall is a gypsum-based wall covering material that is installed in large sheets as a substitute for plaster on interior walls.

DSL (digital subscriber line) (data networking)   A broadband DSL-telephone line technology that transmits voice, data, and video over existing copper telephone wires at very high speeds. See *ADSL*.

DSL modem (data networking)   A type of modem that connects a computer to a DSL network that connects to the Internet. Once connected, DSL modem users usually have a continuous connection to the Internet.

duct (HVAC)   A pipe or enclosed conduit used to control and direct the flow of air from an air-handling device.

ductwork (HVAC)   The system of ducts in a home.

duplex receptacle (electricity)   An electrical outlet that includes two AC power plug-in sockets.

DVD (digital versatile disc) (video)   An optical disc system using MPEG-2 compression technology and the side of a CD-ROM that can store about 133 minutes of digital video.

E

EIA (Electronic Industry Association) (structured wiring)   A trade association of electronic equipment manufacturers that develops and publishes standards.

EIA/TIA 568 (structured wiring)   See *568A* and *568B*.

EIA/TIA 570 (structured wiring)   See *570*.

electrical box (structured wiring)   Also called *outlet box*, a metal or plastic box that is mounted to wall studs to hold electrical receptacles, light switches, and structured wiring jacks and outlets. Structured wiring runs terminate at electrical boxes.

ELV (extra low voltage) (electricity)   Electricity with voltage not exceeding 50 V AC or 120 V DC.

emergency lighting (lighting)   Lighting, typically powered by battery backup, that is used when the normal electrical supply is interrupted and the lighting system is not available.

EMI (electromagnetic interference) (structured wiring)   Interference in signal transmission or a reaction on a cable caused by low-frequency waves emitted from electromechanical devices.

entry delay (security)   A timer in most security system controllers that provides a homeowner time to disarm the security system before an alarm is sounded.

Ethernet (data networking)   A star or bus topology networking technology for computer data communication defined in the IEEE 802.3 standards that operates over twisted-pair, coaxial cable, and RF at speeds up to 1000 Mbps. See *10BaseT*.

exit delay (security)   A timer in most security system controllers that provides a homeowner with time to leave a home after arming the security system without setting off an alarm.

expansion slots (data networking)   Slots or spaces inside a computer or controller that are used to connect additional circuit boards (cards).

F

F-type connector (structured wiring)   A threaded barrel connector used to terminate coaxial cable in video applications.

FDM (frequency division multiplexing) (data networking, communications)   A communications technology that transmits multiple signals over a single communications link, such as cable television systems and wireless networks. Each signal is assigned a separate frequency.

fiber optics (structured wiring)   Plastic or glass cable that carries a large capacity of information using light (modulated light waves) and is immune to electrical noise, lightning, and induced voltages.

firewall (data networking)   Dedicated hardware and/or a software system that protects against intrusion on a network from systems external to the network.

FireWire (general)   A reference to IEEE 1394 1995 standard. A data communication scheme that manages digitization, compression, and synchronization processes.

fish tape (structured wiring)   A coil or steel tape that is used to guide a cable through a wall from above or below.

fixture (lighting)   A permanently installed and connected light or electrical device that consumes electrical power.

fluorescent lamp (lighting)   A low-pressure mercury electric-discharge lamp that has a phosphor coating on the inside of a glass tube to transform UV energy into visible light.

foot-candle (fc) (lighting)   A measurement for the amount of light reaching an object in the United States.

FPS (frames per second) (video)   The number of video frames captured or displayed in one second.

frequency (general)   The number of cycles per second in an electrical signal, measured in Hertz.

FT4 (Fire Type 4) (structured wiring)   A cable jacket material rating for nontoxic, nonflammable materials used for the insulation and outer jackets of low voltage cable, such as speaker wire.

furnace (HVAC)   The part of a heating system that converts gas, oil, or electricity into heat.

fuse (electricity)   A removable device that completes a circuit at the fuse box that will break if the circuit should have an overload or a short occurs on the circuit.

future-proofing (general)   The practice of designing and installing wiring and/ or a system that provides a home with the flexibility, expandability, and adaptability to support new and emerging technologies without requiring new wiring.

G

GA (gauge) (general)   Identifies the physical size of a wire. The lower the AWG (American Wire Gauge) number, the bigger the wire.

gain (audio)   A measure of amplification on a device expressed in dB for the highest frequency of operation.

gateway (structured wiring)   The entry point of services into a residence.

general lighting (lighting)   Uniform ambient lighting of a room or area without using special lighting, such as task lighting or accent lighting.

GFCI (ground fault circuit interrupter) (electricity)   Sometimes called *GFI (ground fault interrupter)*, a specific circuit protection outlet or breaker that protects homeowners from shocks. GFCI outlets are typically installed in kitchens and bathrooms.

ghosting (video)   Positive or negative images displaced in time from the actual image caused by signal interference from multiple paths of signal reception.

gigahertz (GHz) (data networking)   A network frequency of one billion cycles per second.

glare (lighting)   Light coming into an eye directly from a light source that can harm vision and cause visual discomfort. Indirect glare is light reflected into an eye from a nonlight source surface.

glass break sensors (security)   Sensors that detect the sound or vibration of glass breaking and generate a trip signal.

ground (electricity)   A conductive entity with a zero electrical potential that is neither positively nor negatively charged.

ground fault (electricity)   Current that has been misdirected from a hot or neutral lead to a grounding element such as a wire, box, or conductor.

ground wire (electricity)   One of the three common circuit wires. The ground provides a safety route for returning current. The ground circuit is joined with the neutral conductor at the main service panel.

H

HA (home automation) (general)   The use of a computer or microprocessor-based controller to control the functions and scheduling of home systems.

halogen lamp (lighting)   A type of incandescent lamp that contains halogen gases, such as iodine, chlorine, bromine, or fluorine, that impede the degradation of the tungsten filament. Also called a *tungsten halogen lamp* or a *quartz lamp*.

HAN (home area network) (data networking) A local area network (LAN) inside a single home.

handheld remote (general) A portable handheld control device.

hand-over section (security) If the security system detects an entry or exit through the primary entry/exit point, the entry or exit delay feature is engaged. However, if an entry or exit is made through any other point, the alarm is sounded.

hardware (data networking) The physical components of a computer or network system, including the Internet gateway, monitor, hard drive, printer, modem, network adapter, keyboard, and so on.

HDTV (high-definition television) (video) A high-resolution, wide-screen picture format and transmission standard.

heat loss (HVAC) The amount of heat lost from a space to be conditioned, measured in BTUs.

heat pump (HVAC) A compression cycle system that uses the heat in outdoor air to supply heat to a home or to remove heat from the home to cool it.

hertz (general) A unit of signal frequency equal to one cycle per second.

HID (high-intensity discharge) (lighting) Lamps that produce more lumens per watt and have longer lives than most other lamp types. HID lamps include mercury vapor, metal halide, high-pressure sodium, and low-pressure sodium.

high temperature sensor (security) A sensor that detects a rise in the ambient temperature of a room or area beyond a certain preset level and generates a trip signal.

home network (data networking) A peer-to-peer network that allows users to share data, peripheral devices, and Internet resources on a common network inside a home.

homerun (structured wiring) A wiring method where every cable is terminated at a central distribution facility and pulled directly to a single device, hub, or group of devices wired in series.

hot wire (electricity) One of the three common circuit wires with neutral and ground. The current flow travels on the hot wire.

house code (lighting) An alpha character (A–P) setting on an X-10 PLC device that is used to indicate an item or area/zone within the home. This code setting is combined with a Unit Code (1–16) to uniquely identify the X-10 device.

HTI (home technology integration) (general) The integration of a home's control and entertainment, and other systems, based on a structured wiring system, through the use of automated controllers.

HTI+ (general) The certification examinations produced by the Computer Technology Industry Association (CompTIA) that certify the abilities of an HTI technician to install, troubleshoot, and maintain home automated systems.

hub (data networking) A network clustering device that connects several network-ready devices to the network media using a shared bandwidth.

HV (high voltage) (electricity) Electrical lines that carry voltage in excess of 1,000 V AC or 1,500 V DC.

HVAC (heating, ventilation, and air conditioning) (HVAC) The integrated system that heats, cools, and ventilates a home.

I

IDC (insulation displacement connector) (data networking, structured wiring) A type of wiring terminating connection where the insulating jacket is removed from the connector when the wire is inserted/pushed/forced into the split connector with tines. This eliminates the need to strip wires first.

IEC (International Electrotechnical Commission) (general) A non-profit international standards organization that prepares and publishes standards for electrical, electronic, and related technologies.

IEEE (Institute of Electrical and Electronics Engineers) (data networking) A trade organization of engineers, scientists, and students that develops standards for the computer and electronics industry.

impedance (general) The resistance and reactance of a conductor or component measured in ohms. The lower the ohm value, the better the quality of the conductor.

incandescent lamp (lighting) A filament heated to the point of incandescence by an electric current inside of a glass bulb that produces light.

induction (general) Creating an electric current on a circuit from the magnetic influence of an adjacent circuit.

instant start (lighting) A type of fluorescent lamp that starts without the need for preheating the cathodes or a starter.

Internet (data networking) A work of networks around the world that provides access to information, electronic mail, graphics, and other media on content servers connected to the network.

Internet gateway (data networking) Also called a *residential gateway* or a *home gateway*, provides a link between a home network and the Internet.

I/O (input/output) (data networking) The operations of a computer that accept data inputs and transmit data outputs to and from peripheral devices.

IP (Internet Protocol) address (data networking)   A 32-bit binary logical address that identifies a computer on a TCP/IP (Transmission Control Protocol/Internet Protocol) network.

IP telephony (data networking)   The act of using Internet protocols to exchange voice, fax, and other forms of information traditionally carried over dedicated circuit-switched connections of the public switched telephone network.

iPod (audio)   A brand of portable media players manufactured by the Apple Corporation.

IR (infrared) (general)   A transmission technology that uses infrared light to transmit command signals and data. IR signals are also used in motion detectors and IR beam trip sensors.

ISDN (Integrated Services Digital Network) (data networking)   A telephone system of digital voice and data transmission services carried over the PSTN.

ISO (International Organization of Standardization) (standards)   An international membership organization that develops computer and telecommunications standards, among others. ISO is comprised of the national standards institutes of 157 countries. ANSI represents the United States at the ISO.

isolation (video)   The amount of separation or loss between two channels or signals.

ISP (Internet service provider) (data networking)   A company or organization that provides Internet connection services to subscribers.

J

jack (structured wiring)   The female component of a jack and plug connector that is attached to a cable as a terminator at an outlet or interconnect.

jacket (structured wiring)   The outer protection covering of wire or cable that may also provide additional insulation.

K

keypad (general)   User interface and input devices that are used to control the functions of one or more integrated systems. In a security system, a keypad is used to arm or disarm the system. In an audio/video system, keypads are used to select source devices and control volume.

kilobyte (KB) (data networking)   The equivalent of 1,000 bytes of data.

kilohertz (KHz) (data networking)   The equivalent of a frequency of 1,000 cycles per second.

kilowatt (kW) (lighting) The equivalent of 1,000 watts.

kilowatt hour (kWh) (lighting) The amount of kilowatts used by a device in one hour of operation.

knockout (structured wiring) A plug or piece of an electrical box or panel that can be removed to provide a pass-through for cable to enter or exit the box.

L

lamp (lighting) A light source, such as an incandescent, a halogen, a HID, or a fluorescent lamp. Also called a *light bulb*.

LCD (liquid crystal display) (video) Utilizes two transparent sheets of polarizing material with a liquid containing rod-shaped crystals between them that respond to electrical currents and align to create dark images. LCD panels do not emit light, but are often backlit or side lit for better viewing.

LCD projector (video) Utilizes LCD technique, separating red, green, and blue information to three different LCD panels where the appropriate colored light is then passed through and combined before exiting through the projector lens.

lead (structured wiring) A short length of conductor wire loose in a box or service panel.

LED (light-emitting diode) (general) A small electronic device that produces light when electricity is passed through it. LEDs are commonly used as indicator lights on keypads and other control devices.

light fixture (lighting) A complete lighting device that consists of a lamp, housing, and power connection.

line conditioner (general) Contains multiple protection devices in one package to provide electrical noise isolation and voltage regulation.

line doubler (video) Doubles the number of scan lines in a video picture. Fills in the space between the original lines, making them less noticeable and increases the brightness of the picture.

line voltage (electricity) The normal or nominal voltage level of a line. In the United States, the line voltage of a home is typically 120 volts AC.

load (lighting) Applies to all current-carrying devices on a given electrical circuit or feeder.

local area network (LAN) (data networking) A computer network in which two or more computers are connected with a communications medium for the purpose of sharing resources. Local area networks are typically created in a small geographical area, such as a home.

logic circuit control (security)   The system used with PIR devices to analyze changes in signal frequency to generate a trip signal, such as in a motion sensor, to determine movement before sounding an alarm. Also determines whether the object detected is a person or a pet to prevent a false alarm.

loss (general)   The energy dissipated by a transmission line.

louver (lighting)   A diffuser made of opaque or translucent material in a geometric design to prevent a lamp from being viewed directly and to minimize glare.

low temperature sensor (security)   A sensor that detects decreases in the ambient temperature of a room or area to a preset limit and generates a trip signal.

lumen (lighting)   The amount of light produced by a lamp is measure in lumens.

luminaire (lighting)   An architectural lighting effect or fixture.

LV (low voltage) (electricity)   An electrical circuit that carries voltage not exceeding 1,000 volts AC or 1,500 volts DC.

M

MATV (multiple access television) (video)   The method used for broadcasting television signals through the air.

Mbps (megabits per second) (data networking)   The equivalent of one million bits of data transmitted in one second.

MHz (megahertz) (general)   The equivalent of a frequency with one million cycles per second.

mixer (audio)   A device that will mix two or more input signals to form a combined outlet signal.

MMOF (multimode optical fiber) (structured wiring)   Transmission medium that uses glass or plastic strands to carry light impulses.

modem (modulator/demodulator) (data networking)   A telephone communications device that modulates digital data into analog data for transmission over a telephone line and demodulates the analog data into digital data at the receiving end for use by a computer.

modular outlets (structured wiring)   Multiuse outlets that allow for a variety of jacks to be mixed into a single outlet faceplate. Modular jacks are snapped into the faceplate in any pattern desired.

modulation (audio, video, data networking)   Raising a signal to a higher frequency by changing amplitude, frequency, or phase.

motion detector (security, lighting)   A sensor that can detect movement or the presence of a person in a room or area to sound an alarm or merely turn on or off the lights.

mounting bracket (structured wiring)   A bracket attached to a wall stud during rough-in that allows the mounting of a faceplate during trim-out. Also called a *low-voltage mounting bracket.*

mud ring (structured wiring)   A bracket attached to a wall stud during rough-in that ends up mounted flush with the drywall for the attachment of a faceplate during trim-out.

multizone (general)   A home automation or home technology integration system set up that allows separate areas of a home to operate independently of other areas of the home.

N

NEC (National Electric Code) (standards)   A guideline for electricians, electrical contractors, engineers, and electrical inspectors, put out by the NFPA that is generally accepted as the building wiring standard in the United States.

NEMA (National Electrical Manufacturer's Association) (standards)   An association of manufacturers that develops technical standards for electrical products.

network (general)   Two or more computers or peripheral devices connected by a communications medium.

network adapter (data networking)   The device that provides the interconnection and transceiver services to connect a computer or network-ready device to a network.

network cable (data networking)   The physical wire medium used to connect two or more computers or peripheral devices.

neutral wire (electricity)   One of the three common circuit wires. The neutral wire returns current to the power source. The neutral conductor is joined with the ground at the main service panel.

NEXT (near-end crosstalk) (data networking)   Interference caused by the induction of a signal from one wire pair into another pair at the transmitting end of a cable.

NIC (network interface card) (data networking)   A network adapter that is installed in a computer as an expansion card and manages the flow of information over the network.

NID (network interface device) (communications)   The interface device where the telephone company's lines interconnect with the residential wiring. Also called the *demarc.*

NM (nonmetallic) cable (electricity)   An electric service cable that is sheathed in a plastic material.

NMC (nonmetallic, corrosive) (electricity) An electric service cable that is sheathed in a solid plastic jacket for use in wet or corrosive areas, but is not approved for underground use.

node (data networking) Any network device where a network cable terminates.

noise (general) In a cable or circuit, any extraneous signal that tends to interfere with the signal normally present in or passing through the system.

noise reduction (audio, video) Processes used to reduce the amount of noise in an audio or video signal.

normally closed (general) A circuit or switch where the contacts are closed during normal operation.

normally open (general) A circuit or switch where the contacts are open during normal operation.

NTSC (National Television Standards Committee) (video) A color television broadcast signal standard that is used in North America and Japan.

O

occupancy sensor (security, lighting) A control device that detects the presence of a person in a given space. Commonly used to detect intrusion in a security system or control lighting systems and HVAC.

off-air (video) RF signals (typically TV) that can be received by a conventional antenna system, including VHF and UHF broadcast stations.

ohm (general) The unit of measure for the resistance in a conductor.

ohmmeter (general) An instrument for directly measuring resistance in ohms.

P

PAL (phase alternation by line) (video) The television signal format used in Europe and several South American countries.

PAN (data networking) Personal area network.

parallel circuit (general) Circuit interconnection where all components share a common positive and common negative connection.

patch cords (structured wiring) The cabling used to interconnect terminations at the central distribution panel.

patch panel (data networking) An interconnecting device that is used to terminate homerun cabling and connect it to distribution devices using patch cords.

PCI (peripheral component interconnect) (data networking) An internal communications and expansion bus on computers. Most network interface cards are PCI compatible.

PCMCIA (Personal Computer Memory Card International Association) (data networking) A standard for hot-swappable cards developed for use with portable PCs.

peer-to-peer (data networking) A simple kind of network that sets up a conversation between two machines without a middle man.

pendant light (lighting) Lighting fixtures used for either task or general lighting that are suspended from a ceiling.

peripheral device (data networking) External computer devices that are attached to the computer, such as CD-ROM drives, modems, and printers, through an interface cable.

PIP (picture-in-picture) (video) A display of a small picture with a larger picture, each from its own video source.

PIR (passive infrared) sensor (security) A detector device that senses changes in the radiation in the infrared band.

pixel (picture element) (video) A video image is composed of individual dots called pixels that create the image patterns and colors.

PLC (power line carrier) (data networking) The use of electrical AC wiring for networking transmissions of signals.

plenum (general) Airflow space between the actual ceiling and a drop ceiling where ductwork for an HVAC system is installed.

plenum-rated cable (structured wiring) A cable that has a fire retardant coating that complies with local and national building codes and is suitable for installation in air ducts and plenum spaces.

plug pack (security) A transformer that converts 120 or 240 volts AC to 16 volts DC to power a security system controller.

port (data networking) A receptacle on a computer or patch panel.

POTS (plain old telephone system) (communications) Analog telephone service that runs over copper wires, based on the original Bell telephone system.

pre-wire (structured wiring) The installation of structured wiring in a home before the drywall is installed during new construction.

protocol (data networking) A set of rules or guidelines that governs the communication between two applications, computers, or networks.

PSTN (Public Switched Telephone Network) (communications) The switched telephone network that carries long distance calls and point-to-point network communications.

punch-down (structured wiring)   A method for securing wire to a contact where the insulated wire is paced in a terminal groove and pushed down with a special tool. As the wire is seated, the terminal displaces the wire insulation to make an electrical connection.

punch-down block (data networking)   See *110 block*.

punch-down tool (data networking)   A spring-loaded tool that is used to insert conductors into IDC contacts when terminating on a 110 block.

PVC (polyvinyl chloride) (general)   Material most commonly used for the insulation and jacketing of cable.

R

raceway (structured wiring)   A metal or plastic channel used to hold electrical or structured wiring in a floor.

rapid start (lighting)   A fluorescent system without starters that requires one to two seconds of warm-up before beginning to emit light.

rated life (lighting)   The time in which 50 percent of a large quantity of a certain lamp burns out.

reactance (general)   The measure of the combined effects of capacitance and inductance on an alternating current.

recessed downlight (lighting)   A light fixture that is recessed into a ceiling that concentrates its light downward.

refrigerant (HVAC)   The substance used in a refrigerating mechanism that absorbs heat in an evaporator by changing its state from liquid to a gas, and then releases its heat in a condenser as it is returned to a liquid state.

register (HVAC)   A device that combines a grille and damper to cover an air opening.

relay (general)   An electromechanical switching device.

remodel box (structured wiring)   An electrical box designed for use during remodeling projects for installing electrical receptacles such as jacks or light switches in existing walls.

remote alarm (security)   An alarm signal that is transmitted to a remote central monitoring station.

repeater (data networking)   A network device that amplifies and regenerates signals so they can travel for longer distance on a cable.

reset (security, general)   To restore an electrical component or an alarm to its original (normal) condition after improper performance or alarm signal.

residential gateway (data networking)   See *Internet gateway*.

resistance (general)   The amount of opposition a cable has to the flow of electrical current that is measured in ohms.

resolution (video)   The density of lines or dots for a given area that make up an image. Resolution determines the detail and quality in an image.

retrofit (general)   A modification to an existing building.

return air (HVAC)   Air drawn into a heating unit after being circulated in a room by the HVAC system supply.

RF (radio frequency) (general)   Transmission of wireless signals over a high-frequency carrier.

RFI (radio frequency interference) (general)   Interference inducted into a conductor from radio frequency signals on a nearby carrier.

RG6 (radio grade 6) coaxial cable (data networking)   Type of coaxial cable with a 20-gauge center conductor that is the current standard for data communications over coaxial cable as it allows for higher bandwidth than RG59.

RG59 coaxial cable (video)   A type of coaxial cable typically used for video signal transmission.

RGB (red, green, and blue) (video)   The chroma information in a video signal. The basic components of the color television system.

RGB monitor (video)   A color monitor that accepts separate red, green, and blue input signals to produce a high-quality picture.

rheostat (general)   A variable resistor.

ring (communications)   The side of a two-wire circuit that is connected to the negative side of a power source at the telephone company's CO.

RJ-11 (communications)   A modular jack/plug connector that accepts a single pair of conductors. Used for single-line telephones and modems.

RJ-31X (security)   A modular jack/plug connector that is used to interconnect a security system to a telephone distribution panel and allows for seizure of an in-use phone line.

RJ-45 (data networking)   A modular jack/plug connector that is used to terminated twisted-pair cabling per EIA/TIA 568 termination standards.

Romex (electricity)   A brand of nonmetallic-sheathed cable that is also the generic name used for NM sheathed cable.

rough-in (structured wiring)   The phase of a structured wiring project in which the boxes, cables, and in-wall connections are installed. Rough-in occurs before the drywall is installed.

router (data networking)   A device where the basic function is to efficiently route network traffic from one network to another network.

run (structured wiring)   The path of a length of cable from a distribution panel to an outlet or other termination point.

S

SECAM (Systeme Electronique Couleur Avec Memoire) (video)   A color TV standard developed in France.

sensor (security)   A device designed to produce a signal or other indication in response to an event or stimulus within its detection.

serial interface (data networking)   An I/O port that transmits data one bit at a time in contrast to parallel transmission that transmits multiple bits simultaneously. RS-232 is a common serial signaling protocol.

series wiring (structured wiring)   See *daisy chain*.

server (data networking)   An application running on a centralized computer that processes requests from network clients (nodes).

service drop (general)   The overhead conductors between the electrical supply, such as the lat pole and the building being served.

service entrance (SE) (electricity)   The point where the incoming electrical line enters a home.

service lead (electricity)   An incoming electrical line that supplies power to a service panel. Also called *supply lead*.

service loop (structured wiring)   A length of cable coiled near the end of a cable run to facilitate future changes in the wiring system.

service panel (electricity)   The distribution facility that ties the service lead to the interior electrical circuits of a home. The service panel is typically a main circuit breaker panel or a fuse box.

set point (HVAC)   The temperature setting a thermostat is to maintain in a room or area.

setback thermostat (HVAC)   An electronic programmable thermostat that can be set to provide different temperature settings for different times of the day.

set-top box (video)   A generic term for a device connected between the television set and the cable service coming in. It performs selection and decryption processes.

Sheetrock (general)   A brand name for drywall material. See *drywall*.

shield (structured wiring)   A metal braid, mesh, or foil placed around a cable to conduct return current and to prevent signal leakage or interference.

short circuit (general)   The condition caused when a current flow is interrupted short of or before reaching the device terminating the cable. A short circuit is caused when a hot conductor comes into contact with neutral or ground conductors.

shunt (security)   To remove some portion of an alarm system from operation, allowing entry into a protected area without initiating an alarm signal.

signal (security, communications)   Any visible or audible indication that can convey information. Also, the information conveyed through a communications system.

signal strength (general)   The intensity of a signal measured in volts (V), millivolts (mV), microvolts (uV), or dbmV.

silent alarm (security)   A remote alarm without local indication that an alarm has been transmitted.

single-zone (general)   A whole-house system in which all devices operate from a single controller.

siren (security)   A sounding device that emits a harsh and loud sound when a trip signal is received from a directly connected sensor or the security system controller.

skin effect (general)   The tendency of alternating current to travel only on the surface of a conductor as its frequency increases.

SMOF (single-mode optical fiber) (structured wiring)   A type of fiber optic cable that carries a single signal stream over long distances.

smoke detector (security)   A device where an electrical circuit runs through a chamber where two electrodes are placed very close together to allow electricity to cross the gap, completing the circuit. Should smoke particles collect on one or both of the electrodes, the circuit is broken and a trip signal or an alarm is generated.

snow (video)   Visual noise displayed on a television screen caused by excessive signal noise on a circuit.

speaker siren (security)   A siren that receives audio signals from the security system controller for playback.

spike (general)   A momentary increase in electrical current that can damage electrical equipment.

splice (general)   The joining of two or more cables together by connecting the conductors pair to pair.

splitter (video)   A device that divides or combines the RF energy on the coaxial cable to two or more cables. Splitters are also two-way.

star topology (structured wiring)   A wiring pattern where each cable run emanates from a central distribution facility and is terminated at a single device. See *homerun*.

starter (lighting)   The electrical device that works with a ballast to start a fluorescent or HID lamp.

stereo (audio)   A process of using separate signals on separate channels for the left and right audio, thereby giving depth, or dimension, to the sound.

STP (shielded twisted-pair) (structured wiring)   A type of twisted-pair cable that includes a foil shielding around each wire pair.

streaming media (video)   This type of network-download video file allows a user to watch the media content of a file without first downloading the entire file. The user is able to watch the content while the download is in progress.

strobe light (security)   A high-intensity light that strobes when an alarm is activated.

structured wiring (structured wiring)   A system of installing home wiring in which all cable runs are distributed from a central distribution panel using a star topology and homerun cable pulls.

subwoofer (audio)   A loudspeaker that reproduces very low sounds usually in the range of 20 Hz to 1000 Hz.

supply (HVAC)   The ductwork that carries conditioned air to a room.

surge (general)   A rapid rise in current or voltage usually followed by a fall back to a normal level.

surround sound (audio)   A system that separates the various components of the soundtrack, then disperses them to speakers placed around the room. Four to five speakers are incorporated and a surround sound processor is used to create the effect.

SVGA (super video graphics array) (video)   Resolutions higher than VGA (640 × 480). SVGA computer graphics cards have a resolution of 800 × 600 pixels (480,000 pixels) but may be able to output resolutions of up to 1280 × 1024 and 16 million colors.

S-VHS (super video home systems) (video)   A high band video recording process for VHS that increases the picture quality and resolution capabilities.

S-Video (video)   The composite video signal is separated into the lum (Y, black, and white information) and the chroma (C, color information).

switch (data networking)   In addition to several other features, the advantage of a switch over a hub is that each port has its own dedicated bandwidth. A LAN switch is used to efficiently forward messages on a network.

switch (general)   A two position wall-mounted device that toggles between the completion or interruption of a circuit between two devices.

system (general)   A group of electrical devices that processes inputs into outputs, allowing for feedback and control. For example, an audio system includes audio source devices, audio distribution and amplification devices, cabling, speakers, and controls.

systems integration (general)   Having intelligent subsystems that communicate with each other and act upon the information shared.

T

T1 (communications)   A standard for digital transmission in North America. T1 lines are used for connecting networks across remote distances.

tamper sensor (security)   A sensor or switch used to detect the unauthorized tampering with a sensor or contact.

tap (communications)   A device inserted into a communications line that allows the line to be shared.

task lighting (lighting)   Lighting specifically placed to illuminate an area used for a particular activity.

TCP/IP (Transmission Control Protocol/Internet Protocol) (data networking)   The primary protocol suite for networks that use IP addressing.

TDM (time division multiplexing) (data networking)   A communications technology that transmits multiple signals over a single communications link, assigning each signal a certain time slice.

telecommunications (communications)   Any transmission, emission, or reception of signs, signals, writing, images, and sounds or information of any nature by cable, radio, visual, optical, or other electromagnetic systems.

terminator (structured wiring)   A resistive device that is attached to the end of a cable run. A terminator must match the impedance of the cable to which it is attached.

thermostat (HVAC)   A set point device used to control the operation of a HVAC system.

thinnet (data networking)   See *10Base2*.

three-way switch (lighting)   A switch that allows control of power from two or more locations.

THX (video)   A trade name of Lucasfilm, Ltd. for a movie sound enhancement technology that sets the standard of performance for Dolby sound; originally THX represented Tomlinson Holman Experiment.

TIA (Telecommunications Industry Association) (standards)   A trade organization that develops and publishes standards for the telecommunications industry.

TIA/EIA (standards)   Trade associations that collaborate on communications, electronic, and cabling standards. See *EIA* and *TIA*.

tie-wrap (structured wiring)   Plastic or nylon strapping used for binding or bundling cables together or holding them in place. Several styles of tie-wraps are available: cinching, hole-mounted, and adhesive closure.

tip (communications)   A conductor in a two-wire telephone circuit that is attached to the circuit leading to a positive power source at the telephone company's CO.

ton (HVAC)   A cooling system unit of measure that is the equivalent of 12,000 BTUH. Single-family residences typically are equipped with air conditioning units that provide between 2 and 5 tons of cooling.

topology (general)   The physical or logical pattern of a cabling system. These include star, ring, and bus configurations.

touch screen (general)   A visual display terminal screen that responds to instructions as the user touches the screen.

transformer (general)   An electrical device used to reduce or convert the current of an electrical circuit.

traveler wires (lighting)   Wires interconnecting switches when more than one switch can control circuit power independently.

trip signal (security)   A signal generated by a sensor or contact and transmitted to an alarm or the security system controller when an out-of-norm condition occurs.

troffer (lighting)   A large recessed luminaire that is typically flush-mounted on a ceiling.

tuner (audio)   A device used to select signals at a specific radio frequency for amplification and conversion to sound.

TVSS (transient voltage surge suppressor) (general)   A device designed to protect connected devices from transient voltages.

tweeter (audio)   A loudspeaker designed to reproduce high-pitched or treble sounds.

twisted pair (structured wiring)   A communications cable made up of one or more wire pairs that have been looped around each other. An increased number of twists in the pair reduce the vulnerability of the wire pair to external interference and signal radiation.

U

UF (underground feeder) cable (electricity)   A cable designed and rated for underground and outdoor use that is molded into solid plastic.

UHF (ultra high frequency) (video)   Off-air signal frequencies that carry television channels 14 through 69.

UPS (uninterruptible power supply) (general) Provides protection against all power disturbances.

upstream (general) The transfer of data from an in-house device to elsewhere in the home.

USB (universal serial bus) (data networking) A standard high-speed interface mode for attaching peripheral devices to a PC.

USOC (Universal Standards Ordering Code) (communications) A standard coding scheme for registered jacks used in telecommunications.

UTP (unshielded twisted pair) (structured wiring) A type of twisted-pair cable that does not include additional shielding to resist EMI or RFI.

UV (ultraviolet) radiation (general) Invisible light that is composed of electromagnetic radiation with a wavelength of less than 400 nanometers (nm) and greater than 100 nm. UV radiation can be harmful to humans and pets.

V

valves (HVAC) Devices inserted into air ducts that are used to open or restrict the air resistance of a HVAC system.

VHF (very high frequency) (video) Off-air signal frequencies that carry television channels 2 through 13.

VHS (video home service) (video) The half-inch video cassette format originated and developed by JVC and adopted by different manufacturers.

volt (general) Unit of electrical measure that indicates the amount of electrical pressure on a circuit.

voltage drop (general) A loss of the power level of a circuit caused by the electrical resistance of the wire.

voltmeter (general) An instrument designed to measure a difference in electrical potential in volts.

W

wall sconce (lighting) A decorative wall-mounted light fixture.

wall washing (lighting) A lighting technique used to illuminate a wall.

WAN (wide area network) (data networking) A computer network that interconnects LANs over a large geographic area.

watt (general) An electrical unit measure that indicates the amount of electrical power on a circuit.

wattage (lighting) The amount of electricity consumed by a lamp.

WEP (wired equivalent privacy) (data networking) The encryption protocol used to encode data transmitted over an 802.11b wireless network using either 40-bit or 128-bit encryption.

whole-house controller (general) A computer-based system dedicated to integrating and managing all home electronics systems.

whole-house network (general) A network designed to allow any appliances, electronic products, or systems to communicate directly with any other electronic product or system also on the network, regardless of application.

Wi-Fi (wireless fidelity) (data networking) A certification awarded to IEEE 802.11b wireless networking products that meet the standards developed by WECA (Wireless Ethernet Compatibility Alliance) aimed at ensuring interoperability.

window contact (security) A magnetic device used to detect when a window is opened and generate a trip signal to an alarm or the security system controller.

wire (structured wiring) A single solid metal conductor or a multiple strand metal conductor used to carry an electrical signal or a current.

wire clamps (structured wiring) See *cable clamps*.

wire stripper (structured wiring) A tool used to remove portions of insulation from a wire.

wiremold (structured wiring) A brand name for surface-mounted cable raceway.

woofer (audio) A loudspeaker that reproduces bass frequency.

X

X-10 (data networking, security) A popular power line carrier (PLC) technology that transmits signals over AC power lines to transfer data on a network or to control lights, appliances, and other devices.

XLR connector (general) A type of audio connector featuring three leads: two for the signal and one for overall system grounding. A secure connector often found on high quality audio and video equipment, also called a *cannon connector*.

Z

zone (general) A single room, a group of rooms, or an entire house in which automated or centrally located devices are controlled from a single controller. For example, in an audio zone all occupants hear the same audio playback.

CEA-CompTIA DHTI+ Exam Objectives

CEA-CompTIA DHTI+ Exam Objectives

1.0 Networking

- Identify basic networking protocols and their uses and know when / how to apply them.
- Recognize and implement methods of network security.
- Configure setup and maintain a residential LAN (local area network).
- Configure setup and maintain a secure wireless network.
- Identify and define network cabling characteristics and performance.

2.0 Audio/Video

- Implement, maintain, and troubleshoot multiroom audio systems. Identify common interference sources.
- Install, configure, and maintain a residential home theater system.
- Assess, install, and configure content management systems and describe their applications in a residential environment.
- Implement, maintain, and troubleshoot multiroom video systems.

3.0 Telephony/VoIP

- Differentiate and describe POTS versus VoIP delivery. Identify and troubleshoot common issues.
- Describe and define fundamentals of telephone systems.

4.0 Security and Surveillance Systems

- Maintain, configure, and troubleshoot basic security systems and applications.
- Describe basic security terminology and apply installation procedures and methodologies.
- Identify, configure, install, maintain, and troubleshoot security and surveillance cameras.

5.0 Home Control and Management

- Identify user interfaces and their appropriate applications.
- Define and recognize control systems that integrate subsystems in the home.
- Describe the functionality, characteristics, and purpose of a home control system.
- Identify commonly used communication protocols and their application.
- Describe basic HVAC (heating, ventilation, and air conditioning) terminology and install peripheral control devices.
- Describe basic lighting terminology and install peripheral control devices.
- Identify and install component power protection devices.

6.0 Troubleshooting Methodology and Documentation

- Identify and apply the fundamentals of troubleshooting and diagnostics.
- Given a scenario, demonstrate how to apply troubleshooting skills to integrate subsystems.
- List and describe the benefits of verification of installation.
- Deliver appropriate manuals and documentation to the end user upon completion of installation.

Page numbers with *f* denote figures and with *t* denote tables.